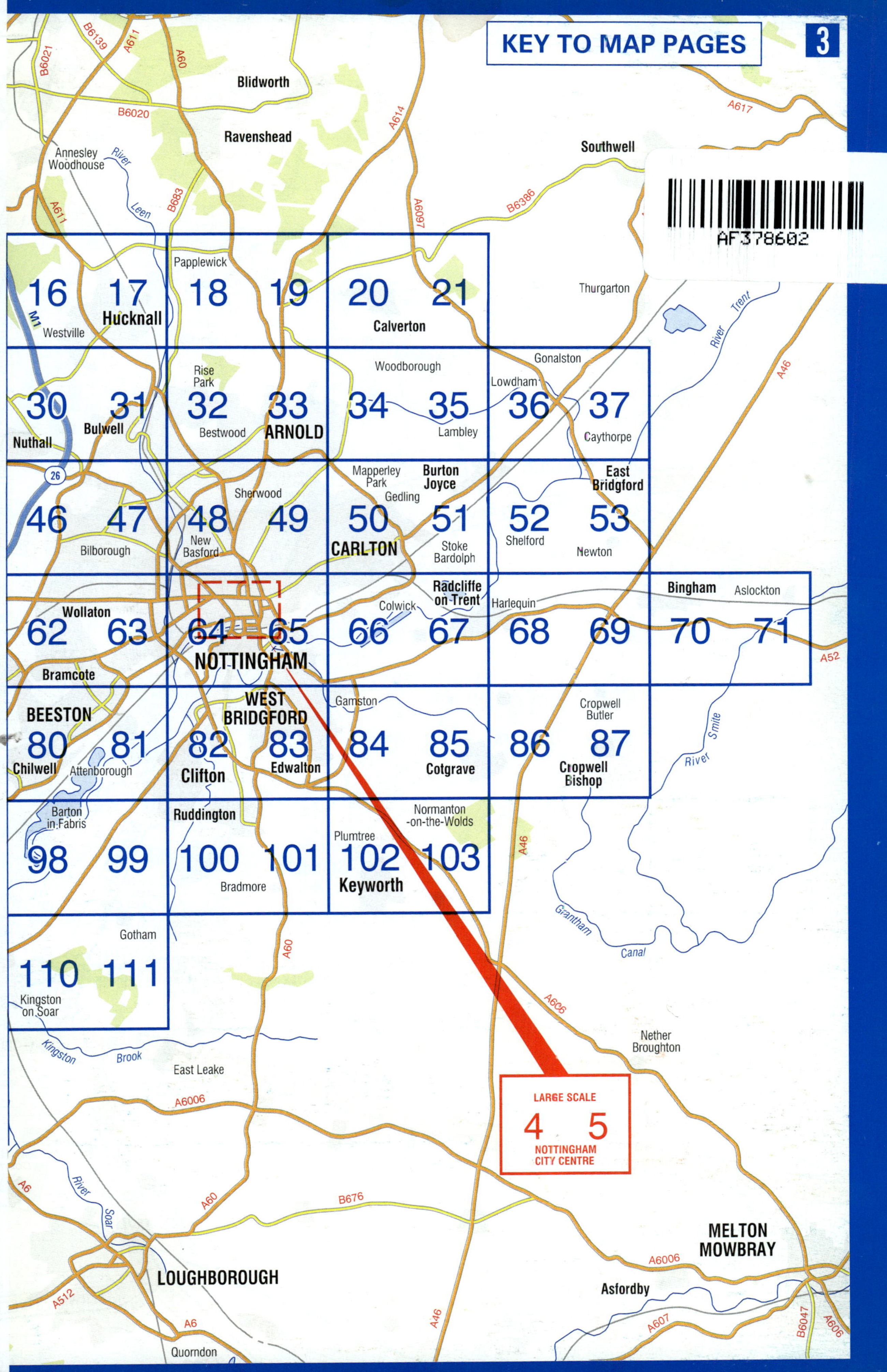

KEY TO MAP PAGES
3
Blidworth
Ravenshead
Southwell
Annesley Woodhouse
Thurgarton
Westville
Papplewick
16
17
Hucknall
18
19
20
21
Calverton
Rise Park
Woodborough
Gonalston
Lowdham
30
31
Bulwell
32
33
34
35
36
37
Nuttall
Bestwood
ARNOLD
Lambley
Caythorpe
Mapperley Park
Burton Joyce
East Bridgford
Sherwood
Gedling
46
47
48
49
50
51
52
53
Bilborough
New Basford
CARLTON
Stoke Bardolph
Shelford
Newton
Wollaton
Radcliffe on Trent
Bingham
Aslockton
Colwick
Harlequin
62
63
64
65
66
67
68
69
70
71
NOTTINGHAM
Bramcote
WEST BRIDGFORD
Gamston
Cropwell Butler
BEESTON
80
81
82
83
84
85
86
87
Chilwell
Attenborough
Clifton
Edwalton
Cotgrave
Cropwell Bishop
Barton in Fabris
Ruddington
Normanton -on-the-Wolds
Plumtree
98
99
100
101
102
103
Bradmore
Keyworth
Gotham
110
111
Kingston on Soar
Nether Broughton
Kingston Brook
East Leake
LARGE SCALE
4
5
NOTTINGHAM CITY CENTRE
MELTON MOWBRAY
LOUGHBOROUGH
Asfordby
Quorndon
AF378602

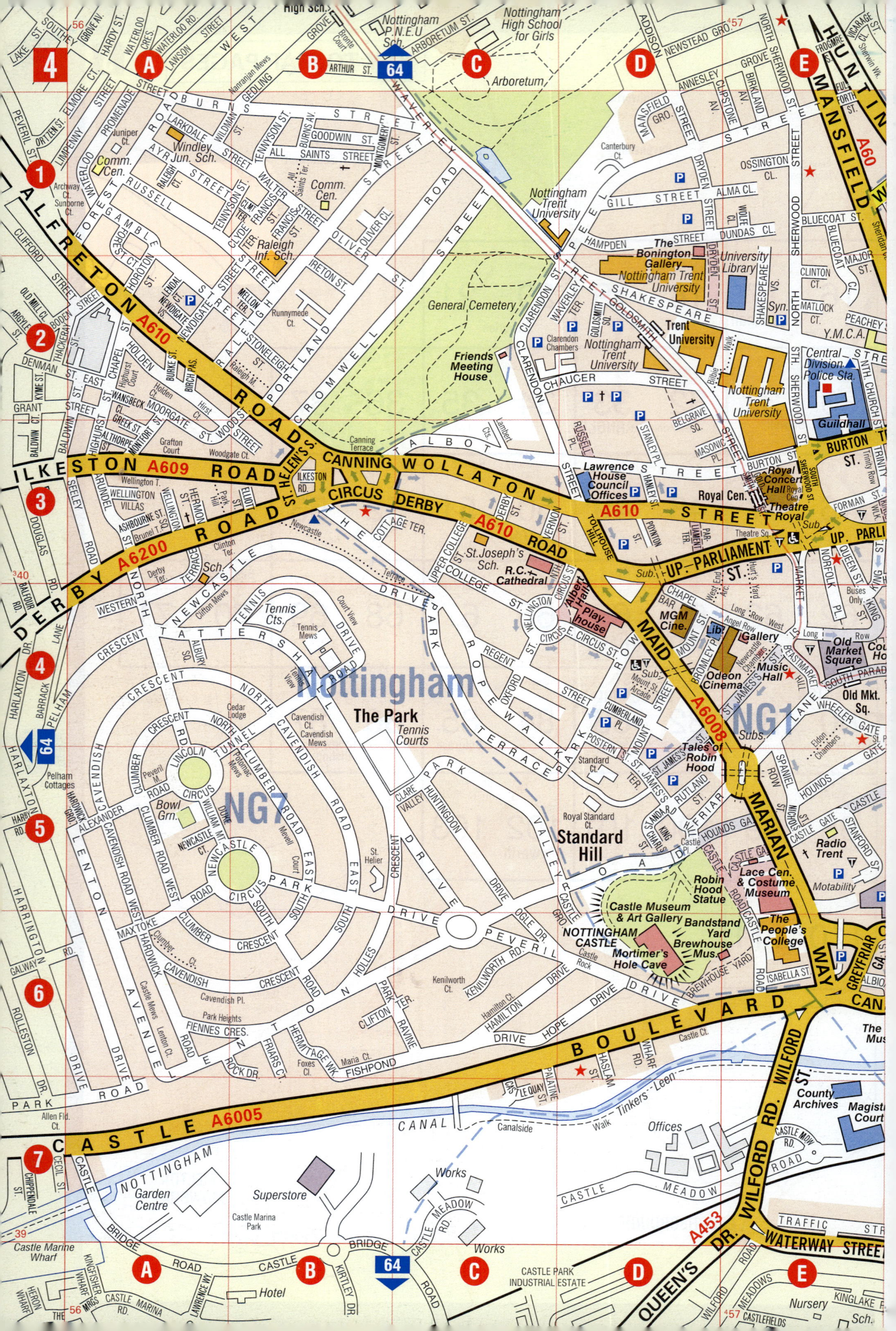

Nottingham
The Park
NG7
NG1
Standard Hill
Nottingham Castle
Castle Museum & Art Gallery
Mortimer's Hole Cave
Robin Hood Statue
Lace Cen. & Costume Museum
The People's College
Bandstand
Brewhouse Yard
Brewhouse Mus.
Castle Rock
Tales of Robin Hood
Old Market Square
Music Hall
Odeon Cinema
MGM Cine.
Playhouse
Theatre Royal
Royal Concert Hall
Royal Cen.
Guildhall
Central Division Police Sta.
Nottingham Trent University
University Library
The Bonington Gallery
Trent University
General Cemetery
Friends Meeting House
Arboretum
Nottingham High School for Girls
Nottingham P.N.E.U. Sch.
High Sch.
R.C. Cathedral
St. Joseph's Sch.
St. Helier
Lawrence House Council Offices
Canterbury
Y.M.C.A.
Cedar Lodge
Bowl Grn.
Pelham Cottages
Garden Centre
Superstore
Castle Marina Park
Hotel
Works
Offices
County Archives
Magistrates Court
Castle Park Industrial Estate
Nursery
Raleigh Inf. Sch.
Comm. Cen.
Windley Jun. Sch.
Larkdale
Tennis Cts.
Tennis Courts
Castle Marine Wharf


ALFRETON
A610
ILKESTON ROAD
A609
DERBY ROAD
A6200
CANNING CIRCUS
DERBY ROAD
A610
WOLLATON STREET
A610
UP. PARLIAMENT ST.
MAID MARIAN WAY
A6008
BURTON ST.
CASTLE BOULEVARD
A6005
CASTLE BOULEVARD
WATERWAY STREET
QUEEN'S DR.
A453
WILFORD RD.
CANAL
Tinkers' Leen
MANSFIELD
A60
HUNTIN
CASTLE ROAD
GREYFRIAR
NORTH SHERWOOD STREET
SOUTH SHERWOOD STREET
SHAKESPEARE STREET
GOLDSMITH STREET
WAVERLEY STREET
GILL STREET
PEEL STREET
CLARENDON STREET
TALBOT STREET
WOLLATON STREET
DRYDEN STREET
ADDISON STREET
64
64
64
64

# A-Z NOTTINGHAM & DERBY

## CONTENTS


Key to Map Pages   2-3

Large Scale Nottingham City Centre   4-5

Large Scale Derby City Centre   6-7

Map Pages   8-117

Index to Streets, Towns, Villages and selected Places of Interest   118-152


## REFERENCE

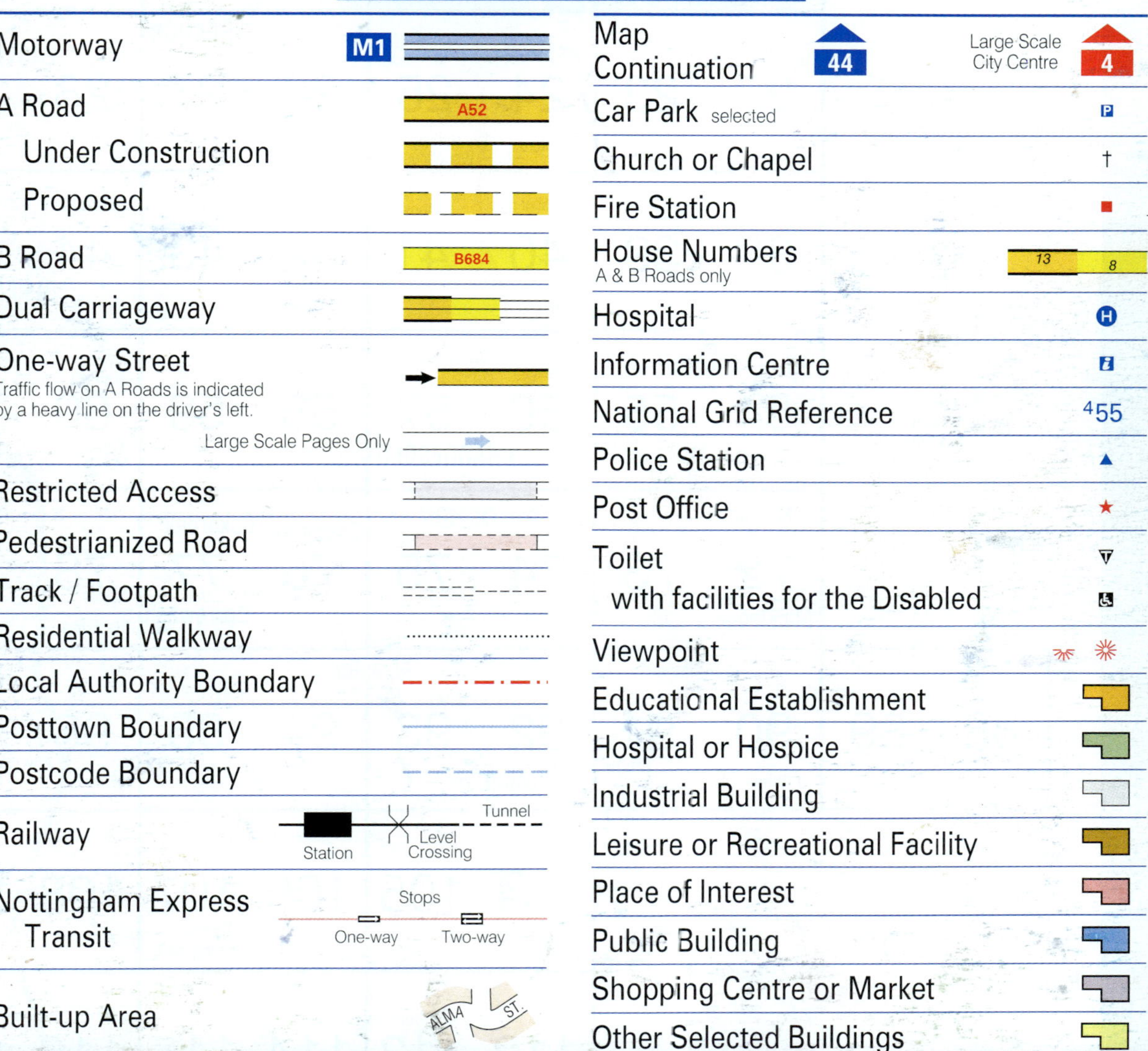

| | |
|---|---|
| Motorway | M1 |
| A Road | A52 |
|    Under Construction | |
|    Proposed | |
| B Road | B684 |
| Dual Carriageway | |
| One-way Street | |
| Traffic flow on A Roads is indicated by a heavy line on the driver's left. | |
| | Large Scale Pages Only |
| Restricted Access | |
| Pedestrianized Road | |
| Track / Footpath | |
| Residential Walkway | |
| Local Authority Boundary | |
| Posttown Boundary | |
| Postcode Boundary | |
| Railway | Station   Level Crossing   Tunnel |
| Nottingham Express Transit | Stops   One-way   Two-way |
| Built-up Area | |

| | |
|---|---|
| Map Continuation | 44   Large Scale City Centre 4 |
| Car Park selected | P |
| Church or Chapel | † |
| Fire Station | ■ |
| House Numbers   A & B Roads only | 13   8 |
| Hospital | H |
| Information Centre | i |
| National Grid Reference | 455 |
| Police Station | ▲ |
| Post Office | ★ |
| Toilet | ▽ |
|    with facilities for the Disabled | |
| Viewpoint | |
| Educational Establishment | |
| Hospital or Hospice | |
| Industrial Building | |
| Leisure or Recreational Facility | |
| Place of Interest | |
| Public Building | |
| Shopping Centre or Market | |
| Other Selected Buildings | |

## SCALE

**Map Pages 8-117**
1:14908 (4¼ inches to 1 mile) 6.7cm to 1km

0   ¼   ½ Mile
0   250   500   750 Metres

**Map Pages 4-7**
1:7454 (8½ inches to 1 mile) 13.4cm to 1km

0   ⅛   ¼ Mile
0   100   200   300 Metres

**Copyright of Geographers' A-Z Map Company Ltd.**


Head Office:
Fairfield Road, Borough Green, Sevenoaks, Kent TN15 8PP
Telephone: 01732 781000 (Enquiries & Trade Sales)
01732 783422 (Retail Sales)
www.a-zmaps.co.uk
Copyright © Geographers' A-Z Map Co. Ltd. 2002

This product includes mapping data licensed from Ordnance Survey® with the permission of the Controller of Her Majesty's Stationery Office.
© Crown Copyright 2001. All rights reserved. Licence number 100017302
Edition 1 2001   Edition 1a 2005 (part revision)

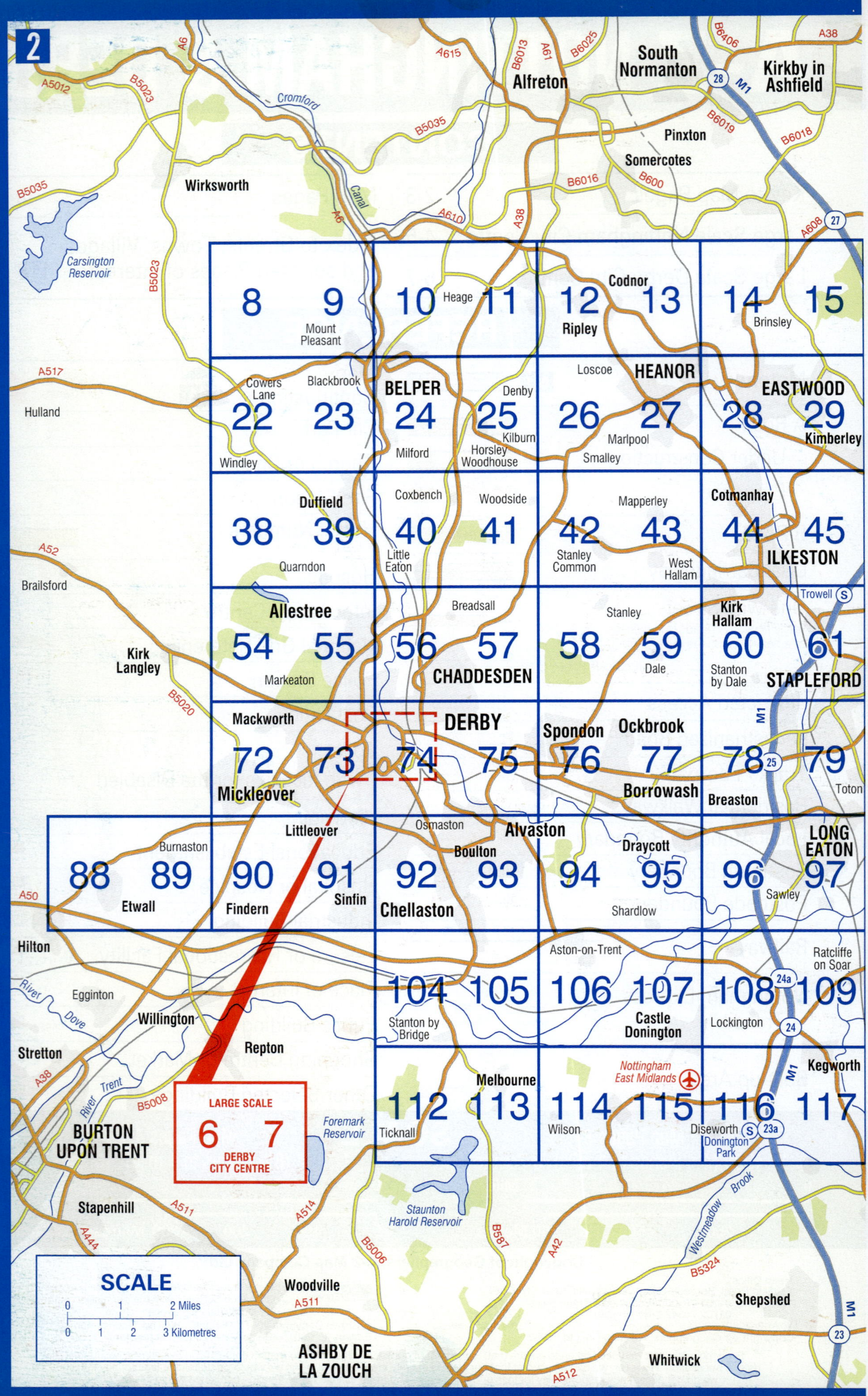

2
Carsington Reservoir
Cromford Canal
South Normanton
Alfreton
Kirkby in Ashfield
Pinxton
Somercotes
Wirksworth
Codnor
Ripley
8
9
10
Heage
11
12
13
14
Brinsley
15
Mount Pleasant
Cowers Lane
Blackbrook
BELPER
Denby
Loscoe
HEANOR
EASTWOOD
22
23
24
25
26
27
28
29
Windley
Milford
Kilburn
Horsley Woodhouse
Marlpool
Smalley
Kimberley
Hulland
Duffield
Coxbench
Woodside
Mapperley
Cotmanhay
38
39
40
41
42
43
44
45
Quarndon
Little Eaton
Stanley Common
West Hallam
ILKESTON
Brailsford
Allestree
Breadsall
Stanley
Kirk Hallam
Trowell
Kirk Langley
54
55
56
57
58
59
60
61
Markeaton
CHADDESDEN
Dale
Stanton by Dale
STAPLEFORD
Mackworth
DERBY
Spondon
Ockbrook
72
73
74
75
76
77
78
79
Mickleover
Borrowash
Breaston
Toton
Littleover
Osmaston
Alvaston
Draycott
LONG EATON
Burnaston
Boulton
88
89
90
91
92
93
94
95
96
97
Etwall
Findern
Sinfin
Chellaston
Shardlow
Sawley
Hilton
Aston-on-Trent
Ratcliffe on Soar
Egginton
104
105
106
107
108
109
Willington
Stanton by Bridge
Castle Donington
Lockington
Stretton
Repton
LARGE SCALE
Nottingham East Midlands
Kegworth
6
7
112
113
114
115
116
117
BURTON UPON TRENT
DERBY CITY CENTRE
Foremark Reservoir
Ticknall
Melbourne
Wilson
Diseworth
Donington Park
Stapenhill
Staunton Harold Reservoir
SCALE
Woodville
Shepshed
0   1   2 Miles
0   1   2   3 Kilometres
ASHBY DE LA ZOUCH
Whitwick

ROAD
Huntingdon Prim. Sch.
Playing Field
St. Ann's
Play. Fld.
Acacia Ct.
Peas Hill Rd.
65
Bellevue
Nugent Gdns.
Blue Bell Hill Rd.
Wigley Cl.
Rodway Rd.
Sketchley Rd.
5
F
G
H
J
K
Southampton St.
Gordon Rd.
St. Matthias Rd.
Bluebell Hill Infant School
Rosehill School
1
Adventure Playground
Melville Gdns.
Jersey Gardens
NG3
Woodhouse St.
Cardiff Lib.
2
Stonebridge City Farm
Road
B686
King Edward Park
3
Sneinton
Sneinton Prim. Sch.
4
York Ho.
Bus Station
A60 GLASSHOUSE STREET
Victoria Shopping Centre
Victoria Market
Mosque
Bingo Halls
St. Mary's Rest Garden
VICTORIA PARK
Robin Hood Industrial Estate
Stonebridge
Stonebridge Court Industrial Est.
MILTON
ROAD
Palais
KING EDWARD ST.
HUNTINGDON ST.
LOWER PARLIAMENT STREET
A60
Arnold & Carlton College
Park View Court
Victoria Leisure Centre
A6008
CLUMBER ST.
CRANBROOK ST.
Arts Theatre
Media Cen.
Lincoln St.
Old Lenton St.
GOOSE GATE
HOCKLEY
SOUTHWELL ROAD
CARLTON
MANVERS
SNEINTON
WALKER STREET
Mus.
Nottingham Social Cen.
William Booth Inf. Sch.
Youth Club
65
The Green
5
Arts Cen.
St. Mary's
Lace Mkt.
Lace Market
WOOLPACK LA.
Bowling Alley
The Nottingham National Ice Centre
Bus Depot
STANHOPE
Lace Market Theatre Mus.
County Ho.
St. Mary's Church
Shire Hall & Comm. Galleries of Justice
Lace Hall Museum
PLUMPTRE
BELLAR GATE
FISHER GATE
PENNYFOOT ST.
LOWER PARLIAMENT ST.
PLOUGH
NEWARK
Beaumont St.
The Caves of Nottingham
Broad Marsh Shopping Centre
Listergate Square
St. Mary's Church
KAYES WALK
CANALS
LONDON RD.
POPLAR ST.
B.B.C. East Midlands
CITY LINK
CRESCENT
Bus Station
CANAL
A6008 ST.
CARRINGTON ST.
Crown & County Courts
Canal Museum
Station Street
Nottingham
CANAL
Works
NOTTINGHAM
A612 STREET
Sneinton Hermitage
Colwick Rd.
6
Ardmore
Gresley Dr.
STATION
Goods Shed
NOTTINGHAM STATION
LONDON ROAD
A6019
A60
Warehouses
NG2
7
QUEENS
SHERIFFS
A6019 ROAD
Works
County Business Park
Meadow Trading Estate
Waste Disposal Unit
MEADOW LA.
WEST
F
G
H
65
Depot Works
J
Clarke Rd.
K
Cattle Market
MEADOW
58
39

Mundy Pleasure Grd.
Whitecross House
Whitecross Gardens
QUARN GDNS.
ELMS
Elm Park Court
KEDLESTON RD.
FIVE LAMPS
St. Nicholas Mews
NICHOLAS
MARGARET
ARTHUR ST.
DARLEY GRO.
ETRURIA GDNS.
CITY
JOHN LOMBE DR.
6
A
Whitecross Nursery Sch.
PARKER STREET
B
Ryecote Centre
C
D
74
E
MANSFIELD
37
BLACKWORTH ROAD
WATSON ST.
WALTER ST.
WHITECROSS
AVENUE
WEST
GARDEN STREET
DUFFIELD ROAD
NORTH
DUFFIELD
HENRY ST.
NORTH PARADE
MARY'S MEWS
Joseph Wright Ter.
DUKE STREET
WELL ST.
BATH ST.
MAPLEBECK CT.
RIVER
MANSFIELD RD.
Markeaton Recreation Ground
1
ST. ANNE'S CL.
WILLIAM ST.
WILLIAM ST.
BROOK GARDENS
LEAPER ST.
QUARN WY.
QUARN ST.
WATSON STREET
PARKER ST.
KING'S MEAD
KING ST.
EDWARD ST.
Adult Ed Cen.
Primary School
MARY'S
RIVER ST.
BUCHANAN ST.
BRITANNIA ST.
ST. MARY'S CT.
BRIDGE
GATE
NOTTINGHAM RD.
FO
Markeaton
Eaton Court
Central Community Nursery School
STREET
LODGE
WILLOW ROW
ST. HELEN'S
ORCHARD
A6
WY.
ST. ALKMUND'S
Subway
STREET
CAUSEY BRIDGE
A52
PHOENIX ST.
STUART ST.
BUCK LAND CL.
UTTOXETER OLD RD.
2
ASHBOURNE RD.
FRIAR GATE
BRICK ST.
MILL ST.
NUNS ST.
BRIDGE ST.
ST. JOHN'S TER.
Friargate Ho. Sch.
Halls of Residence
AGARD STREET
A52
SEARL ST.
Princess Alice Ct.
LITTLE BROOK ST.
BROOK WALK
A52
Halls of Residence
ST. ALKMUND'S STREET
FORD STREET
CATHEDRAL RD.
CATHEDRAL
CHAPEL
Queen St. Gallery
Queen's Leisure Cen.
QUEEN
ST. MICHAEL'S LA.
CHRISTOPHER ST.
Industrial Museum
Silk Mill Park
DERWENT
GREEN WOOD
Slater AV.
Rebecca House
STEPPING
FOWLER ST.
Ashbourne Old Rd.
Clock Wo.
FRIAR GATE
CLARKE ST.
DERBY
Derby Gaol
Pickford's House Mus.
LIME TREE AV.
FRIAR GATE CT.
FRIARY ST.
Roman House
Heritage Gate
Friargate Mews
CAVENDISH ST.
GEORGE ST.
WILLOW ROW
Sports Cen.
Offs.
CATHEDRAL RD.
WALKER LANE
College PL.
Cathedral
Offices
County Hall Mus.
St. Mary's Offices
Bold Lane Ct. Ho.
ST. WERBURGHS CHURCHYARD
St. Werburghs Cloisters
CHEAPSIDE
SADLER GATE
STRAND
IRON GATE
AMEN ALLEY
Magistrates Court
DERWENT ST.
CORPORATION ST.
Ex Bri
3
JAMES CL.
SIMS AV.
73
VERNON GA.
YORK ST.
VERNON ST.
St. James Court
LARGES ST.
AMBROSE TER.
FRIAR GATE
FRIAR GATE CT.
STREET
FRIAR GATE
ST. FRIAR
PONSONBY TER.
GEORGE ST.
CURZON ST.
BRAMBLE ST.
ST. GEORGE
BLACKMORE ST.
SADLER GATE
WARDWICK
Mus. & Liby.
St. Werburghs Churchyard
BECKET ST.
VICTORIA ST.
James St.
MARKET
CORN MARKET
Guildhall Theatre
Market Hall
War Mem.
Assembly Rooms
ALBERT ST.
MORLEDGE
THORNTREE LANE
AUDLEY CEN.
ALBION ST.
CROWN WK.
DERWENT
Council House
Cro. & Co. Co.
DE1
4
Warehouses
Warehouses
NORTHERN ROAD
STAFFORD ST.
FRIARY ST.
FORMAN ST.
CURZON ST.
KENSINGTON ST.
TALBOT STREET
Derwent Ct.
MONK ST.
MACKLIN ST.
NEWLAND
COBURN ST.
BECKET ST.
PICKETWELL
DUCKWORTH SQ.
ST. PETER'S CHURCHYARD
ST. PETER'S WY.
Eagle Shopping Centre
THE SPOT
LONDON
OSMASTON
GREAT
SUDBURY
SUDBURY
NEW ROAD
A516
Bus Depot
DRWRY CT.
DUNKIRK
ALMA ST.
WILSON STREET
CROMPTON STREET
Derby
GERARD CT.
GOWER STREET
BABINGTON LANE
E. BABINGTON LA.
Heritage Centre
Metro Cinema
Darwin St.
BURROWS WK.
5
College
MEWS
336
College Bus. Centre
LAVERSTOKE CT.
DRWRY WARD
JACKSON ST.
BAKEWELL ST.
WOLFA ST.
KING ST.
ALFRED ST.
LANE
STREET
BARN CL.
FORESTER STREET
Swinscoe Ho.
ROSENGRAVE STREET
Sterndale Ho.
Eldon Ho.
DEGGE ST.
BROW ST.
HILL STREET
Univ.
SITWELL ST.
BACK SITWELL ST.
The Maltings
BOURNE ST.
BRADS RETAIL
UTTOXETER
PEEL ST.
OLIVE ST.
LYNTON ST.
WERBURGH STREET
Primary School
PARLIAMENT ST.
EDENSOR SQ.
COPPERLEAF CL.
PELHAM ST.
WEBSTER ST.
HARCOURT STREET
GREEN LANE
ROAD
Govt. Offices
NORMANTON ROAD
SACHEVEREL ST.
Highgates
WILMOT STREET
BOURNE ST.
6
FREEHOLD ST.
Mason Wk.
Parliament St. Mills
PARLIAMENT ST.
Walk
Churchside
Burnage Ct.
Summerbrook Ct.
SPRING STREET
GREY STREET
BAKERS LA.
Derby Coll. of Further Education
LEOPOLD ST.
A5250
CHARNWOOD STREET
THE AVENUE
Ramshaw Wy.
STOCKBROOK
Recreation Ground
DE22
CROWN MS.
MAY STREET
SUN STREET
PITTAR STREET
FARM
ARBOR CL.
PETER BAINES IND. EST.
SPA LANE
Loosdonstone Walk
MOUNT ST.
A5250
SWINBURNE ST.
NORMANTON ROAD
MELBOURNE ST.
CHARNWOOD STREET
DE23
MOSS ST.
7
DEAN ST.
HARRISON ST.
RAVEN ST.
LEMAN ST.
PERCY ST.
SHERWOOD ST.
RIDDINGS ST.
CROWN ST.
WOODS
VALE
MILLS ST.
CHANCEL ST.
Plimsoll Ct.
Boyer Wk.
LIME ELM LANE
ABBEY STREET
A601
GREY ST.
SPA LANE
Longstone Walk
MOUNT STREET
HILL ST.
AVONDALE RD.
HARTINGTON ST.
DE23
LEONARD ST.
Leonard Wk.
Alder Wk.
Grove House
Arboretum
A
73
B
LARGO LE.
WARNER ST.
BURTON ROAD
C
St. Joseph's R.C. Prim. School
MONK ST.
CARMEL ST.
MILL HILL LANE
MILL ST.
D
DASHWOOD ST.
RENALS ST.
SALISBURY ST.
BELGRAVE ST.
GROVE ST.
74
E
TWYFORD
Grove House
Arboretum
FAIRE ST.
BRAMFIELD AV.
Bradbourne Ct.
ARGYLE ST.
LOWE ST.
S. J. C. Inf.

Racecourse Park
74
CARDIGAN
ST.
BEAUFORT
KERRY
CONSLEY
7
Derwent Comm. Prim. School
LOTHIAN PL.
Beaufort Gds.
F
G
H
J
K
37
Day Nursery
DORSET
STREET
1
ST. MARY'S
WHARF RD.
KENTISH CT.
EUSTON DR.
STORES
SIR
Works
MONMOUTH
ESSEX
STREET
PRIME
CHARING
PANCRAS
WATERLOO
CT.
WAY
FRANK
Grand Stand
GRANDSTAND RD.
DERBYSHIRE BUSINESS DEVELOPMENT CENTRE
PRIME ENTERPRISE PARK
THE DERWENT BUSINESS CENTRE
Depot
CLARKE
WHITTLE
Derbyshire County Cricket Ground
WESTMORLAND CL.
GREEN
STREET
2
Landau Forte College
ALICE ST.
KEYS
ROBERT
ST.
STREET
STREET
A61
Pavilion
HUNTINGDON
Derwent Ho. Willow Ho.
HUNTINGDON GRN.
FRANCIS
ROAD
WOOD ST.
NOTTINGHAM
ROAD
ROAD
P
Park Vw. Ho.
NOTTINGHAM
WAYZGOOSE DR.
CHEQUERS
Depot
WAY
STREET
EXETER ST.
THE EASTGATE
Eastgate Bridge
A52
THE PENTAGON
Works
LANE
3
STREET
DARWIN PLACE
UNDERPASS
MEADOW ROAD
EASTGATE
THE PENTAGON
CHEQUERS
CHARTWELL DR.
A52
ROAD
DE21
P
DARWIN PLACE
Exeter Ho.
Bus Depot
CRANMER
HANSARD GATE
ROAD
THE MEADOWS INDUSTRIAL ESTATE
74
Exeter Bridge
MEADOW
A6
A6
WEST MEADOWS IND. EST.
ROAD
ROAD
4
Riverside Gardens
THE COCK PITT
The Holmes
DUNTON CLOSE
ASHLYN
Bowling Green
Subway
County Court
Bus Station
P
Bass's Recreation Ground
RIVER
Sports Ground
Market
THE COCK PITT
Mill Fleam
Derby Junction
5
Derby Playhouse
Sch.
STATION APP.
PRIDE
Viaduct
DERWENT
THEATRE WK.
Copecastle Sq.
SIDDALS
ROAD
SIDDALS RD.
A6
Castle Sq.
STREET
COPELAND
Castle House Flats
Castlefields Main Centre
COPELAND WK.
STREET
STREET
David Lloyd Leisure
Pipe Bridge
Coliseum Centre
LIVERSAGE
STREET
TRAFFIC
A6
STREET
STREET
NEW ST.
APP.
PARKWAY
Sub.
Crafters Mkt. Pl.
HOPE
ST.
JOHN
SHEF-FIELD PL.
Works
6
CASTLE
ROAD
Liversage Ct.
CARRINGTON
DERBY SMALL BUSINESS CEN.
Florence Court
MIDLAND
LEEDS PL.
B6000
RAILWAY TERRACE
The Roundhouse Centre
RIVERSIDE
BRADSHAW WY.
LONDON
LIVERSAGE PL.
ST.
LIVERSAGE RD.
ST.
TRINITY ST.
PARK
Wellington Cdns.
CALVERT
DE24
ROAD
SHAW PARK
Liversage Almshouses
B6000
CHAPEL LA.
CARRINGTON STREET
P
MIDLAND ST.
DERBY STATION
Roundhouse
WHEELWRIGHT
Offices
MARSTON
DERBYSHIRE ROYAL INFIRMARY
ROAD
CANAL
WELLINGTON
NOBLE ST.
NELSON ST.
HUDSON WAY
WAY
Works
7
LITCHURCH ST.
MIDLAND RD.
NELSON ST.
WORKS
LOCOMOTIVE
James of E. Sch.
LEONARD ST.
GROVE ST.
A514
REGENT ST.
OXFORD ST.
LONDON ST.
HULLAND ST.
St. Andrews House
WAY
Works
Arboretum House
ARBOR-ETUM
ARBORETUM ST.
KEBLE CL.
Day Hospital
BLOOMFIELD ST.
CLIFTON ST.
BARLOW ST.
OSBORNE ST.
74
Works
F
G
H
J
K
Royal Crown Derby Works
Oriel Ct.
BLOOM-FIELD
CENTRE CT.
36

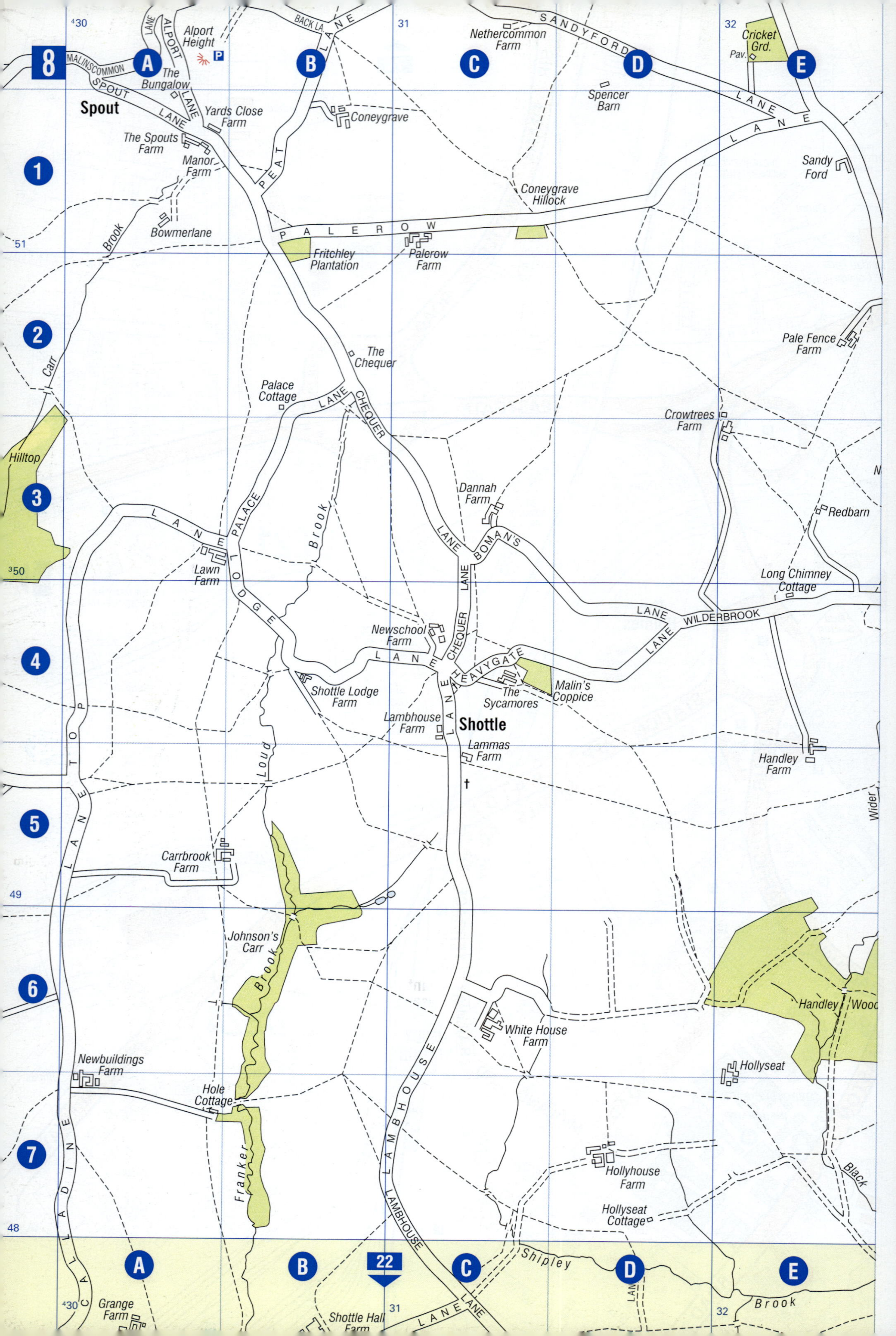

8
A
B
C
D
E
1
2
3
4
5
6
7
430
31
32
Alport Height
BACK LANE
SANDYFORD
Cricket Grd.
Pav.
MALINSCOMMON
The Bungalow
Spout
SPOUT LANE
ALPORT LANE
Yards Close Farm
Coneygrave
Nethercommon Farm
Spencer Barn
The Spouts Farm
Manor Farm
Sandy Ford
Bowmerlane
PEAT LANE
PALEROW
Coneygrave Hillock
51
Brook
Carr
Fritchley Plantation
Palerow Farm
Pale Fence Farm
The Chequer
CHEQUER LANE
Crowtrees Farm
Hilltop
Palace Cottage
PALACE LANE
Brook
Dannah Farm
Redbarn
350
LANE TOP
Lawn Farm
LODGE LANE
BOMANS LANE
Long Chimney Cottage
LANE
Newschool Farm
CHEQUER LANE
WILDERBROOK LANE
Shottle Lodge Farm
HEAVYGATE
The Sycamores
Malin's Coppice
Lambhouse Farm
Shottle
Handley Farm
Loud
Lammas Farm
†
Carrbrook Farm
Wider
49
Johnson's Carr
Brook
Handley Wood
Newbuildings Farm
White House Farm
Hollyseat
Hole Cottage
Franker Brook
LAMBHOUSE LANE
Hollyhouse Farm
Black
Hollyseat Cottage
48
CALLADINE
A
B
22
C
Shipley
D
E
430
31
32
Grange Farm
Shottle Hall Farm
LAMBHOUSE LANE
Brook

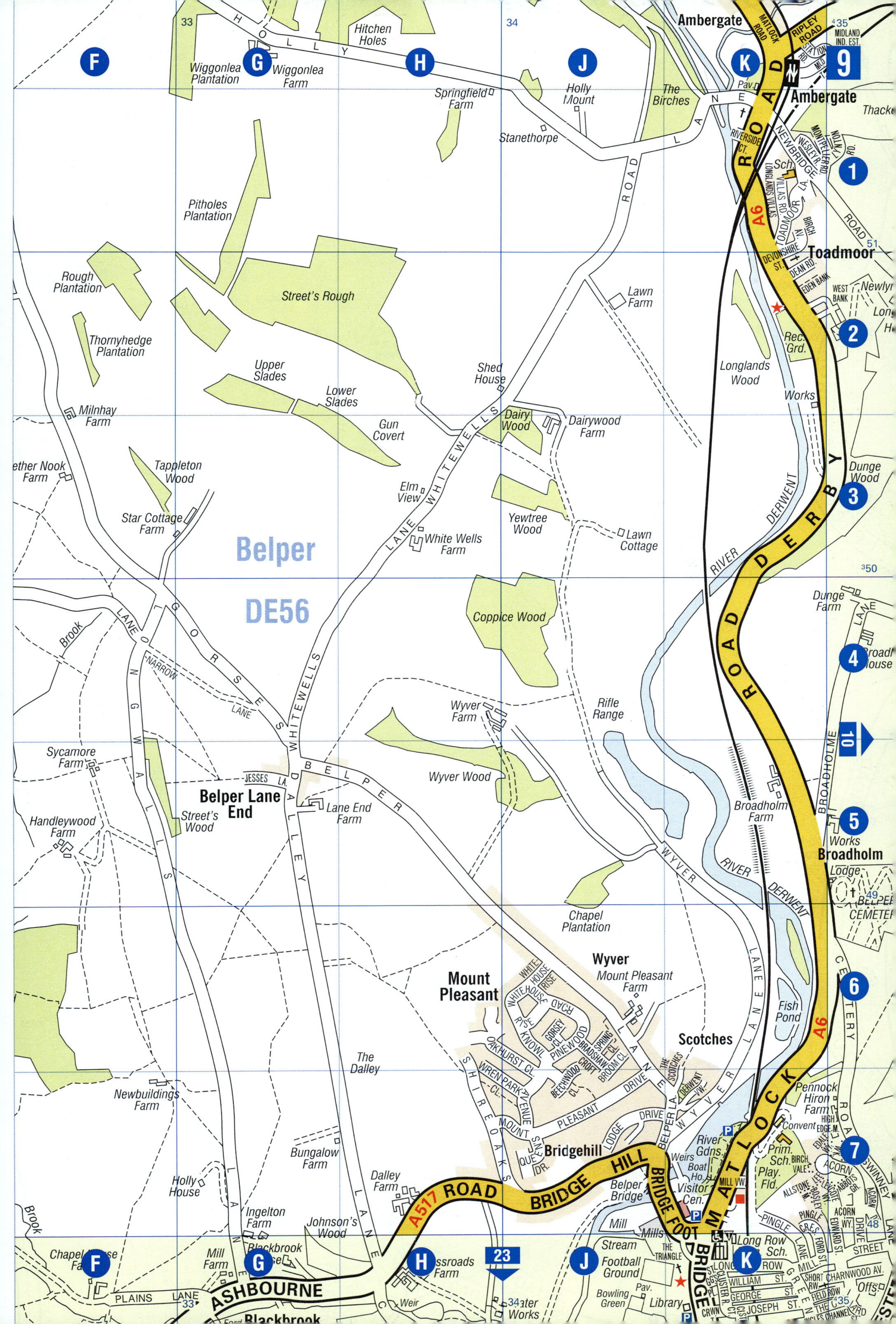
33
34
35
F
G
H
J
K
9
MIDLAND IND. EST.
Ambergate
Ambergate
RIPLEY ROAD
MATLOCK ROAD
STATION
Pav. D.
Thacke
NOLLY RD.
MONTPELIER RD.
WESLEY
Sch
BIRCH
ROAD
Hitchen Holes
HOLLY
Wiggonlea Plantation
Wiggonlea Farm
Springfield Farm
Holly Mount
The Birches
LANE
RIVERSIDE CT.
NEWBRIDGE
LONGLANDS VILLAS
LONGLANDS RD.
QUADDING
BIRCH ROAD
1
Stanethorpe
Road
A6
51
DEVONSHIRE
DEAN RD.
EDEN BANK
WEST BANK
Toadmoor
Newly
Long
Pitholes Plantation
Street's Rough
Lawn Farm
Longlands Wood
Rec. Grd.
Works
2
Rough Plantation
Thornyhedge Plantation
Upper Slades
Lower Slades
Shed House
Dairy Wood
Dairywood Farm
RIVER
DERWENT
Dunge Wood
3
Milnhay Farm
Gun Covert
WHITEWELLS
LANE
Elm View
White Wells Farm
Yewtree Wood
Lawn Cottage
DERBY
350
ether Nook Farm
Tappleton Wood
Star Cottage Farm
Belper
DE56
Coppice Wood
Dunge Farm
LANE
4
Broad House
ROAD
Brook
LANE
GORSES
NARROW LANE
WHITEWELLS
Rifle Range
BROADHOLME
10
Sycamore Farm
NG WALL
S
JESSES LA.
DALLEY
BELPER
Wyver Farm
Wyver Wood
WYVER
Broadholm Farm
RIVER DERWENT
5
Works
Broadholm
Handleywood Farm
Street's Wood
Belper Lane End
Lane End Farm
Lodge
49
BELPER CEMETER
Chapel Plantation
Wyver
Mount Pleasant Farm
LANE END
6
Mount Pleasant
WHITE HOUSE RISE
WHITE HOUSE RISE ROAD
GORSEY CL.
KNOWL
PINEWOOD
SPRING CL.
BRADSHAW
BROOM CL.
Scotches
THE SCOTCHES
Fish Pond
A6
CENTERY
The Dalley
OAKHURST CL.
WRENPARK AVENUE
BEECHWOOD CL.
CROFT
CL.
Pleasant
DRIVE
BELPER LA.
WYVER LA.
River Gdns.
Weirs
Boat Ho.
Visitor Cen.
Pennock
Hiron Farm
HIGH EDGE M.
Convent
Prim. Sch.
BIRCH VALE
ALLSTONE
7
Newbuildings Farm
MOUNT
SHIREOAKS
QUE
DR.
Bridgehill
LODGE
DRIVE
Belper Bridge
BRIDGE FOOT
Play. Fld.
PINGLE
ACORN
EDWARD ST.
ABBOTS DR.
48
Holly House
LA
Bungalow Farm
Dalley Farm
A517 ROAD
BRIDGE HILL
BELPER LA.
MILL
Mill VW.
Long Row Sch.
LONG ROW
ACORN
SWINNEY
Chapel House Fa
Mill Farm
Blackbrook House
Ingelton Farm
Johnson's Wood
23
ssroads Farm
Stream
Mills
Mill
Long Row
WILLIAM
GEORGE
JOSEPH ST.
SHORT ROW
FIELD ROW
CHARNWOOD AV.
Offs
35
Brook
PLAINS LANE
LANE
ASHBOURNE
Weir
34 ater Works
Football Ground
Bowling Green
Pav.
Library
THE TRIANGLE
BRIDGE
CRWN
CLISTER R.
Blackbrook

RIPLEY RD.
Ridgeway
Graves Wood
Prospect Farm
The Cottage
Brickyard Cottage
10
A
Sewage Works
Thacker Hall Farm
B
C
D
E
B6013
ROAD
Ambergate
Thacker's Wood
Ridgeway House
Pea
Ridgeway Farm
The Hollies
Gun Lane Farm
Priory Grange
Heage Hall
The Bungalow
Polzeath
Sunningdale
Glen Brae
Highclere
Valley Farm
ST. CHESTERFIELD
1
Toadmoor
Newlyn
Wynfield
Nodin Hill Farm
Heage Firs
The Firs
Heage Towermill
Windmill House
Bond Lane Farm
Longford
Heage Firs Farm
West View Farm
Four Winds
Factory
Crich View
Nether Heage
Brook Farm
Chapel Farm
Depot
The Gables Farm
ROAD
2
West Bank
Firs Farm
Dunge Wood
Heage Common Farm
Bentfield House
Bent Farm
Heage Prim. Sch.
Playing Field
Heage
Downmeadow Brook
DERBY
3
Sewerage Farm
Random Ridge
Sewage Works
Limb Farm
Pickard
Dunge Farm
Broadholme House Farm
Belper
DE56
Bessalone
West Bank Farm
B6013
Sycamore Farm
4
ROAD
9
Foreclose Farm
The Bent
Parkside Farm
5
Broadholm
Works
Lodge
BELPER CEMETERY
Swinney Wood
Grangewood Farm
Reservoir
Jackson's
Lodge Farm
Boothgate
Boothgate
Laund Farm
CHESTERFIELD ROAD
Far Laund
Brook
Morleyhill Farm
Dale Farm
6
Fish Pond
Lawn Farm
Coppice
Rookery Farm
Morley Pk.
Knob
MATLOCK
St. Johns C. of E. Prim. Sch.
White Moor
Rec. Grd.
Morrell Close Farm
7
Pennock Hiron Farm
Bowling Green
Whitemoor Hall
Morrell Wood Farm
Henmoor
A
B
24
C
Belper School
Belper Sports Cen.
D
E
ROAD
ROAD
KILBO

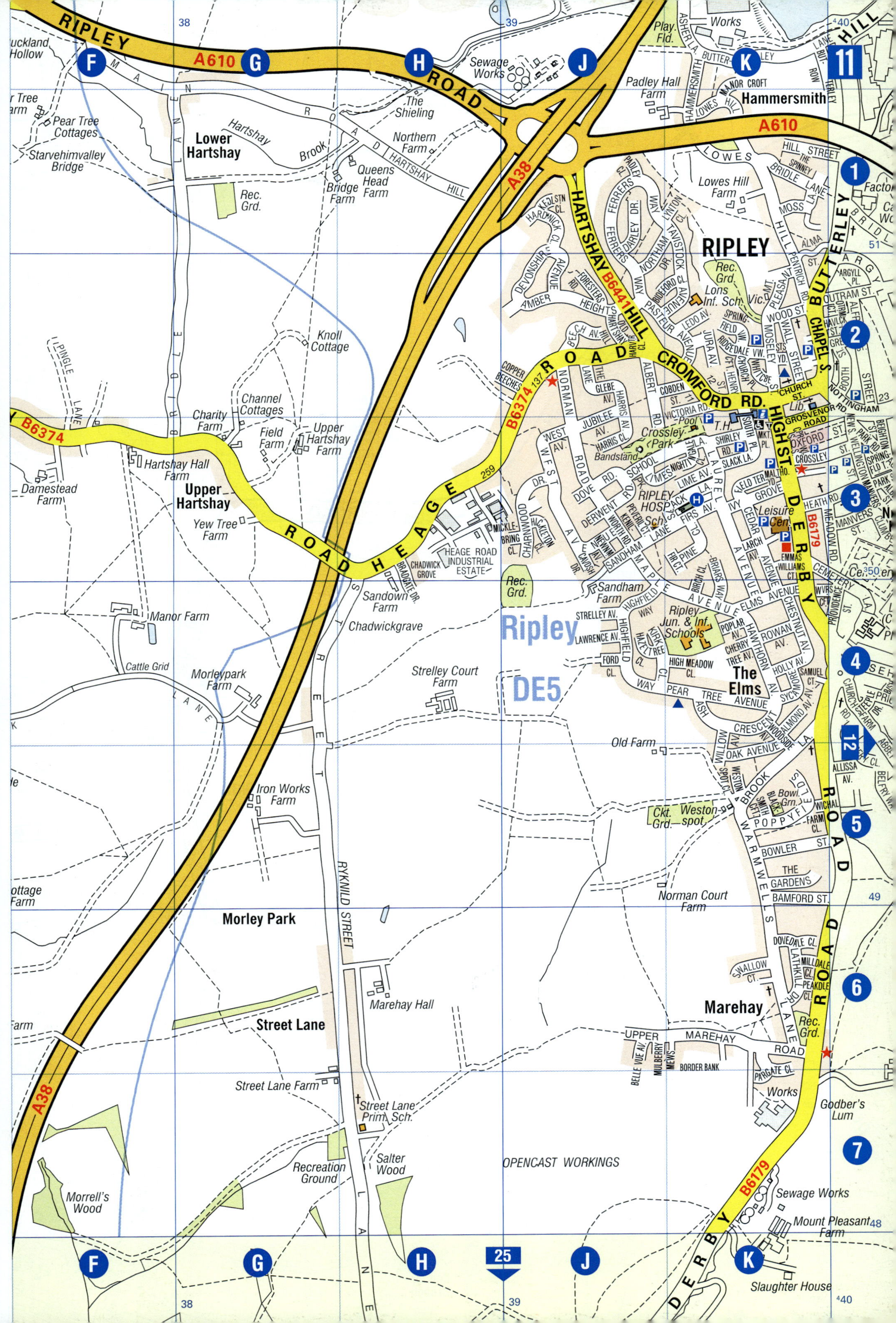

RIPLEY
A610
Buckland Hollow
Pear Tree Farm
Pear Tree Cottages
Starvehimvalley Bridge
Lower Hartshay
Hartshay Brook
The Shieling
Northern Farm
Queens Head Farm
Bridge Farm
Hartshay Hill
Sewage Works
Padley Hall Farm
Hammersmith
A610
HILL
11
Lowes
Lowes Hill Farm
RIPLEY
HILL STREET
The Spinney
Bridle Lane
Moss La.
Alma
1
51
BUTTERLEY
Factory
Argyll Pl.
Outram St.
Alfreton St.
2
Nottingham Street
Oxford
Crossley
3
B6179
Knoll Cottage
Pingle Lane
Channel Cottages
Charity Farm
Field Farm
Upper Hartshay Farm
B6374
Damestead Farm
Hartshay Hall Farm
Upper Hartshay
Yew Tree Farm
HEAGE ROAD
Copper Beeches
137
Norman Lane
The Glebe
Harris Av.
Albert
Cobden St.
West Av.
Jubilee Av.
Harris Cl.
Victoria Rd.
Crossley Park
Bandstand
Pool
T.H.
Shirley Rd.
Slack La.
Lime Av.
RIPLEY HOSP.
DOVE RD.
DERWENT
Aurel
259
CROMFORD RD.
Church St.
Chapel St.
Grosvenor Road
Meadow Rd.
Cemetery
Manvers St.
Mickle Bring
Charnwood
Hicketon
CL.
Heage Road Industrial Estate
Chadwick Grove
Sandown Farm
Chadwickgrave
Rec. Grd.
Sandham Farm
Strelley Av.
Lawrence Av.
Highfield Way
Kirk Cl.
Ford Cl.
Way
Pear Tree Av.
Ash
Ripley Jun. & Inf. Schools
High Meadow Cl.
Poplar Av.
Cherry Tree Av.
Hawthorn Av.
Rowan Av.
Holly Av.
Chestnut Av.
Samuel Ct.
Sycamore
The Elms Avenue
Crescent
Willow
Oak Avenue
Weston
Spot
Brook
Salmond Av.
Woodside La.
Allissa Av.
12
Belfry Way
DERBY ROAD
4
5
Ripley DE5
Manor Farm
Cattle Grid
Morleypark Farm
Iron Works Farm
RYKNILD STREET
Old Farm
Weston spot
Ckt. Grd.
Norman Court Farm
Black Smith Cl.
Poppyfields
Bowl. Grn.
Michael Farm Cl.
Bowler St.
The Gardens
Bamford St.
Warmwells
49
Dovedale Cl.
Lathkill Cl.
Peakdale Cl.
Milldale Cl.
Swallow Ct.
6
Morley Park
Cottage Farm
Farm
Street Lane
Marehay Hall
Street Lane Farm
Street Lane Prim. Sch.
Recreation Ground
Salter Wood
Marehay
Upper Marehay Road
Belle Vue Av.
Mulberry Mews
Border Bank
Pargate Cl.
Works
Godber's Lum
7
B6179
Sewage Works
Mount Pleasant Farm
48
DERBY ROAD
A38
Morrell's Wood
OPENCAST WORKINGS
Slaughter House
A38
440
F
G
H
25
J
K
38
39
440

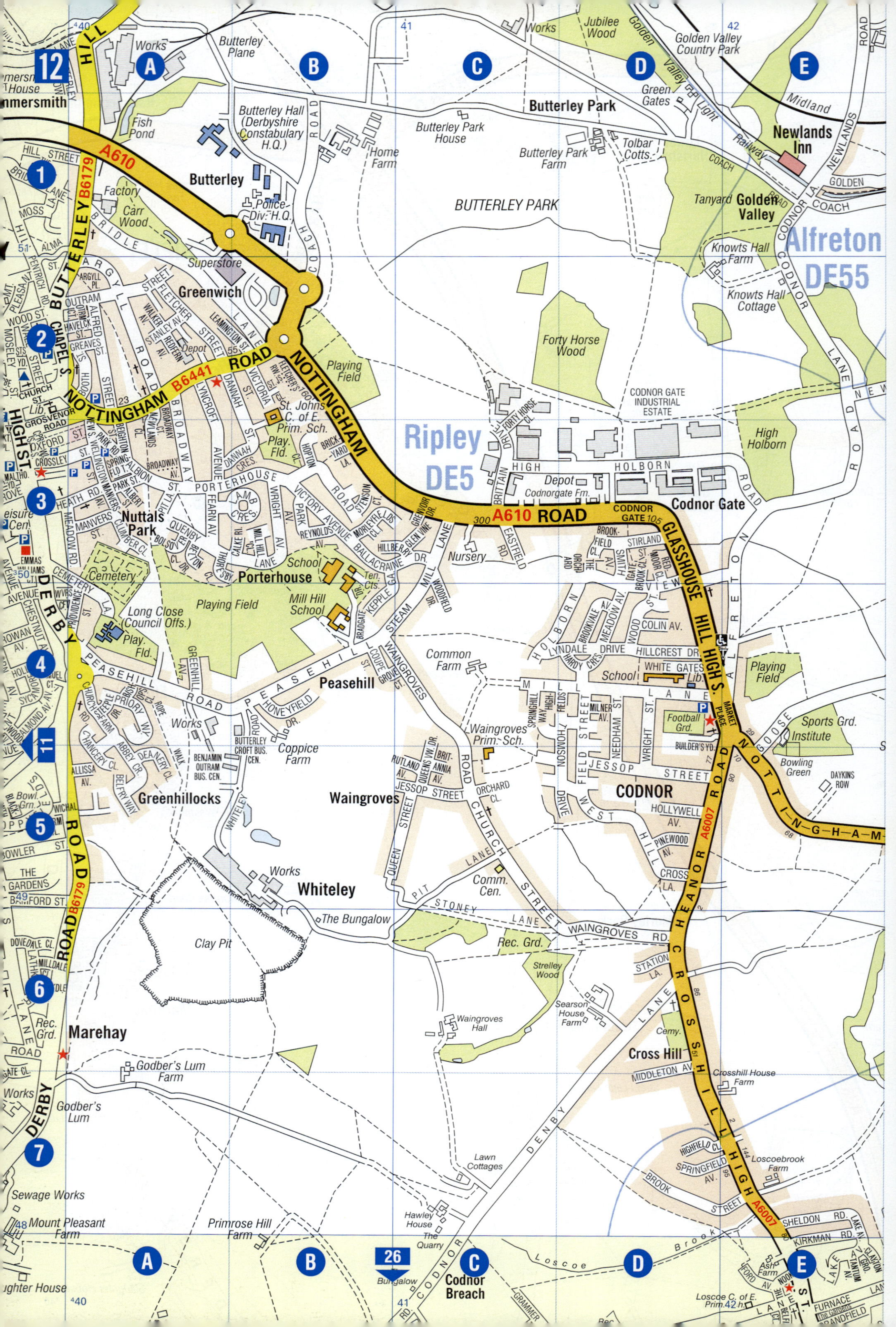
12
Hammersmith
House
Hammersmith
HILL
A610
B6179
Works
A
Butterley
Plane
B
Works
C
Jubilee
Wood
Golden
Valley
Light
Golden Valley
Country Park
D
Midland
E
42
ROAD
Butterley Park
Green
Gates
Tolbar
Cotts.
Newlands
Inn
Railway
Butterley Hall
(Derbyshire Constabulary H.Q.)
Home
Farm
Butterley Park
House
Butterley Park
Farm
COACH
GOLDEN
COACH LA.
Fish
Pond
Butterley
Factory
Carr
Wood
Police
Div. H.Q.
BUTTERLEY PARK
Tanyard
Golden
Valley
Alfreton
DE55
Superstore
Greenwich
ROAD
COACH LANE
Knowts Hall
Farm
Knowts Hall
Cottage
NOTTINGHAM
B6441
ROAD
Depot
St. Johns
C. of E.
Prim. Sch.
Play.
Fld.
BROADWAY
Playing
Field
Forty Horse
Wood
Ripley
DE5
FORTY HORSE CL.
CODNOR GATE
INDUSTRIAL
ESTATE
High
Holborn
CHAPEL ST.
HIGH ST.
CHURCH ST.
Lib.
ROAD
Nuttals
Park
BROADWAY
Cemetery
Porterhouse
Mill Hill
School
VICTORY AVENUE
WRIGHT AV.
School
Ten.
Cts.
NOTTINGHAM ROAD
STENSON
MILL HILL LA.
WOODFIELD DR.
STEAM LANE
Nursery
BRITTAIN DR.
HIGH
HOLBORN
Depot
Codnorgate Fm.
A610 ROAD
CODNOR
GATE 105
Codnor Gate
EASTFIELD RD.
ALFRETON
ROAD
MANVERS RD.
MEADOW RD.
DERBY ROAD
PEASEHILL ROAD
Playing Field
Long Close
(Council Offs.)
Play.
Fld.
Greenhill
Av.
HONEYFIELD DR.
Peasehill
Common
Farm
HOLBORN
VIEW
LYNDALE AV.
BROOKVALE AV.
MEADOW AV.
COLIN AV.
HILLCREST DR.
HARDY CRES.
School
Lib.
GLASSHOUSE HILL HIGH S.
WHITE GATES
Playing
Field
PEASEHILL
ROAD
Works
Butterley
Croft Bus.
Cen.
Benjamin
Outram
Bus. Cen.
Coppice
Farm
WAINGROVES
Waingroves
Prim. Sch.
RUTLAND AV.
QUEENS VW. DR.
BRIT-
ANNIA
AV.
SPRINGHILL
WAY
HIGH-
FIELDS
THOMSON RD.
MILNER
AV.
NEEDHAM ST.
WRIGHT ST.
Football
Grd.
Builder's Yd.
MARKET
PLACE
NOTTINGHAM ROAD
Sports Grd.
Institute
Bowling
Green
DAYKINS
ROW
Greenhillocks
CHANCERY CL.
DEANERY CL.
BELFRIWAY
ALLISSA AV.
PRIORY WY.
WHITELEY
Waingroves
JESSOP STREET
QUEEN STREET
ORCHARD
CL.
ROAD
CHURCH LANE
WEST
FIELD
DRIVE
JESSOP
STREET
CODNOR
HOLLYWELL
AV.
PINEWOOD
AV.
CROSS
HILL
HEANOR ROAD
A6007
NOTTING-H-A-M
Works
Whiteley
The Bungalow
Clay Pit
QUEEN STREET
PIT LANE
STONEY
LANE
Comm.
Cen.
WAINGROVES RD.
Rec. Grd.
Strelley
Wood
STATION
LA.
CROSSHILL ROAD
Cross Hill
Crosshill House
Farm
B6179 ROAD
DOVEDALE CL.
MILLDALE
Marehay
Godber's
Lum
Godber's Lum
Farm
DENBY
Waingroves
Hall
Searson
House
Farm
Cemy.
MIDDLETON AV.
HIGHFIELD CL.
SPRINGFIELD
AV.
Loscoebrook
Farm
DERBY ROAD
Rec.
Grd.
Works
Sewage Works
Mount Pleasant
Farm
Primrose Hill
Farm
26
Bungalow
Codnor
Breach
Hawley
House
The
Quarry
CODNOR
Loscoe
DENBY
BROOK
Lawn
Cottages
CROSS HILL HIGH STREET
A6007
SHELDON RD.
KIRKMAN RD.
Ash
Farm
Furnace
Loscoe C. of E.
Prim. Sch.
A
B
C
D
E
440
41
42

Newlands Farm
Ironville
Centre
Railway
VALLEY ROAD
Codnorpark Reservoir
Codnor Park
MARKET ST.
MARKET PL.
CINDER BANK
Weir
PARKSIDE
PARKSIDE CL.
ARTHURS
VICARAGE
PIPERS CT.
JESSOP AV.
NEW ROAD
RES. (Cov.)
THE PARK
MONUMENT LA.
KESTREL HEIGHTS
MONUMENT
CHEVIOT AV.
CASTLE FIELDS
FORGE ROW
THOMAS CL.
BENJAMIN CT.
LANE
STATION
STONE BR.
OLD BR.
PYE HILL RD.
Wks.
Liby.
SELSTON ROAD
Jacksdale
WAGSTAFF LA.
ALBERT AV.
HAMP SHIRE CT.
YORK AV.
RUTLAND CT.
DIXIE ST.
KENT AV.
MAIN ROAD
War Mem.
SEDGWICK
WESTMORLAND
THE ORCHARDS
CHESHIRE WY. CL.
BRINSLEY ROAD
Nursery
Westwood Farm
Jacksdale Prim. Sch.
CHURCH HILL
ST. MARY'S WK.
Rec. Grd.
Pav.
Cromford Canal (Disused)
ASHFIELD BROXTOWE
AMBER VALLEY
Bagthorpe Brook
Monument Grounds
Jessop's Monument
Wallis's Gorse
Exhibition Plantation
(LONG LANE)
ROAD
MONUMENT
CASTLE
CASTLEHILL
Waterworks Plantation
Kennels Farm
Foxhole Plantation
Codnor Park South Sidings
Castle Plantation
Codnor Castle (Remains)
Castle Farm
Nottingham
NG16
Ormonde Fields
Long Wood
The Spinney
LANE
CASTLE
DRIVE
Corfield Plantation
ORMONDE FIELDS
GOLF COURSE
Club House
Stoneyford Farm
Lower Stoneyford Farm
Stoneyford
Stoneyford
LANE
BOAT
ALDERCAR
RIVER EREWASH
Crowfield
A610
ROAD
CROMFORD
LODGE LANE
LANE
Benty Fields
Woodlinkin
Woodlinkin House
Crow Wood
Park Farm
Aldercar Hall
Toll House
Heanor
DE75
HOGGBARN LANE
Hoggbarn Farm
Bell House
Quarry Houses
ROAD
LANGLEY
MILL
A610
BY-PASS
Loscoe Dam
Playing Fields
Aldercar Inf. Sch.
Aldercar School
CROMFORD
Aldercar
ORMONDE ROAD
DALTONS CL.
TARN CL.
ORMONDE TER.
OAK AV.
PLUMPTRE RD.
Caravan Park
HALL ROAD
Tennis Courts

14
A   B   C   D   E
1
2
3
4
5
6
7
13
28
HAMP-
SHIRE CT.
KENTAV
Prim. Sch.
MORLAND
RUTLAND
DERBYSHIRE AV.
SHROPSHIRE
CHESHIRE WY.
CORNWALL
PALMERSTON STREET
RD.
Westwood
Inf. Sch.
WESTWOOD
GARDENS
Westwood
Bents
Westwood
HILL LA.
BARRONS
FLATTS LANE
Brook
Nursery
Bagthorpe Lane
Yewtree
Farm
Westwood
Farm
Nursery
MAIN
WILHALLOW LANE
WANSLEY LANE
Wansley Hall
Farm
Wansley
Hall
Kill
Dogs
Manor
Farm
Manor Cottage
White
Cottage
Mexborough
House
LANE   LOWER
Bagthorpe
Brookside
Farm
BAGTHORPE
SCHOOL
Football
Grd.
Parsonage
Bagthorpe
Prim. Sch.
Play
Fld.
CHURCH
Bagthorpe
Common
Social
Cen.
Rec.
Grd.
OLD CHAPEL LANE
HANKIN AV.
DESMOND CT.
ROAD
DE MORGAN CL.
ASHBOURNE RD.
WESTBOURNE
SMEATH ROAD
PALMERSTON STREET
SHARRARD CL.
SMALLEY CL.
Pav.
Cricket Grd.
WHEELER GATE
FAIRVIEW AVENUE
BELL CL.
BLUE BELL
PRIM.
RISE
MAIN
Underwood
Hill Farm
Underwood
Hill
Poole
Farm
Rec. Grd.
Underwood
Green
Hill
Farm
ROAD
PLAINSPOT LANE
HINSLEY
Cornfield
Rise
Brook
MAIN
51  50
49
Plain Spot
Farm
Plain
Spot
Underwood C. of E.
Prim. Sch.
WINTER CLOSES
WILLOW CT.
Wilcox Dr.
MANSIDE CRES.
FELLE
ALFRETON LANE
A608
ROAD
Willeylane
End
Willeylane
Plantation
Pollington
House
FRANCES
ST.
Cherry Tree
Farm
HIGH ST.
ST. JOHN'S CL.
CLUMBER AV.
New
Brinsley
Oaktree
Farm
RED
LANE
Works
Depot
NG16
CORDY LANE
A608
B600
WILLEY
Hunt's Hill
Main St.
CLUMBER ROAD
WINDSMOOR
WHITEHEAD DR.
HOBSIC CLOSE
ASH GRO.
BROAD OAK DRIVE
ST. JAMES CL.
CHERRY APPLE
CHERRY TREE CL.
Hobsic
Gin
Farm
Gin
House
Allandale
Farm
Gin House
Brinsley Gin
Sewage
Pumping
Station
LAWRENCE DR.
Wks.
The Moor
Brinsley
Prim. Sch.
MOOR ROAD
GLADSTONE DR.
BRYNSMOOR RD.
QUEENS DR.
KINGS DR.
Rec.
Grd.
Bowl. Grn.
Tennis Ct.
Football
Ground
Saints
Coppice
Farm
Saints
Coppice
Willey Wood
Farm
Hunt's Hill
Cottages
Hall Farm
HALL LANE
WALK
CLINTON AV.
WALTERS AV.
CHURCH WALK
Pear Tree
Farm
Timber
Yard
Brinsley
CHURCH LANE
Manor
Farm
STONEY LANE
New Farm
EREWASH
RIVER
Hall Farm
Coneygrey
Plantation
Coneygrey
Farm
Grange Fields
Farm Cottage
Weir
A608   MANSFIELD ROAD
Brinsley Brook
Nether
Green
COCKERHO
Lodge
Caravan
Park
PLUMPTRE RD.
BROMFD. CL.
LANGLEY   A610   MILL
BY-PASS
HALL   ROAD
STONEY LANE FORD
45   46   47

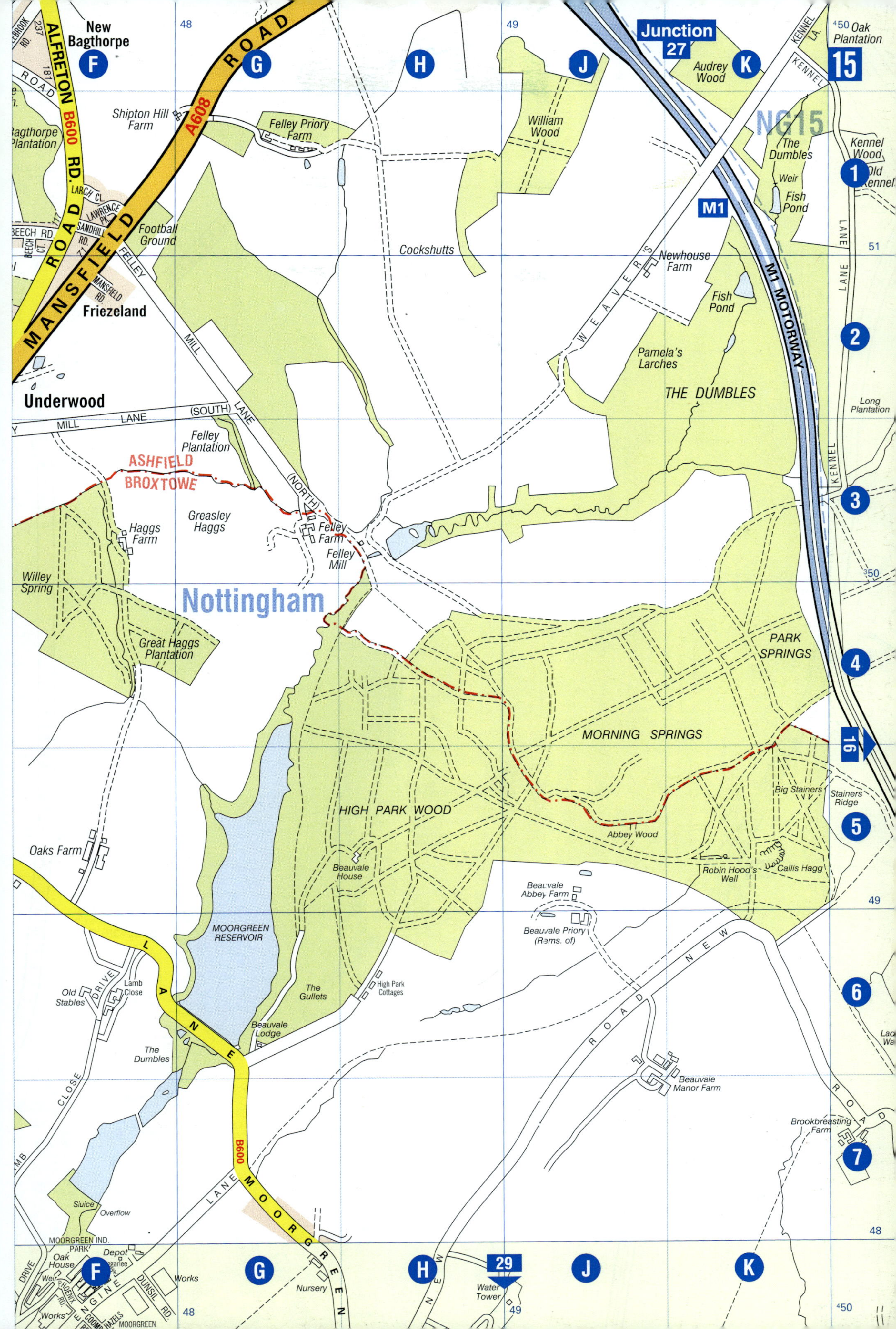
New Bagthorpe
F
G
H
J
Junction 27
K
Oak Plantation
15
ALFRETON ROAD
B600
237
187
Bagthorpe Plantation
ROAD
A608 ROAD
Shipton Hill Farm
Felley Priory Farm
William Wood
Audrey Wood
NG15
Kennel Wood
The Dumbles
Old Kennel
1
LARCH CL.
LAWRENCE PK.
SANDHILL RD.
BEECH RD.
CT.
71
MANSFIELD RD.
MANSFIELD ROAD
FELLEY
Football Ground
MILL
M1
Newhouse Farm
Fish Pond
KENNEL LA.
KENNEL LANE
51
Friezeland
Cockshutts
WEAVERS
Fish Pond
2
Underwood
MILL LANE (SOUTH) LANE
Pamela's Larches
THE DUMBLES
Long Plantation
Felley Plantation
ASHFIELD
BROXTOWE
(NORTH)
KENNEL
3
Greasley Haggs
Felley Farm
Felley Mill
350
Haggs Farm
Willey Spring
Nottingham
PARK SPRINGS
4
Great Haggs Plantation
MORNING SPRINGS
16
Big Stainers
Stainers Ridge
HIGH PARK WOOD
Abbey Wood
Robin Hood's Well
Callis Hagg
5
Oaks Farm
Beauvale House
Beauvale Abbey Farm
49
MOORGREEN RESERVOIR
Beauvale Priory (Rems. of)
NEW
LANE DRIVE
Old Stables
Lamb Close
The Gullets
High Park Cottages
ROAD
6
CLOSE
The Dumbles
Beauvale Lodge
Beauvale Manor Farm
Lady Wa
B600
Sluice
Overflow
Brookbreasting Farm
ROAD
7
MOORGREEN IND. PARK
Oak House
Depot
LANE
MOORGREEN
DUNSIL RD.
HAZELS
Works
Nursery
NEW
Water Tower
29
ROAD
48
F
G
H
J
K
48
49
450

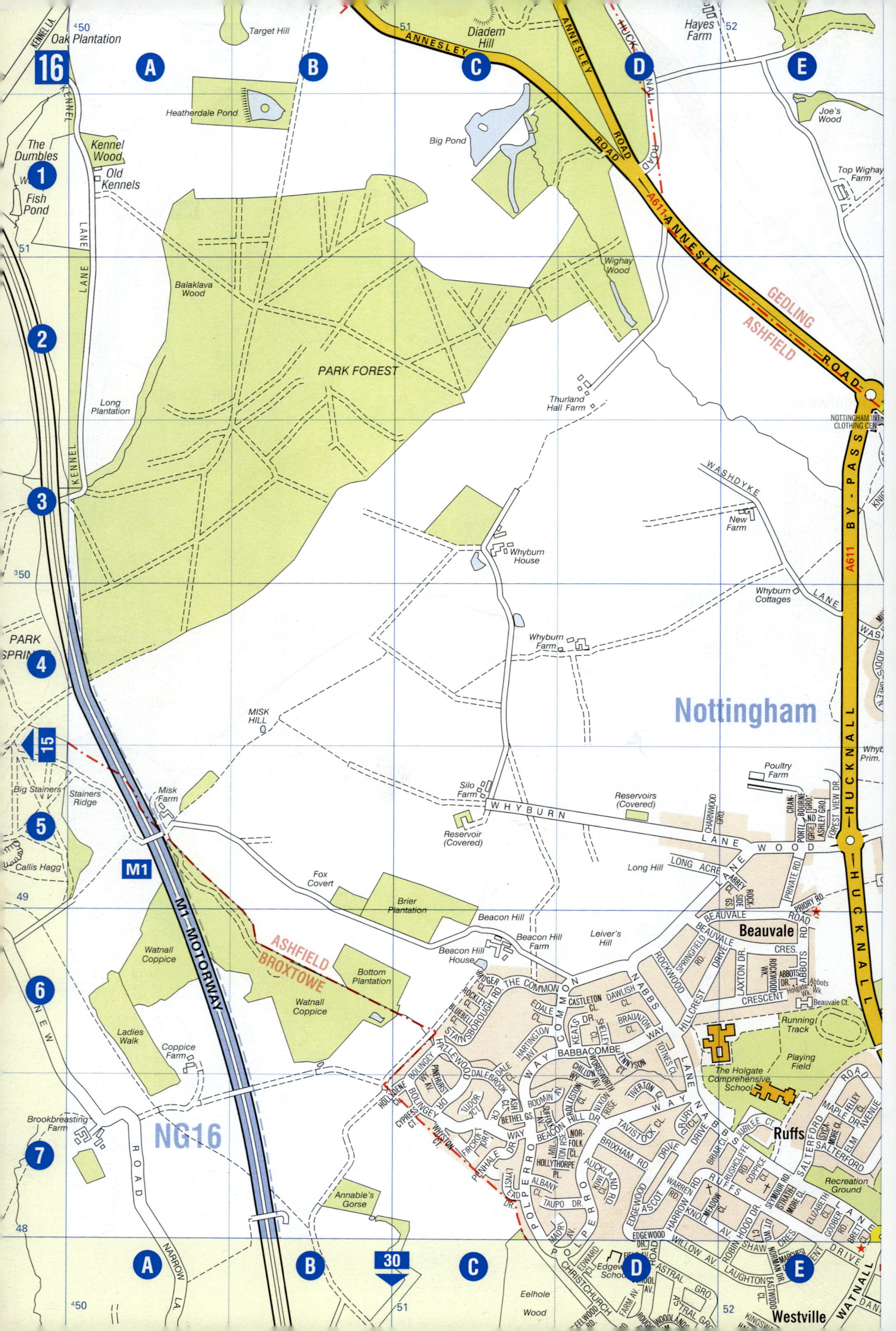

16
Oak Plantation
Target Hill
Diadem Hill
Hayes Farm
Kennel Wood
Heatherdale Pond
Big Pond
Joe's Wood
The Dumbles
Kennel Wood
Old Kennels
Top Wighay Farm
Fish Pond
Kennel Lane
Balaklava Wood
Wighay Wood
Long Plantation
PARK FOREST
Thurland Hall Farm
Nottingham Int Clothing Cen
WASHDYKE
New Farm
Kennel Lane
Whyburn House
Whyburn Cottages
PARK SPRING
Whyburn Farm
Whyburn Lane
MISK HILL
Nottingham
15
Whyb Prim.
Big Stainers
Stainers Ridge
Misk Farm
Silo Farm
Reservoirs (Covered)
Poultry Farm
Reservoir (Covered)
WHYBURN
CHARNWOOD GRO.
CRAN-
PORT-
END
BOURNE GRO.
GREE
ASHLEY GRO.
Callis Hagg
M1
Long Hill
LANE WOOD
Long Hill
LONG ACRE
ABBEY CL.
PRIVATE RD.
FOREST VIEW DR.
Fox Covert
Brier Plantation
Beacon Hill
Beacon Hill Farm
Leiver's Hill
BEAUVALE
ROCKWOOD
SPRINGFIELD RD.
BEAUVALE
PRIORY RD.
Beauvale
ABBEY CL.
ROCK SIDE
BEAUVALE DRIVE
ROCKWOOD WK.
ABBOTS DR.
ABBOTS
CRES.
M1-MOTORWAY
ASHFIELD
BROXTOWE
Watnall Coppice
Bottom Plantation
Beacon Hill House
BADGER RD.
THE COMMON
CASTLETON CL.
DAWLISH CL.
NABBS
HILLCREST
LAXTON DR.
CRESCENT
Beauvale Ct.
Running Track
Watnall Coppice
ROCKLEY
EDALE
CL.
KEALS DR.
SKELLEY CL.
BRAUNTON CL.
WAY
NABBS LANE
Playing Field
NEW
Ladies Walk
Coppice Farm
BLUEBELL CL.
STAINSBOROUGH RD.
HARTINGTON AV.
BABBACOMBE
CHILLON AV.
CONISBOROUGH AV.
TENNYSON
TIVERTON CL.
BURY DRIVE
The Holgate Comprehensive School
NG16
HALLEWOOD DR.
BOLINGEY DR.
PINEHURST
DALEBROOK
DALE CL.
BODMIN AV.
ASH CR.
ROLLISTON DR.
NIXON RISE
COMMON WAY
TAVISTOCK CL.
BRIARCL.
RUSHCLIFFE
MAPLE DR.
AVENUE
Ruffs
Brookbreasting Farm
CYPRESS CT.
WHISTON CT.
TUDOR CT.
FIRCROFT CL.
BETHEL GS.
BEACON CL.
NORFOLK CL.
BRIXHAM RD.
AUCKLAND CL.
EDGEWOOD DRIVE
ASCOT
WARREN RD.
RUFFS DR.
COPPICE CL.
ELM CL.
SALTERFORD
SALTERFORD RD.
ROAD
PENHALE DR.
HOLLYTHORPE PL.
ALBANY CL.
TAUPO DR.
HARROW KNOLL
MEADOW CL.
EDGEWOOD DR.
WILLOW AV.
ROBIN HOOD DR.
SEYMOUR RD.
Recreation Ground
Annable's Gorse
POLPERRO
MAORI DR.
LISNA DR.
EDWARD AV.
CHRISTCHURCH
Edgewood School
ASTRAL GRO.
LAUGHTON AV.
NARROW LA.
ROAD
Eelhole Wood
FARM AV.
Westville
WATNALL
A611-ANNESLEY
ANNESLEY ROAD
HUCKNALL
HUCKNALL ROAD
GEDLING
ASHFIELD
A611 BY-PASS
ANNESLEY ROAD
HUCKNALL

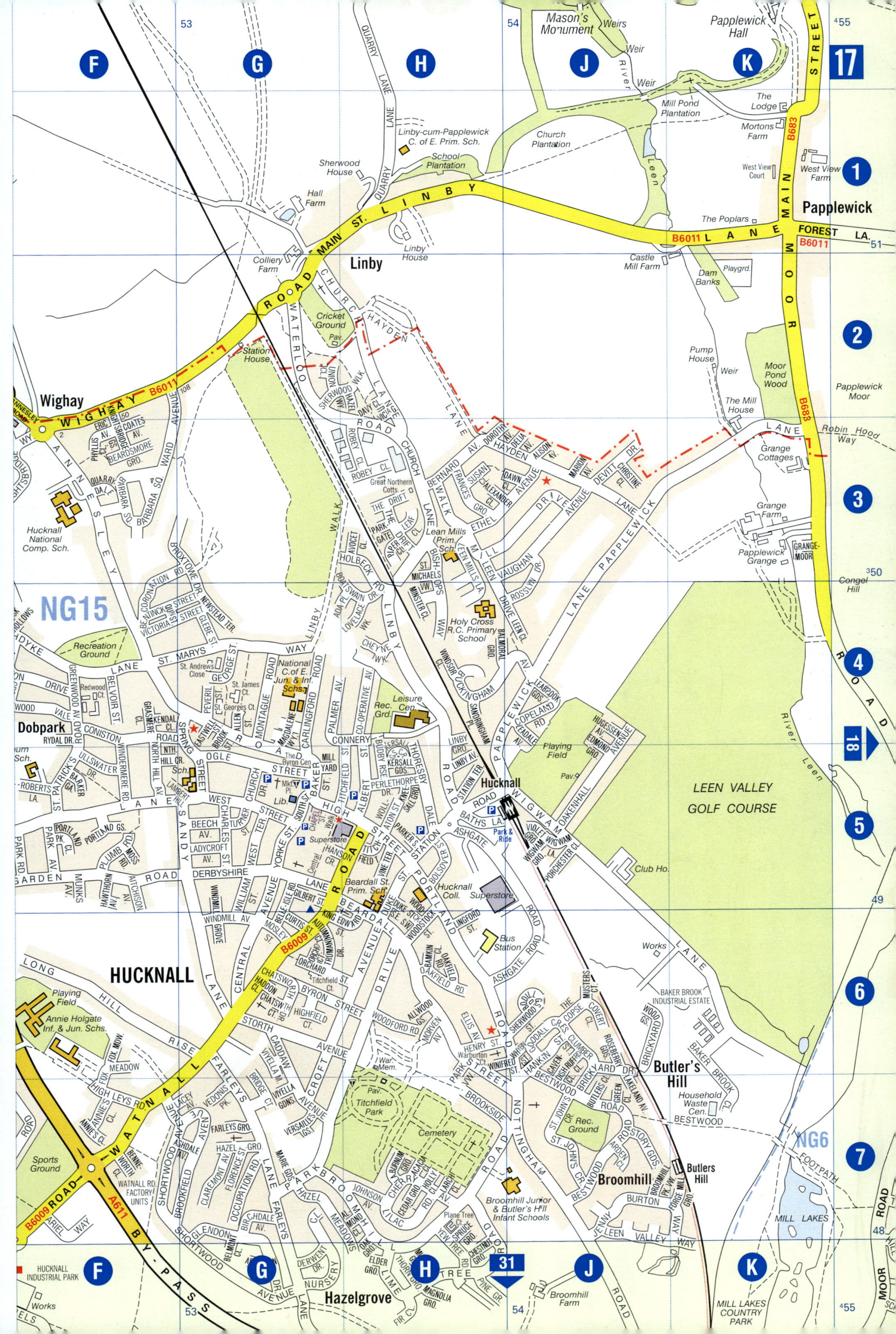

F G H J K 17
455
Mason's Monument
Weirs
Papplewick Hall
STREET
Weir
Weir
The Lodge
Mortons Farm
B683
MAIN
Linby-cum-Papplewick C. of E. Prim. Sch.
Sherwood House
School Plantation
Church Plantation
West View Court
West View Farm
1
Hall Farm
River Leen
The Poplars
Papplewick
MAIN ST. LINBY
ROAD
Colliery Farm
Linby
Linby House
B6011 LANE
FOREST LA.
51
Castle Mill Farm
MOOR
B6011
Dam Banks
Playgrd.
2
WATERLOO
Cricket Ground
Pav.
HAYDEN LANE
CHURCH
Pump House
Weir
Moor Pond Wood
B683
Papplewick Moor
Wighay
Station House
B6011 108
WIGHAY
ANNESLEY WY
ROAD
SHERWOOD
HAZEL
DAW
GRANGE
ROAD
ROBEY CL.
ROBEY CL.
LANGE
BEWALK
CHURCH WALK
DOROTHY AV.
DELIA AV.
HAYDEN
AUSON DR.
MARION AV.
DEVITT CL.
CHRISTINE CL.
LANE
Robin Hood Way
Grange Cottages
ERIC AV.
PHYLLIS AV.
BRIDGE CL.
COATES AV.
BEARDSMORE GRO.
QUARRY DALE
BARBARA SQ.
WARD
AVENUE
Great Northern Cotts.
THE DRIFT
PARK GATE
RIVER DRIFT
LEAF CL.
BERNARD AV.
FRANCES GRO.
SUSAN AV.
ETHEL AV.
DAWN AV.
ALEXANDER GRO.
DRIVE
MILL
AVENUE
PAPPLEWICK
DEVITT
ROSSLYN DR.
Grange Farm
Grange Moor
3
350
Hucknall National Comp. Sch.
SLEY
QUARRY DALE
BROXTOWE RD.
HOLBECK
ADA PL.
BOATSWAIN DR.
LOVELACE WK.
LINBY
Lean Mills (Prim. Sch.)
ST. MICHAELS
VW.
Holy Cross R.C. Primary School
Papplewick Grange
Congel Hill
NG15
WILLOWS
DYKE
GREENWOOD AV.
Recreation Ground
Redwood Ct.
BELVOIR ST.
REINCK STREET
VICTORIA STREET
NEWSTEAD TER.
GLEBE ST.
ST. MARYS
St. Andrews Close
National C. of E. Jun. & Inf. Schs.
GEORGE ST.
St. James Ct.
ST. GEORGES CT.
WAY
MONTAGUE
CARLINGFORD ROAD
PALMER AV.
CO-OPERATIVE AV.
CHEYNE WK.
WINDSOR JKINGHAM
BUCKINGHAM
SANDRINGHAM
BALMORAL GRO.
LEAP DOK GDS.
COPELAND
CADLE
HUGESSEN AV.
EDMOND GRO.
AVENUE
4
DRIVE
WOOD
VALE
GRASMERE
KENDAL CL.
PEVERIL
ALLEN ST.
MAGDALENE WY
Rec. Grd.
Leisure Cen.
PAPPLEWICK
Playing Field
Pav.
River Leen
LEEN VALLEY GOLF COURSE
18
Dobpark
RYDAL DR.
CONISTON
NTH.
NORTH HILL AV.
OGLE STREET
BROOK ST.
ST.
MILL YARD
MkV
KERSALL RSE.
PERLETHORPE DR.
BUDBY RSE.
THORESBY
LINBY GRO.
STATION TER.
Hucknall
ULLSWATER
ST. PATRICK'S GA.
WINDERMERE RD.
SCH.
LAMBERT ST.
CHURCH
MkV
Lib.
BAKER ST.
TITCHFIELD
ALBERT ST.
DALE
Pav.
Club Ho.
5
ROBERTS AV.
LA.
PORTLAND
PARK PK. CL.
PORTLAND CL.
PLUMB RD.
MOSS CL.
AITCHISON AV.
WEST CHARLES STREET
SANDY
LANE
BEECH AV.
LADYCROFT AV.
YORKE ST.
SOUTH ST.
CHAPEL
HIGH
STREET
Superstore
HANSON CR.
Central
PARKER S.
Hucknall
BATHS LA.
WIGWAM
VIOLET WIGWAM GRO.
OAKENHALL
PORCHESTER CL.
Works
49
GARDEN
HAWTHORN AV.
MUNKS AV.
DERBYSHIRE
WILLIAM AVENUE
BELLE ISLE R.
GILBERT ST.
Beardall Prim. Sch.
DUKE ST.
DUKE ST SW
WOODSTOCK
LINGFORD
ASHGATE
WOLL
BOLSOVER
Hucknall Coll.
Superstore
ASHGATE ROAD
LANE
Baker Brook Industrial Estate
BRICKYARD
6
LONG HILL
Playing Field
Annie Holgate Inf. & Jun. Schs.
WATNALL
RISE
FARLEYS
CADDAW AV.
MOSLEY ST.
CURTIS ST.
KING EDW AVENUE
AUTUMN VIEW
DRIVE
BAMKIN
OAKFIELD RD.
Bus Station
ASHGATE ROAD
MUSTERS CT.
COVERT
ROSEBERY GDS.
CLUMBER DR.
CRES
WOOD GS.
Household Waste Cen.
BESTWOOD
Butler's Hill
NG6
HIGH LEYS CL.
FOX MDW.
MEADOW
CENTRAL
CHATSWH
HADDON CL.
CHATSWTH
HIGHFIELD CT.
BYRON STREET
STORTH AVENUE
VIVELLA AV.
BRIDGE
VERSAILLES GS.
WOODFORD RD.
MORVEN
ELLIS AV.
HENRY ST.
Warburton
WINIFRED ST.
SHERWOOD
HANK
ASEN
BESTWOOD RD.
RYE
ST. JOHN'S CR.
BESTWOOD ROAD
ARDEN GDS.
Household Waste Cen.
BESTWOOD
Butlers Hill
7
Sports Ground
ANNIE'S CL.
BONN
WORTH
WATNALL RD. FACTORY UNITS
B6009 ROAD
A611 BY-PASS
ARIEL WAY
SHORTWOOD
BROOKFIELD
CLAREMONT AV.
FLORENCE ST.
OCCUPATION RD.
BIRCHDALE AV.
HAZEL FARLEYS GRO.
HAZEL
Pav.
Titchfield Park
Cemetery
BURNUM
CHERR
ACACIA
HOLLY
LARCH
Plane Tree Ct.
SPRUCE
BROOKSIDE
NOTTINGHAM
ST. JOHN'S
St. John's Rec. Ground
JENNY BURTON
Broomhill
LEEN VALLEY WAY
MILL LAKES
48
455
HUCKNALL INDUSTRIAL PARK
Works
F
HAZELGROVE
53
GLENDON DR.
BELMONT
DERWENT DR.
NURSERY
AVENUE
G
THORNBO RD.
LIME
ELDER GRO.
MAGNOLIA
FGR CL.
PINE GR
H
31
Broomhill Junior & Butler's Hill Infant Schools
War Mem.
J
Broomhill Farm
ROAD
MILL LAKES COUNTRY PARK
K
MOOR ROAD
54
455

18
55
56
57
A
B
C
D
E
King Edward's Plantation
MANSFIELD
New Plantation
NG15
63
1
View Farm
Papplewick
Vincent Plantation
The Woodlands
Vincent Lodge
A60
MAIN STREET
FOREST
Barracks Farm Cottage
Keeper's Cottage
Seven Mile Wood
B6011 LANE
Warren Plantation
Forest Lodge
51
MOOR
Moor Pond Wood
Seven Mile Wood
ROAD
MANSF
BURNTSTUM
SHERWOOD LODGE
2
Way
Seven Mile Plantation
Papplewick Moor
Robin Hood
Stanker Hill Farm
Seven Mile House
North Lodge
LANE
range Cottages
Sherwood Police H
GEDLING
ASHFIELD
The Bungalow
3
range Farm
wick ge
GRANGE-MOOR
South Lodge
50
Congel Hill
Nottingham
4
B683 ROAD
The Duck Ponds
Duke Cotta
River Leen
17
Raceground Hill
Sports Ground
Round Hill Plantation
Pav.
5
Goosedale Farm
Weir
International Model Centre
GOOSEDALE
Sunnyside Poultry Farm
49
Gordon's Farm
NG6
Two Acres
Twelve Acre Farm
LANE
6
Six Ways Pig Farm
SQUARES
AVENUE
Cobbler's Hill Farm
Hundred Acres Farm
Coronation Strip
CHAPMANS WK
DRIVE
SUNRISE
KNIGHTWOOD
Mushroom Farm
CRIMEA PLANTATION
7
Westhouse Farm
Keepers Cottages
BESTWOOD FOOTPATH
B683
THE SPINNEY
MILL LAKES
48
Bestwood Village
LAMINS
MOOR HILL RD.
CORONATION RD.
School
KEEPERS CL.
YEOMANS CL.
BROAD VALLEY
BEESON
Broad Valley Farm
The Old Rectory
LAMINS LANE
A
B
32
C
D
E
The Mount
SCHOOL WLK.
MAYF
HERN
55
56
57
Railway View Farm

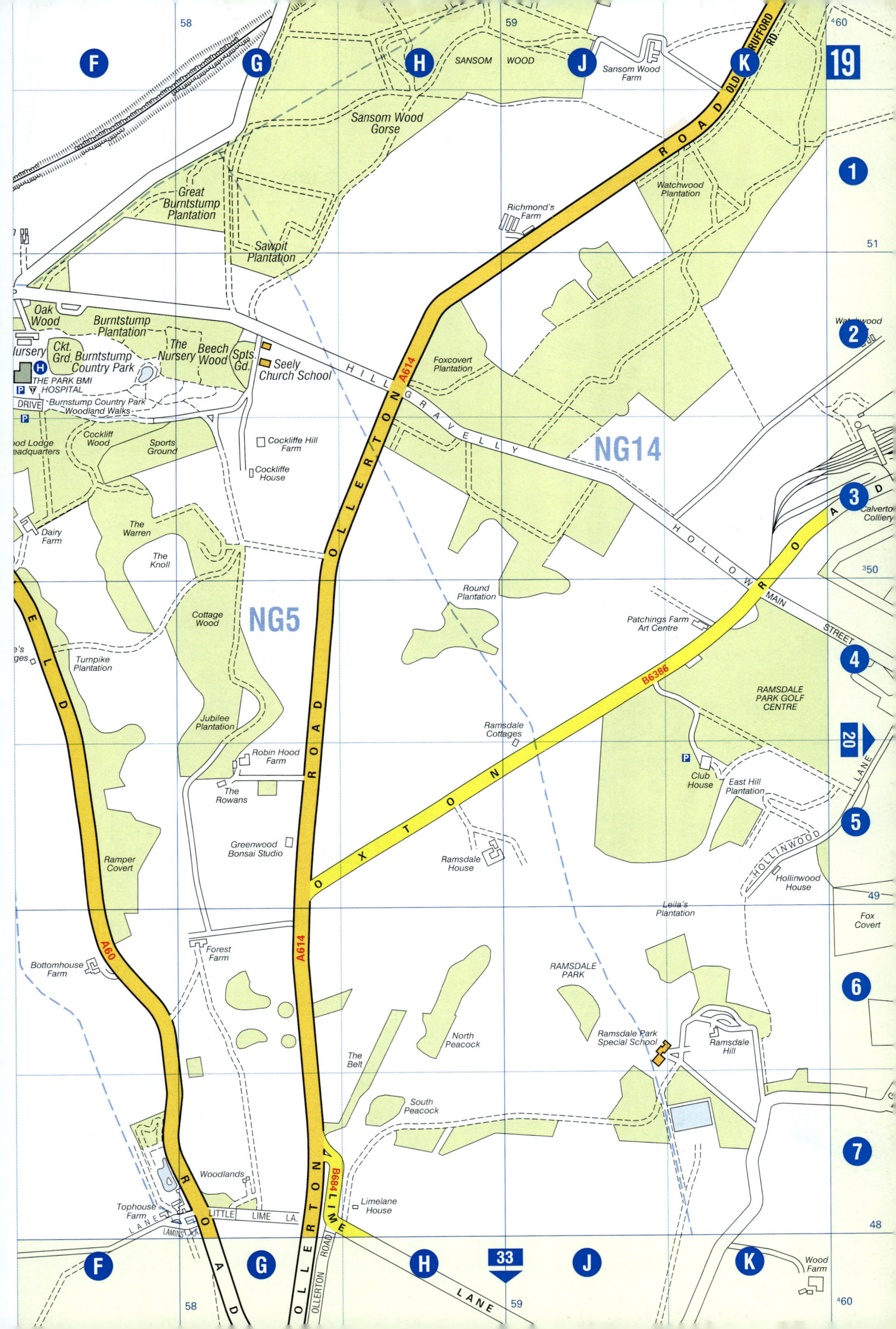

58
59
460
19
1
51
F
G
H
J
K
RUFFORD RD.
OLD
SANSOM WOOD
Sansom Wood Farm
ROAD
Sansom Wood Gorse
Richmond's Farm
Watchwood Plantation
Watchwood
2
Great Burntstump Plantation
Sawpit Plantation
Oak Wood
Burntstump Plantation
Ckt. Grd. Burntstump Country Park
The Nursery
Beech Wood
Spts. Gd.
Seely Church School
HILL GRAVELLY
A614
Foxcovert Plantation
NG14
Nursery
H
THE PARK BMI HOSPITAL
P
Burntstump Country Park Woodland Walks
DRIVE
P
OLLERTON
Cockliffe Hill Farm
Cockliffe House
HOLLOW ROAD
CALVERTO
3
Calverton Colliery
350
Cockliff Wood
od Lodge eadquarters
Sports Ground
Dairy Farm
The Warren
ROAD
Round Plantation
Patchings Farm Art Centre
MAIN
STREET
The Knoll
NG5
Cottage Wood
B6386
RAMSDALE PARK GOLF CENTRE
4
e's ges
Turnpike Plantation
OXTON
Ramsdale Cottages
P
Club House
East Hill Plantation
20
LANE
Jubilee Plantation
Robin Hood Farm
Ramsdale House
HOLLINWOOD
Hollinwood House
5
The Rowans
Greenwood Bonsai Studio
49
Fox Covert
Ramper Covert
A60
Leila's Plantation
6
Bottomhouse Farm
A614
RAMSDALE PARK
Ramsdale Park Special School
Ramsdale Hill
Forest Farm
North Peacock
The Belt
7
48
South Peacock
Woodlands
ROAD
OLLERTON ROAD
B684
Limelane House
LAMINS LA.
Tophouse Farm
LANE
LITTLE LIME LA.
33
Wood Farm
F
G
H
J
K
58
OLLERTON ROAD
LANE
59
460

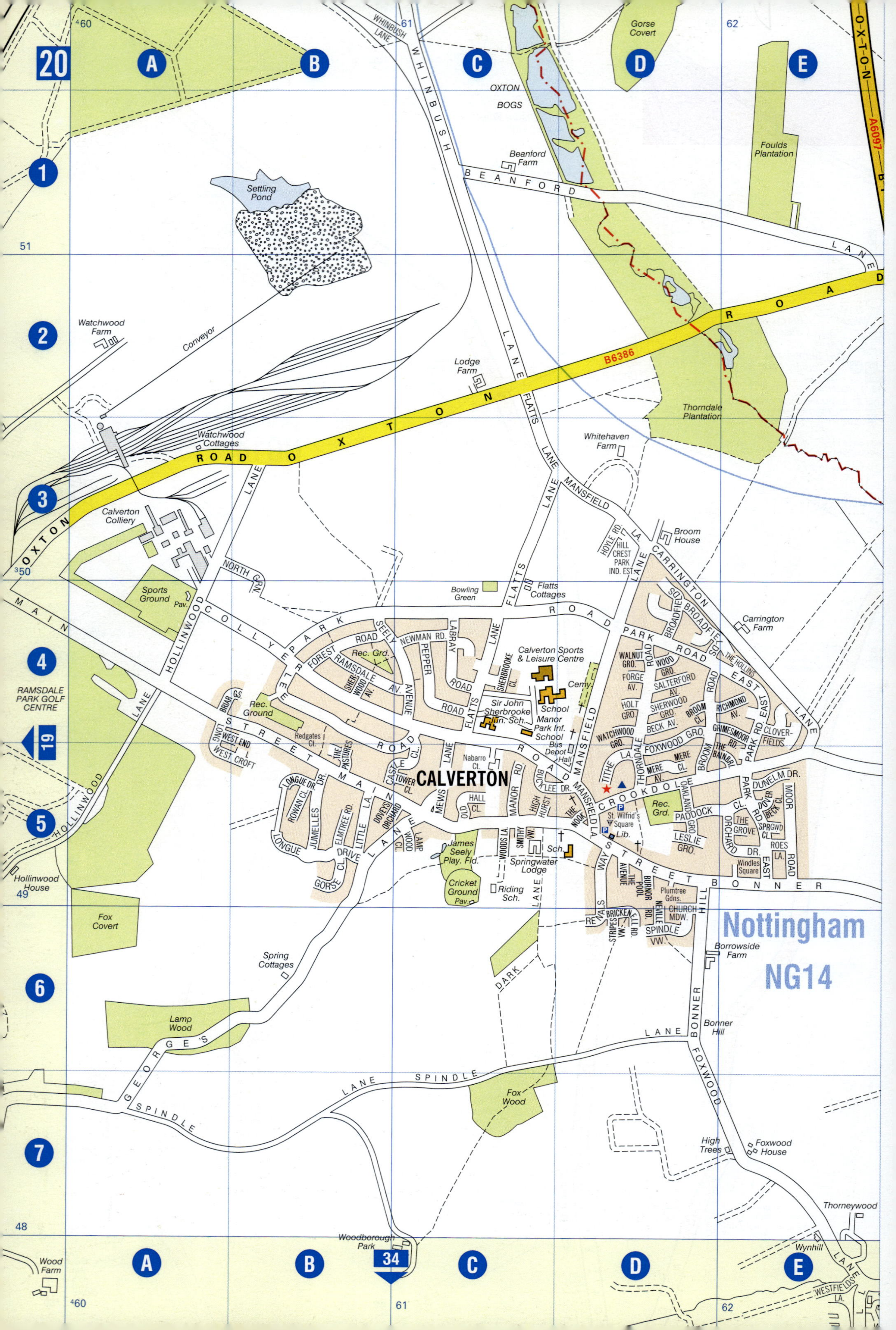

20
A B C D E
1
Settling Pond
51
Watchwood Farm
Conveyor
2
Lodge Farm
OXTON
B6386
ROAD
Gorse Covert
OXTON BOGS
Beanford Farm
Foulds Plantation
LANE
Thorndale Plantation
Whitehaven Farm
Watchwood Cottages
ROAD OXTON
OXTON
3
Calverton Colliery
50
Sports Ground
Pav.
MAIN
Bowling Green
Flatts Cottages
FLATTS
ROAD
MANSFIELD LA.
HOYLE RD.
HILL CREST PARK IND. EST.
Broom House
CARRINGTON
Carrington Farm
BROADFIELD
THE HOLLINS
4
RAMSDALE PARK GOLF CENTRE
NORTH GRN.
HOLLINWOOD
COLLYER
PARK
FOREST
SEELY ROAD
RAMSDALE
SHERWOOD AV.
NEWMAN RD.
PEPPER
LABRAY AVENUE
SHERBROOKE
Calverton Sports & Leisure Centre
Cemy.
WALNUT GRO.
FORGE AV.
HOLT GRO.
SALTERFORD AV.
SHERWOOD GRO.
BROOM GRO.
RICHMOND AV.
GRIMESMOOR RD.
CLOVER-FIELDS
PARK RD. EAST
19
BRIAR G.S.
Rec. Ground
SHERBROOKE
Sir John Sherbrooke Jun. Sch.
School
Manor Park Inf. School
WATCHWOOD GRO.
BECK AV.
FOXWOOD GRO.
MERE
MERE CL.
THE BAINBRI.
DUNELM DR.
5
Redgates Ct.
WEST END
THE PASTURES
WEST CROFT
LONGUE DR.
ROWAN CL.
JUMELLES
ELMTREE RD.
THE DR.
STREET MAIN
LITTLE LA.
DOVE'S
ORCHARD
CASTLE
TOWER CL.
MEWS
OLD HALL CL.
Nabarro Ct.
MANOR RD.
HIGH HURST
BUCK
LEE DR.
THE NOOK
CROOKDOLE
MANSFIELD LA.
St. Wilfrid's Square
Lib.
Rec. Grd.
OAKLANDS
PADDOCK
LESLIE GRO.
THE GROVE
ORCHARD
DR.
SPRGWD CL.
ROES LA.
Windles Square
EAST MOOR ROAD
CALVERTON
49
Hollinwood House
Fox Covert
LAMP WOOD CL.
GORSE
LONGUE DRIVE
James Seely Play. Fld.
Cricket Ground
Pav.
WOODS LA.
SMITHY
Sch.
V.W.
Springwater Lodge
Riding Sch.
WAY
THE STRIPES
BRICKEN
REVAS
STREET HILL
THE AVENUE
BURNOR POOL
NEVILLE RD.
SPINDLE
V.W.
CHURCH MDW.
Plumtree Gdns.
Borrowside Farm
BONNER
6
Spring Cottages
LAMP WOOD
GEORGE'S
SPINDLE
DARK LANE
SPINDLE LANE
Fox Wood
FOXWOOD
Bonner Hill
BONNER
Nottingham NG14
7
34
High Trees
Foxwood House
Thorneywood
48
Wood Farm
A B C D E
Woodborough Park
Wynhill
WESTFIELD
60 61 62

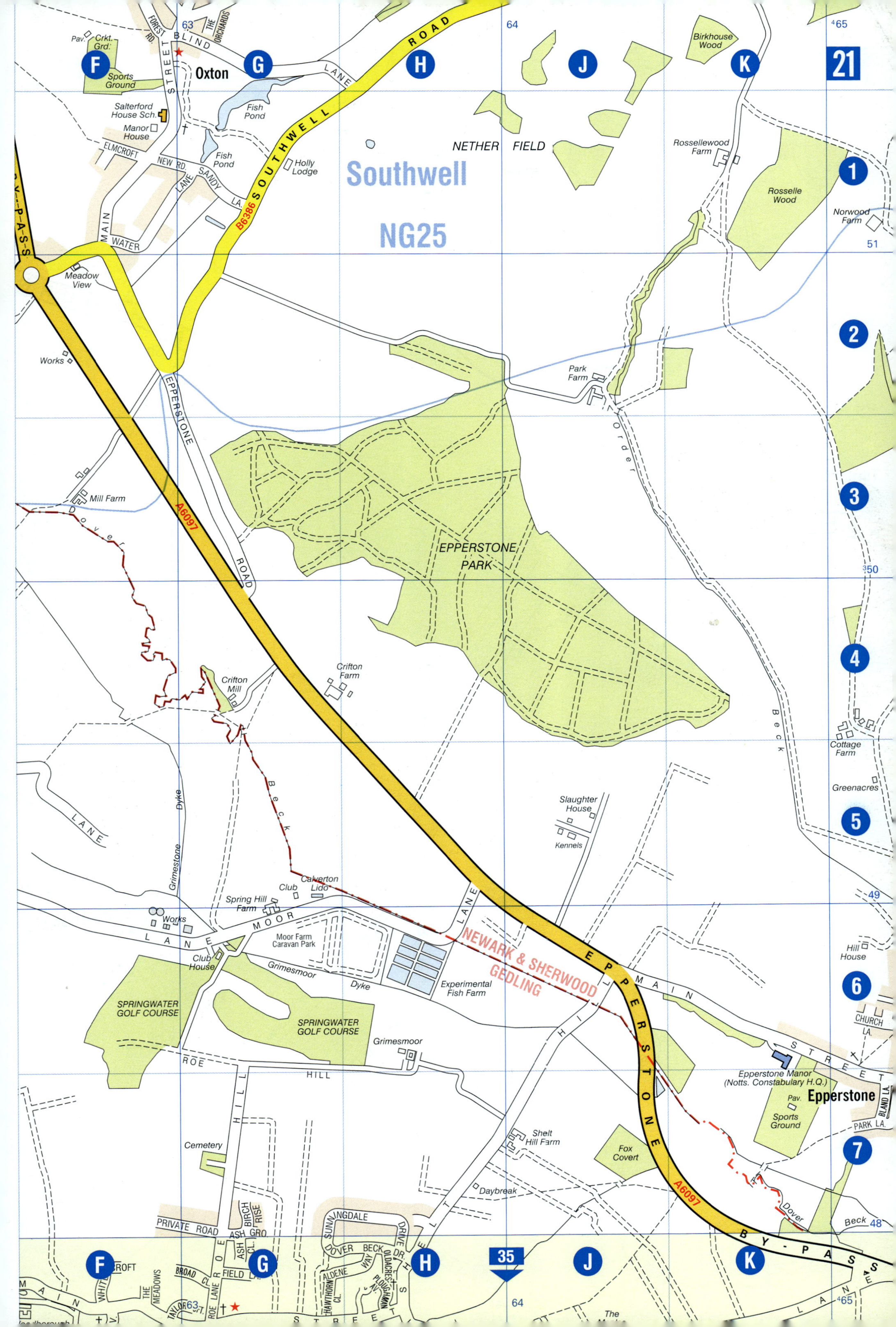
21
F
G
H
J
K
63
64
465
1
2
3
4
5
6
7
51
350
49
48
Oxton
Pav.
Crkt. Grd.
FOREST RD.
THE ORCHARDS
BLIND
Street
Sports Ground
Salterford House Sch.
Manor House
ELMCROFT
NEW RD.
SANDY LA.
MAIN
WATER
Meadow View
Works
Fish Pond
Fish Pond
Holly Lodge
LANE
SOUTHWELL
B6386
BY-PASS
EPPERSTONE
ROAD
A6097
Dover
Mill Farm
Crifton Mill
Crifton Farm
Beck
Dyke
Grimestone
LANE
LANE
MOOR
LANE
ROAD
Southwell
NG25
NETHER FIELD
Birkhouse Wood
Rossellewood Farm
Rosselle Wood
Norwood Farm
Park Farm
Order
Beck
EPPERSTONE PARK
Cottage Farm
Greenacres
Hill House
Slaughter House
Kennels
EPPERSTONE
MAIN
Epperstone Manor (Notts. Constabulary H.Q.)
Pav.
Sports Ground
BLAND LA.
PARK LA.
CHURCH LA.
STREET
Fox Covert
Shelt Hill Farm
Daybreak
Dover
Beck
A6097
BY-PASS
HILL
Calverton Lido
Club
Spring Hill Farm
Works
Club House
Moor Farm Caravan Park
Grimesmoor
Dyke
Experimental Fish Farm
NEWARK & SHERWOOD
GEDLING
SPRINGWATER GOLF COURSE
SPRINGWATER GOLF COURSE
Grimesmoor
ROE
HILL
HILL
Cemetery
PRIVATE ROAD
WHITLOCK
MAIN
BROAD
CROFT
THE MEADOWS
TAYLOR
63
ROE LANE
FIELD CL.
ASH CL.
BIRCH RISE
SUNNINGDALE
DOVER
BECK WAY
ALDENE
HAWTHORN CL.
OLDACRES
PLOUGHMAN
DRIVE
DR.
STREET
35
F
G
H
J
K
64
465
THE

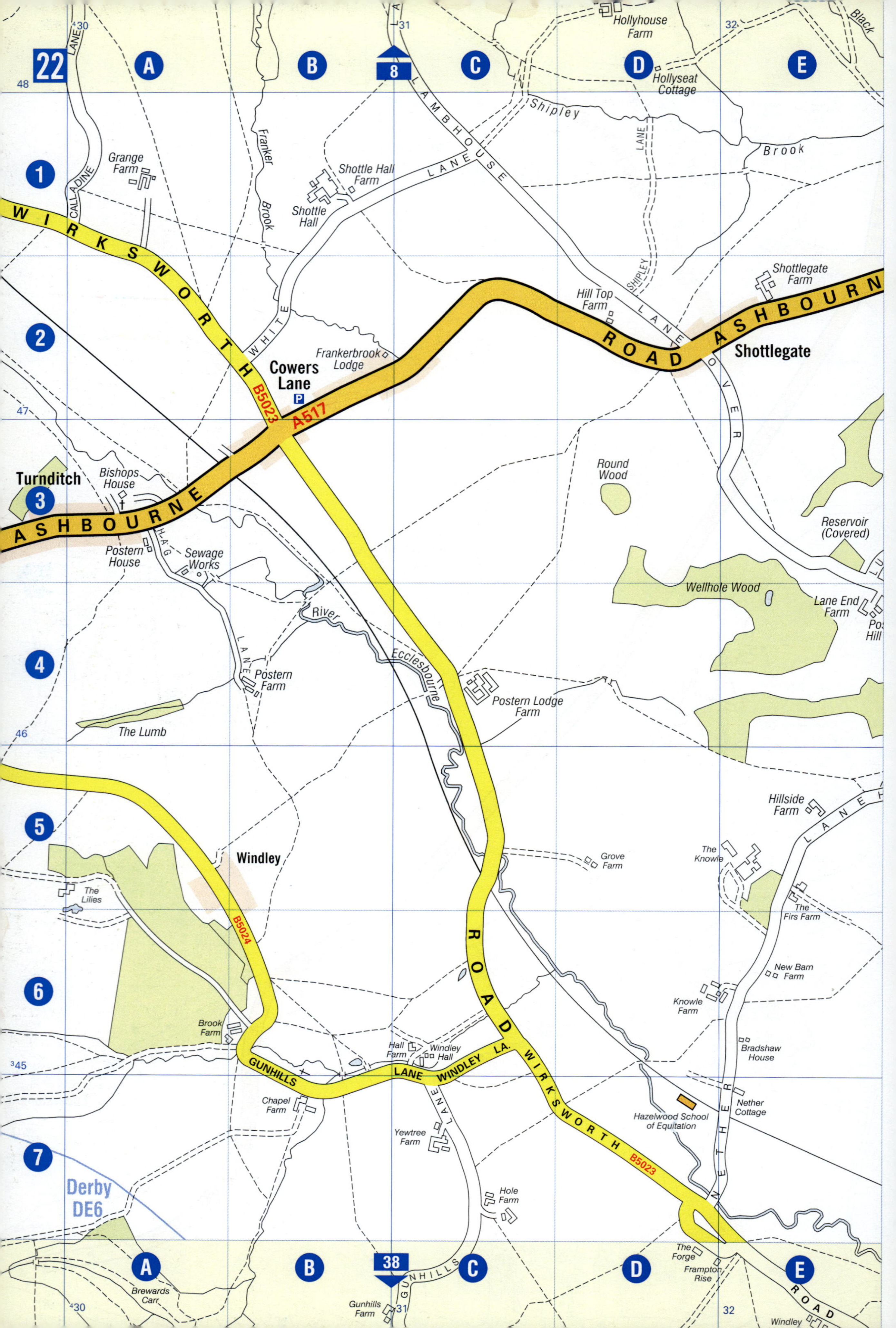

22
A B C D E
8
1
Grange Farm
Franker Brook
White
Shottle Hall Farm
Shottle Hall
Lambhouse Lane
Shipley
Hollyhouse Farm
Hollyseat Cottage
Brook
Shottlegate Farm
2
Frankerbrook Lodge
Cowers Lane
B5023
A517
ROAD ASHBOURNE
Hill Top Farm
Shipley Lane
Dover
Shottlegate
Turnditch
3
ASHBOURNE
Bishops House
Round Wood
Reservoir (Covered)
Postern House
Hag
Sewage Works
Wellhole Wood
Lane End Farm
Pos Hill
4
Lane
Postern Farm
River
Ecclesbourne
Postern Lodge Farm
The Lumb
5
Windley
Grove Farm
Hillside Farm
Lane H
The Knowle
The Lilies
The Firs Farm
B5024
New Barn Farm
6
Brook Farm
Hall Farm
Windley Hall
WINDLEY LA.
WIRKSWORTH ROAD
Knowle Farm
Bradshaw House
Gunhills
LANE WINDLEY
Chapel Farm
Hazelwood School of Equitation
Nether Cottage
WIRKSWORTH B5023
NETHER
7
Derby DE6
Yewtree Farm
Hole Farm
The Forge
Frampton Rise
ROAD
A B C D E
38
Brewards Carr
Gunhills Farm
Windley

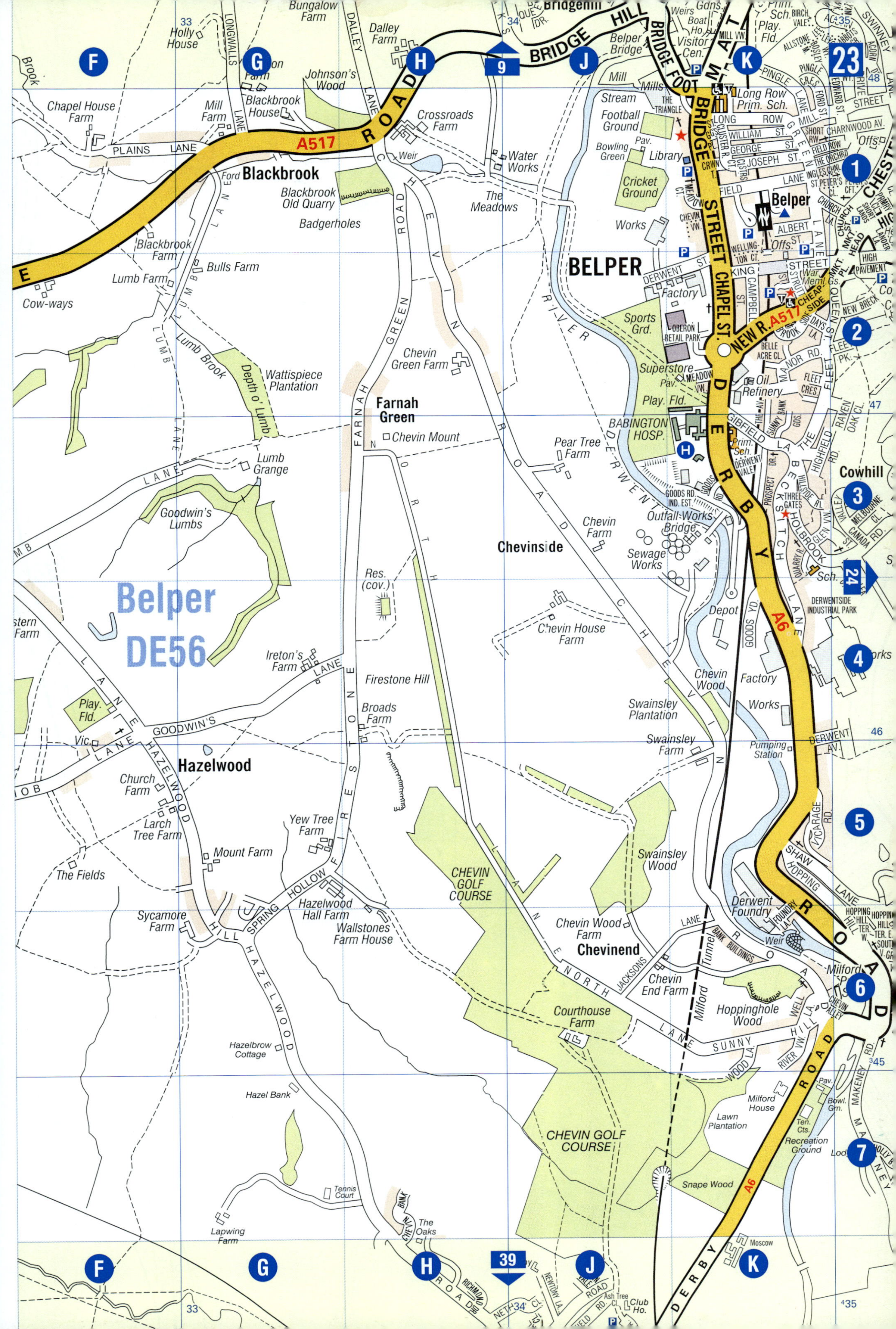
F
G
H
J
K
23
Bungalow Farm
Holly House
Longwalls
Dalley Farm
Bridge Hill
BRIDGE HILL
Belper Bridge
Weirs Boat Ho.
Visitor Cen.
Sch. Birch Vale
Play. Fld.
Allstone
Swinney
Pingle
Long Row Prim. Sch.
Charnwood Av.
Field Row
The Orchard
Chapel House Farm
Mill Farm
Blackbrook House
Johnson's Wood
ROAD
9
BRIDGE FOOT
Mill Stream
THE TRIANGLE
Long Row
William St.
George St.
Joseph St.
St. Peter's
St.
1
PLAINS LANE
A517
ROAD
Crossroads Farm
Weir
Water Works
Football Ground
Bowling Green
Library
Cricket Ground
Works
Albert St.
Church St.
Belper
Offs.
High Pavement
Blackbrook
Ford
Blackbrook Old Quarry
Badgerholes
The Meadows
STREET
CHAPEL ST.
BELPER
Factory
Derwent St.
King St.
Campbell St.
War Meml. Gs.
Cheapside
New Breck
Blackbrook Farm
Bulls Farm
Lumb Farm
Sports Grd.
Oberon Retail Park
NEW R. A517
Belle Acre Cl.
Manor Rd.
Fleet
2
Cow-ways
LUMB LANE
RIVER DERWENT
Superstore
Meadow Vw.
Play. Fld.
Oil Refinery
Fleet Cres.
47
Chevin Green Farm
Lumb Brook
Depth o' Lumb
Wattispiece Plantation
BABINGTON HOSP.
DERBY
Gibfield
Sunny Bank
The Highfield
Hillside
Cowhill
3
Lumb Grange
Farnah Green
Chevin Mount
Pear Tree Farm
Prim. Sch.
Goods Rd. Ind. Est.
Prospect Dr.
Three Gates
Holbrook
24
Goodwin's Lumbs
Res. (cov.)
Chevin Farm
Outfall Works Bridge
Sewage Works
Quarry Hill
Sch.
Derwentside Industrial Park
Belper
DE56
FARNAH GREEN ROAD
Chevinside
Chevin House Farm
Depot
A6
Derwent Av.
4
Ireton's Farm
Firestone Hill
Chevin Wood
Factory
Works
5
Play. Fld.
Vic.
GOODWIN'S LANE
Broads Farm
Swainsley Plantation
Swainsley Farm
Pumping Station
Derwent Av.
46
HAZELWOOD
Church Farm
Larch Tree Farm
Mount Farm
Yew Tree Farm
Swainsley Wood
Shaw
Hopping Lane
Vicarage Rd.
The Fields
HAZELWOOD ROAD
SPRING HOLLOW
Hazelwood Hall Farm
Wallstones Farm House
CHEVIN GOLF COURSE
Chevin Wood Farm
Chevinend
Derwent Foundry
Weir
ROAD
Hopping Hill
6
Sycamore Farm
FIRESTONE LANE
Chevin End Farm
Bank Buildings
Milford Tunnel
NORTH LANE
Courthouse Farm
Hoppinghole Wood
Milford House
CHEVIN DELLEY
345
Hazelbrow Cottage
Milford Lane
Sunny Well
River Vw.
Lawn Plantation
Makeney Rd.
Bowl. Grn.
Hazel Bank
CHEVIN GOLF COURSE
Snape Wood
Recreation Ground
7
Lapwing Farm
Tennis Court
CHEVIN BANK
The Oaks
39
Moscow
DERBY ROAD
A6
F
G
H
J
K

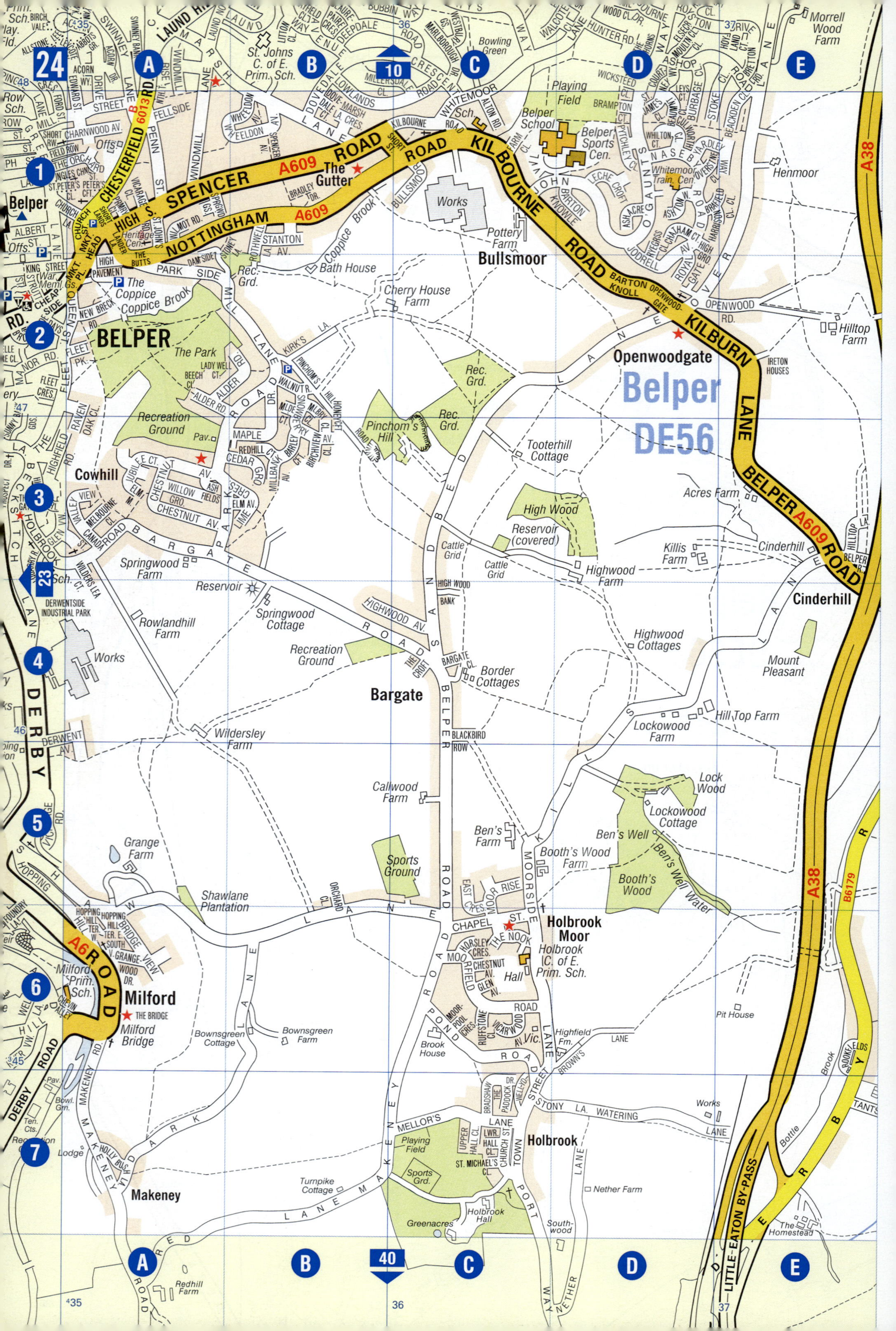
24
Belper
BELPER
Belper DE56
Openwoodgate
Cowhill
Bargate
Bullsmoor
Cinderhill
Milford
Makeney
Holbrook
Holbrook Moor
CHESTERFIELD ROAD B6013
HIGH ST. SPENCER ROAD A609
NOTTINGHAM ROAD A609
SHORT ROAD
KILBOURNE ROAD
KILBURN LANE
BELPER ROAD A609
BARTON KNOLL
OPENWOOD GATE
BELPER LANE
DERBY ROAD
A6 ROAD
LITTLE-EATON BY-PASS
A38
B6179
HIGHWOOD AV.
HIGHWOOD ROAD
BARGATE ROAD
BELPER ROAD
BLACKBIRD ROW
KILLIS LANE
MOORSIDE
MOOR RISE
EAST CRES.
MAKENEY LANE
PARK ROAD
PORT WAY
STONY LANE
WATERING LANE
NETHER LANE
ORCHARD LANE
POND LANE
CHAPEL ST.
THE NOOK
HORSLEY CRES.
CHESTNUT AV.
GLEN AV.
MOORFIELD
MOORPOOL CRES.
RUFFSTONE RISE
VICARWOOD AV.
HIGHFIELD LANE
VIC.
The Park
Recreation Ground
Pav.
Cowhill
Springwood Farm
Reservoir
Rowlandhill Farm
Works
Springwood Cottage
Recreation Ground
Wildersley Farm
Callwood Farm
Grange Farm
Shawlane Plantation
Sports Ground
Ben's Farm
Booth's Wood Farm
Ben's Well
Booth's Wood
Ben's Well Water
Lock Wood
Lockowood Cottage
Lockowood Farm
Hill Top Farm
Highwood Cottages
Highwood Farm
Killis Farm
Acres Farm
High Wood
Reservoir (covered)
Tooterhill Cottage
High Wood Bank
Cattle Grid
Cattle Grid
Border Cottages
Pinchom's Hill
Rec. Grd.
Rec. Grd.
Rec. Grd.
Cherry House Farm
Bath House
Works
Pottery Farm
Bowling Green
Belper School
Belper Sports Cen.
Playing Field
Whitemoor Train. Cen.
Henmoor
Hilltop Farm
Ireton Houses
Morrell Wood Farm
Mount Pleasant
Pit House
Nether Farm
Works
Bottle Brook
The Homestead
Milford Prim. Sch.
THE BRIDGE
Milford Bridge
Bownsgreen Cottage
Bownsgreen Farm
Brook House
Turnpike Cottage
Playing Field
Sports Grd.
ST. MICHAEL'S CL.
UPPER HALL CL.
LWR. HALL CL.
CHURCH ST.
TOWN ST.
BRADSHAW DR.
THE PADDOCK
WELL-HILL DR.
BROWN'S LANE
MELLOR'S LANE
Holbrook Hall
Greenacres
Southwood
Hall
Holbrook C. of E. Prim. Sch.
Highfield Fm.
Redhill Farm
Lodge
Grange Farm
Hopping
Hopping Bridge
Hopping Hill
Foundry
Weir
Pav.
Bowl. Grn.
Ten. Cts.
Recreation
DERBY ROAD
The Coppice
Coppice Brook
Coppice Brook
Mill Lane
Park Side
Dam Side
Honey Lane
Kirk's Lane
Rec. Grd.
Heritage Cen.
MKT. PL.
THE BUTTS
HIGH PAVEMENT
St. Johns C. of E. Prim. Sch.
St. Peter's C. of E. Prim. Sch.
The Gutter
Works
St. Peter's
War Meml. Gdns.
CHEAPSIDE
Sch.
DERWENTSIDE INDUSTRIAL PARK
Wilders' Lea
Sch.
Holbrook
DERBY ROAD
A38
23
40
36
37
10
48
46
45
35
36
37
1
2
3
4
5
6
7
A
B
C
D
E

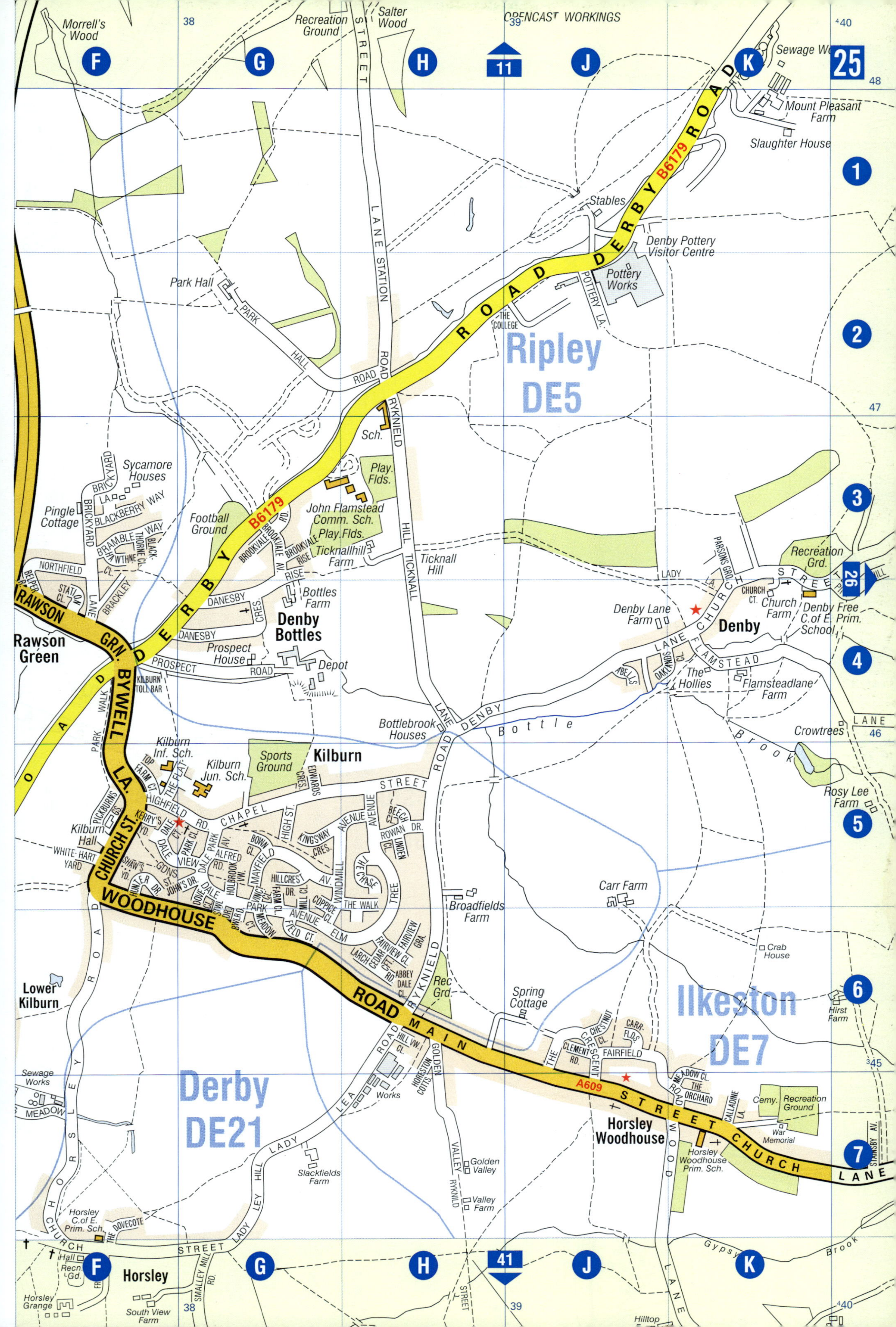

Morrell's Wood
Recreation Ground
Salter Wood
OPENCAST WORKINGS
Sewage Works
25
Mount Pleasant Farm
Slaughter House
Stables
Denby Pottery Visitor Centre
Pottery Works
Park Hall
PARK HALL
Ripley DE5
THE COLLEGE
LANE STATION ROAD
RYKNIELD ROAD
Sch.
Play. Flds.
John Flamstead Comm. Sch. Play. Flds.
Ticknallhill Farm
Ticknall Hill
HILL
Recreation Grd.
26
PARSONS GRO.
LADY LANE
STREET
CHURCH CT.
Church Farm
Denby Free C. of E. Prim. School
B6179
Sycamore Houses
Pingle Cottage
BRICKYARD
BRICKYARD LA.
BLACKBERRY WAY
BRAMBLE WAY
BLACK THORNE CL.
HAWTHNE. CL.
NORTHFIELD
STATION CL.
BRACKLEY
Football Ground
DERBY ROAD
BROOKVALE RD.
BROOKVALE AV.
BROOKVALE RISE
RISE
DANESBY CRES.
Bottles Farm
Denby Bottles
Ticknall Hill
Denby
Denby Lane Farm
CHURCH LANE
FLAMSTEAD LANE
CHURCH CT.
OAKWOOD CL.
ABELL'S
The Hollies
Flamsteadlane Farm
Crowtrees
LANE
RAWSON GRN.
Rawson Green
BYWELL LA.
A609
PROSPECT ROAD
Prospect House
DANESBY
Depot
Kilburn Toll Bar
Bottlebrook Houses
DENBY LANE
Bottle Brook
Rosy Lee Farm
PARK WALK
Kilburn Inf. Sch.
TOP FARM CT.
THE FLAT
HIGHFIELD
Kilburn Jun. Sch.
Sports Ground
EDWARDS CRES.
Kilburn
STREET
AVENUE
AVENUE
BEECH CL.
ROWAN DR.
LINDEN
DR.
Carr Farm
PICKBURNS
KERRY'S YD.
DALE
DALE
PARK CL.
CHAPEL RD.
HIGH ST.
KINGSWAY CRES.
Kilburn Hall
WHITE HART YARD
SHAW'S YD.
DALE GDNS.
PARK VIEW
DALE PARK AV.
ALFRED RD.
BOWN CL.
MAYFIELD
HOLBROOK VW.
HILLCREST DR.
FARM CL.
WINDMILL AV.
THE CHASE
TREE
Broadfields Farm
Crab House
HUNTER DR.
JOHN'S DR.
DOVE DALE
SWILL HILL
CT.
PARK MEADOW CT.
WINDMILL
COPPICE CL.
THE WALK
WOODHOUSE
FIELD CT.
AVENUE ELM
FAIRVIEW CL.
FAIRVIEW GRA.
LARCH CL.
CEDAR CL.
ABBEY DALE CL.
RYKNIELD
Rec. Grd.
Spring Cottage
Ilkeston DE7
Hirst Farm
6
Lower Kilburn
ROAD MAIN
HILL VW. CL.
GOLDEN
HORESTON COTTS.
CHESTNUT CL.
CRESCENT
CLEMENT RD.
CARR. FLDS.
Fairfield
THE ORCHARD
CALLDINE
Cemy.
Recreation Ground
War Memorial
Sewage Works
HORSLEY MEADOW
Derby DE21
A609
Works
LEA
LADY HILL
Slackfields Farm
VALLEY RYKNIELD
Golden Valley
Valley Farm
Horsley Woodhouse
MEADOW CL.
WOOD STREET
Horsley Woodhouse Prim. Sch.
CHURCH LANE
STARBY AV.
Horsley C. of E. Prim. Sch.
THE DOVECOTE
CHURCH STREET
SMALLEY MILL RD.
Horsley
Horsley Grange
South View Farm
Hilltop
GYPSY LANE
Brook

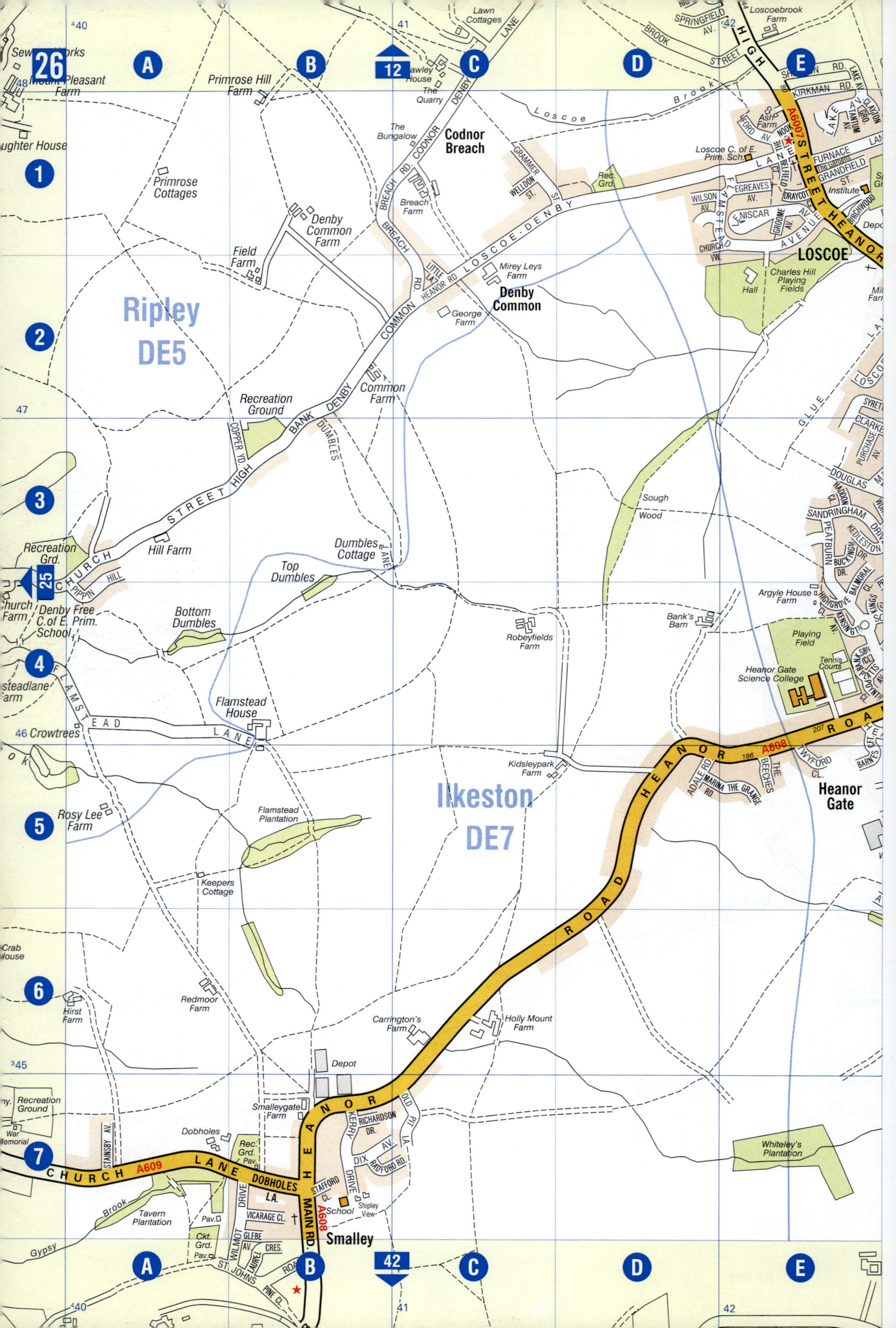
26
40
41
42
A
B
12
C
D
E
Sewage Works
Mount Pleasant Farm
Slaughter House
Primrose Hill Farm
Lawn Cottages
LANE
SPRINGFIELD AV.
BROOK
HIGH
Loscoebrook Farm
STREET
1
Primrose Cottages
The Bungalow
Rawley House
The Quarry
CODNOR
DENBY
Codnor Breach
Loscoe
Brook
KIRKMAN
SHELTON
RD.
LAKE AV.
CLAYTON
TITANIUM AV.
GRO.
A6007
STREET
HEANOR
FORD
ASH
AV.
Farm
NOON
FURNACE
GRANDFIELD
DRAYCOT
Depot
Denby Common Farm
Field Farm
BREACH RD.
Breach Farm
BREACH
Breach
GRAMMER
WELLDON
ST.
LOSCOE-DENBY
ST.
Rec. Grd.
Loscoe C. of E. Prim. Sch.
The Gardens
St. Institute
WILSON
AV.
EGREAVES
AV.
BROOME
ENISCAR
BIRCHWOOD
CHURCH VW.
LOSCOE
2
Ripley DE5
RD.
COMMON
HEANOR RD.
LITTLE
Mirey Leys Farm
George Farm
Denby Common
Hall
Charles Hill Playing Fields
47
Recreation Ground
DENBY
BANK
Common Farm
DUMBLES
FAMSTEAD AVENUE
GLUE
LA.
LOSCOE
SYRETT
CLARKES
PURCHASE AV.
3
COPPER YD.
HIGH
STREET
CHURCH
Hill Farm
PIPPIN HILL
Sough Wood
Argyle House Farm
SANDRINGHAM
PEATBURN
HADDON CL.
KEDLESTON
BUCKING
DR.
HIGHGROVE
KENSINGTON
BALMORAL
KINGS
Recreation Grd.
25
Church Farm
Denby Free C. of E. Prim. School
Bottom Dumbles
Dumbles Cottage
LANE
Top Dumbles
Robeyfields Farm
Bank's Barn
Playing Field
Tennis Courts
Heanor Gate Science College
4
FLAMSTEAD
steadlane Farm
Crowtrees
LANE
Flamstead House
Kidsleypark Farm
ADALE RD.
MARINA
THE GRANGE
A608
207
ROAD
THE BEECHES
TWYFORD CL.
BARNES
46
5
Rosy Lee Farm
Flamstead Plantation
Ilkeston DE7
HEANOR
186
Heanor Gate
ROAD
Keepers Cottage
Crab House
6
Hirst Farm
Redmoor Farm
Carrington's Farm
Holly Mount Farm
Whiteley's Plantation
45
Recreation Ground
War Memorial
Depot
Smalleygate Farm
HEANOR
OLD PIT LA.
KERRY
RICHARDSON DR.
DIX AV.
RADFORD RD.
7
CHURCH
STAINSBY AV.
A609
LANE
DOBHOLES
Dobholes
Rec. Grd.
Pav.
LA.
ROAD
STAFFORD CL.
DRIVE
School
Shipley View
Tavern Plantation
Brook
Pav.
DRIVE
WILMOT
VICARAGE CL.
GLEBE AV.
MAIN RD.
A608
Smalley
Gypsy
Ckt. Grd. Pav.
ST. JOHNS
LAUREL CRES.
PINE CL.
A
B
42
C
D
E
40
41
42

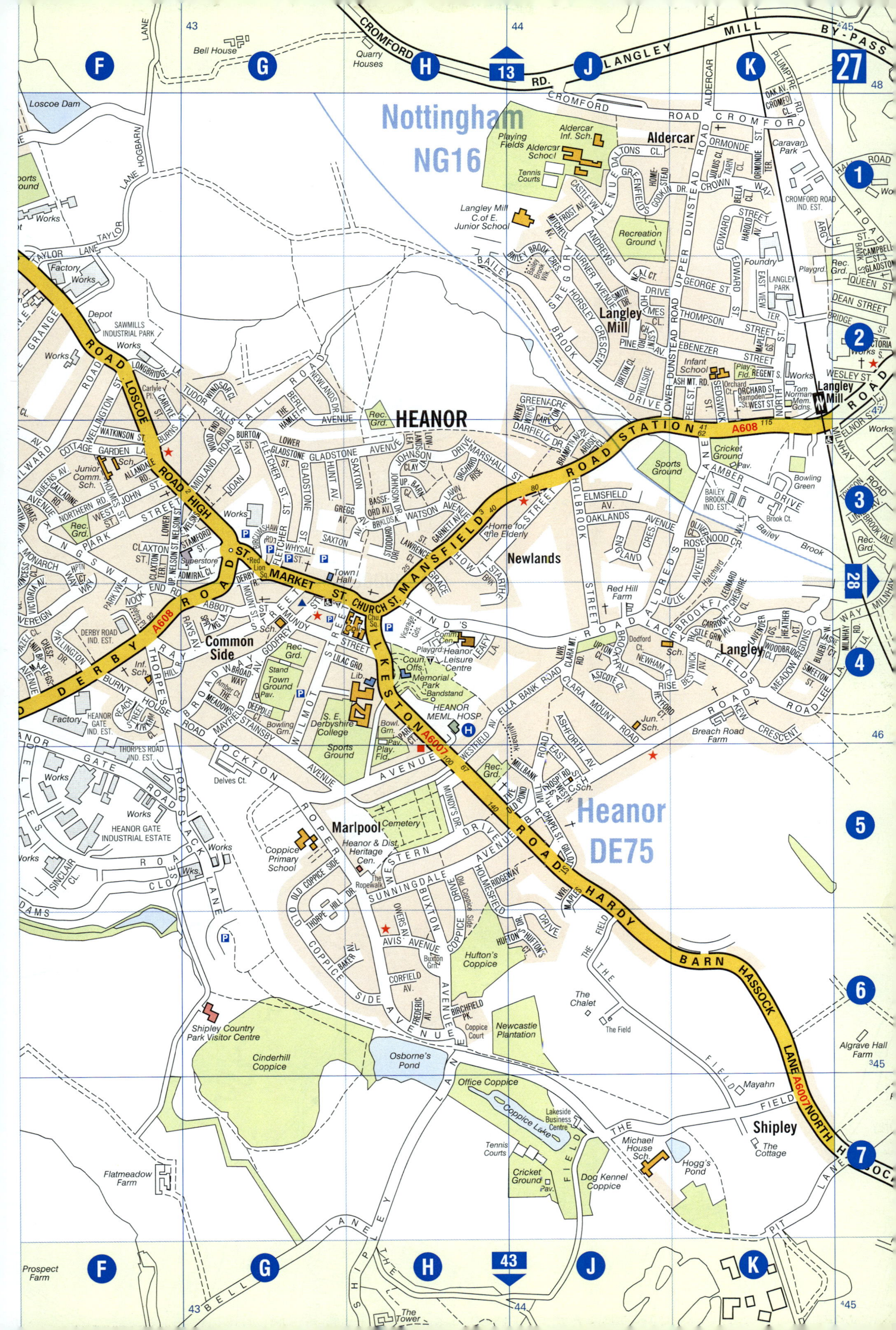

43
44
45
48
CROMFORD MILL LANGLEY BY-PASS
27
F
G
H
13
J
LANGLEY
K
Bell House
Quarry Houses
RD.
CROMFORD
Nottingham
NG16
Loscoe Dam
Playing Fields
Aldercar Inf. Sch.
Aldercar School
Aldercar
ROAD
CROMFORD
Caravan Park
Cromford Road Ind. Est.
1
Tennis Courts
Langley Mill C. of E. Junior School
Langley Mill
Recreation Ground
Langley Park
Dean Street
2
Works
Infant School
Langley Mill
A608
Road Station
Works
3
HEANOR
Sports Ground
Cricket Ground
Bowling Green
Bailey Brook Ind. Est.
Newlands
Home for the Elderly
Red Hill Farm
Langley
4
Common Side
Heanor Leisure Centre
Heanor Meml. Hosp.
Jun. Sch.
Breach Road Farm
Heanor Gate Ind. Est.
S. E. Derbyshire College
Sports Ground
Memorial Park
Heanor DE75
5
Heanor Gate Industrial Estate
Marlpool
Cemetery
Heanor & Dist. Heritage Cen.
Coppice Primary School
Newcastle Plantation
The Chalet
The Field
6
Shipley Country Park Visitor Centre
Cinderhill Coppice
Osborne's Pond
Office Coppice
Algrave Hall Farm
Mayahn
Shipley
The Cottage
7
Flatmeadow Farm
Lakeside Business Centre
Michael House Sch.
Hogg's Pond
Prospect Farm
Tennis Courts
Cricket Ground
Dog Kennel Coppice
A6007 NORTH
F
G
H
43
J
K
The Tower

28
LANGLEY
14
27
A610
A608
MANSFIELD ROAD
Grange Fields Farm Cottage
Weir
Nether Green
Hall Farm
COCKERHOUSE ROAD
Lodge
EASTWOOD HALL
Brinsley Brook
Caravan Park
CROMFORD ROAD IND. EST.
Works
HALL ROAD
ARGYLE ST.
CAMPBELL ST.
BANK ST.
GLADSTONE ST.
QUEEN ST.
Playgrd.
Rec. Grd.
Langley Park
DEAN STREET
BRIDGE
Victoria Works
WESLEY ST.
Tom Norman Mem. Gdns.
Langley Mill
LANGLEY STATION
MILNHAY
ELNOR STREET
Works
DERBY ROAD
A608
Langley Bri.
Works
Slurry Lagoon
Slurry Lagoon
CHRYSALIS WAY
LIMMEL
MILL
BY-PASS
Nether Green Brook
MUSHROOM FM.
MEADOWBANK
Meadowbank Wy.
Works
Works
New Derby Road
NEW DERBY ROAD
ANCHOR
Hall Pk.
Pavilion
Playing Fields
Hall Park Dr.
GREENHILLS ROAD
MOORFIELDS
THORPE RD.
COACH DRIVE
ROBEY DRIVE
Beauvale Brook
Cricket Ground
Pav.
Beauvale
LOWER
THORN TREE
SNUG
CRESCENT
MEADOW CL.
DOROTHY RD.
LYNNCROFT
KIRBY
BEAUVALE
LAMB CLOSE
Eastwood Comp. Sch.
GRANGE VIEW
Charlotte Ct.
GRANGE
Playing Field
Eastwood Comp. (Lwr.) Sch.
D.H. Lawrence 'Sons & Lovers' Cottage
Lynncroft Prim. Sch.
Tennis Cts.
THE CRES.
Bowling Green
TOWSON AV.
LIME AV.
Rec. Grd.
Langley Mill
DERBY ROAD
A608
DERBY ROAD
Superstore
BAILEY GROVE
Sewage Works
Erewash
Bailey
MILNHAY ROAD
BROOKFIELD
HEATHER CT.
MILNHAY
LEE LA.
WAY
MEADOW ROAD LEE LANE
BROOKVALE RD.
Works
OLD DERBY RD.
Superstore
FERN AV.
PARK AV.
WOODSIDE RD.
Tennis Cts.
KELHAM WY.
MANSFIELD ROAD
NOTTINGHAM ROAD
Princes
VICTORIA ST.
ALBERT ST.
Hopkins Ct.
The Hollies
WELLINGTON ST.
GROSVENOR
ATHERFIELD GDNS.
KING'S
Liby.
THREE TUNS
PERCY STREET
COMET ST.
NURSERIES
EDWARD ROAD
Eastwood Jun. & Inf. Sch.
DEVONSHIRE DR.
CHURCH ST.
Tennis Courts
ALEXANDRA ST.
QUEENS ST.
OXFORD ST.
WELLINGTON ST.
Offs.
RATCLIFFE ST.
BISHOP ST.
HOGGS FLD.
AVENUE
Pav.
CASTLE ST.
Football Ground
BAILEY ST.
GREAT NORTHERN CL.
SCALBY CL.
COP PICE CT.
BLACKTHORN
OAK WK.
LARCH CR.
WOODLAND DRIVE
Rectory
IVY LANE
WOOD ST.
PINE TREE WK.
RYE
SOUTH STREET
FARRINGTON
EASTWOOD
CHURCH STREET
EASTWOOD
SWIFT CT.
MIDLAND RD.
PICKERING AV.
SUTTON
WILLIAM
PLUMPTRE
Ten. Cts.
Coronation Park
Brookhill Leys Jun. Sch.
Brookhill Leys Inf. Sch.
Parkside School
CHEWTON
PHILIP AV.
RAGLAN
GREY ST.
ROCKLEY AV.
Cemetery
Playgrd. Rec. Ground
CHAPEL ST.
MAIN ST.
Cockfield Fm.
Brae Mar Rd.
New Eastwood
PRIORY RD.
ROBIN
QUEENS ROAD
SEYMOUR RD.
SHERWOOD
QUEENS ROAD STH.
RISE
CRESCENT
NEWTHORPE
DAWSON
ORCHARD CL.
CLOSE
COMMONS
HALLS LANE
HALLS LA.
MERCIA CL.
WESSEX CL.
SUSSEX CL.
BACON ST.
BRANDRETH DR.
LUDLAM
Works
NEWMANLEYS ROAD
BY-PASS
NEWMANLEYS ROAD (STH.)
A610
KIMBERLEY
EASTWOOD
TINSLEY
SUDBURY MEWS
BROOKHILL
SYCAMORES
ADDISON RD.
CHAPEL LEYS
Stanley Ct.
LINWOOD
WEBSTER
Factory
A610
KIMBERLEY EASTWOOD
Sports Ground
Playing Field
Pavilion
Works
Erewash River
Nottingham Canal
Swing Bridge
Eastwood Lock
(Disused)
Lacey Fields Farm
Weir
Shipley Lock
Shipley Gate
Boat Inn Farm
ERE WASH
BROXTOWE CANAL
Heanor DE75
Algrave Hall Farm
Purdy House Farm
Bentley's Plantation
AMBER VALLEY
EREWASH
LONG LANE
Poplars Farm
The Bungalow
Towing Path
Ilkeston DE7
NORTH HASSOCK LANE
A6007
SOUTH HASSOCK LANE
Rec. Grd.
Cotmanhay Wood
AMERICAN ADVENTURE THEME PARK
BEAUVALE
MILLERSDALE
DOVEDALE
LATHKILL AV.
BIRCHOVER
SKEAVINGTONS LANE
CANON
PAVILION
DRIVE
Pav.
Rec. Grd.
Woodlands Farm
44
45
46
47
48
1
2
3
4
5
6
7

Nottingham NG16
48  49  15  50  29  48
F  G  H  J  K
1  2  3  4  5  6  7
30  45
MOORGREEN IND. PARK
Oak House
Apple Ash Ct.
Beggarlee Pk.
Depot
Works
High Ct.
Moorgreen Business Park
Lower Beauvale
Nursery
Manor House
Nursery
Moorgreen
Dicks Lane
Poplar Farm
Water Tower
Gas Valve Compound
Greasley House
Cemetery
Hall
St. Mary's Church
Earthwork
Greasley
GREASLEY CASTLE (Rems. of)
Greasley Castle Fm.
Fish Ponds
Beauvale
Greasley Beauvale D.H. Lawrence Infants Sch.
Greasley Beauvale Jnr. Sch.
Greasley Sports & Comm. Cen.
Rec. Gnd.
BEAUVALE ROAD
B6010
Hill Top
DOVECOTE
CHARLES
NOTTINGHAM ROAD
Mary Road
Glen Cl.
Mansell Cl.
Wheeler Av.
EAST NOTTINGHAM
Newthorpe
Greenacres Cl.
Hollyfarm Ct.
Hemingway Cl.
Depot
Nottingham NG16
Opencast Workings
Bogend
Quarry Wood
Hall Farm
WATNALL WOOD
Reckoning House
ROLLESTON CR.
LANCELOT
ROLLESTON DRI.
MAIN ROAD
B600
NARROW LANE
CHURCH ROAD
Sledder Wood
Crow Farm
Newthorpe Common
Pinfold
Stamford St.
Stamford St.
Robin Hood
Giltbrook Cr.
South St.
Giltbrook
GILTBROOK IND. EST.
Works
Depot
Warehouse
IKEA WAY
Superstore
Subway
BY-PASS
Gilt Brook
A6096
GIN CLOSE WAY
Sewage Works
Works
Depot
Depot
Ponderosa
Glasshouse Yard
Barlows Cotts.
The Meadows
MEADOW RD.
MAIN STREET
DOUGLAS AV.
Playing Field
Gilt Hill Farm
Gilthill Prim. Sch.
AMBER TRAD. CEN.
ARTIC WAY
Recycling Centre
Depot
Football Gnd.
GILT HILL
VALLEY RD.
JUBILEE
DIGBY
BROXTOWE
HALEY CL.
EASTWOOD LANE
GOODWIN DR.
Gilt Briggs Farm
AWSWORTH
Crabcroft Farm
KIMBERLEY EASTWOOD
BY-PASS
A610
KIMBERLEY
The Fives
Eastwood & Kimberley Community College
Council Depot
Recreation Grnd.
Brewery
Watnall Cantelupe
Watnall Road
ACACIA GDS.
CARMAN CL.
BELSFORD CL.
Lychgate Ct.
FLEMING DR.
Hollywell Prim. Sch.
The Firs
Kimberley Prim. Sch.
Superstore
Manor Farm
MAIN STREET
HIGH STREET
NEWDIGATE
CHAPEL
BY-PASS

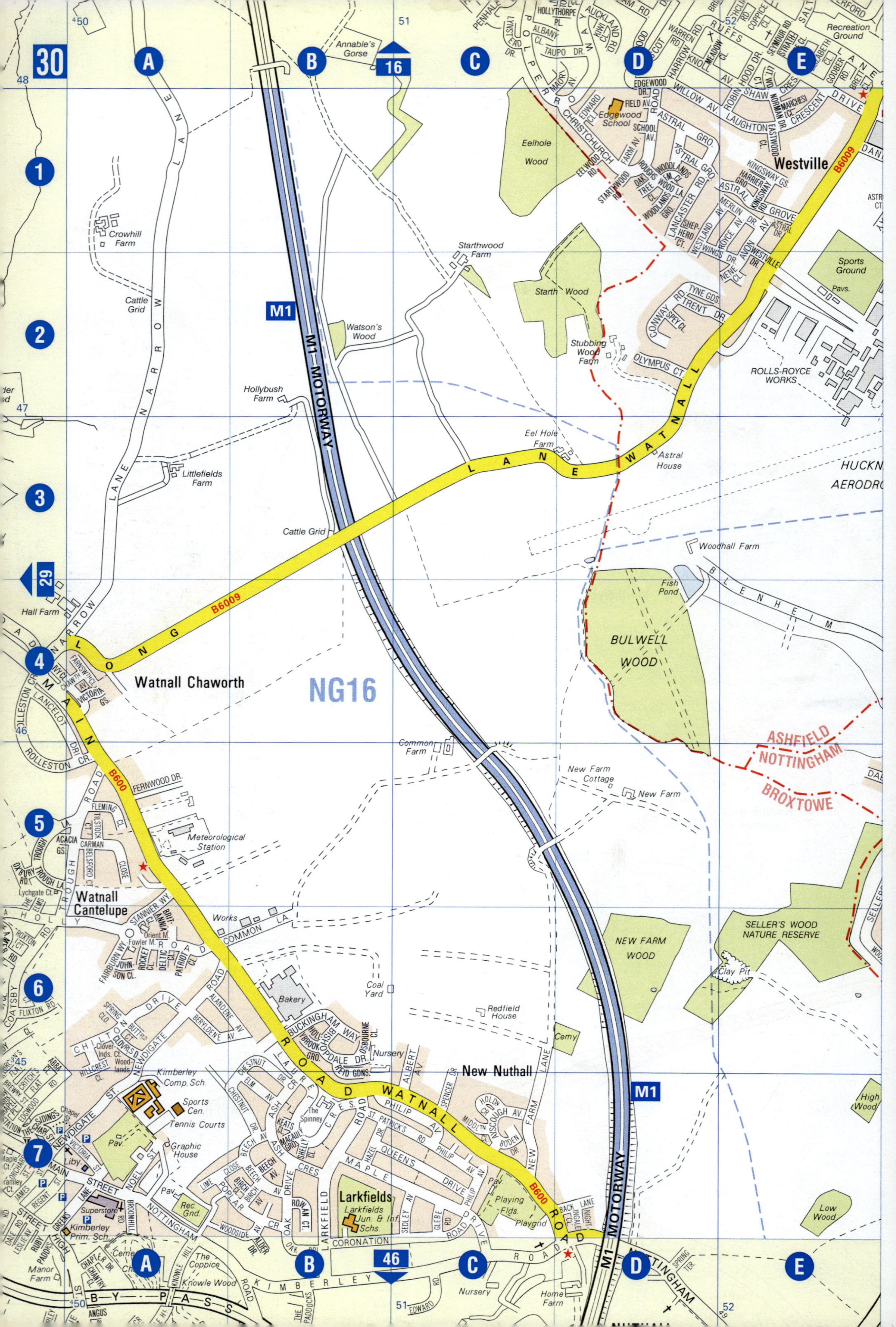

30
A
B
16
C
D
E
1
2
47
3
29
Hall Farm
4
46
5
45
6
7
A
B
46
C
D
E
Crowhill Farm
Cattle Grid
Littlefields Farm
Annable's Gorse
M1
M1 MOTORWAY
Watson's Wood
Hollybush Farm
Cattle Grid
B6009
LONG
NARROW
LANE
MAIN
NARROW LANE
ROAD
Watnall Chaworth
NG16
Meteorological Station
B600
FERNWOOD DR.
FLEMING
TILSTOCK CT.
CARMAN
BELSFORD CL.
ACACIA GS.
TROUGH
OXBURY RD.
TROUGH LA.
Lychgate Ct.
THE ELMS
Watnall Cantelupe
HOLLY
ROXTON CT.
Works
COMMON LA.
STANNIER WY.
ANNAH
ORIENT M.
Fowler M.
ROCKET CL.
DELTIC CL.
PATRIOT CL.
JOHN-SON CL.
FAIRBURN WY.
Bakery
Coal Yard
Redfield House
Cemy
ALMONDE AV.
BERYLDENE AV.
BUCKINGHAM WY.
HOLLYBROOKE DR.
BISHOPDALE DR.
OSBOURNE CL.
Nursery
FIELD GDNS.
New Nuthall
CHESTNUT DR.
ELM AV.
ASH CRES.
BEECH AV.
KEATS CL.
MACAULAY
SHELLEY CL.
St. PATRICK'S RD.
CRESCENT
St.
ALBERT
SPENCER
PHILIP AV.
HOLDEN
KINSBOROUGH AV.
MIDDLETON
BODEN DR.
LAUREL
WATNALL
ROAD
QUEEN'S
DRIVE
PHILIP
Playing Flds.
Playgnd
Pav.
B600
BACK LANE
NEW FARM LANE
ROAD
M1 MOTORWAY
NOTTINGHAM
NEW FARM WOOD
SELLER'S WOOD NATURE RESERVE
Clay Pit
High Wood
Low Wood
Common Farm
New Farm Cottage
New Farm
ASHFIELD
NOTTINGHAM
BROXTOWE
BULWELL WOOD
Fish Pond
BLENHEIM
Woodhall Farm
HUCKN
AERODRO
Eel Hole Farm
Astral House
WATNALL
LANE
Stubbing Wood Farm
OLYMPUS CT.
CONWAY
SPEY CL.
TRENT DR.
TYNE GDS.
Starth Wood
Starthwood Farm
CHRISTCHURCH
Eelhole Wood
EELHOLE RD.
STARTHWOOD RD.
Edgewood School
EDGEWOOD DR.
FIELD AV.
EDWARD
WILLOW AV.
ROBIN SHAW CL.
NORMAN DR.
EASTWOOD
LAUGHTON AV.
ASTRAL GRO.
ASTRAL GRO.
ASTRAL GRO.
WOODLANDS
DAM
TREE
WOOD
LANCASTER
SHEP-HERD
WINGS
WESWING
ROYCE DR.
MERLIN DR.
AVON DR.
NENE CL.
KINGSWAY GS.
WESTVILLE
Westville
B6009
DRIVE
Sports Ground
Pavs.
ROLLS-ROYCE WORKS
HARRIER
HARROW
Sports Cen.
Tennis Courts
Graphic House
Kimberley Comp. Sch.
NEWDIGATE
VICTORIA
Pav.
Pav.
Rec. Gnd.
Superstore
Kimberley Prim. Sch.
NOTTINGHAM
BROOMHILL
HIGH
GREENS
MAIN STREET
NOEL
LIME
POPLAR
BIRCH
OAK
ROWAN CL.
WOODSIDE CL.
ALDER DR.
CORONATION
Larkfields
Larkfields Jun. & Inf. Schs.
LARKFIELD
SEDLEY AV.
GLEBE
KIMBERLEY
ROAD
BY-PASS
The Paddocks
Nursery
Home Farm
The Coppice
Knowle Wood
Manor Farm
CHAPEL
SPRING CLO.
BUTT RD.
CHILTON DRIVE
HILLCREST CL.
Clovers Inds. Ct.
Woodlands
COATSBY
FLIXTON RD.
HILL
Hall Farm
ROLLESTON DR.
ROLLESTON CR.
LANCELOT
DILLESTON CR.
VICTORIA GS.
FARNSWORTH AV.
MAPLE
SPINNEY
HAZEL
CHESTNUT
BEECH AV.
30
1
2
3
4
5
6
7
50
51
52
48
47
46
45
50
51
52
29
16
46

31
Sports Ground
Broomhill
Butlers Hill
Hucknall
HUCKNALL
HUCKNALL INDUSTRIAL PARK
Works
NG15
Hazelgrove
Farleys
Farleys Farm
A611 BY-PASS
Broomhill Farm
Broomhill Junior & Butler's Hill Schools
Mill Lakes
Mill Lakes Country Park
The Oaks
Sports Grd.
Pav.
River Leen
Weirpool
Old Mill Close
Old Mill Cl.
ASHFIELD
GEDLING
NOTTINGHAM ROAD
MOOR ROAD
Home Wood
Playing Field
Fish Ponds
Nottingham
Nurseries
The Screen
Bulwell Hall Park
Playing Field
Allcock's Wood
Playground
NOTTINGHAM CITY (PUBLIC) GOLF COURSE
Barker's Wood
Cricket Ground
Pav.
Moor Bridge
Park & Ride
Caravan Park
Moor Bridge
Weir
Springfield Prm. Sch.
Lawton Dr.
Play. Fld. Pav.
NG5
NG6
Blenheim
Blenheim Villas
BLENHEIM INDUSTRIAL ESTATE
Works
A6002 ROAD
SANDHURST ROAD
Blenheim
Blenheim Cottages
Playing Fld.
T.A. Centre
Alderman Derbyshire Sch.
St. Mary's C. of E. Prim. Sch.
Depot
Bulwell Forest
Weir
WILLOW INDUSTRIAL ESTATE
HUCKNALL
FOREST VIEW INDUSTRIAL & RETAIL EST.
Springfield Retail Park
Superstore
Leen Dr.
Ken Martin Pool & Lido
Naomi Crescent
BESTWOOD
BULWELL FOREST (Public) GOLF COURSE
Bulwell Forest
Stanstead Primary School
Stanstead
Camberley Road
Snape Wood
Snape Wood Prim. Sch.
Rufford Jun. & Inf. Schs.
St. Andrews
Minerva St.
Carey Rd.
Cantrell Prim. Sch.
Playing Field
NORTHERN CEMETERY
BULWELL BUSINESS CENTRE
Bulwell
BULWELL
Chap.
Lodge
Works
MAIN ST.
HIGH ROAD
MONTAGUE ST.
Montague St.
Works
Bulwell Library
HIGHBURY
Town Pk.
Recreation Ground
Soldier's Hill
Potter's Hollow
Bowling Grn.
Rec. Gnd. Pav.
Northern Cemetery
Sandfield Bradford
Comm. Cen.
Hempshill Inf. & Jun. Schs.
Coventry
Chatham Ct.
Henrietta Street
Logan Street
Repton
Piccadilly
Playing Fields
Highbury Vale
Hempshill Vale
Hempshill Hall Prim. Sch.
Highbury Hospital
Henry Mellish Comp. Sch.
Prim. Terr.
Coventry Ct.
Comm. Cen.
Charles Way
A6002 WOOD ROAD

32
455
MILL 48
Westhouse Farm
56
18
CRIMEA PLANTATION
Keepers Cottages
57
A B C D E
Bestwood Village
LAMINS LANE
LAMINS
MILL LAKES COUNTRY PARK
1
CORONATION RD.
Primary School
The Old Rectory
NG6
The Oaks
Sports Grd.
Pav.
Reservoir
Broad Valley Farm
DRIVE
Alexandra Lodges
Warrenhill Plantation
Violet Hill
2
MOOR RD.
GOLD MILL CL.
47
BESTWOOD COUNTRY PARK
BIG WOOD
3
MOOR ROAD
The Warren
Warren Ho.
Playing Field
Tennis Court
Playing Field
Gaunts Hill
Fire Brigade H.Q.
Bestwood Country Park
Moyra Plantation
Queens Bower
Sports Ground
Big Wood Comp. Sch.
Warren Prim. Sch.
31
GEDLING
NOTTINGHAM
Rise Park
St. Albans Rd.
Bestwood Lodge
The Strip
Old Lodge
4
BESTWOOD PARK DRIVE
DUNVEGAN
BRACADALE
BESTWOOD PARK DRIVE WEST
Church Field Plantations
Churchfield Way
Pavilion
WOODCHURCH
Tennis Courts
Rise Park Jun. & Inf. Schs.
Top Valley Comp. Sch. & Lib.
Recreation Area
BESTWOOD ROAD
46
Stanstead Primary School
Top Valley
Westglade Jun. & Inf. Sch.
BROADWOOD
St. Margaret Clitherow R.C. Prim. Sch.
5
HUCKNALL
COURSE
ALBERT BALL Comm. Centre
Playground
Playing Field
Southglade Jun. & Inf. Schs.
Glade Hill Prim. Sch.
Glade Hill
BECKHAMPTON
PEDMORE VALLEY
QUEENS BOWER
6
A611
Superstore
Southglade Park
Miniature Golf Course
BESTWOOD
Robin Hood Inf. & Jun. Schs.
Swimming Pool
Burford Prim. Sch.
B6004
SHERBROOK
345
Recreation Ground
Soldier's Hill
Potter's Hollow
Southglade Sports Centre
Tennis Cts.
Playground
EASTGLADE
Playing Field
The Beckhampton Centre
Hall
OXCLOSE
ROAD
7
ST. ALBANS ROAD
NG6
SOUTHGLADE
ANDOVER ROAD
LEYBOURNE
RAYMEDE
Tennis Courts
Bestwood Comm. Sch.
Henry Whipple Jun. & Inf. Schs.
Playing Fields
Community Centre
Playing Field
Hawthorns
CHIPPENHAM ROAD
EDWARDS LANE
Haywood Comp. School
BEDALE
455
A B C D E
TEVIOT
GAINSFORD ROAD
48
High Pavement Sixth Form College Playing Fields
ARNOLD
56's
57
RIDSDALE

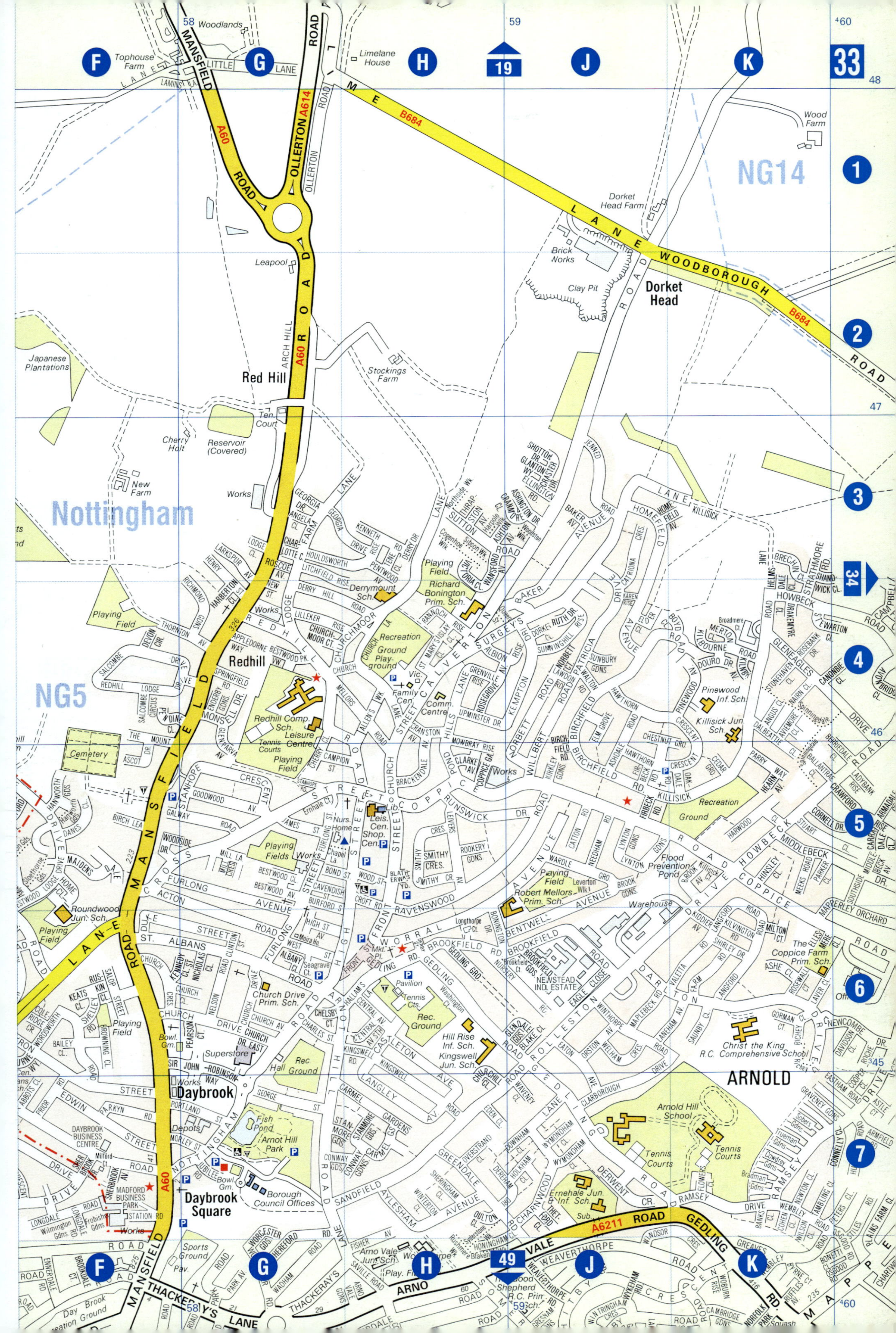

33
NG14
NG5
Nottingham
Arnold
Daybrook
Daybrook Square
Redhill
Red Hill
Dorket Head
Woodlands
Tophouse Farm
Limelane House
Wood Farm
Dorket Head Farm
Brick Works
Clay Pit
Japanese Plantations
Stockings Farm
New Farm
Cherry Holt
Reservoir (Covered)
Leapool
Ten. Court
Works
Playing Field
MANSFIELD ROAD
OLLERTON ROAD
A60
A614
B684
WOODBOROUGH LANE
WOODBOROUGH ROAD
ARCH HILL
ME LANE
Cemetery
Roundwood Jun. Sch.
Playing Field
Redhill Comp. Sch.
Leisure Centre
Tennis Courts
Playing Field
Recreation Ground Playground
Family Cen.
Comm. Centre
Derrymount Sch.
Richard Bonington Prim. Sch.
Playing Field
Pinewood Inf. Sch.
Killisick Jun. Sch.
Recreation Ground
Flood Prevention Pond
Robert Mellors Prim. Sch.
Warehouse
Nenstead Ind. Estate
The Coppice Farm Prim. Sch.
Christ the King R.C. Comprehensive School
Arnold Hill School
Tennis Courts
Church Drive Prim. Sch.
Superstore
Rec. Ground
Hall Ground
Hill Rise Inf. Sch.
Kingswell Jun. Sch.
Pavilion
Tennis Cts.
Rec. Ground
Daybrook Business Centre
Madford Business Park
Sports Ground
Fish Pond
Arnot Hill Park
Borough Council Offices
Shepherd R.C. Prim.
Arno Vale Jun. Sch.
Ernehale Jun. Inf. Sch.
Playing Field
Day Brook Recreation Ground
MANSFIELD ROAD
THACKERAY'S LANE
ARNO VALE ROAD
GEDLING ROAD
A6211
RAMSEY DRIVE
19
34
49
F G H J K
1 2 3 4 5 6 7
58 59 60
48 47 46 45

34
48
60
61
62
A
B
20
C
D
E
FOXWOOD
Wood Farm
1
Thorne
Wynhill
WESTFIELDS
LA.
Southwood
The Bank
Stoup Hill Farm
Bank Farm
Bank Hill Cottage
2
WOODBOROUGH
Arnold Lodge
NG14
ROAD BANK
B684
LANE
47
PLAINS
NOTTINGHAM
Wood Barn Farm
Works
Lambley House
3
HUNGERHILL
LBREC
MORE
SHANDWICK CL.
Howbeck Clo.
HELMS
33
Barn Farm
HOWBECK
CAMPBELL
FIRTH CL.
LANE
DRAKEMYRE
EWARTON
BANK
Mellish Rugby Football Club
4
GLENEAGLES DRIVE
MUIR BRIDGE ROAD
HAMILTON
CROMDALE CL.
Fox Covert
Nottingham
46
CANONBIE CL.
BRUECDALE
LADYBANK RISE
NG5
CAT FOOT
Foxhill Farm
HOWBECK
CRAWFORD DR.
CARRA DALE AV.
ARMADALE CL.
Coppice Farm
Nursery
Cottage Farm
LANE
Nursery
5
CORNELL DR.
SPORT
MIDDLEBECK
MIDDLE BECK AV.
PARKER
Nursery
Play Area
The Firs
CATFOOT
MEWS ROAD
SOUTHSIDE
MAPPERLEY
Highclere House
COPPICE
ORCHARD ROAD
DRIVE
DRIVE
PLAINS
6
The Coppice Farm Prim. Sch.
Offices
Middlebeck Farm
GORMAN CL.
NEWCOMBE DR.
DAVISON CL.
Lambley Dumble
45
School
Springlane Farm
LD
STOLLE CL.
GRAVENEY GDNS.
EASTHAM ROAD
CROPER CT.
ASTLE CT.
SPRING
HATHER LEIGH CR.
DUNSFORD DR.
AVENUE
Chicken Farm
7
CONNELLY
ARMFIELD RD.
HUNTER
OKEHAMPTON CR.
OKEHAMPTON DR.
THURLESTONE DR.
KINGSLEY DR.
CHEDINGTON DR.
LYFORD CL.
NG3
Crimea Farm
Factory
WEMBLEY
TAMBLING CL.
WINSTON
PETERS RD.
PLAINS FARM CL.
WINSTON CL.
PODDER LANE
COPSE
ASHWATER DR.
WOOLACOMB CL.
SPENCER AV.
LANE
SPRING
MEADOW
A
B
50
C
D
E
MAPPERLEY
60
61
62
Hill Top

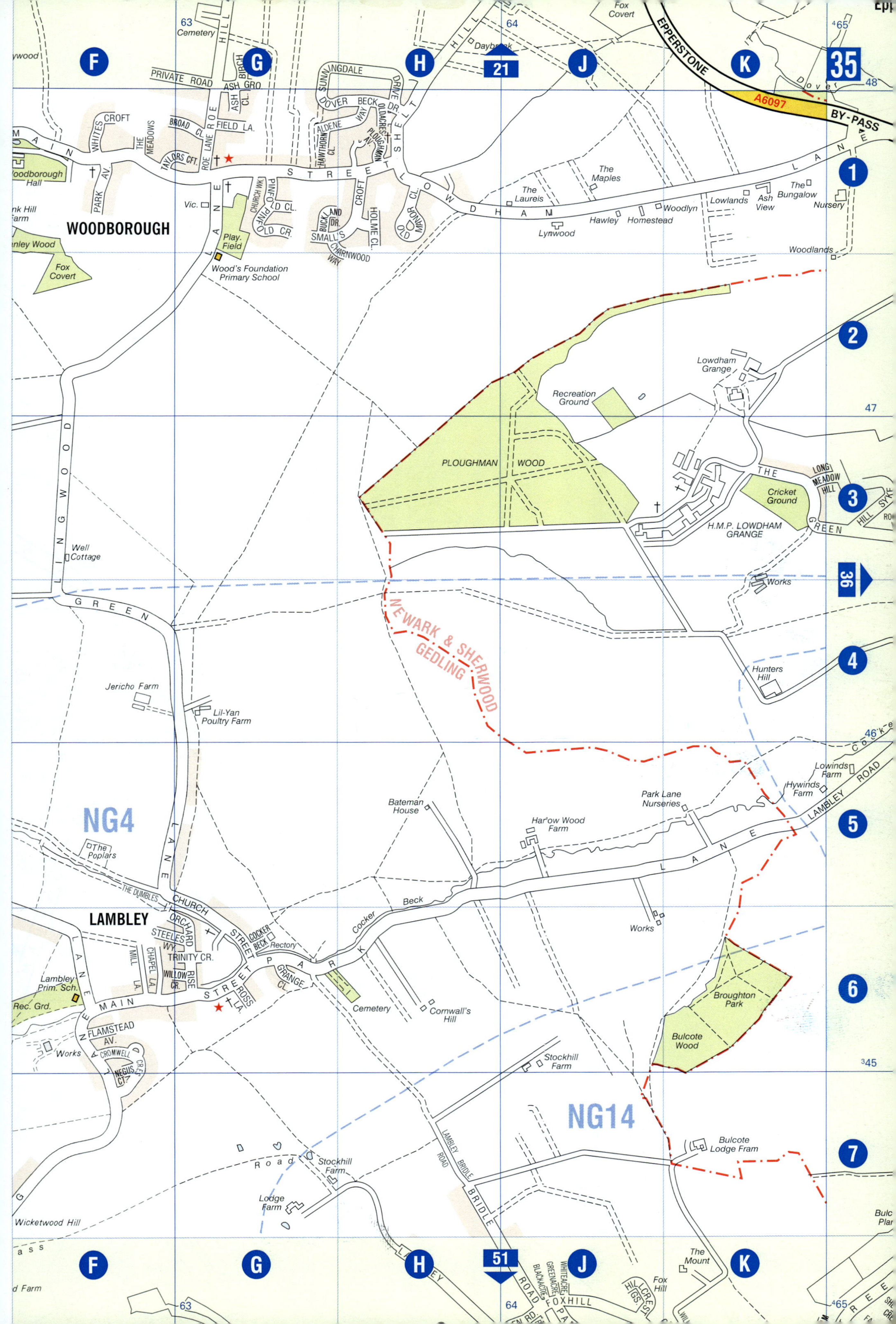
35
F G H J K
Epp
Fox Covert
EPPERSTONE
A6097
BY-PASS
Dover
63 Cemetery
HILL
64
Daybrook
21
48
65
1
PRIVATE ROAD
ASH GRO
BIRCH
ASH CL.
FIELD LA.
BROAD CL.
ROE LANE
TAYLORS CFT.
SUNNINGDALE
DOVER BECK
OLDACRES
ALDENE CL.
HAWTHORN CL.
DRIVE
PLOUGHMAN DR.
BECK WAY
STREET
LOWDHAM LANE
The Maples
The Laurels
The Bungalow
Nursery
WHITES CROFT
THE MEADOWS
MAIN
PARK AV.
Woodborough Hall
Woodborough
CHURCH WK.
PINFOLD CL.
PINFOLD CR.
Vic.
BUCKLAND DR.
SMALL'S
HOLME CL.
CROFT
MANOR CL.
OLD
LOWDHAM STREET
The Lauris
Hawley
Homestead
Woodlyn
Lowlands
Ash View
Woodlands
Lynwood
WOODBOROUGH
ank Hill Farm
anley Wood
Fox Covert
CHARNWOOD WAY
Play. Field
Wood's Foundation Primary School
2
Lowdham Grange
47
LINGWOOD
Recreation Ground
PLOUGHMAN WOOD
THE GREEN
LONG MEADOW HILL
HILL SYKE
RO
3
Well Cottage
Cricket Ground
H.M.P. LOWDHAM GRANGE
GREEN
Works
36
NEWARK & SHERWOOD
GEDLING
Hunters Hill
4
Jericho Farm
Lil-Yan Poultry Farm
46
Lowinds Farm
Hywinds Farm
LAMBLEY ROAD
NG4
Bateman House
Park Lane Nurseries
5
The Poplars
Har'ow Wood Farm
LANE
Cocker Beck
Works
THE DUMBLES
CHURCH
ORCHARD
STEELES WY.
COCKER BECK
Rectory
PARK
Cocker Beck
LAMBLEY
LAMBLEY
MILL LA.
CHAPEL LA.
TRINITY CR.
WILLOW CR.
STREET
GRANGE CL.
Broughton Park
6
Lambley Prim. Sch.
Rec. Grd.
LANE
MAIN
RISE
CROSS LA.
Cemetery
Cornwall's Hill
Bulcote Wood
FLAMSTEAD AV.
CROMWELL
NEGUS CT.
CRFT.
NG14
Stockhill Farm
45
Road
Stockhill Farm
LAMBLEY ROAD
LAMBLEY BRIDLE
Bulcote Lodge Fram
7
Works
Wicketwood Hill
Lodge Farm
Bulc Plar
ass
d Farm
F G H J K
51
LAMBLEY
WHITEACRE
GREENACRE
BLACKACRE
FOXHILL
HILLCRES
The Mount
Fox Hill
63
64
65

36
48
65
A
B
C
D
E
Order Beck
ROAD
Village Hall Pav.
Epperstone Playing Field
GONALSTON
Netherfield Farm House
Wash Bridge
Dover
LOWDHAM LA.
Beck
EPPERSTONE
1
LOWDHAM LA.
The Bungalow
Ash View
Nursery
OLD
EPPERSTONE
A6097
Old Mill House
Car Holt Farm
ROAD
GEDLING
NEWARK & SHERWOOD
Woodlands
Weir
Lela Dun
Car Holt
2
Eliment Hill Farm
Nurseries
West End Villas
ROAD
Lowdham Mill
Vicarage
Dover
47
THE
LONG MEADOW HILL
HILL SYKE
Crick Grou
GREEN
HILL
ROCKLEYS VIEW
The Hut
Cemetery
Orchard Nurseries
Brookfield
EPPERSTONE RD.
MOUNT PLEASANT
THE LEYS
C. of E. Sch.
MAIN
RIDGE HILL
Nottingham
Barker Hill
Hill House
3
OHAM
Greenacres
Grove Farm
CHURCH LA.
The Old Hall
THE PRIORS
NURSERY GDS.
St. Mary's CL.
Lib.
THE FORGE
FRANKLIN RD.
BARKER HILL
ROGERS AV.
The Beck House
ROAD
Beck
Nursery
STONEY LA.
BANK
TON LA.
BLACK-THORNE DR.
LANE
LOWDHAM
35
Low Meadow
Hunters Hill
Cocker
LAMBLEY
RED
PLOUGH
ELM TREE Farm
MANOR HOUSE CL.
Hall Rec. Grd.
A6097
CRANLEIGH DR.
NEIGHBOURS
SOUTH
4
Worlds End
LANE
BROOKSIDE
STREET
MORLEY'S CL.
REC. Grd.
THE CORNER
War Mem.
MAGNA
WILLOW HOLT
MERE VALE CL.
LIME TREE
NEWTON CL.
WOR
LEICESTER CL.
ROSS AV.
46
Lowinds Farm
Hywinds Farm
BYPASS
NOTTINGHAM STATION RD.
LIME TREE GDS.
BLENHEIM AV.
BLACKBECK
WOR.
SIDINGS
Char Ho
Lowdham
5
SKITHORNE RISE
Brakes Farm
VICTORIA AV.
MOOR AV.
LONG TRD.
THE DROPS
GUNTHORPE RD.
PAVILION
ROAD
Marlock Bridge
Lowdham Lodge
NG14
CT.
LOWDHAM
6
COTTAGE PASTURE LA.
Little Marlock
45
Slurry Pond
Cocker
Gran Far
OLD
Hill Farm
Sunny Bank
Sibthorpe House
A612
Beecroft Farm
Tall Trees Nurseries
7
Riding School
NOTTINGHAM
The Manor House
The Lodge
OLD MAIN RD.
The Cottage
Lake
Lake
Ce
Bulcote Hill Plantation
OLD
REDMAN'S DR.
MAIN RD.
Bulcote
52
Bulcote Crossing
Bulcote Farm
Gran Far
65
ROAD
SHAFTESBURY AV.
SHELFORD CRES.
THE RIDINGS
SPIN
THE LEAS
Corporation Cottages
A
B
C
D
E
66
67

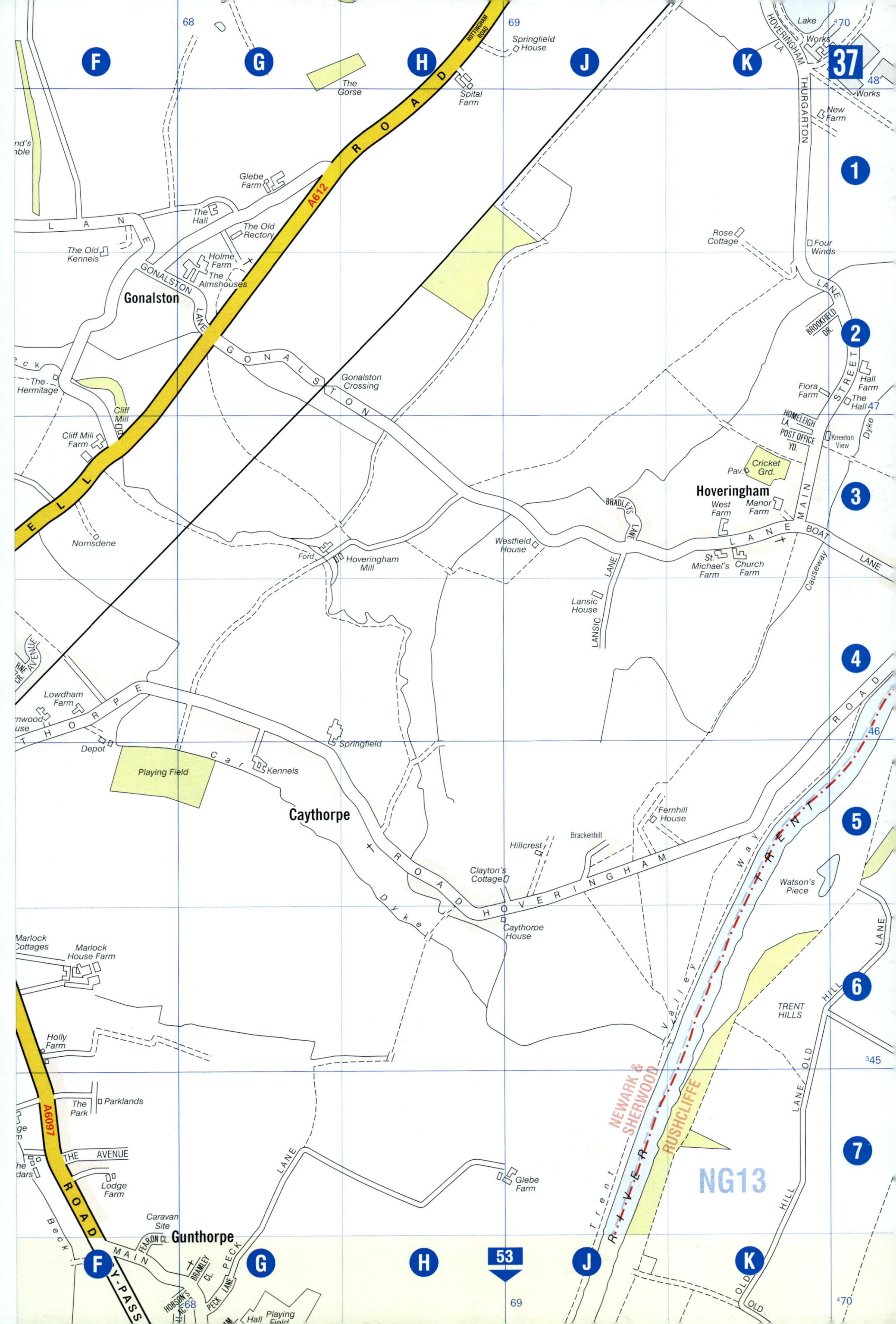

F
G
H
J
K
37
48
68
69
70
NOTTINGHAM ROAD
Springfield House
Lake
Works
HOVERINGHAM LA.
THURGARTON
New Farm
Works
1
The Gorse
Spital Farm
ROAD
Rose Cottage
Four Winds
LANE
Glebe Farm
A612
The Hall
The Old Rectory
BROOKFIELD DR.
2
nd's nble
LANE
The Old Kennels
Holme Farm
The Almshouses
Hall Farm
Flora Farm
STREET
The Hall 47
GONALSTON
Gonalston
GONALSTON LANE
Gonalston Crossing
HOMELEIGH LA.
POST OFFICE YD.
Kneeton View
The Hermitage
Peck
Cliff Mill
Cricket Grd.
Pav.
Hoveringham
3
Cliff Mill Farm
Norrisdene
BRADLEYS LANE
West Farm
Manor Farm
MAIN LANE
BOAT
LANSIC LANE
St. Michael's Farm
Church Farm
Causeway
LANE
Westfield House
Ford
Hoveringham Mill
Lansic House
4
AVENUE
ROAD
46
TRENT
Lowdham Farm
nwood use
THORPE
Depot
Car
Kennels
Springfield
Fernhill House
Brackenhill
Way
Watson's Piece
5
Playing Field
Caythorpe
Hillcrest
Clayton's Cottage
HOVERINGHAM
TRENT
Valley
HILL
6
Marlock Cottages
Marlock House Farm
ROAD DYKE
Caythorpe House
TRENT HILLS
OLD LANE
Holly Farm
NEWARK & SHERWOOD
RUSHCLIFFE
45
A6097
The Park
Parklands
LANE
Trent
RIVER
RUSHCLIFFE
NG13
7
THE AVENUE
Lodge Farm
ROAD
Glebe Farm
HILL
Beck
MAIN
Caravan Site
PECK LANE
Gunthorpe
F
BY-PASS
FEARON CL.
BRAMLEY CL.
HORSON'S
68
G
Hall
Playing Field
53
69
H
J
K
OLD LANE
70

38
30
31
22
WIRKSWORTH
32
A
B
C
D
E
Hole Farm
The Forge
Frampton Rise
B5023
Windley Meadows
1
Brewards Carr
Gunhills Farm
The Clouds
Gun Hills
44
GREEN LANE
Moseyley
GUNHILLS LANE
WOODFALL
Windleyhill Farm
2
Weir
BURLAND
Ivyhouse Farm
Newlands
Champion Carr
Spring Carr
3
43
Burland-green Plantation
DE6
Draycott Plantation
4
Sugar Loaf
Derby
Marplas Pantation
Cocks-hut-hill
DE22
Blind Brook
Ireton Rough
5
GOODWINS
Hall Close
Northfield Plantation
Newkennel Plantation
42
Oak Wood
Kennels
Gothic Temple
Beech Aven Cottages
6
Frost Covert
Ireton Gardens
Ireton Farm
CUMBERHILLS LANE
KEDLESTON
Stonequarry Plantation
BEECH
Brick-kiln Covert
Blindbrook Bridges
GOODWINS LANE
Ireton Lodge
HAY WOOD
North Lodge
Park N Wood
Cutler Brook
MERCASTON
The Smithy
Park House
Deer Cote
Saw Mill
7
41
Weir
South Lodge
Weir
KEDLESTON
Weir
Rectory
LODGE LANE
A
B
54
Weir
C
D
KEDLESTON PARK
King
E
Boat House
GOLF CLUB
ROAD
Club House
30
31
32

CHEVIN GOLF COURSE
Snape Wood
Lodge
Ground
39
F G H 23 J K
Lapwing Farm
Tennis Court
Newtony
Moscow
Moscow Farm
1
CHEVIN VALE ROAD
Ash Tree Cl.
Club Ho.
Chevin
NETHER CL.
Newtony La.
Chadfield Rd.
Avenue Road
Richmond Rd.
Hazeldene
Cemy.
Castle (remains of)
DERBY A6
RIVER DERWENT
44
Brook House
River Ecclesbourne
Duffield Meadows
Meadows Farm
Lime Road
Castle Hill
Vicarage
Prim. Sch.
St. Alkmunds
Mayfair Ct.
Castle Vw.
Station Rd.
Orchard Rd.
Castle App.
Pipe Bridge
2
Belper
DE56
Ecclesbourne
Sefton Way
Moulbourn Cl.
Cornhill Cl.
William Cl.
MEADOWS HOLLOWAY RD.
Philips St.
The Pastures
Champion St.
Hilt Cl.
King Street
Milford Road
Duffield
Halcyon
Rec. Grd.
Mill Green
Orchard Cotts.
Crown St.
Tamworth Lane
Fisher
Playing Field
Pav.
Cricket Grd.
Duffieldbank House
DUFFIELD
Snake Lane
Duck Island
De Ferrers Court
Curzon Ct.
The Park
The Mews
Street
Tennis Courts
Donald
3
Duffield Meadows Prim. Sch.
Meadow Dr.
Ferrers
Meadows Croft
Tennis Court
The Kirkstyles
Farnah House
Spring-field Dr.
Old Hall Av.
Hill View
Hazel
Ecclesbourne School
Tennis Courts
Ecclesbourne Av.
Ash Tree Farm
Library
Duffield Bridge
43
ROAD
Fairlawns
Vale
Wirksworth
Park
Old Hall Road
Marsden Lane
Lodge Cl.
Oak Cl.
Curzon La.
Devonshire Lane
Scarsdale Rd.
Granville Cl.
Melbourn Cl.
Ronan's Cl.
Duffield Hall
Makeney
ROAD
Cumberhill Farm
Caven-dish Cl.
Devonshire Dr.
New Zealand
Hall Farm
Gilbert Cres.
Chestnut Av.
Chestnut Cl.
Church Wlk.
Way
War Meml.
Westwind
4
Champion Farm
Works
Eaton Ct.
B5023
STREET DERBY
40
CUMBERHILLS
Park Leys
Celadon
ROAD WAY
Laundry
Depot
Hayley Croft
Flaxholme Av.
5
Cumberhill Farm
ROAD
Flaxholme
A6
Burley Meadows
Sewage Works
Bullpit Lane
Reservoir
Botany Farm
Quarndon Hill
Burleywood Farm
6
Park Nook Farm
AVENUE
THE
Park Nook
Park Nook House
The Elms
Quarndon House
Burley Wood
Bunker's Hill
ROAD
Burley Hill
7
Cricket Field
Pav.
The Plantation
AMBER VALLEY
DERBY
DUFFIELD
Quarndon Common
COACH DR.
The Edge
Suleys Fld.
Montpelier
COMMON ROAD
WOODLANDS LANE
BURLEY LANE
Holmwood Selworthy
Burley Grange
Carr Hole
Burley
Brook
41
Field Farm
The Curzon C. of E. Prim. Sch.
Sunnyside
F G H 55 J K
The Grange
33 34 35

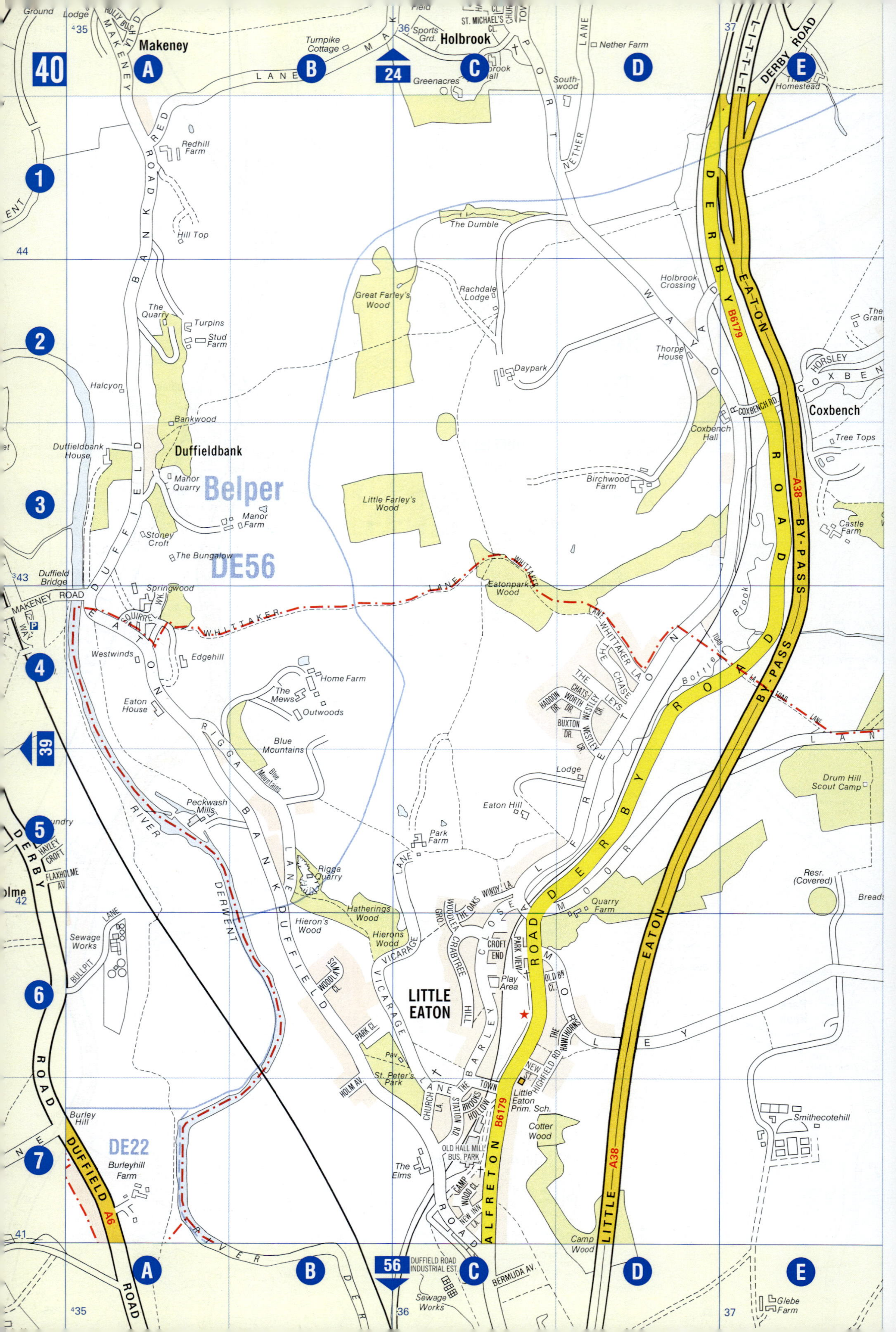

Ground
Lodge
HOLLY BUSH D
MAKENEY
Makeney
35
40
A
B
24
C
Field
Sports Grd.
St. Michael's CL.
Holbrook
TOV
CHURCH
36
D
37
E
LITTLE
DERBY ROAD
Turnpike Cottage
LANE
MAKE
Greenacres
Brook Hall
LANE
Nether Farm
Homestead
Southwood
NETHER
RED
ROAD
BANK
Redhill Farm
1
44
Hill Top
The Dumble
WAY
PORT
Holbrook Crossing
E-A-T-O-N
B6179
The Grang
2
The Quarry
Turpins
Stud Farm
Great Farley's Wood
Rachdale Lodge
Daypark
Thorpe House
DERBY
Coxbench Hall
HORSLEY
COXBEN
Coxbench
Halcyon
Bankwood
Little Farley's Wood
COXBENCH RD.
Birchwood Farm
ROAD
Tree Tops
Duffieldbank House
Duffieldbank
Belper
Manor Quarry
3
43
DE56
Manor Farm
Stoney Croft
The Bungalow
A38
Castle Farm
BY-PASS
Duffield Bridge
Springwood
SQUIRRE WK.
WHITTAKER
LANE
Eatonpark Wood
WHITTAKER
Brook
Makeney ROAD
WAY
P
EATON
Westwinds
Edgehill
LANE
THE CHASE
THE LEYS
Bottle
39
Eaton House
RIGGA
Home Farm
The Mews
Outwoods
HADDON DR.
CHATSWORTH DR.
WESTLEY CR.
WESTLEY CR.
BUXTON DR.
LANE
ROAD
BY-PASS
LANE
Drum Hill Scout Camp
5
undry
HAYLEY CROFT
FLAXHOLME AV.
DERBY
RIVER
BANK
Peckwash Mills
Blue Mountains
Blue Mountains
LANE
DUFFIELD
Rigga Quarry
Lodge
Eaton Hill
Eaton Hill
Park Farm
FOR
DERBY
Resr. (Covered)
42
olme
DERWENT
Hatherings Wood
Hieron's Wood
Hierons Wood
WINDY LA.
The OAKS
WOODLE
CROFT
Quarry Farm
EATON
Breads
Sewage Works
LANE
WOODLA CL.
VICARAGE
CRABTREE
CLOSE
Park View
ROAD
MOORLEY
6
Bullpit
VICARAGE
CROFT END
Play Area
OLD BN CL.
LITTLE EATON
HILL
BARLEY
THE HAWTHORNS
New HIGHFIELD RD.
Smithecotehill
ROAD
Burley Hill
DE22
PARK CL.
HOLM AV.
St. Peter's Park
Pav.
CHURCH LA.
The BROOKS
TOWN
HOLLOW
Little Eaton Prim. Sch.
Cotter Wood
7
41
DUFFIELD
Burleyhill Farm
A6
The Elms
STATION RD.
B6179
ALFRETON
Camp Wood
Camp Wood CL.
NEW INN
LA.
Old Hall Mill BUS. PARK
ROAD
A38
LITTLE
A
56
B
C
D
E
35
DUFFIELD ROAD INDUSTRIAL EST.
BERMUDA AV.
36
Sewage Works
37
Glebe Farm

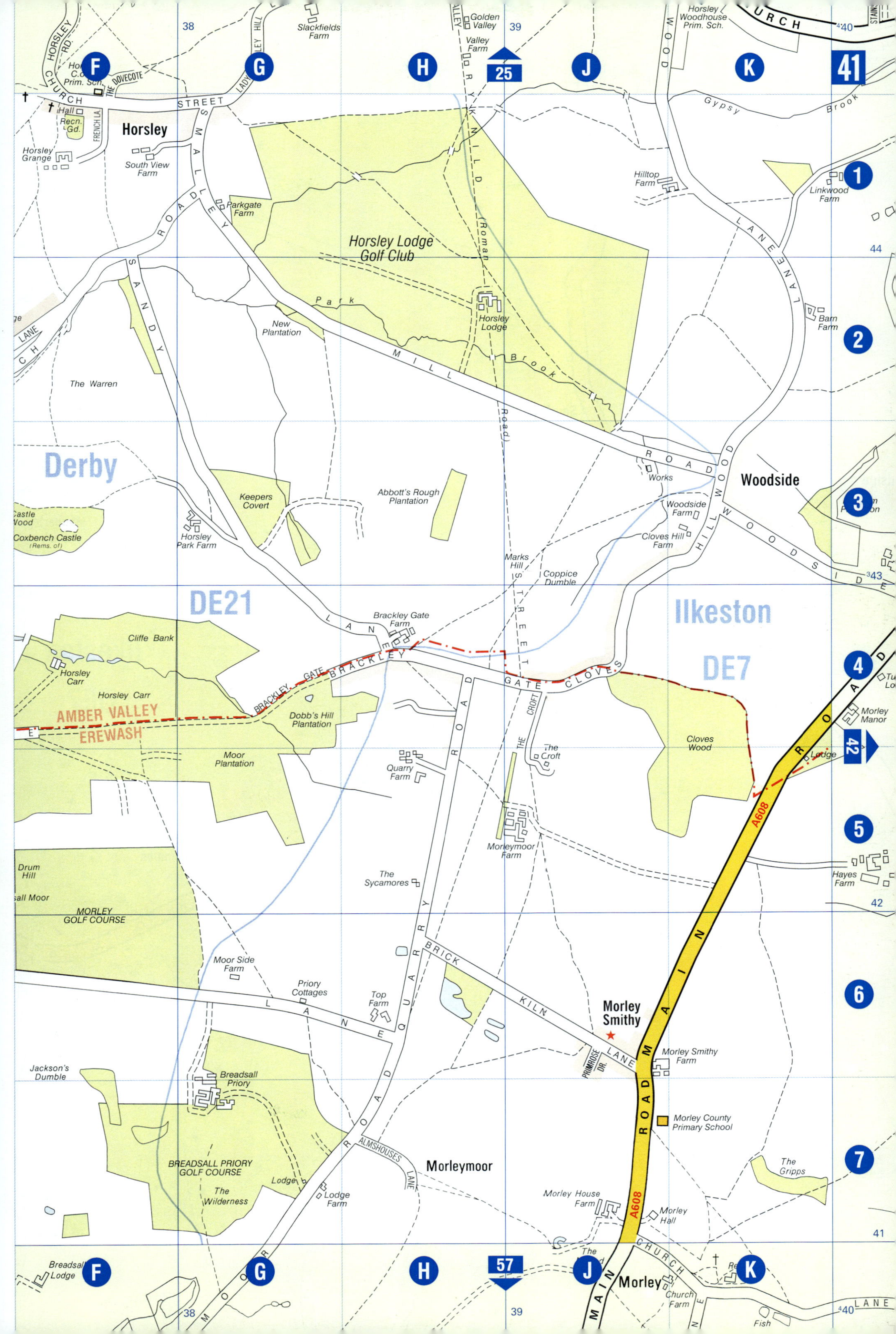

Horsley
Horsley C. of E. Prim. Sch.
CHURCH
Hall
Recn. Gd.
Horsley Grange
South View Farm
THE DOVECOTE
FRENCH LA.
CHURCH ST.
STREET
HORSLEY RD.
LADY HILL
Slackfields Farm
38
Golden Valley
Valley Farm
39
25
Horsley Woodhouse Prim. Sch.
DOOM LANE
CHURCH
40
STAINS
41
GYPSY Brook
Hilltop Farm
Linkwood Farm
1
44
Barn Farm
2
SANDY ROAD
MALLEY
Parkgate Farm
New Plantation
Horsley Lodge Golf Club
Park
MILL Brook
Roman Road
ROAD
Works
Woodside
HILL WOOD
WOODSIDE
3
43
Derby
The Warren
Castle Wood
Coxbench Castle (Rems. of)
Keepers Covert
Horsley Park Farm
Abbott's Rough Plantation
Marks Hill
Coppice Dumble
Woodside Farm
Cloves Hill Farm
Ilkeston
DE7
DE21
Cliffe Bank
Horsley Carr
Horsley Carr
AMBER VALLEY EREWASH
Dobb's Hill Plantation
Moor Plantation
Brackley Gate Farm
BRACKLEY GATE
BRACKLEY
LANE
GATE
CLOVES
THE CROFT
The Croft
Cloves Wood
Morley Manor
Lodge
42
A608
ROAD
4
Drum Hill
sall Moor
MORLEY GOLF COURSE
Quarry Farm
Morleymoor Farm
The Sycamores
Hayes Farm
5
42
6
Jackson's Dumble
Moor Side Farm
Priory Cottages
Top Farm
QUARRY LANE
BRICK KILN LANE
Morley Smithy
Morley Smithy Farm
PRIMROSE DR.
MAIN ROAD
A608
Breadsall Priory
LANE
Lodge Farm
ALMSHOUSES LANE
Morleymoor
Morley County Primary School
Morley House Farm
Morley Hall
The Gripps
7
41
Breadsall Priory Golf Course
The Wilderness
Lodge
MOOR ROAD
Breadsall Lodge
F
G
38
H
57
39
J
Morley
MAIN
CHURCH
Church Farm
Fish
K
40
LANE

42
A B C D E
Smalley
26
Plantation
42
Two Elms
Brook
Linkwood Farm
Stainsby House
Widdowson's Plantation
Barn Farm
Manchester Wood
The Bungalow
The Lodge
Whitehouse Farm
Abbot's Rough
Leys Houses
Smalley Hall
Ratcliffe Plantations
Long Plantation
The Wickets
Bell Lane Farm
West Meadow Farm
Smalley Green
A608
Mapperley Park
Mill Dam Plantation
Yew Tree Farm
Smalley Green Farm
Park Hall Farm
WOODSIDE
Ilkeston
DE7
Birch Cottage
Simonfield
Ilkeston
A609 ROAD
BELPER
Feran Hayes
Tudor Lodge
Club Room Farm
Morley Manor
41
Amber Valley Erewash
THE ROPEWALK
Stanley Common
Willow Cl.
Spencer St.
Andrews Dr.
Glendon St.
Blunt St.
Oakfield St.
Simon Fields Cl.
Tangley Av.
Smalley Common
Morleyhayes Wood
Stanley Common C. of E. Prim. Sch.
The Brickyard
Beaumont
Hayes Farm
Hayes Wood Lodge Farm
Hill Cl.
Hayes Av.
Valley View Dr.
Wood Rd.
Barker Cl.
Rec. Grd.
Crown Hill Wy.
Oakfield Farm
Little Wood
Hayeswood Farm
Stanley Lodge Farm
Crescent
Brough Farm
NEWGATE ST.
STATION
West Hallam Common
Valley Cottage
Bagot Farm
BAGOT ST.
Hayes Park Farm
Park Farm
Hilltop Farm
Briggswood Farm
The Gripp
MOSES LANE
COMMON
Rostrevor
CORONATION
Playing
58
41

43
Heanor
DE75
F G H J K
27
Flatmeadow Farm
Prospect Farm
The Tower
Shipley Hill
SHIPLEY COUNTRY PARK
Shipley Lake
THE AMERICAN ADVENTURE THEME PARK
Courts
Cricket Ground
Pav.
Dog Kennel Coppice
Hogg's Pond
Cottage
HASSOC
Rose Co
Mapperley Reservoir Nature Trail
Square Wood
Pond House
Mapperley Reservoir
Lodge Farm
Shipley Common
Mapperley Pond
Mapperley Wood
Park Hall
PARK HALL LANE
Rec. Grd.
THE LIMES
Mapperley
COACH WAYS
SYCAMORE CL.
Sch.
ROAD
SLACK
Head House Farm
Mapperley Farm
MAIN ST.
CORNIN RD.
CORONATION RD.
New Church Farm
Woodlands
MAPPERLEY
Mapperley Park Wood
Brook
The Brook
MAPPERLEY BROOK
HALL LANE
Brook Plantation
Brook Farm
Coppice Farm
West Hallam
A609
LANE
WEST HIGH
LANE
CENTRAL HIGH
LANE A609
Rec. Grd.
KILN CL.
Rec. Grd.
EWCOTE LA.
Rec. Grd.
CHATSWORTH CT.
SURBITON CL.
WHITTON CR.
HARTINGTON CL.
DERBYSHIRE
RIBER CL.
DERBY AV.
BRASS
SHIRE
CRESCENT
AVENUE
The Tinklers
LECHLADE CL.
HYSON
WALTON
MARLOW CR.
HAYE'S CL.
CHILTERN DR.
BURGO WAY
DERWENT
DARLEY
PICKINGTON CL.
GRINDSLOW
FERNILEE CL.
Paddock Farm
ETON CT.
HALLAM
HENLEY CL.
RICHMOND
EARNHAM
ELIZABETH
WEYBRIDGE WALK
PEVERIL
HARDWICK AV.
LATHKILL CL.
Whitefurrows
HAM CL.
BURN CL.
CHERTSEY CT.
ASHFORD CL.
KINGSTON CT.
HURLEY WALK
CAVERSHAM WAY
HAMPTON CL.
HARLOW CT.
SCARGILL
Greenacres
ROAD
SUNNINGHILL CL.
NURSERY
HOLME CFT.
ST. WILFRID'S
AVENUE
Sports Ground
Rec. Grd.
Pav.
Scargill C. of E. Prim. Sch.
ASCOT CL.
BURNT OAK CL.
ROAD
BEECH LANE
THE VILLAGE
Beechcroft
DALES SHOP. CEN.
The Spinney
Glebe Farm
EAST
Works
The Rookery
ORCHARD CL.
SCHOOL SQ.
HALL CT.
The Dell
Newdigates New Covert
Thacker Barn Cottages
Stanley
Brook
St. John House R.C. Scho
Station House
The Grange
Ordnance House
59
Newdigates New Covert
Thacker Barn
ABBOT
PRIORY
42
41
1
2
3
4
44
5
6
7

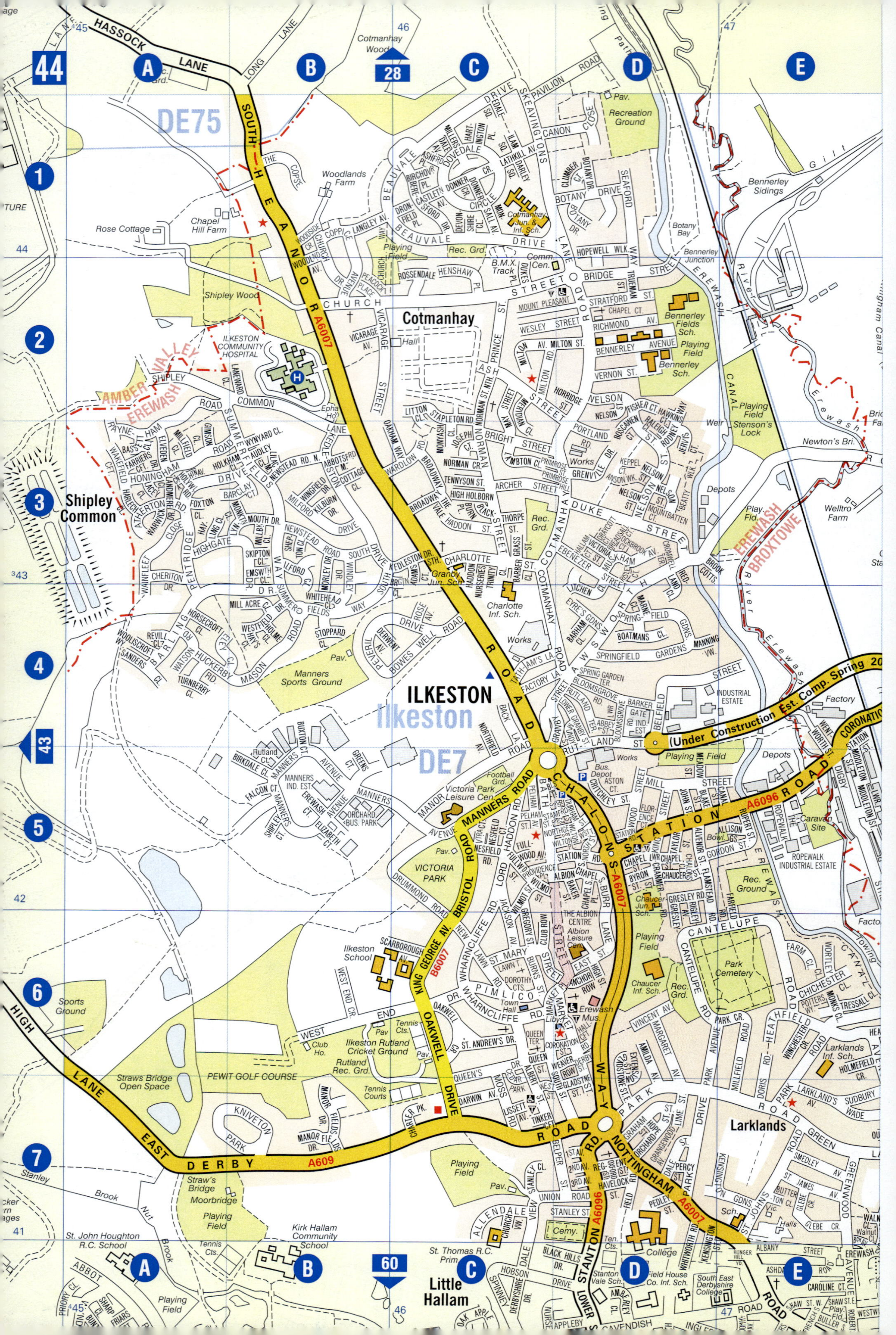
44
DE75
Cotmanhay
Shipley Common
ILKESTON
Ilkeston
DE7
Little Hallam
Larklands
AMBER VALLEY
EREWASH
EREWASH
BROXTOWE
HEANOR ROAD
A6007
SOUTH STREET
CHURCH STREET
SUMMERFIELDS
STATION ROAD
A6096
NOTTINGHAM ROAD
A6007
DERBY ROAD
A609
HIGH LANE EAST
BRISTOL ROAD
KING GEORGE AV
B6007
OAKWELL DRIVE
MANNERS ROAD
BATH STREET
CHALONS WAY
CANTELUPE ROAD
CORONATION ROAD
Ilkeston Community Hospital
Shipley Wood
Shipley Common
Rose Cottage
Chapel Hill Farm
Woodlands Farm
Ilkeston School
Victoria Park
Victoria Park Leisure Cen.
Manners Sports Ground
Pewit Golf Course
Straws Bridge Open Space
Straw's Bridge Moorbridge Playing Field
Ilkeston Rutland Cricket Ground
Rutland Rec. Grd.
Park Cemetery
Park Cemetery
Ropewalk Industrial Estate
Industrial Estate
Recreation Ground
Bennerley Sidings
Bennerley Junction
Botany Bay
Stenson's Lock
Welltro Farm
Newton's Bri.
St. John Houghton R.C. School
Kirk Hallam Community School
St. Thomas R.C. Prim
South East Derbyshire College
Larklands Inf. Sch.
Cotmanhay Jun. & Inf. Sch.
Bennerley Fields Sch.
Bennerley Sch.
Charlotte Inf. Sch.
Granby Jun. Sch.
Chaucer Jun. Sch.
Chaucer Inf. Sch.
Field House Co. Inf. Sch.
Sports Ground
Town Hall
Erewash Mus.
Albion Leisure
The Albion Centre
Gill
River Erewash
Nottingham Canal
Erewash Canal
45
46
47
44
43
42
41
28
60

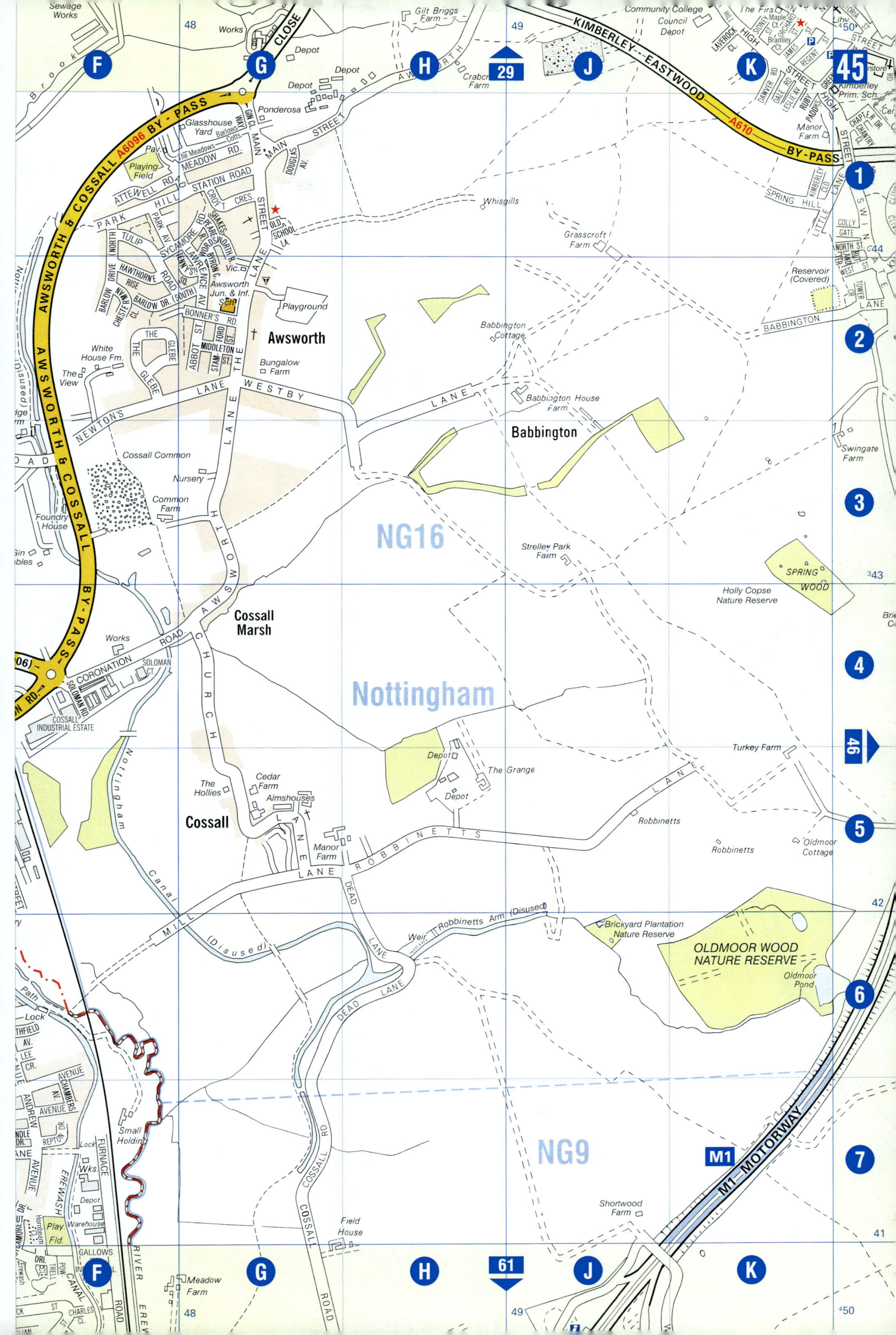

Sewage Works
Works
CLOSE
Gilt Briggs Farm
KIMBERLEY - EASTWOOD
Community College Council Depot
The First
LAVEROCK CL.
HIGH STREET
SIDNEY ST.
Bramley
Maple Ct.
VICTORIA STREET
45
Depot
Depot
Depot
Crabtree Farm
29
J
A610
BY-PASS
Manor Farm
DAWKER RD.
DALE RD.
LESLIE AV.
RUBY PADDOCKS
ORCHARD
CHANTRY
Kimberley Prim. Sch.
1
Works
Ponderosa
Glasshouse Yard
Barlow Cotts.
GIN CL.
MAIN STREET
DOUGLAS AV.
Whisgills
SPRING HILL
KIMBERLEY CLO.
LITTLE LANE
SWINGATE
AWSWORTH & COSSALL A6096 BY-PASS
The Meadows
MEADOW RD.
Station Road
PARK HILL
ATTEWELL RD.
Playing Field
Pav.
Grasscroft Farm
COLLY GATE
NORTH ST.
44
SYCAMORE
CROFT CRES.
SHAKESWORTH CL.
WORDSWORTH RD.
OLD SCHOOL LA.
Reservoir (Covered)
TOWER LANE
PARK AV.
TULIP
BARLOW NTH.
HAWTHORNE RISE
CHESTER CL.
LAWRENCE AV.
BYRON C.
PENNY SQ.
Vic.
Awsworth Jun. & Inf. Sch.
BABBINGTON
2
BARLOW DRIVE NORTH
BARLOW DR. (SOUTH)
BONNER'S RD.
T.S.
STAM. ST.
MIDDLETON ST.
ABBOT
Playground
Babbington Cottage
Swingate Farm
White House Fm.
THE GLEBE
Awsworth
The View
NEWTON'S ROAD
FORD ST.
Bungalow Farm
WESTBY
LANE
Babbington House Farm
Babbington
3
43
Foundry House
Gin Stables
Cossall Common
Nursery
AWSWORTH LANE
THE LANE
Common Farm
NG16
Strelley Park Farm
Holly Copse Nature Reserve
SPRING WOOD
Brier
Works
CHURCH ROAD
Cossall Marsh
Nottingham
4
CORONATION
SOLOMAN CT.
SOLOMAN RD.
06
NOTTINGHAM RD.
COSSALL INDUSTRIAL ESTATE
Nottingham Canal (Disused)
Cedar Farm
The Hollies
Almshouses
Depot
The Grange
Depot
Turkey Farm
46
5
Cossall
Manor Farm
LANE
ROBBINETTS
Robbinetts
Robbinetts
Oldmoor Cottage
42
MILL
DEAD LANE
Weir
Robbinetts Arm (Disused)
Brickyard Plantation Nature Reserve
OLDMOOR WOOD NATURE RESERVE
NORTHFIELD AV.
LEE CR.
Lock
Path
Oldmoor Pond
6
CHAMBERS
AVENUE
ANDREW
AVENUE
PRIOR RD.
RANDLE
REPTON
LANE
Lock
Small Holding
COSSALL RD.
NG9
M1 MOTORWAY
7
FURNACE ROAD
EREWASH
Wks
Depot
Warehouse
Play Fld.
RIVER EREWASH CANAL
Field House
Shortwood Farm
41
GALLOWS
DRI.
POW TRELL
CHARLES CL.
ST.
Meadow Farm
COSSALL ROAD
48
49
50

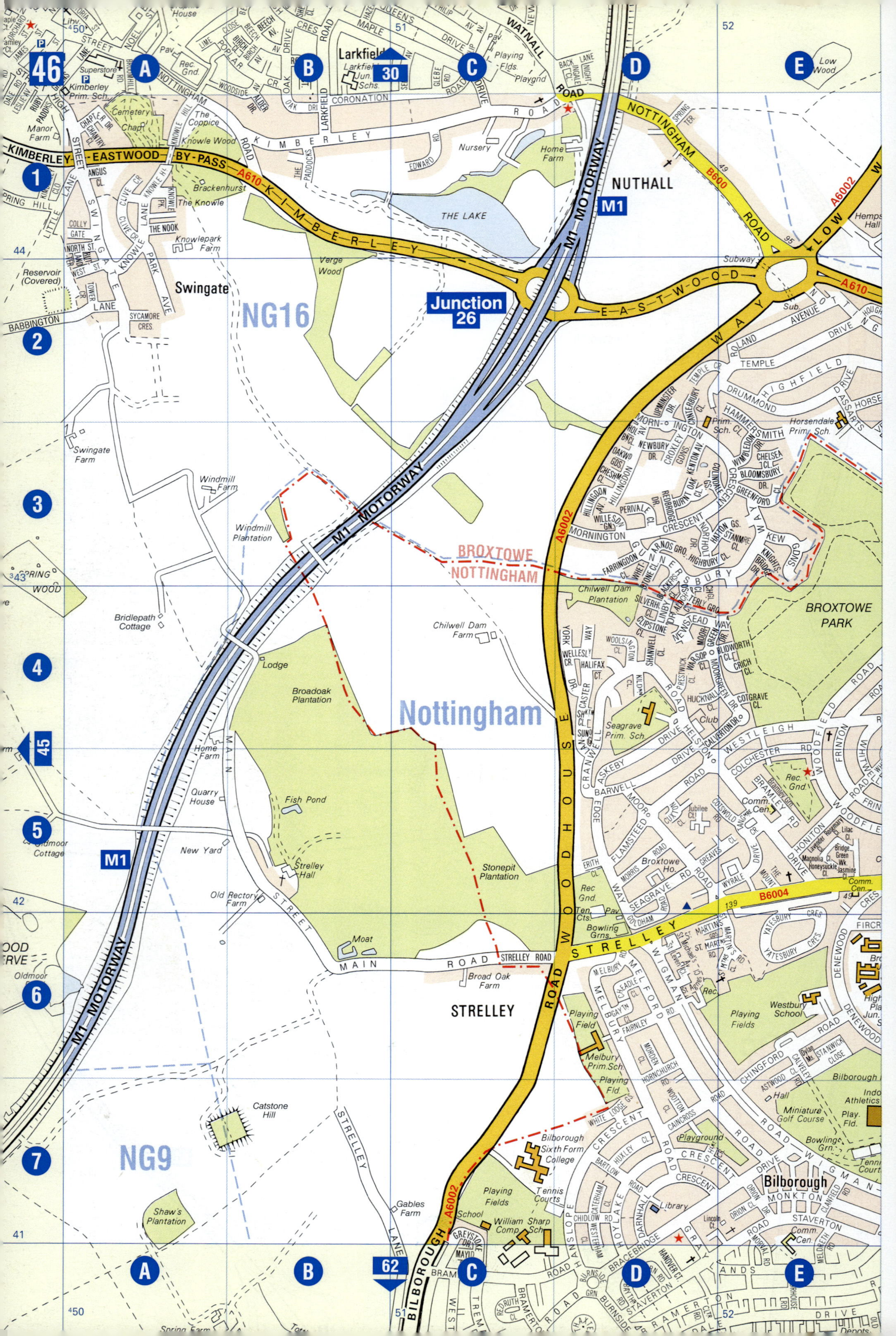

46
KIMBERLEY - EASTWOOD - BY - PASS
A610 KIMBERLEY ROAD
NG16
Swingate
Larkfield
Larkfield Jun. Schs.
30
Kimberley Prim. Sch.
Cemetery
Chapl.
The Coppice
Knowle Wood
Brackenhurst
The Knowle
THE NOOK
Knowlepark Farm
Swingate Farm
Windmill Farm
Windmill Plantation
Reservoir (Covered)
BABBINGTON
SPRING WOOD
Bridlepath Cottage
M1 MOTORWAY
Junction 26
THE LAKE
Nursery
Home Farm
NUTHALL
M1
EASTWOOD WAY
Subway
NOTTINGHAM ROAD
B690
LOW WOOD
A6002
Hempshill Hall
Low Wood
BROXTOWE NOTTINGHAM
Chilwell Dam Plantation
Chilwell Dam Farm
Lodge
Broadoak Plantation
Nottingham
Home Farm
Quarry House
New Yard
Fish Pond
Strelley Hall
Old Rectory Farm
Moat
MAIN STREET
MAIN ROAD
STRELLEY ROAD
Broad Oak Farm
STRELLEY
Stonepit Plantation
Oldmoor Cottage
M1
Oldmoor
NG9
Catstone Hill
Shaw's Plantation
STRELLEY LANE
Gables Farm
BILBOROUGH ROAD
A6002
Bilborough Sixth Form College
Playing Fields
School
William Sharp Comp. Sch.
62
WOODHOUSE WAY A6002
BROXTOWE PARK
Horsendale Prim. Sch.
Seagrave Prim. Sch.
Broxtowe Ho.
STRELLEY ROAD
B6004
Melbury Prim. Sch.
Westbury School
Playing Fields
Miniature Golf Course
Indoor Athletics
Bilborough
Library
Tennis Courts
Playing Fields

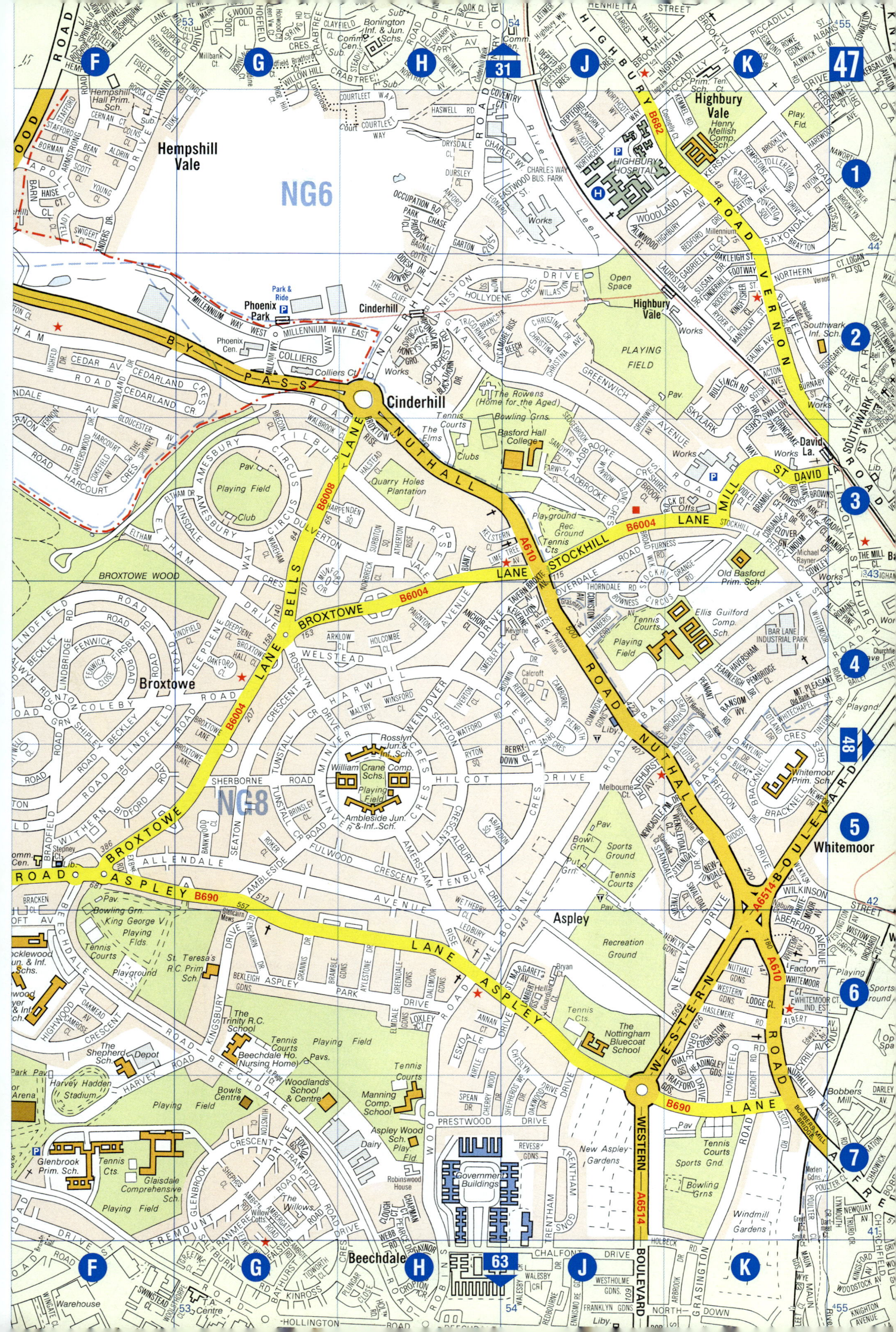

47
31
63
48
NG6
NG8
Hempshill Vale
Cinderhill
Highbury Vale
Broxtowe
Whitemoor
Aspley
Beechdale
Phoenix Park
Park & Ride
Phoenix Cen.
Colliers
Millennium Way West
Millennium Way East
Highbury Hospital
Highbury Vale
Playing Field
Open Space
Basford Hall College
The Rowens (Home for the Aged)
Bowling Grns.
Quarry Holes Plantation
Playing Field
Broxtowe Wood
William Crane Comp. Schs.
Rosslyn Jun. & Inf. Sch.
Ambleside Jun. & Inf. Sch.
Ellis Guilford Comp. Sch.
Bar Lane Industrial Park
Whitemoor Prim. Sch.
Old Basford Prim. Sch.
David La.
Southwark Inf. Sch.
Henry Mellish Comp. Sch.
Mt. Pleasant
The Nottingham Bluecoat School
Recreation Ground
Aspley Wood Sch. Play Fld.
The Trinity R.C. School
St. Teresa's R.C. Prim. Sch.
The Shepherd Sch.
Beechdale Ho. (Nursing Home)
Woodlands School & Centre
Manning Comp. School
Harvey Hadden Stadium
Glenbrook Prim. Sch.
Glaisdale Comprehensive Sch.
Government Buildings
Robinswood House
New Aspley Gardens
Windmill Gardens
Bobbers Mill
The Mill
Playing Field
Stockhill
NUTHALL ROAD
STOCKHILL LANE
BROXTOWE LANE
ASPLEY LANE
WESTERN BOULEVARD
BELLS LANE
BY-PASS ROAD
NUTHALL ROAD
VERNON ROAD
SOUTHWARK STREET
CHURCH STREET
MILL STREET
DAVID LANE
A610
A6514
B690
B6004
B6008
B682

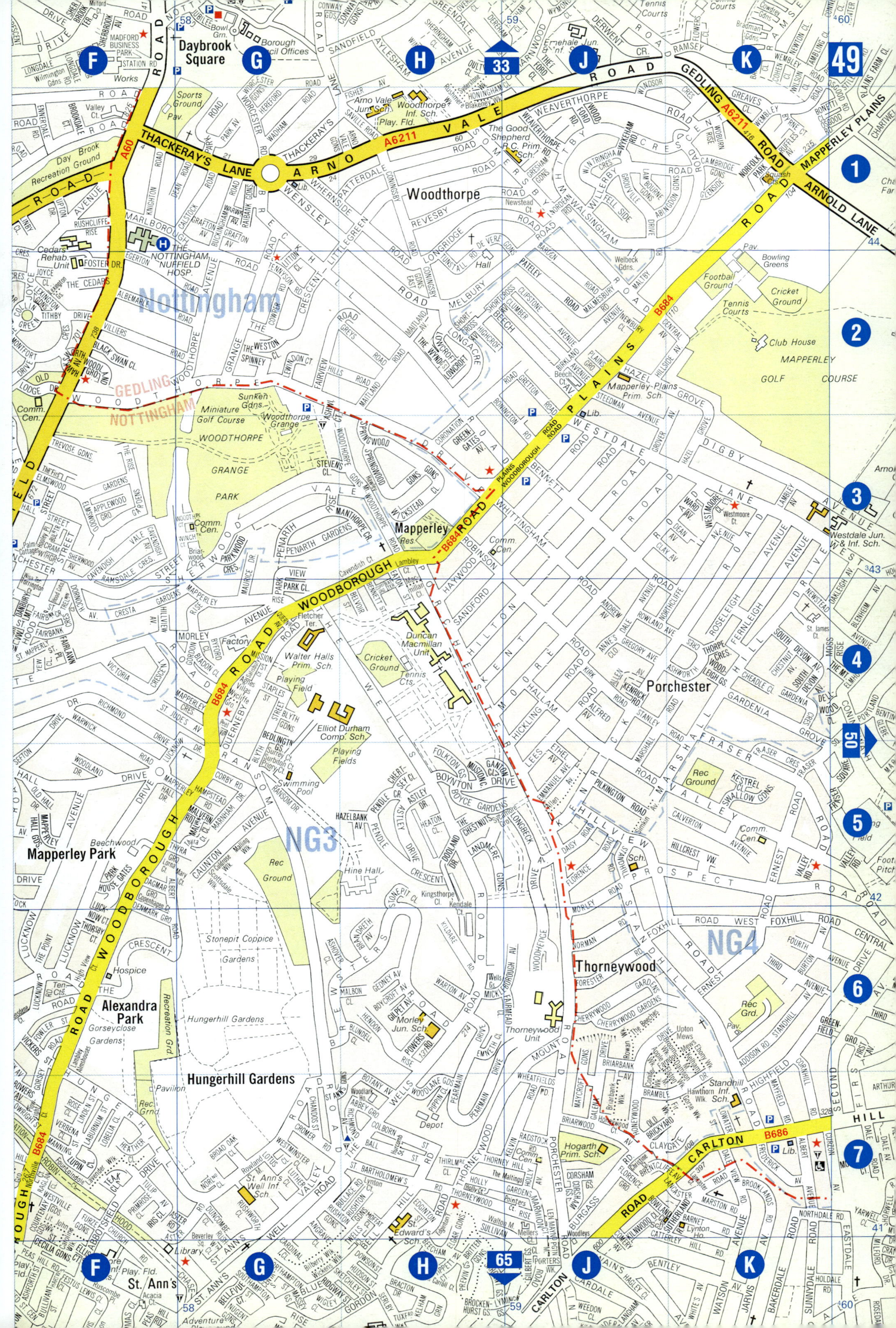

49
F
G
H
33
J
K
Daybrook Square
Woodthorpe
Mapperley Plains
Arnold Lane
THACKERAY'S LANE
A6211
ARNO VALE ROAD
GEDLING A6211 ROAD
B684
The Nottingham Nuffield Hosp.
Nottingham
Gedling Nottingham
Woodthorpe Grange Park
Mapperley
Mapperley Plains
MAPPERLEY GOLF COURSE
Club House
Cricket Ground
Football Ground
Bowling Greens
Tennis Courts
Westdale Jun. & Inf. Sch.
WOODBOROUGH ROAD
B684
Duncan Macmillan Unit
Walter Halls Prim. Sch.
Cricket Ground
Tennis Cts.
Elliot Durham Comp. Sch.
Swimming Pool
Porchester
Rec Ground
NG3
NG4
Mapperley Park
WOODBOROUGH ROAD
B684
Alexandra Park
Hospice
Thorneywood
West Foxhill Road
Foxhill Road
Rec Grd.
Green-field
Hungerhill Gardens
Morley Jun. Sch.
Thorneywood Unit
Standhill Inf. Sch.
Hogarth Prim. Sch.
CARLTON ROAD B686
HILL
St. Ann's
St. Ann's Well Inf. Sch.
Library
F
G
H
65
J
K
1
2
3
4
50
5
6
7
A60

50
MAPPERLEY B684
NG3
NG4
Crimea Farm
Hill Top Nursery
Chase Farm
ARNOLD A6211
Bowling Greens
Cricket Ground
Club
MAPPERLEY GOLF COURSE
Wood Farm
Glebe Farm
Harvey's Plantation
Scotgrave Farm
Household Waste and Recycling Centre
Gedling Wharf
Playing Field
Kennels
Glebe Farm Vw
Arnold & Carlton College
Carlton Digby Sch.
Westdale Jun. & Inf. Sch.
Digby Hall Dr.
Gedling Stanhope Prim. Sch.
The Playing Field
The Gedling Comp. Sch.
Liby
Gedling
Rec. Ground
Westdale Avenue
Drive
Holyoake Rd.
West Avenue
Cavendish
Highgate
Wheldon Road
Cemetery
Willow Farm Prim. Sch.
St. James
Cookson Av.
Cavendish Av.
Rufford Av.
Orchard Ct.
Perlethorpe Cres.
Perlethorpe Av.
Phoenix Avenue
Queens Avenue
Marion Murdoch Ct.
Marwood Cres.
Glendale Cl.
Haddon Prim. Sch.
Grassing Dale Cl.
Welbeck Av.
Besecar Av.
Cantley Avenue
St. Michael's Avenue
St. Mary's Avenue
Newcastle Av.
Imperial Av.
Phoenix Av.
Phoenix Inf. Sch.
The Wheldon Comp. Sch.
Comm. Cen.
Violet Road
Violet Rd.
Veronica
Lavender Gro.
Heather Rd.
Hartington
Baslow Avenue
Carlton Castleton Av.
Priory Jun. Sch.
All Hallows Prim. Sch.
Bramble Cl.
Gedling Manor
Youth Cen.
Carlton Forum Leisure Centre North
Playing Field
Football Pitch
Belper Road
Buxton Avenue
Crimford
Pierrepont Av.
Addolton Av.
Barons Cl.
Priory Cres.
Hardy's Dr.
First Av.
Second Av.
Tennyson Avenue
Duncroft Av.
The Orchard
SHEARING HILL A6211
Valley Rd.
Prospect Road
Foxhill
Winster Pave.
Ramsdale Cres.
Oxford
Westdale Av.
Darley
Chestnut
Albert St.
Victoria St.
Ranmoor Rd.
Vernon Av.
Burton Dr.
Brooklands Dr.
Brook Lands Cr.
Pav.
Recreation Ground
COLWICK
Carlton Forum Leisure Centre South
The Richard Herrod Bowls Centre
Comm. Cen.
Rushcliffe Av.
Carnarvon
Cambridge Street
Burlington
St. Austins Dr.
St. Austins Ct.
Redland Grove
Gedling Rd.
Orlando Drive
Dowerbridge Rd.
Ouse Bridge Dr.
Council Offices
Highclere Dr.
Freemans Rd.
Willow Cr.
Conway Cr.
Green Field
Middle Av.
Third Av.
Campbell Drive
Foxhill
Lilac Gro.
Myrtle Gro.
Campbell Gro.
Grove
Deep Furrow Av.
Beck
Worth
Garden City
East Road
CARLTON
T.A. Cen.
Carlton Cemetery
Allwood Dr.
Badger Dr.
Carlisle Av.
Ian Gro.
Park Av.
Redland Av.
Eastholme
Midland
Netherfield Jun. Sch.
Belvoir Green
Works
Highfield
Mayfield
Arthur St.
Hastings S.
Lambley Rd.
Forrester St.
Celia Dr.
Central Inf. Sch.
Central Jun. Sch.
Chesterfield St.
Gladstone St.
Cromwell
Church Rd.
Superstore
Station
Carlton Sq.
Elm Av.
Manor Lib.
Crown Walk
Carlton Business Centre
Carlton
Bowl. Grn. Rec. Ground
Youth Cen.
Nozi Kotz
Morris St.
Recreation Ground
Carlton Grange
Kirk Bldgs.
Sacred Heart R.C. Prim. Sch.
Southcliffe Rd.
Southdale Dr.
Mount Pleasant
Shipley Rise
Newgate Cl.
Fearn Chase Ct.
Greenland Cres.
St. John's Ct.
Kensington
Parkdale Prim. Sch. Playing Field
Avondale
South Dale Dr.
Cliff
Trentdale Rd.
Oakdale Road
Woodlane
Whimsey Park
The
Victoria Rd.
Meadow
Britannia
Netherfield
CARLTON HILL B686
B686
HILLBURTON B686
Priory Road
Main Road
Jessops

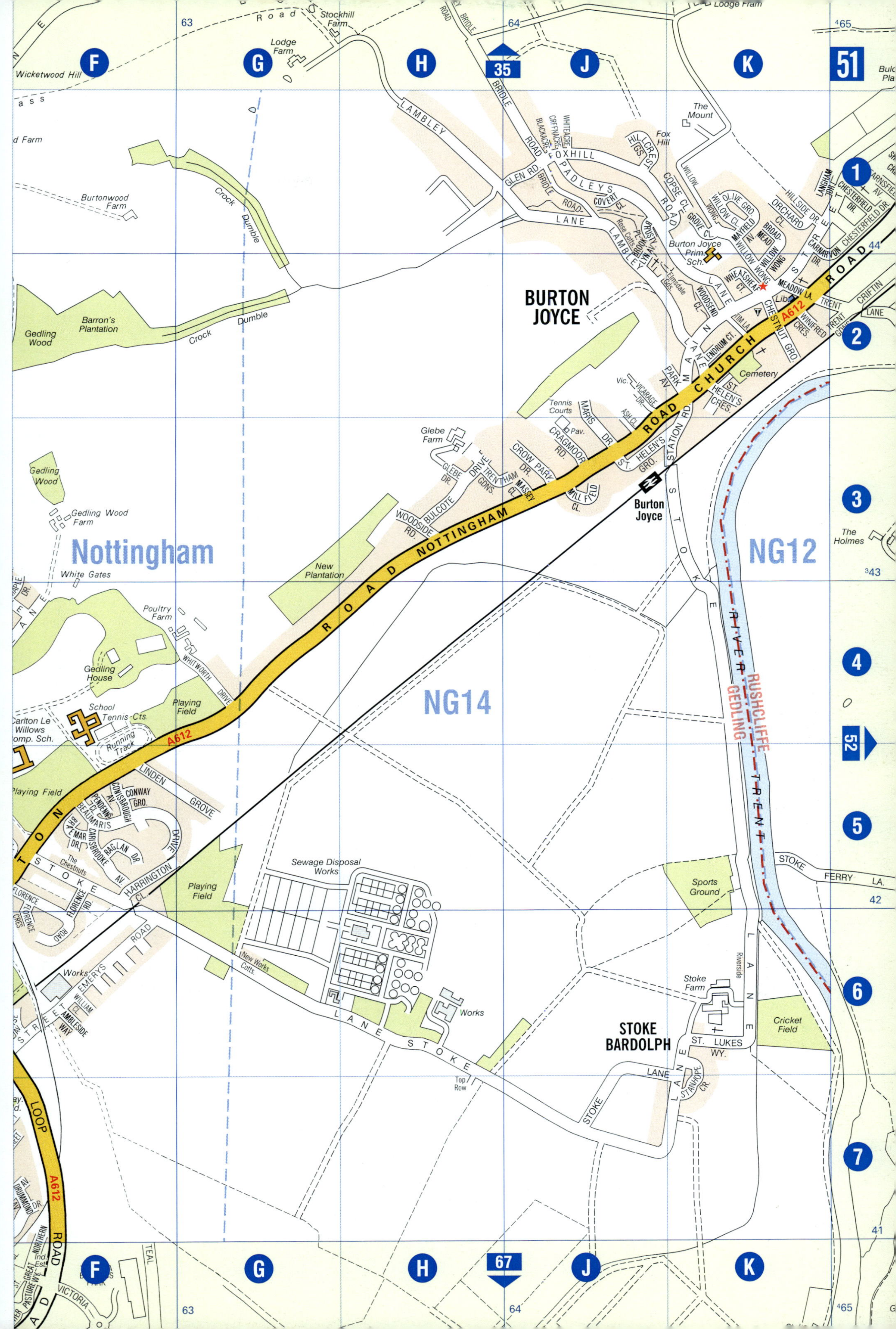

Wicketwood Hill
Stockhill Farm
Road
Lodge Farm
Lodge Farm
F
G
H
35
J
K
51
d Farm
Burtonwood Farm
Crock Dumble
The Mount
BRIDLE
LAMBLEY
FOXHILL
WHITEACRE
CLIFFNACRE
HILLCREST
Fox Hill
WILLOW
The Mount
1
GLEN RD
PADLEYS
COVERT
COPSE CL
OLIVE GRO
MAYFIELD
BROAD
ORCHARD
HILLSIDE DR
LANGHAM
CHESTERFIELD DR
CHESTERFIELD DR
Barron's Plantation
Gedling Wood
BRIDLE
ROAD
LANE
CRESTY MAY CL
Rose Cottes
Eastdale Gdns
WILLOW CL
GROVE CT
WILLON WONG
WILLOW WONG
MEAD
CARNARVON DR
TRENT GONS
CRIFTIN
LANE
44
Crock Dumble
LAMBLEY
Burton Joyce Prim. Sch.
WHEATSHEAF CT
WOODSEND
MEADOW LA.
Lib.
WINIFRED CRES
TRENT
2
BURTON JOYCE
LENDRUM CT
A612
Cemetery
ST. HELEN'S CRES
Vic.
VICARAGE
PARK AV
ROAD
CHURCH
ST. HELEN'S
STATION RD
Tennis Courts
MARIS DR
CRAGMOOR RD.
ASH CL.
GRO.
3
Glebe Farm
Pav.
CROW PARK DR.
MASSEY CT
ROAD
NG12
The Holmes
Nottingham
GLEBE DR
DRIVE
TRENTHAM GDNS.
WILL FYELD CL.
Burton Joyce
343
White Gates
WOODSIDE RD.
BULCOTE
NOTTINGHAM
4
Gedling Wood
Gedling Wood Farm
New Plantation
RIVER
RUSHCLIFFE
GEDLING
52
Poultry Farm
WHITWORTH DRIVE
NG14
TRENT
Gedling House
Playing Field
5
School
Tennis Cts.
A612
Carlton Le Willows Comp. Sch.
Running Track
STOKE
STOKE FERRY LA.
42
Playing Field
LINDEN GROVE
Sports Ground
LINTON
CONWAY GRO.
PENDINE AV.
CONSBROUGH AV.
BEAUMARIS DR.
RAGLAN DR.
HARRINGTON CL.
Playing Field
Sewage Disposal Works
LANE
6
Playing Field
BRA MAR DR.
CARISBROOKE AV.
The Chestnuts
FLORENCE RD.
FLORENCE CRES
ROAD
Riverside
Stoke Farm
Cricket Field
Works
New Works Cotts.
Works
STOKE BARDOLPH
ST. LUKES WY.
Works
EMERYS
WILLIAM
AMBLESIDE WAY
LANE
STOKE
Top Row
LANE
STOKE
STANHOPE CR.
7
LOOP
A612
ROAD
VICTORIA
DRUMMOND
NORTHERN
F
G
H
67
J
K
63
64
465
41
465

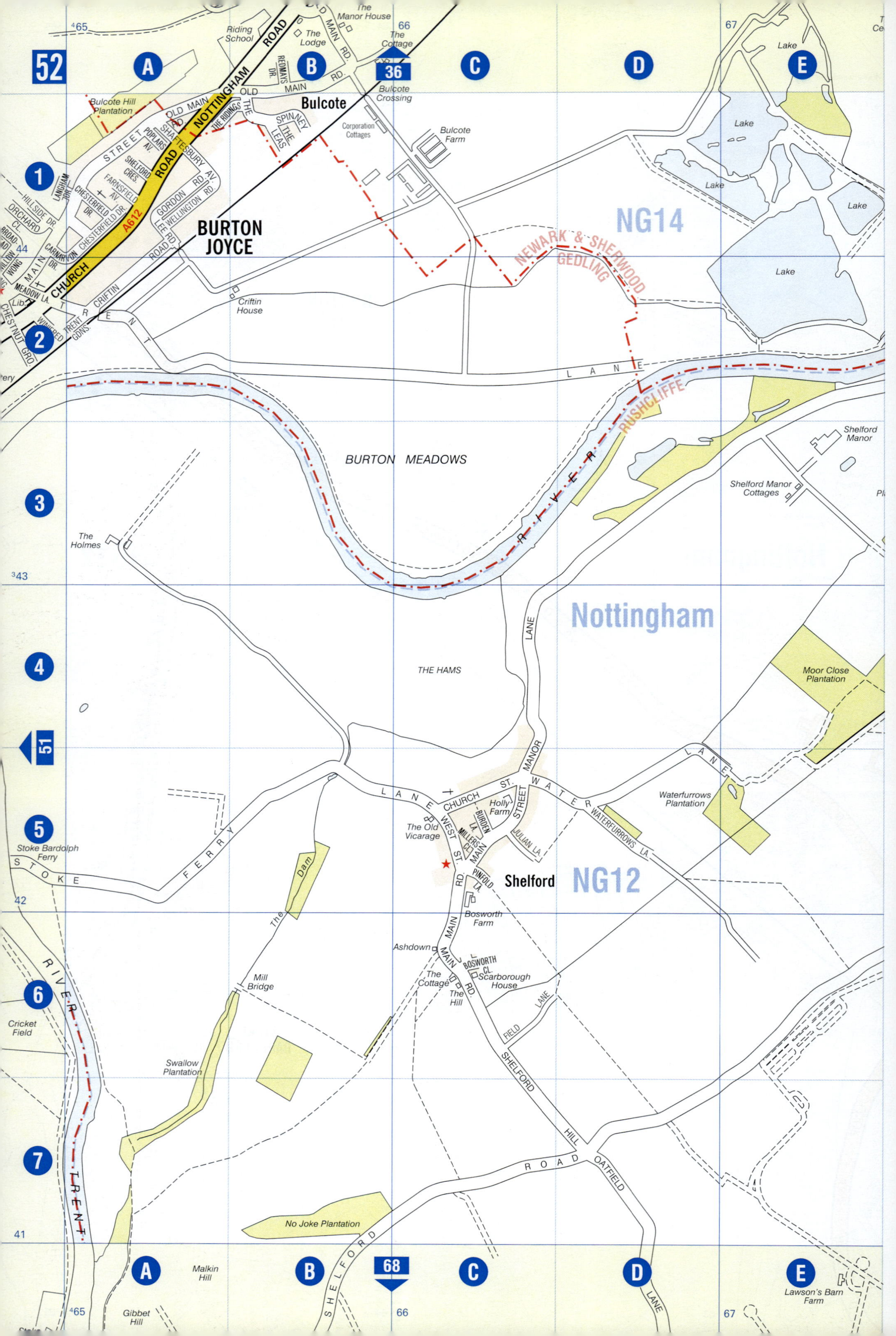

52
A
B
C
D
E
1
2
3
4
5
6
7
465
66
67
44
43
42
41
Riding School
ROAD
The Lodge
MAIN RD.
The Manor House
The Cottage
36
Bulcote Crossing
Bulcote
REDMAY'S DR.
MAIN RD.
OLD
SPINNEY
THE LEAS
THE RIDINGS
NOTTINGHAM
SHAFTESBURY AV.
POPLARS AV.
STREET
OLD MAIN RD.
Bulcote Hill Plantation
Corporation Cottages
Bulcote Farm
NG14
SHELFORD CRES.
FARNSFIELD AV.
CHESTERFIELD DR.
CHESTERFIELD DR.
GORDON RD.
WELLINGTON RD.
LEE RD.
LANGHAM DR.
HILLSIDE DR.
ORCHARD CL.
A612
ROAD
CHURCH
CARNARVON DR.
CRIFTIN
NEWARK & SHERWOOD
GEDLING
BURTON JOYCE
MEADOW LA.
Lib.
CHESTNUT GRO.
WINNIPEG
TRENT GDNS.
Criftin House
RIVER
RUSHCLIFFE
BURTON   MEADOWS
Shelford Manor
Shelford Manor Cottages
The Holmes
Nottingham
51
THE HAMS
Moor Close Plantation
LANE
MANOR
WATER
LANE
Stoke Bardolph Ferry
FERRY
STOKE
The Dam
CHURCH ST.
STREET
Holly Farm
BURDON
MILLERS CL.
MAIN
WATERFURROWS LA.
JULIAN LA.
Waterfurrows Plantation
The Old Vicarage
WEST ST.
Shelford
NG12
Mill Bridge
RIVER
Cricket Field
Ashdown
The Cottage
MAIN RD.
PINFOLD LA.
Bosworth Farm
BOSWORTH CL.
Scarborough House
The Hill
FIELD LANE
Swallow Plantation
SHELFORD
TRENT
No Joke Plantation
HILL
ROAD
OATFIELD
Malkin Hill
68
SHELFORD RD.
LANE
Gibbet Hill
Lawson's Barn Farm
465
66
67
Lake
Lake
Lake
Lake
Lake

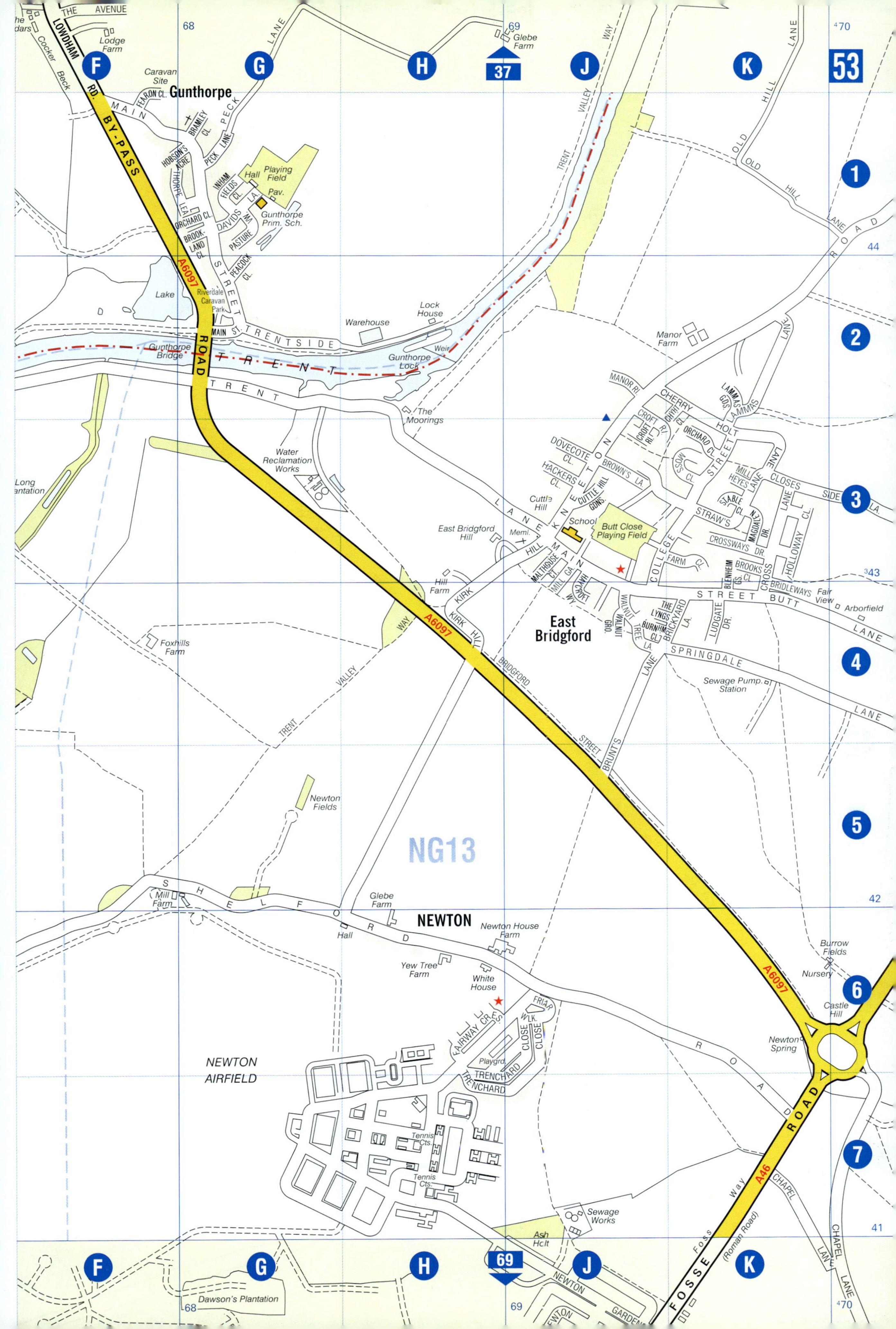
53
37
69
Gunthorpe
East Bridgford
Newton
NEWTON AIRFIELD
NG13
LOWDHAM
THE AVENUE
Cedars
Cocker Beck
Lodge Farm
Caravan Site
Heaton Cl.
Bramley Cl.
Hobson's Acre
Thorpe Lea
Orchard Cl.
Brook Land
Main Road
By-Pass
A6097
Peck Lane
Inham Fields Cl.
Hall
Davids La.
Pasture
Peacock Cl.
Playing Field
Pav.
Gunthorpe Prim. Sch.
Lake
Riverdale Caravan Park
Gunthorpe Bridge
Trentside
Warehouse
Lock House
Gunthorpe Lock
Weir
Trent
The Moorings
Water Reclamation Works
Long Plantation
Foxhills Farm
Trent Valley Way
A6097
Hill Farm
Kirk Hill
Bridgford Street
Lane
East Bridgford Hill
Meml.
School
Cuttle Hill
Malthouse Ct.
Mill Ga.
Haycroft
Kenneth
Dovecote Cl.
Hackers Cl.
Cuttle Hill Gdns.
Brown's La.
Croft Rd.
Croft Rl.
Cherry
Orchard Cl.
Holt
Lammas Gds.
Lammas
Street
Sow Cl.
Mill
Heyes Lane
Closes
Side La.
Sable Cl.
Straw's
Magdala Dr.
Crossways Dr.
Holloway Cl.
Butt Close Playing Field
College Farm
Brooks
Blenheim Cts.
Cross
Bridleways
Fair View
Arborfield
Butt Lane
Walnut Gro.
Walnut Tree La.
The Lyngs
Burnham Cl.
Brickyard La.
Ludgate Dr.
Springdale
Brunt's Lane
Sewage Pump Station
Street
Shelford Road
Mill Farm
Newton Fields
Glebe Farm
Hall
NEWTON
Newton House Farm
Yew Tree Farm
White House
Fairway
Cres.
Friar Wlk.
Close
Orchard Close
Trenchard
Playgrd.
Tennis Cts.
Tennis Cts.
Sewage Works
Ash Holt
Newton Gardens
Burrow Fields
Nursery
Castle Hill
Newton Spring
A46
Fosse Way
Chapel Lane
A6097
Road
Fosse (Roman Road)

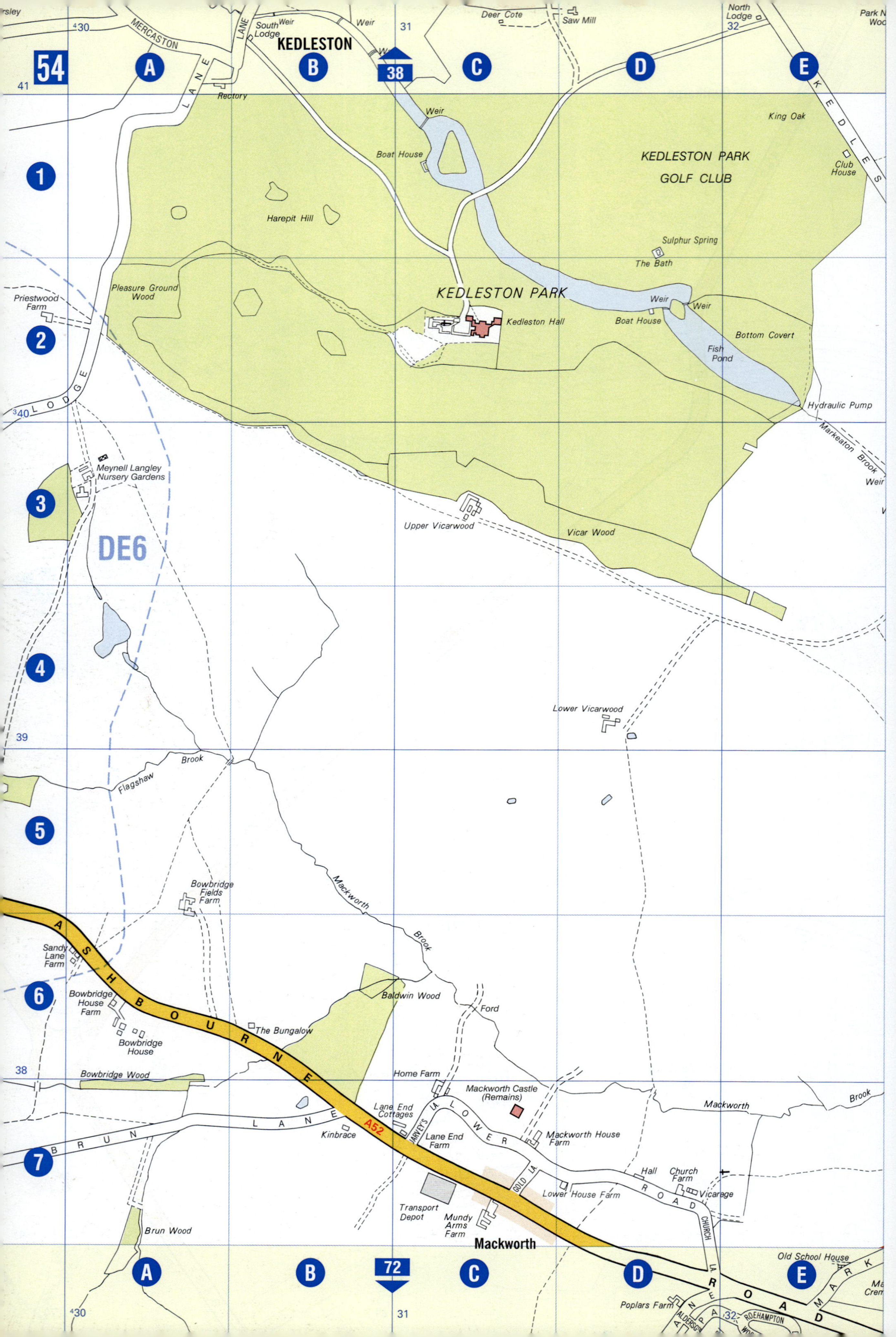

54
41
430
31
32
A
B
C
D
E
MERCASTON
LANE
South Lodge
Weir
Weir
KEDLESTON
Rectory
Deer Cote
Saw Mill
North Lodge
Park N Wood
38
W
Weir
Boat House
KEDLESTON PARK
GOLF CLUB
King Oak
Club House
1
Harepit Hill
Sulphur Spring
The Bath
KEDLESTON PARK
Kedleston Hall
Boat House
Weir
Weir
Bottom Covert
Priestwood Farm
Pleasure Ground Wood
Fish Pond
2
340
LODGE
Hydraulic Pump
Markeaton Brook
Weir
Meynell Langley Nursery Gardens
Upper Vicarwood
Vicar Wood
3
DE6
Lower Vicarwood
4
39
Flagshaw
Brook
5
Mackworth
Bowbridge Fields Farm
Brook
Sandy Lane Farm
Baldwin Wood
Ford
ASHBOURNE
6
Bowbridge House Farm
The Bungalow
Home Farm
Mackworth Castle (Remains)
Mackworth
Brook
Bowbridge House
LANE
Lane End Cottages
HARVEY'S LA
LOWER
Mackworth House Farm
38
Bowbridge Wood
A52
Lane End Farm
GOLD LA
Hall Farm
Church Farm
BRUN
Kinbrace
Vicarage
ROAD
7
LANE
Lower House Farm
CHURCH LA
Transport Depot
Mundy Arms Farm
Brun Wood
Mackworth
Old School House
A
B
72
C
D
MARK
E
430
31
32
Poplars Farm
ROEHAMPTON
ROAD
ALDERSG

Quarndon Common
Burley Grange
Burley
Burley Lane
55
F
G
H
39
J
K
Coach Dr.
The Edge
Suiters
Montpelier
Burley Dr.
Field
Holmwood
Sunnyside
Carr Hole
The Curzon C. of E. Prim. Sch.
Woodlands
Burley Brook
Club House
Allestree Hall
1
The Grange
Lodge
Bath Plantation
Big Wood
Allestree Park
Barn
Quarndon Hall
Old Gravel Pit
Allestree Park Nature Trail
Gorses
QUARNDON
Landing Stage
Cannon Hill
White House
Lake
Allestree Park (Public) Golf Course
Weir
2
The Mount
Chalybeate Well
Old Sand Pit
Allestree Firs
Evans Avenue
Old Croft House
Old Vicarage
The Old Vicarage
Old Brook Cottage
Imperial Ct.
Grove
West Bank
Main Avenue
Short Av.
Poplar Link
The Poplars
Lime Cft.
Church Walk
Derwe
Crescent
3
Church
Brook Cl.
Brook House
AMBER VALLEY DERBY
Laburnum
Elm Gro.
Tamar Av.
Liskeard Dr.
Portway Inf. Sch.
Riddings
Ladycroft Paddock
Ladycroft
Cornhill
Park View Cl.
St. Edmunds Cl.
Kingscroft
Gisborne
Duffield Road
56
Tennis Courts
Woodlands Comm. Sch. & Allestree Adult Educ. Cen.
Sports Ground
Sports Ground
Blenheim Pde. Dr.
Robin
Portway Jun. Sch.
Charter Hames
Stone
Foxes La.
Park
Pav.
Recreation Ground
Pav.
Tennis Courts
Pav.
ALLESTREE
Crabtree
Avenue
Askerfield
Woodstock
Lockwood
Ash
Park Cl.
Road
Portreath
Riddings Road
A38
Ravensdale Rd.
Ashbrook Cl.
Hardwick Av.
Kingsley Hollies
Larch Cl.
Sycamore
Lane
Wilderness
Rydal Cl.
Devonshire
Baslow Dr.
Birchover Ho.
North Av.
The Old Vicarage Sch.
Derby DE22
Garside Cl.
Scarsdale
Quarn
Harewood
Welwyn
Beaufter
Thirlmere
Windermere Cr.
Rannoch Av.
Calder
Tay
Cavendish
Birchover Roundabout
South
Church La.
Spinney
Somme Road
Memorial
Rossmount Ct.
Netherwood Ct.
Quarndon Vw.
Clifton Cl.
St. John's Cl.
Birchover Way
Portreath Drive
Windermere Cr.
Chatsworth Cr.
Barden Drive
The Close
A6
Thatch
Friars
Leafen
Meynell
Lens
Kewin
St. Nicholas Cl.
Fairway
Crescent
Abbey Hill
Bank Side
The Rise
Tresillian
Maltby Cl.
Foxlands Drive
Finningley
Slack Lane
Duffield Road
Walter Evans C. of E. Prim. Sch.
5
Abbey
St. Hugh's Cl.
St. Matthew's Cl.
Darley
Ypres
Bellingham
Otterburn Dr.
Ribblesdale Cl.
Widdybank Cl.
Lilac Way
Ashover Road
Beeley Cl.
Ferrers Way
Finningley Rd.
The Crest
Canons Wk.
Willow Row
Lavender Row
Coppice Cl.
Abbey
Old
Stoodley Pike
Lambley Cl.
Carsington
Park Farm Cen.
Lib.
Norbury Cl.
Whiteway
West Bank
East Bank
St. Benedict Sch. & Sixth Form Centre
Vicarwood Av.
Windley
Darley
Belper
6
Rugby Football Ground
Club Ho.
Melbourne
Longford Cl.
Longford Cl.
Norbury Cl.
Lawn Prim. Sch.
Lanscombe
Berry Park
Alstonfield Dr.
Marchington
Darley Abbey
Playing Field
St. Benedict Sch. & Sixth Form Centre
Cricket Ground
Markeaton Stones
Dovedale
Findern Cl.
Jacksdale Cl.
Kedleston Crescent
Hilland View
Thorpelands Av.
Carsington Cr.
Ten. Cts.
Play Fld.
St. Philomena's Convent
Beechwood
Catherine McAuley Houses
Darley Park Dr.
Darley Abbey Park Tree Tr.
7
Osierbed Wood
Stables
Fulams Wood
Gravelpit Wood
Weir
Kedleston Road
Carsington
Dovedale Cr.
University of Derby Kedleston Road Campus
Sports Ground
Markeaton Bowls Club
Leylands Road
Penny Long Lane
Broadfields
Norfolk Gdns.
Beech Dr.
Stanley Ho.
Stanley Cl.
Darley View
Derwent Park
Belper Road
MARKEATON
Old Forge
Mundy Children's Play Centre
Markeaton Craft Village
Miniature Railway
The Farm
Weir
Maxwell Av.
Kedleston Road
Greenway
Markeaton Prim. Sch.
School Resources Centre
Queens
Broadway
Sherwin
Woodland Rd.
Wheeldon Manor
Bank Ct.
Victor Rd.
Burleigh Dr.
Highfield
Robin
South Dr.
Chevin
F
G
H
73
J
K
MARKEATON PARK
Markeaton Lake
Woodside
Markeaton Crematorium
Pitch & Putt Golf Courses
Weir
Playing Field
Watson
Brookside
Statham
Ruskin Rd.
Kingston St.

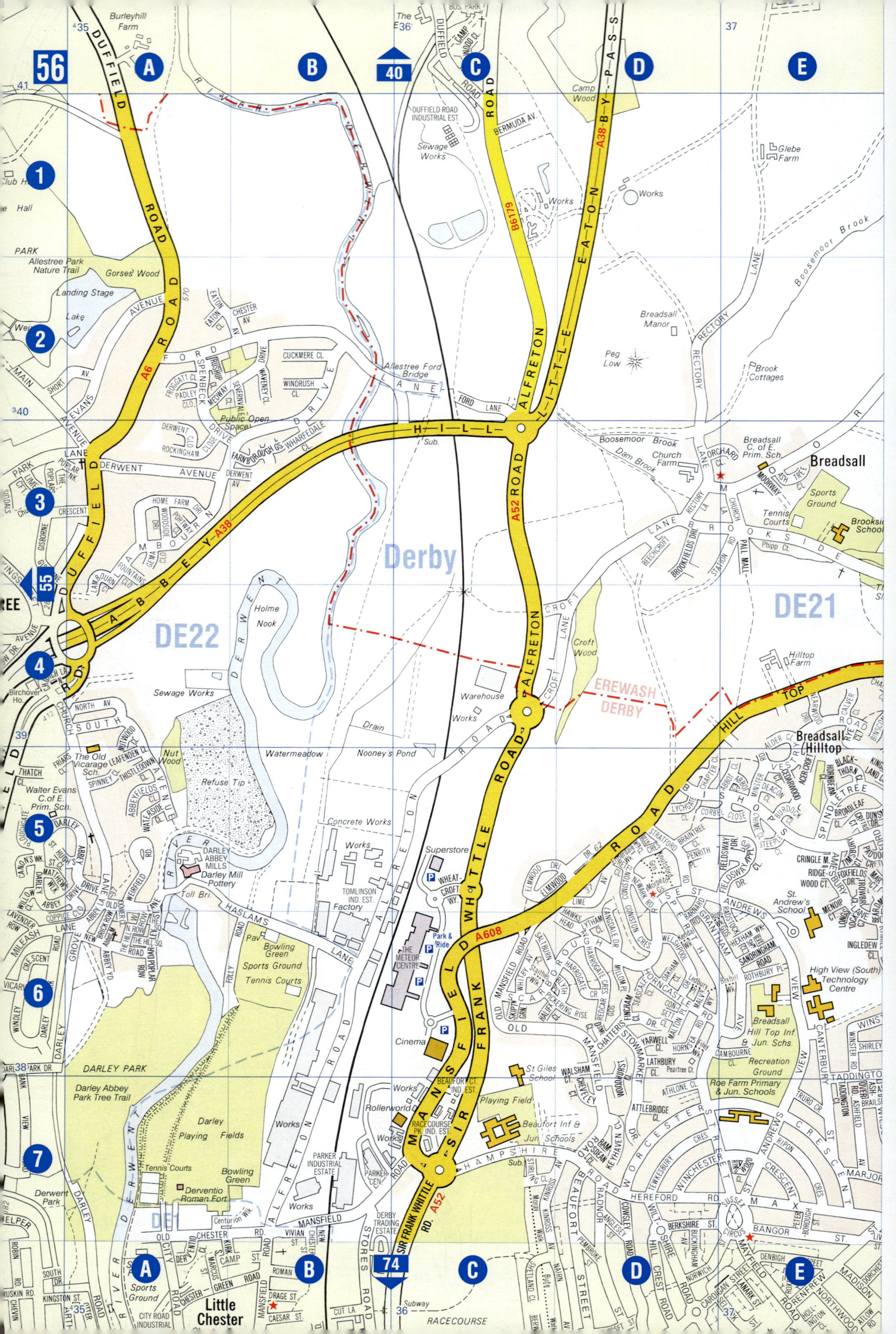
56
A
B
40
C
D
E
35
Burleyhill Farm
The E36
BUS PARK
DUFFIELD
CAMP WOOD CL.
DUFFIELD ROAD
Club H.
e Hall
1
PARK
41
DUFFIELD ROAD INDUSTRIAL EST.
Sewage Works
Works
BERMUDA AV.
B6179
Camp Wood
Works
Glebe Farm
37
Allestree Park Nature Trail
Gorses' Wood
Landing Stage
Lake
Weir
2
MAIN
SHORT
AV.
EVANS
AVENUE
AVENUE
ROAD
A6
FORD
SPENBECK
FROGGATT CL.
TRUSLEY
PADLEY CLO.
EATON CL.
CHESTER AV.
DRIVE
WAVENEY CL.
CUCKMERE CL.
WINDRUSH CL.
WHARFEDALE
Allestree Ford Bridge
FORD LANE
LANE
Sub.
Breadsall Manor
Peg Low
RECTORY
RECTORY LANE
Brook Cottages
Boosemoor Brook
340
3
PARK
POPLAR
LANE
GISBORNE
LIME CRFT.
POPLARS
CRESCENT
SPENBECK
DERWENT AVENUE
HOME FARM DR.
WOODSIDE
PORTWAY
DERWENT AV.
FARNBOROUGH GDS.
LITTLE
EATON
ALFRETON ROAD
A52 ROAD
HILL
Sub.
Boosemoor Brook
Dam Brook
Church Farm
ORCHARD CL.
ASH TREE CL.
MOWBRAY
RECTORY LANE
BEECHCROFT
BROOKFIELDS DR.
STATION RD.
PALL MALL
Phipp Ct.
Breadsall C. of E. Prim. Sch.
Breadsall
Sports Ground
Brookside School
A38
ABBEY
Derby
KINGS
55
28
FOUNTAINS
LAMBOURN CLO.
GEMA
ROCKINGHAM
CLO.
DERWENT
B
M
Holme Nook
DE22
DE21
Hilltop Farm
Breadsall (Hilltop)
39
412
North Dr.
Birchover Ho.
4
CHURCH
SOUTH
NORTH AV.
NUTWOOD
Sewage Works
Watermeadow
Drain
Nooney's Pond
Warehouse
Works
ALFRETON
CROFT LANE
Croft Wood
CROFT
EREWASH DERBY
HILL TOP
HILL TOP ROAD
Breadsall Hilltop
ALDER CL.
VESTRY RD.
CEDARWOOD
BLACKTHORN
HORNBEAM
SPINDLETREE
5
FRIARS
The Old Vicarage Sch.
Walter Evans C. of E. Prim. Sch.
THATCH
LEAFENDEN CL.
SPINNEY
THISTLEDOWN
WATERSIDE
ABBEYFIELDS CL.
Nut Wood
Refuse Tip
RIVER
Concrete Works
Works
Superstore
WHEATCROFT WY.
ELMWOOD DRI.
ELMWOOD
LIME AV.
STRATFORD CRES.
PENRITH CL.
BRAINTREE CL.
FIELDSWAY DR.
STEEPLES
CRINGLE M.
RIDGE AV.
WOOD CT.
FOXFIELDS DR.
St. Andrew's School
MENDIP
INGLEDEW CL.
6
DARLEY
ST. HUGH'S CL.
MATLOCK
CANON'S WK.
WILLOW
ABBEY
LAVENDER ROW
MILEASH
CRESCENT
VICARY
WINDLEY
DARLEY
ABBEY
DRIVE
WEIRFIELD RD.
OLD VICARAGE CL.
N. ROW
N. ROW
THE HILL
SQ.
COPPICE CLO.
GROVE
NEW ROW
OLD ROW
POPLAR ROW
FOLLY
HAPPORLANE
HASLAMS LANE
DARLEY ABBEY MILLS
Darley Mill Pottery
Toll Bri.
Pav.
Bowling Green
Sports Ground
Tennis Courts
TOMLINSON IND. EST.
Factory
THE METEOR CENTRE
Park & Ride
P
A608
MANSFIELD ROAD
WHITTLE
SIR FRANK WHITTLE ROAD
OLD MANSFIELD ROAD
HAWKS HEAD
LYTHAM
SALTBURN
WHITBY
STAITHES
BLYTH
HARROGATE CRES.
REDCAR
CARTMEL
SEASCALE
MILTON
CONISTON CRES.
HORNCASTLE
CHATTERIS
STOWMARKET
YARWELL CL.
LATHBURY CL.
Peartree Cl.
ANDREWS
GRANTHAM
HEXHAM WK.
SANDRINGHAM ROAD
ROTHBURY PL.
High View (South) Technology Centre
Breadsall Hill Top Inf. & Jun. Schs.
Recreation Ground
CANTERBURY
WINSTER
SHIRLEY
7
Derwent Park
DARLEY PARK
Darley Abbey Park Tree Trail
Tennis Courts
Bowling Green
Darley Playing Fields
Works
Works
Rollerworld
Cinema
P
RACECOURSE PK IND. ESTATE
Works
Derby Trading Estate
PARKER INDUSTRIAL ESTATE
PARKER CEN.
Derventio Roman Fort
Centurion Wk.
CHESTER RD.
VIVIAN ST.
MANSFIELD RD.
NEW CHESTER RD.
ALFRETON ROAD
STORES ROAD
SIR FRANK WHITTLE RD.
A52
HAMPSHIRE
Sub.
St Giles School
WALSHAM CL.
CHEVELEY
WINDOWHURST
ATHLONE CL.
ATTLEBRIDGE CL.
Beaufort Inf & Jun Schools
Playing Field
BEAUFORT ROAD
RADNOR
COWLEY
HEREFORD
WINCHESTER RD.
BERKSHIRE
BUCKINGHAM
NORWICH
Roe Farm Primary & Jun. Schools
WORCESTER
CRES.
WILTSHIRE
PEMBROKE
BANGOR
DENBIGH
RENFREW
TADDINGTON
MARJOR
RIPON
ANDREWS CRESCENT
TRURO CR.
MAX
CRESCENT
MADISON
NORTHWOOD
36
74
C
D
E
A
B
Little Chester
Sports Ground
CITY ROAD INDUSTRIAL
Subway
ROMAN
CAESAR ST.
CUT LA.
RACECOURSE
357
DE1
35
Derwent Park
BANK VIEW
KINGSTON ST.
RUSKIN RD.
SOUTH DR.
ROBIN
PETER ST.
CHEVIN
DRAGE ST.
CAMP
GREEN
MARCUS ST.
38
ELPER

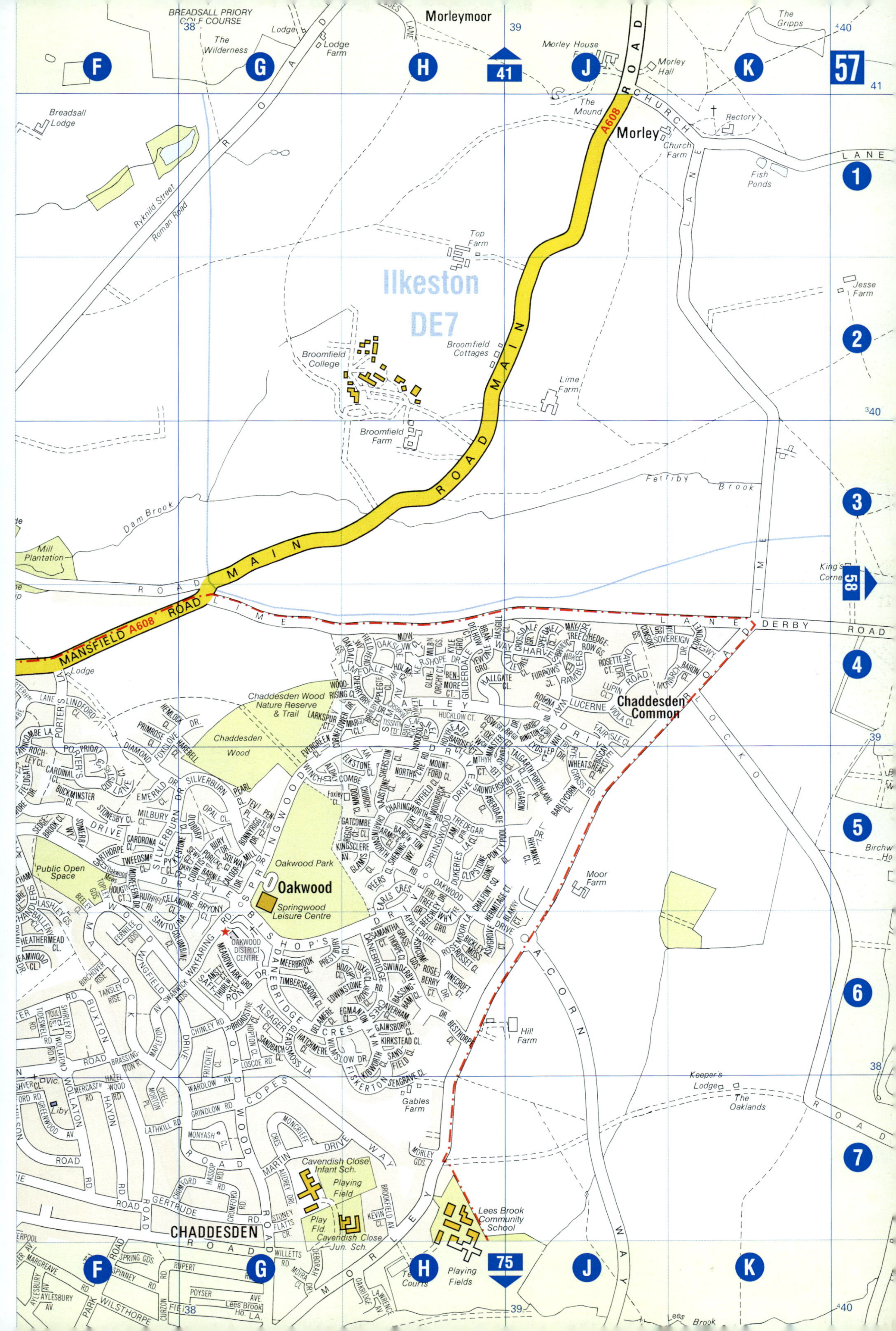

BREADSALL PRIORY GOLF COURSE
Morleymoor
The Gripps
The Wilderness
Lodge
Lodge Farm
Morley House
Morley Hall
F G H J K
57
Breadsall Lodge
The Mound
Rectory
A608
Morley
Church Farm
Fish Ponds
LANE
Ryknild Street
Roman Road
Top Farm
1
Jesse Farm
Ilkeston DE7
Broomfield College
Broomfield Cottages
2
ROAD MAIN
Lime Farm
Fetliby Brook
3
Dam Brook
King's Corner
58
Mill Plantation
MANSFIELD A608 ROAD
LIME LANE
DERBY ROAD
4
Lodge
Chaddesden Wood Nature Reserve & Trail
Chaddesden Common
Sovereign
Consort
Chaddesden Wood
PORTER'S LA.
LINDFORD CL.
HEMLOCK DR.
PRIMROSE CL.
HAREBELL
FOXGLOVE
LARKSPUR CT.
Hucklow Ct.
Lucerne
Viola Cl.
39
BUCKMINSTER
STONESBY
EMERALD DR.
SILVERBURN DR.
PEARL
OPAL CL.
RUBY
WINCH CL.
ELKSTONE
NORTHACRE RD.
MOUNTFORD CL.
Tredegar
Wheatsheaf
Grass Rd.
5
Public Open Space
TWEEDSMUIR
CARDRONA
MILBURY
CALDER
SILVERBURN DR.
SPRINGWOOD
Oakwood Park
CHARINGWORTH DR.
SPRINGWOOD
Birchw Ho
HEATHERMEAD CL.
CELANDINE CL.
BRYONY CL.
SANTOLINA
COLUMBINE
WAYFARING RD.
Oakwood
Springwood Leisure Centre
Oakwood District Centre
BISHOP'S DR.
Moor Farm
6
FERNLEA GDNS.
WINGFIELD RD.
MEADOWLARK GRO.
SAFFRON
MEERBROOK CL.
DANEBRIDGE
TIMBERSBROOK CL.
PRESTBURY
SWINDERBY
APPLEDORE
PINECROFT DR.
Hill Farm
ACORN
BIRCHOVER RISE
TANSLEY RISE
SWANWICK
CHINLEY RD.
BROADSIDE
ALSAGER
EDWINSTOWE RD.
GAINSBOROUGH
BESTHORPE
BUXTON ROAD
MAPLETON
FRITCHLEY
SANDBACH
GLADSMOSS LA.
WILMSLOW DR.
KIRKSTEAD CL.
BASSING
SAND FIELD
Keeper's Lodge
The Oaklands
38
SHIRLEY RD.
TIDESWELL RD.
WOLLATON
HAZELWOOD
WARDLOW RD.
GRINDLOW RD.
COPES
WOOD
FISKERTON CL.
SEAGRAVE CL.
Gables Farm
7
GREENWOOD AV.
MERCASTON
HAYDN
CHELMORTON PL.
LATHKILL RD.
MONYASH
MONCRIEFF CRES.
AUDREY DRI.
MARTIN DRIVE
MORLEY GDS.
Morley GDS.
ROAD
Cavendish Close Infant Sch.
Playing Field
Lees Brook Community School
CHADDESDEN
HASSOP RD.
CROMFORD RD.
GERTRUDE RD.
STONEY FLATTS CR.
Play Fld.
Cavendish Close Jun. Sch.
KEVIN CL.
BROOMFIELD AV.
MORLEY
SPRING GDS.
RUPERT RD.
WILLETTS RD.
MOIRA RD.
DEBORAH DRI.
F G H J K
75
Tennis Courts
Playing Fields
AYLESBURY AV.
MARGREAVE
SPINNEY
POYSER AVE.
PARK WILSTHORPE
Lees Brook Ho. LA.
OAKRIDGE
LAWRENCE
Lees Brook
38 39 40

58
The Gripps
40
41
A
B
42
C
D
E
Rostrevor
CHURCH LANE
MOSES LANE
1
Spring Oak Farm
MORLEY
CORONATION
Playing Field
QUEENS AV.
PARK AV.
HURST DR.
ROAD
Brook House Farm
Whitehouse Farm
Stanley Farm
The Hall
Stanley
GLEBE CRES
NEW ST.
Jesse Farm
2
STATION ROAD
St. Andrews C. of E. Prim. Sch.
DALE
ROAD
340
Manor Farm
Sough Farm
3
Hill Farm
57
King's Corner
Home Farm
Lodge
DERBY ROAD
DERBY ROAD
4
39
Fish Pond
Locko Grange Farm
Hollies Farm
Birch Wood
Fish Pond
Locko Rookery
5
Birchwood House
LOCKO PARK
LOCKO ROAD
Crow Wood Farm
DE21
DEER PARK
Dunnshill
6
Boat House
Lodge Farm
Boat House
The Lake (Fish Pond)
Crow Wood
ROAD
38
Weirs
Derby
Lodge
Weir
Bartlewood Lodge
DALE ROAD
7
Weir
Lees Brook
A6096
Bartlewood Farm
A
B
76
C
D
E
40
41
42
Brunswood Farm
Spondonwood Farm

ROAD
VILLAGE
SCHOOL
The Spinney
Glebe Farm
Stanley
Brook
44
45
ORCHARD CL.
HALL CT.
F
G
The Dell
H
43
J
K
Thacker Barn Cottages
59
St. John Hough R.C. School
Works
The Rookery
ABBOT
Station House
The Grange
Thacker Barn
PRIORY CL.
SHARP
FRIARS
1
Ordnance House
WYNDALE
DUMBLES
Newdigates New Covert
BANKFIELD DR.
DRIVE
CROSSHILL DR.
CAT AND
Stanley Grange
TDG PINNACLE (STORAGE PARK)
HIGHFIELD DR.
SUNNINGDALE DR.
SUNNINGDALE
GOD
Depot
RIDGEWAY DR.
DRIVE
Brook
Moat Wood
Moat
ROAD
Baldock Mill Cottage
Rose Cottage
Stanley
HILLARY PL.
RD.
2
A6096
WIRKSWORTH
AMBLESDALE PL.
DALE RD.
ASCOT
FIDDLE
Lower Hagg Farm Cottages
Foxhole Farm
40
LADYWOOD
GLENDA RD.
Ilkeston
Cat & Fiddle Farm
Ladywood Lodge Farm
Ladywood Lodge
HAGG
DE7
LANE
Lady Wood
3
Dale Abbey Cat & Fiddle Postmill
Ladywood Farm
Lower Hagg Farm
Upper Hagg Farm
60
LANE
Bassett Farm
4
Ashtree Farm
Sow
Brook
A6096
HAGG
Arbour Hill
39
LANE
ARBOUR
Arbour Hill
Burial Grd.
LANE
Ford
Stanton Grove
Flourish Farm
HILL
MOOR
CROSS
Brook
WOODPECKER
Furnace Pond Farm
5
The Flourish
THE
LEA
Dale
Sow
Dale Moor
Furnace Pond
CROFT CL.
Waterlog Farm
Close Farm
VILLAGE
Dale Abbey (remains of)
HILL
ROAD
TATTLE
HILL
Moorfield Farm
Columbine Farm
DALE
LANE
Hermit's Wood
Bagu Wo
Underhill
Ockbrook Wood
HILL
POTATO
6
Dale Hills
Dalemoor Farm
Burnwood
Malthouse
PIT
38
Boyah Grange
Sandiacre Lodge
HIXON'S
The Spots
LANE NO
The Spots Plantation
DE72
MAN'S
7
Black Plantation
Overdale
LANE
Near Park Farm
F
G
H
77
J
K
43
44
45
Risley Park Farm

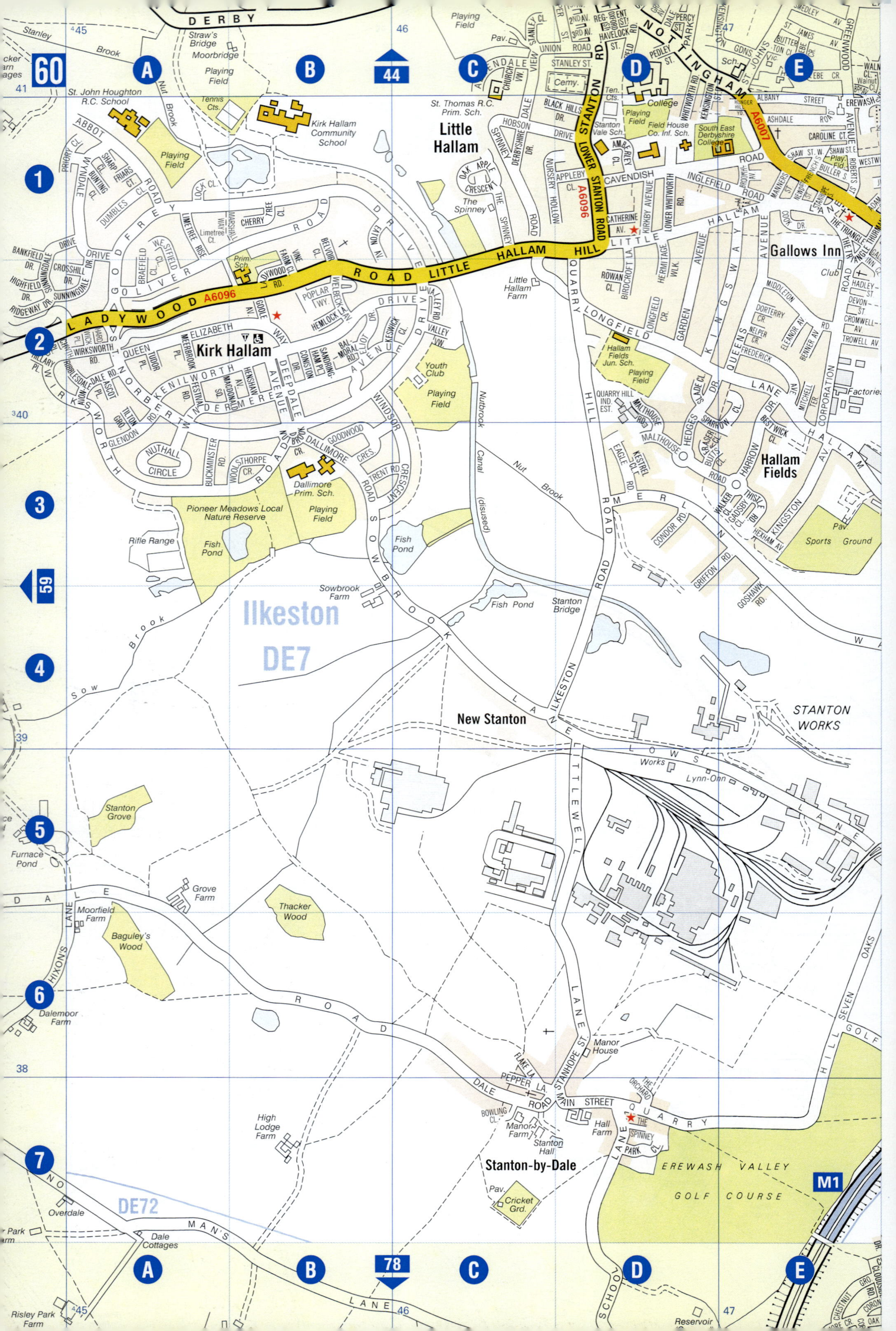

60
DERBY
44
59
45
46
47
A
B
C
D
E
1
2
3
4
5
6
7
Stanley
St John Houghton R.C. School
Straw's Bridge Moorbridge
Playing Field
Tennis Cts.
Kirk Hallam Community School
Little Hallam
St. Thomas R.C. Prim. Sch.
NOTTINGHAM
College
South East Derbyshire College
Field House Co. Inf. Sch.
Stanton Vale Sch.
Cemy.
Stanley St.
Union Road
Stanton Road
Lower Stanton Road
A6096
A6096
A6007
Ashdale
Caroline Ct.
Gallows Inn
Club
Playing Field
ABBOT
Godfrey Road
Olive Grove
Drive
Crosshill Dr.
Highfield Dr.
Ridgeway Dr.
Sunningdale
Bankfield Dr.
Braefield
Westfield
Dumbles
Wyndale
Sharp Cl.
Friars
Bunting Cl.
Marshall Wk.
Cherry Tree Cl.
Limetree Rise
Limetree Ct.
Ladywood Road
Prim. Sch.
Ladywood Rd.
Farm Cl.
Vine Cl.
Belvoir Cl.
Poplar Wy.
Welbeck La.
Hemlock La.
Goole Av.
Kirk Hallam
LADYWOOD
ROAD
LITTLE
HALLAM
HILL
Little Hallam Farm
Youth Club
Playing Field
Nutbrook Canal (disused)
Nut Brook
Quarry Hill
Longfield
Hallam Fields Jun. Sch.
Playing Field
Quarry Hill Ind. Est.
Malthouse
Malthouse Road
Merlin Road
Hallam Fields
Hexham Cl.
Pav
Sports Ground
Wirksworth Rd.
Queen
Tudor Pl.
Norbert Way
Kenilworth Rd.
Deepdale Avenue
Festival Rd.
Windsor Road
Balmoral Rd.
Eliot Dr.
Keswick Cl.
Coniston
Henshaw Av.
Maidmore Rd.
Valley Rd.
Valley Vw.
Dale Rd.
Ascot
Tilton Gro.
Glendon
Nuthall Circle
Buckminster
Woolsthorpe Cr.
Dallimore Cr.
Goodwood Cres.
Trent Rd.
Sowbrook Road
Dallimore Prim. Sch.
Playing Field
Pioneer Meadows Local Nature Reserve
Rifle Range
Fish Pond
Fish Pond
Sowbrook Farm
Fish Pond
Fish Pond
Stanton Bridge
Ilkeston DE7
Sow Brook
Ilkeston Lane
New Stanton
STANTON WORKS
Littlewell Lane
Works
Lynn-Onn
Stanton Grove
Furnace Pond
Grove Farm
Thacker Wood
Moorfield Farm
Baguley's Wood
Hixon's Lane
Dale Lane
Dalemoor Farm
Road
High Lodge Farm
Stanton Hall
Stanton-by-Dale
Manor House
Flake La.
Pepper La.
Stanhope St.
Stanton Grove
Dale Road
Main Street
Bowling Cl.
Manor Farm
Hall Farm
The Spinney
Orchard
Quarry
Stanton Park
EREWASH VALLEY GOLF COURSE
Seven Oaks
Golf Hill
M1
School Lane
Pav.
Cricket Grd.
78
DE72
Man's Lane
Overdale
Dale Cottages
Risley Park Farm
Reservoir
Gallows Inn Lane
45
46
47

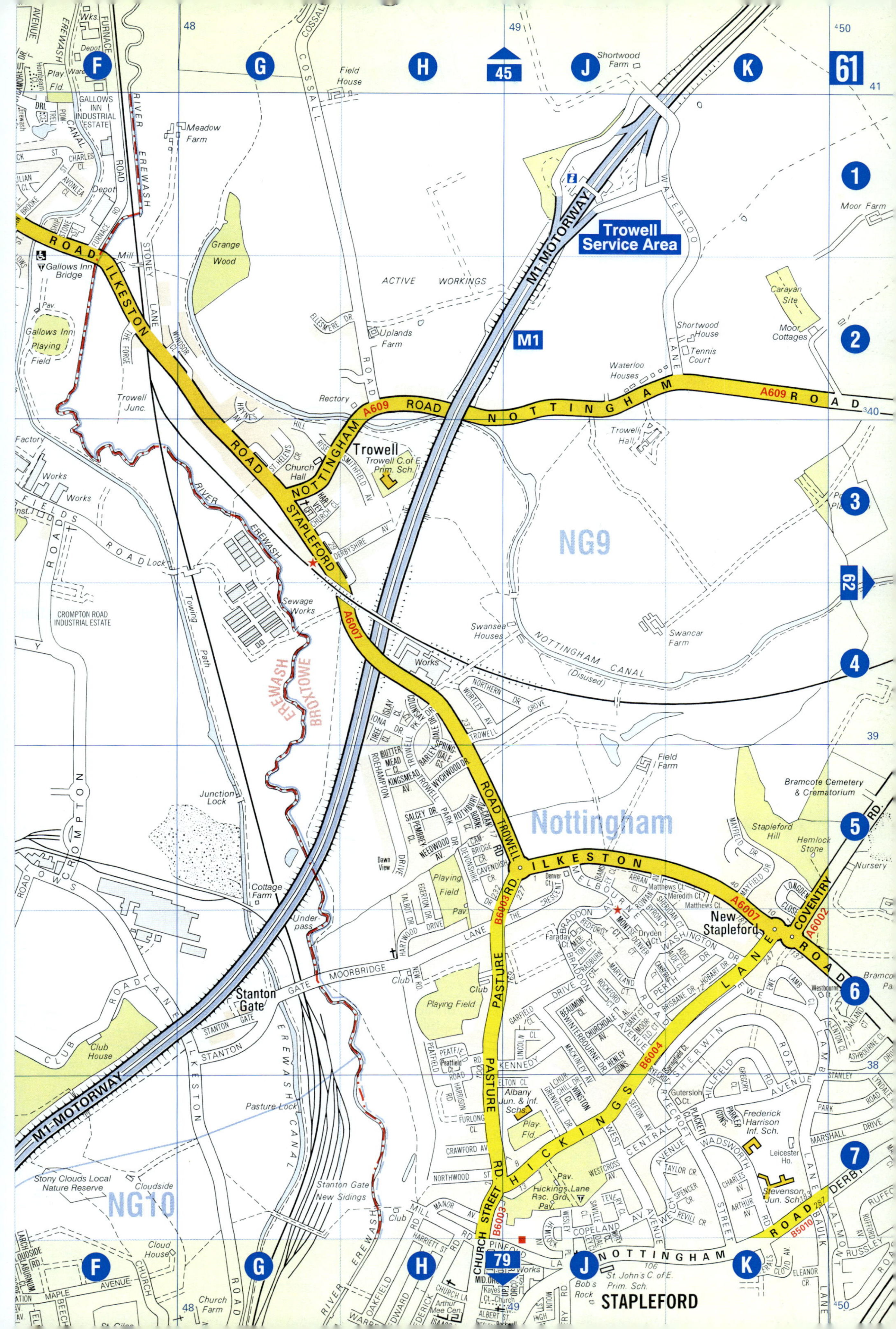

Wks
FURNACE
Depot
Play Fld
AVENUE
EREWASH
Hornbeam
DRI
POW
RELL
ST
BROOKE
CHARLES CL
AVONLEA
JULIAN CL
FURNACE RD
RIVER EREWASH
ROAD
ILKESTON
Meadow Farm
Grange Wood
STONEY LANE
WINDSOR CL
THE FORGE
Depot
Mill
Gallows Inn Bridge
GALLOWS INN INDUSTRIAL ESTATE
Pav
Gallows Inn Playing Field
Trowell Junc.
HAYNES WAY
HILL RISE
ST HELEN'S CR
SMITHFIELD AV
Rectory
A609 ROAD
NOTTINGHAM
ROAD
STAPLEFORD
Church Hall
Trowell
Trowell C. of E. Prim. Sch.
HARR... CL
VIC... CHURCH
DERBYSHIRE AV
Factory
Works
Works
FIELDS
Inst
ROADS
ROAD
Lock
CROMPTON ROAD INDUSTRIAL ESTATE
Sewage Works
TOWING PATH
EREWASH
BROXTOWE
Junction Lock
A6007
Works
Swansea Houses
NOTTINGHAM CANAL (Disused)
Swancar Farm
NORTHERN DR
WORTLEY AV
GROVE
SLAY
IONA CL
TREE CL
ROEHAMPTON
BUTTER MEAD CL
KINGSMEAD
BARLEY
SPRING DALE GDNS
WYCHWOOD DR
TROWELL
SALCEY DR
PEMBREY CL
PARK
ROTHBURN
BOURNE
NEEDWOOD DR
CAM...
DEVONSHIRE
CAVENDISH
Dawn View
DRIVE
Playing Field
Pav
TALBOT DR
EGGERTON DR
HARTWOOD DR
NEW RD
MOORBRIDGE
Club
ROAD TROWELL
ILKESTON
Nottingham
Field Farm
Bramcote Cemetery & Crematorium
Stapleford Hill
Hemlock Stone
Nursery
MAYFIELD DR
A6007
COVENTRY ROAD
A6002
New Stapleford
DENVER CL
MELBOURNE
ARRAN
MATTHEWS CT
MEREDITH CT
Matthews Ct
ROWAN
BYRON CT
STEFODA CT
DRYDEN CT
WASHINGTON DR
ADEL DR
PERTH
HOBART DR
BRISBANE DR
LONGDEN CLOSE
MAYFIELD
Bramcote Pa
WESTBOURNE CL
TRENTON CL
OAKLAND
ASHBOURNE
STANLEY
MARSHALL DRIVE
CRANDALE
PARKER GDNS
HILLFIELD
GREGORY RD
SHERWIN ROAD
RYECROFT ST
GUTERSLOH CT
PACKETT
Frederick Harrison Inf. Sch.
Leicester Ho.
Stevenson Jun. Sch.
B5010
DERBY ROAD
RUFF...
RUSSLEY
BAULK LANE
VALMONT AV
CLO...
ELEANOR CR
B6004
KINGS
HICKINGS
WEST CENTRAL AVENUE
WESTCROSS AV
TAYLOR CR
SPENCER CR
REVILL CR
SAVILLE
ARTHUR STREET
CHARLES
Hickings Lane Rec. Grd.
Pav
B6003 RD
PASTURE
GARFIELD CL
BEAUMONT CL
BEWINTERBOURNE DR
CHURCHDALE AV
HENLEY CL
LINCOLN CL
MACKINLEY AV
PEATFIELD
PEATFIELD CT
KENNEDY
ELTON CL
Albany Jun. & Inf. Schs
GRANVILLE CL
WINSTON
CHILL DR
SEFTON DR
Play Fld
FURLONG CL
FELTON RD
CRAWFORD AV
NORTHWOOD ST
CHURCH STREET
B6003
MILL RD
MANOR AV
HARRIETT ST
OAKFIELD
EDWARD
DERRICK RD
Church Farm
MAPLE
BEECH AV
ST GILES
LABURNUM RD
CLOUDSIDE RD
Cloud House
Stony Clouds Local Nature Reserve
NG10
Cloudside
Stanton Gate New Sidings
PASTURE LOCK
ERE WASH CANAL
ILKESTON ROAD
STANTON GATE
STANTON
Club House
M1 MOTORWAY
CROMPTON ROAD
Club
Underpass
Cottage Farm
Stanton Gate
MOORBRIDGE GATE
RIVER EREWASH
M1 MOTORWAY
M1
ACTIVE WORKINGS
ELLESMERE DR
Uplands Farm
ROAD
Field House
COSSALL
Shortwood Farm
Trowell Service Area
WATERLOO LANE
Shortwood House
Tennis Court
Waterloo Houses
Trowell Hall
NOTTINGHAM
A609 ROAD
NG9
Moor Farm
Caravan Site
Moor Cottages
P... Pla...
Bob's Rock
St John's C. of E. Prim. Sch.
NOTTINGHAM
STAPLEFORD
Club
WESLEY
PINFOLD
Kayes
Mee Cen.
CHURCH LA
COPELAND
HEMLOCK
SAVILLE
MONTROSE CT
BEDFORD CT
BRADDON
FARADAY CT
MARYLAND CT
ROCKFORD
RADBURN CT
CAMBRIDGE
MOOR RD CL
BRADDON LANE
THE
BRAIDEN
PELTON CL
FURLONG
NORTHWOOD
WADSWORTH RD

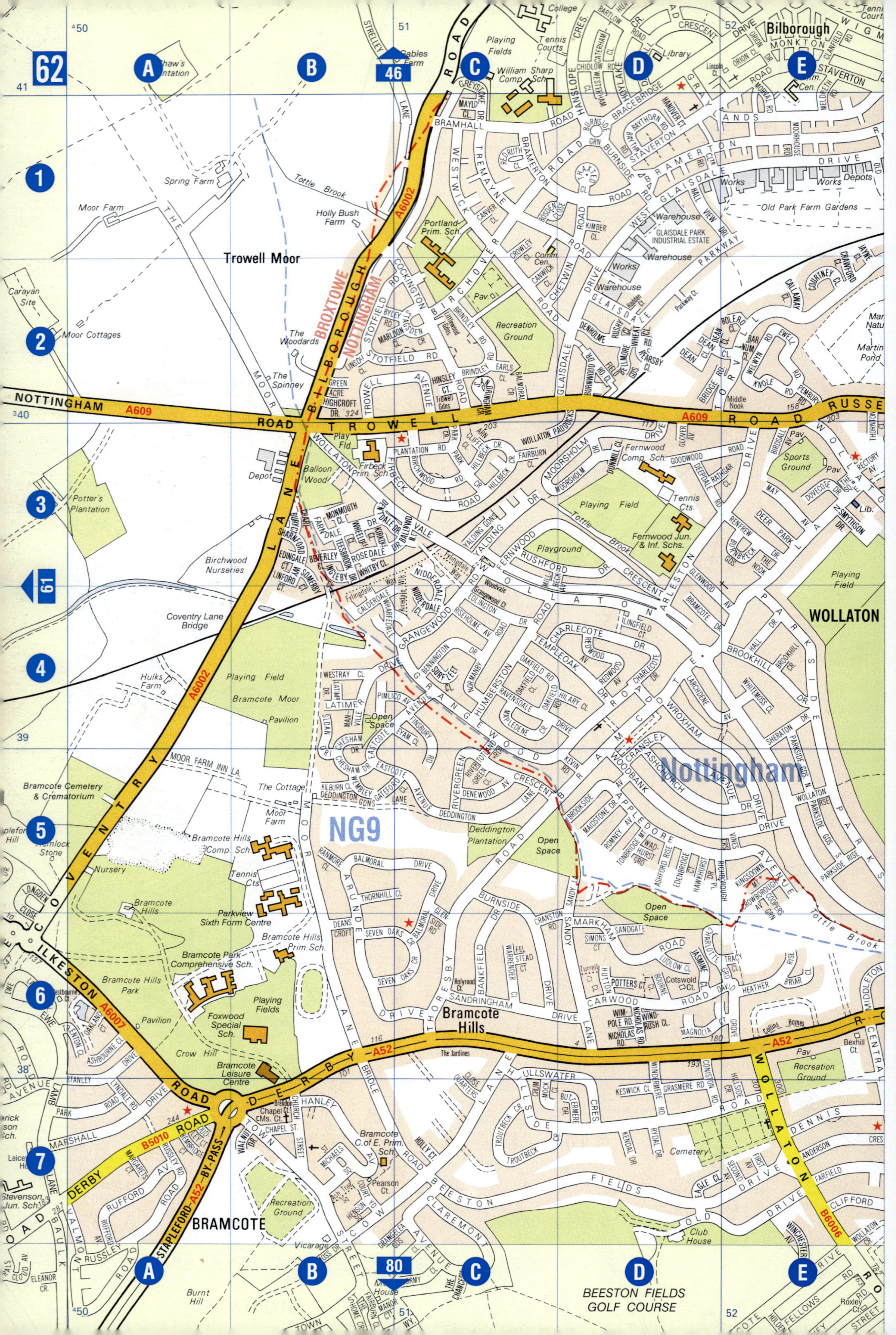

62
Trowell Moor
Moor Farm
Spring Farm
Tottle Brook
Holly Bush Farm
Caravan Site
Moor Cottages
The Woodards
The Spinney
Green Acre
Highcroft Dr. 324
NOTTINGHAM
A609
ROAD TROWELL
Potter's Plantation
Birchwood Nurseries
Coventry Lane Bridge
Hulks Farm
Playing Field
Bramcote Moor
Pavilion
Moor Farm Inn La.
Bramcote Cemetery & Crematorium
Hemlock Stone
Nursery
The Cottage
Moor Farm
NG9
Bramcote Hills Comp. Sch.
Tennis Cts.
Parkview Sixth Form Centre
Bramcote Hills Prim. Sch.
Bramcote Hills Park
Bramcote Park Comprehensive Sch.
Foxwood Special Sch.
Playing Fields
Crow Hill
Pavilion
Bramcote Leisure Centre
STAPLEFORD A52 BY-PASS
DERBY
ROAD
B5010
244
Chapel St.
Bramcote C. of E. Prim. Sch.
Recreation Ground
Vicarage
BRAMCOTE
Burnt Hill
BROXTOWE
NOTTINGHAM
Cables Farm
46
STRELLEY
LANE
ROAD
Greyshke Dr.
Bramhall
Mayld Dr.
Portland Prim. Sch.
WESTWICK
TREMAYNE
BIRCHOVER
ROAD
COCKINGTON
STOTFIELD
MARLDON
AVENUE
Play Fld.
WOLLATON
Firbeck Prim. Sch.
Balloon Wood
Depot
MONMOUTH
CL.
FAIRDALE
BEVERLEY
ROSEDALE
WHITBY CL.
DALES DR.
NIDDERDALE
GRANGEWOOD
FILINGDALE
CALDERDALE
WESTRAY CL.
LATIMER
PIMLICO AV.
CHESHAM DR.
SLOAN
MANVILLE
EASTCOTE
KILBURN CL.
DEDDINGTON
WRELY
GATEFORD
CHESHAM
DENEWOOD
AVENUE DEDDINGTON
RIVERGREEN
DEDDINGTON LANE
RANMORE
BALMORAL
DRIVE
ARUNDEL
THORNHILL CL.
DEANS CROFT
SEVEN OAKS
SEVEN OAKS CR.
BALMORAL RD.
GLEN
SIDE RD.
BURNSIDE
CRANSTON RD.
THORESBY
LANE
SANDRINGHAM
Bramcote Hills
DERBY
A52
The Jardines
BRIDLE LANE
HANLEY
CHURCH ST.
St. Michaels
HOLLY CL.
BEESTON
CLAREMONT
AVENUE
HINSLEY CT.
BRINDLEY
EARLS CT.
Recreation Ground
WOLLATON PADDOCKS
FAIRBURN
MOORSHOLM
Playing Field
Fernwood Comp. Sch.
Fernwood Jun. & Inf. Schs.
Playground
RUSHFORD
Woodvale
CHARLECOTE
TEMPLEOAK AV.
RAVENSDALE
HUMBERSTON
NUP MANBY
OAKFIELD RD.
HILARY CL.
WOODBANK
ASHCHURCH
CRANSLEY
Nottingham
WROXHAM
Deddington Plantation
Open Space
MAIDSTONE DR.
BROOKSIDE
APPLEDORE
ROMNEY
TONBRIDGE
ASHFORD RISE
EDENBRIDGE
HAWKHURST
MARKHAM ROAD
SANDGATE
HUTTIN
POTTERS CT.
CARWOOD
Open Space
KINGSDOWN
Tottle Brook
WINCHESTER
B6006
Beeston Fields Golf Course
WOLLATON
Sports Ground
DEER PARK
Playing Field
Old Park Farm Gardens
GLAISDALE PARK INDUSTRIAL ESTATE
Warehouse
Works
PARKWAY
BILBOROUGH
STAVERTON
MONKTON
RUSSELL
Martins Pond
BROOKHILL
WHITEMOSS CL.
SHERATON
PARKSIDE
Recreation Ground
CENTRAL
DENNIS
WINCHESTER DRIVE
Cemetery
KESWICK CL.
GRASMERE RD.
ULLSWATER
TROUTBECK
WINTHORPE
MAGNOLIA
HEATHER
BRIAR

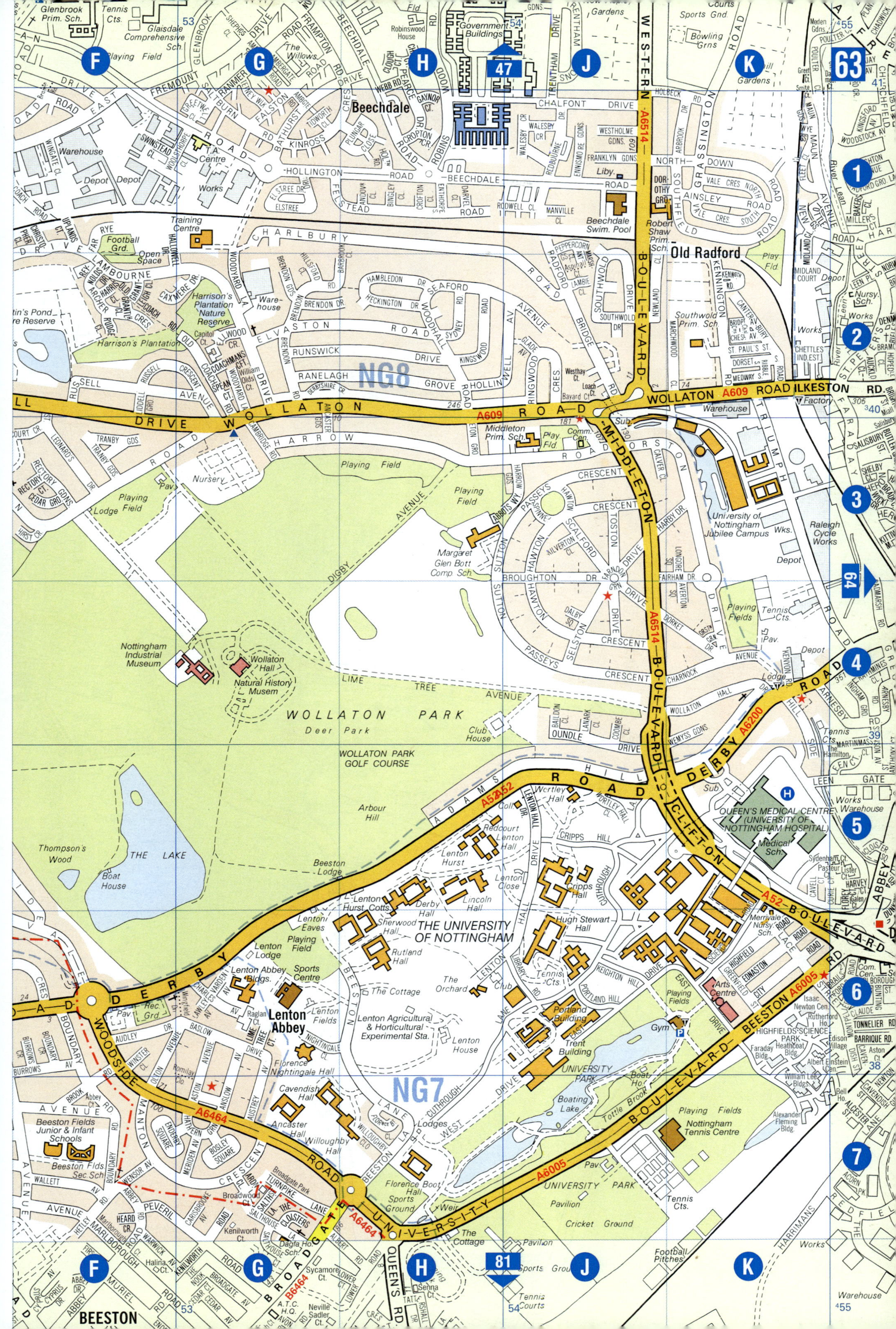
63
BEESTON
Glenbrook Prim. Sch.
Tennis Cts.
Glaisdale Comprehensive Sch.
Playing Field
Beechdale
Government Buildings
Robinswood House
Old Radford
Beechdale Swim. Pool
Robert Shaw Prim. Sch.
Southwold Prim. Sch.
Midland Court Depot
Harrison's Plantation Nature Reserve
Harrison's Plantation
Training Centre
Football Grd.
Open Space
Warehouse
Depot
Works
NG8
Martin's Pond Nature Reserve
Nursery
Playing Field
Lodge
WOLLATON DRIVE
WOLLATON ROAD A609
ILKESTON RD.
Middleton Prim. Sch.
Play Fld.
Comm. Cen.
University of Nottingham Jubilee Campus
Raleigh Cycle Works
Depot
Playing Field
Margaret Glen Bott Comp. Sch.
DIGBY AVENUE
Nottingham Industrial Museum
Wollaton Hall
Natural History Musem
WOLLATON PARK
Deer Park
LIME TREE AVENUE
Club House
WOLLATON PARK GOLF COURSE
Playing Fields
Tennis Cts.
Depot
Lodge
Wollaton Hall
Queen's Medical Centre (University of Nottingham Hospital)
Medical Sch.
Works Warehouse
Arbour Hill
Thompson's Wood
THE LAKE
Boat House
Beeston Lodge
A52 A52
ADAMS HILL ROAD
Redcourt Lenton Hall
Lenton Hurst
Lenton Close
Lincoln Hall
Cripps Hall
Hugh Stewart Hall
DERBY ROAD
CLIFTON BOULEVARD
DERBY A6200
Sub
The Hamilton
THE UNIVERSITY OF NOTTINGHAM
Derby Hall
Sherwood Hall
Rutland Hall
The Orchard
Tennis Cts.
Portland Building
Portland Hill
Highfield City
Arts Centre
Isaac Newton Cen.
HIGHFIELDS SCIENCE PARK
Faraday Heathcoat Bldg.
Albert Einstein Bldg.
William Lee Bldg.
Lenton Lodge
Lenton Abbey Bldgs.
Sports Centre
LENTON ABBEY
Raglan Hall
Lenton Fields
Playing Field
Lenton Eaves
Lenton Hurst Cotts.
Lenton Agricultural & Horticultural Experimental Sta.
Lenton House
NG7
Trent Building
UNIVERSITY PARK
Boating Lake
Tottle
Nottingham Tennis Centre
Playing Fields
Alexander Fleming Bldg.
A6464 DERBY ROAD
Beeston Fields Junior & Infant Schools
Beeston Flds. Sec. Sch.
BOUNDARY ROAD
WOODSIDE ROAD
Rec. Grd.
Pav.
Florence Nightingale Hall
Cavendish Hall
Ancaster Hall
Willoughby Hall
Broadgate Park
TURNPIKE LANE
THE CLOISTERS
A6464
BROADGATE
UNIVERSITY BOULEVARD A6005
Florence Boot Hall Sports Ground
University Park
Pavilion
Cricket Ground
Football Pitches
The Cottage
Sports Ground
Tennis Courts
QUEEN'S RD.
BEESTON
A.T.C. H.Q.
Neville Sadler Ct.
Warehouse
Works
81
47
54
55

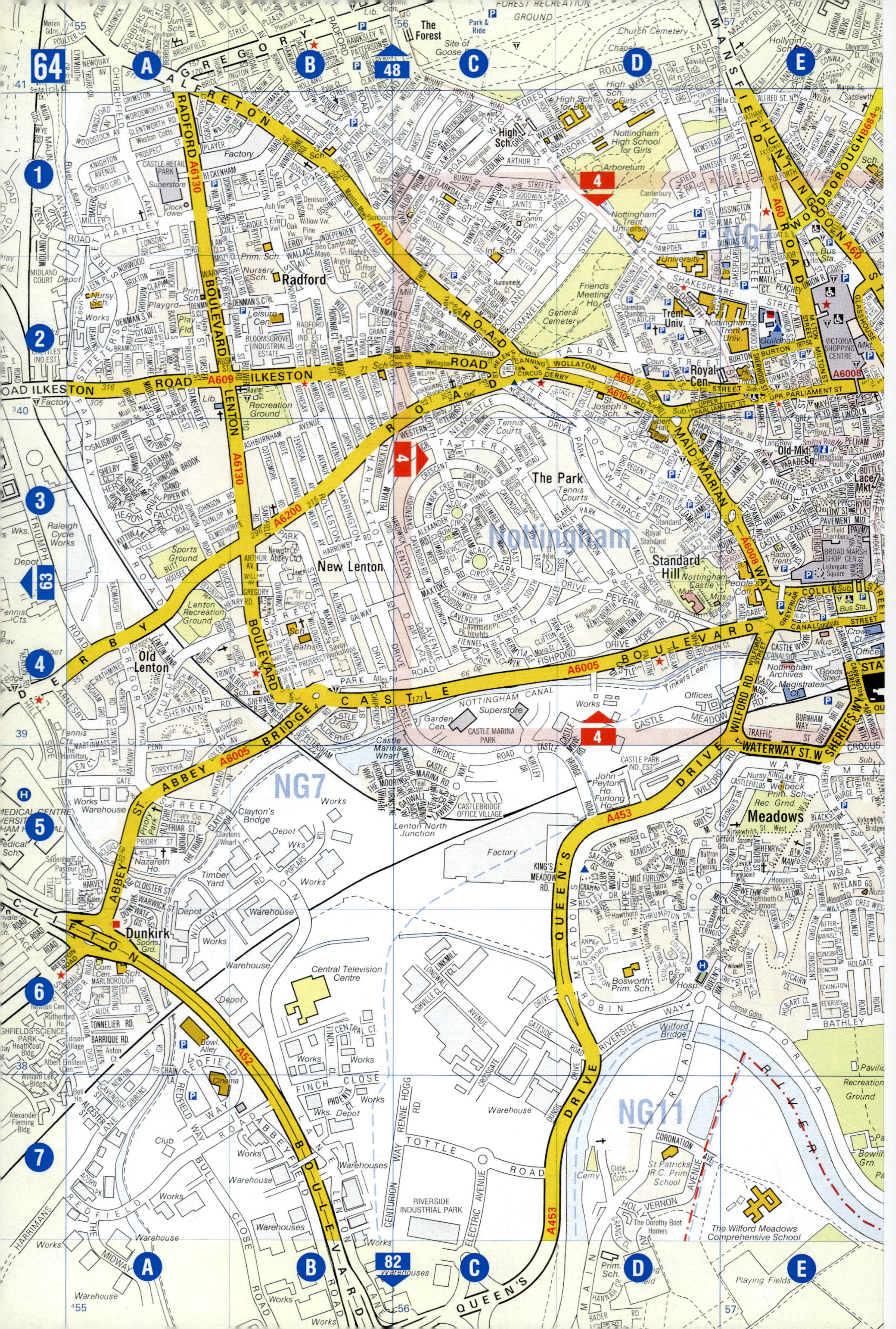

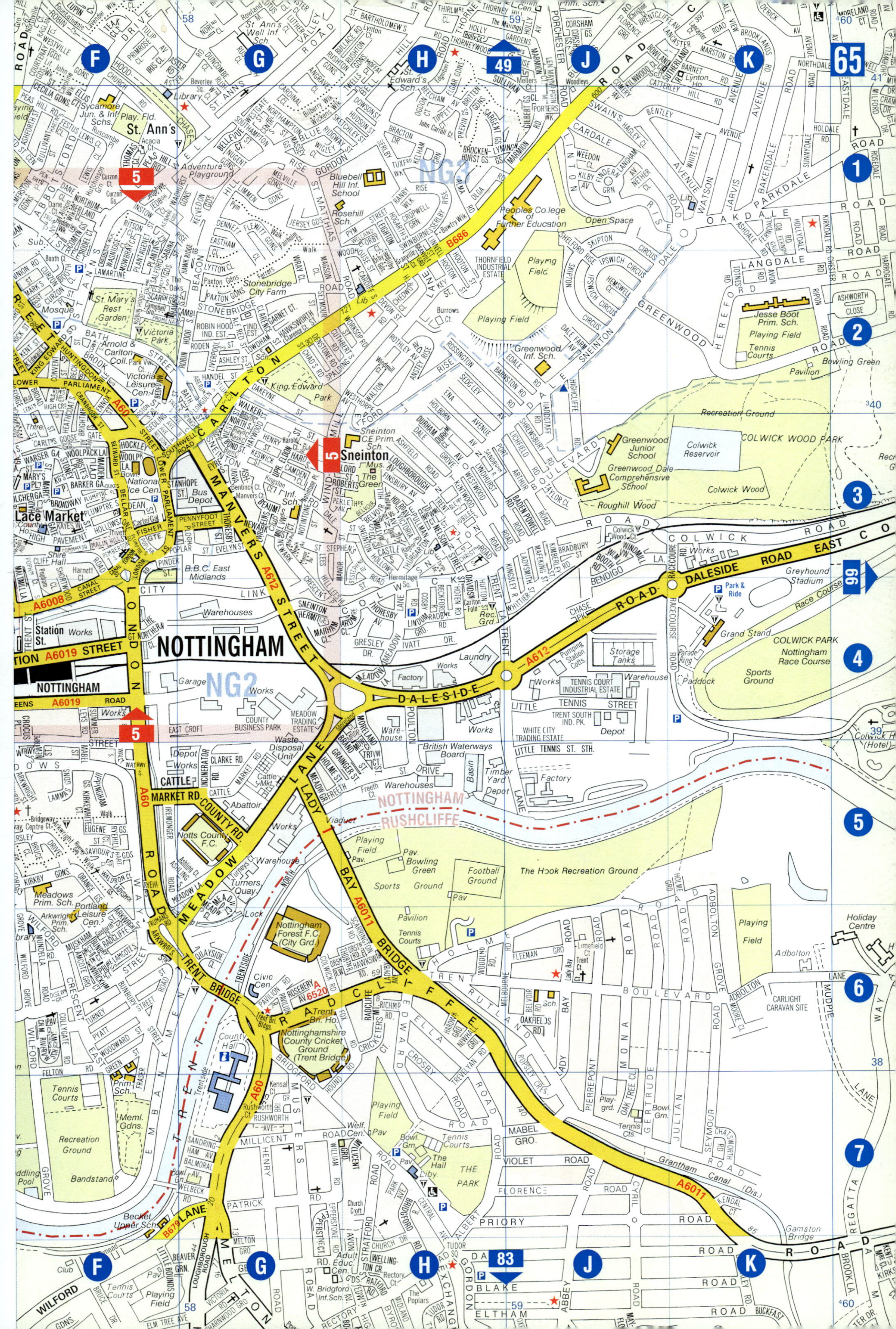

65
NOTTINGHAM
NG2
NG3
Sneinton
Lace Market
St. Ann's
COLWICK WOOD PARK
Colwick Wood
Colwick Reservoir
Colwick Park
Nottingham Race Course
Grand Stand
Greyhound Stadium
Race Course
DALESIDE ROAD EAST
DALESIDE ROAD
CARLTON ROAD
LONDON ROAD
MANVERS STREET
MEADOW LANE
RADCLIFFE ROAD
TRENT BRIDGE
COUNTY RD
CATTLE MARKET RD
A60
A612
A6011
A6008
A6019
B686
B679
Peoples Co-llege of Further Education
Thornfield Industrial Estate
Greenwood Junior School
Greenwood Dale Comprehensive School
Jesse Boot Prim. Sch.
Bowling Green
Pavilion
Recreation Ground
Colwick Wood
Roughill Wood
Playing Field
Tennis Courts
B.B.C. East Midlands
National Ice Cen.
Bus Depot
Victoria Leisure Cen.
King Edward Park
Sneinton CE Prim. Sch.
The Green
Bluebell Hill Inf. School
Rosehill Sch.
Adventure Playground
Stonebridge City Farm
St. Mary's Rest Garden
Mosque
Arnold & Carlton Coll.
St. Ann's
Sycamore Jun. & Inf. Schs.
Library
Nottingham
NG2
Meadow Trading Estate
County Business Park
East Croft
Waste Disposal Unit
Cattle Mkt.
Abattoir
Notts County F.C.
Nottingham Forest F.C. (City Grd.)
Turners Quay
Lock
Bowling Green
Football Ground
Sports Ground
The Hook Recreation Ground
NOTTINGHAM RUSHCLIFFE
British Waterways Board
Timber Yard
White City Trading Estate
Trent South Ind. Pk.
Tennis Court Industrial Estate
Storage Tanks
Pumping Station Cotts.
Laundry
Park & Ride
Paddock
Sports Ground
Holiday Centre
Carlight Caravan Site
Adbolton
Playing Field
BOULEVARD
ADBOLTON LANE
MUDPIE WAY
REGATTA WAY
Grantham Canal (Dis.)
Gamston Bridge
THE PARK
Nottinghamshire County Cricket Ground (Trent Bridge)
Trent Bridge
County Hall
Civic Cen.
Rosebery A A6520
Trent Br. Ho.
Embankment
Meml. Gdns.
Recreation Ground
Bandstand
Tennis Courts
Meadows Prim. Sch.
Portland Leisure Cen.
WILFORD
The Hall
Lady Bay
Violet Road
Mabel Gro.
Florence
Priory
Blake
Eltham
TUDOR
49
83
66
59
58
60
41
40
39
38
Colwick H. (Hotel)
F  G  H  J  K
1  2  3  4  5  6  7

66
A
B
50
C
D
E
Carlton
Southcliffe
Sacred Heart R.C. Prim. Sch.
Shipley
Kensington
Netherfield
Bakers Fields
Parkdale Prim. Sch. Playing Field
Colwick Vale
Colwick Industrial Estate
Netherfield
NG3
Works
Depot
Bowling Green
Pavilion
Playing Field
Three Hills
Colwick Business Park
Churchill Park
Colwick Vale
Works
Depot
NG4
Colwick Industrial Estate
Colwick Wood Park
Recreation Grd.
Mile End Rd.
Meadow
Colwick
COLWICK
A612
GEDLING NOTTINGHAM
Sports Ground
Works
Daleside Rd. Colwick Rd. A612
East
Colwick Road
Race Course
65
Colwick Lake
Drain
Water Ski Lagoon
Colwick Park
Nottingham Race Course
COLWICK COUNTRY PARK
Holme Sluices
RUSHCLIFFE
Holme Cut
Holme Lock
Rowing Course
HOLME PIERREPONT COUNTRY PARK
Colwick Marina
Canoe Slalom Course
Colwick Hall (Hotel)
Colwick Hall
West Lake
HOLME PIERREPONT
NG2
River Trent
Sports Ground
Holme Pierrepont National Watersports Centre & Country Park
Jetties
Polser Brook
Holiday Centre
Hostel
Adbolton
Bolton Lane
Holme Grange
Cattle Grid
Carlight Caravan Site
Adbolton La.
Greenacres Caravan Park
Polser Bridge
Holme Pierrepont C.E. Primary Sch.
Gamston Bridge
Regatta Way Lane
A52 Road
A52
Radcliffe
Holme Lane
Bassingfield
RATCLIFFE
Council Yard
A
B
84
C
D
E
Lea Farm
Holly Farm
Cherry Tree Cottage
Smallholding
Manor Farm

F
G
H
51
J
K
67
R
63
64
465
41
ROAD
DR
NORTHERN
GREAT
PASTURE WY.
Ind. Est.
VICTORIA
BUSINESS
PARK
A612
VICTORIA
PARK-
WAY
TEAL
CLOSE
DRAKE ROAD
MALLARD RD
PINTAIL CL.
NG14
Ouse Dyke
Sludge Beds
Stoke
Lock
1
Slack
Hollow
THE AVENUE
CLIFFS
ROAD 3
PRIVATE ROAD 5
PRIVATE ROAD 4
Depot
Works
TRENT
RIVER
TRENT
Viaduct
Trent Field
Plantation
Brook
2
TRENT VW.
GDS.
Hallow
Well
CLIFF
DRIVE
HOPEWELL
CL.
340
WAKEFIELD
WEST-
CLIFFE
CLIFF
ROCKLEY
AV.
PARK
RD
ROAD
3
Craig
Moray
Birkin
AV.
FRANCIS
MALKIN
CLIFF CRES
GRANDFIELD
WAY
GRANDFIELD
AV.
HAMILTON
DR.
QUEEN'S
RD.
CHESTNUT
Nottingham
Polser
Brook
Cricket
Grd.
Pav.
LANE
HOLME
Nottingham
SUMMER
WAY
OAK AV.
CENTRE
WY.
OAK AV.
FERNWOOD
OAK TREE
DR.
STAN-
FORD
GDS.
RICHM.
Recreation
Grd.
Radcliffe
Lodge
Radcliffe
68
BROOKFIELD
Holme
Pierrepont
Hall
The Firs
RADCLIFFE
ON TRENT
Manor
Ho.
The Chestnuts
WHARF LANE
WALNUT
GRO.
SHELFORD
ROAD
Station Lib.
RUSHCLIFFE
AV.
LORNE
GRO.
BINGHAM
ROAD
NEW
CLOSE
GATCOMBE
ROAD
CLOSE
4
Welby's Yd.
Richmond Ter.
ALBERT
ST.
LINCOLN GRO.
VICTORIA
ST.
CROPWELL
GLEBE LA.
Bowl.
Grn.
39
CROP.
WELL GDS.
Home Farm
The Rectory
SANDY
LANE
THE GREEN
GREEN
WAY
LAMCOTE
MS.
LAMOTTE CONS.
YEW TREE CL.
Lamcote
House
Lamcote
Ms.
W End
Vs.
SYDNEY GRO.
PINFOLD
HOGG
LA.
THE WOODLANDS
WATER
LANE
TALBOT CL.
SHADWELL
GRO.
HALL
CL.
CHURCH
VICARAGE
LA.
LIME
GRO.
MAPLE
CL.
BEECH CL.
SYCAMORE
CL.
WILLOW
CL.
Radcliffe on Trent
Junior Sch.
Cemetery
CHERRY TREE
R.S.P.C.A.
Animal Shelter
NG12
PADDOCK CL.
BAILEY LA.
ST.
PRINCE
EDWARD
CRES.
BARR-
INGTON
CL.
Bailey
Ct.
VANCOUVER
AV.
WHITWORTH
BOULEVARD
AVENUE
DRIVE
ROAD
A52
38
NOTTINGHAM
ROAD
GRANTHAM
ROAD
RADCLIFFE
ROAD
LANE
STRAGGLETHORPE
Holme
House
LEES
BARN
ROAD
Lees Barn
Lamcote
Field
6
Works
7
Landfill Waste Site
Thornton's Holt
Farm
Shepherd's
Houses
MAIN
ROAD
Cockcchat
Plantation
North
Farm
F
G
H
85
J
K
63
64
465
Stragglet

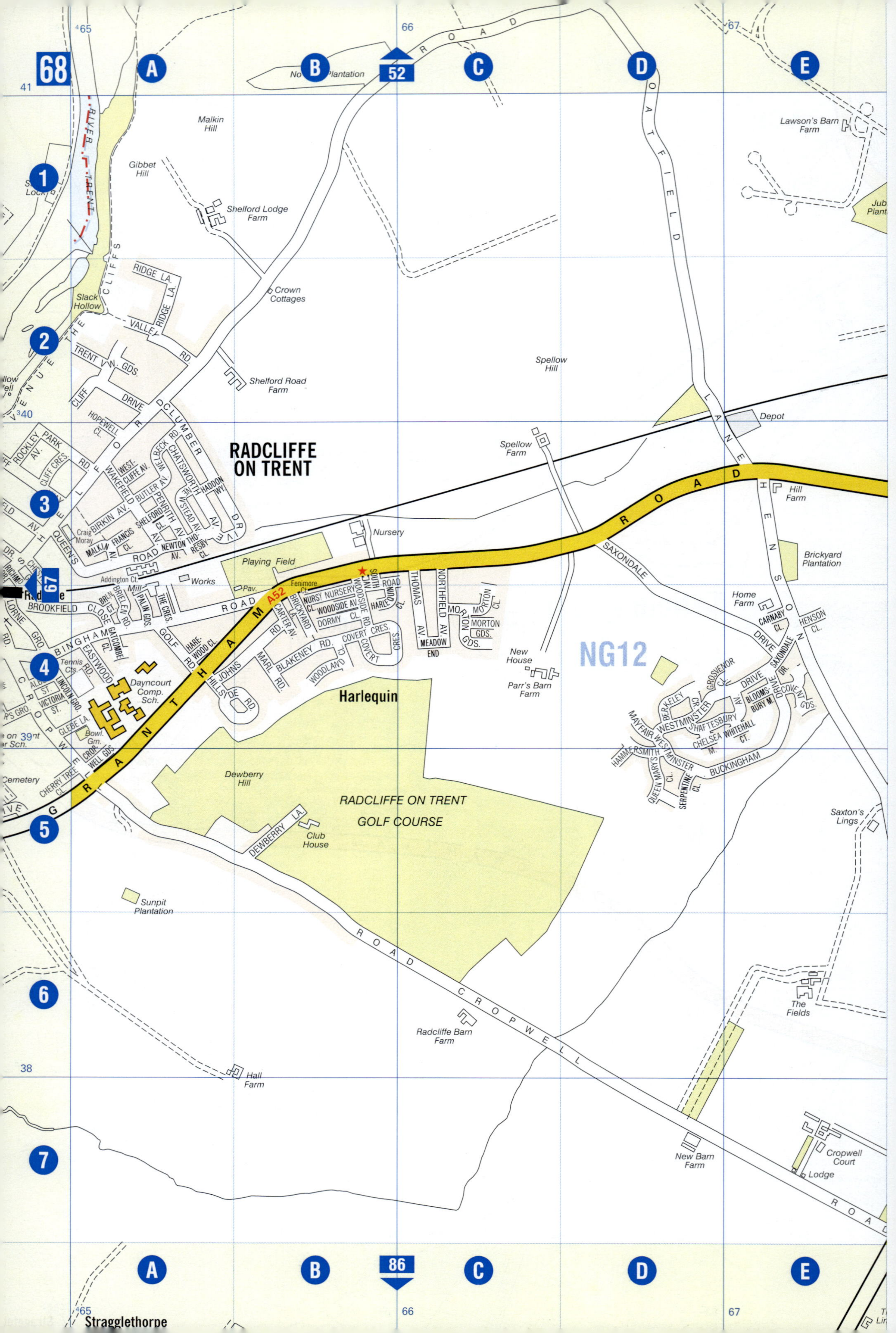

68
65
41
66
52
67
A
B
C
D
E
1
40
2
3
67
4
39
5
6
38
7
Malkin Hill
Gibbet Hill
Shelford Lodge Farm
Crown Cottages
Slack Hollow
Lock
RIVER TRENT
THE CLIFFS
RIDGE LA.
RIDGE LA.
VALLEY RD.
TRENT VW. GDS.
CLIFF DRIVE
CLUMBER RD.
HOPEWELL CL.
Shelford Road Farm
RADCLIFFE ON TRENT
Spellow Hill
Spellow Farm
Depot
Hill Farm
Lawson's Barn Farm
Brickyard Plantation
LANE
OAT FIELD
ROAD
Nursery
Saxondale
ROAD
Home Farm
HENSON
CARNABY
HENSON CL.
Playing Field
Works
Pav.
Fenimore
A52
Nursery
Nurst CL.
Woodside Av.
Woodside Rd.
South La.
King Road
Thomas Av.
Northfield Av.
Morton Av.
Morton Gdns.
MORTON GDNS.
Morton CL.
MEADOW END
New House
Parr's Barn Farm
NG12
Harle CL.
HARLE CRES.
Covert CL.
Covert CRES.
DORMY CL.
Blakeney Rd.
Woodland CL.
Marl Rd.
Carter Av.
Brickyard
St. Johns DE RD.
Hills RD.
GRANTHAM RD.
Golf RD.
Hare Wood CL.
The CRES.
PALIN GDS.
MILL
CLOSE
BRIELEY RD.
BRUN RD.
GATCOMBE CL.
EASTWOOD RD.
BINGHAM RD.
LINCOLN GRO.
VICTORIA ST.
LORNE RD.
ALBERT ST.
GLEBE LA.
CROPWELL RD.
Bowl. Grn.
CROP WELL GDS.
CHERRY TREE
Tennis Cts.
Dayncourt Comp. Sch.
Cemetery
BROOKFIELD
Craig Moray
MALKIN AV.
FRANCIS AV.
SHELFORD AV.
PENRITH AV.
NEWTON AV.
RESBY CL.
THO. CL.
BIRKIN AV.
ROAD
HADDON WY.
WILBECK AV.
CHATSWORTH AV.
WELBECK AV.
DRIVE
BUTLER CL.
WAKEFIELD
WEST CLIFFE AV.
QUEENS
ROCKLEY PARK
CLIFF CRES.
AV.
RD.
Addington Ct.
Harlequin
Dewberry Hill
DEWBERRY LA.
Club House
Sunpit Plantation
RADCLIFFE ON TRENT GOLF COURSE
ROAD
CROPWELL
Radcliffe Barn Farm
Hall Farm
New Barn Farm
The Fields
Saxton's Lings
Cropwell Court
Lodge
ROAD
SAXONDALE DRIVE
BUCKINGHAM
GROSVENOR DRIVE
BERKELEY CR.
SHAFTESBURY AV.
WESTMINSTER
MAYFAIR
HAMMERSMITH
QUEEN MARY'S CL.
SERPENTINE CL.
CHELSEA
WHITEHALL CT.
BLOOMS BURY M.
COVENT GDNS.
BURY M.
A
B
86
C
D
E
65
66
67
Stragglethorpe

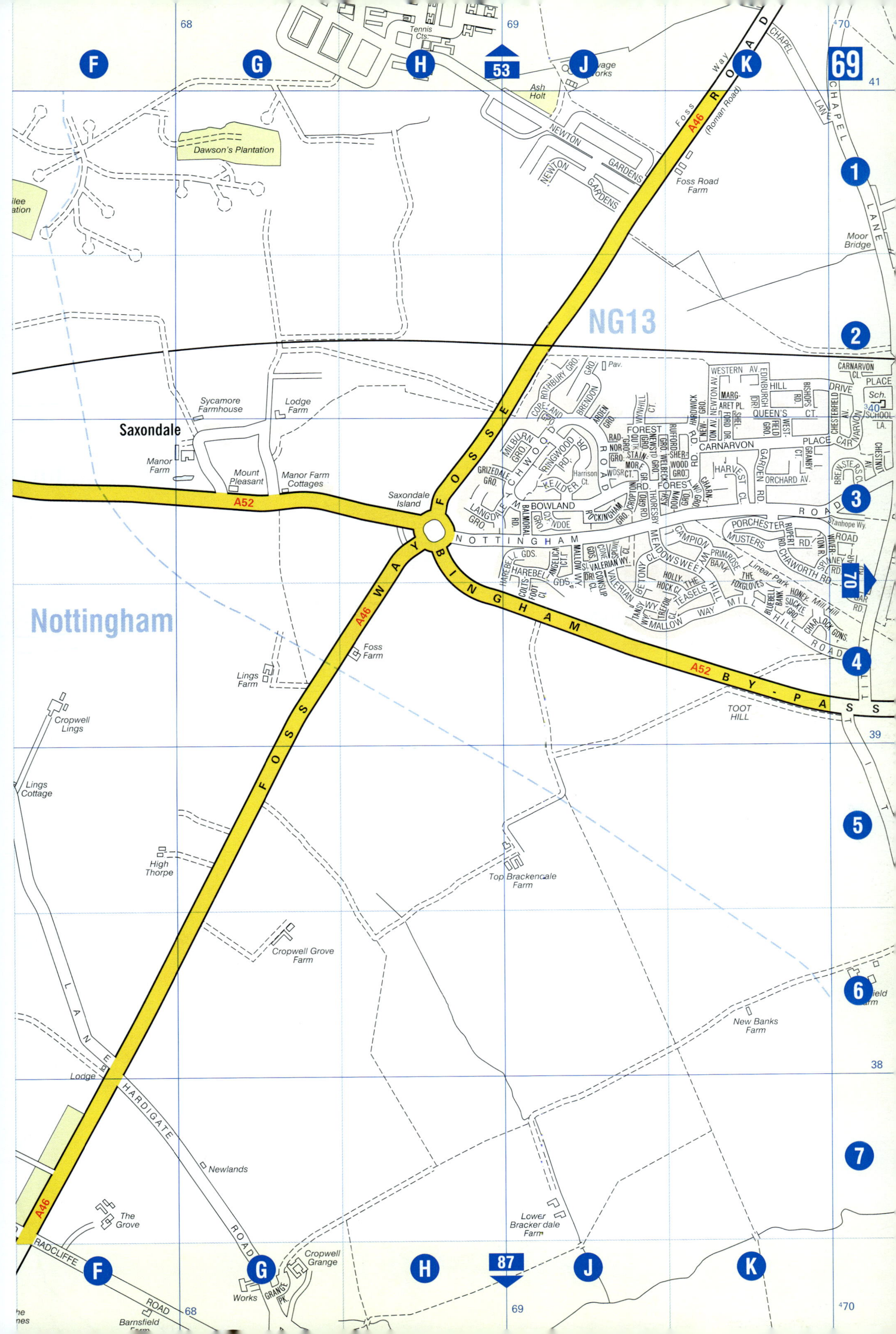

68
69
470
69
41
F
G
H
53
J
K
Tennis Cts.
Savage Works
Ash Holt
Foss Way
Chapel Lane
1
Newton Gardens
A46 (Roman Road)
Foss Road Farm
Moor Bridge
Dawson's Plantation
NG13
2
Carnarvon Cl
Carnarvon Place
Pav.
Western Av.
Edinburgh Dr.
Hill Rd.
Bishops Ct.
Chesterfield Drive
Sch.
340 School La.
Saxondale
Rothbury Gro.
Gro.
Copeland
Brendon
Arden Gro.
Hawick
Marg-aret Pl.
Newton Av.
Sher-ford Dr.
Queen's Place
West Place
Granby Ct.
Chestnut Av.
Sycamore Farmhouse
Lodge Farm
Milburn Gro.
Beech Gro.
Ringwood Rd.
Forest Rad- Gro.
Newstd Gro.
Rufford Gro.
Welbeck Gro.
Thoresby Gro.
Sher-wood Gro.
Rd.
Carnarvon
Harvest Cl.
Garden Gro.
Orchard Av.
Brewsters Cl.
3
Manor Farm
Mount Pleasant
Manor Farm Cottages
A52
Grizedale Gro.
Keilder Gro.
Nor. Gro.
Stain-Gro.
Mor. Ct.
Wdsr. Ct.
Gr.
Forest Esy.
Chaworth Rd.
Road
Stanhope Wy.
Langdale Gro.
Balmoral Rd.
Bowland
Rockingham Gro.
Porchester Musters
Rupert Rd.
Road
Saxondale Island
Nottingham
Wyndoe
Harrison Ct.
Meadowsweet
Campion
Primrose Bank
River St.
70
Harebel Gds.
Angelica Ct.
Mallow Gro.
Cone Cl.
Valerian Wy.
Cowslip Cl.
Betony
Linear Park
Honey Suckle Gro.
Mill Hill
Foss Way
Harebell
Foot Cl.
Cl.
Gds.
Dr.
Holly Hock Cl.
The Teasels
The Foxgloves
Bluebell Bank
Char- lock Gdns.
Mill Hill Road
Coltsfoot Ct.
Tansy Wy.
Treefell Cl.
Mallow
Way
Nottingham
A52 BY-PASS
4
Foss Farm
TOOT HILL
39
Lings Farm
5
Cropwell Lings
Lings Cottage
High Thorpe
Top Brackendale Farm
6
New Banks Farm
38
Cropwell Grove Farm
Lodge
Hardigate Road
7
Newlands
Lower Bracker dale Farm
Lane
The Grove
A46
Radcliffe
F
Works
Grange Pk.
Cropwell Grange
G
H
87
J
K
Road
68
69
470
Barnsfield Farm

70
41
40
39
38
470
71
72
A
B
C
D
E
1
2
3
4
5
6
7
CHAPEL LANE
Moor Bridge
Moorbridge Ct.
MOORBRIDGE
MOORBRIDGE RD.
BINGHAM INDUSTRIAL PARK
Parson's Hill
Tennis Ct.
Playing Field
Pav.
Bingham
Car Dyke
Car Dyke
Holme Farm
Nottingham
CARNARVON CL.
CARNARVON PLACE
KIRKHILL
GILLOTS CL.
MOOR LA.
Old Mill Ct.
LANGTREE GDS.
STATION ST.
ST. MARYS
ROAD
LANE
PRIORS CL.
BROWNES RD.
VICTORIA
NURSERY RD.
CARR RD.
DOUGLAS RD.
BANES RD.
Sch.
Offs.
Robert Miles Jun. Sch.
CHURCH RD.
ABBEY
ROAD
DRIVE
CHESTERFIELD AV.
CARNARVON
NEWGATE ST.
SCHOOL
NEEDHAM ST.
MARKET PL.
Library
Eaton Place
CHURCH ST.
CHURCH ST.
RUTLAND GROVE
EAST ST.
EAST GRO.
HOLME RD.
BUTT RD.
Playgrd.
Carnarvon Primary School
BISHOPS CT.
HILL
GREEN
WEST PLACE
GRANBY CT.
ORCHARD AV.
BREWSTERS CL.
CHESTNUT
NOTTINGHAM RD.
THE CROFTS
WALKERS CL.
THE PADDOCK
Bowl Grn.
CHERRY ST.
Ct.
FOSTERS
LONG ACRE
MANOR RD.
CROW CT.
COGLEY LA.
Oak Lodge
Beech Lodge
ASPEN CL.
WILLOW RD.
LARCH
POPLAR CL.
OAK AV.
HOLLY
HAZEL
VIPER
BLACKTHORN
GDS.
Nursery
UNION
PORCHESTER RD.
STANTON RD.
RUPERT RD.
PINXTON
LANGAR RD.
SPINNEY RD.
LANGAR RD.
MELVYN DR.
BANKS CL.
BANKS CRES.
FISHER LA.
BANKS PADDOCK
BEETHAM CL.
LONG ACRE EAST
JEBB'S LA.
PINFOLD
PERRY GRO.
DARK LA.
RAYMOND DR.
ROWAN CL.
ASH CL.
WILLOW RD.
MAPLE CL.
BEECH AV.
SYCAMORE CL.
ELM AV.
CEDAR CL.
WILLOW ROAD
DERBY LA.
Stanhope Wy.
THE
ROAD
Sports Centre
Cemy.
Belvoir Vale Centre
MALLARD CL.
WADES CL.
GOLDCREST CL.
NIGHTINGALE WAY
BLUEBELL BANK
SUCKLE GRO.
CHARLOCK GDS.
DOVE MILL HILL
MILL HILL
Toot Hill Comp. Sch.
Tennis Courts
KESTREL DRIVE
ALLSOP CL.
PIPE CL.
DOVE CL.
TIT CL.
WINDOVER CL.
AVOCET CL.
BY-PASS
GRANTHAM
A52
Playing Field
Playing Fld.
Sports Arena
SKYLARK CL.
ALLOW
BINGHAM
A52
TITHBY ROAD
Sub.
39
Starnhill Cottages
Starnhill Farm
Sta. Plan
Whitefield Farm
Crown Cottages
Spring Farm
38
NG12
Tithby Grange Cottages
Tithby Grange
Crane's Covert
RIVER
470
71
72

F
G
H
J
K
71
73
74
475
41
1
2
40
3
39
4
5
6
38
7
475
Mill Field
Hill Farm
Cliff Holme
Cemetery
Corner Farm
Holme View
MEADOW CL.
Spinney Corner
CHAPEL LA.
The Fields
ST. THOMAS DR.
DAWN'S LA.
Saucer Farm
Football Ground
Blackberry Hill
Malthouse
NOBLE LA.
WALNUT
Sch
ABBEY CL.
FIELDS DR.
THE CAPES
SCH. LA.
Aslockton
Aslockton
VALE CL.
The Abbey
Sewage Works
MOOR
LANE
ABBEY
LANE
NEW
Crossing House
The Hall
Brocker Farm
NG13
BEVERLEY'S
GREEN WLK.
AV.
DARK LANE
MAIN
SMITE CL.
COTTAGE
AVENUE
AZIMGHUR RD.
Cricket Ground
Pav.
Fish Pond
RIVER
SMITE
RIVERSIDE LA.
CHURCH WLK.
Manor Farm
The Grange
BURTON
SUNBEAM
MAIN ST.
Whipling Farm
The Gables
SCHOOL LA.
CHURCH STREET
Hollies Farm
Whatton Bridge
OLD
GRANTHAM
ORSTON
LANE
Whatton
The Lawns
IVY ROW
ROAD
H.M. Young Offender Institution
Sewage Works
BELVOIR CL.
CROMWELL RD.
CRANMER
AVENUE
ROAD
GRAN
BY
Aslockton Grange
CONERY
GARDENS
Whatton Towermill
CONERY
Greenacres
A52
Whatton Lodge Farm
Starnhill Cottages
Thorough Bridge
rnhill tation
SMITE
Long Meadow
Butlers Cottage
CONERY
HALL LANE
Vicars Croft
Keeper's Cottage
Playhouse Plantation
Whatton Barn
Lane Plantations
Whipling
River
Whatton Fields
Whatton Manor
Pond Plantation
Manor Lodge
Front Plantation
The Rookery
Middle Covert
New Covert
Long Plantation
Whipling Covert
Moor Dyke
F
G
H
J
K
73
74
475
MILL
Gutter
LANE
The
LANE
STREET
CLIFF HILL
LANE
LANE
Spinney
RIVER
River
LANE

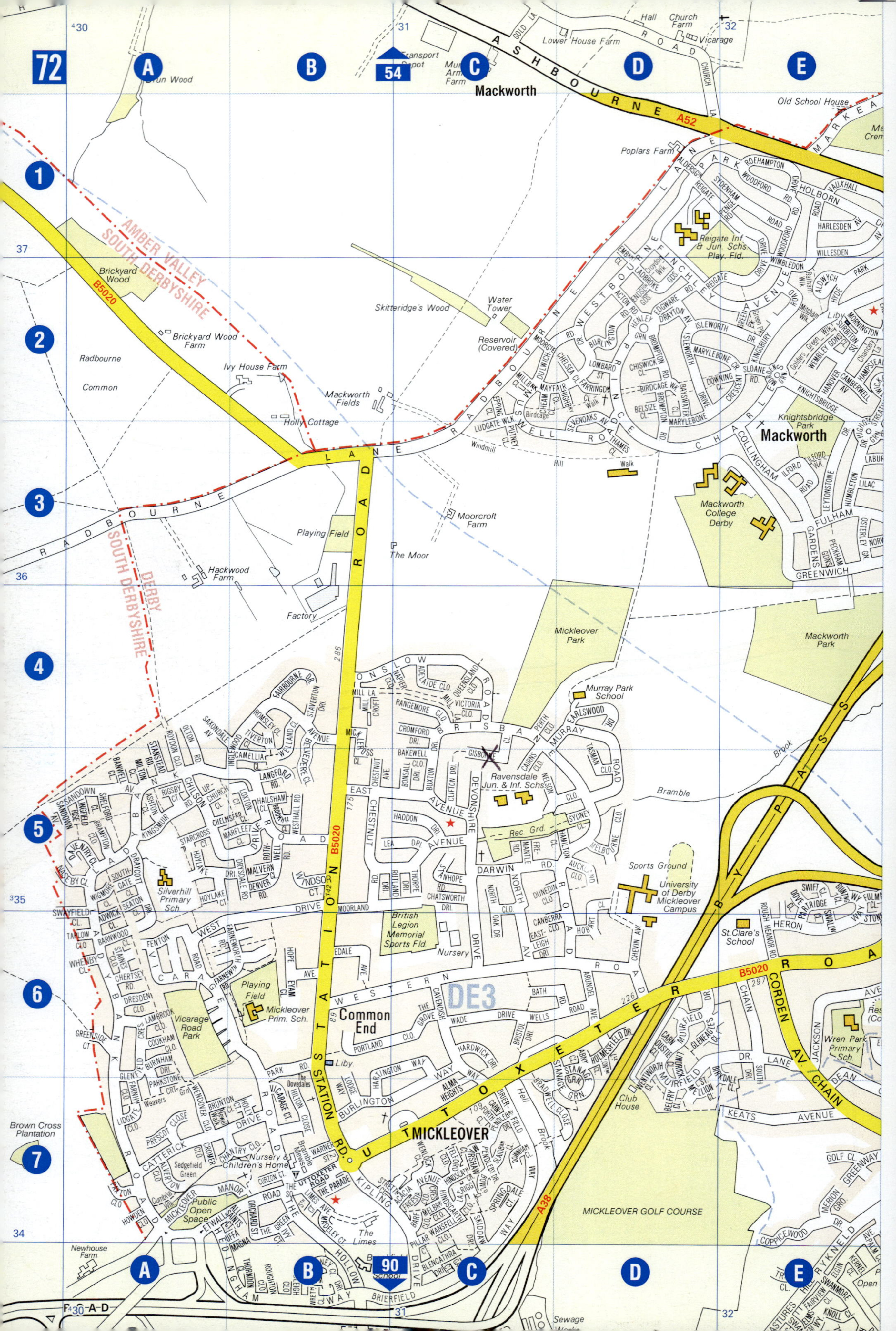

72
30
31
32
A
B
C
D
E
54
Mackworth
ASHBOURNE ROAD
A52
Lower House Farm
Hall
Church Farm
Vicarage
Old School House
Transport Depot
Murray Arms Farm
Poplars Farm
Reigate Inf. & Jun. Schs Play. Fld.
1
37
AMBER VALLEY
SOUTH DERBYSHIRE
Brickyard Wood
B5020
Skitteridge's Wood
Water Tower
Mackworth
2
Radbourne Common
Brickyard Wood Farm
Ivy House Farm
Reservoir (Covered)
Mackworth Fields
Holly Cottage
Windmill Hill
Walk
Knightsbridge Park
Mackworth College Derby
3
36
RADBOURNE LANE
Hackwood Farm
Playing Field
Moorcroft Farm
The Moor
Factory
Greenwich
4
Mickleover Park
Mackworth Park
Murray Park School
Mickleover Park
Brook
Bramble
5
35
SWAYFIELD
Silverhill Primary Sch.
Ravensdale Jun. & Inf. Schs.
Gisborne
Rec. Grd.
Darwin
Sports Ground
University of Derby Mickleover Campus
St. Clare's School
B5020
EAST AVENUE
B5020
6
British Legion Memorial Sports Fld.
Nursery
DE3
Common End
UTTOXETER ROAD
Club House
B5020
CORDEN AVENUE
Wren Park Primary Sch.
Mickleover Prim. Sch.
Playing Field
Vicarage Road Park
Keats Avenue
Brown Cross Plantation
7
34
Newhouse Farm
Nursery Children's Home
Sedgefield Green
Public Open Space
The Parade
The Limes
MICKLEOVER
A38
MICKLEOVER GOLF COURSE
90 School
BRIERFIELD
Sewage Works
A
B
C
D
E
30
31
32

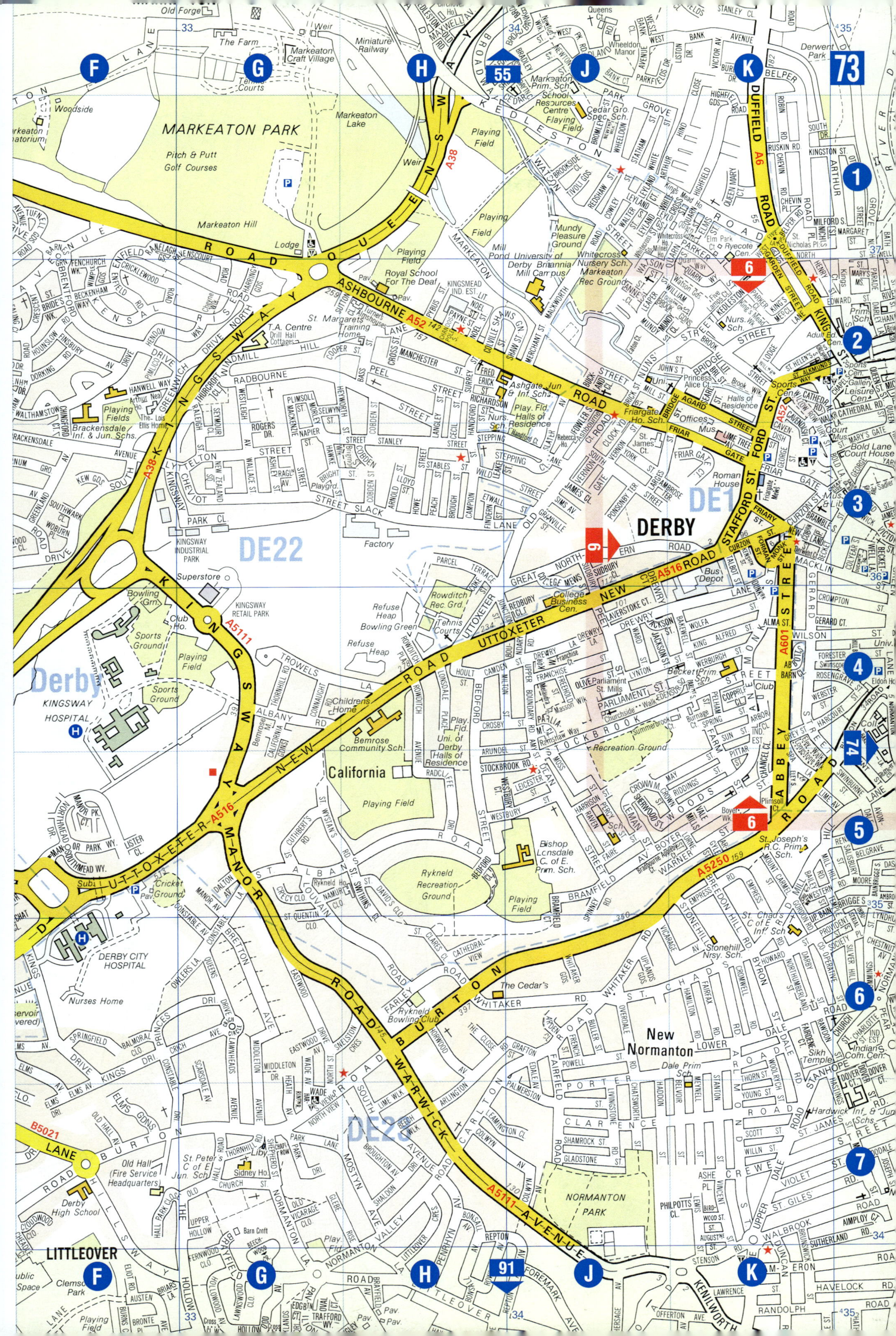

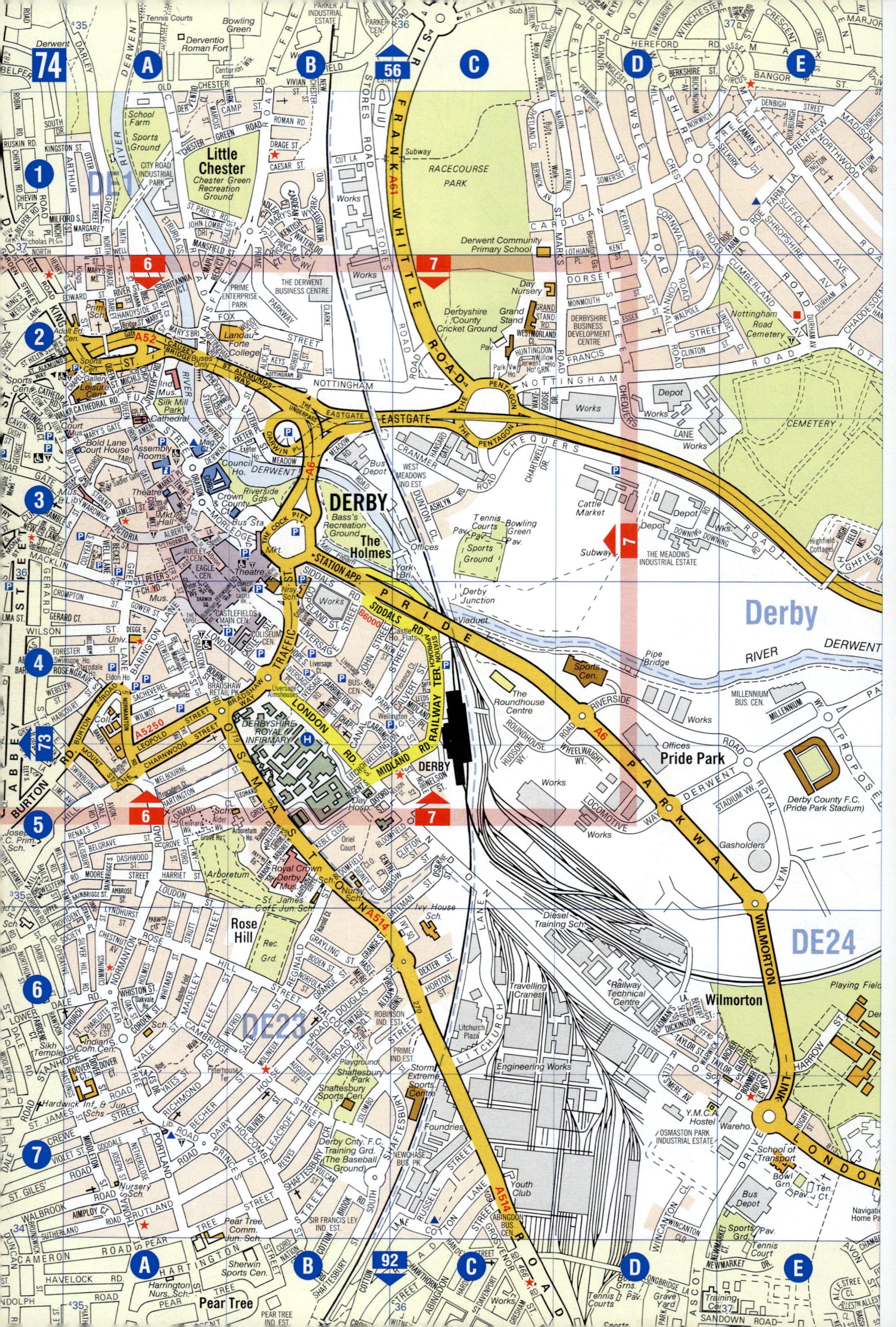

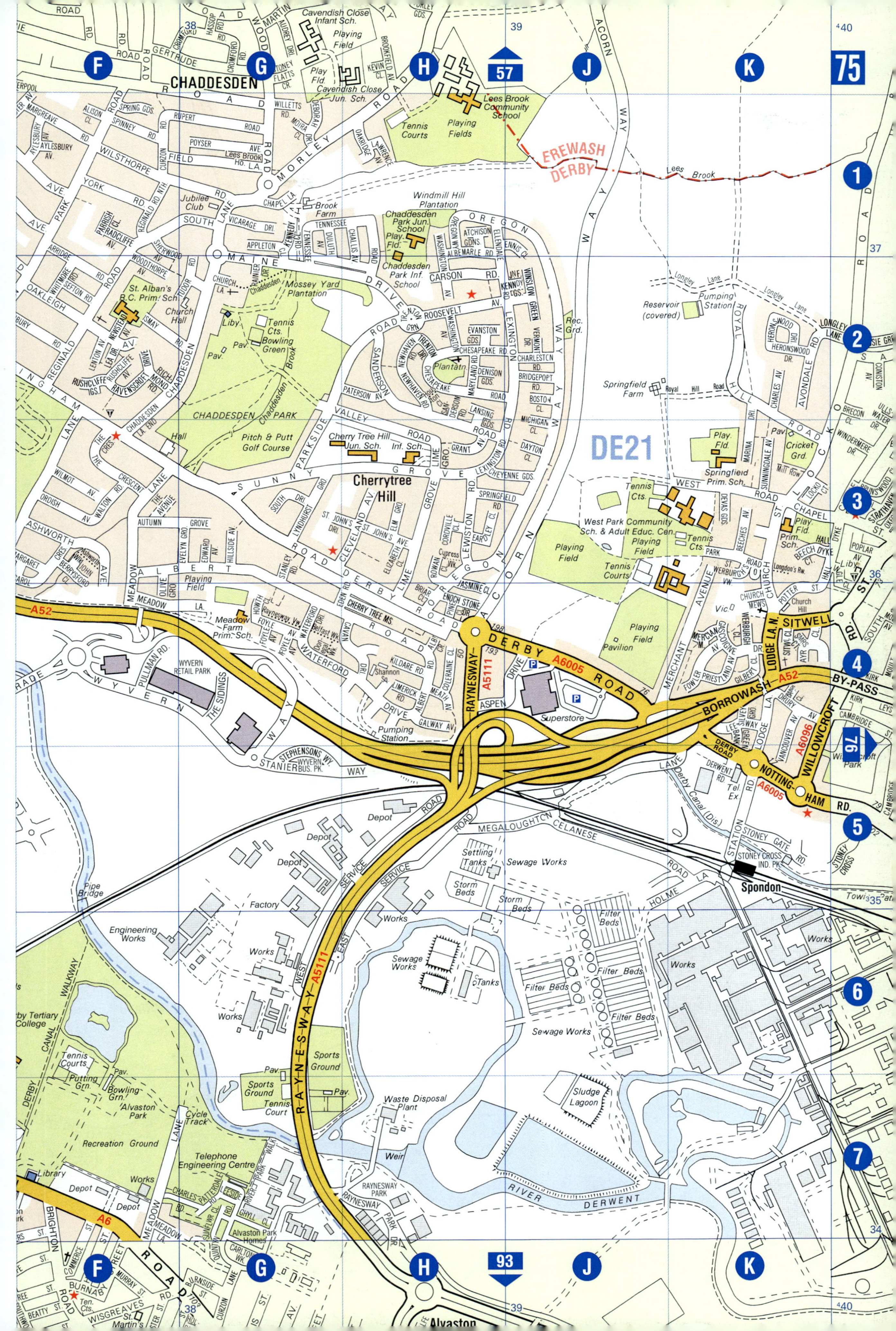

CHADDESDEN
F  G  H  57  J  K  75
Cavendish Close Infant Sch.
Playing Field
Lees Brook Community School
Tennis Courts
Playing Fields
EREWASH
DERBY
Lees Brook
ACORN WAY
1
Windmill Hill Plantation
Brook Farm
Chaddesden Park Jun. School Play. Fld.
Chaddesden Park Inf. School
OREGON
Reservoir (covered)
Pumping Station
Longley Lane
Longley Lane
2
St. Alban's R.C. Prim. Sch.
Church Hall
Mossey Yard Plantation
Rec. Grd.
Springfield Farm
Royal Hill Road
HERONSWOOD
LONGLEY LANE
Liby
Tennis Cts. Bowling Green
Pav.
Chaddesden Brook
Trenton Grn.
Roosevelt
DE21
Springfield Prim. Sch.
Play. Fld.
Cricket Grd.
3
CHADDESDEN PARK
Pitch & Putt Golf Course
Hall
Cherry Tree Hill Jun. Sch.   Inf. Sch.
Cherrytree Hill
West Park Community Sch. & Adult Educ. Cen.
Playing Field
Tennis Cts. Park
WEST ROAD
SITWELL
Play. Fld. Prim. Sch.
BEECH DYKE
CHURCH
Tennis Courts
Vic.
Church Hill
A52
MEADOW
Playing Field
Meadow Farm Prim. Sch.
Cherry Tree Ms.
Playing Field Pavilion
MERCHANT AVENUE
LODGE LA. N.
SITWELL
BY-PASS
4
WYVERN RETAIL PARK
The Sidings
Pumping Station
RAYNESWAY
DERBY  A6005  ROAD
A5111
Superstore
A52
BORROWASH
A6096
WILLOWCROFT
76
Willowcroft Park
STEPHENSONS WY.
STANIER
WYVERN WAY
WAY
DERBY ROAD
NOTTINGHAM RD.
A6005
5
Depot
Depot
Depot
MEGALOUGHTON
CELANESE
Settling Tanks
Sewage Works
Storm Beds
Storm Beds
STATION ROAD
STONEY GATE
STONEY CROSS IND. PK.
Spondon
Factory
SERVICE ROAD
Works
Filter Beds
Works
6
Engineering Works
Works
Sewage Works
Tanks
Filter Beds
Filter Beds
Filter Beds
Works
Works
RAYNESWAY
A5111
EAST
WEST
Derby Tertiary College
Tennis Courts
Putting Grn.
Bowling Grn.
Alvaston Park
Cycle Track
Sports Ground
Sports Ground
Tennis Court
Pav.
Waste Disposal Plant
Sludge Lagoon
7
Recreation Ground
Telephone Engineering Centre
Library
Depot
Depot
Weir
RAYNESWAY PARK DR.
RAYNESWAY
RIVER  DERWENT
A6
BRIGHTON
Alvaston Park Homes
F  G  H  93  J  K
Alvaston

76
40
41
58
42
A
B
C
D
E
1
Brunswood Farm
Spondonwood Farm
SPONDON WOOD
Moor Lane Farm
Ladywood
Poplar Farm
37
2
Longley Lane
Heronswood Dr.
Charles Av.
Avondale
Longley Lane
Lousie Greaves La.
Sancroft
Coniston Av.
Chapel La.
Brecon Cl.
Ulls Water Lane
Windermere Dr.
Reader St.
Stone Cl.
Chesterton Av.
Nicholas Cl.
Chesterton Rd.
Stewart Cl.
Frazer Cl.
Orchard Ct.
Hamilton
Croft Cl.
Gerard
Hill Ct.
Field Ho.
Fellside
Deer Park Vw.
Goldcrest Dr.
Chaf. Finch Cl.
Green Cl.
Badger Cl.
Linnet Cl.
Huntley Av.
Dolphin Cl.
Lland Cl.
Hazel Dri.
Birch Cl.
Wood Rd.
Windsor Av.
Huntley Av.
Pheasant Field House
Pheasant Field
Dale Road
Moor
Road
A6096
OCKBROOK
The Cottage
3
Play Fld. Prim. Sch.
Hall
Beech Dyke
Landon's Rw.
Chapel
Chapel Side
Stratham Ct.
Poplar Av.
Sycamore Ct.
Antony Cl.
Wingerworth Pk. Rd.
Gravel
Brockley
Gladstone Rd.
Oxford
St. Dale
Moor End
Brackley Drive
Cemy.
Lawnside
Farningham Cl.
Ludlow
Arundel
Clover
Larkrise
Nursery
Beaumaris
Caernarvon Cl.
Holyrood Cl.
Haplech Cl.
Hampton Cl.
Rannoch
Borrow Wood Jun. & Inf. Schools
Playing Field
Dale Road Park
Burrow Wood Farm
Playing Field
Bakehouse Lane
Ockbrook Sch.
Ockbrook Grange
Wesley La.
Sisters La.
Settlement
Home Farm
Bare Green
Top Manor Cl.
Oak Cl.
Cedar
Playing Fld.
Redh Prim.
36
Potter St.
Church St.
St.
A6096
Sitwell
Chapel Hill
Sitwell
Sitwell Cl.
Louise La. N.
Willow-croft Rd.
Borrowash
South Av.
Meadow Av.
Moult Av.
The Covert
Recreation Ground
Hillside
Hillside Cr.
Goldstone Ct.
Pit
Andringham Dr.
Bankfield Dr.
Burnside
Orms Kirk Rise
Sundew Cl.
Lochinvar Cl.
Lane
DE21
EREWASH
DERBY
The Paddocks
Hillcroft Dr.
Croft St.
Flood Rd.
New Church St.
Victoria Avenue
Collier
Lane
Cricket Grd.
Orchard Cl.
Cole
Birchfield
Ock Brook
4
75
Van
Kirk Leys Av. North
Kirk Leys Av. South
Cambridge
Belper Ho.
Heanor Ho.
Craddock
Matlock Ho.
Melbourne Ho.
Arnhem
Chester Ct.
Langley Rd.
Vincent Av.
Ripley Rd.
Dovedale Rd.
Edmund
Monsal Dri.
Kirkdale Avenue
Kirkdale Av.
Wesley Dr.
Edale Rd.
Terrace
Haddon Dri.
Vernon Rd.
Dale Vw.
Aster Cl.
Trevor's La.
Beres Ford Dri.
Ladybower
Borrowash
By-pass
A52
Subway
Asterdale Prim. Sch.
Play Fld.
Derby Golf Centre
Field Cl.
Greenway Cl.
Hawthorne
Beech Av.
Chestnut Gro.
Chevin Av.
Vicarage
Church Hall
Borrow-a
Derwent Avenue
5
Nottingham
A6005
Cross
Stony La.
Gate Rd.
Cross Pk.
Willowcroft Park
Cambridge
Borrowfield
Silverhill Rd.
Litton Dri.
Milldale
Deep-dale Rd.
Lock Way
Derby
Road
Borrow W. Fld.
Tennis Courts
The Asterdale
The Asterdale Sports Grd.
Pav.
Nursery
Ashbrook Jun. & Inf. Sch.
Rec. Grd.
Deans Drive
Hermitage
Peveril Av.
Woodland Av.
Rutland Av.
335
Towing Path
Anglers
Council Yard
Works
Works
Road
Derby
Road
Borrowash House
Kimberley
Ladysmith Rd.
Victoria
Ashbrook Av.
Devonshire Av.
Harrington Av.
Charnwood
BORROWASH
6
Works
Works
Works
Works
River Derwent
Works
Weir
Manor
Princess Dr.
Dovecote Dr.
Cumberland Cres.
Manor Park Road
Elm St.
Very Cl.
Chapel Rw.
Belmont Dr.
Nottingham
Road
Balmoral
Rose Cl.
Windsor Cl.
Cemetery
7
34
Works
The Stryne
Mill Race
Weirs
Sluices
Mill Stream
Little Stryne
Station
B5010
Borrowash Bridge
Central
St. Stephens Cl.
Gordon
Royal Cl.
Robins Tow.
Lock
Borrowfld.
Ashmeadow
Mere
Bellevue
Avenue
Mill Cl.
Way
Acres
Pollards Dr.
Brook
Fosse Cl.
Roman
Shacklecross
Newbold
Hook's Farm
Draycott
A6005
40
41
42
A
B
C
D
E
94

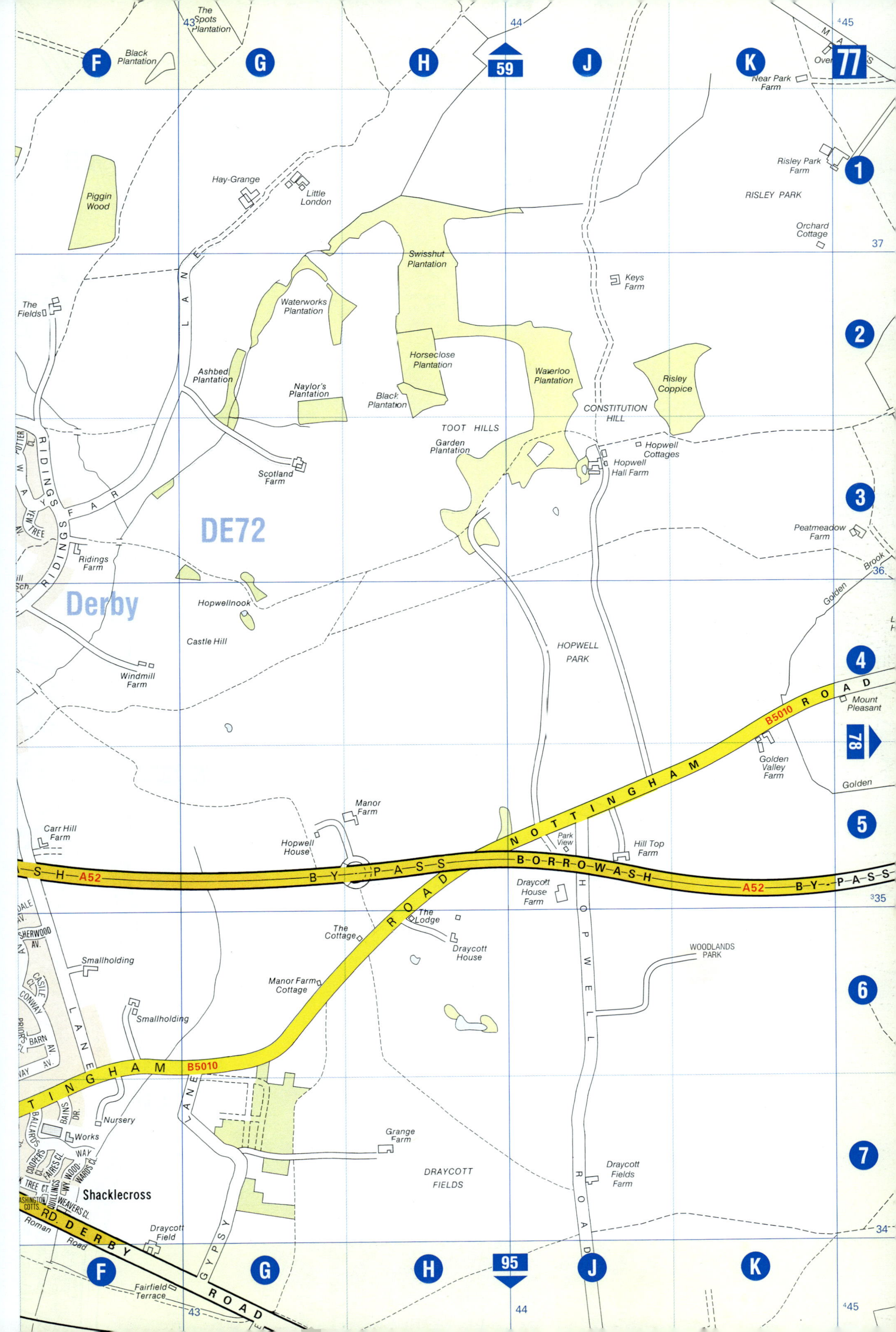
F
G
H
59
J
K
77
The Spots Plantation
43
44
45
Black Plantation
Near Park Farm
Over
Risley Park Farm
1
Hay-Grange
Little London
RISLEY PARK
37
Piggin Wood
Orchard Cottage
Swisshut Plantation
Keys Farm
2
The Fields
Waterworks Plantation
Risley Coppice
Horseclose Plantation
Waterloo Plantation
Ashbed Plantation
Naylor's Plantation
Black Plantation
CONSTITUTION HILL
RIDINGS WAY
FAR
YEW TREE
TOOT HILLS
Hopwell Cottages
Garden Plantation
Hopwell Hall Farm
3
Scotland Farm
DE72
Peatmeadow Farm
Ridings Farm
Brook
36
Derby
Hopwellnook
Golden
Castle Hill
HOPWELL PARK
4
Windmill Farm
B5010 ROAD
Mount Pleasant
78
Golden Valley Farm
Golden
Manor Farm
5
Carr Hill Farm
Park View
Hill Top Farm
NOTTINGHAM
Hopwell House
BY PASS
BORROWASH
A52
BY PASS
35
DALE AV.
SHERWOOD AV.
Draycott House Farm
Draycott House
The Lodge
The Cottage
WOODLANDS PARK
CASTLE CL.
CONWAY AV.
PRIORS CL.
BARN AV.
Smallholding
Manor Farm Cottage
HOPWELL
6
Smallholding
LANE
BAINS DR.
BALLARDS
B5010
Nursery
Works
Grange Farm
Draycott Fields Farm
7
LOOPERS CL.
CAIPES CL.
LWY. WOOD
WARDS CL.
WAY
DRAYCOTT
WEAVERS CL.
DRAYCOTT FIELDS
ROAD
34
Shacklecross
QUILLINGS
WASHINGTON COTTS.
RD. DERBY
Roman Road
Draycott Field
GYPSY LANE
F
G
H
95
J
K
Fairfield Terrace
ROAD
43
44
45

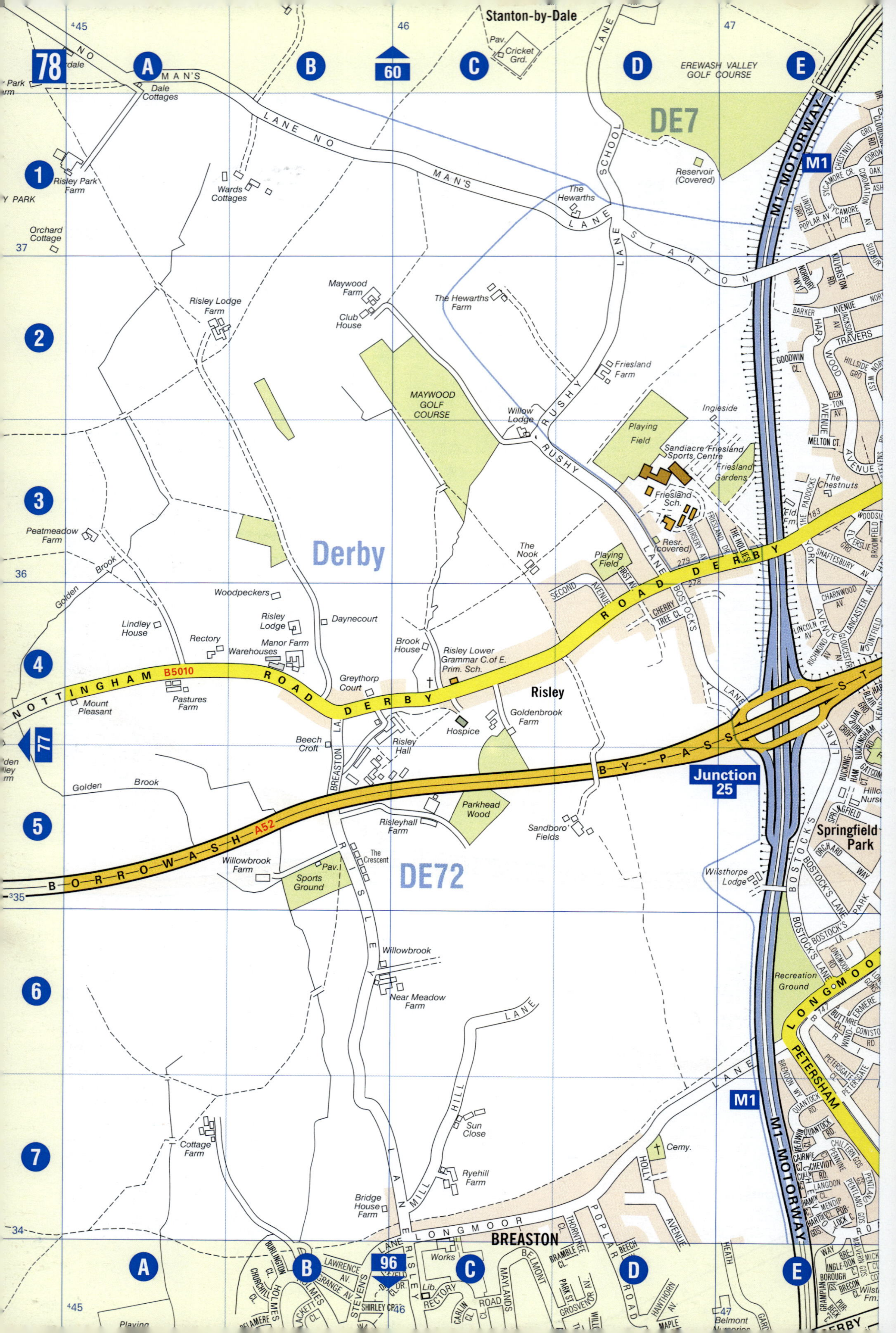

78
Stanton-by-Dale
A
B
60
C
D
EREWASH VALLEY GOLF COURSE
E
DE7
M1
Risley Park Farm
Wards Cottages
Reservoir (Covered)
The Hewarths
Orchard Cottage
37
Maywood Farm
Club House
The Hewarths Farm
Friesland Farm
Risley Lodge Farm
MAYWOOD GOLF COURSE
Willow Lodge
RUSHY
RUSHY
Ingleside
Playing Field
Sandiacre Friesland Sports Centre
Friesland Gardens
Friesland Sch.
Peatmeadow Farm
Derby
The Nook
Playing Field
Resr. (covered)
279
278
The Chestnuts
36
Golden Brook
Woodpeckers
Risley Lodge
Daynecourt
Brook House
Risley Lower Grammar C.of E. Prim. Sch.
CHERRY TREE CL.
BOSTOCK'S
Fld Fm
The Paddocks
WOODSID
Lindley House
Rectory
Manor Farm
Warehouses
NOTTINGHAM
B5010
ROAD
DERBY
ROAD DERBY
Risley
Mount Pleasant
Pastures Farm
Greythorp Court
Goldenbrook Farm
77
Hospice
Beech Croft
Risley Hall
BREASTON LA.
BY-PASS
Junction 25
Golden Brook
Parkhead Wood
Sandboro' Fields
Springfield Park
BORROWASH
A52
Risleyhall Farm
Wilsthorpe Lodge
BOSTOCK'S LANE
35
Willowbrook Farm
Pav.
Sports Ground
The Crescent
RISLEY
DE72
Recreation Ground
LONGMOOR
PETERSHAM
M1 MOTORWAY
Willowbrook
Near Meadow Farm
LANE
HILL LANE
6
Sun Close
Cemy.
HOLLY LANE
7
Cottage Farm
Ryehill Farm
Bridge House Farm
MILL LANE
RISLEY LANE
LONGMOOR
BREASTON
POPLAR AVENUE
BEECH AVENUE
M1 MOTORWAY
34
45
A
B
96
C
D
E
LAWRENCE AV.
Works
Lib.
Rectory
MAYLANDS
BELMONT
BRAMBLE CL.
SHIRLEY CR.
46
47
DERBY
Playing

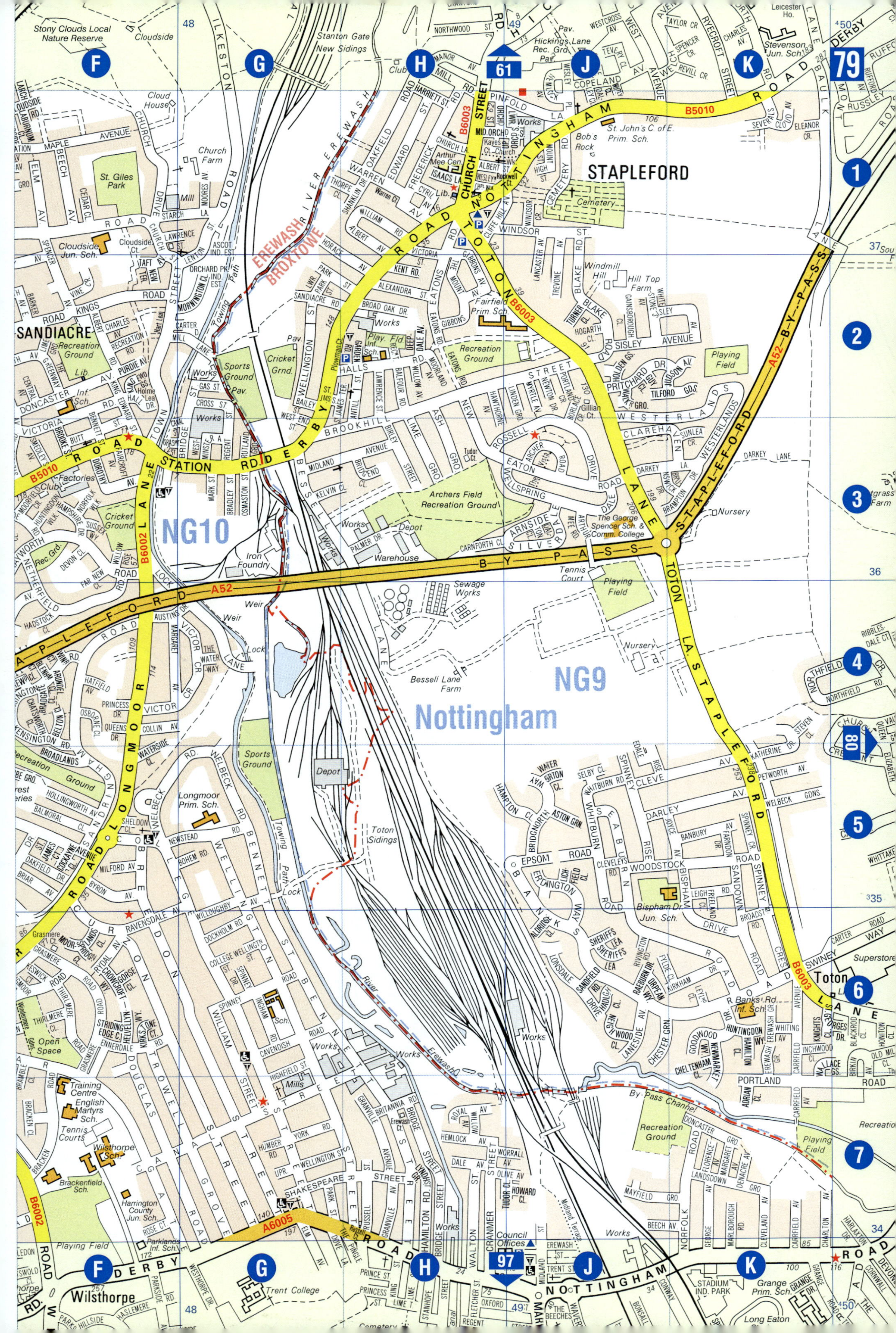
79
STAPLEFORD
SANDIACRE
NG10
NG9
Nottingham
Wilsthorpe
Stony Clouds Local Nature Reserve
EREWASH BROXTOWE
A52 BY-PASS
A52-STAPLEFORD
TOTON LA STAPLEFORD
BY-PASS
A52
B5010
B6003
B6002
B5010
B6003
B6002
A6005
Toton
Toton Sidings
Trent College
Council Offices
RIVER EREWASH

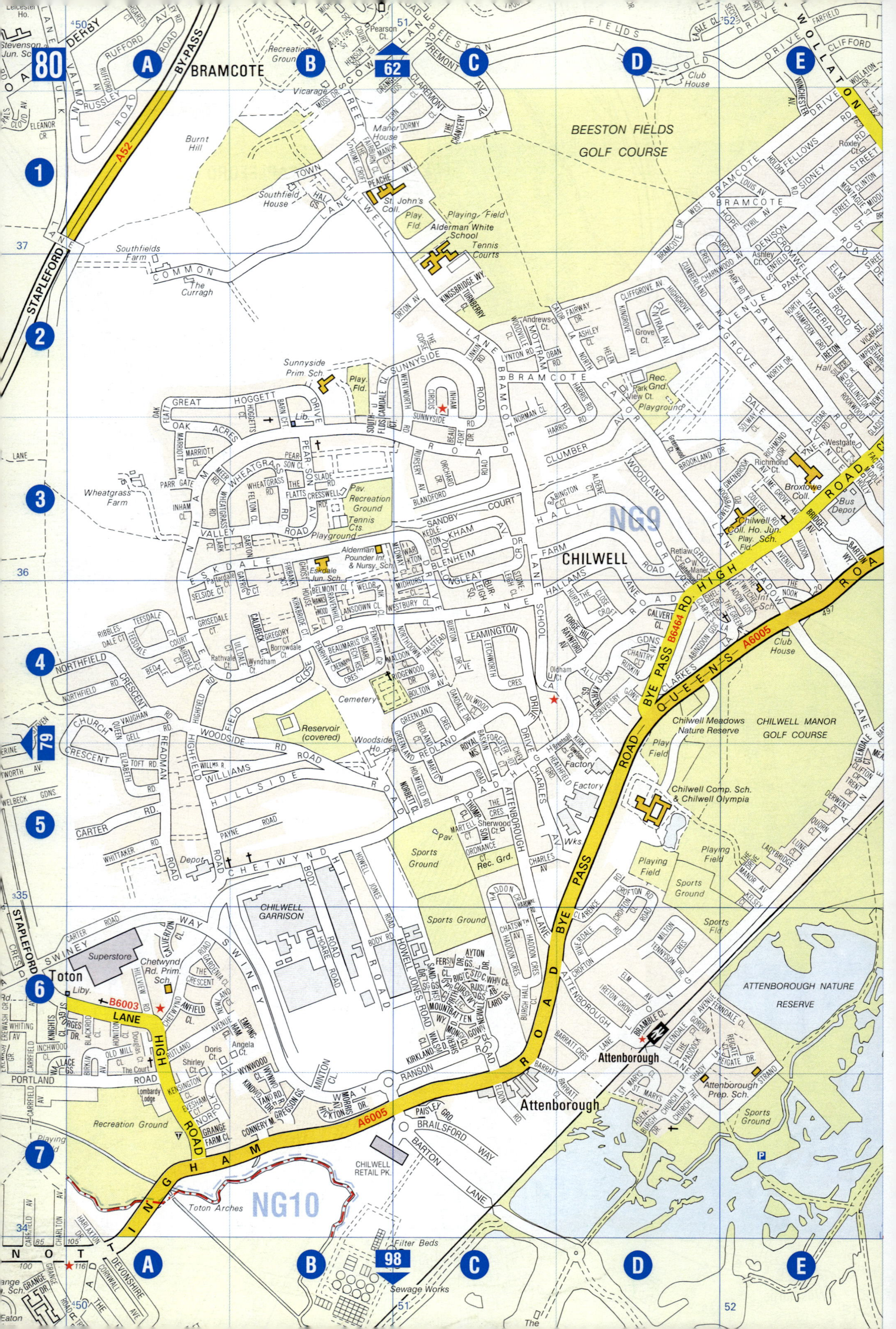

80
BRAMCOTE
BEESTON FIELDS GOLF COURSE
CHILWELL
NG9
Toton
NG10
Toton Arches
CHILWELL GARRISON
CHILWELL RETAIL PK.
Attenborough
ATTENBOROUGH NATURE RESERVE
CHILWELL MANOR GOLF COURSE
Chilwell Meadows Nature Reserve
Chilwell Comp. Sch. & Chilwell Olympia
STAPLEFORD
DERBY ROAD BY-PASS
A52
A6005
QUEENS ROAD
HIGH ROAD
BYE PASS ROAD
NOTTINGHAM ROAD
Sewage Works
Filter Beds

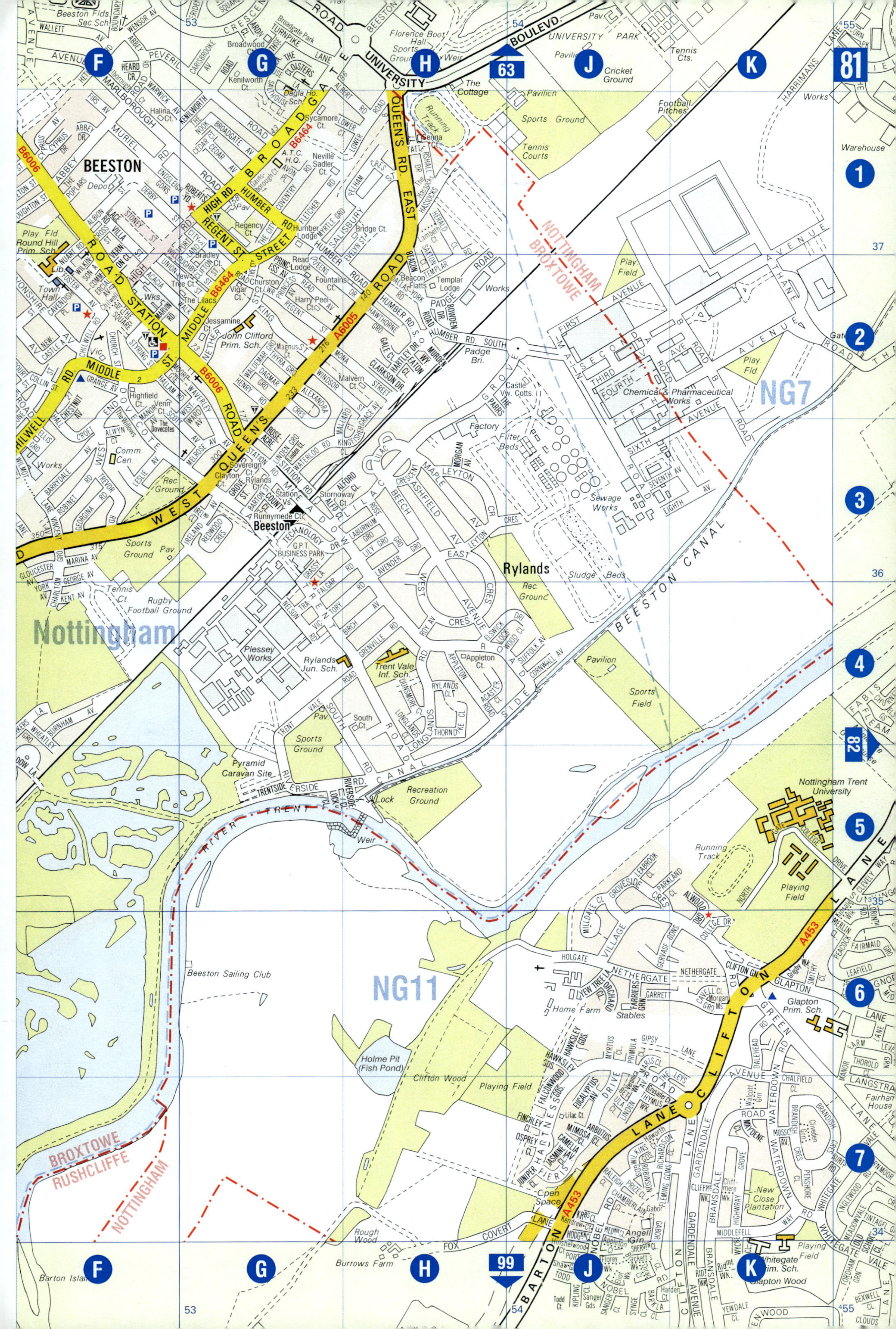
Beeston Flds Sec Sch
BOULEVD
University Park
81
Nottingham Broxtowe
BEESTON
Road Station
NG7
Humber Road
Queen's Road East
Broadgate
Warehouse
Chemical & Pharmaceutical Works
Sewage Works
Sludge Beds
Beeston Canal
Rylands
Nottingham
Trentside
River Trent
Weir
Recreation Ground
82
Nottingham Trent University
Running Track
Playing Field
A453
Clifton Lane
Glapton
NG11
Beeston Sailing Club
Holme Pit (Fish Pond)
Clifton Wood
Playing Field
Broxtowe Rushcliffe
Nottingham
Barton Island
99
Barton Lane
Clifton Lane
F  G  H  J  K

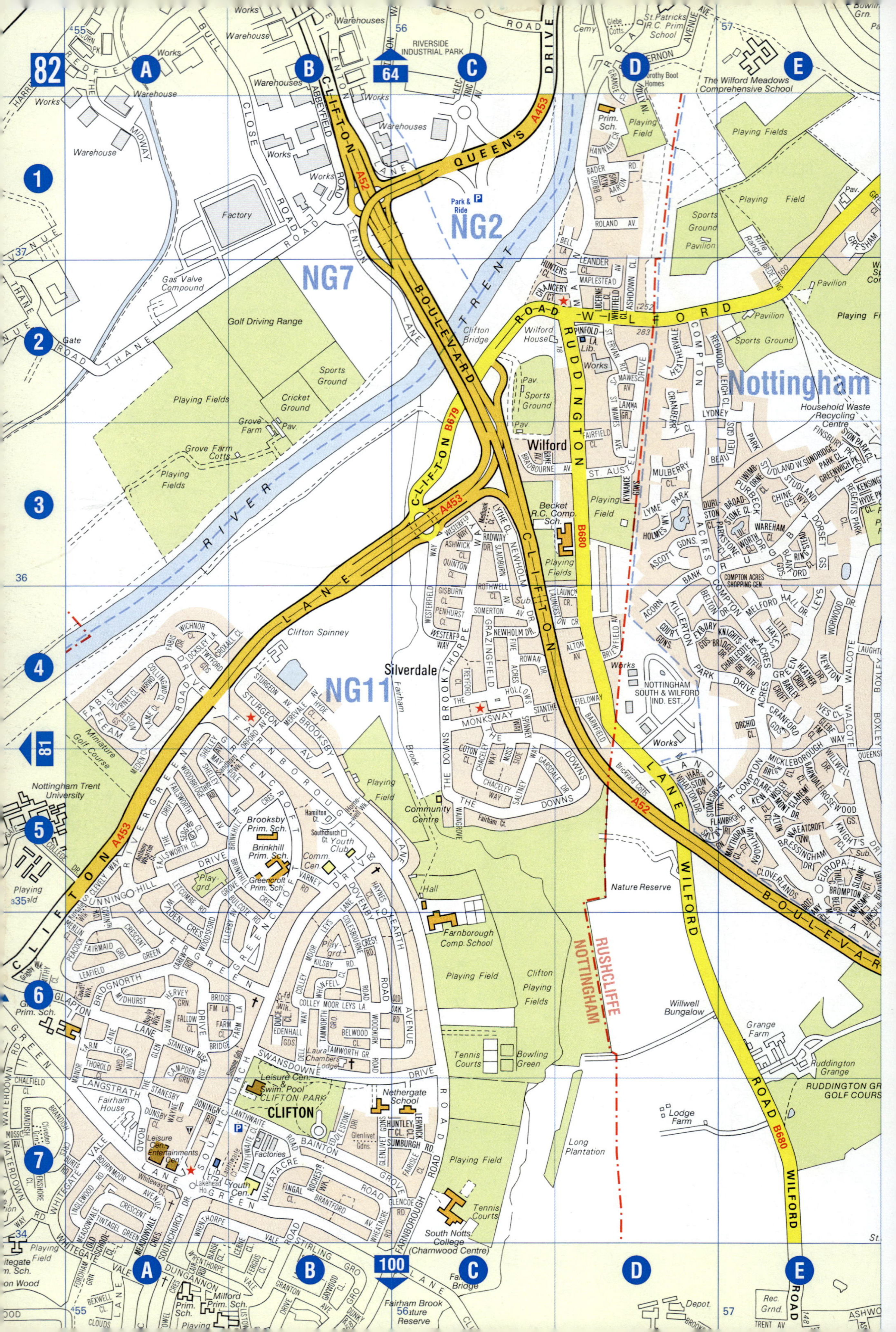

NG2
WEST BRIDGFORD
NG12
Wilford Hill
RADCLIFFE
LOUGHBOROUGH ROAD
MELTON ROAD
A60
A606
A52
A6011
SOUTHERN CEMETERY
EDWALTON MUNICIPAL GOLF COURSES
Sharphill Wood
Sharp Hill
Mickleborough Hill
Landmere Farm
Home Farm
Hall Farm
Ruddington Hall
Olgalans Lodge
Roberts Farm
Toll Bar House
Hill Farm House
Rushcliffe Arena
Rushcliffe Comp. Sch. & Leisure Centre
South Nottingham College
West Bridgford School Playing Fields
Jesse Gray Primary Sch.
Heymann Prim. Sch.
Abbey Road Prim. Sch.
St. Edmund Campion R.C. Prim. Sch.
St. Peter's C. of E. Junior School
Crematorium
Garden of Remembrance
Jewish Cemy.
Grosvenor Sch
Grainger St
Becket Upper Sch.
West Park
West Bridgford Inf. Sch.
THE PARK
Public Open Space
Gamston Bridge
Grantham Canal
83
84
85
101
65
59
58
A52
A60
A606

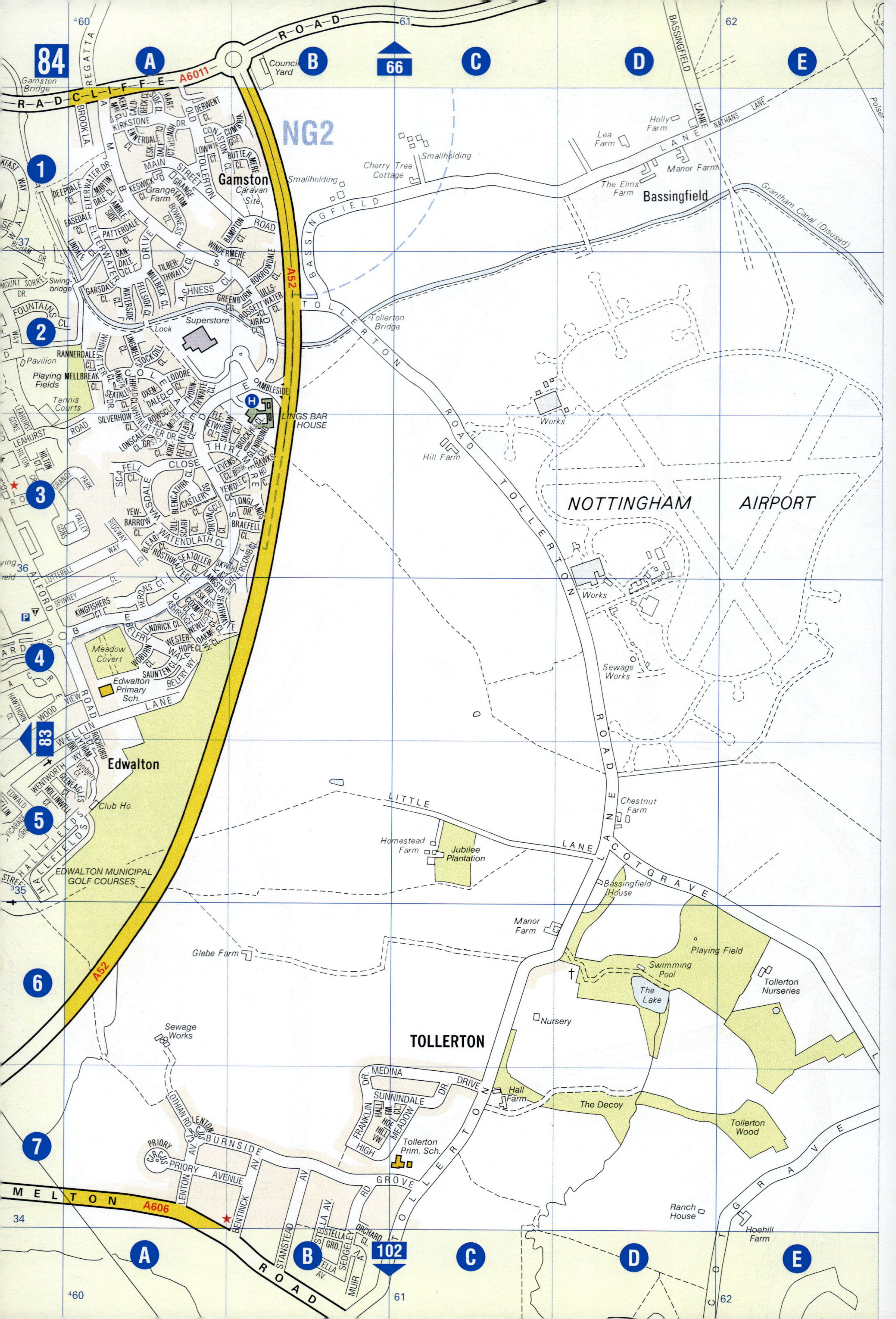
84
Gamston Bridge
RADCLIFFE
REGATTA
ROAD
A6011
A
Council Yard
B
66
C
D
BASSINGFIELD
E
NG2
Gamston
Smallholding
Cherry Tree Cottage
Smallholding
Smallholding
BASSINGFIELD
Lea Farm
Holly Farm
LANEE
Manor Farm
NATHANS LANE
The Elms Farm
Bassingfield
Grantham Canal (Disused)
Polser
Caravan Site
WINDERMERE CL.
BORROWDALE
A52
Grange Farm
Deepdale CL.
Elterwater Dr.
Kirkstone
Martindale CL.
Ennerdale CL.
Esk Dale
Low Wir
Coniston
Cumbria
Butter-mere CL.
Old Derwent CL.
Hart-
Kent CL.
Beck CL.
Grange
Main Street
Tollerton
Bowness CL.
ROAD
1
37
Bigham
Easedale
Undale
Patterdale
Elterwater
San Dale
Millbeck CL.
Tilber-thwaite CL.
Fellside CL.
Greenburn
Rossett Water CL.
AIRA CL.
BASSINGFIELD
TOLLERTON
Tollerton Bridge
Works
MOUNT SORREL Dr.
Swing-bridge
FOUNTAINS CL.
WAY
2
Pavilion
RANNERDALE
LATTER
Stockgill
Limemere CL.
Oxen-
Dale CL.
Lodore CL.
Thorn CL.
Tywaite CL.
Ambleside
Superstore
Lock
Playing Fields
MELLBREAK
Tennis Courts
Silverhow
Seatallan
Longscale
Dale CL.
Bowscale
Feel Fellow
Gasto
Kirk CL.
H
LINGS BAR HOUSE
Hill Farm
ROAD
Works
Leahurst
Leahurst
GDNS.
HILTON
GRANGE PARK
Yew-barrow CL.
Fel CL.
SC4
Blencathra
Castler
Thirlmere
Levens CL.
Bowes
Yewdec CL.
Hawks-
Head Rd.
CLOSE
NOTTINGHAM      AIRPORT
3
ALFORD
LUTTERGILL
SPINNEY
Ridgeway
Yew-barrow CL.
Bleaberry
Rosthwaite CL.
Seatoller CL.
Watendlath CL.
Skiddaw CL.
Longlands
Braefell CL.
Works
36
P
Kingfishers Ct.
Herons Ct.
Meadow Covert
Lindrick CL.
Belfry
Wester
Woburn CL.
Saunten CL.
Hope CL.
Belfry Wy.
Ashridge CL.
Newlyn CL.
Oakme CL.
Coxm
Sewage Works
4
HAWTHORN
WOOD
VIEW ROAD
Edwalton Primary Sch.
RICHBORO
LYTHAM
LANE
ROAD
Chestnut Farm
5
WELLIN
83
Wentworth
Hollinwell
Geneagles
EDWALD
WYCHMERE
Edwalton
Club Ho.
HALLFIELDS
LITTLE
Homestead Farm
Jubilee Plantation
LACOTGRAVE
Bassingfield House
6
HALLFIELDS
STREET
35
EDWALTON MUNICIPAL GOLF COURSES
A52
Glebe Farm
Manor Farm
Swimming Pool
The Lake
Playing Field
LANE
Tollerton Nurseries
Sewage Works
Nursery
TOLLERTON
The Decoy
7
LOTHAN RD.
LENTON
CIRCUS
BURNSIDE
PRIORY CIRCUS
PRIORY AV.
LENTON AVENUE
MEDINA
Dr.
SUNNINDALE
DRIVE
Hall Farm
Tollerton Wood
FRANKLIN
HALL
HOF
HILL
MEADOW
Tollerton Prim. Sch.
STELLA AV.
TOLLERTON
GRAVE
MELTON
A606
Bentinck
STANSTEAD
AV.
STELLA AV.
STELLA GRO.
SEDGELEY
ORCHARD
GROVE
Ranch House
Hoehill Farm
A
B
102
ROAD
C
D
E
60
61
62

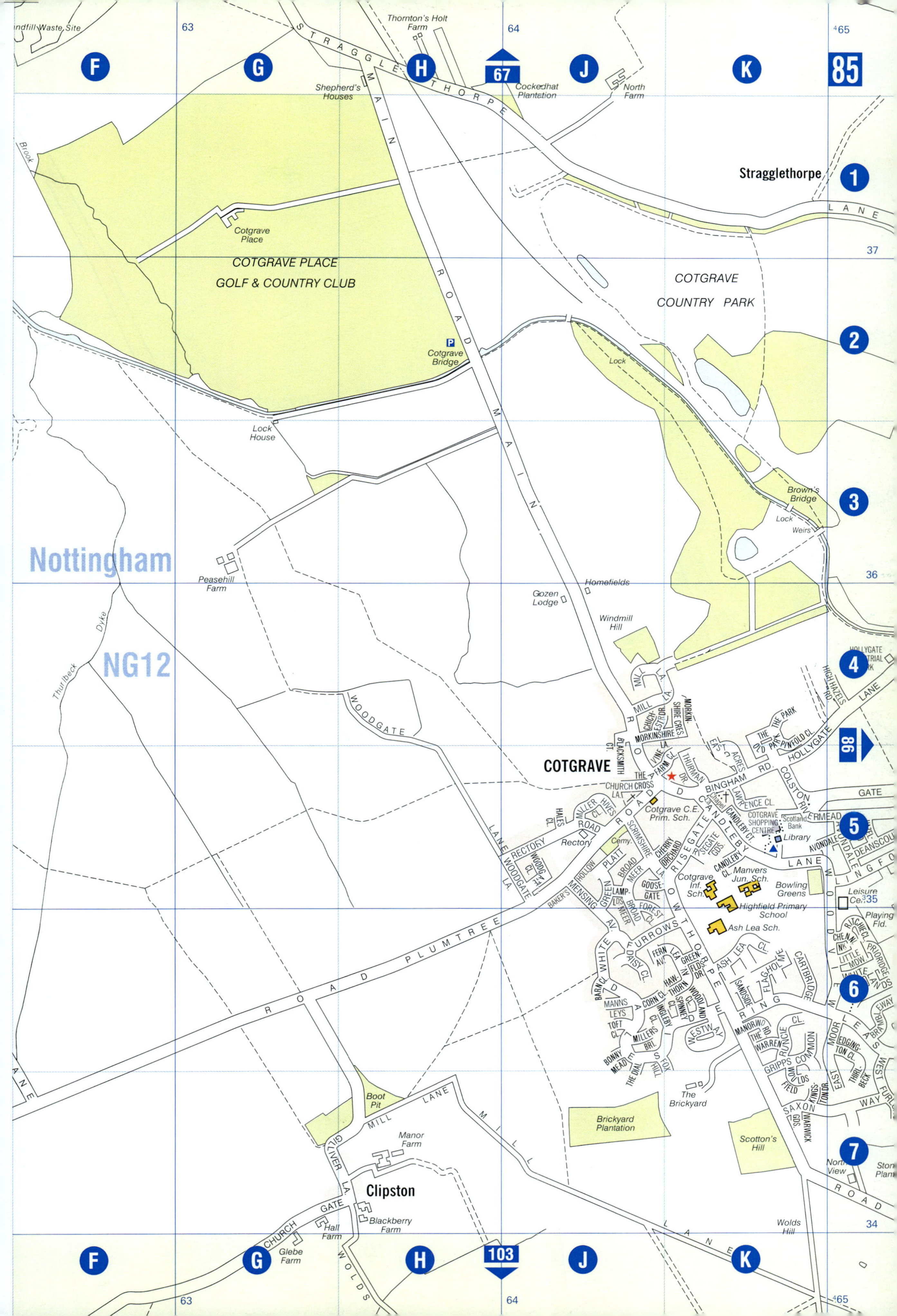

F
G
H
J
K
85
67
Landfill Waste Site
63
64
65
Thornton's Holt Farm
Stragglethorpe
Cockedhat Plantation
North Farm
Shepherd's Houses
Stragglethorpe
1
37
Brook
Cotgrave Place
COTGRAVE PLACE
GOLF & COUNTRY CLUB
COTGRAVE
COUNTRY PARK
Lock
2
Cotgrave Bridge
Lock House
Brown's Bridge
3
Lock Weirs
Nottingham
Peasehill Farm
36
Homefields
Gozen Lodge
Windmill Hill
HOLLYGATE INDUSTRIAL PARK
4
NG12
Thurlbeck Dyke
WOODGATE
MILL LA.
MORKINSHIRE CRES.
THE PARK
THE PARK
PINFOLD CL.
HIGH HAZELS RD.
LANE
HOLLYGATE
86
KNOCK LA.
ESTHER DRI.
MORKINSHIRE CL.
FARM DR.
VINE CL.
EAST RD.
THE OLD PARK
ACRES RD.
COLSTON RI.
GATE
COTGRAVE
BLACKSMITH CT.
THURMAN
BINGHAM
LAWRENCE CL.
CHURCH CROSS
The RD.
LAWRENCE CL.
COTGRAVE SHOPPING CENTRE
Scotland Bank
Library
5
MILLER CL.
HIVES CL.
Cotgrave C.E. Prim. Sch.
CANDLEBY CT.
CANDLEBY
SEGATE GDS.
RIVERMEAD
AVONDALE
DEANSCOU
HALES CL.
RECTORY
Rectory
Cemy.
CHERRY ORCHARD
RISEGATE
CANDLEBY LANE
LINGFO
SORMSHIRE RD.
PLATT
BROAD MEER
Manvers Jun. Sch.
Bowling Greens
Leisure Ce. 335
WOODGATE LA.
WOODGATE CL.
ROLLOW
GREEN
LAMP. LDS.
GOOSE GATE
FOREST
Cotgrave Inf. Sch.
CANDLEBY CL.
Highfield Primary School
Playing Fld.
BAKER'S
MENSING AV.
BROAD MEER
BROAD LDS.
Ash Lea Sch.
RATCHEL CL.
LITTLE MOW.
NK.
335
FURROWS
FERN AV.
ASH LEA CL.
CARTBRIDGE
CHENI
PLURIDGE RDS.
BARRA CL.
WHITE RD.
DAISY CL.
GREEN.
FLOS DR.
WOODLAND
FLAGHOLME
SANDSIDE
WEST
E. WAY
PLUMTREE
MANNS LEYS
TOFT CL.
CORN CL.
HAW THORN
INGLEBY CL.
SPINNEY
WESTWAY
MANOR WD.
WARREN CL.
GRIPPS COMMON
MOOR
EDGINGTON CL.
EAST FURLONG
THE GOSL
BONNY MEAD
THE DIAL
MILLERS BRI.
S. FOX
RUNCLE FIELD
RUM LDS.
SAXON GDS.
WARWICK GDS.
THIRL BECK
WEST FURLONG
WAY
Boot Pit
Manor Farm
The Brickyard
Brickyard Plantation
Scotton's Hill
North View
Stont Plant
7
34
LANE
MILL LANE
OLIVER LA.
Clipston
CHURCH GATE
Hall Farm
Blackberry Farm
Glebe Farm
WOLDS
Wolds Hill
ROAD
63
64
65
F
G
H
103
J
K

86
65
66
68
67
A
B
C
D
E
1
Stragglethorpe
STRAGGLETHORPE
37
COTGRAVE
COUNTRY PARK
Paddock Cottages
New Barn Farm
Cropwell Court
Lodge
ROAD
A46
2
Brown's Cotts.
Foss Bridge
Berry Hill
LANE
Hollygate Farm
3
Lock
Weirs
36
Mann's Bridge
Nottingham
NG12
Canal
(Disused)
NOTTINGHAM
A46
Grantham
HOLLYGATE
INDUSTRIAL
PARK
Hollygate Bridge
HIGH HAZIES RD.
HILLYGATE
4
The Paddocks
THE PARK
COL
85
The Bungalow
STON
The Park
RD.
CL.
5
RIVERMEAD
TROUT BECK
GLENBROOK
Play. Fld.
GATE
HAZEL WOOD
AVONDALE
RNG
AVONDALE
DEANSCOURT
WINGFORD
GRASSMERE
FIR
WILLOWDENE
DALE
SPRING MEADOW
CROSSHILL
LANE
Foss House
FOSSE
35
Bowling Greens
Leisure Centre
THORNS CL.
COTGRAVE
Foss Cottages
Field Primary School
Sch.
Playing Fld.
RITCHER CL.
CHENIN
Nr.
PRIORIDGE
LITTLE MDW.
WHITE LAN
WOODHAMS
Smith's Round Hill
Long Plantation
Groundwells Farm
FLAGHOLME
CARTER
RNG
MOOR
DOVE
EDGING-TON CL.
BURHILL
F'WAY
BR'N
CLOVERDALE
FLAX
FENDALE
EASTWOLD
Fosse Nk.
Wolds Farm
6
LAWRENCE CL.
RUNCLE CL.
GRIPPS COMMON
COMMONS
WOLDS
EAST FIELD
KINGS
THIRL BECK
WEST FURLONG
MARI
WOOD
BRIAR GATE
LEAS
Three Corner Plantation
Cotgrave Copse
CL.
SAXON GDS.
WARWICK
HICKLING WY.
WAY
Firdale Holt
CROPWELL WOLDS
son's
7
North View
Stone Pit Plantation
OWTHORPE
34
Ids Hill
NE
A46
Bells Stud Farm
ROAD
THE
Taylors Wold
Fox Holes
Fish Ponds
A
B
C
D
E
465
66
67

Newlands
68
HARDIGATE
69
70
87
F
The Grove
G
H
69
Lower Brackendale Farm
J
K
RADCLIFFE
Cropwell Grange
ROAD
GRANGE PK.
Works
MAIN
1
Barnsfield Farm
ROAD
BLACK
The Court
Cropwell Butler
OLD SCHOOL HOUSE CL.
Rookery Farm
Manor Farm
Tithby
37
Meadow Court
LANE
THE POSTS
CARPENTERS CL.
CARPENTERS CL.
The Rookery
TITHBY
ROAD
Holly Tree Farm
2
CLOSE
Cemetery
Rookery Cottages
ROAD
Lych Gate
Millfield Cottage
MEADOW
BUTLER
Millfield House
HOE
Stratford House
BISHOP
3
Hoe Hill
Grantham
Canal (disused)
RD. CROPWELL
36
LANE
HOE
ROAD
VIEW
PARKING CL.
COPPER CL.
SALMON
ROAD
THURLBY CL.
BUTLER
ETHELDENE
HARDY'S CL.
Sewage Works
4
VIEW
COPPER CL.
NEW-BERRY CL.
KENDAL
HALL DR.
SQUIRES CL.
STREET
OLD
Cropwell Bishop
Spring Hill
Fern Hill
Fern Hill Cottage
BROWNHILL CL.
ST. GILES
THE MALTINGS
WY.
SPRINGFIELD
Rawlings Ct.
Cropwell Bishop Primary School
MERCIA AV.
MARSHALL
RD.
SMITHS CL.
STOCKWELL LA.
Playing Field
CLARKE
HOE
MILLIA
CHURCH
DOBBIN CL.
ROAD
Fern Hill Farm Cottages
Cropwell Bridge
Hall CL.
OLD
LENTON CL.
NOOK
FIELD
BARRATT
FERN
MANOR CT.
CROPWELL
Fern Hill Farm
5
RICHARDS CL.
Home Farm
PASTURE
Mill Hill
ROAD
35
KINOULTON
Works
LANE
6
Reecy Plantation
Edmondthorpe Lodge
COLSTON
Blue Hill
Old Brickyard Plantation
Home Farm
7
Limekiln Farm
Colston Bridge
ROAD
Home Farm Cottages
WASH
Bellevue Spinney
Spring Hill Cottages
Smite
34
Swabbs Farm
SWABBS LANE
Grantham Canal (Disused)
Blanche's Gorse
NEW
Bellevue
PIT
Adam Spring Spinney
F
68
G
Old Gorse
H
69
J
LANE
K
70
China Bridge
River

88
25
26
27
34
33
32
31
A
B
C
D
E
1
2
3
4
5
6
7
Rectory
Dalbury
Dizzybeard
Plantation
Gamekeepers
Cottage
Baldfields
Farm
Trusley
Brook
Highfield
Ash
Gorse
Highway
Lodge
Baldfield
Covert
Highfields
Highfield
Cottages
Arbourfield
Covert
Ash
Farm
Brook
Lab.
Co.
Bridge
House
Ash
Cottages
Hepnalls
Heage
Etwall
Ivy House
Farm
Garden
Cottage
Brook
DE65
BY-PASS
Park Farm
Cottages
Pond
Cottage
Marsh
Cottage
Farm
Th.
Ma.
Park
Farm
Ashe
Hall
Holly Bush
Farm
Willowpit
Lane
Primrose
Bank
Burna
Sutton
Lane
Etwall Leisure
Centre
Church Hill
Street
Lawn
Park Av.
Slade
Cl.
Sandypits
ALMSHOUSES
Blenheim M.
Kvn. Croft
Roystone
House
Tennis
Courts
John Port
School
Land
St.
Port
Cl.
John Port
Cl.
Lodge
Cl.
Etwall Lodge
ETWALL
Hilton
Pear Tree
Ct.
Oaklands
Road
Lib.
King
George's
Field
Friary Farm
Bank
Ho.
Main
Road
Gerard
Gro.
Sycamore
Cl.
Hayes Croft
Meadow
Wy.
Way
Etwall
Prim. Sch.
Pine
Cl.
Ash
View
Beech
Cl.
Laburnum
Rd. Wy.
The Mill
Wy.
The
Blake
Dr.
Bancroft
Chestnut
Grove
Windmill
Court
Land
Etwall Hay.
Road
Lodge
Hilton
Lodge
A516
Park Lodge
Junction 5
Bancroft
BELFIELD
Belfield
Ct.
Belfield
Ter.
Elms
Gro.
Springfield Rd.
Melville
Ct.
Springfield
Ct.
Sewage
Works
FOSTON/HATTON/HILTON
BY-PASS
A50
DERBY
Egginton
Gro.
A5132
DERBY
Pecks
Rmws.
Lucas
Rd.
Monty
Normandy
Wy.
Utah
Bren
Wy.
Shaef
Cl.
Way
HILTON
Jacksons
La.
Broomhill
Cottages
Derby
Rd.
Elm
Dr.
New
Rd.
Mulberry Wy.
Chhll.
Cl.
Sherman
Cl.
Enfield
Cl.
Lane
Elm Tree
Farm
Hargate
Lodge
SOUTHERN
Tynefield
Court & Mews
Blakeley
Lodge
Egginton
Road
Egginton
Sch.
Ban-
croft
Cl.
Oak
Eggington
Rd.
Witham Cl.
The
Mease
EGGINTON
RD.
Hargate House
Farm
Etwell
Brook
A50
Avon Wy.
Calder
Cl.
Welland
Rd.
Alders Brook
Huntspill
Rd.
Marston Brook
Dale
Brook
Fleem
A5
36

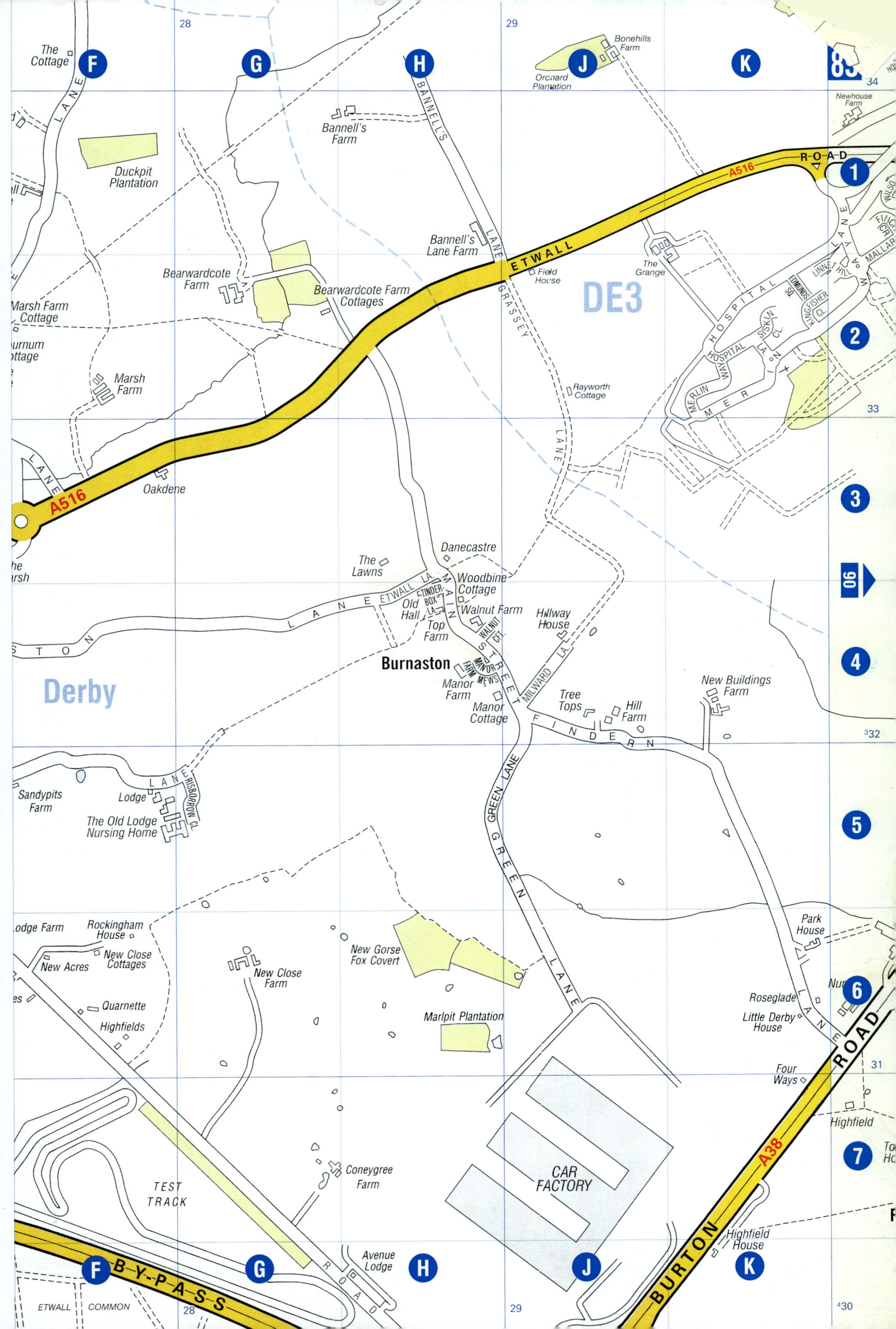

The Cottage
F
G
H
J
Bonehills Farm
Orchard Plantation
K
85
34
Newhouse Farm
Duckpit Plantation
Bannell's Farm
ROAD
A516
1
Bannell's Lane Farm
ETWALL
Field House
The Grange
DE3
2
Bearwardcote Farm
Bearwardcote Farm Cottages
Marsh Farm Cottage
Rayworth Cottage
33
urnum ottage
Marsh Farm
3
he arsh
A516
Oakdene
90
Danecastre
The Lawns
Woodbine Cottage
4
Old Hall
TINDER BOX
Walnut Farm
Hillway House
New Buildings Farm
ETWALL LA
MAIN STREET
Top Farm
WALNUT CFT.
Burnaston
Derby
Manor Farm
MANOR FARM MEWS
Tree Tops
32
Manor Cottage
Hill Farm
MILWARD LA.
Sandypits Farm
Lodge
RISBORROW CL.
FINDERN
5
The Old Lodge Nursing Home
GREEN LANE
Park House
Lodge Farm
Rockingham House
New Close Cottages
New Acres
New Gorse Fox Covert
GREEN LANE
Roseglade
Nur
6
New Close Farm
Little Derby House
ROAD
Quarnette
Highfields
Marlpit Plantation
Four Ways
31
Highfield
BURTON
A38
7
To Ho
TEST TRACK
Coneygree Farm
CAR FACTORY
Highfield House
F
BY-PASS
G
ROAD
Avenue Lodge
H
J
K
ETWALL COMMON
28
29
30

90
A B 72 C D E
34 30
31
32
Sedgefield Green
Children's Home
Public Open Space
Newhouse Farm
ETWALL ROAD
A516
MICKLEOVER GOLF COURSE
Brookfield Primary School
BRIERFIELD
THE HOLLOW
Sewage Works
Littleover Community School
Playing Field
Milverton
Meadow Croft
PASTURES GOLF COURSE
DE3
Haven Baulk Lane Park
BAULK
BAULK LANE
East Midlands Grammar Sch. for Boys
EAST MIDLANDS NUFFIELD HOSPITAL
HOLLYBROOK
Heatherton
Stakerfield
White Lodge
BURGHLEY WY.
RYKNELD WAY
DERBY
SOUTH DERBYSHIRE
Hilltop
Staker House
A38 M
Micklemeadow
Highfields Farm
LANE MOOR WAY
STAKER LANE
RYKNELD
89
Thurston
Blakemere Farm
DE65
BURTON ROAD
Park House
Depot
FINDERN
Fields Farm
Depot
Brook
Hell
Stenson Fields
Nursery
Derby House
DOLES
Four Ways
BURTON
A38
Highfield
Mill Farm
Wallfield House
BARN CL.
CARDALES CL.
Ash Plantation
Tower House
FINDERN
HILLSIDE
Longlands Cottage
A B C D E SOUTHERN
DERBY
30 31 32

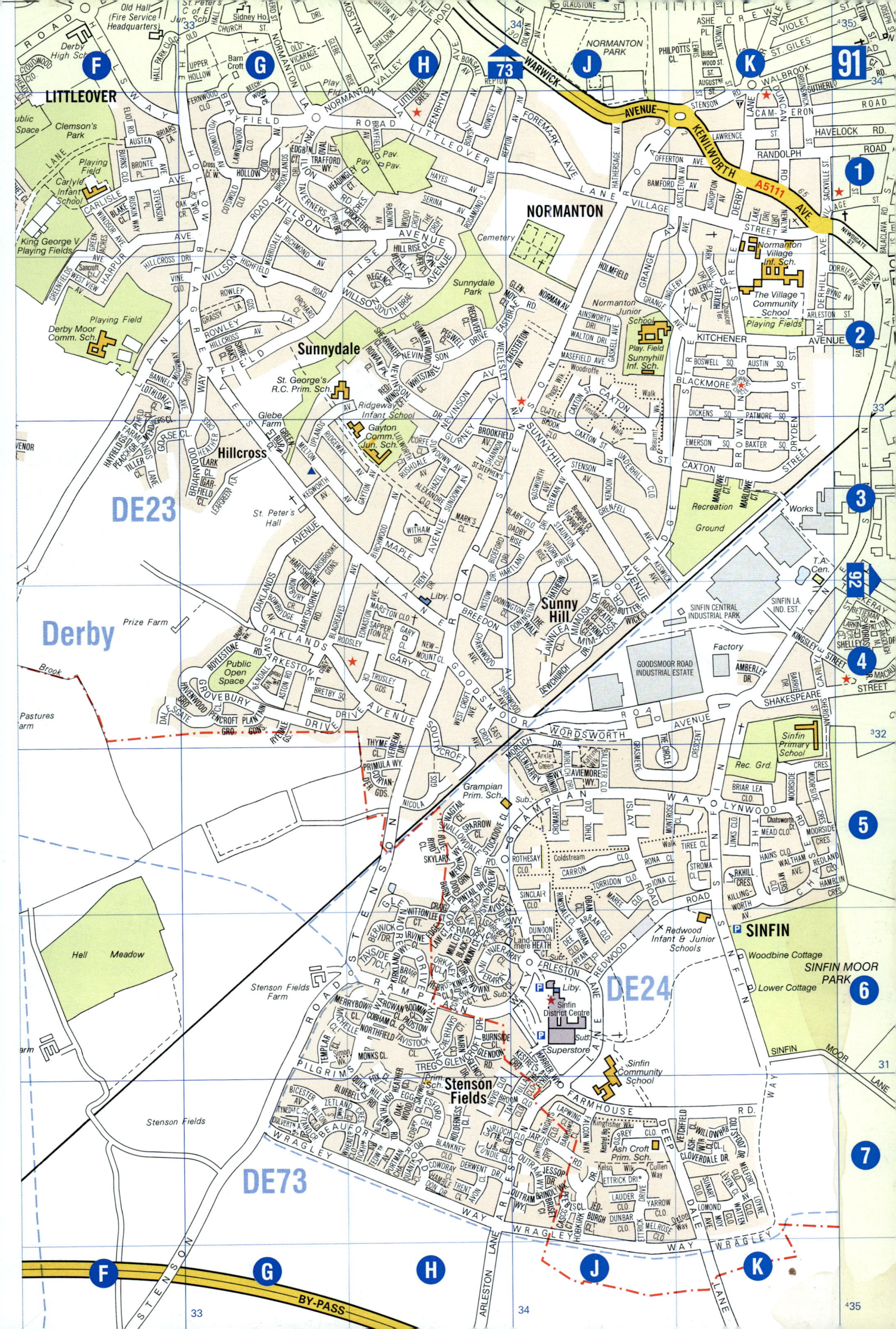

92
DE23
Pear Tree
Peartree
Osmaston
Allenton
Shelton Lock
Sinfin Moor
Sinfin Moor Park
Sinfin Municipal Golf Course
Osmaston Park
DE24
DE73
Moor Plantation
Whitehouse Farm Park
Sports Ground
Foundry
Foundry
Rolls-Royce Works
Works
Cottons Farm
Club House
Moor Farm
Lea Farm
Moorbridge Farm
Homefields
Baltimore Bridge
Fullen's Lock Park
Derby Canal Walkway
Sinfin Lane Ind. Est.
Tannery
Sports Ground
Works
Cinema
Forester's Leisure Park
Ten-Pin Bowling
Superstores
Dairy
Peak Park
Osmaston Park Industrial Estate
Osmaston Park Industrial Estate
Factories
Works
Works
Training Centre
Sandown Road
Haydock
Newmarket
Newbury
Wetherby
Bus Depot
School of Transport
Tennis Court Dr.
Merril College
Merril Moor Prim.
Nursery
Recreation Ground
Playground
Allenton Mkt.
Allenpark Inf. Sch.
Allenton Comm. Prim. Sch.
Lord Street Community Sch.
Swimming Pool
Moorways Sports Complex
Sports Centre
Elm Wood
Tennis Courts
Bowling Grns Pav.
Tennis Courts
Pav.
Putting Green
Ash Wood
Playground
Engineering Works
Sir Francis Ley Ind. Est.
Sherwin Sports Cen.
Harrington Nurs. Sch.
Pear Tree Comm. Jun. Sch.
Nursery Sch.
Pear Tree Ind. Est.
Rec. Grd.
Jun. & Inf. Schs.
Jun. & Inf. Schs.
Bowl. Grns.
Grave Yard
Tennis Courts
Sports Ground
Sports Grd.
Training Grd. (The Baseball Ground)
Newchase Bus. Pk.
Youth Club
Abingdon Bus. Cent.
Training Centre
Longbridge La.
Shelton Jun. & Inf. Schs.
Playing Field
Playing Field
Saddleworth Walk
Sinfin Primary School
Sinfin La. Ind. Est.
Moor Lane
OSMASTON ROAD
A5111
A514
A514
HARVEY ROAD
VICTORY ROAD
MERRILL ROAD
CHELLASTON ROAD
BOULTON
WAY
CARLTON AVENUE
SINFIN
AVENUE
91
74
104

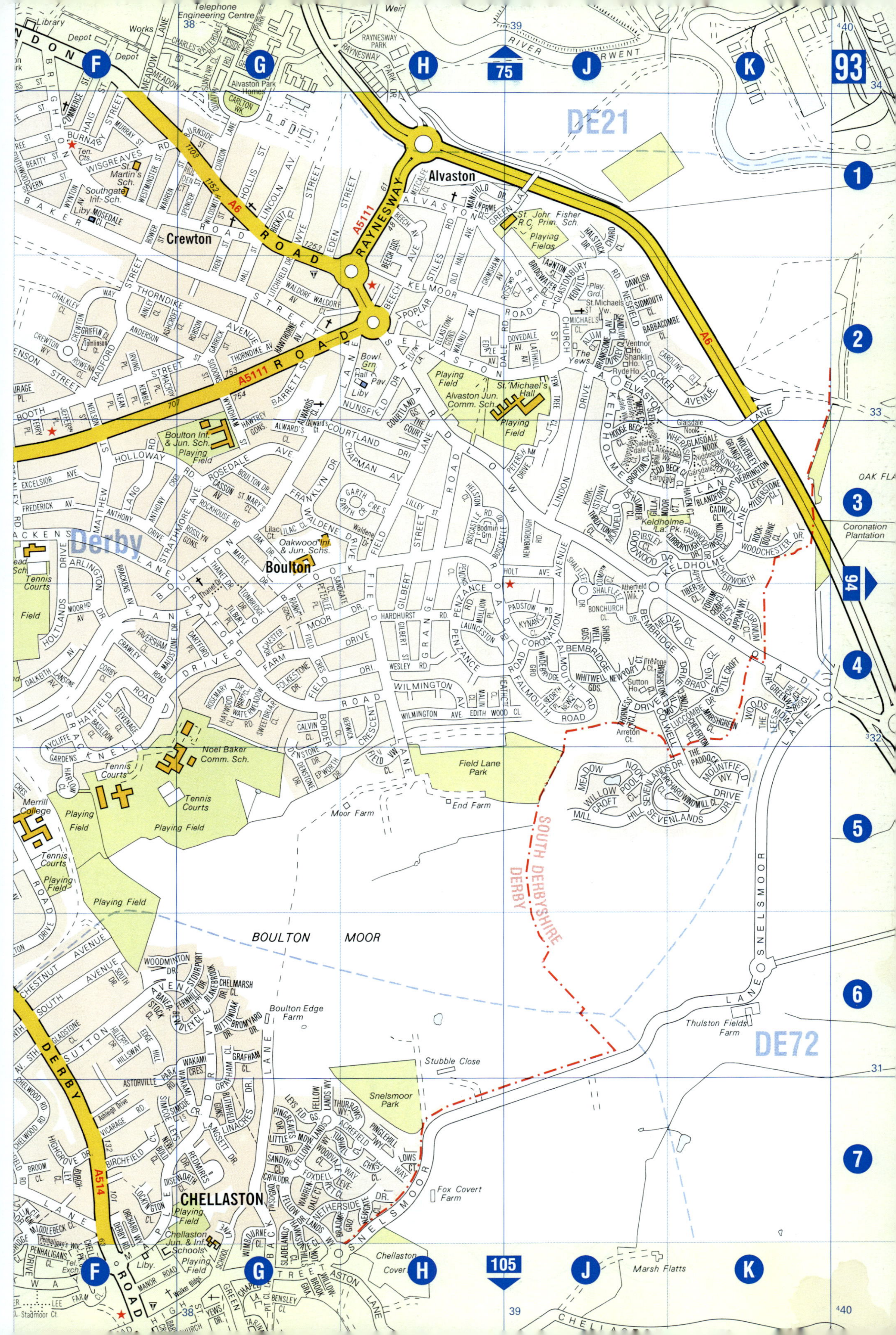

94
A  B  76  C  D  E
34
DE21
Weir
DERBY
1
The Stryne
Mill Race
Weirs
Sluices
Mill Stream
Little Stryne
STATION ROAD
BOROWASH BRIDGE
B5010 LANE
Mill
Works
ST. STEPHEN'S CL.
BROWFLDS
LOCK LEA
MERE
42
BROOK
POLLARKS DR.
ASH MEADOW
RAYCOTT
NEWBOLD
CROSS CL.
ROMAN WY.
FOSSE ROW
Hook's Farm
RIVER  EREWASH
SOUTH DERBYSHIRE
Works
Home Farm
Harrington Villas
Field House
33
2
DE24
THE PARK
The Lake
Fox Covert
Caravan Site
ELVASTON CASTLE COUNTRY PARK & MUSEUM
Park Cottage
ELVASTON CASTLE
The Kennels
OAK FLAT
Cricket Ground
The Cottage
Drive Lodge
Elvaston  Avenue
Derby
3
Coronation Plantation
Coronation Cottage
Golden Gate Lodge
BORROWASH
MAIN  ROAD
CASTLE CT.
ELVASTON
93
A6
Avenue Farm
CASTLE CT.
SILVER LANE
AMBASTON  LANE
AMBASTON
4
THE GREENWAY
MIDWAY
LEES AVE.
BALL  B5010 LA.
ROAD
AMBASTON
LANE
Grange Farm
Ambaston Lane Farm
32
HANS
GROVE CL.
BROOK RD.
LYNW.
THE PINFOLD
GROVE
GROVE
STURGES LA.
GROVE CT.
OAK  BROAD  LANE
EHLM AVE.
Thulston
5
London Road Lodge
The Grove
White Lodge
Thurlaston Grange
Bellington Wood (Fox Covert)
DERBY
SOUTHERN
31
6
Bellington Barn
DERBY
7
Glebe Farm
Playing Field
Pav.
B-Y-P-A-S-S
A6
DERBY
SOUTHERN
A50
BY-PASS
Brickyard Plan
Foxcovert Farm
BROAD  ROAD
A  B  106  C  D  E
40
41
Bird's Nest Farm
42
Aston Moor
Junction 2

Shacklecross
DRAYCOTT FIELDS
Draycott Fields Farm
95
DERBY ROAD
A6005
GYPSY LANE
Draycott Field
Fairfield Terrace
Roman Road
Works
Melbourne House
NOONING LANE
DRAYCOTT
WEST AV.
ARTHUR ST.
WALTER ST.
MAPLETON RD.
Pav.
Sports Grd.
Prim. Sch.
LIME GRO.
LIME GRO.
THORESBY CRES.
GERTRUDE ST.
CLEVELAND AV.
GARFIELD AV.
MARYS AV.
QUEENS ST.
MILNER AV.
CLEVELAND AV.
NEW ST.
Factory
VICTORIA RD.
MARKET
WALK
VICTORIA
SYDNEY RD.
MILLS
BARNES CT.
WALLIS CL.
TOWN END RD.
MEADOW CL.
ELVASTON ST.
VILLA ST.
HARRINGTON ST.
A6005
STATION ROAD
DRAYCOTT RD.
Brooklyn
Cemetery
Works
HOPWELL
STEVENSON AV.
HILLS RD.
GREGORY
HIND
ALBERT ST.
HAXES
FESTIV
Attewell House
The Elms
SAWLEY
PINES
FOWLER CT.
MILLHSE
DONECT
ATTEWELL CL.
LODGE ST.
SOUTH
NEW ST.
McNEIL CT.
HOLLY CL.
ST. CHADS CL.
DERWENT ST.
THE CROFT
GILLVER GDS.
ST. WILNE
The Boathouse
RIVER DERWENT
DERWENT ROAD
WILNE ROAD
Works
Works
Yew Tree Cottage
Ambaston
MAIN STREET
Meadow Farm
Winfield's Farm
AMBASTON LANE
Works
DE72
Dungeon Hole
Armiston Cottages
New Delight
Church Wilne
Church Wilne
96
Ambaston Grange
Bellington Hill
Weir
Works
Wilne Bridge
Great Wilne
LONG ROW
Moor Farm Cottage
Shardlow Moor
Bottom Wood
Moor Farm
LONDON LANE
Shardlow County Primary School
CLOVER CT.
GLENN WY.
ALIS CT.
WOOK WY.
WEST
ENN
COWLISHAW LA.
WAKELYN CL.
Elms Farm
The Manor Farm
THE GROVE HOSPITAL
Shardlow
Shardlow Hall
107
Shardlow Nurseries
CAVENDISH
THE WHARF
MILLFIELD
WHARF ROAD
WILNE LANE
KINGS
F  G  H  J  K  95
F  G  H  J  K

96
A
B
C
D
E
1
2
3
4
5
6
7
45
46
47
34
33
32
31
78
95
108
BREASTON
DE72
Derby
Wilne Cross
Netherlands
Sawley Grange
Church Wilne Water Sports Club
Fox Covert
New Delight
Church Wilne
Ivy House Farm
Works
Sawley
Poplar Farm
Breaston Fields Farm
Belmont Nurseries
Recreation Ground
Sawley Park Play. Fld.
Sawley Infant & Junior Schools
Top Barn
RIVER DERWENT
RIVER TRENT
EREWASH
SOUTH DERBYSHIRE
Aqueduct
Long Horse Bridge
Midshires Way
Weir
Lock
Harrington Bridge
Church Farm
Sawley Bridge Marina
Sawley Basin
Warren La.
Derwent Mouth Lock
Porter's Bridge
Works
Crowder's Eaves
TAMWORTH LANE
M1 MOTORWAY
M1
B65-40
DRAYCOTT A6005
MAIN STREET
WILSTHORPE ROAD DERBY
A6005
Playing Field
Tennis Cts.
Playing Field
Council Depot
Festival
Works
West Farm
Ryehill Farm
Bridge House Farm
MILL LANE
LONG MOOR LANE
POPLAR LANE
HOLLY LANE
HEATH AVENUE
Rec. Grd.
Lib.
RECTORY
Firfield Prim. Sch.
Golden Brook
Reservoir
Reservoir
Works
DERBY ROAD
WILNE LANE
DRAYCOTT ROAD
Sawley Park
Lodge
Atte House
The Elms
The Firs
BRIDGE FIELD
Works
Gregory Av.
Hind Av.
Hills Rd.
Stevenson Av.
Albert Av.
Hayes Av.
Spring
Burlington Cl.
Churchill Cl.
Holmes Cl.
Holmes
Grange Av.
Delamere Cl.
Earlswood Cl.
Far Croft
Plackett Cl.
Lawrence Av.
Kirk Dale Dr.
Risley Lane
Stevens Rd.
Ward's Lane
Shirley Cres.
Manor Ct.
Manor Leigh
Sawley Road
Blind Lane
Green Church Cl.
Meadow Cl.
Carlin Cl.
Cherry Cl.
Road
Maylands Avenue
Belmont Cl.
Bramble Cl.
Park St.
Grosvenor
The Grove
Willoughby Cl.
Maple Gro.
Maxwell St.
Mount Street
Orchard Cl.
Harrimans Dr.
Heather Cl.
Field
Birchwood Cl.
Fearn Cl.
Richmond
Woodland
Grampian Way
Brecon
Mendip
Pennine
Belmont Gardens
The Plantations
Grange
Eaton
Crown
Shilling
Pennyfields
Cranleigh
Fulwood
Moor
Borrowdale Dri.
Avondale
Calderdale
Dovedale
Langdale Dr.
Tynedale
Stourdale Cl.
Bishopdale Cl.
Wharfedale
Teesdale
Kingsdale Cl.
Ribblesdale
Overdale Cl.
Peakdale Cl.
Farndale
Deepdale
Lathkilldale
Meadow Crescent
Osmaston Rd.
Baslow Cl.
Rowsley Av.
Peveril
Matlock Ct.
Hathersage Way
Duffield
Darley
Beresford Ho.
Wilmot Ho.
Cromford Cl.
Keddleston
Ingleby
Twyford Cl.
Hilton Cl.
Meadow Ct.
Hardwick Ct.
Haddon Way
Sudbury Cl.
Repton Rd.
Weston Cr.
Ladybay Rd.
Weston
Cliffro Cl.
Shirley Street
Plant
Arnold Cr.
Towle St.
Firs Cl.
Grosvenor St.
Clarke Dr.
Chantry Cl.
Fairfield
Portland
Trent Ho.
Arnold Av.
Wilne Rd.
Attewell

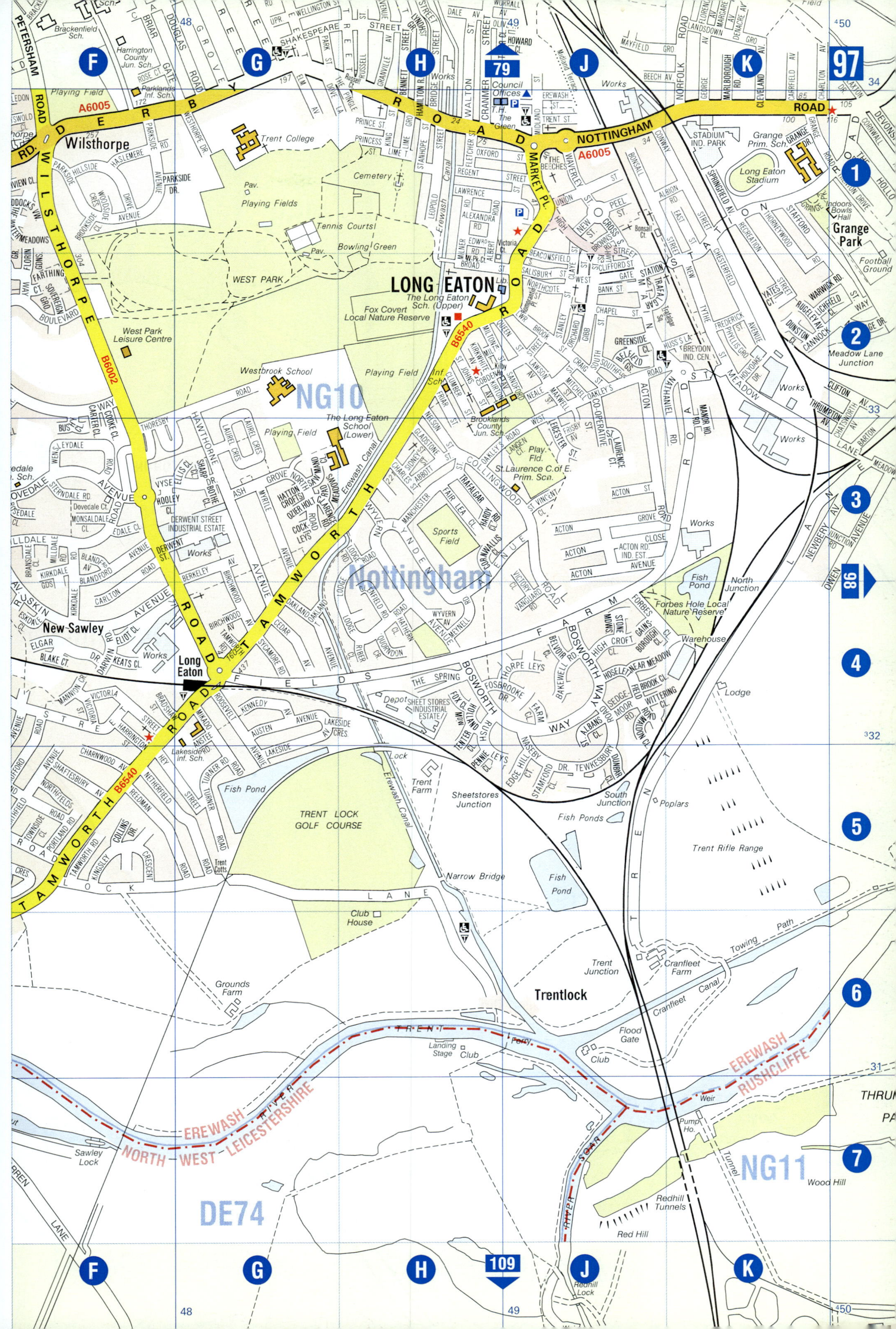

97
Wilsthorpe
LONG EATON
Grange Park
New Sawley
Long Eaton
Nottingham
Trentlock
TRENT LOCK GOLF COURSE
Trent Rifle Range
NG10
NG11
DE74
DERBY ROAD
A6005
NOTTINGHAM ROAD
A6005
MARKET PL
TAMWORTH ROAD
WILSTHORPE ROAD
B6002
B6540
Trent College
West Park
West Park Leisure Centre
Westbrook School
The Long Eaton School (Upper)
The Long Eaton School (Lower)
Fox Covert Local Nature Reserve
Long Eaton Stadium
Grange Prim. Sch.
Football Ground
Brooklands County Jun. Sch.
St. Laurence C. of E. Prim. Sch.
Sports Field
Meadow Lane Junction
Forbes Hole Local Nature Reserve
Fish Pond
North Junction
Sheetstores Junction
South Junction
Trent Junction
Cranfleet Farm
Cranfleet Canal
Erewash Canal
RIVER TRENT
Trent Lock
Narrow Bridge
Fish Ponds
Grounds Farm
Club House
Sawley Lock
Redhill Tunnels
Red Hill
Redhill Lock
Wood Hill
EREWASH RUSHCLIFFE
EREWASH NORTH WEST LEICESTERSHIRE
Poplars
Towing Path
Trent Cotts
Trent Farm
Lodge
Warehouse
Council Offices
The Green
79
86
98
109

Field
450
ROAD
CHILWELL RETAIL PK.
51
WAY
52
P
98
34
85
A
Toton Arches
B
80
C
D
E
100
105 NOTTINGHAM
116
CARTERFIELD AV
CHILWELL
DR
Filter Beds
HARLAXTON
Sewage Works
The Warren
Grange Sch.
GRANGE
GRANGE DR.
DEVONSHIRE
1
Eaton ilium
STATION
CORNWALL AVE
THE HOLLOWS
AVENUE
SOMERSET CL.
Filter Beds
NG9
FRENTON DRIVE
GRANGE
STAFFORD
HONEYWOOD
RD
Indoors Bowls Hall
Grange Park
River Erewash
Barton Ferry
BROXTOWE
RUSHCLIFFE
The Bungalow
Football Ground
Playing Field
WARWICK RD.
2
RUGELEY AV
LICHFIELD
ST WAY
Golden Brook
Attenborough Junction
TRENT
Grange Farm
GATES CT.
STREET
I DR
CANNOCK
ARMITAGE DR.
Meadow Lane Junction
LANE
CHESTNUT
CLIFTON
AVE
RD
BARTON-IN-
FABIS
Works
33
THRUMPTON AV.
CHATSWORTH AV.
Trent Meadows
BROWN
THE SWITE
LANE
Old Farm
NEW ROAD
MEADOW
BARTON
Works
LANE
MEADOW
CHURCH LA.
Manor Farm
3
NEWBERY RD
JUNCTION
AVENUE
LANE
RECTORY PL.
RECTORY PL.
97
OWEN
Home Farm
PASTURE
LITTLE LUNNON
MANOR
TRENT
NG10
Nottingham
4
32
LANE
5
RIVER
EREWASH
RUSHCLIFFE
Path
TRENT
LANE
CHURCH LANE
Fields Farm
GREEN
Towing
LANE
Ferry Farm
6
Thrumpton Hall
The Manor Ho.
The Grange
CHURCH LANE
Thrumpton
New Buildings
A453
Manor Farm
31
Church Farm
Pav.
CHURCH
The Lindens
LANE
Wood Farm
THRUMPTON
PARK
Old Wood
7
Wood Hill
Wright's Hill Plantation
Twenty Lands Plantation
Hillside Cottage
GOTHAM HILL WOOD
Wright's Hill
BARTON
Cottagers Hill
A
B
110
C
D
E
450
51
Cottagers Hill Spinney
52

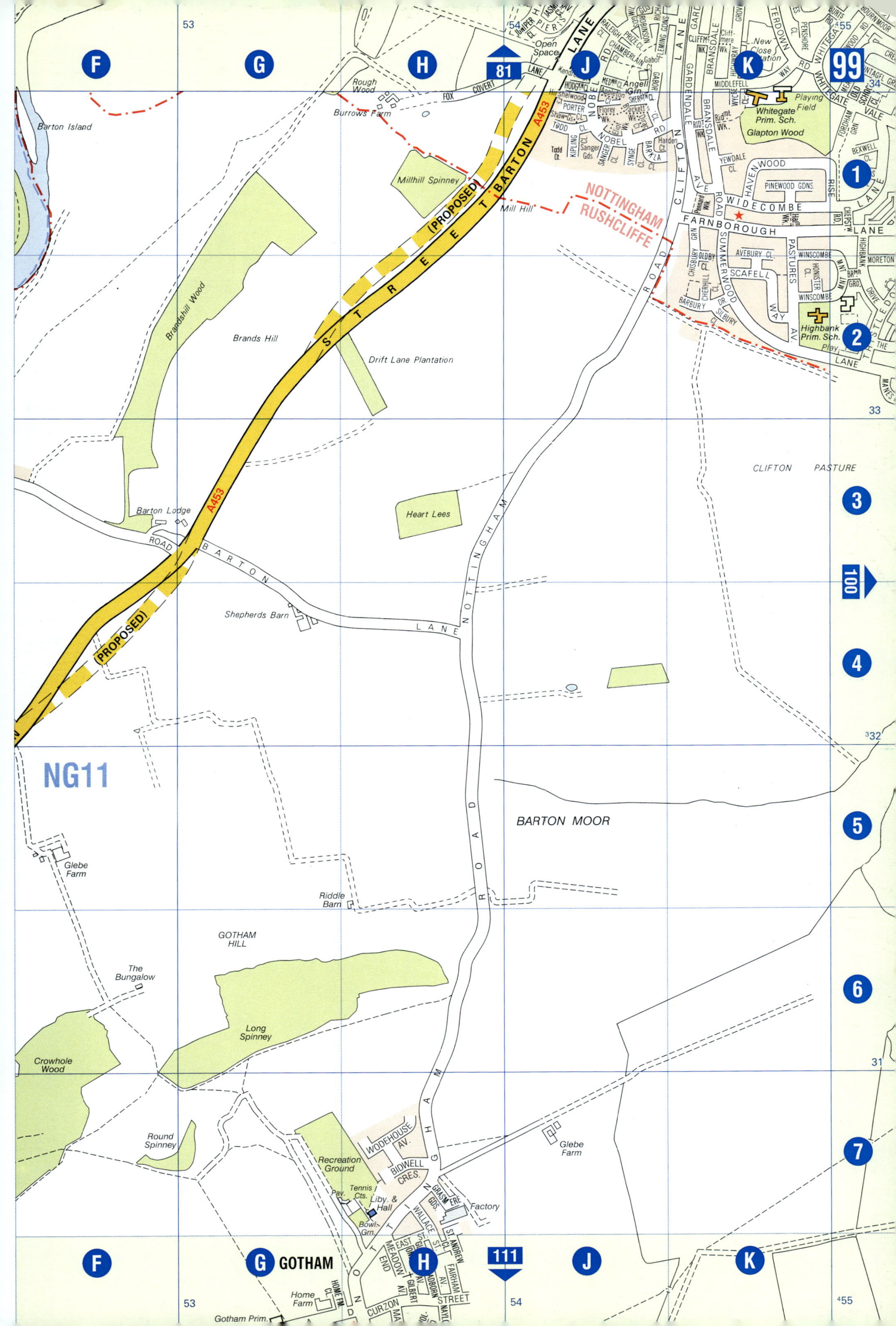

53
54
55
F
G
H
J
K
99
81
Open Space
PIERS
LANE
JUNIPER
JASM. AV.
RALEIGH
ROBINSON
FLEMING GDNS.
GARD.
TERDOWN
BURTS RD.
PENSHORE
BOURNMOOR
Rough Wood
FOX COVERT
CHAMBERLAIN
CL.
WK.
NEW
BRANSDALE
Clift.
mere
WK.
VINTAGFL.
VALE
34
Burrows Farm
Kendr.
Angell Grn.
GARDENDALE
Whitegate
WHITEGATE
CHEPSTW.
RD.
Shelwood CL.
HODGEN CL.
PRIZE CL.
GABOR
GOR.
BRANSDALE
Close
Station
New
FORDHAM GRN.
Millhill Spinney
PORTER CL.
APPLETON
RID.
Whitegate
Prim. Sch.
MORETON
Mill Hill
SHAW GS. CL.
BRMA.
Glapton Wood
Playing
Field
BEXWELL
CL.
TODD CT.
KIPLING
SANGER GDS.
ELIOT
WK.
RIDMT. WK.
1
PROPOSED
BARTON
STREET
NOBEL
SYNGE
CL.
YEWDALE
HAVEN WOOD
HIGHBANK
NOTTINGHAM
RUSHCLIFFE
CL.
PINEWOOD GDNS.
RISE
LANE
CHISBURY
WIDECOMBE
Pernard Wk.
Brandshill Wood
A453
FARNBOROUGH
CHEPSTW.
Brands Hill
CLIFTON
OLDBY
AVEBURY CL.
PASTURES
WINSCOMBE
CL.
SCAFELL
HONISTER
MORETON
Drift Lane Plantation
CHERHILL
SUMMERWOOD
2
BARBURY
SILBURY
DR.
WINSCOMBE
Highbank
Prim. Sch.
Play.
WAY
LANE
MAN'S
33
ROAD
Heart Lees
CLIFTON
PASTURE
A453
3
Barton Lodge
BARTON
NOTTINGHAM
ROAD
100
Shepherds Barn
LANE
4
PROPOSED
32
NG11
BARTON
MOOR
5
Glebe
Farm
Riddle
Barn
ROAD
GOTHAM
HILL
The
Bungalow
6
GOTHAM
Long
Spinney
31
Crowhole
Wood
NOTTINGHAM
Round
Spinney
Glebe
Farm
7
WODEHOUSE
AV.
Recreation
Ground
BIDWELL
CRES.
Factory
Tennis
Cts.
Pav.
Liby. &
Hall
GRASMERE
WALLACE ST.
ST. ANDREW GDS.
GILBERT
FAIRHAM AV.
Bowl-
Grn.
EAST ST.
AUBORN
F
G
GOTHAM
H
111
J
K
53
54
55
Home
Farm
HOME FM. CL.
CURZON
GILBERT AV.
FAIRHAM
STREET
Gotham Prim.

100
55
56
57
A
B
82
C
D
E
34
Playing Field
Whitegate Prim. Sch.
Clifton Wood
Whitegate
Youth Cen.
Lakehead Ho.
Green
WHITEWORTH CRES
Whiteways Ct.
Cen.
Lib.
LANE
WHEATACRE
WHARTON
FINGAL
ROCHESTER
BRANTFORD
AV
GROVE
ROAD
Playing Field
Tennis Courts
South Notts. College (Charnwood Centre)
Fairham Bridge
Fairham Brook Nature Reserve
Brook Hill
Depot.
BROOKSIDE GDNS
Brookside
Rec. Grnd.
TRENT AV
PAGET CRES
WILFORD
Pinewood Wse Station
HAZELWOOD
HALE
Pinewood Rise
High Bk.
WIDECOMBE
Meadowvale
Tintagel Green
Wrenthorpe
Dungannon
Milford Prim. Sch.
Prim. Sch.
Playing Field
Blase Ct.
Cerne Cl.
Listowel
Holbrook
Ferrus Vale
Stirling Gro.
Lansing
Granton Cl.
Graywood Cl.
Dunk.
Vale
Stirling Gro
Camelot
Grenay
Lyons
Brookside
Birkin Av
Grange Av
Bradmore Av
Savages
Wilford Cres
Ashworth Av
Ashworth
Cordham Vale
Bexwell Cl.
Southchurch
Clouds Hill
Listowel
Glenloch
Bradley Wlk.
Cres
Road
Lane
Fairham Community College
NOTTINGHAM
RUSHCLIFFE
Samson Ct.
Shelton Ct.
Cres
Camelot Cres
Templeman Cl.
North
Clifton
St. Johns
St. Marys
Pear Tree Orchard
Easthorpe
Pastures
Farnborough
Winscombe Cl.
Honister Cl.
Highbank
Moreton Rd.
Chedor.
Road
Lane
Lane
Clifton
Mike Powers Pottery
Park
Road
Cumberland Cl.
St. John's
Winscombe Way
Highbank Prim. Sch.
Play. Flds
The Glade
Clarewood
Breckswood
Conifer
Conifer Cres
Killerton
Road
Drive
Manor
Manor Pk.
Drive
Manor
James Peacock Infant School
Ruddington Village Mus.
Vicarage
Church
Woodley St.
Wilsons Ct.
Thistle Down
Manesty
Summerwood La.
Summerwood
Summerwood Cres
Brecks Plantation
Spring Grn.
Grove
Station Works
Tall Trees Farm
Sports Ground
Westerham Rd.
Churchill
Bladon
Spencer
St. Peters Cr.
Charles St.
Shaw
Cemetery
Peacock Cl.
Barton Cl.
Rd.
Malting Cl.
Chapel St.
Mus.
The Green
Youth & Comm. Cen.
Carter Av
Elms
Gdns
SUMMERWOOD
33
Printing Works
Western Fields
Musters
Sandbury
Rainham Gdns
But. Cl.
Distillery
Gdns
Sutton
Fuller
Top R.
Asher
East
Leys
Dunblane Rd.
Moor
Sheepfold
Sellars Av.
CLIFTON  PASTURE
99
Sewage Works
PASTURE
Road
Leys Ct.
Wheatley
Barley Fields Cl.
Lane
Lane
32
Fields Farm Cottages
Great Central Railway (Nottingham)
Leys Farm
NG11
RUSHCLIFFE COUNTRY PARK
Nottingham Heritage
P
West End
Asher
Ruddington Fields Farm
Moorend Farm Cottages
Moorend Farm
Moor Farm
31
RUDDINGTON MOOR
Fairham Brook
BRADMORE MOOR
A
GOTHAM  MOOR
B
C
D
E
55
56
57
KIRK
HIGH ST.
WILFORD ROAD
B680

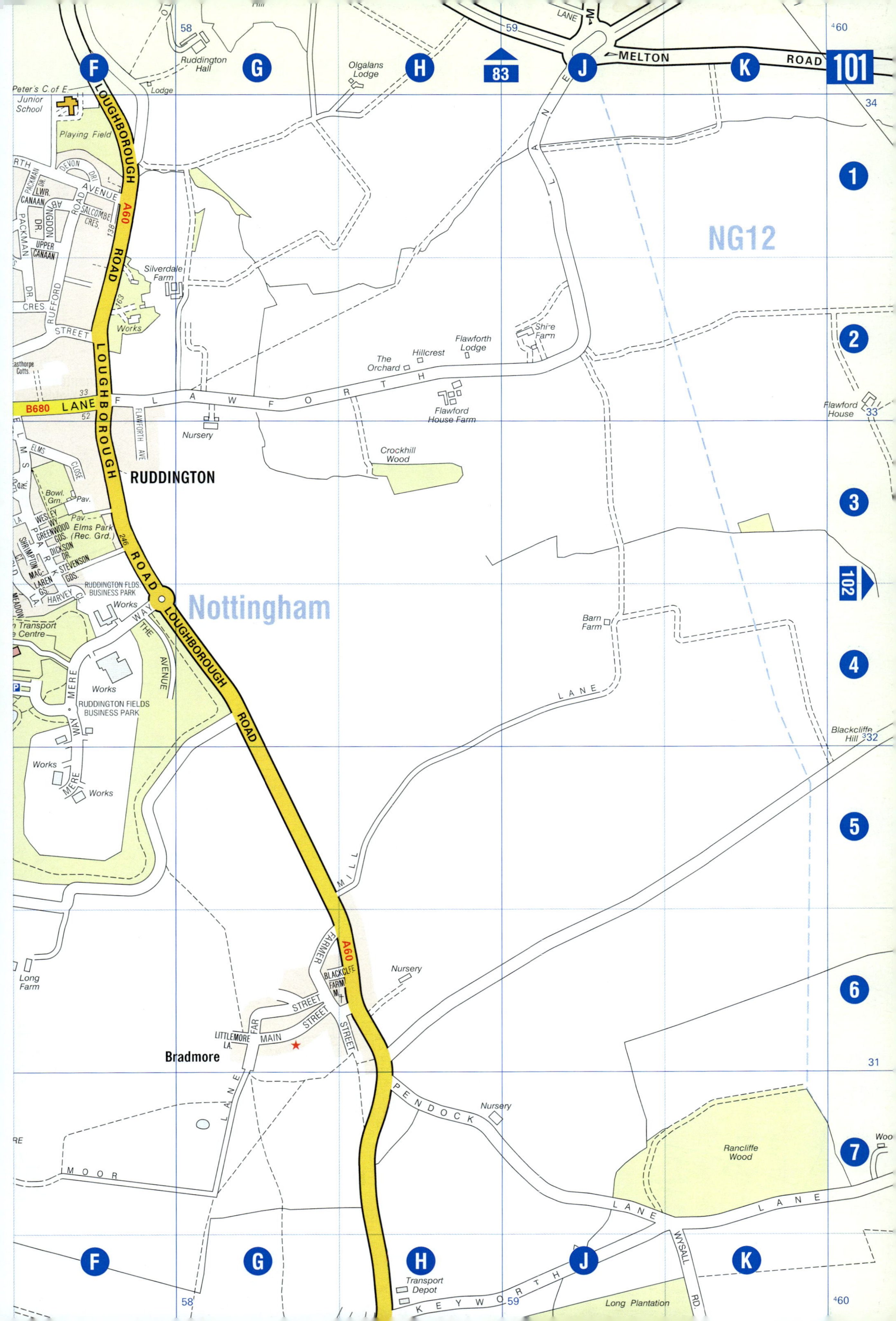
58
59
60
101
34
F
G
H
83
J
MELTON
K
ROAD
Ruddington Hall
Olgalans Lodge
Lodge
St. Peter's C. of E. Junior School
Playing Field
PACKMAN
DEVON DR.
ABINGDON ROAD
LWR. CANAAN
UPPER CANAAN
DR.
PACKMAN DR.
CRES.
SALCOMBE CRES.
A60
LOUGHBOROUGH ROAD
1
NG12
Silverdale Farm
Works
RUFFORD STREET
Easthorpe Cotts.
B680
LANE
52
33
FLAWFORTH
Flawforth Ave.
Nursery
The Orchard
Hillcrest
Flawforth Lodge
Shire Farm
2
Flawford House Farm
Flawford House
33
ELMS
ELMS CLOSE
RUDDINGTON
Nursery
Crockhill Wood
3
Bowl. Grn.
Pav.
WESLEY WY
GREENWOOD GDS.
Pav.
Elms Park (Rec. Grd.)
DICKSON DR.
STEVENSON GDS.
SHRIMPTON
MAC-LAREN GDS.
HARVEY
MEADOW LA.
RUDDINGTON FLDS. BUSINESS PARK
Works
102
246
LOUGHBOROUGH ROAD
Barn Farm
4
n Transport e Centre
THE AVENUE
MERE WAY
Works
LANE
Works
RUDDINGTON FIELDS BUSINESS PARK
Blackcliffe Hill
32
Works
MERE WAY
Works
5
MILL
Long Farm
FARMER STREET
A60
Nursery
BLACKCLIFE FARM M
6
LITTLEMORE LA.
FAR LANE
MAIN STREET
STREET
STREET
Bradmore
PENDOCK
Nursery
31
MOOR
Rancliffe Wood
Woo
7
WYSALL RD.
LANE
LANE
F
G
H
J
K
Transport Depot
KEYWORTH
Long Plantation
58
59
60

102
34
33
32
31
460
61
62
A B C D E
1 2 3 4 5 6 7
84
101
A606
MELTON ROAD
MAIN ROAD
OLD MELTON ROAD
COTGRAVE ROAD
CLIPSTON LANE
THE LEYS
Normanton-on-the-Wolds
Hoe Hill
Hoe Hill Cottages
Hoehill Farm
Ranch House
Weir
The Lawns
Manor House
Normanton House
Avenue Farm
BLACK LANE
Plumtree
Plumtree Sch.
Plumtree Park
Town End
Manor Farm
Hall Farm
CHURCH LA.
FELLOWS YD.
BRADLEYS YD.
CHURCH HILL
SADDLERS YARD
ROAD STATION LANE
THE POPLARS
Cricket Grd.
Pav.
Chestnut Farm
Flawford House
Blackcliffe Hill
BRADMORE
Cotton's Plantation
Greenhays Farm
Woodfields
Lynwood
Wheatcroft Farm
KEYWORTH LA.
BUNNY
Sewage Works
Burial Grd.
The Bungalow
WYSALL LA.
KEYWORTH
Crossdale Drive Prim. Sch.
HILLCREST RD.
DELVILLE AV.
HIGHBURY RD.
RANCLIFFE AV.
DEBDALE LANE
HIGHFIELD RD.
ABBOT CL.
BISHOPS CL.
SIDMOUTH CL.
BEAUMONT CL.
BELVEDERE CL.
CROSSDALE DRIVE
BROCKDALE GDS.
BROCKWOOD CRS.
BRIAR CL.
ROSE GRO.
VILLA RD.
FRANKLYN GDS.
ADAMS HILL
CLIFFORD RD.
FEIGNIES CT.
COMBE RD.
NORMANTON LANE
LOWLANDS DR.
WYNBRECK DR.
ASHLEY CRES.
ASHLEY RD.
WALTON DR.
RANNOCK GDS.
BRANTOCK GDS.
PARK RD.
PARK AV.
ROAD TER.
PARK GDS.
POPLARS CL.
GREEN CL.
PARKSIDE
RODNEY CL.
DRIVECKER
COVERT CL.
WOLDS RISE
MOUNT PLEASANT
HIGH VIEW AV.
MEADOW DR.
THE RIDINGS
CHERRY HILL
PLEASANT MOUNT
British Geological Survey
Sheltons Houses
Firs Farm
PLATT LANE
SPINNEY RD.
FAIRHAM RD.
FURGORSE RD.
HAYES RD.
PLANTATION RD.
INTAKE RD.
CROFT RD.
PARK AV. WEST
MANOR ROAD
THELDA RD.
DALE RD.
ROSE HILL
BARNT CT.
CHURCH DRIVE
ASHLEY RD.
NOTTINGHAM ROAD
SELBY LANE
EAST AV.
EAST CL.
WEST CL.
LEIGH RD.
CHANTRY CL.
Keyworth Prim. Sch.
Recreation Grd.
Hall
Liby.
Taylor Ct.
South Wolds Comp. Sch.
Playing Fld.
ELM AV.
ELM CL.
WINDMILL CT.
BEECH AV.
LAUREL CL.
LIMETREE CL.
ASH GRO.
LILAC CL.
WILLOW LANE
AVENUE
PLEASANT MOUNT
ALDER AV.
PLEASANT AV.
LABURNUM WY.
LARCH WY.
ROWAN DR.
MAPLE CL.
COMMERCIAL RD.
MAIN STREET
The Square
BROOK VIEW
HAWTHORN CL.
HIGH ORCHARD
HOLMFIELD RD.
BARROW SLADE
FAIR PASTURES
ROSELAND CL.
CEDAR DR.
BROOK VW. CT.
Avenue
Stanstead Av.
Stella Gro.
Stella Av.
Sedgeley
Orchard Cl.
Muir
Bentinck
Lenton Av.
Priory Circus
Priory Avenue
Osburnside Av.
Tollerton Prim. Sch.
Grove Rd.
Tollerton Lane
High

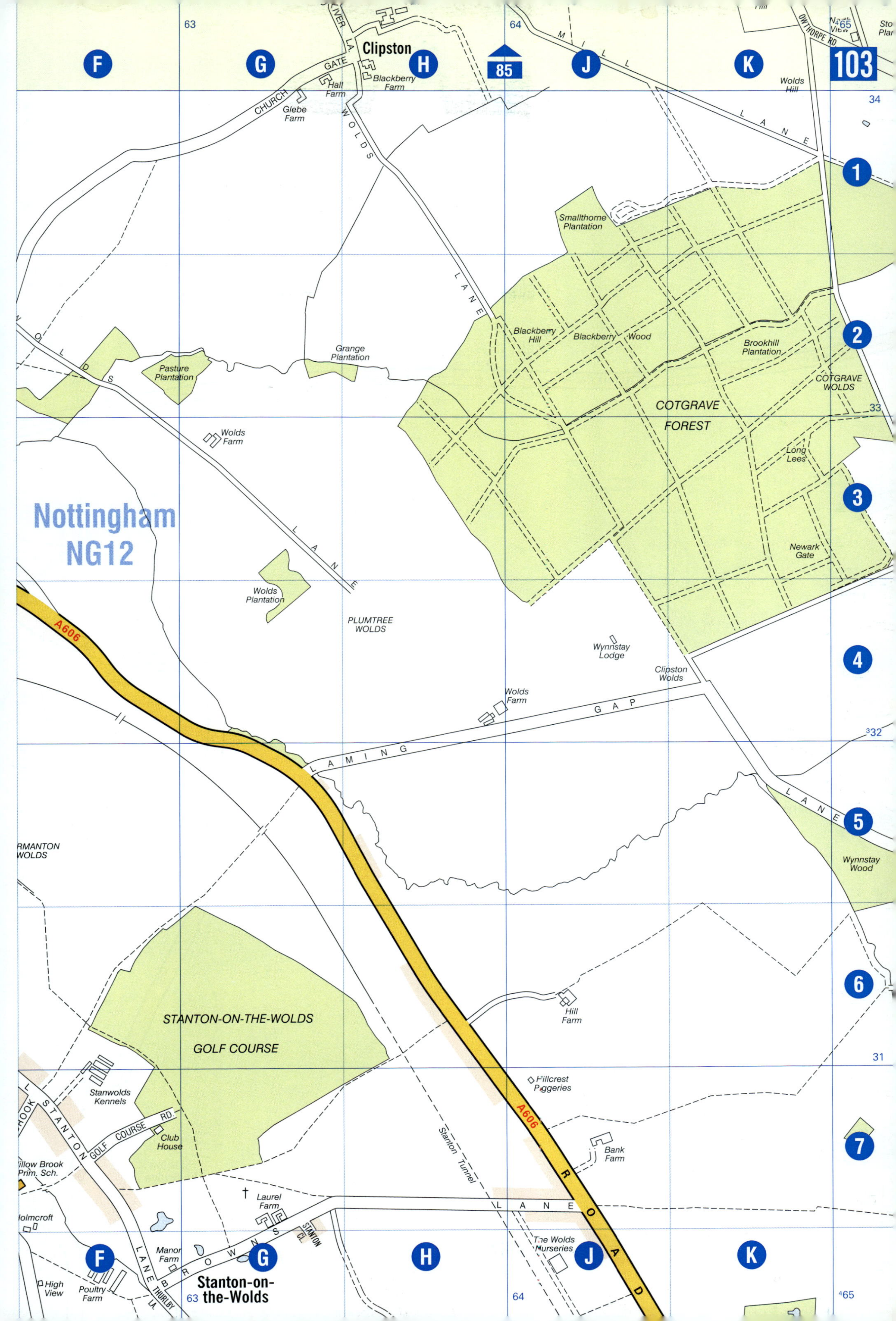

103
63
64
F
G
H
J
K
Clipston
85
34
Church Gate
Wolds Lane
Hall Farm
Blackberry Farm
Glebe Farm
River Wolds
Mill Lane
Owthorpe Rd
Wolds Hill
Nantee View
Stockwell Plantation
1
Smallthorne Plantation
2
Blackberry Hill
Blackberry Wood
Brookhill Plantation
Cotgrave Wolds
33
Grange Plantation
Pasture Plantation
Cotgrave Forest
Wolds Farm
Long Lees
Nottingham NG12
Newark Gate
3
Wolds Plantation
Plumtree Wolds
Wynnstay Lodge
Clipston Wolds
4
32
Laming Gap
Wolds Farm
Lane
5
Wynnstay Wood
Ormanton Wolds
Stanton-on-the-Wolds Golf Course
Hill Farm
6
31
Hillcrest Piggeries
7
Stanwolds Kennels
Golf Course Rd
Club House
Brook
Stanton Lane
Willow Brook Prim. Sch.
Holmcroft
Laurel Farm
Manor Farm
Stanton Cl
Browns
Stanton Tunnel
A606
Lane Road
Bank Farm
The Wolds Nurseries
F
G
H
J
K
High View
Poultry Farm
Lane Thurlby
Stanton-on-the-Wolds
63
64
65

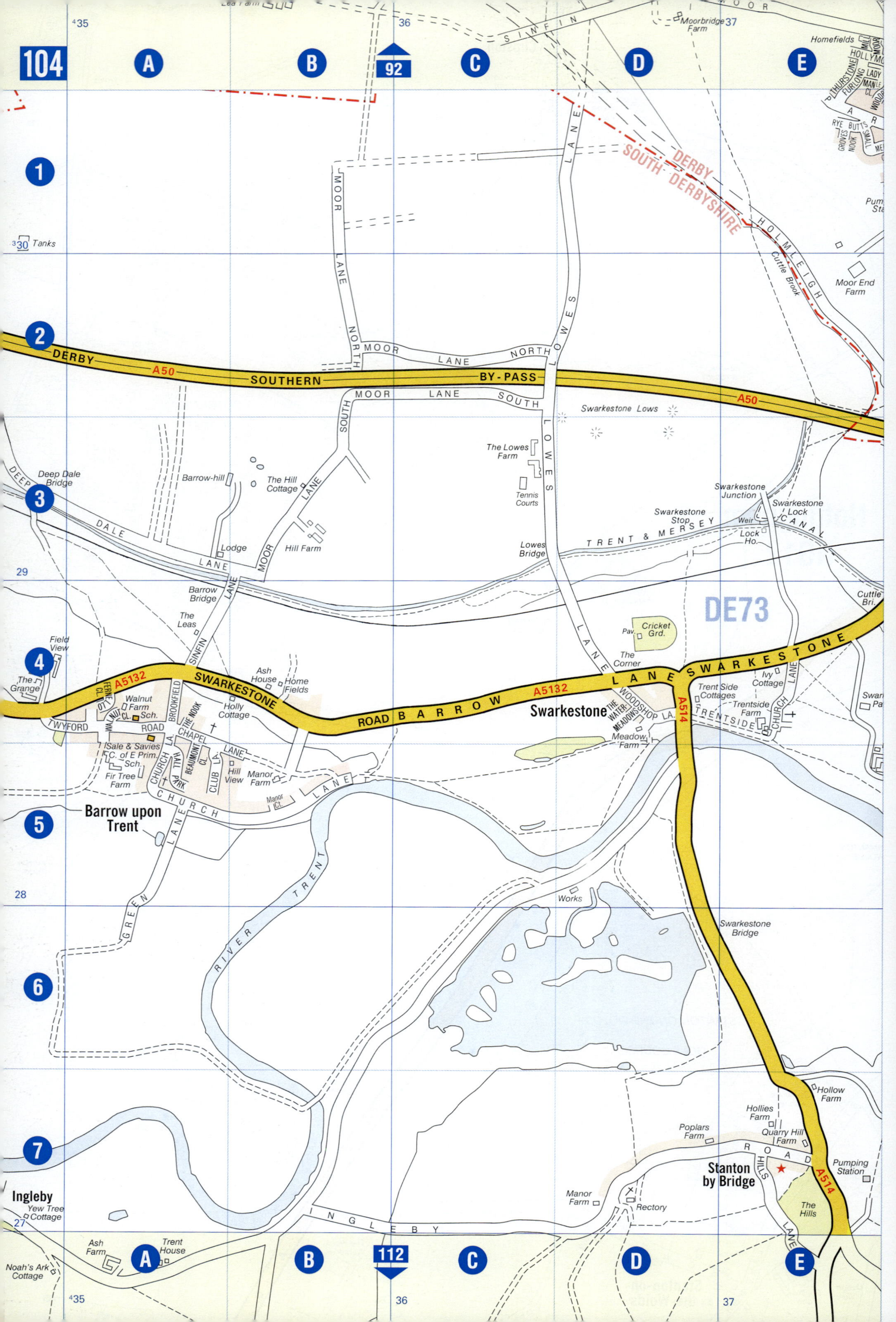
104
A B 92 C D E
1
30 Tanks
2 DERBY A50 SOUTHERN BY-PASS A50
MOOR LANE NORTH
MOOR LANE NORTH
LOWES LANE
SINFIN
DERBY
SOUTH DERBYSHIRE
HOLMLEIGH
Moorbridge Farm 37
Homefields
Cuttle Brook
Moor End Farm
Pump Sta
MOOR LANE SOUTH
Swarkestone Lows
The Lowes Farm
Tennis Courts
Lowes Bridge
Swarkestone Stop
Swarkestone Junction
Swarkestone Lock
Weir
Lock Ho.
TRENT & MERSEY
CANAL
Cuttle Bri.
DE73
Deep Dale Bridge
Barrow-hill
The Hill Cottage
Lodge
Hill Farm
MOOR LANE
SOUTH LANE
DEEP DALE LANE
3
29
Barrow Bridge
The Leas
SINFIN LANE
Field View
The Grange
TWYFORD
A5132 SWARKESTONE ROAD BARROW A5132
Swarkestone
LANE SWARKESTONE
Cricket Grd.
Pav.
The Corner
The Water Meadows
Meadow Farm
WOODSHOP LA.
A514
Trent Side Cottages
Ivy Cottage
Trentside Farm
TRENTSIDE
CHURCH LANE
Swar Pa
4
Walnut Farm Cl.
Sch.
FERNEY CL.
WALNUT CL.
Brookfield
THE NOOK
Ash House
Home Fields
Holly Cottage
CHAPEL LANE
BEAUMONT CL.
CLUB LA.
Hill View
Manor Farm
Sale & Savies C. of E Prim. Sch.
Fir Tree Farm
CHURCH LANE
Manor Cl.
CHURCH LANE
PARK
LANE
5
Barrow upon Trent
28
RIVER TRENT
GREEN LANE
Works
Swarkestone Bridge
6
Hollow Farm
Hollies Farm
Poplars Farm
Quarry Hill Farm
ROAD HILLS
Pumping Station
A514
7
Ingleby
Yew Tree Cottage
27
INGLEBY
Manor Farm
Rectory
Stanton by Bridge
The Hills
Ash Farm
Trent House
Noah's Ark Cottage
A B 112 C D E
35 36 37

105
39
40
105
F
G
H
93
J
K
Fox Covert Farm
Chellaston Jun. & Inf. Schools
Playing Field
Chellaston Covert
Marsh Flatts
CHELLASTON
1
Liby.
Manor Road
Playing Field
Recreation Ground
Pav
CHELLASTON
CHELLASTON
Tel. Exch.
Rec. Ground
Brick Works
Precast Concrete Works
30
Weston Fields Farm
CHELLASTON
Bowling Grn.
Tennis & Netball Cts.
Chellaston School
Playing Fields
SOUTHERN
2
A50
Meadow Way
Woodgate
Woodlands Farm
Chellaston Hill
Mill House
Windmill Cottage
Windmill
DERBY
BY-PASS
Fox Covert
3
Junction 3
Spring Farm
29
Cuttle Bri. Cott.
Glebe Farm
DE72
SWARKESTONE
Cuttle Brook
Derby
4
Swarkestone Pavilion
Old Hall Farm
106
Massey's Bridge
Chellaston Cottages
5
28
Melome
LANE
6
Sarson's Bridge
Westonhill Farm
Weston Cliff
Tarasiyka Youth Centre
Rectory
Rectory Mews
ROAD
TRENT
BRIDGE
Weston House
CANAL
Stanton Barn
Cliff Wood
Old Cliff House
Black Pool
MERSEY
7
Basin
RIVER
TRENT
27
F
G
H
113
J
K
39
38
40

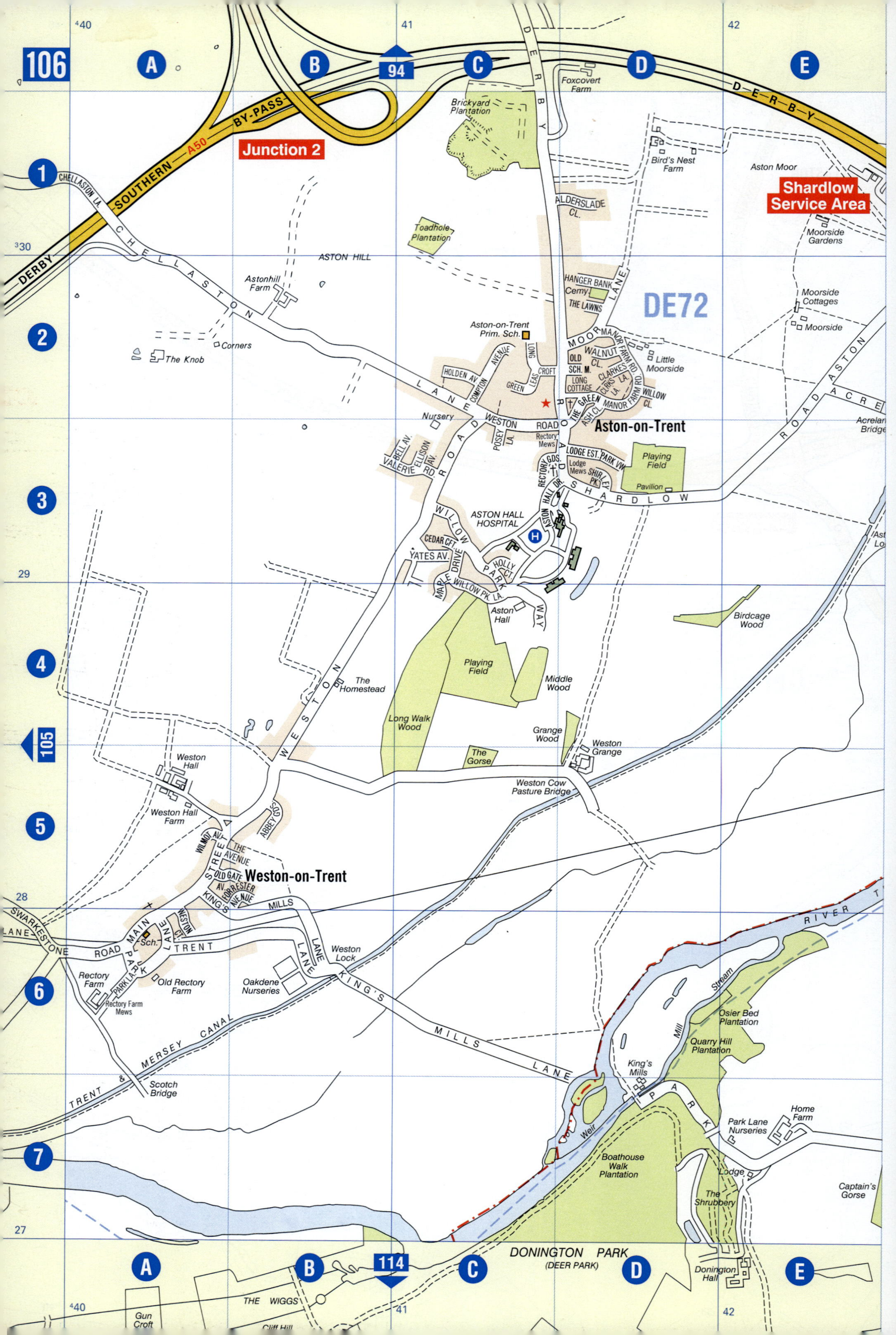

106
A B 94 C D E
Junction 2
A50 SOUTHERN BY-PASS
DERBY
CHELLASTON LA.
CHELLASTON LANE
DERBY
Foxcovert Farm
Brickyard Plantation
Bird's Nest Farm
Aston Moor
Shardlow Service Area
Moorside Gardens
ALDERSLADE CL.
Toadhole Plantation
ASTON HILL
Astonhill Farm
HANGER BANK
Cerny
THE LAWNS
DE72
Moorside Cottages
Moorside
Corners
The Knob
MOOR LANE
MANOR FARM RD.
Little Moorside
ROAD
ASTON
ACRE
Aston-on-Trent Prim. Sch.
AVENUE
LONG CROFT
OLD SCH. M.
WALNUT CL.
CLARKES CL.
HOLDEN AV.
COMPTON
LEAS
GREEN
LONG COTTAGE
CLERKS LA.
MANOR FARM RD.
WILLOW CL.
Acreland Bridge
Nursery
THE GREEN
ASH CL.
Aston-on-Trent
WESTON        ROAD
Rectory Mews
BELL AV.
VALERIE
ELLISON RD.
PARK AV.
POSEY LANE
Rectory GDS.
LODGE EST. PARK VW.
Lodge Mews
SHIRLEY PK.
SHARDLOW
Playing Field
Pavilion
WESTON ROAD
WILLOW
ASTON HALL DR.
Aston Hall Hospital
H
CEDAR CFT.
YATES AV.
HOLLY CT.
PARK
Birdcage Wood
MAPLE DRIVE
WILLOW PK. LA.
WAY
Aston Hall
The Homestead
Playing Field
Middle Wood
Long Walk Wood
Grange Wood
Weston Grange
105
Weston Hall
The Gorse
Weston Cow Pasture Bridge
Weston Hall Farm
ABBEY GDS.
WILMOT AV.
THE AVENUE
STREET
OLD GATE AV.
FORRESTER AVENUE
KING'S
MILLS
Weston-on-Trent
SWARKESTONE LANE
MAIN
ROAD
PARK LANE
WESTON CT.
TRENT
LANE
Sch.
Weston Lock
LANE
KING'S
Rectory Farm
Old Rectory Farm
Oakdene Nurseries
MILLS
LANE
River
RIVER
Rectory Farm Mews
Mill Stream
Osier Bed Plantation
TRENT & MERSEY CANAL
Quarry Hill Plantation
Scotch Bridge
King's Mills
PARK
Weir
Park Lane Nurseries
Home Farm
Lodge
Boathouse Walk Plantation
The Shrubbery
Captain's Gorse
A B 114 C DONINGTON PARK (DEER PARK) D Donington Hall E
THE WIGGS
Gun Croft
Cliff Hill

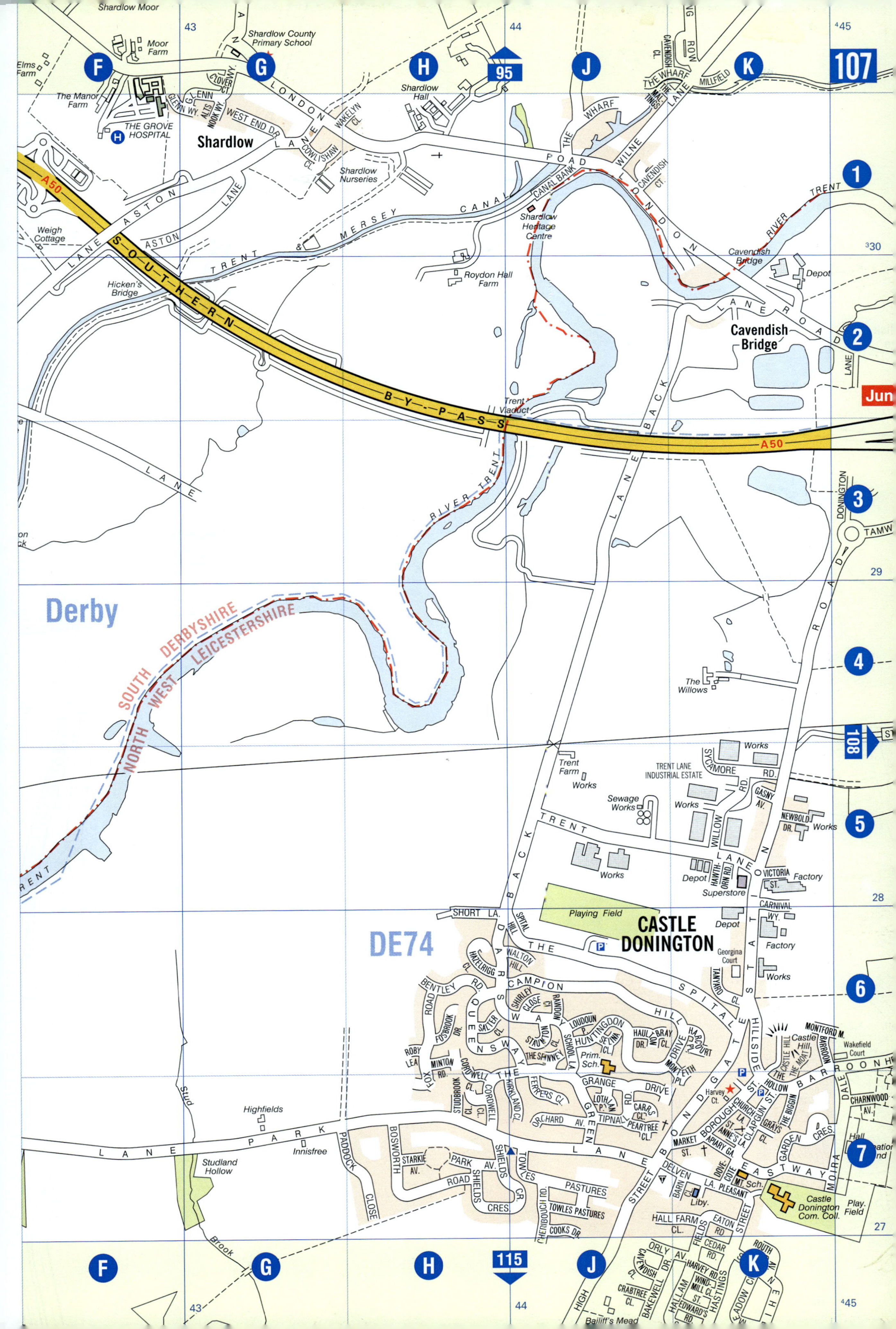

107
95
108
115
Shardlow Moor
Moor Farm
Shardlow County Primary School
Elms Farm
The Manor Farm
THE GROVE HOSPITAL
Shardlow
CLOVER CT.
GLENN WY.
NOOK WY.
ALIS
WEST END DR.
WAKELYN CL.
COWLISHAW CL.
WEST END DR.
LONDON LANE
GLENN WY.
Shardlow Hall
THE WHARF
CAVENDISH ROW
THE WHARF
MILLFIELD
KINGS
CL.
CAVENDISH CT.
Weigh Cottage
ASTON LANE
ASTON LANE
SOUTHERN
Shardlow Nurseries
TRENT & MERSEY CANAL
CANAL BANK
Shardlow Heritage Centre
ROAD
WILNE
CAVENDISH
LONDON
RIVER TRENT
1
Cavendish Bridge
Depot
2
Cavendish Bridge
Jun
Hicken's Bridge
Roydon Hall Farm
Trent Viaduct
BY-PASS
A50
LANE BACK
LANE
3
DONINGTON ROAD
TAMW
LANE
RIVER TRENT
Derby
SOUTH DERBYSHIRE
NORTH WEST LEICESTERSHIRE
TRENT
The Willows
4
108
S
5
Trent Farm
Works
Works
Sewage Works
Works
TRENT LANE INDUSTRIAL ESTATE
SYCAMORE RD.
RD.
GASNY AV.
NEWBOLD DR.
Works
BACK LANE
TRENT LANE
WILLOW
HAWTHORN RD.
Works
Depot
Superstore
VICTORIA ST.
Factory
CARNIVAL
Depot
Factory
Georgina Court
Works
6
Playing Field
CASTLE DONINGTON
SHORT LA.
SPITAL HILL
THE
DE74
HAZELRIGG RD.
BENTLEY ROAD
FOSBROOK DR.
QUEENSWAY
SALTER CL.
DARRS
WALTON HILL
CAMPION
SHIRLEY CLOSE
RAWDON
LOUDOUN CL.
HUNTINGDON
SE ZINA
SCHOOL LA.
HAUL
DR.
BRAY CL.
HILL
HARCOURT
MONTEITH
DRIVE
SPITAL
HILLSIDE
TANYARD CL.
STATION
MONTFORD M.
Castle Hill
Castle Hill
BARROON
Wakefield Court
ROBY LEA
FOX
MINTON RD.
CORDWELL
THE SPINNEY
Prim. Sch.
GRANGE
LOTH...
RD.
CARRS
TIPNAL
PEARTREE CL.
DELVEN LANE
Harvey Ct.
Church
BOROUGH ST.
ST. ANNE'S LA.
CLAPGUN ST.
GRAYS
THE RIGGIN
THE MORT
CASTLE HILL
THE HOLLOW
CHARNWOOD AV.
Hall
7
Highfields
Innisfree
Studland Hollow
LANE PARK
Stud
STUDBROOK CL.
CORDWELL CL.
BOSWORTH CLOSE
PADDOCK CLOSE
FERRERS CL.
ORCHARD AV.
THE GREEN
STARKIE AV.
PARK AV.
SHIELDS RD.
SHIELDS CR.
TOWLES PASTURES
TOWLES PASTURES
CHENBOUGH RD.
COOKS DR.
Market
APIARY GA.
Liby.
MT. Sch.
L.A. PLEASANT
DOVE COTE
BARN LA.
Hall Farm CL.
EATON FIELDS
STREET
STREET
GARDEN CRES.
EASTWAY
MOIRA DALE
Castle Donington Com. Coll.
Play Field
CRABTREE CL.
HIGH
ORLY AV.
CEDAR RD.
HARVEY RD.
WIND. MILL CL.
HASTINGS
ROUTH
HALLAM ST.
BAKEWELL ST.
EDWARD'S RD.
HEATH
MEADOW
Bailiff's Mead
CAVENDISH DR.
DAVENS
HIGH
F 43   G   H 44   J   K 45
F   G   H 115   J   K

108
45
Works
Derwent Mouth Lock
Long Horse Bridge
46
96
Porter's Bridge
A
B
C
D
ROAD
Works
Marina
47
E
1
30
RIVER
TRENT
SOUTH
NORTH WEST
DERBYSHIRE
LEICESTERSHIRE
DE72
Crowder's Eaves
B6540
The Cottage
Hemington Fields House
LANE
M1 MOTORWAY
M1
Lockington Grounds Farm
2
Depot
LONDON LANE
ROAD
Junction 1
TAMWORTH
Conveyors
Sand and Gravel Pit
A50
NETHERFIELD
Derby
3
DONINGTON ROAD
TAMWORTH
RYECROFT ROAD
ROAD
Hemington Hole
Junction 24a
WARREN
Warren Farm
29
4
STATION
STATION
107
RYECROFT STREET
New Delight Cottages
DE74
M1 MOTORWAY
5
Works
NEW DR.
ROAD
GRANGE CL. FM.
Hemington
LOCKINGTON
ROAD
HEMINGTON
STREET
LOCKINGTON PARK
Rec. Grd.
Lockington Hall
A50
VICTORIA
Factory
28
CARNIVAL
Y.
actory
Hemington Prim. Sch.
Halfway House
Hemington Court
MAIN
DALEACRE
KINGSGATE
LANE
Post Office Farm
Lockington
Daleacre Hil
CHURCH LA.
6
Works
Post Office Farm
THE HORSE SHOES
CHURCH LA.
HILL
CHURCH
Daleacre Farm
Daleacre House
MAIN ST.
CHURCH STREET
Hall Farm
A50
Hemington House Farm
MONTFORD M.
Castle Hill
BARROON
Wakefield Court
BARROON HEMINGTON
THE MOAT
The Dumps
STREET
LOW
THE BIGGIN
DALE
CHARNWOOD AV.
Cemetery
Hemington Hill
7
27
GARDEN CRES.
MOIRA
WAY
Hall Recreation Ground
Castle Donington Com. Coll.
Play. Field
King Street Plantation
A453
A
B
116
C
D
E
45
46
47

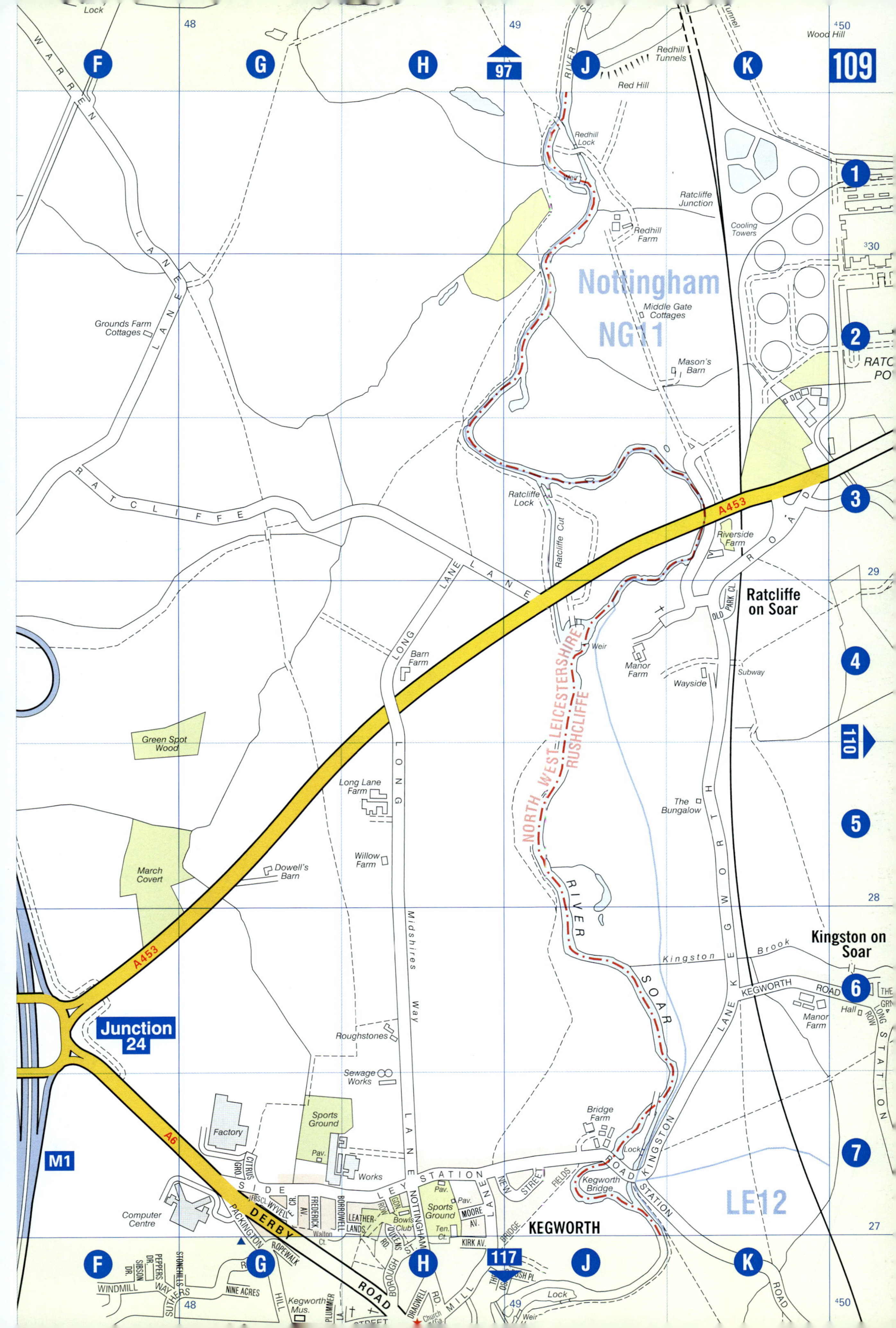
F
G
H
97
J
K
109
Lock
48
49
50
Wood Hill
River Soar
Redhill Tunnels
Red Hill
Redhill Lock
Weir
1
Ratcliffe Junction
Redhill Farm
Cooling Towers
30
RATC
PO
Nottingham
NG11
Middle Gate Cottages
Mason's Barn
2
Grounds Farm Cottages
Ratcliffe Lock
Ratcliffe Cut
A453
Riverside Farm
3
RATCLIFFE LANE
29
Ratcliffe on Soar
Old Park Cl.
Weir
Manor Farm
Wayside
Subway
4
LONG LANE
Barn Farm
NORTH WEST LEICESTERSHIRE
RUSHCLIFFE
RIVER SOAR
The Bungalow
110
Green Spot Wood
Long Lane Farm
5
A453
March Covert
Dowell's Barn
Willow Farm
28
River Soar
KEGWORTH LANE
Kingston Brook
Kingston on Soar
M1
Junction 24
Midshires Way
Roughstones
Kingston Road
KEGWORTH ROAD
Manor Farm
Hall
LONG STATION ROW
THE GRN
6
A6
Factory
Sewage Works
Sports Ground
Pav.
Works
Bridge Farm
Lock
7
M1
Computer Centre
SIDE
DERBY
PACKINGTON
ROPEWALK
GRO
CITRUS
WYVELL CR.
FREDERICK AV.
BORROWELL
LEATHER-LANDS
Walton Ct.
STATION
LEY
NOTTINGHAM LANE
Pav.
Bowls Club
Sports Ground
Ten. Ct.
MOORE AV.
Pav.
NEW STREET
FIELDS
Kegworth Bridge
Lock
Station Road
KINGSTON
LE12
KEGWORTH
F
WINDMILL
PEPPERS DR.
SIBSON DR.
STONEHILLS WAY
SUTHERS
NINE ACRES
PLUMMER
HILL
Kegworth Mus.
G
ROAD
BOROUGH
QUEENS RD.
RD.
DRAGWELL
117
H
BRIDGE MILL LANE
Church
Lock
Weir
J
KIRK AV.
RUSH PL.
49
50
K
KINGSTON ROAD
27

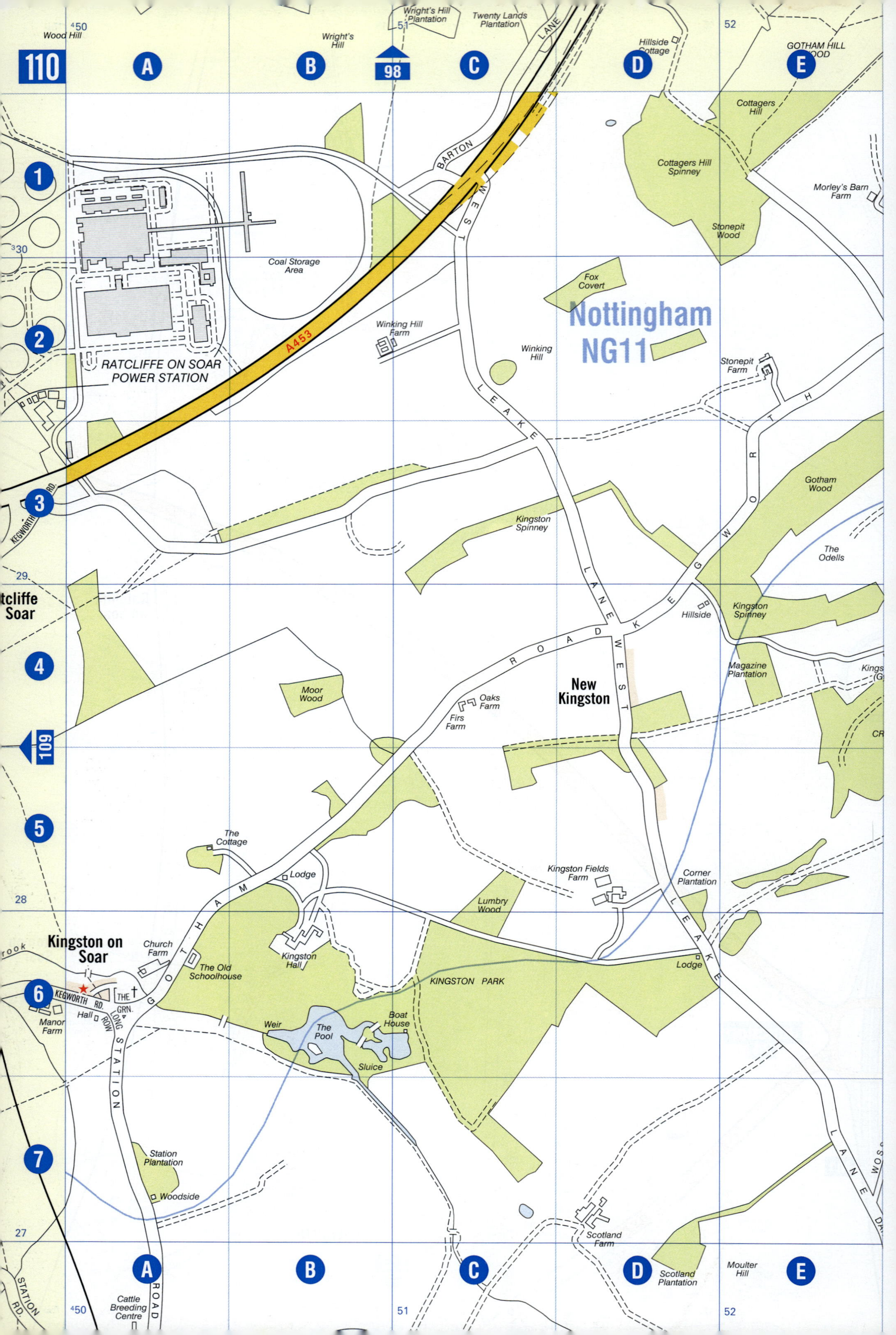

110
50
51
52
A
B
98
C
D
E
Wood Hill
Wright's Hill
Wright's Hill Plantation
Twenty Lands Plantation
Hillside Cottage
GOTHAM HILL WOOD
1
Cottagers Hill
30
Cottagers Hill Spinney
Morley's Barn Farm
Stonepit Wood
Coal Storage Area
Fox Covert
Nottingham NG11
2
A453
RATCLIFFE ON SOAR POWER STATION
Winking Hill Farm
Winking Hill
Stonepit Farm
KEGWORTH RD.
3
29
Kingston Spinney
Gotham Wood
Ratcliffe on Soar
The Odells
LEAKE LANE WEST
Hillside
Kingston Spinney
ROAD
Moor Wood
4
Magazine Plantation
Kings (G
109
Oaks Farm
New Kingston
Firs Farm
The Cottage
5
Kings (G
CR
28
Lodge
Kingston Fields Farm
Corner Plantation
Kingston on Soar
Church Farm
The Old Schoolhouse
Kingston Hall
Lumbry Wood
LEAKE LANE
Lodge
KEGWORTH RD.
6
THE GRN.
Manor Farm
Hall
LONG ROW
GOTHAM ROAD
STATION
KINGSTON PARK
Weir
The Pool
Boat House
Sluice
Station Plantation
7
27
Woodside
Scotland Farm
Scotland Plantation
Moulter Hill
STATION RD.
A
B
C
D
E
50
Cattle Breeding Centre
ROAD
51
52

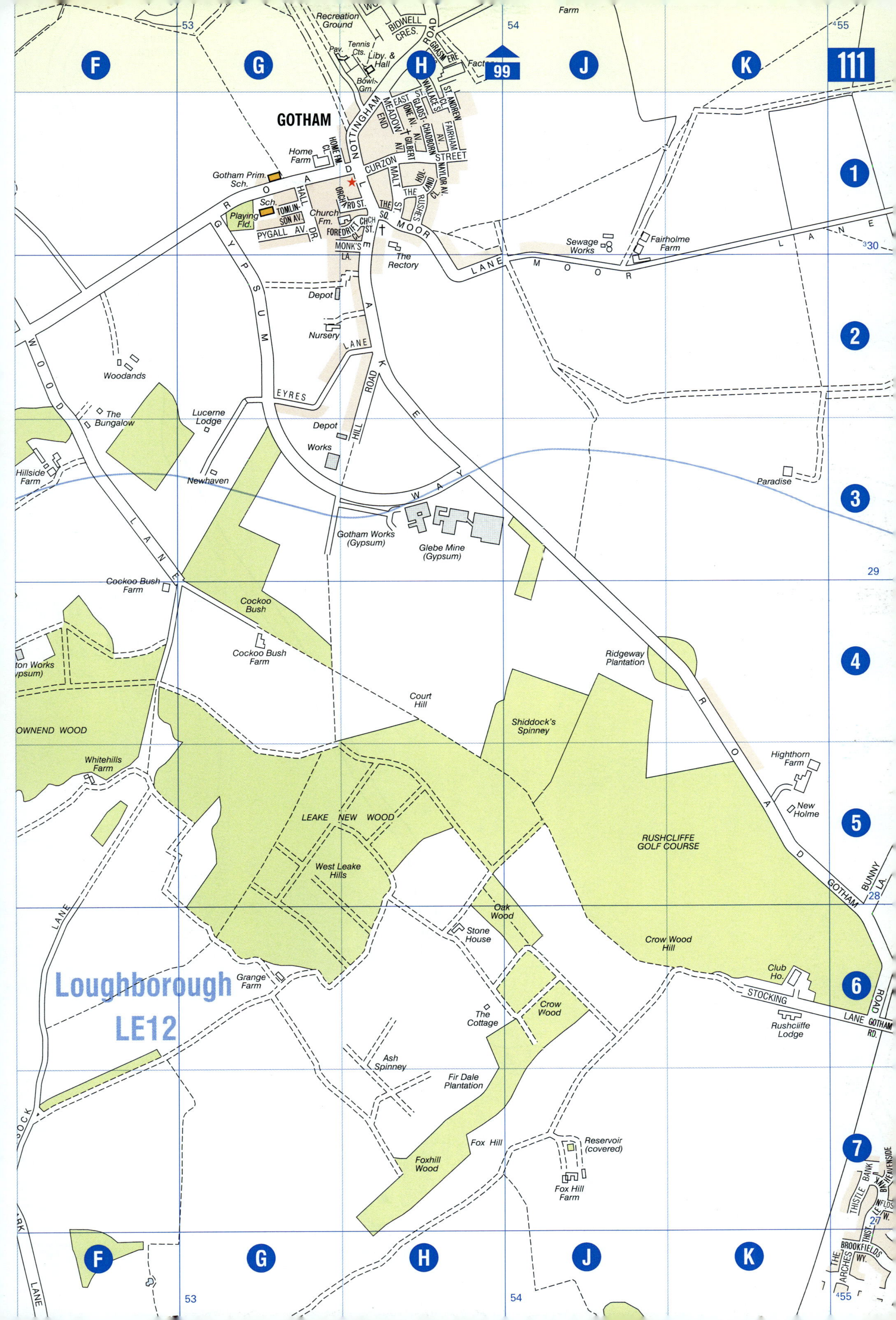

F
G
H
99
J
K
111
GOTHAM
Recreation Ground
Pav.
Tennis Cts. Liby. & Hall
Bowl. Grn.
BIDWELL CRES.
Farm
Factory
GRASMERE
St. ANDREW
WALLACE'S
EAST END
ONE AV.
GLADSTONE AV.
GILBERT AV.
CHADBORN AV.
FAIRHAM AV.
NAYLOR AV.
STREET
Home Farm
HOME FM. CL.
Gotham Prim. Sch.
Sch.
TOMLINSON AV.
Playing Fld.
PYGALL AV.
CURZON
MALT
ST.
GILBERT AV.
THE RUSHES
THE SQ.
Church Fm.
CH.CH. ST.
FOREDRIFT CL.
MONK'S LA.
ORCHARD ST.
The Rectory
Depot
Nursery
NOTTINGHAM ROAD
MEADOW
GYPSUM LANE
Sewage Works
Fairholme Farm
LANE MOOR
Woodlands
The Bungalow
Lucerne Lodge
Hillside Farm
Newhaven
EYRES
HILL ROAD
KEGWORTH ROAD
Depot
Works
Paradise
WAY
Gotham Works (Gypsum)
Glebe Mine (Gypsum)
Cockoo Bush Farm
Cockoo Bush
Cockoo Bush Farm
...ton Works (Gypsum)
Ridgeway Plantation
Highthorn Farm
New Holme
OWNEND WOOD
Whitehills Farm
Court Hill
Shiddock's Spinney
LEAKE NEW WOOD
West Leake Hills
RUSHCLIFFE GOLF COURSE
GOTHAM ROAD
BUNNY LA.
LANE
Oak Wood
Stone House
Crow Wood Hill
Club Ho.
STOCKING LANE
Loughborough LE12
Grange Farm
Crow Wood
The Cottage
Rushcliffe Lodge
GOTHAM RD.
Ash Spinney
Fir Dale Plantation
Fox Hill
Foxhill Wood
Reservoir (covered)
Fox Hill Farm
THISTLE BANK
LANE
BR. HEAVENSIDE
FNFLDS WY.
THISTLE
THE ARCHES
BROOKFIELDS WY.
53
54
55
30
29
28
27
1
2
3
4
5
6
7

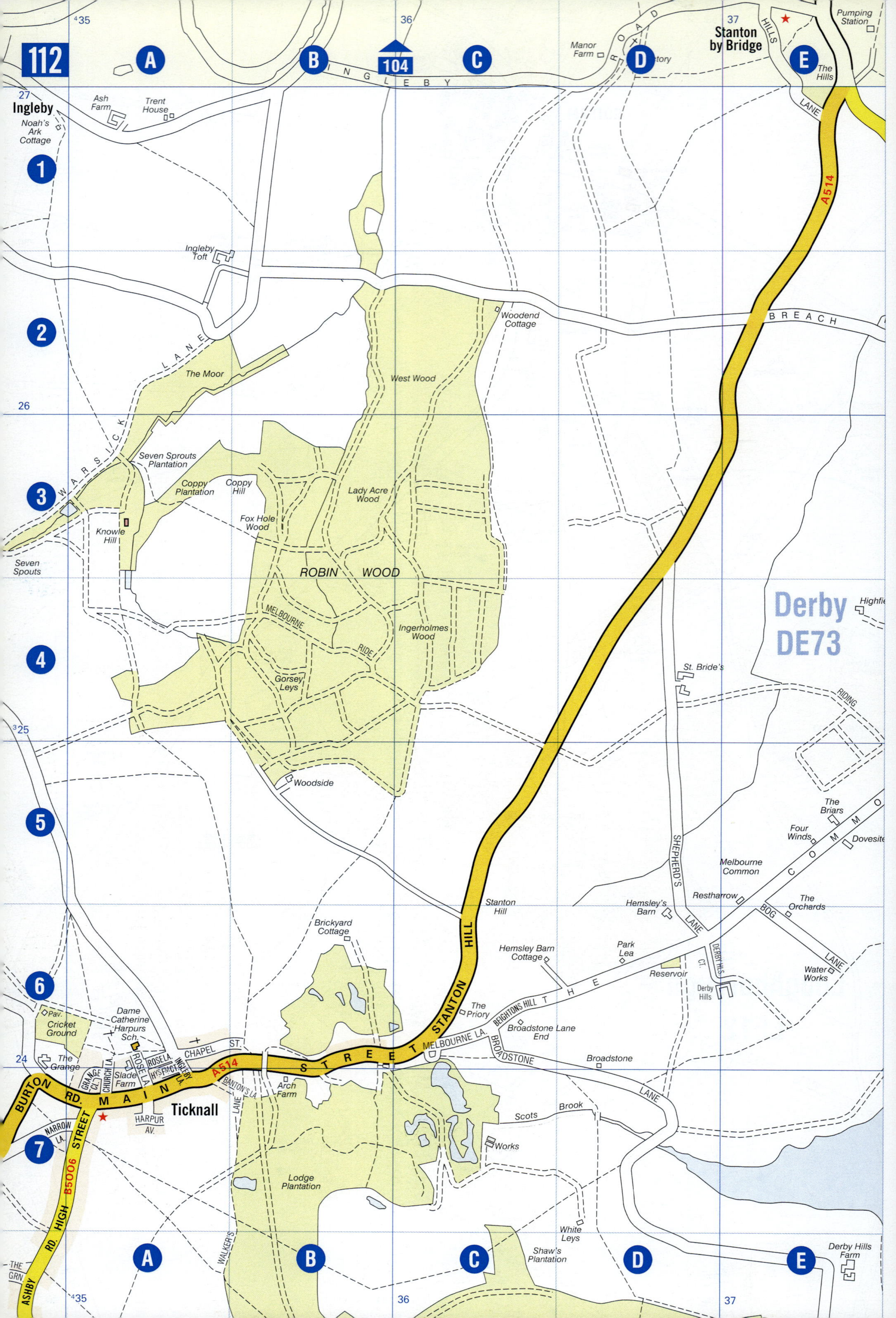
112
435
36
104
37
Stanton by Bridge
A
B
C
D
E
Ingleby
Noah's Ark Cottage
Ash Farm
Trent House
Pumping Station
ROAD
Manor Farm
tory
HILLS
The Hills
1
BREACH
Ingleby Toft
INGLEBY
LANE
A514
2
26
Woodend Cottage
West Wood
The Moor
WARSICK LANE
Seven Sprouts Plantation
Coppy Plantation
Coppy Hill
Lady Acre Wood
3
Fox Hole Wood
Knowle Hill
Seven Spouts
ROBIN WOOD
Derby DE73
Highfie
MELBOURNE
Ingerholmes Wood
St. Bride's
RIDING
4
325
RIDE
Gorsey Leys
The Briars
Woodside
SHEPHERD'S LANE
Four Winds
Dovesit
COMMO
5
Melbourne Common
Restharrow
The Orchards
Stanton Hill
Hemsley's Barn
BOG LANE
DERBY HLS. CT.
Brickyard Cottage
Hemsley Barn Cottage
Park Lea
Water Works
6
Pav.
Cricket Ground
Dame Catherine Harpurs Sch.
STANTON HILL
Reservoir
Derby Hills
24
The Grange
GRANGE CL.
CHURCH LA.
ROSELA
ROSELA
HY SFM CL.
INGLEBY LA.
CHAPEL ST.
A514
MAIN STREET
Melbourne La.
The Priory
Beightons Hill
THE
Broadstone Lane End
BROADSTONE LANE
Broadstone
BURTON RD.
MAIN STREET
NARROW LA.
Slade Farm
Ticknall
HARPUR AV.
BANTON'S LA.
Arch Farm
Scots Brook
7
THE GRN
ASHBY RD. HIGH STREET
B5006
WALKER'S LA.
Lodge Plantation
Works
White Leys
Shaw's Plantation
Derby Hills Farm
A
B
C
D
E
435
36
37

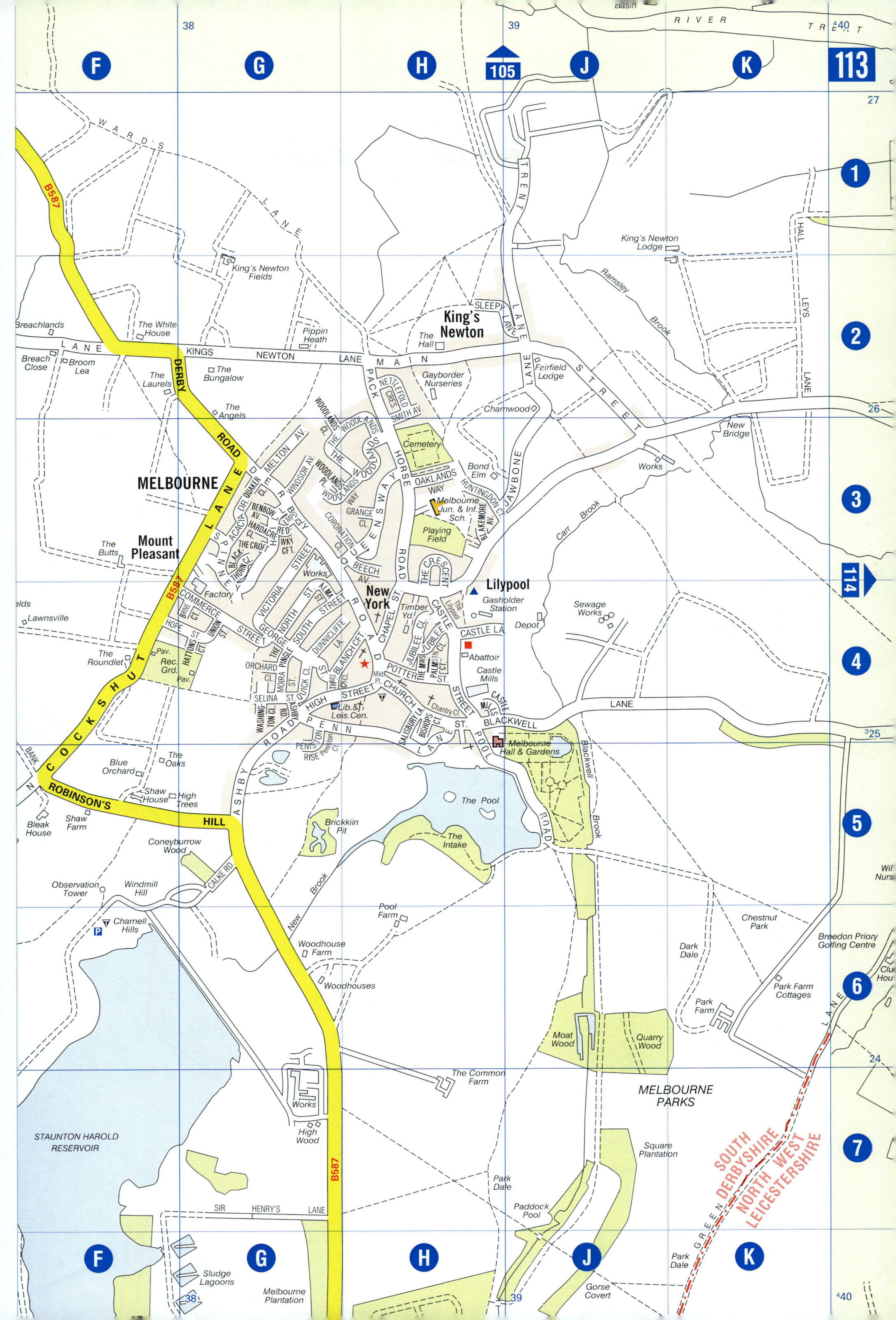
113
105
114
38
39
40
27
26
25
24
F G H J K
1 2 3 4 5 6 7
RIVER TRENT
Basin
WARDS LANE
B587
DERBY ROAD
LANE
King's Newton Fields
Breachlands
The White House
Breach Close
Broom Lea
The Laurels
The Bungalow
The Angels
KINGS NEWTON LANE
MAIN STREET
Pippin Heath
King's Newton
The Hall
Netherfield Cres.
Gayborder Nurseries
SLEEPY LANE
King's Newton Lodge
Ramsley Brook
Charnwood
Feirfield Lodge
JAWBONE LANE
New Bridge
Works
MELBOURNE
Mount Pleasant
The Butts
PINE LANE
ASPEN
MELTON AV.
WINDSOR AV.
DR. QUAKER CL.
BENBOW AV.
ACACIA CL.
HARDACRE CL.
THE CROFT
BLACK THORN CZ.
RED CFT.
IMPD
CLY
THE WOODLANDS
WOODLANDS CL.
WOODLANDS PL.
WOODLANDS WAY
GRANGE CL.
CORONATION CL.
BEECH AV.
QUEENSWAY
HORSE SHOE
OAKLANDS WAY
Cemetery
SMITH AV.
PACK HORSE ROAD
HUNTINGDON CL.
BLAKEMORE CL.
Melbourne Jun. & Inf. Sch.
Bond Elm
Playing Field
Carr Brook
Lilypool
Gasholder Station
Works
Sewage Works
The Lilypool
New York
Victoria Street
George Street
North Street
South Street
DUNNICLIFFE LA.
NINE ST.
PINGLE ST.
Works
THE CRESCENT
CASTLE ST.
JUBILEE ST.
THE MILLS
PALMISTO CT.
CASTLE LA.
Abattoir
Castle Mills
Depot
Lawnsville
fields
COMMERCE ST.
HOPE ST.
UNION ST.
HATTONS CT.
BRNE CT.
Factory
The Roundlet
Pav. Rec. Grd.
Pav.
Pav.
ORCHARD CL.
MOIRA ST.
QUICK CL.
SELINA ST.
WASHING-TON CL.
ASHBY ROAD
HIGH STREET
BLANCH CFT.
THIS
CFCL
Mkt Pl.
CHURCH STREET
Chantry Cl.
BISHOPS CT.
SALISBURY LA.
ST.
POTTER STREET
CASTLE STREET
POOL
CASTLE MILLS
BLACKWELL
Melbourne Hall & Gardens
Chapel St.
Timber Yd.
Lib. & Leis. Cen.
PENN
PENISTON RISE
Painton CT.
Blackwell Brook
The Oaks
Blue Orchard
Shaw House
High Trees
LANE
BANK
ROBINSON'S HILL
Bleak House
Shaw Farm
Coneyburrow Wood
CALKE RD.
Windmill Hill
Observation Tower
Charnell Hills
P
STAUNTON HAROLD RESERVOIR
Brickkiln Pit
New Brook
The Pool
The Intake
Pool Farm
Woodhouse Farm
Woodhouses
Works
High Wood
SIR HENRY'S LANE
B587
The Common Farm
MELBOURNE PARKS
Moat Wood
Quarry Wood
Park Farm
Dark Dale
Chestnut Park
Breedon Priory Golfing Centre
Park Farm Cottages
Club Hou
Wil Nurs
Square Plantation
Park Dale
Paddock Pool
Gorse Covert
Park Dale
GREEN LANE
SOUTH DERBYSHIRE
NORTH WEST LEICESTERSHIRE
Melbourne Plantation
Sludge Lagoons
Melbourne Plantation

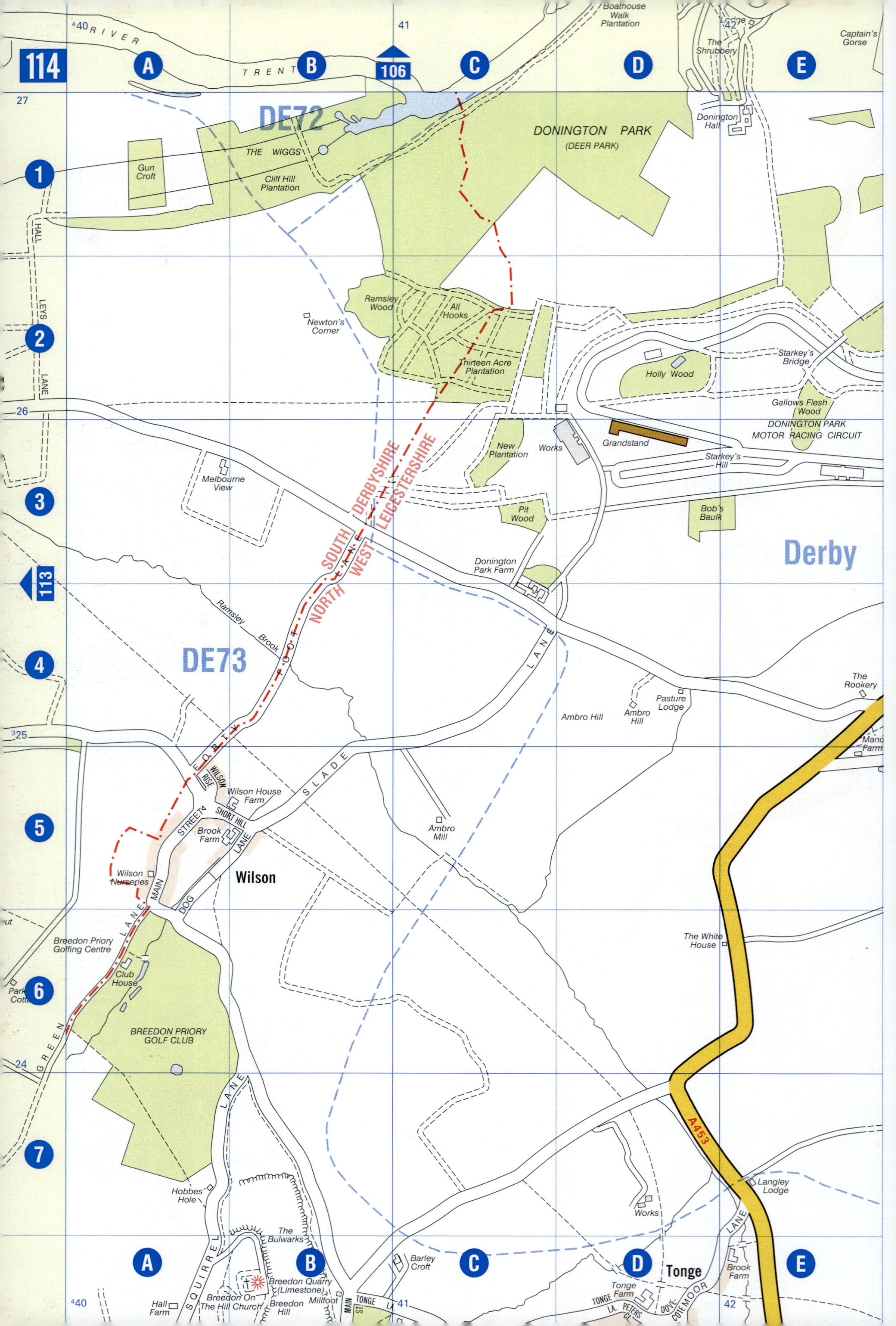
114
106
113
A B C D E
1 2 3 4 5 6 7
40 41 42
27 26 25 24
RIVER TRENT
DE72
THE WIGGS
Gun Croft
Cliff Hill Plantation
HALL LEYS LANE
Newton's Corner
Ramsley Wood
All Hooks
Thirteen Acre Plantation
DONINGTON PARK
(DEER PARK)
Boathouse Walk Plantation
Captain's Gorse
The Shrubbery
Donington Hall
Starkey's Bridge
Holly Wood
Gallows Flesh Wood
DONINGTON PARK MOTOR RACING CIRCUIT
New Plantation
Works
Grandstand
Starkey's Hill
Pit Wood
Bob's Baulk
Melbourne View
SOUTH DERBYSHIRE
NORTH WEST LEICESTERSHIRE
FOOT LANE
Ramsley Brook
DE73
Derby
Donington Park Farm
LANE
Pasture Lodge
Ambro Hill
Ambro Hill
The Rookery
Manor Farm
SLADE LANE
Ambro Mill
Wilson House Farm
WILSON RISE
SHORT HILL
STREET
Brook Farm
Wilson
Wilson Nurseries
MAIN LANE
DOG LANE
GREEN LANE
Breedon Priory Golfing Centre
Club House
Park Cotts
BREEDON PRIORY GOLF CLUB
The White House
A453
Hobbes' Hole
The Bulwarks
SQUIRREL LANE
Barley Croft
Works
Langley Lodge
Tonge
Brook Farm
Tonge Farm
COTEMOOR LANE
DOVE
Hall Farm
Breedon On The Hill Church
Breedon Quarry (Limestone)
Breedon Hill
Millfoot
MAIN ST
TONGE LANE
LA. PETERS CL.

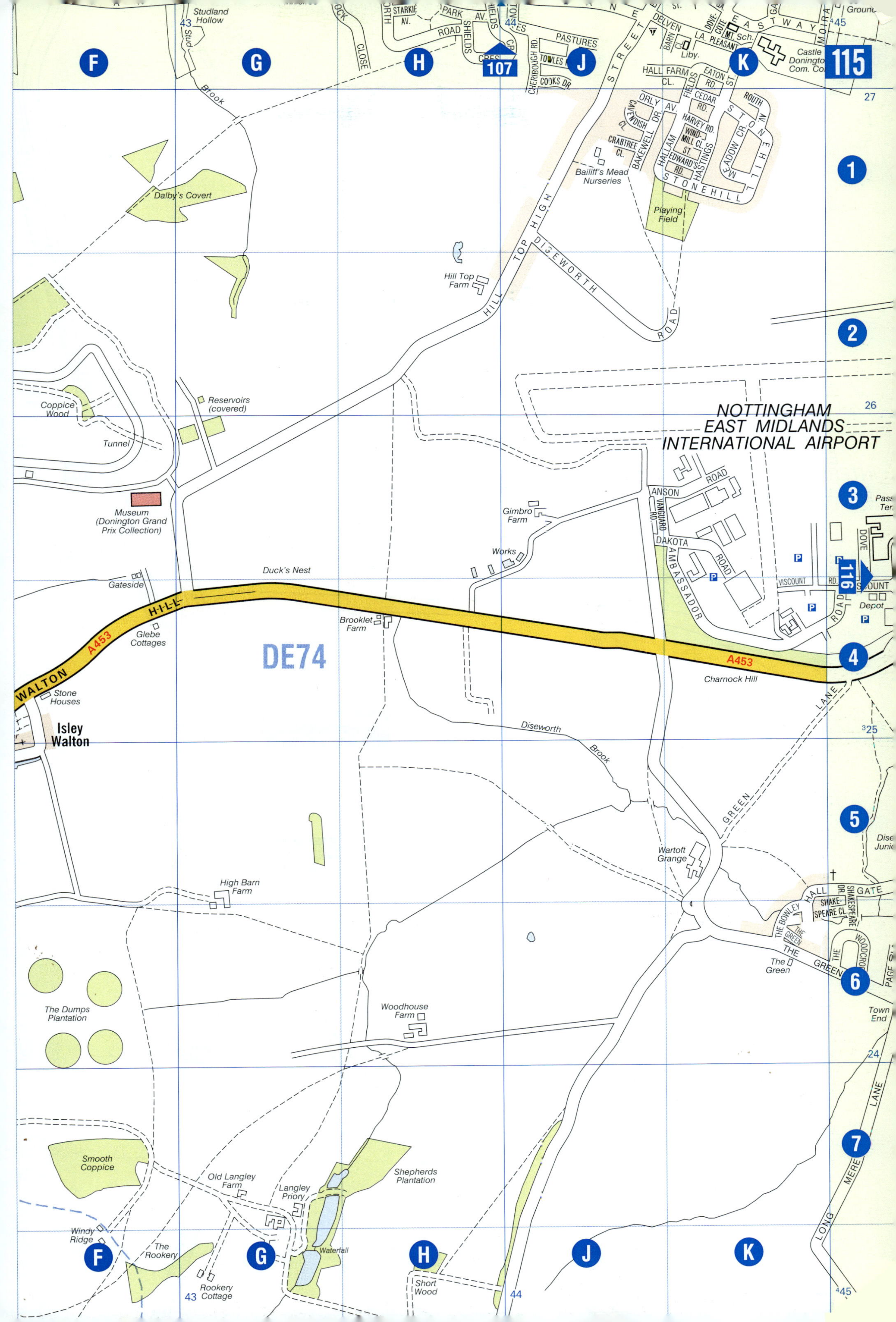

Studland Hollow
43
F
G
H
STARKIE AV.
PARK AV.
ROAD
SHIELDS
FIELDS
CRES.
TOWLES
44
PASTURES
CHERRBOROUGH RD.
COOKS DR.
J
STREET
DELVEN
DOVE-
COTE
LA. PLEASANT
BARN CL.
MT. Sch.
Liby.
EASTWAY
MOIRA
Ground
45
K
Castle Donington Com. Co
115
27
HALL FARM CL.
FIELDS
EATON RD.
CEDAR RD.
STONEHILL
ROUTH AV.
1
CAVENDISH DR.
ORLY AV.
BAKEWELL DR.
HARVEY RD.
WIND. MILL CL.
HALLAM ST.
EDWARD RD.
HASTINGS
STONEHILL
MEADOW CR.
CRABTREE CL.
Bailiff's Mead Nurseries
Playing Field
STONEHILL
Dalby's Covert
Hill Top Farm
HILL TOP HIGH
DISEWORTH
ROAD
2
26
NOTTINGHAM
EAST MIDLANDS
INTERNATIONAL AIRPORT
Coppice Wood
Reservoirs (covered)
Tunnel
ANSON ROAD
VANGUARD RD.
DAKOTA
AMBASSADOR ROAD
Gimbro Farm
Works
Pass Ter
3
DOVE ST
P
VISCOUNT
P
116
UNT
Museum (Donington Grand Prix Collection)
Duck's Nest
Gateside
HILL
Brooklet Farm
A453
A453
Charnock Hill
Depot
P
4
WALTON
Glebe Cottages
DE74
Stone Houses
Isley Walton
Diseworth Brook
LANE
3 25
High Barn Farm
Wartoft Grange
GREEN
5
Dise Junc
The Dumps Plantation
Woodhouse Farm
HALL GATE
SHAKE-SPEARE CL.
SHAKESPEARE DR.
THE BOWLEY
THE GREEN
WOODCROFT
THE GREEN
The Green
PAGE
6
Town End
24
Smooth Coppice
Old Langley Farm
Shepherds Plantation
Langley Priory
MERE LANE
7
Windy Ridge
The Rookery
Waterfall
Short Wood
LONG LANE
F
G
H
J
K
Rookery Cottage
43
44
45

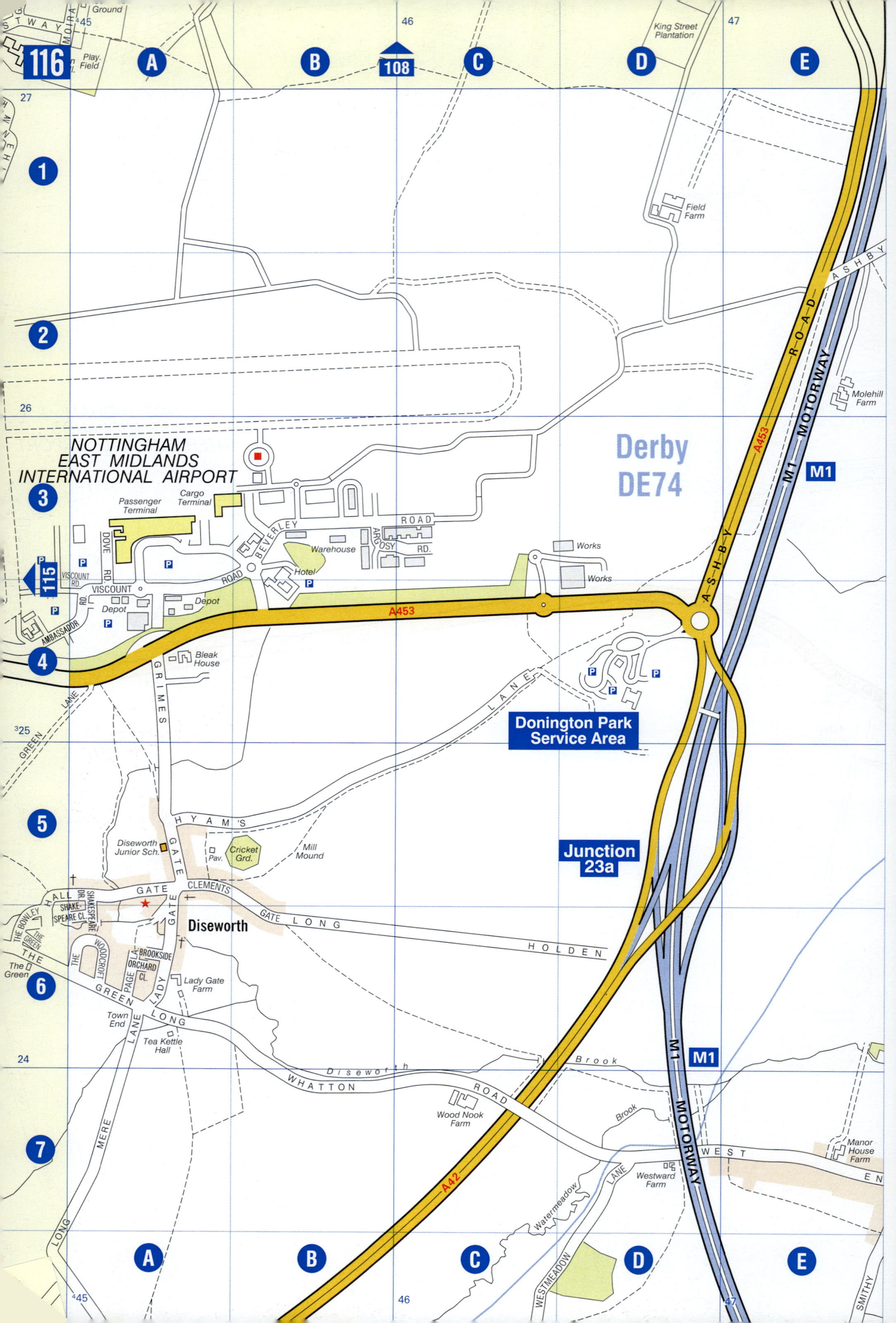
116
A B 108 C D E
45 MOIRA Ground Play. Field King Street Plantation 47
46
THE CHANNEL 27
1
Field Farm
2
26
Derby DE74
Molehill Farm
NOTTINGHAM EAST MIDLANDS INTERNATIONAL AIRPORT
3
Passenger Terminal
Cargo Terminal
BEVERLEY ROAD
Warehouse
ARGOSY RD.
Works
Works
115
DOVE RD.
VISCOUNT RD.
VISCOUNT
Hotel
Depot
Depot
AMBASSADOR
A453
Bleak House
GRIMES LANE
ROAD
Donington Park Service Area
A453
M1 MOTORWAY
M1
ASHBY ROAD
GREEN LANE
325
HYAM'S GATE
5
Diseworth Junior Sch.
Pav.
Cricket Grd.
Mill Mound
Junction 23a
THE BOWLEY
HALL
SHAKESPEARE CL.
SHAKESPEARE DR.
GATE
GATE
CLEMENTS
GATE LONG
Diseworth
HOLDEN
THE GREEN
THE
WOODCROFT
PAGE LA.
ORCHARD CL.
BROOKSIDE
LADY GATE
6
The Green
Lady Gate Farm
GREEN LANE
LONG
Town End
Tea Kettle Hall
MERE LANE
24
Diseworth Brook
WHATTON ROAD
Brook
M1 MOTORWAY
M1
Wood Nook Farm
Brook
Manor House Farm
7
A42
Westward Farm
WEST EN
WATERMEADOW LANE
SMITHY
A B 46 C WESTMEADOW D 47 E
445
445

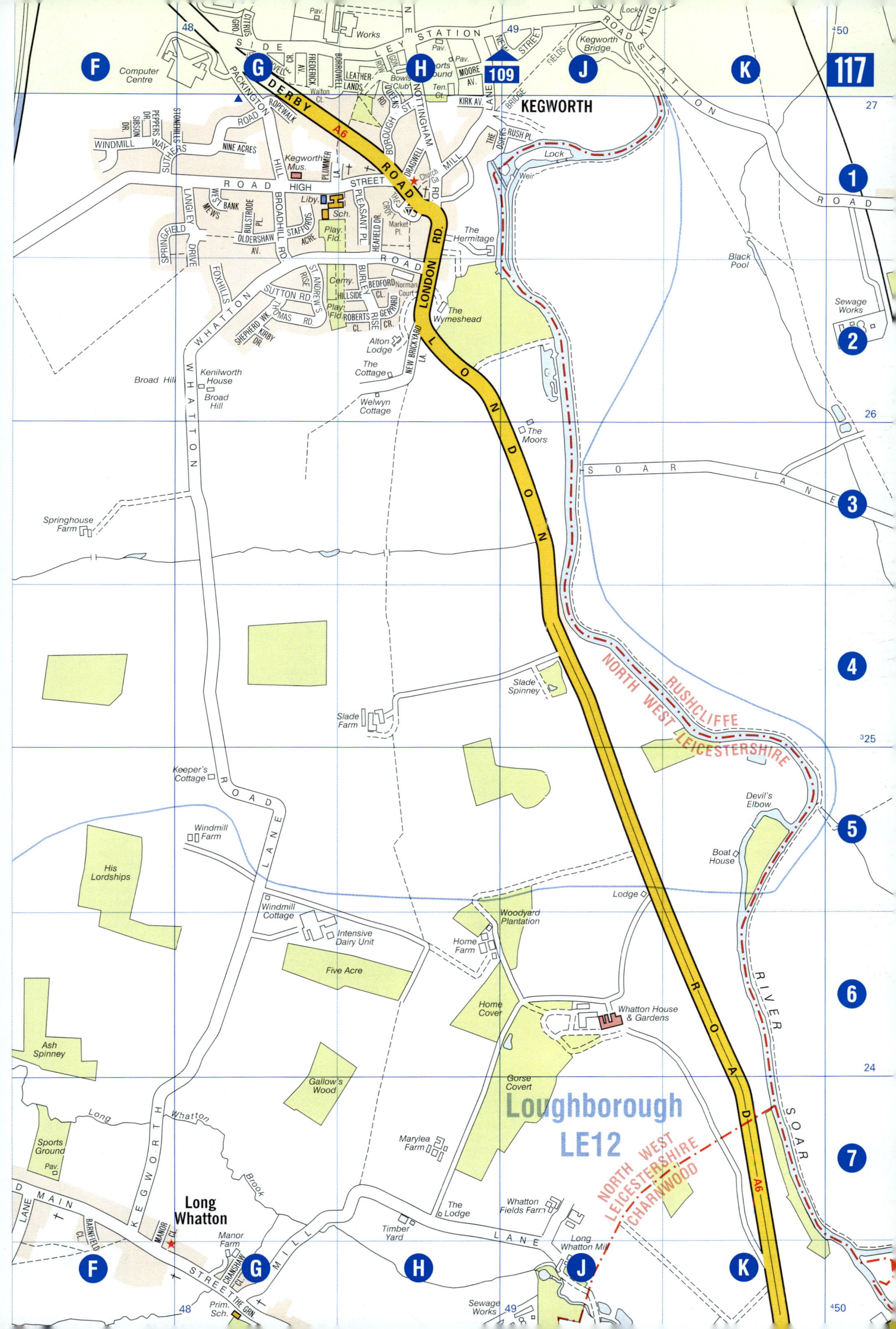

117
KEGWORTH
Loughborough LE12
Long Whatton
Computer Centre
Kegworth Bridge
Kegworth Mus.
Kegworth Station
Derby Road
A6
Packington Hill
Ropewalk
Windmill Way
Suthers Road
Peppers Dr.
Sibson Dr.
Stonehills
Nine Acres
West Bank
Langley Mews
Springfield Drive
Bulstrode Pl.
Broadhill Rd.
Stafford Acre
Oldershaw Av.
Foxhills
Whatton Road
Sutton Rd.
St. Andrew's Rise
Hillside
Thomas Rd.
Shepherd Wk.
Kirby Dr.
Burley Cl.
Bedford Cl.
Norman Court
Roberts Cl.
Geyward Cr.
High Street
Citrus Gro.
Frederick Av.
Borrowell Cr.
Walton Ct.
Leather-lands
Borough Rd.
Queens St.
Nottingham Rd.
Bowls Club
Ten. Ct.
Sports Ground
Pav.
Moore Av.
Kirk Av.
New Bridge
The Oshers
Station Fields
King Road
Lock
Mill
Dragwell
Church Ga.
Church Ga Rd.
The Croft
Market Pl.
Sch.
Liby.
Play. Fld.
Plummer La.
Heather Dr.
Pleasant Pl.
London Rd.
London Road
The Hermitage
The Wymeshead
Alton Lodge
New Brickyard La.
The Cottage
Welwyn Cottage
The Moors
Rush Pl.
Lock
Weir
Black Pool
Sewage Works
Soar Lane
Springhouse Farm
Broad Hill
Kenilworth House
Broad Hill
Whatton Road
Keeper's Cottage
Windmill Farm
His Lordships
Windmill Cottage
Intensive Dairy Unit
Five Acre
Slade Farm
Slade Spinney
Woodyard Plantation
Home Farm
Home Cover
Lodge
Whatton House & Gardens
Rushcliffe
North West Leicestershire
Devil's Elbow
Boat House
River Soar
Ash Spinney
Sports Ground
Pav.
Long Whatton
Main Lane
Barnfield Cl.
Manor Cl.
Cransmoor
The Grn.
Prim. Sch.
Kegworth Street
Mill Street
Long Whatton Brook
Manor Farm
Timber Yard
Gallow's Wood
Marylea Farm
The Lodge
Whatton Fields Farm
Long Whatton Mill
Gorse Covert
North West Leicestershire
Charnwood
Sewage Works
A6
109

# INDEX

Including Streets, Industrial Estates, Selected Subsidiary Addresses
and Selected Places of Interest.

## HOW TO USE THIS INDEX

1. Each street name is followed by its Posttown or Postal Locality and then by its map reference; e.g. Aaron Clo. *Nott* —1D **82** is in the Nottingham Posttown and is to be found in square 1D on page **82**. The page number being shown in bold type. A strict alphabetical order is followed in which Av., Rd., St., etc. (though abbreviated) are read in full and as part of the street name; e.g. Abbotsbury Clo. appears after Abbot Rd. but before Abbots Clo.

2. Streets and a selection of Subsidiary names not shown on the Maps, appear in the index in *Italics* with the thoroughfare to which it is connected shown in brackets; e.g. *Albert Sq. Nott* —4A **64** (off Church St.)

3. An example of a selected place of interest is **Albion Leisure Cen. —6D 44**

4. Map references shown in brackets; e.g. Abbey St. *Der*—5K **73** (7C **6**) refer to entries that also appear on the large scale pages 4-7.

## GENERAL ABBREVIATIONS

| | | | | |
|---|---|---|---|---|
| All : Alley | Cir : Circus | Gt : Great | M : Mews | Sq : Square |
| App : Approach | Clo : Close | Grn : Green | Mt : Mount | Sta : Station |
| Arc : Arcade | Comn : Common | Gro : Grove | Mus : Museum | St : Street |
| Av : Avenue | Cotts : Cottages | Ho : House | N : North | Ter : Terrace |
| Bk : Back | Ct : Court | Ind : Industrial | Pal : Palace | Trad : Trading |
| Boulevd : Boulevard | Cres : Crescent | Info : Information | Pde : Parade | Up : Upper |
| Bri : Bridge | Cft : Croft | Junct : Junction | Pk : Park | Va : Vale |
| B'way : Broadway | Dri : Drive | La : Lane | Pas : Passage | Vw : View |
| Bldgs : Buildings | E : East | Lit : Little | Pl : Place | Vs : Villas |
| Bus : Business | Embkmt : Embankment | Lwr : Lower | Quad : Quadrant | Vis : Visitors |
| Cvn : Caravan | Est : Estate | Mc : Mac | Res : Residential | Wlk : Walk |
| Cen : Centre | Fld : Field | Mnr : Manor | Ri : Rise | W : West |
| Chu : Church | Gdns : Gardens | Mans : Mansions | Rd : Road | Yd : Yard |
| Chyd : Churchyard | Gth : Garth | Mkt : Market | Shop : Shopping | |
| Circ : Circle | Ga : Gate | Mdw : Meadow | S : South | |

## POSTTOWN AND POSTAL LOCALITY ABBREVIATIONS

| | | | | |
|---|---|---|---|---|
| *Altn* : Allenton | *Chad* : Chaddesden | *Heag* : Heage | *Melb* : Melbourne | *Sin* : Sinfin |
| *Alst* : Allestree | *Chel* : Chellaston | *Hean* : Heanor | *Mick* : Mickleover | *Smal* : Smalley |
| *Alv* : Alvaston | *Clif* : Clifton | *H'ton* : Hemington | *Milf* : Milford | *Snei* : Sneinton |
| *Ambtn* : Ambaston | *Clip* : Clipston | *Hilt* : Hilton | *M'ly* : Morley | *Spon* : Spondon |
| *Ambgt* : Ambergate | *Cod* : Codnor | *Holb* : Holbrook (Belper) | *N'fld* : Netherfield | *Stan* : Stanley |
| *Ann* : Annesley | *Cols B* : Colston Bassett | *H'brk* : Holbrook (Sheffield) | *Neth H* : Nether Heage | *Stan C* : Stanley Common |
| *Arn* : Arnold | *Colw* : Colwick | *Hol P* : Holme Pierrepont | *New B* : New Basford | *Stan B* : Stanton-by-Bridge |
| *Asl* : Aslockton | *Colw I* : Colwick Ind. Est. | *Hors* : Horsley | *Newt* : Newthorpe | *Stan D* : Stanton-by-Dale |
| *Ast T* : Aston-on-Trent | *Colw P* : Colwick Park | *Hors W* : Horsley Woodhouse | *Nwtn* : Newton | *S'fd* : Stapleford |
| *Att* : Atterton | *Coss* : Cossall | *Hov* : Hoveringham | *Nott* : Nottingham | *Sten F* : Stenson Fields |
| *Aws* : Awsworth | *Cotg* : Cotgrave | *Huck* : Hucknall | *Nun* : Nuneaton | *Stock* : Stockhill |
| *Bagt* : Bagthorpe | *Cox* : Coxbench | *Ilk* : Ilkeston | *Nut* : Nuthall | *Strel* : Strelley |
| *Bar T* : Barrow-on-Trent | *C Bis* : Cropwell Bishop | *Iron* : Ironville | *Oak* : Oakwood | *Sun* : Sunnyhill |
| *Bar F* : Barton-in-Fabis | *C But* : Cropwell Butler | *Jack* : Jacksdale | *Ock* : Ockbrook | *Sut B* : Sutton Bonington |
| *Bees* : Beeston | *Dal A* : Dale Abbey | *Keg* : Kegworth | *Old B* : Old Basford | *Swar* : Swarkestone |
| *Belp* : Belper | *Dar A* : Darley Abbey | *Keyw* : Keyworth | *Oxt* : Oxton | *T'wd* : Thorneywood |
| *Belt* : Belton | *Day* : Daybrook | *Klbrn* : Kilburn | *Pap* : Papplewick | *Thrum* : Thrumpton |
| *B Vil* : Bestwood Village | *Den* : Denby | *Kimb* : Kimberley | *Park T* : Park, The | *Thul* : Thulston |
| *Bilb* : Bilborough | *Den V* : Denby Village | *King S* : Kingston-on-Soar | *Pear T* : Pear Tree | *Thurl* : Thurlaston |
| *Bing* : Bingham | *Der* : Derby | *Kgswy* : Kingsway | *Plum* : Plumtree | *Tickn* : Ticknall |
| *Black* : Blackbrook | *Dis* : Diseworth | *Kirk L* : Kirk Langley | *Plun* : Plungar | *Toll* : Tollerton |
| *Blen I* : Bleneim Ind. Est. | *Dray* : Draycott | *Lamb* : Lambley | *Pri P* : Pride Park | *Trow* : Trowell |
| *Borr* : Borrowash | *Duf* : Duffield | *Lan M* : Langley Mill | *Quar* : Quarndon | *Turn* : Turnditch |
| *Boul M* : Boulton Moor | *E Bri* : East Bridgford | *Lent* : Lenton | *Quar H* : Quarry Hill Ind. Est. | *Und* : Underwood |
| *Bradm* : Bradmore | *E Leak* : East Leake | *Lent L* : Lenton Lane Ind. Est. | *Q Dri* : Queens Drive Ind. Est. | *Wain* : Waingroves |
| *Bramc* : Bramcote | *Eastw* : Eastwood | *L'by* : Linby | *Rad T* : Radcliffe-on-Trent | *Wat* : Waterthorpe |
| *Bread* : Breadsall | *Edw* : Edwalton | *L Eat* : Little Eaton | *Rat S* : Ratcliffe-on-Soar | *Watn* : Watnall |
| *Breas* : Breaston | *Egg* : Egginton | *L'ver* : Littleover | *Red* : Redhill | *W Bri* : West Bridgford |
| *Bree H* : Breedon-on-the-Hill | *Epp* : Epperstone | *Locki* : Lockington | *Ridd* : Riddings | *W Hal* : West Hallam |
| *Brins* : Brinsley | *Etw* : Etwall | *Long E* : Long Eaton | *Rip* : Ripley | *W Leak* : West Leake |
| *Bul* : Bulcote | *Find* : Findern | *Long W* : Long Whatton | *Ris* : Risley | *W Mead* : West Meadows Ind. Est. |
| *Bulw* : Bulwell | *For F* : Forest Fields | *Los* : Loscoe | *Rud* : Ruddington | *Wstn T* : Weston-on-Trent |
| *Bun* : Bunny | *Fos* : Foston | *Low* : Lowdham | *Sand* : Sandiacre | *W'wd* : Westwood |
| *Burna* : Burnaston | *Gam* : Gamston | *Lwr H* : Lower Hartshay | *Shard* : Shardlow | *What* : Whatton |
| *Bur J* : Burton Joyce | *Ged* : Gedling | *Lwr K* : Lower Kilburn | *Shelf* : Shelford | *Wilf* : Wilford |
| *But* : Butterley | *Gilt* : Giltbrook | *Mack* : Mackworth | *Shel L* : Shelton Lock | *Wind* : Windley |
| *C'tn* : Calverton | *Got* : Gotham | *Mak* : Makeney | *Sher* : Sherwood | *Woll* : Wollaton |
| *Cltn* : Carlton | *Greas* : Greasley | *Man I* : Manners Ind. Est. | *Sher R* : Sherwood Rise | *Wdbgh* : Woodborough |
| *Carr* : Carrington | *Gun* : Gunthorpe | *M'ley* : Mapperley (Ilkeston) | *Ship* : Shipley | *Wd'p* : Woodthorpe |
| *Cas D* : Castle Donington | *Hatt* : Hatton | *Map* : Mapperley (Nottingham) | *Shot* : Shottle | |
| *Cay* : Caythorpe | *H'wd* : Hazelwood | *Mare* : Marehay | *Shot G* : Shottle Gate | |

## INDEX


**A**aron Clo. *Nott* —1D **82**
Abba Clo. *Kimb* —6K **29**
Abbey Bri. *Nott* —5A **64**
Abbey Cir. *W Bri* —1J **83**
Abbey Clo. *Asl* —2H **71**
Abbey Clo. *Huck* —5E **16**
Abbey Ct. *Bees* —7F **63**
Abbey Ct. *Nott* —3B **64**
Abbey Dale Clo. *Klbrn* —6H **25**
*Abbeydale Wlk. Alv* —3K **93**
  (off Elvaston La., in two parts)
Abbey Dri. *Bees* —1F **81**
Abbeyfield Rd. *Nott* —7B **64**
Abbeyfields Clo. *Dar A* —5A **56**
Abbey Gdns. *Wstn T* —5B **106**

Abbey Gro. *Nott* —7H **49**
Abbey Hill. *Alst & Bread* —4A **56**
Abbey Hill Rd. *Alst* —5H **55**
Abbey La. *Asl* —2G **71**
Abbey La. *Dar A* —6A **56**
Abbey Rd. *Bees* —7F **63**
Abbey Rd. *Bing* —2C **70**
Abbey Rd. *Eastw* —3F **29**
Abbey Rd. *W Bri* —1J **83**
Abbey St. *Der* —5K **73** (7C **6**)
Abbey St. *Ilk* —4D **44**
Abbey St. *Nott* —5A **64**
Abbey Yd. *Dar A* —6A **56**
Abbot Clo. *Keyw* —5C **102**
Abbot Clo. *Oak* —5E **56**

Abbot M. *Dar A* —6A **56**
Abbot Rd. *Ilk* —1A **60**
Abbotsbury Clo. *Nott* —4K **31**
Abbots Clo. *Day* —7F **33**
Abbots Dri. *Huck* —6E **16**
Abbotsford Dri. *Nott*
  —1F **65** (1G **5**)
Abbotsford M. *Ilk* —3B **44**
Abbots Gro. *Belp* —7A **10**
Abbots Rd. *Huck* —6E **16**
Abbot St. *Aws* —2G **45**
Abbots Wlk. *Huck* —6E **16**
Abbots Way. *Nott* —3H **63**
Abbotts Barn Clo. *Der*
  —4K **73** (5C **6**)

Abbott St. *Hean* —4G **27**
Abbott St. *Long E* —3H **97**
Abells. *Den V* —4J **25**
Abercarn Clo. *Nott* —6H **31**
Aberdare Clo. *Oak* —5H **57**
Aberdeen St. *Nott* —2G **65** (3J **5**)
Aberford Av. *Nott* —6K **47**
Abingdon Bus. Cen. *Der* —7C **74**
Abingdon Dri. *Rud* —1F **101**
Abingdon Gdns. *Bees* —4D **80**
Abingdon Gdns. *Wd'p* —1J **49**
Abingdon Rd. *W Bri* —1J **83**
Abingdon Sq. *Nott* —5H **47**
Abingdon St. *Der* —2B **92**
Ablard Gdns. *Bees* —6C **80**

Abney Clo. *Mick* —6D **72**
Acacia Av. *Mick* —7C **72**
Acacia Clo. *Huck* —7H **17**
Acacia Ct. *Nott* —1F **65** (1H **5**)
Acacia Cres. *Cltn* —6D **50**
Acacia Dri. *Melb* —3G **113**
Acacia Gdns. *Watn* —5K **29**
Acacia Wlk. *Bees* —2F **81**
Academy Clo. *Nott* —3K **47**
Acaster Clo. *Bees* —4H **81**
Acer Cft. *Oak* —5E **56**
Acle Gdns. *Nott* —4H **31**
Acorn Av. *Gilt* —5F **29**
Acorn Bank. *W Bri* —4D **82**
Acorn Clo. *Shel L* —6E **92**

Acorn Dri. *Belp* —7K **9**
Acorn Av. *Ged* —3E **50**
Acorn Pk. *Lent L* —7A **64**
Acorn Way. *Belp* —7A **10**
Acorn Way. *Der* —6J **57**
Acott Hill. *Ilk* —1K **11**
Acourt St. *Nott* —1B **64**
Acrefield Way. *Chel* —7H **93**
Acre La. *Shard* —2E **106**
Acton Av. *Long E* —3J **97**
Acton Av. *Nott* —2K **47**
Acton Clo. *Long E* —3J **97**
Acton Gro. *Long E* —3J **97**
Acton Rd. *Arn* —5F **33**
Acton Rd. *Der* —2D **72**
Acton Rd. *Long E* —2J **97**
Acton Rd. Ind. Est. *Long E*
—3J **97**
Acton St. *Long E* —3J **97**
Adale Rd. *Smal* —5D **26**
Adams Clo. *Hean* —5F **27**
Adams Ct. *Ilk* —3C **44**
Adams Hill. *Keyw* —6D **102**
Adams Hill. *Nott* —5H **63**
Adam St. *Ilk* —1E **60**
Adbolton Av. *Ged* —5C **50**
Adbolton Gro. *W Bri* —5K **65**
Adbolton La. *W Bri & Hol P*
—6K **65**
Adbolton Lodge. *Cltn* —1C **66**
Adderley Clo. *Nott* —7C **32**
Addington Ct. *Rad T* —3A **68**
Addington Rd. *Nott* —1B **64**
Addison Dri. *Huck* —4E **16**
Addison Rd. *Cltn* —6K **49**
Addison Rd. *Der* —1B **92**
Addison St. *Nott* —7D **48** (1D **4**)
Addison Vs. *Eastw* —4C **28**
(in two parts)
Adelaide Clo. *Mick* —4C **72**
Adelaide Clo. *S'fd* —6K **61**
Adelaide Gro. *Nott* —5A **32**
Adel Dri. *Ged* —4C **50**
Adelphi Clo. *L'ver* —3E **90**
Adenburgh Dri. *Bees* —7D **80**
Adler Ct. *Der* —1B **74**
Admiral Clo. *Hean* —3G **27**
Adrian Clo. *Bees* —7K **79**
Adrian St. *Der* —3D **92**
Adwick Clo. *Mick* —6A **72**
Aeneas Ct. *Nott* —6D **48**
Agard St. *Der* —2K **73** (2B **6**)
Agnes Vs. *Nott* —4G **49**
Aidan Gdns. *Nott* —3C **32**
Aimploy Ct. *Der* —7A **74**
Ainley Clo. *Alv* —2F **93**
Ainsdale Cres. *Nott* —3G **47**
Ainsley Rd. *Nott* —1K **63**
Ainsworth Dri. *Der* —2J **91**
Ainsworth Dri. *Nott* —6D **64**
Aintree Clo. *Kimb* —6J **29**
Aira Clo. *Gam* —2B **84**
Airedale Clo. *Long E* —3E **96**
Airedale Ct. *Bees* —4A **80**
Airedale Wlk. *Alv* —3J **93**
Airedale Wlk. *Nott* —4C **62**
Aitchison Av. *Huck* —5F **17**
Alandene Av. *Watn* —6A **30**
Albany Clo. *Arn* —6G **33**
Albany Clo. *Huck* —7C **16**
Albany Ct. *S'fd* —6J **61**
Albany Rd. *Der* —4G **73**
Albany Rd. *Nott* —6C **48**
Albany St. *Ilk* —1E **60**
Albemarle Rd. *Chad* —1H **75**
Albemarle Rd. *Wd'p* —2F **49**
Alberta Ter. *Nott* —6C **48**
Albert Av. *Cltn* —7K **49**
Albert Av. *Jack* —1K **13**
Albert Av. *Nott* —6K **47**
Albert Av. *Nut* —6C **30**
Albert Av. *S'fd* —1H **79**
Albert Ball Clo. *Nott* —5B **32**
Albert Cres. *Chad* —4H **75**
Albert Einstein Cen. *Nott* —6K **63**
Albert Gro. *Nott* —2B **64**
**Albert Hall. —4D 4**
Albert Rd. *Bees* —7G **63**
Albert Rd. *Breas* —2K **95**
Albert Rd. *Chad* —3F **75**
Albert Rd. *Lent* —4B **64**
Albert Rd. *Long E* —1H **97**
Albert Rd. *Nott* —5F **49**
Albert Rd. *Rip* —2J **11**
Albert Rd. *Sand* —2F **79**
Albert Rd. *W Bri* —7H **65**
*Albert Sq. Nott* —4A *64*
(off Church St.)
Albert St. *Belp* —1K **23**

Albert St. *Der* —3A **74** (4E **6**)
Albert St. *Eastw* —2D **28**
(in two parts)
Albert St. *Ged* —5D **50**
Albert St. *Huck* —5H **17**
Albert St. *Ilk* —6C **44**
Albert St. *Nott* —3E **64** (4F **5**)
Albert St. *Rad T* —4K **67**
Albert St. *Rip* —3A **12**
Albert St. *S'fd* —1H **79**
Albion Cen., The. *Ilk* —6D **44**
**Albion Leisure Cen. —6D 44**
Albion Ri. *Arn* —4H **33**
Albion Rd. *Long E* —1K **97**
Albion St. *Bees* —1F **81**
Albion St. *Der* —3A **74** (4E **6**)
Albion St. *Ilk* —5D **44**
Albion St. *Nott* —4E **64** (6E **4**)
Albion St. *Rip* —3A **12**
Albrighton Av. *Sten F* —7H **91**
Albury Dri. *Nott* —5H **47**
Albury Sq. *Nott* —3C **64** (4A **4**)
Alcester Rd. *Nott* —7A **64**
Aldene Ct. *Bees* —3D **80**
Aldene Way. *Wdbgh* —1G **35**
Aldercar La. *Lan M* —1K **27**
Alder Clo. *Oak* —4E **56**
Alderfen Clo. *Shel L* —6D **92**
Alder Gdns. *Nott* —6G **31**
Alderley Ct. *Oak* —5G **57**
Aldermens Clo. *Nott* —5E **64**
Alderney St. *Nott* —4B **64**
Alder Rd. *Belp* —2A **24**
Alders Brook. *Hilt* —7A **88**
Aldersgate. *Der* —1D **72**
Alderslade Clo. *Ast T* —1D **106**
Aldersley Clo. *Find* —7A **90**
Alderton Rd. *Nott* —7E **32**
Alder Wlk. *Der* —5A **74** (7E **6**)
Alder Way. *Keyw* —7E **102**
Aldgate Clo. *Nott* —5G **31**
Aldred's La. *Hean & Lan M* —4J **27**
Aldridge Clo. *Bees* —6J **79**
Aldrin Clo. *Nott* —1F **47**
Aldworth Clo. *Nott* —7D **32**
Aldwych. *Der* —2E **72**
Aldwych Clo. *Arn* —4C **32**
Aldwych Clo. *Nut* —4D **46**
Alexander Clo. *Huck* —3H **17**
Alexander Fleming Building. *Nott*
—7K **63**
Alexander Rd. *Nott*
—3C **64** (5A **4**)
Alexandra Cres. *Bees* —2G **81**
Alexandra Gdns. *Der* —6B **74**
Alexandra Gdns. *Nott* —5D **48**
Alexandra M. *Nott* —6D **48**
Alexandra Rd. *Long E* —1H **97**
Alexandra St. *Eastw* —3D **28**
Alexandra St. *Nott* —6D **48**
Alexandra St. *S'fd* —2H **79**
Alexandre Clo. *L'ver* —3H **91**
Alford Clo. *Bees* —3G **81**
(in two parts)
Alford Rd. *W Bri & Edw* —2K **83**
Alfred Av. *Nott* —4J **49**
Alfred Clo. *Nott* —1E **64**
Alfred Rd. *Klbrn* —5G **25**
Alfred St. *Rip* —2A **12**
Alfred St. Central. *Nott*
—1E **64** (1F **5**)
Alfred St. N. *Nott* —1E **64**
Alfred St. S. *Nott* —2G **65** (2J **5**)
Alfreton Rd. *Bread & L Eat*
—4C **56**
Alfreton Rd. *Cod* —4E **12**
Alfreton Rd. *Der* —7B **56**
Alfreton Rd. *Nott* —7A **48** (1A **4**)
Alfreton Rd. *Und* —1F **15**
Alice St. *Der* —2B **74** (2F **7**)
Alison Av. *Huck* —3J **17**
Alison Clo. *Chad* —1F **75**
Alison Wlk. *Nott* —1F **65** (1G **5**)
Allan Av. *L'ver* —1C **90**
Allandale Rd. *Hean* —3F **27**
Allen Av. *Nott* —5J **49**
(in two parts)
Allendale. *Ilk* —7C **44**
Allendale Av. *Bees* —6D **80**
Allendale Av. *Nott* —5F **47**
Allen Fld. Ct. *Nott* —4B **64** (7A **4**)
Allen St. *Altn* —4E **92**
Allen St. *Huck* —4G **17**
Allen's Wlk. *Arn* —4H **33**
Allestree Clo. *Der* —1E **92**
Allestree La. *Der* —5H **55**
**Allestree Pk. —1K 55**
**Allestree Pk. Golf Course.**
**—2J 55**

Allestree St. *Der* —1E **92**
All Hallows Dri. *Ged* —4D **50**
Allington Av. *Nott* —4B **64**
Allison Gdns. *Bees* —4D **80**
Allison Gdns. *Ilk* —5E **44**
Allissa Av. *Rip* —5A **12**
All Saints Ct. *Mick* —7B **72**
All Saints St. *Nott* —1C **64** (1B **4**)
All Saints Ter. *Nott* —1C **64** (1B **4**)
Allstone Lee. *Belp* —7K **9**
Allwood Dri. *Cltn* —6C **50**
Allwood Gdns. *Huck* —6H **17**
Alma Clo. *Ged* —4E **50**
Alma Clo. *Nott* —1E **64** (1E **4**)
Alma Heights. *Mick* —7C **72**
Alma Hill. *Kimb* —5J **29**
Alma Rd. *Nott* —1H **65**
Alma St. *Der* —4K **73** (5C **6**)
Alma St. *Melb* —4G **113**
Alma St. *Nott* —6C **48**
Alma St. *Rip* —1K **11**
Almond Av. *Rip* —4K **11**
Almond Clo. *Huck* —7H **17**
Almond Clo. *Kimb* —6J **29**
Almond Ct. *Nott* —5E **64**
Almond St. *Der* —6A **73**
Almond Wlk. *Ged* —4E **50**
Almshouses. *Etw* —4D **88**
Almshouses La. *M'ly* —7H **41**
Alnwick Clo. *Nott* —7K **31**
Alpha Ter. *Nott* —1D **64**
Alpine Cres. *Cltn* —6C **50**
Alpine St. *Nott* —4A **48**
Alport Clo. *Belp* —7B **10**
**Alport Height. —1A 8**
Alport La. *Shot* —1A **8**
Alsager Clo. *Oak* —6G **57**
Alstonfield Dri. *Alst* —6J **55**
Althorpe St. *Nott* —2C **64** (3A **4**)
Alton Av. *Nott* —4D **82**
Alton Clo. *Alst* —4H **55**
Alton Clo. *W Bri* —5E **82**
Alton Dri. *Gilt* —5F **29**
Alton Rd. *Belp* —1C **24**
Alts Nook Way. *Shard* —1G **107**
Alum Clo. *Alv* —2J **93**
Alum Ct. *Nott* —5B **32**
Alvaston Pk. Homes. *Der* —7G **75**
Alvaston St. *Alv* —1H **93**
Alvenor St. *Ilk* —5D **44**
Alverstone Rd. *Nott* —5E **48**
Alverton Clo. *Mick* —7A **72**
Alvey Ter. *Nott* —2A **64**
Alward's Clo. *Alv* —3G **93**
Alward's Ct. *Alv* —3G **93**
Alwood Gro. *Nott* —5K **81**
Alwyn Ct. *Bees* —3F **81**
Alwyn Rd. *Nott* —4F **47**
Alyth Ct. *Nott* —3B **48**
Ambassador Rd. *Dis* —3K **115**
Ambaston La. *Thul & Shard*
—4C **94**
Amber Ct. *Belp* —6A **10**
Amber Ct. *Hean* —4G **27**
Amber Dri. *Lan M* —3K **27**
Ambergate Rd. *Nott* —7G **47**
(in two parts)
Amber Heights. *Rip* —2J **11**
Amber Hill. *Nott* —6D **32**
Amberley Clo. *Ilk* —1D **60**
Amberley Dri. *Sin* —4K **91**
Amber Rd. *Alst* —6H **55**
Amber St. *Der* —2C **92**
Amber Trad. Cen. *Kimb* —6H **29**
Ambervale Clo. *L'ver* —3E **90**
Ambleside. *Gam* —1A **84**
Ambleside Dri. *Eastw* —2B **28**
Ambleside Rd. *Nott* —5G **47**
Ambleside Way. *Ged* —6F **51**
Ambrose St. *Der* —5A **74**
Ambrose Ter. *Der* —3J **73** (3A **6**)
Amen All. *Der* —3A **74** (3D **6**)
**American Adventure Theme Pk.**
**—1A 44**
Amersham Ri. *Nott* —5H **47**
Amesbury Cir. *Nott* —3G **47**
Amesbury La. *Oak* —5E **56**
Amilda Av. *Ilk* —6D **44**
Ampthill Ri. *Nott* —2D **48**
Amy St. *Der* —4J **73**
Ancaster Gdns. *Nott* —2G **63**
Anchor Clo. *Nott* —6D **32**
Anchor Ct. *Nott* —6D **32**
Anchor Fold. *Der* —6A **74**
Anchor Row. *Ilk* —6D **44**
Anders Dri. *Nott* —1F **47**
Anderson Ct. *Nott* —5C **32**
Anderson Cres. *Bees* —7E **62**

Anderson St. *Alv* —2F **93**
Andover Clo. *Nott* —1H **63**
Andover Rd. *Nott* —7A **32**
Andrew Av. *Ilk* —7F **45**
Andrew Av. *Nott* —4J **49**
Andrew Clo. *L'ver* —2C **90**
Andrews Ct. *Bees* —2C **80**
Andrews Dri. *Lan M* —1J **27**
Andrews Dri. *Stan C* —5C **42**
Anfield Clo. *Bees* —6A **80**
Anford Clo. *Nott* —1H **47**
**Angear Vis. Cen. —6K 63**
Angela Clo. *Arn* —3G **33**
Angela Ct. *Bees* —6B **80**
Angel All. *Nott* —3F **65** (4G **5**)
Angelica Ct. *Bing* —3J **69**
Angel Row. *Nott* —3E **64** (4E **4**)
**Angel Row Gallery. —4E 4**
Anglers' La. *Spon* —5A **76**
Anglesey St. *Der* —7D **56**
Angletarn Clo. *W Bri* —2A **84**
Angrave Clo. *Nott* —7G **49**
Angus Clo. *Arn* —4K **33**
Angus Clo. *Kimb* —1A **46**
Anmer Clo. *Nott* —6D **64**
Annan Ct. *Nott* —6H **47**
Anne Potter Clo. *Ock* —3F **77**
Anne's Clo. *Nott* —4J **49**
Annesley Gro. *Nott*
—1D **64** (1D **4**)
Annesley Rd. *Huck* —1D **16**
Annesley Rd. *W Bri* —1H **83**
Anslow Av. *Bees* —7G **63**
Anson Rd. *Dis* —3J **115**
Anson Ter. *Nott* —7B **48**
Anstee Rd. *Long E* —4G **97**
Anstey Ct. *Oak* —6G **57**
Anstey Ri. *Nott* —2H **65**
Anthony Cres. *Alv* —3F **93**
Anthony Dri. *Alv* —3F **93**
Anthony Wharton Ct. *Nott* —5A **82**
Antill St. *S'fd* —2H **79**
Antony Ct. *Spon* —3A **76**
Apiary Ga. *Cas D* —7K **107**
Apollo Dri. *Nott* —1F **47**
Appian Clo. *Borr* —7E **76**
Appian Way. *Alv* —3K **93**
(in two parts)
Appleby Clo. *Ilk* —1D **60**
Appleby Ct. *Der* —5J **73** (7B **6**)
Applecross Ct. *Sin* —6H **91**
Appledore Av. *Nott* —5D **62**
Appledore Dri. *Oak* —6H **57**
Appledorne Way. *Arn* —4G **33**
Applegate Clo. *Oak* —4H **57**
Applemead Clo. *Der* —5E **56**
Apple Pl. *Brins* —4C **14**
Appleton Clo. *Chad* —1G **75**
Appleton Clo. *Nott* —1J **99**
Appleton Ct. *Bees* —4H **81**
Appleton Dri. *Belp* —6B **10**
Appleton Rd. *Bees* —4H **81**
Appletree Clo. *Borr* —7E **76**
Apple Tree Clo. *Edw* —4J **83**
Appletree La. *Ged* —4D **50**
Applewood Clo. *Belp* —7B **10**
Applewood Gro. *Nott* —3F **49**
Arbor Clo. *Der* —4K **73** (6C **6**)
Arboretum Ho. *Der* —5B **74** (7F **7**)
Arboretum Sq. *Der* —5B **74** (7F **7**)
Arboretum St. *Der* —5B **74** (7F **7**)
Arboretum St. *Nott*
—1D **64** (1C **4**)
Arbour Hill. *Dal A* —4G **59**
Arbrook Dri. *Nott* —1K **63**
Arbutus Clo. *Nott* —7J **81**
Archdale Rd. *Nott* —7E **32**
Archer Cres. *Nott* —2F **63**
Archer Rd. *S'fd* —3J **79**
Archer St. *Der* —6E **74**
Archer St. *Ilk* —3C **44**
Arches, The. *E Leak* —7K **111**
Arch Hill. *Red* —2G **33**
Archibald All. *Duf* —2J **39**
Archway Ct. *Nott* —1A **4**
Arden Clo. *Bees* —7G **63**
Arden Clo. *Der* —6J **73**
Arden Clo. *Huck* —7J **17**
Arden Gro. *Bing* —2J **69**
Ardleigh Clo. *Mick* —1B **90**
Ardleigh Clo. *Nott* —4K **31**
Ardmore Clo. *Nott* —4H **65** (6K **5**)
Ardsley Clo. *Hean* —3J **27**
Argosy Rd. *Dis* —3B **116**
Argyle Ct. *Nott* —2B **64**
Argyle St. *Der* —5K **73** (7B **6**)
Argyle St. *Lan M* —1K **27**

Argyle St. *Nott* —2B **64** (2A **4**)
Argyll Clo. *Spon* —3B **76**
Argyll Pl. *Rip* —2A **12**
Argyll Rd. *Rip* —2A **12**
Ariel Clo. *Nott* —1B **48**
Arkendale Wlk. *Alv* —3J **93**
Arkers Clo. *Nott* —3K **47**
Arkle Grn. *Sin* —5J **91**
Arklow Clo. *Nott* —4G **47**
Arkwright Av. *Belp* —6C **10**
Arkwright St. *Der* —2C **92**
Arkwright St. *Nott* —5F **65** (7G **5**)
(in two parts)
Arkwright St. N. *Nott*
—4E **64** (7F **5**)
Arkwright St. S. *Nott* —6F **65**
Arkwright Wlk. *Nott* —5E **64**
(in two parts)
Arleston Dri. *Nott* —4D **62**
Arleston La. *Der* —7H **91**
Arleston La. *Sten F* —6J **91**
Arleston St. *Der* —2K **91**
Arlington Clo. *Huck* —1G **31**
Arlington Dri. *Alv* —3F **93**
Arlington Dri. *Nott* —5E **48**
Arlington Rd. *Der* —7H **73**
Armadale Clo. *Arn* —5A **34**
Armfield Rd. *Arn* —7A **34**
Armitage Dri. *Long E* —2A **98**
Armscote Clo. *Oak* —5H **57**
Armstrong Rd. *Nott* —1F **47**
Arncliffe Clo. *Nott* —3C **62**
Arndale Rd. *Nott* —1E **48**
Arne Ct. *Nott* —6E **64**
Arnesby Rd. *Nott* —4K **63**
Arnhem Ter. *Spon* —4A **76**
Arno Av. *Nott* —6D **48**
Arnold Av. *Long E* —5E **96**
Arnold Cres. *Long E* —5E **96**
Arnold La. *Ged & Ged* —1K **49**
Arnold Rd. *Nott* —2A **48**
Arnold St. *Der* —3H **73**
Arnos Gro. *Nut* —3D **46**
Arnot Hill Rd. *Arn* —6G **33**
*Arnot House. Cltn* —6C *50*
(off Foxhill Rd. E.)
Arno Va. Gdns. *Wd'p* —1H **49**
Arno Va. Rd. *Wd'p* —1G **49**
Arnside. *S'fd* —3J **79**
Arnside Clo. *Nott* —1D **48**
Arnside Rd. *Nott* —1C **48**
A Rd. *Lent* —2J **81**
Arran Clo. *Sin* —6J **91**
Arran Clo. *S'fd* —5J **61**
Arreton Ct. *Alv* —4J **93**
Arridge Rd. *Chad* —1F **75**
Arthur Av. *Nott* —3B **64**
Arthur Av. *S'fd* —7K **61**
Arthur Ct. *Der* —6B **74**
Arthur Cres. *Cltn* —7A **50**
Arthur Hind Clo. *Der* —1J **73**
Arthur Mee Rd. *S'fd* —3J **79**
Arthur Neal Ho. *Der* —2F **73**
Arthur St. *Der* —1A **74** (1D **6**)
Arthur St. *Dray* —1H **95**
Arthur St. *N'fld* —1E **66**
Arthur St. *Nott* —1C **64** (1B **4**)
Arthurs Vw. *Iron* —1H **13**
Artic Way. *Kimb* —6H **29**
**Arts Cen. —(4G 5)**
**(Nottingham)**
Arundel Av. *Mick* —6D **72**
Arundel Clo. *Sand* —4F **79**
Arundel Dri. *Bees* —5B **62**
Arundel Dri. *Spon* —3B **76**
Arundel St. *Der* —5H **73**
Arundel St. *Nott* —2C **64** (3A **4**)
Ascot Av. *Kimb* —6J **29**
Ascot Clo. *W Hal* —7F **43**
Ascot Dri. *Der* —2D **92**
Ascot Dri. *Huck* —7D **16**
Ascot Dri. *Red* —5F **33**
Ascot Ind. Est. *Sand* —1G **79**
Ascot Pl. *Ilk* —2A **60**
Ascot Rd. *Nott* —7K **47**
Ascott Gdns. *W Bri* —3D **82**
Ashacre. *Belp* —1D **24**
Ashborne Rd. *Der* —1D **72**
Ashbourne Clo. *Bees* —6A **62**
Ashbourne Ct. *Der* —3J **73** (3A **6**)
Ashbourne Ct. *Nott* —7F **31**
*Ashbourne Ho. Spon* —4A *76*
(off Arnhem Ter.)
Ashbourne Rd. *Kirk L & Mack*
—6A **54** (2A **6**)
Ashbourne Rd. *Shot* —3A **22**
Ashbourne Rd. *Und* —2E **14**
Ashbourne St. *Nott*
—2C **64** (3A **4**)

Ashbrook Av. *Borr* —6E **76**
Ashbrook Clo. *Alst* —4G **55**
Ashburnham Av. *Nott* —3B **64**
Ashby Rd. *Keg* —4D **116**
Ashby Rd. *Melb* —4G **113**
Ashby Rd. *Tickn* —7A **112**
Ashby St. *Altn* —3E **92**
Ashchurch Dri. *Nott* —5D **62**
Ash Clo. *Alst* —3H **55**
Ash Clo. *Ast T* —2D **106**
Ash Clo. *Bing* —3C **70**
Ash Clo. *Bur J* —2J **51**
Ash Clo. *Huck* —7C **16**
Ash Clo. *Wdbgh* —1G **35**
Ashcombe Gdns. *Oak* —6H **57**
Ash Ct. *Cltn* —7B **50**
Ash Cres. *Nut* —7B **30**
Ash Cres. *Rip* —4K **11**
Ashcroft Clo. *Alv* —2F **93**
Ashdale Av. *Huck* —7G **17**
Ashdale Rd. *Arn* —5J **33**
Ashdale Rd. *Ilk* —1E **60**
Ashdale Rd. *Nott* —1K **65**
Ashdene Gdns. *Belp* —7C **10**
Ashdown Clo. *Wilf* —2D **82**
Ashdown Gro. *Bing* —3K **69**
Ashe Clo. *Arn* —6K **33**
Ashe Pl. *Der* —7K **73**
Asher La. *Rud* —3E **100**
Ashfield Av. *Bees* —3H **81**
Ashfield Av. *Chad* —7E **56**
Ashfield Rd. *Nott* —3H **65**
Ashford Ct. *W Hal* —6F **43**
Ashford Pl. *Ilk* —1C **44**
Ashford Ri. *Belp* —6C **10**
Ashford Ri. *Nott* —5D **62**
Ash Forth Av. *Hean* —4J **27**
Ashforth St. *Nott* —1F **65** (1G **5**)
Ashgate Rd. *Huck* —6H **17**
Ash Gro. *Brins* —4B **14**
Ash Gro. *Keyw* —7D **102**
Ash Gro. *Long E* —3G **97**
Ash Gro. *Sand* —1E **78**
Ash Gro. *S'fd* —2H **79**
Ash Gro. *Wdbgh* —7G **21**
Ashgrove Ct. *Oak* —6H **57**
Ashiana. *Nott* —3G **65** (4J **5**)
Ashington Dri. *Arn* —3J **33**
Ash La. *Etw* —2A **88**
Ash Lea Clo. *Cotg* —6K **85**
Ashleigh Dri. *Chel* —7F **93**
Ashley Clo. *Bees* —2D **80**
Ashley Ct. *Bees* —2E **80**
Ashley Cres. *Keyw* —6D **102**
Ashley Gro. *Huck* —5E **16**
Ashley Rd. *Keyw* —6C **102**
Ashley St. *Der* —3G **73**
Ashley St. *Nott* —2G **65** (3J **5**)
Ashling Ct. *Nott* —5G **65**
Ashling St. *Nott* —5F **65**
Ashlyn Rd. *W Mead*
　　　　　—3C **74** (4H **7**)
Ashmeadow. *Borr* —7D **76**
Ash Mt. Rd. *Lan M* —2K **27**
Ashness Clo. *Gam* —2A **84**
Ashop Rd. *Belp* —7D **10**
Ashopton Av. *Der* —1K **91**
Ashover Clo. *Chad* —7F **57**
Ashover Clo. *Nott* —6G **49**
Ashover Rd. *Alst* —5H **55**
Ashover Rd. *Chad* —7E **56**
Ashridge Way. *Edw* —4A **84**
Ash St. *Ilk* —2C **44**
Ashton Av. *Arn* —3H **33**
Ashton Clo. *Mick* —5A **72**
Ashton Way. *Belp* —1D **24**
Ashtree Av. *Der* —3B **92**
Ash Tree Clo. *Bread* —3E **56**
Ash Tree Clo. *Duf* —1J **39**
Ash Tree Sq. *Bees* —7B **62**
Ash Vw. *Nott* —1B **64**
Ash Vw. Clo. *Etw* —5D **88**
Ashview Clo. *Long E* —1F **97**
Ash Vs. *Nott* —5D **48**
Ashville Clo. *Q Dri* —6C **64**
Ashwater Clo. *Sin* —7K **91**
Ashwater Dri. *Nott* —7B **34**
Ashwell Ct. *Wd'p* —2G **49**
Ashwell Gdns. *Nott* —6A **48**
Ashwell St. *N'fld* —1D **66**
Ashwick Clo. *Nott* —3C **82**
Ashworth Av. *Chad* —3F **75**
Ashworth Av. *Rud* —1E **100**
Ashworth Clo. *Nott* —2A **66**
Ashworth Cres. *Nott* —4K **49**
Ashworth Wlk. *Chad* —3F **75**
Askeby Dri. *Nott* —5D **46**
Askerfield Av. *Alst* —3G **55**
Aslockton Dri. *Nott* —4K **47**

Aspen Clo. *Bing* —3C **70**
Aspen Dri. *Spon* —4H **75**
Aspen Rd. *Nott* —7F **31**
Asper St. *N'fld* —7E **50**
Aspinall Ct. *Nott* —2J **63**
Aspley La. *Nott* —5F **47**
Aspley Pk. Dri. *Nott* —6G **47**
Aspley Pl. *Nott* —1B **64**
Assarts Lodge. *Nut* —2D **46**
Assarts Rd. *Nut* —2E **46**
Assembly Rooms. —3E **6**
Astcote Clo. *Hean* —4J **27**
Asterdale Vw. *Spon* —4B **76**
Aster Rd. *Nott* —7F **49**
Astle Ct. *Arn* —7A **34**
Astley Dri. *Nott* —5H **49**
Astlow Dri. *Belp* —6B **10**
Aston Av. *Bees* —7G **63**
Aston Clo. *Chel* —2G **105**
Aston Ct. *Ilk* —5D **44**
Aston Ct. *Nott* —6A **64**
Aston Dri. *Nott* —3J **31**
Aston Grn. *Bees* —5J **79**
Aston Hall Dri. *Ast T* —3C **106**
Aston La. *Chel* —1H **105**
Aston La. *Shard* —2E **106**
　(in two parts)
Aston Rd. *L'ver* —4G **91**
Astorville Pk. Rd. *Chel* —7F **93**
Astral Dri. *Huck* —1E **30**
Astral Gro. *Huck* —1D **30**
　(in two parts)
Astrid Gdns. *Nott* —7B **32**
Astwood Clo. *Nott* —7E **46**
Atchison Gdns. *Chad* —1H **75**
Atherfield Gdns. *Eastw* —2D **28**
Atherfield Wlk. *Alv* —4J **93**
Atherton Ri. *Nott* —3H **47**
Atherton Rd. *Ilk* —3A **44**
Athlone Clo. *Der* —7D **56**
Athol Clo. *Sin* —5J **91**
Atholl Clo. *Nott* —3B **48**
Athorpe Gro. *Nott* —3B **48**
Atlow Rd. *Chad* —1E **74**
Attenborough La. *Bees* —6D **80**
Attenborough La. N. *Bees* —5C **80**
　(in two parts)
Attenborough Nature Reserve.
　　　　　—5F **81**
Attercliffe Ter. *Nott* —6E **64**
Attewell Clo. *Dray* —2K **95**
Attewell Rd. *Aws* —1F **45**
Attlebridge Clo. *Der* —7D **56**
Atworth Gro. *L'ver* —3D **90**
Aubrey Av. *Nott* —3G **65** (5K **5**)
Aubrey Rd. *Nott* —4D **48**
Aubyn Clo. *Stan C* —6D **42**
Auckland Clo. *Mick* —5D **72**
Auckland Clo. *Nott* —2A **64**
Auckland Rd. *Huck* —7D **16**
Audley Cen. *Der* —3A **74** (4E **6**)
Audley Clo. *Ilk* —3B **44**
Audley Dri. *Bees* —6F **63**
Audon Av. *Bees* —3E **80**
Audrey Dri. *Chad* —7G **57**
Augusta St. *Der* —6B **74**
Augustine Gdns. *Nott* —4C **32**
Aults Clo. *Find* —7A **90**
Austen Av. *L'ver* —1F **91**
Austen Av. *Long E* —4G **97**
Austen Av. *Nott* —7C **48**
Austins Dri. *Sand* —4F **79**
Austin Sq. *Der* —2K **91**
Austin St. *Nott* —6J **31**
Austrey Av. *Bees* —7G **63**
Autumn Ct. *Huck* —6G **17**
Autumn Gro. *Chad* —3F **75**
Avalon Clo. *Nott* —7A **32**
Avebury Clo. *Nott* —1K **99**
Avenue A. *Nott* —3F **65** (4H **5**)
Avenue B. *Nott* —3F **65** (4H **5**)
Avenue C. *Nott* —3G **65** (4H **5**)
Avenue Clo. *Nott* —5B **32**
Avenue D. *Nott* —3G **65** (4J **5**)
Avenue E. *Nott* —2G **65** (3J **5**)
Avenue Rd. *Duf* —1J **39**
Avenue, The. *Belp* —3K **23**
Avenue, The. *C'tn* —5D **20**
Avenue, The. *Chad* —3F **75**
Avenue, The. *Der* —4A **74** (6E **6**)
Avenue, The. *Gun* —7F **37**
Avenue, The. *Rad T* —3K **67**
Avenue, The. *Rud* —4F **101**
Avenue, The. *Wstn T* —5B **106**
Averham Clo. *Oak* —6H **57**
Averton Sq. *Nott* —4K **63**
Aviemore Clo. *Arn* —4K **33**
Aviemore Way. *Sin* —5J **91**
　(in two parts)
Avis Av. *Hean* —6H **27**
Avocet Clo. *Bing* —4C **70**

Avocet Ct. *Sin* —5H **91**
Avocet Wharf. *Nott* —5C **64**
Avon Av. *Huck* —2E **30**
Avonbridge Clo. *Arn* —4A **34**
Avon Clo. *Sten F* —7H **91**
Avondale. *Cotg* —5A **86**
Avondale Clo. *Long E* —3E **96**
Avondale Rd. *Cltn* —1B **66**
Avondale Rd. *Der* —5A **74** (7D **6**)
Avondale Rd. *Ilk* —2A **60**
Avondale Rd. *Spon* —2K **75**
Avon Gdns. *W Bri* —1H **83**
Avonlea Clo. *Ilk* —1F **61**
Avonmouth Dri. *Alv* —1E **92**
Avon Pl. *Bees* —1G **81**
Avon Rd. *Ged* —4D **50**
Avon Rd. *Nott* —2K **65**
Avon St. *Der* —1E **92**
Avon Way. *Hilt* —7A **88**
Awsworth & Cossall By-Pass. *Aws*
　　　　　—2F **45**
Awsworth La. *Coss* —4G **45**
Awsworth La. *Kimb* —7H **29**
Awsworth Rd. *Ilk & Aws* —4D **44**
Axford Clo. *Ged* —4D **50**
Aycliffe Gdns. *Alv* —4F **93**
Aylesbury Av. *Chad* —1F **75**
Aylesham Av. *Arn* —7H **33**
Aylestone Dri. *Nott* —6H **47**
Ayr Clo. *Spon* —4K **75**
Ayr St. *Nott* —1C **64** (1A **4**)
Ayscough Av. *Nut* —7C **30**
Ayton Clo. *Nott* —5D **64**
Ayton Gdns. *Bees* —6C **80**
Azalea Ct. *Gilt* —5G **29**
Azimghur Rd. *What* —3J **71**

**B**abbacombe Clo. *Alv* —2J **93**
Babbacombe Dri. *Nott* —7D **32**
Babbacombe Way. *Huck* —6D **16**
Babbington Cres. *Ged* —4C **50**
Babbington La. *Kimb* —2K **45**
Babington Ct. *Bees* —3C **80**
Babington La. *Der* —4A **74** (6D **6**)
　(in two parts)
Back La. *Cas D & Shard* —5J **107**
Back La. *Chel* —1G **105**
Back La. *C But* —3E **102**
Back La. *Hean* —4G **27**
Back La. *Ilk* —4C **44**
Back La. *Nut* —7D **30**
Bk. Sitwell St. *Der* —4A **74** (5E **6**)
Bk. Wyver La. *Belp* —7K **9**
Bacon Clo. *Gilt* —5E **28**
*Baconsfield Ho. Chad* —4H **75**
　(off Coleraine Clo.)
Bacton Av. *Nott* —5H **31**
Bacton Gdns. *Nott* —5H **31**
Baden Powell Rd. *Nott* —3J **65**
Bader Rd. *Nott* —1D **82**
Badger Clo. *Cltn* —6D **50**
Badger Clo. *Huck* —6C **16**
Badger Clo. *Spon* —2B **76**
Bagnall Av. *Arn* —7E **32**
Bagnall Cotts. *Nott* —1H **47**
Bagnall Rd. *Nott* —2H **47**
Bagot St. *W Hal* —6E **42**
Bagshaw St. *Der* —1E **92**
Bagthorpe Clo. *Nott* —3C **48**
Baildon Clo. *Nott* —4J **63**
Bailey Brook Cres. *Lan M* —1J **27**
Bailey Brook Dri. *Lan M* —2J **27**
Bailey Brook Ind. Est. *Lan M*
　　　　　—3K **27**
Bailey Brook Wlk. *Lan M* —2J **27**
Bailey Clo. *Day* —6F **33**
Bailey Ct. *N'fld* —7E **50**
Bailey Ct. *Rad T* —5J **67**
Bailey Gro. Rd. *Eastw* —3B **28**
Bailey La. *Rad T* —5J **67**
Bailey St. *Der* —5K **73**
Bailey St. *N'fld* —7E **50**
Bailey St. *Nott* —4A **48**
Bailey St. *S'fd* —2G **79**
Bainbridge, The. *C'tn* —5E **20**
Bainbridge St. *Car* —3A **108**
Bains Dri. *Borr* —7F **77**
Bainton Gro. *Nott* —7B **82**
Bakeacre La. *Find* —7B **90**
Bakehouse La. *Ock* —3D **76**
Baker Av. *Arn* —4J **33**
Baker Av. *Hean* —6H **27**
Baker Brook Ind. Est. *Huck*
　　　　　—6K **17**
Bakerdale Rd. *Nott* —1K **65**
Baker Rd. *Gilt & Newt* —5G **29**
Bakers Clo. *Nott* —1A **64**
Bakers Hill. *Heag* —3E **10**

Baker's Hollow. *Cotg* —5J **85**
Bakers La. *Der* —4A **74** (6D **6**)
Baker St. *Alv* —1F **93**
Baker St. *Huck* —5G **17**
Baker St. *Ilk* —5D **44**
Baker St. *Nott* —7D **48**
Bakewell Av. *Cltn* —5C **50**
Bakewell Clo. *Mick* —5C **72**
Bakewell Dri. *Cas D* —1J **115**
Bakewell Dri. *Nott* —6A **32**
Bakewell Rd. *Long E* —4J **97**
Bakewell St. *Der* —4K **73** (5B **6**)
Balaclava Rd. *Der* —1A **92**
Bala Dri. *Nott* —6C **32**
Baldwin Ct. *Nott* —2B **64** (3A **4**)
Baldwin St. *Newt* —4G **29**
Baldwin St. *Nott* —2B **64** (3A **4**)
Balfour Rd. *Der* —1A **92**
Balfour Rd. *Nott* —2B **64** (4A **4**)
Balfour Rd. *S'fd* —2H **79**
Balfron Gdns. *Nott* —5D **64**
Balham Wlk. *Der* —2E **72**
Ballacraine Dri. *Rip* —3B **12**
Ballantrae Clo. *Arn* —5K **33**
Ballards Way. *Borr* —7F **77**
Ballater Clo. *Sin* —5J **91**
Balleny Clo. *Oak* —6F **57**
Ballerat Cres. *Nott* —5A **32**
Ball La. *Thurl* —4C **94**
Ballon Wood N. *Nott* —3C **62**
Ball St. *Nott* —7H **49**
Balmoral Av. *W Bri* —7G **65**
Balmoral Clo. *Hean* —4E **26**
Balmoral Clo. *L'ver* —6F **73**
Balmoral Clo. *Sand* —5F **79**
Balmoral Cres. *Nott* —2C **62**
Balmoral Dri. *Bees* —5B **62**
Balmoral Gro. *Colw* —1D **66**
Balmoral Gro. *Huck* —4H **17**
Balmoral Rd. *Bing* —3J **69**
Balmoral Rd. *Borr* —7E **76**
Balmoral Rd. *Colw* —1D **66**
Balmoral Rd. *Ilk* —2B **60**
Balmoral Rd. *Nott* —1D **64**
Bamburgh Clo. *Spon* —4K **75**
Bamford Av. *Der* —1J **91**
Bamford St. *Rip* —5K **11**
Bamkin Clo. *Huck* —6H **17**
Bampton Ct. *Gam* —1A **84**
Banbury Av. *Bees* —5K **79**
Bancroft Dri. *Alst* —3G **55**
Bancroft St. *Nott* —6J **31**
Bancroft, The. *Etw* —5D **88**
Banes Rd. *Bing* —3D **70**
Bangor St. *Der* —7E **56**
Bangor Wlk. *Nott* —7E **48**
Bank Bldgs. *Milf* —6K **23**
Bank Ct. *Der* —7J **55**
Bankfield Dri. *Bees* —6C **62**
Bankfield Dri. *Ilk* —1K **59**
Bankfield Dri. *Spon* —4B **76**
Bank Hill. *Wdbgh* —2D **34**
Bankholmes Clo. *Sten F* —7J **91**
Bank Pl. *Nott* —3E **64** (4F **5**)
Banksburn Clo. *Hean* —4E **26**
Banks Clo. *Arn* —7K **33**
Banks Cres. *Bing* —3A **70**
Bank Side. *Dar A* —5J **55**
Banks Paddock. *Bing* —3B **70**
Banks Rd. *Bees* —5J **79**
Banks, The. *Bing* —3A **70**
Bank St. *Lan M* —1A **28**
Bank St. *Long E* —2J **97**
Bank Vw. Rd. *Der* —7K **55**
Bank Vw. Rd. *Neth H* —2C **10**
Bankwood Clo. *Nott* —5G **47**
*Bank Yd. Bulw* —6H **31**
　(off Main St.)
Bannell's La. *Mick* —1H **89**
Bannels Av. *L'ver* —2F **91**
Bannerman Rd. *Nott* —7J **31**
Banton's La. *Tickn* —7A **112**
Banwell Clo. *Mick* —5A **72**
Barbara Sq. *Huck* —3F **17**
Barber Clo. *Ilk* —3C **44**
Barber St. *Eastw* —3E **28**
Barbor St. *Der* —3A **108**
Barbrook Clo. *Nott* —2H **63**
Barbury Dri. *Nott* —2K **99**
Barcheston Clo. *Oak* —5H **57**
Barclay Ct. *Ilk* —3B **44**
Barden Dri. *Alst* —5K **55**
Barden Rd. *Nott* —2J **49**
Bardfield Gdns. *Nott* —3K **31**
Bardney Dri. *Nott* —5G **31**
Bardsey Ct. *Oak* —4H **57**
Bardsey Gdns. *Nott* —6C **32**
Bare La. *Ock* —3E **76**
Barent Clo. *Nott* —7B **32**

　(in two parts)
Barent Wlk. *Nott* —7B **32**
Barf Clo. *Mick* —7C **72**
Bargate Clo. *Belp* —4C **24**
Bargate Rd. *Belp* —3A **24**
Barker Av. E. *Sand* —2F **79**
Barker Av. N. *Sand* —2E **78**
Barker Clo. *Stan C* —5D **42**
Barker Ga. *Huck* —5F **17**
Barker Ga. *Ilk* —4D **44**
Barker Ga. *Nott* —3F **65** (4G **5**)
Barker Hill. *Low* —3D **36**
Barker's La. *Bees* —4F **81**
Barkla Clo. *Nott* —1J **99**
Bar La. *Nott* —4J **47**
Bar La. Ind. Pk. *Nott* —4K **47**
Barley Clo. *L Eat* —6C **40**
Barleycorn Clo. *Oak* —5J **57**
Barley Cft. *Belp* —3B **24**
Barley Cft. *Chel* —1F **105**
Barley Cft. *W Bri* —4E **82**
Barleydale Dri. *Trow* —5H **61**
Barleylands. *Rud* —3E **100**
Barling Dri. *Ilk* —4A **44**
Barlock Rd. *Nott* —2A **48**
Barlow Dri. N. *Aws* —2F **45**
Barlow Dri. S. *Aws* —2F **45**
Barlows Cotts. *Aws* —1G **45**
Barlow St. *Der* —5B **74** (7H **7**)
Barnard Rd. *Der* —5D **56**
Barnby Wlk. *Nott* —1E **48**
Barn Clo. *Cas D* —7K **107**
Barn Clo. *Cotg* —6J **85**
Barn Clo. *Find* —7B **90**
Barn Clo. *Nott* —1F **47**
Barn Clo. *Quar* —1G **55**
Barn Cft. *Bees* —2B **80**
Barn Cft. *Der* —7G **73**
Barndale Clo. *W Bri* —5E **82**
Barnes Cft. *Hean* —5E **26**
　(Heanor Ga. Rd.)
Barnes Cft. *Hean* —3H **27**
　(Johnson Dri.)
Barnes Grn. *Der* —1F **73**
Barnes Rd. *Nott* —5B **32**
Barnet Rd. *Nott* —7K **49**
Barnett Ct. *Keyw* —6C **102**
Barnfield. *Nott* —4D **82**
Barnfield Clo. *Long W* —7F **117**
Barnham Clo. *Ilk* —4D **44**
Barnhill Gro. *L'ver* —2E **90**
Barnsley Ter. *Nott* —6E **64**
Barnston Rd. *Nott* —2H **65**
Barnum Clo. *Nott* —2E **62**
Barnwood Clo. *Mick* —6A **72**
Baron Clo. *Oak* —4K **57**
Barons Clo. *Ged* —5C **50**
Baroon. *Cas D* —7K **107**
Barrack La. *Nott* —3B **64** (4A **4**)
Barra M. *Nott* —5D **64**
Barratt Clo. *Bees* —7D **80**
Barratt Clo. *C Bis* —4G **87**
Barratt Cres. *Bees* —6D **80**
Barratt La. *Bees* —6C **80**
Barrett St. *Alv* —2G **93**
Barrhead Clo. *Nott* —4A **32**
Barrie Dri. *Sin* —4K **91**
Barrington Clo. *Rad T* —5J **67**
Barrique Rd. *Nott* —6A **64**
Barrons Way. *Borr* —7E **76**
Barrow La. *Swar* —4C **104**
Barrow Slade. *Keyw* —7C **102**
Barrydale Av. *Bees* —3F **81**
Barry St. *Nott* —6H **31**
Bartlow Rd. *Nott* —7D **46**
Barton Clo. *Rud* —3D **100**
Barton Clo. *Spon* —2B **76**
Barton Knoll. *Belp* —2D **24**
Barton Knowle. *Belp* —1D **24**
Barton La. *Bar F* —3G **99**
Barton La. *Bees* —7C **80**
Barton La. *Nott* —1H **99**
Barton La. *Thrum* —1C **110**
Barton Rd. *Long E* —3A **98**
Bartons Clo. *Newt* —3G **29**
Barton St. *Bees* —3G **81**
Barwell Dri. *Nott* —5D **46**
Basa Cres. *Nott* —5B **32**
Basford Rd. *Nott* —5K **47**
Basildon Clo. *Alv* —4F **93**
Baskin La. *Bees* —4C **80**
Baslow Av. *Cltn* —5B **50**
Baslow Clo. *Long E* —4E **96**
Baslow Dri. *Alst* —4K **55**
Baslow Dri. *Bees* —6G **63**
Bassett Clo. *Ilk* —3A **44**
Bassett Clo. *Kimb* —6J **29**
Bassford Av. *Hean* —3H **27**

Bassingfield La. *Gam & Rad T* —2B **84**
Bassingham Clo. *Oak* —6H **57**
Bass St. *Der* —2H **73**
Bastion St. *Nott* —2A **64**
Bateman Gdns. *Nott* —7B **48**
Bateman St. *Der* —6C **74**
Bathley St. *Nott* —6E **64**
Bath Rd. *Mick* —6C **72**
Baths. —6B **48**
(New Basford)
Baths La. *Huck* —5H **17**
Bath St. *Der* —1A **74** (1D **6**)
Bath St. *Ilk* —5C **44**
Bath St. *Nott* —2F **65** (2G **5**)
Bathurst Dri. *Nott* —1G **63**
Baulk La. *S'fd* —7K **61**
Baverstock Clo. *Chel* —6F **93**
Bawtry Wlk. *Nott* —1H **65**
Baxter Sq. *Der* —3K **91**
Bayard Ct. *Nott* —2J **63**
Bayleaf Cres. *Oak* —4H **57**
Bayliss Rd. *Ged* —3B **50**
Bayswater Clo. *Der* —2D **72**
Bayswater Rd. *Kimb* —6K **29**
Baythorn Rd. *Nott* —1D **62**
Beackden Clo. *Belp* —1E **24**
Beacon Flatts. *Bees* —2H **81**
Beacon Hill Dri. *Huck* —7C **16**
Beacon Hill Ri. *Nott*
—2G **65** (2J **5**)
Beacon Rd. *Bees* —2H **81**
Beaconsfield St. *Long E* —2J **97**
Beaconsfield St. *Nott* —6B **48**
Beamwood Clo. *Oak* —6F **57**
Bean Clo. *Nott* —1F **47**
Beanford La. *Oxt* —1C **20**
Beardall St. *Huck* —5H **17**
Beardmore Clo. *Oak* —6E **56**
Beardsley Gdns. *Nott* —5D **64**
(in two parts)
Beardsmore Gro. *Huck* —3F **17**
Beastmarket Hill. *Nott*
—3E **64** (4E **4**)
Beatty St. *Alv* —1F **93**
Beatty Wlk. *Ilk* —3D **44**
Beauclerk Dri. *Nott* —5A **32**
Beaufort Ct. *W Bri* —5E **82**
Beaufort Cliffe Ind. Est. *Der* —7C **56**
Beaufort Dri. *Bees* —3C **80**
Beaufort Gdns. *Der*
—1D **74** (1K **7**)
Beaufort Rd. *Sten F* —7G **91**
Beaufort St. *Der* —1D **74** (1K **7**)
Beaulieu Gdns. *W Bri* —3E **82**
Beaumaris Ct. *Spon* —3B **76**
Beaumaris Dri. *Bees* —4B **80**
Beaumaris Dri. *Ged* —5F **51**
Beaumont Clo. *Bar T* —5A **104**
Beaumont Clo. *Belp* —1D **24**
Beaumont Clo. *Keyw* —5C **102**
Beaumont Clo. *S'fd* —6J **61**
Beaumont Gdns. *W Bri* —4F **83**
Beaumont St. *Nott* —3G **65** (5K **5**)
Beaumont Wlk. *Der* —3J **91**
Beaurepaire Cres. *Belp* —7B **10**
Beaureper Av. *Alst* —4J **55**
Beauvale. *Newt* —3G **29**
Beauvale Ct. *Huck* —6E **16**
Beauvale Cres. *Huck* —6D **16**
Beauvale Dri. *Ilk* —1B **44**
Beauvale Priory. —6J **15**
(remains of)
Beauvale Ri. *Eastw* —2F **29**
Beauvale Rd. *Huck* —6D **16**
Beauvale Rd. *Nott* —6E **64**
Beaver Grn. *W Bri* —1F **83**
Becher St. *Der* —7A **74**
Beck Av. *C'tn* —4D **20**
Beckenham Rd. *Nott* —1A **64**
Beckenham Way. *Der* —2F **73**
Becket St. *Der* —3K **73** (4C **6**)
Beckett Ct. *Ged* —3B **50**
Becketwell La. *Der* —3A **74** (4D **6**)
Beckford Rd. *Nott* —4H **65**
Beckhampton Rd. *Nott* —5D **32**
Beckitt Clo. *Alv* —1G **93**
Beckley Rd. *Nott* —4F **47**
Beckside. *Gam & Gam* —4A **84**
Beckside. *Low* —4E **36**
Becksitch Ct. *Belp* —3K **23**
(off Holbrook Rd.)
Becksitch La. *Belp* —3K **23**
Beck St. *Cltn* —6B **50**
Beck St. *Nott* —2F **65** (3G **5**)
Bedale Ct. *Bees* —4A **80**
Bedale Rd. *Nott* —1E **48**
Bedarra Gro. *Lent* —3A **64**
Bede Clo. *Nott* —4C **32**

Bede Ling. *W Bri* —2E **82**
Bedford Clo. *Der* —5H **73**
Bedford Clo. *Keg* —2H **117**
Bedford Ct. *Nott* —6B **48**
Bedford Ct. *S'fd* —6J **61**
Bedford Gro. *Nott* —1K **47**
Bedford Row. *Nott*
—2F **65** (3H **5**)
Bedford St. *Der* —4H **73**
Bedlington Gdns. *Nott* —4G **49**
Beecham Av. *Nott* —1H **65**
Beech Av. *Alv* —1H **93**
Beech Av. *Bees* —3H **81**
Beech Av. *Bing* —3C **70**
Beech Av. *Borr* —5E **76**
Beech Av. *Breas* —1D **96**
Beech Av. *Huck* —5G **17**
Beech Av. *Keyw* —7D **102**
Beech Av. *Long E* —7J **79**
Beech Av. *Map* —2H **49**
Beech Av. *Melb* —3H **113**
Beech Av. *N'fld* —1D **66**
Beech Av. *New B* —6C **48**
Beech Av. *Nut* —7B **30**
Beech Av. *Quar* —6E **38**
Beech Av. *Rip* —2J **11**
Beech Av. *Sand* —1F **79**
Beech Clo. *Belp* —2A **24**
Beech Clo. *Edw* —4K **83**
Beech Clo. *Klbrn* —5H **25**
Beech Clo. *Nott* —2J **47**
Beech Clo. *Rad T* —5K **67**
Beech Ct. *Map* —2J **49**
Beech Ct. *Spon* —3K **75**
Beech Ct. *Und* —1F **15**
Beechcroft. *Bread* —3D **56**
Beechcroft. *W Hal* —7G **43**
Beechdale Rd. *Nott* —6F **47**
Beechdale Swimming Pool.
—1J **63**
Beech Dri. *Der* —7K **55**
Beech Dri. *Etw* —5E **88**
Beech Dri. *Find* —7C **90**
Beeches Av. *Spon* —3K **75**
Beeches, The. *Long E* —1J **97**
Beeches, The. *Nott* —6J **49**
Beeches, The. *Smal* —5E **26**
Beech Gdns. *Alv* —2H **93**
Beech La. *W Hal* —7F **43**
Beechley Dri. *Oak* —6H **57**
Beech Lodge. *Bing* —3C **70**
Beech Rd. *Und* —1F **15**
Beech Wlk. *L'ver* —7H **73**
Beechwood Clo. *Belp* —7J **9**
Beechwood Cres. *L'ver* —7G **73**
Beechwood Rd. *Arn* —5J **33**
Beeley Clo. *Alst* —5H **55**
Beeley Clo. *Belp* —6C **10**
Beeley Clo. *Chad* —5F **57**
Beeston Clo. *B Vil* —1A **32**
Beeston Ct. *Nott* —6K **31**
Beeston Fields Dri. *Bees* —7C **62**
Beeston Fields Golf Course.
—1D **80**
Beeston La. *Nott* —7H **63**
Beeston Rd. *Nott* —6K **63**
Beethan Clo. *Bing* —3B **70**
Beightons Hill. *Tickn* —6C **112**
Beighton St. *Rip* —3A **12**
Belconnen Rd. *Nott* —1B **48**
Belfast Wlk. *Chad* —4G **75**
Belfield Ct. *Etw* —6D **88**
Belfield Ct. *Los* —1E **26**
Belfield Gdns. *Long E* —2J **97**
Belfield Rd. *Etw* —6D **88**
Belfield St. *Ilk* —4D **44**
Belfield Ter. *Etw* —6E **88**
Belford Clo. *Nott* —5F **31**
Belfry Clo. *Mick* —7D **72**
Belfry Way. *Edw* —4A **84**
Belgrave Clo. *Belp* —7C **10**
Belgrave M. *W Bri* —5E **82**
Belgrave Rd. *Nott* —6G **31**
Belgrave Sq. *Nott* —2D **64** (3D **4**)
Belgrave St. *Der* —5A **74** (7D **6**)
Bellar Ga. *Nott* —3F **65** (4H **5**)
Bell Av. *Ast T* —3C **106**
Belle Acre Clo. *Belp* —2K **23**
Belle-Isle Rd. *Huck* —6G **17**
Belleville Dri. *Nott* —6D **32**
Belle Vue Av. *Rip* —6J **11**
Bellevue Ct. *Nott* —1G **65** (1J **5**)
Belle Vue Ter. *Borr* —7D **76**
Bell Ho. *Nott* —7A **64**
Bellingham Ct. *Alst* —5G **55**
Bell La. *Smal & Ship* —2B **42**
Bell La. *Wilf* —1D **82**
Bellmore Gdns. *Nott* —2D **62**
Bells La. *Nott* —4G **47**

Bell St. *Cltn* —6B **50**
Bell Ter. *Nott* —2A **48**
Belmont Av. *Breas* —1C **96**
Belmont Av. *Nott* —6J **31**
Belmont Clo. *Bees* —4B **80**
Belmont Clo. *Huck* —1G **31**
Belmont Dri. *Borr* —6D **76**
Belper Av. *Cltn* —5B **50**
Belper Cres. *Cltn* —5B **50**
Belper Ho. *Spon* —5A **76**
Belper La. *Belp* —5G **9**
Belper Rd. *Belp & Holb* —4C **24**
Belper Rd. *Der* —7K **55** (1C **6**)
Belper Rd. *Klbrn* —3E **24**
(in two parts)
Belper Rd. *Nott* —7B **48**
Belper Rd. *Stan C & W Hal*
—4B **42**
Belper Sports Cen. —4D **74**
Belper St. *Ilk* —7D **44**
Belsay Rd. *Nott* —6C **32**
Belsford Ct. *Watn* —5A **30**
Belsize Clo. *Der* —2D **72**
Belton Clo. *Sand* —4F **79**
Belton Dri. *Rip* —3A **12**
Belton Dri. *W Bri* —4D **82**
Belton St. *Nott* —6B **48**
Belvedere Av. *Nott* —6B **48**
Belvedere Clo. *Keyw* —5C **102**
Belvedere Clo. *Mick* —4B **72**
Belvoir Clo. *Breas* —2B **96**
Belvoir Clo. *Ilk* —1B **60**
Belvoir Clo. *Long E* —4J **97**
Belvoir Clo. *What* —4G **71**
Belvoir Hill. *Nott* —3H **65** (5K **5**)
Belvoir Lodge. *Cltn* —1C **66**
Belvoir Rd. *N'fld* —7E **50**
Belvoir Rd. *W Bri* —6J **65**
Belvoir St. *Der* —7K **73**
Belvoir St. *Huck* —4F **17**
Belvoir St. *Nott* —4H **49**
Belvoir Ter. *Nott* —3H **65** (5K **5**)
Belward St. *Nott* —3F **65** (4H **5**)
Belwood Clo. *Nott* —6B **82**
Bembridge Ct. *Bees* —7A **62**
Bembridge Dri. *Alv* —4G **93**
Bembridge Dri. *Nott* —7D **32**
(in two parts)
Bemrose M. *Der* —4G **73**
Bemrose Rd. *Altn* —2E **92**
Benbow Av. *Melb* —3G **113**
Bendall Grn. *L'ver* —4G **91**
Bendigo La. *Nott* —4J **65**
Benedict Ct. *Nott* —4C **32**
Benjamin Outram Bus. Cen. *Rip*
—4A **12**
Ben Mayo Ct. *Nott* —1B **64**
Benmore Ct. *Oak* —4H **57**
Benner Av. *Ilk* —2E **60**
Bennerley Av. *Ilk* —2D **44**
Bennerley Ct. *Nott* —5F **31**
Bennerley Rd. *Blen I* —5F **31**
Bennett Rd. *Nott* —3J **49**
Bennett St. *Altn* —4D **92**
Bennett St. *Long E* —5G **79**
Bennett St. *Nott* —4H **49**
Bennett St. *Sand* —3F **79**
Benneworth Clo. *Huck* —7F **17**
Bennington Dri. *Nott* —4C **62**
Bensley Clo. *Chel* —1G **105**
Benson St. *Alv* —2F **93**
Ben St. *Nott* —1B **64**
Bentfield Rd. *Neth H* —2C **10**
Bentinck Av. *Toll* —7B **84**
Bentinck Ct. *Nott* —3G **65** (4J **5**)
Bentinck Rd. *Cltn* —4A **50**
Bentinck Rd. *Nott* —1B **64**
Bentinck St. *Huck* —4F **17**
Bentley Av. *Nott* —1J **65**
Bentley Rd. *Cas D* —6H **107**
Bentley St. *Altn* —3E **92**
Bentwell Av. *Arn* —6J **33**
Beresford Dri. *Ilk* —1C **44**
Beresford Dri. *Spon* —4A **76**
Beresford Ho. *Long E* —4D **96**
Beresford Rd. *Long E* —4E **96**
Beresford St. *Nott* —2A **64**
Berkeley Av. *Long E* —3G **97**
Berkeley Av. *Nott* —6E **48**
Berkeley Clo. *L'ver* —2H **91**
Berkeley Ct. *Nott* —5E **48**
Berkeley Cres. *Rad T* —4D **68**
Berkshire St. *Der* —7D **56**
Berle Av. *Hean* —2G **27**
Bermuda Av. *L Eat* —1C **56**
Bernard Av. *Huck* —3H **17**
Bernard St. *Nott* —5D **48**
Bernard Ter. *Carr* —5D **48**
Bernisdale Clo. *Nott* —4B **32**

Berridge Rd. Central. *Nott*
—6B **48**
Berridge Rd. E. *Nott* —6C **48**
Berridge Rd. W. *Nott* —7A **48**
Berriedale Clo. *Arn* —5A **34**
Berrydown Clo. *Nott* —5J **47**
Berry Hill Gro. *Ged* —4C **50**
Berry Pk. Clo. *Alst* —6J **55**
Belper Av. *Cltn* —5B **50**
Berwick Av. *Der* —1C **74**
Berwick Clo. *Alv* —4H **93**
Berwick Clo. *Nott* —7E **32**
Berwick Dri. *Sten F* —6H **91**
Berwin Clo. *Long E* —7E **78**
Beryldene Av. *Watn* —6A **30**
Besecar Av. *Ged* —4C **50**
Besecar Clo. *Ged* —4C **50**
Bessalone Dri. *Belp* —6A **10**
Bessell La. *S'fd* —3G **79**
Besthorpe Clo. *Oak* —6H **57**
Bestwick Av. *Hean* —4K **27**
Bestwick Clo. *Ilk* —3E **60**
Bestwood Av. *Arn* —5G **33**
Bestwood Clo. *Arn* —5G **33**
Bestwood Country Pk. —2B **32**
Bestwood Footpath. *Huck & B Vil*
—7K **17**
Bestwood Lodge Dri. *Arn* —4E **32**
Bestwood Pk. Dri. *Nott* —4D **32**
Bestwood Pk. Dri. W. *Nott*
—4K **31**
Bestwood Pk. Vw. *Arn* —4G **33**
Bestwood Rd. *Huck* —6J **17**
Bestwood Rd. *Nott* —5J **31**
Bestwood Swimming Pool.
—7D **32**
Bestwood Ter. *Nott* —5J **31**
Bethel Gdns. *Huck* —7C **16**
Bethnal Wlk. *Nott* —6H **31**
Bethule Rd. *Der* —1A **92**
Betjeman Sq. *Sin* —4A **92**
Betony Clo. *Bing* —4J **69**
Betula Clo. *Nott* —7J **81**
Bevel St. *Nott* —7B **48**
Beverley Clo. *Nott* —3B **62**
Beverley Dri. *Kimb* —6J **29**
Beverley Gdns. *Ged* —5D **50**
Beverley Rd. *Dis* —3B **116**
Beverley's Av. *What* —3H **71**
Beverley Sq. *Nott* —7G **49**
Beverley St. *Der* —6D **74**
Bewcastle Rd. *Nott* —4C **32**
Bewdley Clo. *Chel* —6G **93**
Bewick Dri. *Nott* —2A **66**
Bexhill Ct. *Bees* —6E **62**
Bexhill Wlk. *Der* —6E **56**
Bexleigh Gdns. *Nott* —6G **47**
Bexwell Clo. *Nott* —1A **100**
Biant Clo. *Nott* —3H **47**
Bible Wlk. *Nott* —2D **64** (2D **4**)
Bicester Av. *Sten F* —7G **91**
Bickley Moss. *Oak* —6H **57**
Bideford Clo. *Rip* —2J **11**
Bideford Dri. *Sun* —3H **91**
Bidford Rd. *Nott* —5F **47**
Bidwell Cres. *Got* —7H **99**
Biggart Clo. *Bees* —6C **80**
Biggin, The. *Cas D* —7K **107**
Biko Sq. *Nott* —6B **48**
Bilberry Wlk. *Nott* —1G **65**
Bilborough Rd. *Nott* —2B **62**
Bilby Gdns. *Nott* —2H **65**
Billesdon Dri. *Nott* —2B **48**
Bingham By-Pass. *Bing* —3H **69**
Bingham Ind. Pk. *Bing* —2A **70**
Bingham Leisure Cen. —3B **70**
Bingham Rd. *Cotg* —5K **85**
(in two parts)
Bingham Rd. *Nott* —4E **48**
Bingham Rd. *Rad T* —4K **67**
Bingham St. *Altn* —3E **92**
Bingley Clo. *Nott* —1H **63**
Binscombe La. *Oak* —4E **56**
Birch Av. *Ambgt* —1K **9**
Birch Av. *Bees* —4H **81**
Birch Av. *Cltn* —7B **50**
Birch Av. *Ilk* —7E **44**
Birch Av. *Nut* —7B **30**
Birch Clo. *Nut* —7B **30**
Birch Clo. *Rip* —4K **11**
Birch Clo. *Spon* —2C **76**
Birchdale Av. *Huck* —7G **17**
Birches Rd. *Alst* —4H **55**
Birchfield Clo. *Chel* —7F **93**
Birchfield Pk. *Hean* —6H **27**
Birchfield Rd. *Arn* —6J **33**
Birch Lea. *Red* —5F **33**
Birchover Ho. *Dar A* —4K **55**
Birchover Ho. *Der* —7H **55**
Birchover Pl. *Ilk* —1C **44**

Birchover Ri. *Chad* —6F **57**
Birchover Rd. *Nott* —2C **62**
Birchover Way. *Alst* —6G **55**
Birch Pas. *Nott* —2C **64** (2A **4**)
Birch Ri. *Wdbgh* —7G **21**
Birch Va. *Belp* —7K **9**
Birchview Clo. *Belp* —3B **24**
Birchwood. *Los* —1E **26**
Birchwood Av. *Breas* —2D **96**
Birchwood Av. *L'ver* —3H **91**
Birchwood Av. *Long E* —3G **97**
Birchwood Rd. *Nott* —3C **62**
Bircumshaw Rd. *Hean* —3G **27**
Birdcage Wlk. *Der* —2C **72**
(in two parts)
Birdcroft La. *Ilk* —2D **60**
Birdsall Av. *Nott* —3E **62**
Birdwood St. *Der* —7K **73**
Birkdale Clo. *Edw* —5J **83**
Birkdale Clo. *Man I* —5B **44**
Birkdale Clo. *Mick* —6E **72**
Birkdale Way. *Nott* —5B **32**
Birkin Av. *Bees* —6A **80**
Birkin Av. *Nott* —7B **48**
Birkin Av. *Rad T* —3A **68**
Birkin Av. *Rud* —1E **100**
Birkland Av. *Map* —2J **49**
Birkland Av. *Nott* —1E **64** (1E **4**)
Birley St. *S'fd* —3H **79**
Birling Clo. *Nott* —6F **31**
Birrell Rd. *Nott* —6C **48**
Biscay Ct. *Oak* —5J **57**
Bisham Dri. *W Bri* —1K **83**
Bishopdale Clo. *Long E* —3E **96**
Bishopdale Dri. *Watn* —6B **30**
Bishop Pl. *Belp* —7J **9**
Bishops Clo. *Keyw* —5C **102**
Bishops Ct. *Melb* —4H **113**
Bishop's Dri. *Oak* —5D **56**
Bishops Rd. *Bing* —2K **69**
Bishop St. *Eastw* —3D **28**
Bishops Way. *Huck* —3H **17**
Bispham Dri. *Bees* —5K **79**
Blaby Clo. *Sun* —3J **91**
Blackacre. *Bur J* —1J **51**
Blackberry Way. *Klbrn* —3F **25**
Blackbird Row. *Belp* —4C **24**
Blackburn Pl. *Ilk* —3C **44**
Blackcliffe Farm M. *Bradm*
—6G **101**
Blackett's Wlk. *Nott* —1J **99**
Blackfriars Clo. *Nut* —4D **46**
Blackhill Dri. *Cltn* —6D **50**
Black Hills Dri. *Ilk* —1C **60**
Black La. *C But* —1G **87**
Blackmore St. *Der* —2K **91**
Blackmount Ct. *Sin* —6H **91**
Blackrod Clo. *Bees* —6A **80**
Blacksmith Ct. *Cotg* —4J **85**
Blackstone Wlk. *Nott* —5E **64**
Black Swan Clo. *Wd'p* —2F **49**
Blackthorn Clo. *Bing* —3C **70**
Blackthorn Clo. *Melb* —3G **113**
Blackthorn Clo. *Oak* —5E **56**
Blackthorn Dri. *Eastw* —3C **28**
Blackthorn Dri. *Nott* —2H **47**
Blackthorne Clo. *Klbrn* —3F **25**
Blackthorne Dri. *Low* —3D **36**
Blackwell La. *Melb* —4H **113**
Bladon Clo. *Nott* —4G **49**
Bladon Rd. *Rud* —2D **100**
Blagreaves Av. *L'ver* —4G **91**
Blagreaves La. *L'ver* —2G **91**
Blair Ct. *Nott* —6E **64**
Blair Gro. *Sand* —4E **78**
Blaise Clo. *Nott* —1A **100**
Blakebrook Dri. *Chel* —6G **93**
Blake Clo. *Arn* —6J **33**
Blake Ct. *Long E* —4F **97**
Blakelow Dri. *Etw* —6D **88**
Blakemore Av. *Melb* —3H **113**
Blakeney Ct. *Oak* —6J **57**
Blakeney Rd. *Rad T* —4B **68**
Blakeney Wlk. *Arn* —1H **49**
Blake Rd. *S'fd* —2J **79**
Blake Rd. *W Bri* —1H **83**
Blake St. *Ilk* —5D **44**
Blanch Cft. *Melb* —4G **113**
Blandford Av. *Long E* —3F **97**
Blandford Clo. *Alv* —3K **93**
Blandford Rd. *Bees* —3C **80**
Bland La. *Epp* —7K **21**
Blanford Gdns. *W Bri* —3E **82**
Blankney Clo. *Sten F* —7H **91**
Blankney St. *Nott* —2A **48**
Blantyre Av. *Nott* —4A **32**
Blatherwick's Yd. *Arn* —5H **33**
Bleaberry Clo. *W Bri* —3A **84**
Bleachers Yd. *Nott* —5B **48**

Bleasby St. *Nott* —3H **65**
Bleasdale Clo. *Ged* —4E **50**
Blencathra Clo. *W Bri* —3A **84**
Blencathra Dri. *Mick* —1C **90**
Blenheim Av. *Low* —4E **36**
Blenheim Av. *Nott* —4A **50**
Blenheim Clo. *Rud* —2D **100**
Blenheim Ct. *Belp* —7D **10**
Blenheim Ct. *Sand* —4F **79**
Blenheim Dri. *Alst* —4G **55**
Blenheim Dri. *Bees* —3C **80**
Blenheim Gdns. *E Bri* —4K **53**
Blenheim Ind. Est. *Nott* —5F **31**
Blenheim La. *Nott* —3D **30**
Blenheim M. *Etw* —5E **88**
Blenheim Pde. *Alst* —3H **55**
Blidworth Clo. *Strel* —4E **46**
Blind La. *Breas* —1B **96**
Blind La. *Oxt* —1G **21**
Blithfield Gdns. *Chel* —7G **93**
Bloomfield Clo. *Der*
—5B **74** (7G **7**)
Bloomfield St. *Der* —5B **74** (7G **7**)
Bloomsbury Dri. *Nut* —3E **46**
Bloomsbury M. *Rad T* —4E **68**
Bloomsgrove Ind. Est. *Nott*
—2B **64**
Bloomsgrove Rd. *Ilk* —4D **44**
Bloomsgrove St. *Nott* —2B **64**
Bluebell Bank. *Bing* —4K **69**
Bluebell Clo. *Huck* —6C **16**
Bluebell Clo. *Sten F* —7G **91**
Blue Bell Clo. *Und* —2D **14**
Blue Bell Hill Rd. *Nott*
—1G **65** (1K **5**)
Bluebell Way. *Hean* —4K **27**
Bluebird Clo. *Sin* —5H **91**
Bluecoat Clo. *Nott* —1E **64** (1E **4**)
Bluecoat St. *Nott* —1E **64** (1E **4**)
Blue Mountains. *Duf* —5B **40**
Blundell Clo. *Nott* —6H **49**
Blunt St. *Stan C* —4C **42**
Blyth Gdns. *Nott* —4G **49**
Blyth Pl. *Der* —6D **56**
Blyth St. *Nott* —5G **49**
Blyton Wlk. *Nott* —6D **32**
Boat La. *Hov* —3K **37**
Boat La. *Jack* —5H **13**
Boatmans Clo. *Ilk* —4D **44**
Bobbers Mill Bri. *Nott* —7K **47**
Bobbers Mill Rd. *Nott* —7A **48**
Boden Dri. *Nut* —7C **30**
Boden St. *Der* —6B **74**
Boden St. *Nott* —2B **64** (2A **4**)
Bodmin Av. *Huck* —7C **16**
Bodmin Clo. *Sten F* —6H **91**
Bodmin Dri. *Nott* —4J **47**
Bodmin Grn. *Alv* —3H **93**
Body Rd. *Bees* —5B **80**
Bog La. *Tickn* —6E **112**
Bohem Rd. *Long E* —5G **79**
Bolcote Ho. *Cltn* —6C **50**
(off Foxhill Rd. E.)
Bold Clo. *Nott* —5H **31**
Bold La. *Der* —3A **74** (3D **6**)
Bolero Clo. *Nott* —2E **62**
Bolingey Way. *Huck* —6C **16**
Bolsover Clo. *Rip* —3A **12**
Bolsover St. *Huck* —5H **17**
Bolton Av. *Bees* —4C **80**
Bolton Clo. *W Bri* —2J **83**
Bolton Ter. *Rad T* —4K **67**
Boman's La. *Shot* —3C **8**
Bonchurch Clo. *Alv* —4J **93**
Bondgate. *Cas D* —7J **107**
Bond La. *Heag* —2E **10**
Bond St. *Arn* —5G **33**
Bond St. *Nott* —3G **65** (4J **5**)
Bonetti Clo. *Arn* —1K **49**
Boniface Gdns. *Nott* —4C **32**
Bonington Dri. *Arn* —6H **33**
**Bonington Gallery, The.** —1D **4**
Bonington Rd. *Nott* —2H **49**
Bonner Hill. *C'tn* —6D **20**
Bonner La. *C'tn* —5E **20**
Bonner's Rd. *Aws* —2G **45**
Bonnington Clo. *Nott* —7G **31**
(in three parts)
Bonnington Cres. *Nott* —2E **48**
Bonny Mead. *Cotg* —6J **85**
Bonnyrigg Dri. *Oak* —5G **57**
Bonsall Av. *Der* —7H **73**
Bonsall Ct. *Long E* —1J **97**
Bonsall Dri. *Mick* —5C **72**
Bonsall St. *Long E* —1J **97**
Bonser Clo. *Cltn* —7C **50**
Booth Clo. *Nott* —2F **65** (2G **5**)
Boothgate. *Belp* —5E **10**
Booth St. *Alv* —2F **93**

Booth St. *Rip* —2A **12**
Border Bank. *Rip* —6K **11**
Border Cres. *Alv* —4G **93**
Borlace Cres. *S'fd* —2J **79**
Borman Clo. *Nott* —1F **47**
Borough St. *Cas D* —7K **107**
Borough St. *Keg* —1H **117**
Borrowash Bri. *Borr* —1C **94**
Borrowash By-Pass. *Spon & Borr*
—4K **75**
Borrowash La. *Thurl* —3C **94**
Borrowash Rd. *Spon* —5B **76**
Borrowdale Clo. *Gam* —2B **84**
Borrowdale Ct. *Bees* —4B **80**
Borrowdale Dri. *Long E* —3E **96**
Borrowell. *Keg* —7G **109**
Borrowfield Rd. *Spon* —5A **76**
Borrowfields. *Borr* —7D **76**
Boscastle Rd. *Alv* —3H **93**
Boscawen Ct. *Ilk* —3D **44**
Bosden Clo. *Nott* —1C **62**
Bosley M. *Belp* —7K **9**
Bosley Sq. *Bees* —7G **63**
Bostock's La. *Ris* —4D **78**
Bostock's La. *Sand* —5E **78**
Boston Clo. *Chad* —2J **75**
Boston M. *Nott* —3B **48**
Boston St. *Nott* —2F **65** (3H **5**)
Boswell Sq. *Der* —2K **91**
Bosworth Av. *Sun* —3J **91**
Bosworth Clo. *Shelf* —6C **52**
Bosworth Dri. *Newt* —2F **29**
Bosworth Rd. *Cas D* —7H **107**
Bosworth Wlk. *Nott* —6D **64**
Bosworth Way. *Long E* —4J **97**
Botany Av. *Nott* —7H **49**
Botany Clo. *W Bri* —5E **82**
Botany Dri. *Ilk* —1D **44**
Bothe Clo. *Long E* —3G **97**
Bottle La. *Nott* —3E **64** (4F **5**)
Boulton Dri. *Alv* —3G **93**
Boulton La. *Der* —4E **92**
(in two parts)
Boundary Cres. *Bees* —6F **63**
Boundary La. *Lan M* —2A **28**
Boundary Rd. *Bees* —6F **63**
Boundary Rd. *Der* —4J **73**
Boundary Rd. *W Bri* —4G **83**
Bourne Clo. *Bees* —6D **62**
Bourne Ct. *Melb* —4G **113**
Bourne M. *N'fld* —1E **66**
Bourne Sq. *Breas* —1C **96**
Bourne St. *Der* —4A **74** (6E **6**)
Bourne St. *N'fld* —1E **66**
Bournmoor Av. *Nott* —7A **82**
Bovill St. *Nott* —1B **64**
Bowbank Clo. *L'ver* —3E **90**
Bowbridge Av. *L'ver* —4G **91**
Bowden Clo. *Nott* —3E **48**
Bowden Dri. *Bees* —2H **81**
Bowers Av. *Nott* —7F **49**
Bower St. *Der* —1F **93**
Bowes Well Rd. *Ilk* —4C **44**
Bowland Clo. *Mick* —7C **72**
Bowland Clo. *Nott* —7J **49**
Bowland Rd. *Bing* —3J **69**
Bowlees Ct. *L'ver* —2C **90**
Bowler Dri. *Klbrn* —6G **25**
Bowler St. *Rip* —5K **11**
Bowley, The. *Dis* —6K **115**
Bowling All. *Heag* —3E **10**
Bowling Clo. *Stan D* —7C **60**
Bowlwell Av. *Nott* —5B **32**
Bowmer Rd. *Der* —7E **74**
Bown Clo. *Klbrn* —5G **25**
Bowness Av. *Nott* —4J **47**
Bowness Clo. *Gam* —1A **84**
Bowscale Clo. *W Bri* —3A **84**
Boxley Dri. *W Bri* —4E **82**
Boxmoor Clo. *L'ver* —2D **90**
Boyce Gdns. *Nott* —5H **49**
Boycroft Av. *Nott* —6H **49**
Boyd Clo. *Arn* —4K **33**
Boyd Gro. *Chel* —2G **105**
Boyer St. *Der* —5J **73** (7B **6**)
Boyer Wlk. *Der* —5K **73** (7B **6**)
Boylestone Rd. *L'ver* —4G **91**
Boynton Dri. *Nott* —5H **49**
Bracadale Rd. *Nott* —4B **32**
Bracebridge Dri. *Nott* —1D **62**
Bracey Ri. *W Bri* —5G **83**
Bracken Clo. *Cltn* —4B **50**
Bracken Clo. *Long E* —7F **79**
Bracken Clo. *Nott* —5F **31**
Brackendale Av. *Arn* —5H **33**
Brackenfield Dri. *Gilt* —6F **29**
Brackenhill. *Cay* —5J **37**
Bracken Rd. *Long E* —7F **79**
Brackens Av. *Alv* —3F **93**

Brackensdale Av. *Der* —3F **73**
Bracken's La. *Alv* —3E **92**
Brackley Dri. *Spon* —3A **76**
Brackley Ga. *M'ly* —4G **41**
Bracknell Cres. *Nott* —5K **47**
Bracknell Dri. *Alv* —4F **93**
Bracton Dri. *Nott* —1H **65**
Bradbourne Av. *Nott* —3C **82**
Bradbourne Ct. *Der*
—5J **73** (7A **6**)
Bradbury Clo. *Borr* —7E **76**
Bradbury St. *Nott* —3J **65**
Braddock Clo. *Lent* —3A **64**
Braddon Av. *S'fd* —6J **61**
Bradfield Rd. *Nott* —5F **47**
Bradford Ct. *Nott* —7G **31**
Bradgate Clo. *Sand* —4F **79**
Bradgate Ct. *Der* —3J **91**
Bradgate Dri. *Rip* —4B **12**
Bradgate Rd. *Nott* —6C **48**
Brading Clo. *Alv* —4K **93**
Bradley Ct. *Bees* —2G **81**
Bradley Dri. *Belp* —1B **24**
Bradleys Orchard. *Hov* —3J **37**
Bradley St. *Der* —7J **55**
Bradley St. *Sand* —3G **79**
Bradleys Yd. *Plum* —2C **102**
Bradley Wlk. *Nott* —1B **100**
Bradman Gdns. *Arn* —7K **33**
Bradmoor Gro. *Chel* —7G **93**
Bradmore Av. *Rud* —1E **100**
Bradmore Ri. *Nott* —4H **49**
Bradshaw Cft. *Belp* —6J **9**
Bradshaw Dri. *Holb* —7C **24**
Bradshaw Retail Pk. *Der*
—4A **74** (6E **6**)
Bradshaw St. *Long E* —4F **97**
Bradshaw Way. *Der*
—4B **74** (6F **7**)
Bradwell Clo. *Gilt* —5G **29**
Bradwell Clo. *Mick* —7C **72**
Bradwell Dri. *Nott* —5B **32**
Bradwell Way. *Belp* —7B **10**
Braefell Clo. *W Bri* —3B **84**
Braefield Clo. *Ilk* —2A **60**
Braemar Av. *Eastw* —5D **28**
Braemar Clo. *Sten F* —6H **91**
Braemar Dri. *Ged* —5F **51**
Braemar Rd. *Nott* —6J **31**
Brafield Clo. *Belp* —1D **24**
Braidwood Ct. *Nott* —7B **48**
Brailsford Rd. *Chad* —7E **56**
Brailsford Rd. *Nott* —6A **64**
Brailsford Way. *Bees* —7C **80**
Braintree Clo. *Der* —5D **56**
Braithwell Clo. *Alst* —5K **55**
Bramber Gro. *Nott* —2A **100**
Brambleberry Ct. *Oak* —4H **57**
Bramble Clo. *Bees* —6D **80**
Bramble Clo. *Long E* —7F **79**
Bramble Clo. *Nott* —3K **47**
Bramble Ct. *Ged* —5D **50**
Bramble Dri. *Nott* —7J **49**
Bramble Gdns. *Nott* —6G **47**
Bramble M. *Mick* —7B **72**
Bramble St. *Der* —3K **73** (4C **6**)
Brambleway. *Cotg* —6A **86**
Bramble Way. *Klbrn* —3F **25**
Bramblewick Dri. *L'ver* —3E **90**
Bramcote Av. *Bees* —2C **80**
Bramcote Dri. *Bees* —1E **80**
Bramcote Dri. *Nott* —4D **62**
Bramcote Dri. W. *Bees* —2D **80**
Bramcote La. *Bees* —2C **80**
Bramcote La. *Nott* —3C **62**
**Bramcote Leisure Cen.** —6B **62**
Bramcote Rd. *Bees* —1E **80**
Bramcote St. *Nott* —2A **64**
Bramcote Wlk. *Nott* —2A **64**
Bramerton Rd. *Nott* —1C **62**
Bramfield Av. *Der* —5J **73** (7A **6**)
Bramfield Ct. *Der* —5J **73**
Bramhall Rd. *Nott* —1C **62**
Bramley Clo. *Gun* —1G **53**
Bramley Clo. *Oak* —4J **57**
Bramley Ct. *Kimb* —7K **29**
Bramley Grn. *Nott* —5E **46**
Bramley Rd. *Nott* —5E **46**
Brampton Av. *Hean* —3J **27**
Brampton Clo. *Mick* —5A **72**
Brampton Ct. *Belp* —1D **24**
Brampton Dri. *S'fd* —3K **79**
Brancaster Clo. *Nott* —2H **47**
Brandelhow Dri. *Oak* —4H **57**
Brandish Cres. *Nott* —7K **81**
Brandreth Av. *Nott* —6H **49**
Brandreth Dri. *Gilt* —5E **28**
Brand St. *Nott* —5H **65** (7K **5**)

Branklene Clo. *Kimb* —6J **29**
Branksome Av. *Alv* —2J **93**
Branksome Wlk. *Nott* —5E **64**
Bransdale Clo. *Long E* —3F **97**
Bransdale Rd. *Nott* —7K **81**
Branston Gdns. *W Bri* —4F **83**
Branston Wlk. *Nott* —2E **48**
Brantford Av. *Nott* —7B **82**
Brassington Clo. *Gilt* —6F **29**
Brassington Clo. *W Hal* —6G **43**
Brassington Rd. *Chad* —6F **57**
Braunton Clo. *Huck* —6D **16**
Brayfield Av. *L'ver* —1H **91**
Brayfield Rd. *L'ver* —1G **91**
Brayton Cres. *Nott* —1F **47**
Breach La. *Melb* —2E **112**
Breach Rd. *Den V* —1B **26**
Breach Rd. *Hean* —5J **27**
Breadsall Ct. *Ilk* —3D **44**
**Breadsall Priory Golf Course.**
—7G **41**
*Breaston Ct. Nott* —5C **32**
(off Erewash Gdns.)
Breaston La. *Ris* —5B **78**
Brechin Clo. *Arn* —3K **33**
Breckhill Rd. *Wd'p & Map*
—1G **49**
Breckswood Dri. *Nott* —2A **100**
Brecon Clo. *Long E* —1E **96**
Brecon Clo. *Nott* —2G **47**
Brecon Clo. *Spon* —2A **76**
Bredon Clo. *Long E* —1E **96**
Breedon Av. *L'ver* —4H **91**
Breedon Hill Rd. *Der* —5K **73**
**Breedon Priory Golf Club.**
—6A **114**
Breedon St. *Long E* —5F **79**
Brendon Ct. *Bees* —7B **62**
Brendon Dri. *Kimb* —6K **29**
Brendon Dri. *Nott* —2G **63**
Brendon Gdns. *Nott* —2G **63**
Brendon Gro. *Bing* —2J **69**
Brendon Rd. *Nott* —2G **63**
Brendon Way. *Long E* —6E **78**
Brentcliffe Av. *Nott* —7J **49**
Brentford Dri. *Der* —2F **73**
Brentnall Ct. *Bees* —5D **80**
Bren Way. *Hilt* —4A **88**
Bressingham Dri. *W Bri* —5E **82**
Bretby Sq. *L'ver* —4G **91**
Brett Clo. *Huck* —7E **16**
Bretton Av. *L'ver* —6G **73**
Bretton Rd. *Belp* —7E **10**
Brewery St. *Kimb* —7K **29**
**Brewhouse Mus.** —6E **4**
Brewhouse Yd. *Nott*
—4D **64** (6D **4**)
Brewsters Clo. *Bing* —3A **70**
Brewsters Rd. *Nott* —6G **49**
Breydon Clo. *Shel L* —5D **92**
Breydon Ind. Cen. *Long E* —2K **97**
Briar Av. *Sand* —5F **79**
Briarbank Av. *Nott* —6J **49**
Briarbank Wlk. *Nott* —7J **49**
Briar Clo. *Bees* —6E **62**
Briar Clo. *Borr* —6E **76**
Briar Clo. *Chad* —4H **75**
Briar Clo. *Huck* —7D **16**
Briar Clo. *Keyw* —5C **102**
Briar Ct. *Nott* —6D **64**
Briar Gdns. *C'tn* —4A **20**
Briar Ga. *Cotg* —6A **86**
Briar Ga. *Long E* —6E **78**
Briar Lea Clo. *Sin* —5K **91**
Briar Rd. *Newt* —5F **29**
Briarsgate. *Alst* —5H **55**
Briars La. *Der* —2E **90**
(in two parts)
Briars Way. *Rip* —3K **11**
Briarwood Av. *Nott* —7J **49**
Briarwood Ct. *Sher* —3G **49**
Briarwood Way. *L'ver* —3G **91**
Brickenell Rd. *C'tn* —6D **20**
Brick Kiln La. *M'ly* —6H **41**
Brick Row. *Dar A* —6A **56**
Brick St. *Der* —2J **73** (2A **6**)
Brickyard. *Huck* —6J **17**
Brickyard Cotts. *Nott* —5D **82**
Brickyard Dri. *Huck* —7J **17**
Brickyard La. *E Bri* —4K **53**
Brickyard La. *Klbrn* —3F **25**
Brickyard La. *Rad T* —4B **68**
Brickyard La. *Rip* —3B **12**
**Brickyard Plantation Nature
Reserve.** —6J **45**
Brickyard, The. *Stan C* —5D **42**
Bridge Av. *Bees* —3E **80**
Bridge Ct. *Bees* —1H **81**
Bridge Ct. *Huck* —7G **17**

Bri. Farm La. *Nott* —6A **82**
Bridge Field. *Breas* —2A **96**
Bridge Fields. *Keg* —7J **109**
Bridge Foot. *Belp* —7J **9**
Bridge Ga. *Der* —2A **74** (1D **6**)
Bridge Grn. Wlk. *Nott* —5E **46**
Bridge Gro. *W Bri* —7G **65**
Bridge Hill. *Belp* —7J **9**
Bridge La. *Wstn T* —7J **105**
Bridgend Clo. *S'fd* —3H **79**
Bridgend Ct. *Oak* —4J **57**
Bridgeness Rd. *L'ver* —3D **90**
Bridgeport Rd. *Chad* —2J **75**
Bridge Rd. *Nott* —2D **62**
Bridge St. *Belp* —1K **23**
Bridge St. *Der* —2K **73** (2A **6**)
(in two parts)
Bridge St. *Ilk* —2D **44**
Bridge St. *Lan M* —2A **28**
Bridge St. *Long E* —7H **79**
Bridge St. *Sand* —3G **79**
Bridge, The. *Milf* —6A **24**
Bridge Vw. *Milf* —6A **24**
Bridgeway Cen. *Nott* —5E **64**
Bridgeway Ct. *Nott* —5F **65**
Bridgeway Rd. *W Bri* —6G **65**
Bridgford St. *E Bri* —4J **53**
Bridgnorth Dri. *Nott* —6A **82**
Bridgnorth Way. *Bees* —5J **79**
Bridgwater Clo. *Alv* —2J **93**
Bridle Clo. *Chel* —2G **105**
Bridle La. *Heag* —2G **11**
Bridle La. *Rip* —1K **11**
(in two parts)
Bridle Rd. *Bees* —6B **62**
Bridle Rd. *Bur J* —7H **35**
Bridlesmith Ga. *Nott*
—3E **64** (4F **5**)
Bridleways. *E Bri* —4K **53**
Bridlington St. *Nott* —7A **48**
Bridport Av. *Nott* —2K **63**
Brielen Ct. *Rad T* —4A **68**
Brielen Rd. *Rad T* —4A **68**
Brierfield Av. *Nott* —4D **82**
Brierfield Way. *Mick* —7C **72**
Brierley Grn. *N'fld* —7E **50**
Brigden Av. *Altn* —2E **92**
Brighstone Clo. *Alv* —4J **93**
Brightmoor Ct. *Nott*
—3F **65** (4G **5**)
Brightmoor St. *Nott*
—3F **65** (4G **5**)
Brighton Rd. *Alv* —7F **75**
Bright St. *Der* —3G **73**
Bright St. *Ilk* —3C **44**
Bright St. *Nott* —2A **64**
Brigmor Wlk. *Der* —3H **73**
Brindley Ct. *Altn* —3E **92**
Brindley Rd. *Nott* —2C **62**
Brindley Wlk. *Sten F* —7J **91**
Brinkhill Cres. *Nott* —5B **82**
Brinsley Clo. *Nott* —5G **47**
Brinsley Hill. *Jack* —2A **14**
Brisbane Dri. *Nott* —5A **32**
Brisbane Dri. *S'fd* —6K **61**
Brisbane Rd. *Mick* —4C **72**
Briset Clo. *Sten F* —7J **91**
Bristol Dri. *Mick* —6C **72**
Bristol Rd. *Ilk* —5C **44**
Britannia Av. *Nott* —2A **48**
Britannia Av. *Wain* —5C **12**
Britannia Ct. *Der* —2A **74** (1D **6**)
(in two parts)
Britannia Ct. *N'fld* —1E **66**
Britannia Rd. *Long E* —7H **79**
Brittain Dri. *Rip* —3C **12**
Britten Gdns. *Nott* —1H **65**
Brixham Rd. *Huck* —7D **16**
Brixton Rd. *Nott* —2A **64**
B Rd. *Lent* —2K **81**
Broad Bank. *Der* —7J **55**
Broad Clo. *Wdbgh* —1F **35**
Broad Eadow Rd. *Nott* —6F **31**
Broadfields. *C'tn* —4D **20**
Broadfields Clo. *Der* —7K **55**
Broadgate. *Bees* —1G **81**
Broadgate Av. *Bees* —1G **81**
Broadgate Pk. *Bees* —7G **63**
Broadhill Rd. *Keg* —1G **117**
Broadholme La. *Belp* —5K **9**
Broadholme St. *Nott* —4B **64**
Broadhurst Av. *Nott* —4K **47**
Broadlands. *Sand* —5F **79**
Broad La. *Brins* —3C **14**
Broad La. *Thul* —5B **94**
Broadleaf Clo. *Oak* —5E **56**
Broadleigh Clo. *W Bri* —5E **82**
Broad Marsh Shop. Cen. *Nott*
—3E **64** (5F **5**)

Broadmead. *Bur J* —1K **51**
Broad Meer. *Cotg* —5J **85**
Broadmere Ct. *Arn* —4K **33**
Broad Oak Clo. *Nott* —7G **49**
Broad Oak Dri. *Brins* —3B **14**
Broad Oak Dri. *S'fd* —2H **79**
Broadstairs Rd. *Bees* —6K **79**
Broadstone Clo. *Chad* —6G **57**
Broadstone Clo. *W Bri* —3E **82**
Broadstone La. *Tickn* —6C **112**
Broad St. *Long E* —2H **97**
Broad St. *Nott* —2F **65** (3G **5**)
Broad Valley Dri. *B Vil* —1A **32**
Broad Wlk. *Nott* —3J **47**
Broadway. *Der* —7H **55**
Broadway. *Duf* —3H **39**
Broadway. *Hean* —4G **27**
Broadway. *Ilk* —3C **44**
Broadway. *Nott* —3F **65** (5G **5**)
Broadway. *Rip* —2A **12**
Broadway Av. *Rip* —3A **12**
Broadway E. *Cltn* —1B **66**
**Broadway Media Cen. —3G 5**
Broadway Pk. Clo. *Nott* —7J **55**
Broadwood Ct. *Bees* —7G **63**
Broadwood Rd. *Nott* —5D **32**
Brockdale Gdns. *Keyw* —5C **102**
Brockenhurst Gdns. *Nott*
—1H **65**
Brockhall Ri. *Hean* —4J **27**
Brockhole Clo. *W Bri* —3B **84**
Brockley. *Spon* —3A **76**
Brockley Rd. *W Bri* —1K **83**
Brockwood Cres. *Keyw* —5C **102**
Bromfield Clo. *Nott* —7A **50**
Bromley Clo. *Nott* —7H **31**
Bromley Pl. *Nott* —3D **64** (4D **4**)
Bromley Rd. *W Bri* —2G **83**
Bromley St. *Der* —1J **73**
Brompton Clo. *Arn* —3C **32**
Brompton Rd. *Der* —2D **72**
(in two parts)
Brompton Way. *W Bri* —5E **82**
Bromyard Dri. *Chel* —6G **93**
Bronte Clo. *Long E* —2E **96**
Bronte Ct. *Nott* —1C **64** (1B **4**)
Bronte Pl. *L'ver* —1F **91**
Brook Av. *Arn* —5K **33**
Brook Clo. *Find* —7B **90**
Brook Clo. *Long E* —4J **97**
Brook Clo. *Newt* —4F **29**
Brook Clo. *Nott* —7H **31**
Brook Clo. *Quar* —3G **55**
Brook Cotts. *Ilk* —3D **44**
Brook Ct. *Lan M* —3K **27**
Brookdale Ct. *Nott* —1F **49**
Brooke St. *Ilk* —1F **61**
Brooke St. *Sand* —3F **79**
Brookfield. *Bar T* —4A **104**
Brookfield Av. *Chad* —7H **57**
Brookfield Av. *Huck* —7F **17**
Brookfield Av. *Sun* —3H **91**
Brookfield Clo. *Cod* —3D **12**
Brookfield Clo. *Rad T* —4K **67**
Brookfield Ct. *Arn* —6J **33**
Brookfield Ct. *Nott* —5E **64** (7F **5**)
Brookfield Dri. *Hov* —2K **37**
Brookfield Gdns. *Arn* —6J **33**
Brookfield Rd. *Arn* —6H **33**
Brookfields. *Klbrn* —6E **24**
Brookfields Dri. *Bread* —3D **56**
Brookfields Way. *E Leak* —4K **111**
Brookfield Way. *Hean* —4K **27**
Brook Gdns. *Arn* —5J **33**
Brook Gdns. *Der* —2J **73** (1A **6**)
Brookhill Cres. *Nott* —4E **62**
Brookhill Dri. *Nott* —4E **62**
Brookhill Leys Rd. *Eastw* —4C **28**
Brookhill St. *S'fd* —3G **79**
Brookhouse St. *Altn* —4D **92**
Brookland Clo. *Gun* —1G **53**
Brookland Dri. *Bees* —3D **80**
Brooklands Av. *Hean* —3H **27**
Brooklands Cres. *Ged* —5E **50**
Brooklands Dri. *Ged* —5E **50**
Brooklands Dri. *L'ver* —1G **91**
Brooklands Rd. *Nott* —7K **49**
Brook La. *Gam* —1A **84**
Brook La. *Rip* —5K **11**
Brooklyn Av. *Bur J* —2J **51**
Brooklyn Clo. *Nott* —1K **47**
Brooklyn Rd. *Nott* —7K **31**
Brook Rd. *Bees* —7F **63**
Brook Rd. *Borr* —7E **76**
Brook Rd. *Thul* —5B **94**
Brooksby La. *Nott* —4B **82**
Brooks Clo. *E Bri* —3K **53**
Brooks Hollow. *L Eat* —7C **40**
Brook Side. *Belp* —2K **23**

Brookside. *Dis* —6A **116**
Brookside. *Eastw* —1D **28**
Brookside. *Huck* —7H **17**
Brookside. *Low* —4D **36**
Brookside Av. *Nott* —5D **62**
Brookside Clo. *Der* —4H **17**
Brookside Clo. *Long E* —1F **97**
Brookside Gdns. *Rud* —1D **100**
Brookside Rd. *Bread* —3D **56**
Brookside Rd. *Rud* —1D **100**
Brook St. *Der* —2K **73** (1B **6**)
Brook St. *Heag* —3E **10**
Brook St. *Huck* —4G **17**
Brook St. *Los* —7D **12**
Brook St. *Neth H* —2C **10**
Brook St. *Nott* —2F **65** (3G **5**)
Brookthorpe Way. *Nott* —4C **82**
Brookvale Av. *Cod* —4D **12**
Brookvale Av. *Den* —3G **25**
Brookvale Ri. *Den* —3G **25**
Brookvale Rd. *Den* —3G **25**
Brook Va. Rd. *Lan M* —3A **28**
Brook Vw. Ct. *Keyw* —7C **102**
Brook Vw. Dri. *Keyw* —7C **102**
Brook Wlk. *Der* —2K **73** (2B **6**)
Brookwood Cres. *Cltn* —7A **50**
Broom Clo. *Belp* —7F **93**
Broom Clo. *C'tn* —4D **20**
Broom Clo. *Chel* —7F **93**
Broom Clo. *Duf* —3H **39**
Broom Clo. *Sten F* —7H **91**
Broomfield Clo. *Sand* —3E **78**
Broomhill Av. *Ilk* —1E **60**
(in two parts)
Broomhill Clo. *Mick* —5B **72**
Broomhill Pk. Vw. *Huck* —7J **17**
Broomhill Rd. *Huck* —7G **17**
Broomhill Rd. *Kimb* —7A **30**
Broomhill Rd. *Nott* —7J **31**
Broom Rd. *C'tn* —5D **20**
Broom Wlk. *Nott* —6J **49**
Brora Rd. *Nott* —6K **31**
Brough St. *Der* —3H **73**
Broughton Av. *Der* —7H **73**
Broughton Clo. *Ilk* —3C **44**
Broughton Dri. *Nott* —3J **63**
Broughton St. *Bees* —1F **81**
Brownes Rd. *Bing* —2C **70**
Brownhill Clo. *C Bis* —4G **87**
Browning Circ. *Der* —2K **91**
Browning Clo. *Day* —6F **33**
Browning Ct. *Nott* —3D **48**
Browning St. *Der* —3K **91**
Brown La. *Bar F* —3E **98**
Brownlow Dri. *Nott* —4K **31**
Browns Cft. *Nott* —3K **47**
Brown's Flat. *Kimb* —6K **29**
Brown's La. *E Bri* —3J **53**
Brown's La. *Holb* —6D **24**
Browns La. *Keyw* —7F **103**
Brown's Rd. *Long E* —1J **97**
Brown St. *Nott* —7B **48**
Broxtowe Av. *Kimb* —7H **29**
Broxtowe Av. *Nott* —4J **47**
Broxtowe Dri. *Huck* —3G **17**
Broxtowe Hall Clo. *Nott* —4G **47**
Broxtowe Ho. *Nott* —5D **46**
Broxtowe La. *Nott* —5F **47**
**Broxtowe Pk. —4E 46**
Broxtowe Ri. *Nott* —3H **47**
Broxtowe St. *Nott* —4E **48**
Bruce Clo. *Nott* —5F **65**
Bruce Dri. *W Bri* —1F **83**
Brunel Av. *Newt* —1F **29**
Brunel Ter. *Nott* —2C **64** (3A **4**)
Brunswick Dri. *S'fd* —3J **79**
Brunswick St. *Der* —7K **73**
Brunswood Clo. *Spon* —3A **76**
Brunton Clo. *Mick* —7A **72**
Brunt's La. *E Bri* —5J **53**
Brushfield St. *Nott* —7A **48**
*Brussells Ter. Ilk* —5C **44**
(off Bath St.)
Brusty Pl. *Bur J* —1J **51**
Bryan Ct. *Nott* —6J **47**
Brynsmoor Rd. *Brins* —5C **14**
Bryony Clo. *Oak* —5G **57**
Buchanan St. *Der* —2A **74** (1D **6**)
Buchan St. *Der* —2D **92**
Buckfast Way. *W Bri* —1J **83**
Buckingham Av. *Der* —7D **56**
Buckingham Av. *Huck* —4H **17**
Buckingham Clo. *Hean* —3E **26**
Buckingham Ct. *Sand* —5E **78**
Buckingham Dri. *Rad T* —5D **68**
Buckingham Rd. *Sand* —5E **78**
Buckingham Rd. *Wd'p* —1G **49**
Buckingham Way. *Watn* —6B **30**
Buckland Clo. *Der* —2J **73** (2A **6**)

Buckland Dri. *Wdbgh* —1G **35**
Bucklee Dri. *C'tn* —5C **20**
Bucklow Clo. *Nott* —5K **47**
Buckminster Clo. *Oak* —5F **57**
Buckminster Rd. *Ilk* —3A **60**
Budby Ri. *Huck* —4H **17**
Bulcote Dri. *Bur J* —3H **51**
Bulcote Rd. *Nott* —5B **82**
Bullace Rd. *Nott* —7H **49**
Bull Clo. Rd. *Lent* —7A **64**
Buller Ct. *Der* —6J **73**
Buller St. *Ilk* —1E **60**
Buller Ter. *Nott* —3F **49**
Bullfinch Rd. *Nott* —2K **47**
Bullins Clo. *Nott* —4E **32**
Bullivant St. *Nott* —1F **65** (1G **5**)
Bullpit La. *Duf* —6A **40**
Bullsmoor. *Belp* —1C **24**
Bulstrode Pl. *Keg* —1G **117**
Bulwell Bus. Cen. *Nott* —6G **31**
**Bulwell Forest Golf Course.**
**—5K 31**
Bulwell High Rd. *Nott* —6H **31**
Bulwell La. *Nott* —2K **47**
Bulwer Rd. *Nott* —2B **64**
Bunbury St. *Nott* —6F **65**
Bunny La. *E Leak* —5K **111**
Bunny La. *Keyw* —7A **102**
Bunting Clo. *Ilk* —1A **60**
Bunting Clo. *Mick* —5E **72**
Buntings La. *Cltn* —7A **50**
Bunting St. *Nott* —6A **64**
Burbage Clo. *Belp* —1D **24**
Burbage Pl. *Alv* —2F **93**
Burcot Clo. *W Hal* —6G **43**
Burden La. *Shelf* —5C **52**
Burdock Clo. *Oak* —5E **56**
Burford Rd. *Nott* —6B **48**
Burford St. *Arn* —5G **33**
Burgass Rd. *Nott* —7J **49**
Burge Clo. *Nott* —5E **64**
Burgh Hall Clo. *Bees* —6C **80**
Burghley Clo. *Chel* —7F **44**
Burghley Way. *L'ver* —3C **90**
Burhill. *Cotg* —6A **86**
Burke St. *Nott* —2C **64** (2A **4**)
Burleigh Clo. *Cltn* —7D **50**
Burleigh Dri. *Der* —7K **55**
Burleigh Rd. *W Bri* —2H **83**
Burleigh Sq. *Bees* —4C **80**
Burleigh St. *Ilk* —5D **44**
Burley Dri. *Quar* —7J **39**
Burley Hill. *Alst* —7A **40**
Burley La. *Quar* —7H **39**
Burley Ri. *Keg* —2H **117**
Burlington Av. *Nott* —3D **48**
Burlington Clo. *Breas* —1B **96**
Burlington Ct. *Nott* —3E **48**
Burlington Rd. *Cltn* —6C **50**
Burlington Rd. *Der* —2D **72**
Burlington Rd. *Nott* —3E **48**
Burlington Way. *Mick* —7B **72**
Burnaby St. *Der* —1F **93**
Burnaby St. *Nott* —2K **47**
Burnage Ct. *Der* —4K **73** (6B **6**)
Burnaston La. *Etw* —4E **88**
Burnbank Clo. *W Bri* —3B **84**
Burnbreck Gdns. *Nott* —3E **62**
Burncroft. *W Hal* —7G **43**
Burndale Wlk. *Nott* —5A **32**
Burneham Clo. *E Bri* —4J **53**
Burnham Av. *Bees* —4F **81**
Burnham Clo. *W Hal* —6F **43**
Burnham Dri. *Mick* —6A **72**
Burnham Lodge. *Nott* —4A **32**
Burnham St. *Nott* —4E **48**
Burnham Way. *Nott*
—4E **64** (7F **5**)
Burnor Pool. *C'tn* —5D **20**
Burns Av. *Nott* —1C **64** (1B **4**)
Burns Clo. *L'ver* —1F **91**
Burns Ct. *Nott* —3D **48**
Burnside Clo. *Sten F* —6H **91**
Burnside Dri. *Bees* —5C **62**
Burnside Dri. *Spon* —4B **76**
Burnside Grn. *Nott* —1D **62**
Burnside Gro. *Toll* —7A **84**
Burnside Rd. *Nott* —1D **62**
Burnside Rd. *W Bri* —3G **83**
Burnside St. *Der* —1G **93**
Burns St. *Hean* —3F **27**
Burns St. *Ilk* —6C **44**
Burns St. *Nott* —1C **64** (1A **4**)
Burnt Ho. Rd. *Hean* —4F **27**
Burnt Oak Clo. *Nut* —3D **46**
**Burntstump Country Pk. —2F 19**
**(Woodland Walks)**
Burntstump Hill. *Arn & C'tn*
—2E **18**

Burrwood Dri. *Nott* —2D **62**
Burr La. *Ilk* —5D **44**
Burrowfield M. *Der* —6B **76**
Burrows Av. *Bees* —6F **63**
Burrows Ct. *Nott* —2H **65**
Burrows Cres. *Bees* —6F **63**
Burrows Wlk. *Der* —4A **74** (5E **6**)
Burtness Rd. *Nott* —7A **82**
Burton Av. *Cltn* —6K **49**
Burton Clo. *Cltn* —5E **50**
Burton Dri. *Bees* —4C **80**
Burton La. *What* —3K **71**
Burton Manderfield Ct. *Nott*
—5E **64**
Burton Rd. *Cltn* —6D **50**
Burton Rd. *Egg & Find* —7K **89**
Burton Rd. *L'ver* —7F **73** (7B **6**)
Burton Rd. *Tickn* —7A **112**
Burton St. *Hean* —3G **27**
Burton St. *Nott* —2E **64** (3E **4**)
Burwell St. *Nott* —1B **64**
Bushy Clo. *Nott* —5B **32**
Bushy Clo. *Long E* —3F **97**
Bute Av. *Nott* —3B **64**
Bute Wlk. *Der* —1C **74**
Butler Av. *Rad T* —3A **68**
Butler Clo. *C But* —2G **87**
Butlers Clo. *Huck* —7J **17**
Butler St. *Nott* —3A **64**
Butterfield Ct. *Watn* —6A **30**
Butterley Cft. Bus. Cen. *Rip*
—4B **12**
Butterley Hill. *Rip* —2K **11**
Butterley La. *Rip* —1K **11**
**Butterley Pk. —1C 12**
Butterley Row. *Rip* —1K **11**
Buttermead Clo. *Trow* —5H **61**
Buttermere Clo. *Gam* —1B **84**
Buttermere Clo. *Long E* —6E **78**
Buttermere Ct. *Nott* —4E **48**
Buttermere Dri. *Alst* —4J **55**
Buttermere Dri. *Bees* —7D **62**
Butterton Clo. *Ilk* —7E **44**
Butterwick Clo. *Sun* —4J **91**
Butt Houses. *Nott* —3A **64**
Butt La. *E Bri* —4K **53**
Buttonoak Dri. *Chel* —6G **93**
Buttrey Gdns. *Rud* —3E **100**
Butt Rd. *Bing* —3C **70**
Butts Clo. *Ilk* —3D **60**
Butts, The. *Belp* —2A **24**
Butt St. *Sand* —3F **79**
Buxton Av. *Cltn* —5B **50**
Buxton Av. *Hean* —5H **27**
Buxton Ct. *Ilk* —4B **44**
Buxton Dri. *L Eat* —4D **40**
Buxton Dri. *Mick* —5C **72**
Buxton Grn. *Hean* —6H **27**
Buxton Ho. *Spon* —4A **76**
(off Arnhem Ter.)
Buxton Rd. *Chad* —6F **57**
Bye Pass Rd. *Bees* —6D **80**
Byard La. *Nott* —3E **64** (5F **5**)
Byfield Clo. *Nott* —1B **64**
Byfield Clo. *Oak* —5H **57**
Byford Clo. *Nott* —4G **49**
Byley Rd. *Nott* —2B **62**
Byng Av. *Der* —2K **91**
By-Pass Rd. *Gun* —1F **53**
Byrne Ct. *Arn* —1K **49**
Byron Av. *Long E* —5F **79**
Byron Ct. *Nott* —3G **65** (4J **5**)
Byron Ct. *S'fd* —6J **61**
Byron Cres. *Aws* —2G **45**
Byron Gro. *Nott* —3E **48**
Byron Rd. *W Bri* —1H **83**
Byron St. *Day* —6F **33**
Byron St. *Der* —6K **73**
Byron St. *Huck* —6G **17**
Byron St. *Ilk* —5D **44**
Bywell La. *Klbrn* —4F **25**

**C** abot Clo. *Belp* —7E **10**
Caddaw Av. *Huck* —6G **17**
Cadgwith Dri. *Der* —4J **55**
Cadlan Clo. *Nott* —6C **32**
Cadlan Ct. *Nott* —6C **32**
Cadwell Clo. *Alv* —3K **93**
Caerhays Ct. *Sten F* —6H **91**
Caernarvon Clo. *Spon* —3B **76**
Caernarvon Pl. *Bees* —4B **80**
Caesar St. *Der* —1B **74**
Caincross Rd. *Nott* —7D **46**
Cairngorm Dri. *Arn* —3D **32**
Cairnsdale Clo. *Der* —1B **74**
Cairns Clo. *Mick* —5C **72**
Cairns Clo. *Nott* —1C **48**
Cairnsmore Clo. *Long E* —7E **78**

Cairns St. *Nott* —2E **64** (2F **5**)
Cairo St. *Nott* —5B **48**
Caister Rd. *Nott* —1A **100**
Caithness Ct. *Nott* —5D **48**
Caladine La. *Hors W* —7K **25**
Calcroft Clo. *Nott* —4J **47**
Caldbeck Clo. *Gam* —1A **84**
Caldbeck Ct. *Bees* —4B **80**
Caldbeck Wlk. *Nott* —6D **32**
Calder Clo. *Alst* —4J **55**
Calder Clo. *Hilt* —4A **88**
Calderdale. *Nott* —4B **62**
Calderdale Dri. *Long E* —3E **96**
Calderhall Gdns. *Nott* —5E **32**
Caldermill Dri. *Oak* —5G **57**
Calder Wlk. *Nott* —6H **31**
Caldon Grn. *Nott* —3J **31**
Caledon Rd. *Nott* —3D **48**
California Gdns. *Der* —4G **73**
Calke Ri. *Rip* —3B **12**
Calke Rd. *Melb* —5G **113**
Calladine Ct. *Nott* —7G **31**
Calladine La. *Shot* —1A **22**
Calladine Rd. *Hean* —3F **27**
Callaway Clo. *Nott* —2E **62**
Callow Hill. *L'ver* —3B **90**
Callow Hill Way. *L'ver* —2D **90**
Calstock Rd. *Wd'p* —1G **49**
Calveley Rd. *Nott* —6E **46**
Calver Clo. *Belp* —6B **10**
Calver Clo. *Nott* —3J **63**
Calver Clo. *Oak* —4E **56**
Calvert Clo. *Bees* —4D **80**
Calverton Av. *Cltn* —5K **49**
Calverton Clo. *Bees* —6A **80**
Calverton Clo. *Shel L* —6E **92**
Calverton Dri. *Strel* —4D **46**
Calverton Rd. *Arn* —4H **33**
**Calverton Sports & Leisure Cen.**
**—4C 20**
Calvert St. *Der* —4C **74** (6H **7**)
Calvin Clo. *Alv* —4G **93**
Camberley Ct. *Nott* —5G **31**
Camberley Rd. *Nott* —5G **31**
Camberwell Av. *Der* —2E **72**
Camborne Dri. *Nott* —4J **47**
Cambourne Clo. *Der* —6E **56**
Cambria M. *Nott* —7E **48**
Cambridge Ct. *Nott* —1B **64**
Cambridge Cres. *S'fd* —5H **61**
Cambridge Gdns. *Wd'p* —1K **49**
Cambridge Rd. *Nott* —3G **63**
Cambridge Rd. *W Bri* —1J **83**
Cambridge St. *Cltn* —5C **50**
Cambridge St. *Der* —6A **74**
Cambridge St. *Spon* —4A **76**
Camdale Clo. *Bees* —2B **80**
Camden Clo. *Nott* —3G **65** (4K **5**)
Camden St. *Der* —4H **73**
Camelia Av. *Nott* —7J **81**
Camellia Clo. *Mick* —5B **72**
Camelot Av. *Nott* —4C **48**
Camelot Cres. *Rud* —1D **100**
Camelot St. *Rud* —1D **100**
Cameo Clo. *Colw* —1D **66**
Cameron Rd. *Der* —1K **91**
Cameron St. *Nott* —4A **48**
Camomile Clo. *Nott* —6A **32**
Camomile Gdns. *Nott* —7A **48**
Campbell Dri. *Cltn* —6A **50**
Campbell Gdns. *Arn* —4A **34**
Campbell Gro. *Nott*
—2F **65** (2H **5**)
Campbell St. *Belp* —2K **23**
Campbell St. *Der* —2D **92**
Campbell St. *Lan M* —1A **28**
Campbell St. *Nott* —2G **65** (2J **5**)
Campden Grn. *Nott* —6A **82**
Campion Hill. *Cas D* —1J **107**
Campion St. *Arn* —5G **33**
Campion St. *Der* —3H **73**
Campion Way. *Bing* —3K **69**
Campsie Ct. *Sin* —6H **91**
Camp St. *Der* —1A **74**
(in two parts)
Camp Wood Clo. *L Eat* —7C **40**
Camrose Clo. *Nott* —6F **47**
Canada St. *Belp* —3A **24**
Canal Bank. *Shard* —1J **107**
**Canal Mus., The. —6F 5**
Canal Side. *Bees* —5H **81**
Canal Side. *Chel* —6E **92**
Canalside. *Nott* —4E **64** (6F **5**)
Canalside Wlk. *Nott*
—4E **64** (7C **4**)
Canal St. *Der* —4B **74** (6G **7**)
Canal St. *Ilk* —5E **44**
Canal St. *Long E* —7F **79**
Canal St. *Nott* —4E **64** (6E **4**)

Canal St. *Sand* —3F **79**
Canberra Clo. *Mick* —6C **72**
Canberra Clo. *S'fd* —6J **61**
Canberra Cres. *W Bri* —4F **83**
Canberra Gdns. *W Bri* —5F **83**
Candleby Clo. *Cotg* —5K **85**
Candleby Ct. *Cotg* —5K **85**
Candleby La. *Cotg* —5K **85**
Candle Mdw. *Colw P* —2B **66**
Canning Cir. *Nott* —2C **64** (3B **4**)
Canning Ter. *Nott* —2C **64** (3B **4**)
Cannock Way. *Long E* —2K **97**
Cannon St. *Nott* —3E **48**
Canonbie Clo. *Arn* —4A **34**
Canon Clo. *Ilk* —1C **44**
Canon's Wlk. *Dar A* —5K **55**
Cantabury Av. *Nott* —6B **48**
Cantelupe Rd. *Ilk* —6D **44**
Canterbury Clo. *Duf* —3H **39**
Canterbury Clo. *Nut* —2D **46**
Canterbury Ct. *Nott*
—1D **64** (1D **4**)
Canterbury Rd. *Nott* —2K **63**
Canterbury St. *Chad* —6E **56**
Cantley Av. *Ged* —4C **50**
Cantley Clo. *Shel L* —6D **92**
Cantrell Rd. *Nott* —7J **31**
Canver Clo. *Nott* —1C **62**
Canwick Clo. *Nott* —2C **62**
Capenwray Gdns. *Nott* —5E **32**
Capes, The. *Asl* —3H **71**
Capitol Ct. *Nott* —2G **63**
Caporn Clo. *Nott* —1J **47**
Cardale Rd. *Nott* —1J **65**
Cardales Clo. *Find* —7B **90**
Cardean Clo. *Der* —1B **74**
Cardiff St. *Nott* —2H **65** (2K **5**)
Cardigan St. *Der* —1C **74** (1J **7**)
Cardinal Clo. *Nott* —1G **65**
Cardinal Clo. *Oak* —5F **57**
Cardington Clo. *Nott* —4A **32**
Cardrona Clo. *Oak* —5F **57**
Cardwell St. *Nott* —6B **48**
Carew Rd. *Nott* —6A **82**
Carey Rd. *Nott* —5J **31**
Carisbrooke Av. *Bees* —7G **63**
Carisbrooke Av. *Ged* —5F **51**
Carisbrooke Av. *Nott* —5E **48**
Carisbrooke Dri. *Nott* —5E **48**
Carisbrooke Gdns. *L'ver* —3G **91**
Carlight Cvn. Site. *W Bri* —6K **65**
Carlin Clo. *Breas* —1C **96**
Carlingford Rd. *Huck* —5G **17**
Carlin St. *Nott* —6H **31**
Carlisle Av. *L'ver* —1F **91**
Carlisle Av. *Nott* —6J **31**
Carlisle Rd. *Cltn* —6C **50**
Carlswark Gdns. *Nott* —4B **32**
Carlton Av. *Shel L* —5E **92**
Carlton Bus. Cen. *Cltn* —7D **50**
Carlton Clo. *Hean* —2J **27**
Carlton Dri. *Shel L* —6E **92**
Carlton Fold. *Nott* —4H **65**
**Carlton Forum Leisure**
**Cen. South. —6A 50**
Carlton Gdns. *Shel L* —5E **92**
Carlton Grange. *Cltn* —7A **50**
Carlton Hill. *Cltn* —7K **49**
Carlton M. *Cltn* —7A **50**
Carlton Rd. *Der* —7H **73**
Carlton Rd. *Long E* —4F **97**
Carlton Rd. *Nott* —3G **65** (4J **5**)
Carlton Sq. *Cltn* —7C **50**
Carlton St. *Nott* —3F **65** (4G **5**)
Carlton Va. *Cltn* —5B **50**
Carlton Wlk. *Alv* —1G **93**
Carlyle Pl. *Hean* —2F **27**
Carlyle Rd. *W Bri* —1G **83**
Carlyle St. *Hean* —2F **27**
Carlyle St. *Sin* —4K **91**
Carman Clo. *Watn* —5A **30**
Carmel Gdns. *Arn* —7H **33**
Carnaby Clo. *Rad T* —4E **68**
Carnarvon Clo. *Bing* —2A **70**
Carnarvon Dri. *Bur J* —1K **51**
Carnarvon Gro. *Cltn* —6B **50**
Carnarvon Gro. *Ged* —5D **50**
Carnarvon Pl. *Bing* —3K **69**
Carnarvon Rd. *W Bri* —2H **83**
Carnarvon St. *N'fld* —1E **66**
Carnegie St. *Der* —1A **92**
Carnforth Clo. *Mick* —7C **72**
Carnforth Clo. *S'fd* —3H **79**
Carnforth Ct. *Nott* —5E **32**
Carnival Way. *Cas D* —5K **107**
Carnoustie Clo. *Mick* —6D **72**
Carnwood Rd. *Nott* —7C **32**
Carol Cres. *Chad* —3F **75**
Caroline Clo. *Alv* —2K **93**

Caroline Ct. *Ilk* —1E **60**
Caroline Wlk. *Nott* —7F **49**
Carpenters Clo. *C But* —2H **87**
(in two parts)
Carradale Clo. *Arn* —5A **34**
Carrfield Av. *Bees* —6K **79**
Carrfield Av. *Long E* —7K **79**
Carrfields. *Hors W* —6J **25**
Carrington Ct. *Nott* —5E **48**
Carrington La. *C'tn* —3D **20**
Carrington St. *Der* —4B **74** (6G **7**)
(in two parts)
Carrington St. *Nott* —4E **64** (6F **5**)
(in three parts)
Carrock Av. *Hean* —4K **27**
Carroll Gdns. *Nott* —6E **64**
Carron Clo. *Sin* —5J **91**
Carr Rd. *Bing* —2D **70**
Carrs Clo. *Cas D* —7J **107**
Carsington Cres. *Alst* —5H **55**
Carsington Ho. *Alst* —5H **55**
Carsington M. *Alst* —6J **55**
Carson Rd. *Chad* —2H **75**
Cartbridge. *Cotg* —6K **85**
Carter Av. *Rad T* —4B **68**
Carter Av. *Rud* —3E **100**
Carter Clo. *Long E* —2F **97**
Carter Dri. *Sand* —2G **79**
Carter Ga. *Nott* —3F **65** (5H **5**)
Carter Rd. *Bees* —5A **80**
(Readman Rd.)
Carter Rd. *Bees* —6A **80**
(Swiney Way)
Carter St. *Altn* —3D **92**
Carterswood Dri. *Nut* —3F **47**
Carver St. *Nott* —6B **48**
Carwood Rd. *Bees* —6D **62**
Cascade Gro. *L'ver* —2E **90**
Casper Ct. *Nott* —5C **32**
(off Birkdale Way)
Casson Av. *Alv* —3G **93**
Castellan Ri. *Nott* —5E **32**
Casterton Rd. *Nott* —5D **32**
Castings Rd. *Nott* —1B **92**
Castle Boulevd. *Nott*
—4B **64** (7A **4**)
Castlebridge Office Village. *Nott*
—5C **64**
Castle Bri. Rd. *Nott* —4C **64** (7A **4**)
Castle Clo. *Borr* —6F **77**
Castle Clo. *C'tn* —5B **20**
Castle Ct. *Nott* —4D **64** (6D **4**)
Castle Ct. *Thul* —4B **94**
Castle Ct. *Thurl* —3C **94**
Castlecraig Ct. *Sin* —7J **91**
Castle Cft. *Alv* —4K **93**
Castlefields. *Iron* —1H **13**
Castlefields. *Nott* —5E **64** (7E **4**)
Castlefields Main Cen. *Der*
—4A **74** (5F **7**)
Castle Gdns. *Nott* —4B **64**
Castle Ga. *Nott* —3E **64** (5E **4**)
(in three parts)
Castle Gro. *Nott* —3D **64** (5D **4**)
Castle Hill. *Cas D* —6K **107**
Castle Hill. *Duf* —2J **39**
Castle Hill. *Find* —7B **90**
Castle Ho. Flats. *Der*
—4C **74** (5H **7**)
Castle La. *Iron* —2G **13**
Castle La. *Melb* —4H **113**
Castle Marina Pk. *Nott*
—4C **64** (7B **4**)
Castle Marina Rd. *Nott*
—5C **64** (7A **4**)
Castle Mdw. Rd. *Nott*
(in two parts)    —5D **64** (7C **4**)
Castle M. *Nott* —4C **64** (6A **4**)
Castle Mills. *Melb* —4H **113**
**Castle Mus. & Art Gallery.—6D 4**
Castle Orchard. *Duf* —2J **39**
Castle Pk. Ind. Est. *Nott*
—5D **64** (7C **4**)
Castle Pl. *Nott* —3D **64** (5D **4**)
Castle Quay. *Nott* —4D **64** (7C **4**)
Castle Retail Pk. *Nott* —1A **64**
Castlerigg Clo. *W Bri* —3A **84**
Castle Rd. *Nott* —3E **64** (5D **4**)
Castle Rock. *Nott* —4D **64** (6D **4**)
Castleshaw Dri. *L'ver* —2C **90**
Castle St. *Der* —4B **74** (5F **7**)
Castle St. *Bees* —1G **81**
Castle St. *Eastw* —4E **28**
Castle St. *Melb* —4H **113**
Castle St. *Nott* —3H **65**
Castleton Av. *Arn* —6H **33**
Castleton Av. *Cltn* —5C **50**
Castleton Av. *Der* —1K **91**
Castleton Av. *Ilk* —1C **44**

Castleton Clo. *Huck* —6D **16**
Castleton Clo. *Nott* —5D **64**
Castleton Ct. *Nott* —7F **31**
Castle Vw. *Duf* —2J **39**
Castle Vw. *Lan M* —1J **27**
Castle Vw. *W Bri* —2F **83**
Castle Vw. Cotts. *Bees* —2J **81**
Castle Vs. *Nott* —3H **65**
Castle Wlk. *Der* —4B **74** (5F **7**)
Castle Wlk. *Nott* —7B **48**
Cat & Fiddle La. *W Hal* —1F **59**
Caterham Clo. *Nott* —7D **46**
Cathedral Rd. *Der* —2K **73** (2C **6**)
Cathedral Vw. *Der* —6H **73**
Catherine Av. *Ilk* —1D **60**
Catherine Clo. *Nott* —6G **31**
Catherine McAuley Houses. *Der*
—7K **55**
Catherine St. *Der* —6B **74**
Catherine St. *Nott* —6G **31**
Catkin Dri. *Gilt* —5G **29**
Catlow Wlk. *Nott* —5E **32**
Cator Clo. *Ged* —3B **50**
Cator La. *Bees* —2D **80**
Cator La. N. *Bees* —2D **80**
Catriona Cres. *Arn* —3J **33**
Catterick Dri. *Mick* —7A **72**
Catterley Hill Rd. *Nott* —7J **49**
Cattle Mkt. Rd. *Nott*
—5F **65** (7J **5**)
Catton Rd. *Arn* —5J **33**
Caulton St. *Nott* —1B **64**
Caunton Av. *Nott* —5G **49**
Causeway. *Dar A* —5J **55**
Causeway M. *Nott* —5D **64**
Causey Bri. *Der* —2A **74** (2E **6**)
Cavan Ct. *Nott* —6E **64**
Cavan Dri. *Chad* —4H **75**
Cavell Clo. *Nott* —6K **81**
Cavell Ct. *Nott* —5K **63**
Cavendish Av. *Alst* —4K **55**
Cavendish Av. *Ged* —4D **50**
Cavendish Av. *Nott* —3F **49**
Cavendish Clo. *Cas D* —1J **115**
Cavendish Clo. *Duf* —4H **39**
Cavendish Clo. *Huck* —7J **17**
Cavendish Clo. *Shard* —7J **95**
Cavendish Ct. *Der* —2K **73** (2C **6**)
Cavendish Ct. *Nott* —3H **49**
Cavendish Ct. *Park T*
—3C **64** (4B **4**)
Cavendish Ct. *Shard* —1J **107**
Cavendish Cres. *Cltn* —4A **50**
Cavendish Cres. *S'fd* —5H **61**
Cavendish Cres. N. *Nott*
—3C **64** (5A **4**)
Cavendish Cres. S. *Nott*
—4C **64** (6B **4**)
Cavendish Dri. *Cltn* —6C **50**
Cavendish Dri. *Rip* —3J **11**
Cavendish Ho. *Cltn* —6C **50**
(off Foxhill Rd. E.)
Cavendish M. *Nott* —3C **64** (4B **4**)
Cavendish Pl. *Bees* —2F **81**
Cavendish Pl. *Nott* —4C **64** (6A **4**)
Cavendish Rd. *Cltn* —4A **50**
Cavendish Rd. *Ilk* —1D **60**
Cavendish Rd. *Long E* —6G **79**
Cavendish Rd. E. *Nott*
—3C **64** (4B **4**)
Cavendish Rd. W. *Nott*
—3C **64** (5A **4**)
Cavendish St. *Arn* —5G **33**
Cavendish St. *Der* —3K **73** (3C **6**)
Cavendish St. *Lent L* —6A **64**
Cavendish Va. *Nott* —3F **49**
Cavendish Way. *Mick* —6C **72**
Caversfield Clo. *L'ver* —1E **90**
Caversham Way. *W Hal* —6F **43**
Cawdron Wlk. *Nott* —6A **82**
Cawston Gdns. *Nott* —5H **31**
Caxmere Dri. *Nott* —2H **63**
Caxton Clo. *N'fld* —7E **50**
Caxton St. *Der* —2J **91**
Caythorpe Cres. *Nott* —2E **48**
Caythorpe Ri. *Nott* —2E **48**
Caythorpe Rd. *Low* —5E **36**
Cecil St. *Der* —3H **73**
Cecil St. *Nott* —4B **64** (7A **4**)
Cedar Av. *Bees* —1G **81**
Cedar Av. *Long E* —4G **97**
Cedar Av. *Nut* —2F **47**
Cedar Av. *Rip* —3K **11**
Cedar Clo. *Bing* —3C **70**
Cedar Clo. *Sand* —1F **79**
Cedar Ct. *Bees* —1G **81**
Cedar Cft. *Ast T* —3C **106**

Cedar Cft. *Klbrn* —6H **25**
Cedar Dri. *Keyw* —7C **102**
Cedar Dri. *Ock* —4E **76**
Cedar Gro. *Arn* —5K **33**
Cedar Gro. *Belp* —3B **24**
Cedar Gro. *Huck* —7H **17**
Cedar Gro. *Nott* —3F **63**
Cedarland Cres. *Nut* —2F **47**
Cedar Lodge. *Nott* —3C **64** (4B **4**)
Cedar Pk. *Ilk* —6C **44**
Cedar Rd. *Bees* —3E **80**
Cedar Rd. *Cas D* —1K **115**
Cedar Rd. *Nott* —6C **48**
Cedars, The. *Nott* —2F **49**
Cedar St. *Der* —1J **73**
Cedar Tree Rd. *Arn* —4D **32**
Cedarwood Ct. *Oak* —5E **56**
Celandine Clo. *Nott* —6A **32**
Celandine Clo. *Oak* —5F **57**
Celandine Gdns. *Bing* —3J **69**
Celanese Rd. *Der* —5J **75**
Celia Dri. *Cltn* —7B **50**
Cemetery La. *Rip* —3K **11**
Cemetery Rd. *Belp* —6A **10**
Cemetery Rd. *S'fd* —1J **79**
Central Av. *Arn* —6H **33**
Central Av. *Bees* —2D **80**
(Bramcote Av.)
Central Av. *Bees* —6E **62**
(Derby Rd.)
Central Av. *Borr* —7D **76**
Central Av. *Huck* —6G **17**
Central Av. *Map* —2K **49**
Central Av. *New B* —5C **48**
Central Av. *Sand* —2F **79**
Central Av. *S'fd* —7J **61**
Central Av. *W Bri* —7H **65**
Central Av. S. *Arn* —6H **33**
Central Ct. *Nott* —6B **64**
Central St. *Nott* —1G **65**
Central Wlk. *Huck* —5G **17**
Centre Ct. *Der* —5B **74** (7G **7**)
Centre Way. *Rad T* —3J **67**
Centurion Wlk. *Der* —7A **56**
Centurion Way. *Nott* —7B **64**
Cernan Ct. *Nott* —1F **47**
Cerne Clo. *Nott* —1B **100**
Chaceley Way. *Nott* —5C **82**
Chadborn Av. *Got* —1H **111**
Chaddesden. *Der* —2G **75**
Chaddesden La. *Der* —2F **75**
Chaddesden La. End. *Der* —3F **75**
**Chaddesden Pk. —2G 75**
Chaddesden Pk. Rd. *Der* —2E **74**
Chaddesden, The. *Nott* —7E **48**
Chadfield Rd. *Duf* —1J **39**
Chad Gdns. *Nott* —3C **32**
Chadwick Av. *Altn* —4E **92**
Chadwick Gro. *Rip* —3H **11**
Chadwick Rd. *Nott* —7A **48**
Chaffinch Clo. *Spon* —2B **76**
Chain La. *L'ver* —7E **72**
Chain La. *Mick & L'ver* —6E **72**
(in two parts)
Chain La. *Nott* —6A **64**
Chalfield Clo. *Nott* —7K **81**
Chalfont Dri. *Nott* —1J **63**
Chalfont Sq. *Oak* —5H **57**
Chalkley Clo. *Alv* —2F **93**
Challis Av. *Chad* —1H **75**
Challond Ct. *Nott* —5D **32**
Chalons Clo. *Ilk* —5D **44**
Chalons Way. *Ilk* —5D **44**
Chamberlain Clo. *Nott* —7J **81**
Chambers Av. *Ilk* —7F **45**
Chambers St. *Der* —1F **92**
Champion Av. *Ilk* —3A **44**
Champion Hill. *Duf* —2J **39**
Chancel Pl. *Der* —5K **73** (7C **6**)
Chancery Ct. *Wilf* —2C **82**
Chancery La. *Der* —2E **72**
Chancery, The. *Bees* —1C **80**
Chandlers Ford. *Oak* —6F **57**
Chandos Av. *N'fld* —6E **50**
Chandos Pole St. *Der* —2H **73**
Chandos St. *N'fld* —7E **50**
Chandos St. *Nott* —7G **49**
Chandres Ct. *Alst* —3J **55**
Chantrey Rd. *W Bri* —1G **83**
Chantry Clo. *Bees* —4D **80**
Chantry Clo. *Kimb* —1A **46**
Chantry Clo. *Long E* —5E **96**
Chantry Clo. *Melb* —4H **113**
Chantry Clo. *Mick* —7B **72**
Chapel Bar. *Nott* —3D **64** (4D **4**)
Chapel Ct. *Ilk* —2D **44**
Chapel La. *Arn* —5G **33**
Chapel La. *Asl* —2J **71**
Chapel La. *Bar T* —4A **104**

Chapel La. *Bing* —7K **53**
Chapel La. *Chad* —1G **75**
Chapel La. *Chel* —1G **105**
Chapel La. *Cotg* —5K **85**
Chapel La. *Der* —4B **74** (6G **7**)
Chapel La. *Lamb* —6F **35**
Chapel La. *Spon* —2A **76**
Chapel M. Ct. *Bramc* —7B **62**
Chapel Pl. *Kimb* —7K **29**
Chapel Row. *Borr* —6D **76**
Chapel Row. *L'ver* —7G **73**
Chapel Side. *Spon* —3A **76**
Chapel St. *Bees* —7B **62**
Chapel St. *Belp* —2K **23**
Chapel St. *Der* —2A **74** (2C **6**)
Chapel St. *Duf* —3K **39**
Chapel St. *Eastw* —4D **28**
Chapel St. *Hean* —5J **27**
Chapel St. *Holb* —6C **24**
Chapel St. *Huck* —5G **17**
Chapel St. *Ilk* —5D **44**
(in two parts)
Chapel St. *Klbrn* —5G **25**
Chapel St. *Kimb* —7K **29**
(in two parts)
Chapel St. *Long E* —2J **97**
Chapel St. *Melb* —4H **113**
Chapel St. *Nott* —2C **64** (2A **4**)
Chapel St. *Rip* —2K **11**
Chapel St. *Rud* —3E **100**
Chapel St. *Spon* —3K **75**
Chapel St. *Tickn* —6A **112**
Chapel St. Pl. *Ilk* —5D **44**
Chapman Av. *Alv* —3H **93**
Chapman Ct. *Nott* —7H **47**
Chapmans Wlk. *B Vil* —6D **18**
Chapter Clo. *Oak* —5D **56**
Chapter Dri. *Kimb* —1A **46**
Chard St. *Nott* —4B **48**
Chard Ter. *Nott* —4B **48**
Charing Ct. *Der* —1B **74** (1F **7**)
Charingworth Rd. *Oak* —5H **57**
Chariot Clo. *Alv* —4K **93**
Charlbury Clo. *L'ver* —1E **90**
Charlbury Ct. *Bees* —3B **62**
Charlbury Rd. *Nott* —1G **63**
Charlecote Dri. *Nott* —4C **62**
Charlecote Pk. Dri. *W Bri* —4E **82**
Charles Av. *Bees* —6G **63**
(Derby Rd.)
Charles Av. *Bees* —5C **80**
(High Rd.)
Charles Av. *Eastw* —3F **29**
Charles Av. *Sand* —2F **79**
Charles Av. *Spon* —2K **75**
Charles Av. *S'fd* —7K **61**
Charles Clo. *Ged* —4D **50**
Charles Clo. *Ilk* —1F **61**
Charles Rd. *Alv* —7F **75**
Charles St. *Arn* —6G **33**
Charles St. *Huck* —5G **17**
Charles St. *Long E* —3H **97**
Charles St. *Rud* —2E **100**
Charleston Rd. *Chad* —2J **75**
Charlestown Dri. *Alst* —3H **55**
Charles Way. *Bulw* —1H **47**
Charles Way Bus. Pk. *Bulw*
—1J **47**
Charlesworth Av. *Nott* —6A **48**
Charlock Clo. *Nott* —6A **32**
Charlock Gdns. *Bing* —4K **69**
Charlotte Clo. *Arn* —3G **33**
Charlotte Ct. *Eastw* —2D **28**
Charlotte Gro. *Bees* —6D **62**
Charlotte St. *Der* —6A **74**
Charlotte St. *Ilk* —3C **44**
Charlton Av. *Long E* —7K **79**
Charlton Gro. *Bees* —4F **81**
Charnock Av. *Nott* —4K **63**
Charnwood Av. *Bees* —2D **80**
Charnwood Av. *Belp* —1A **24**
Charnwood Av. *Borr* —6E **76**
Charnwood Av. *Cas D* —7A **108**
Charnwood Av. *Keyw* —7C **102**
Charnwood Av. *L'ver* —4H **91**
Charnwood Av. *Long E* —5F **97**
Charnwood Av. *Sand* —4E **78**
Charnwood Dri. *Rip* —3J **11**
Charnwood Gdns. *Nott* —5D **48**
Charnwood Gro. *Bing* —3K **69**
Charnwood Gro. *Huck* —5D **16**
Charnwood Gro. *W Bri* —1G **83**
Charnwood La. *Arn* —7D **34**
Charnwood St. *Der* —5A **74** (7E **6**)
Charnwood Way. *Wdbgh* —1G **35**
Charta M. *Low* —4E **36**
Charterhouse Clo. *Oak* —4E **56**
Charter Pk. *Ilk* —7C **44**
Charterstone La. *Alst* —3J **55**

Chartwell Av. Rud —2D 100
Chartwell Dri. W Mead —3C 74 (3J 7)
Chartwell Gro. Nott —1A 50
Chase Clo. Chel —7H 93
Chase Pk. Nott —4J 65
Chase, The. Klbrn —5H 25
Chase, The. L Eat —4D 40
Chase, The. Sin —5K 91
Chatham Ct. Belp —1D 24
Chatham Ct. Nott —7J 31
Chatham St. Der —1A 92
Chatham St. Nott —1E 64
Chatsworth Av. Bees —6C 80
Chatsworth Av. Cltn —6C 50
Chatsworth Av. Long E —3A 98
Chatsworth Av. Nott —4B 48
Chatsworth Av. Rad T —3A 68
Chatsworth Clo. Sand —4F 79
Chatsworth Ct. Huck —6G 17
Chatsworth Ct. Sin —5K 91
Chatsworth Ct. W Hal —6F 43
Chatsworth Cres. Alst —4K 55
Chatsworth Dri. Huck —6G 17
Chatsworth Dri. L Eat —4D 40
Chatsworth Dri. Mick —5C 72
Chatsworth Pl. Ilk —2K 59
Chatsworth Rd. W Bri —7K 65
Chatsworth St. Der —7J 73
Chatteris Dri. Der —6D 56
Chaucer St. Ilk —5D 44
Chaucer St. Nott —2D 64 (2C 4)
Chaucer Ter. Der —2K 91
Chaworth Av. Watn —4A 30
Chaworth Rd. Bing —3K 69
Chaworth Rd. Colw —1D 66
Chaworth Rd. W Bri —2G 83
Cheadle Clo. Bilb —6D 46
Cheadle Clo. L'ver —7F 73
Cheadle Clo. Map —4K 49
Cheam Clo. Der —2C 72
Cheapside. Belp —2K 23
Cheapside. Der —3A 74 (3D 6)
Cheapside. Nott —3E 64 (4F 5)
Cheddar Rd. Nott —1A 100
Chedington Av. Nott —7B 34
Chediston Va. Nott —5D 32
Chedworth Clo. Nott —2H 65
Chedworth Dri. Alv —3K 93
Chellaston La. Ast T & Ast T —1J 105
Chellaston Pk. Ct. Chel —1F 105
Chellaston Rd. Altn —4E 92
(in two parts)
Chelmarsh Clo. Chel —6G 93
Chelmorton Pl. Chad —7F 57
Chelmsford Clo. Mick —5A 72
Chelmsford Rd. Nott —4B 48
Chelmsford Ter. Nott —4B 48
(off Chelmsford Rd.)
Chelsbury Ct. Arn —6G 33
Chelsea Clo. Der —2D 72
Chelsea Clo. Nut —3E 46
Chelsea M. Rad T —4D 68
Chelsea St. Nott —5B 48
Cheltenham Clo. Bees —6K 79
Cheltenham St. Nott —2A 48
Chelwood Rd. Chel —7F 93
Chennel Nook. Cotg —6A 86
Chepstow Rd. Nott —1A 100
Chequer La. Shot —2B 8
Chequers La. Der —2D 74 (2K 7)
Chequers Rd. Der —3C 74 (3J 7)
Cherhill Clo. Nott —2K 99
Cheribough Rd. Cas D —7J 107
Cheriton Dri. Ilk —3A 44
Cheriton Gdns. L'ver —2C 90
Cherry Av. Huck —7H 17
Cherrybrook Dri. Oak —4H 57
Cherry Clo. Arn —5G 33
Cherry Clo. Breas —1C 96
Cherry Hill. Keyw —6D 102
Cherryholt Clo. E Bri —2K 53
Cherry Holt La. E Bri —2K 53
Cherry Orchard. Cotg —5J 85
Cherry Orchard Mt. Nott —7D 32
Cherry St. Bing —3B 70
Cherry Tree Av. Belp —6A 10
Cherry Tree Av. Rip —4K 11
Cherry Tree Clo. Brins —4C 14
Cherrytree Clo. Brins —4C 14
Cherry Tree Clo. Ilk —1B 60
Cherry Tree Clo. Rad T —5K 67
Cherry Tree Clo. Ris —4D 78
Cherry Tree La. Edw —5K 83
Cherry Tree M. Chad —4H 75
Cherry Wood Dri. Nott —7H 47
Cherrywood Gdns. Nott —6J 49
Chertsey Clo. Nott —5H 49

Chertsey Ct. W Hal —6F 43
Chertsey Rd. Mick —6A 72
Cherwell Ct. Nott —7F 31
Chesapeake Rd. Chad —2H 75
Chesham Clo. Nut —3D 46
Chesham Dri. Bees —4B 62
Chesham Dri. Nott —4D 48
Cheshire Ct. W Bri —3F 83
Cheshire St. Altn —4E 92
Cheshire Way. W'wd —1A 14
Chesil Av. Nott —2K 63
Chesil Cotts. Nott —2K 63
Cheslyn Dri. Nott —6J 47
Chesnuts, The. Ged —5F 51
Chester Av. Alst —2B 56
Chester Ct. Spon —5A 76
Chesterfield Av. Bing —3A 70
Chesterfield Av. Ged —3B 50
Chesterfield Av. Long E —2K 97
Chesterfield Ct. Ged —3B 50
Chesterfield Dri. Bur J —1A 52
Chesterfield Ho. Spon —4A 76
(off Arnhem Ter.)
Chesterfield Rd. Belp —1A 24
Chesterfield Rd. Heag —2E 10
(Church St.)
Chesterfield Rd. Heag —5C 10
(Far Laund)
Chesterfield St. Cltn —7B 50
Chesterford Ct. L'ver —3D 90
Chester Grn. Bees —6J 79
Chester Grn. Rd. Der —1A 74
(in two parts)
Chesterman Dri. Aws —2F 45
Chester Rd. Nott —2A 66
Chesterton Av. Sun —2J 91
Chesterton Rd. Spon —2A 76
Chestnut Av. Bees —2F 81
Chestnut Av. Belp —3A 24
Chestnut Av. Bing —3A 70
Chestnut Av. Chel —6F 93
Chestnut Av. Der —6A 74
Chestnut Av. Holb —6C 24
Chestnut Av. Mick —5B 72
Chestnut Av. Nott —4K 49
Chestnut Av. Rip —4K 11
Chestnut Bank. Hean —4F 27
Chestnut Clo. Duf —4J 39
Chestnut Clo. Hors W —6J 25
Chestnut Dri. Nut —6B 30
Chestnut Gro. Arn —4J 33
Chestnut Gro. Borr —5E 76
Chestnut Gro. Bur J —2K 51
Chestnut Gro. Etw —5D 88
Chestnut Gro. Ged —5D 50
Chestnut Gro. Huck —1H 31
Chestnut Gro. Nott —7E 48
Chestnut Gro. Rad T —3K 67
Chestnut Gro. Sand —1E 78
Chestnut Gro. W Bri —1F 83
Chestnut La. Bar F —3E 98
Chestnut Rd. Lan M —2J 27
Chestnuts, The. Long E —1E 96
Chestnuts, The. Nott —5H 49
Chestnut, The. Rad T —4J 67
Chettles Ind. Est. Nott —2K 63
Chetwin Rd. Nott —2C 62
Chetwynd Rd. Bees —6A 80
(High Rd.)
Chetwynd Rd. Bees —5B 80
(Highfield Rd.)
Cheveley Ct. Oak —7D 56
Cheverton Clo. Alv —4K 93
Cheverton Ct. Nott —7E 48
Chevin All. Milf —6A 24
Chevin Av. Borr —6E 76
Chevin Av. Mick —6D 72
Chevin Bank. Duf —1H 39
Chevin Gdns. Nott —5C 32
Chevin Golf Course. —6J 23
Chevin Pl. Der —1K 73
Chevin Rd. Belp —1H 23
Chevin Rd. Der —1K 73
Chevin Rd. Duf —1J 39
Chevin Va. Duf —1J 39
Chevin Vw. Belp —1K 23
Cheviot Av. Iron —1H 13
Cheviot Clo. Arn —3D 32
Cheviot Ct. Bees —5C 80
Cheviot Dri. Nott —5F 31
Cheviot Rd. Long E —7E 78
Cheviot St. Der —3G 73
Chewton Av. Eastw —4E 28
Chewton St. Eastw —4D 28
Cheyenne Gdns. Chad —3H 75
Cheyne Wlk. Der —2G 73
Cheyny Clo. Nott —6E 64
Chichester Clo. Ilk —6E 44
Chichester Clo. Nott —6A 32

Chichester Dri. Cotg —4J 85
Chidlow Rd. Nott —7D 46
Chigwell Clo. Nut —4D 46
Chillon Way. Huck —6D 16
Chilson Dri. Mick —5A 72
Chiltern Clo. Arn —3D 32
Chiltern Dri. W Hal —6G 43
Chiltern Gdns. Long E —7E 78
Chiltern Way. Nott —7D 32
Chilton Dri. Watn —6A 30
Chilvers Clo. Nott —6C 32
Chilwell Ct. Nott —6K 31
Chilwell La. Bees —1B 80
Chilwell Manor Golf Course. —4E 80
Chilwell Meadows Nature Reserve. —4D 80
Chilwell Retail Pk. Bees —7B 80
(in two parts)
Chilwell Rd. Bees —3F 81
(in two parts)
Chilwell St. Nott —4B 64
Chime Clo. Oak —5E 56
Chine Gdns. W Bri —3E 82
Chingford Ct. Der —2F 73
Chingford Rd. Nott —6E 46
Chinley Rd. Chad —6G 57
Chippendale St. Nott —4B 64 (7A 4)
Chippenham Rd. Nott —7D 32
Chisbury Grn. Nott —2K 99
Chisholm Way. Nott —7C 32
Chiswick Clo. Der —2D 72
Chiswick Ct. Nott —3E 48
Christchurch Ct. Nott —2A 74 (2D 6)
Christchurch Rd. Huck —1D 30
Christina Av. Nott —2J 47
Christina Cres. Nott —2J 47
Christine Clo. Huck —3J 17
Christine Ct. Nott —7J 49
Christopher Clo. Nott —1F 63
Chrysalis Way. Eastw —2A 28
Church Av. Day —6G 33
Church Av. Long E —5E 96
Church Av. Nott —4B 64
Church Clo. Bing —2B 70
Church Clo. Chel —1G 105
Church Clo. Day —6G 33
Church Clo. Nott —1E 64 (1F 5)
Church Clo. Trow —3G 61
Church Ct. Cotg —4J 67
Church Cres. Bees —4A 80
Church Cres. Day —6F 33
Church Cft. Rip —2K 11
Church Cft. W Bri —7H 65
Churchdale Av. S'fd —6J 61
Churchdown Clo. Oak —5H 57
Church Dri. Day —6F 33
Church Dri. Huck —5G 17
Church Dri. Ilk —1B 44
Church Dri. Keyw —6C 102
Church Dri. Nott —5D 48
Church Dri. Sand —1F 79
Church Dri. W Bri —1H 83
Church Dri. E. Day —6G 33
Churchfield Ct. Nott —4C 32
Churchfield La. Nott —7A 48
Churchfield Ter. Nott —4A 48
Churchfield Way. Nott —4C 32
Church Ga. Cols B —1G 103
Church Ga. Keg —1H 117
Church Gro. Nott —4A 64
Church Hill. Etw —4D 88
Church Hill. Jack —1K 13
Church Hill. Kimb —7K 29
Church Hill. Plum —3C 102
Church Hill. Spon —3K 75
Churchill Av. Ilk —6F 45
Churchill Clo. Arn —7H 33
Churchill Clo. Breas —1B 96
Churchill Ct. Bread —3D 56
Churchill Dri. Hilt —7A 88
Churchill Dri. Rud —2D 100
Churchill Dri. S'fd —7J 61
Churchill Pk. Colw —2D 66
Church La. Arn —4G 33
Church La. Bar T —5A 104
Church La. Bar F —3E 98
Church La. Bees —7D 80
Church La. Belp —1K 23
Church La. Bing —3B 70
Church La. Bread —3E 56
Church La. Brins —6C 14
Church La. Bulw —6J 31
Church La. Cas D —7K 107
Church La. Chad —2G 75
Church La. Coss —4G 45
Church La. Cotg —5J 85

Church La. Dar A —4K 55
Church La. Der —7D 54
Church La. Epp —6K 21
Church La. H'ton —6B 108
Church La. Hors W —7K 25
Church La. L'by & Huck —2G 17
Church La. L Eat —7C 40
Church La. Locki —6D 108
Church La. Low —3C 36
Church La. M'ly —1J 57
Church La. Plum —2C 102
Church La. S'fd —1H 79
Church La. Swar —4E 104
Church La. Thrum —6B 98
Church La. Tickn —7A 112
Church La. Und —1E 14
Church La. N. Dar A —4K 55
Church Mdw. C'tn —6D 20
Church M. Nott —6F 65
Church M. Spon —4K 75
Churchmoor Ct. Arn —4G 33
Churchmoor La. Arn —4G 33
Church Rd. B Vil —1A 32
Church Rd. Bur J —2K 51
Church Rd. Greas —3J 29
Church Rd. Newt —1H 29
Church Rd. Nott —7F 49
Church Rd. Quar —3G 55
Churchside Gdns. Nott —6A 48
Churchside Wlk. Der —4J 73 (6A 6)
Church Sq. Hean —4H 27
Church Sq. Nott —4B 64
Church St. Alv —2J 93
Church St. Arn —5H 33
Church St. Bees —7B 62
(Derby Rd.)
Church St. Bees —2F 81
(Middle St.)
Church St. Belp —1A 24
Church St. Bing —3B 70
Church St. Cltn —7C 50
Church St. C Bis —4G 87
Church St. Den V —4K 25
Church St. Der —6A 74
Church St. Eastw —4C 28
Church St. Got —1H 111
Church St. Heag —2D 10
Church St. Hean —4H 27
Church St. Holb —7C 24
Church St. Hors —7F 25
Church St. Ilk —2B 44
Church St. Klbrn —5F 25
Church St. Lamb —5G 35
Church St. Lent —4A 64
(in two parts)
Church St. L'ver —7G 73
Church St. Locki —6D 108
Church St. Melb —4H 113
Church St. Ock —4E 76
Church St. Old B —4A 48
Church St. Rip —2K 11
Church St. Rud —2E 100
Church St. Sand —1F 79
Church St. Shelf —5C 52
Church St. Spon —4K 75
Church St. S'fd —1H 79
Church St. Wain —5C 12
Church St. What —4K 71
Church Vw. Breas —2B 96
Church Vw. Ged —5D 50
Church Vw. Ilk —7C 44
Church Vw. Los —1D 26
Church Vw. Clo. Arn —4D 32
Church Wlk. Alst —3K 55
Church Wlk. Brins —6C 14
Church Wlk. Cltn —7C 50
Church Wlk. Der —5K 73
Church Wlk. Eastw —3D 28
Church Wlk. S'fd —1H 79
Church Wlk. What —3J 71
Church Wlk. Wdbgh —1G 35
Church Way. Ilk —2B 44
Church Wilne Water Sports Club. —4B 96
Churnet Clo. Nott —4A 82
Churston Ct. Bees —2G 81
Cincerhill Footway. Nott —2K 47
Cincerhill Gro. Ged —4C 50
Cincerhill Rd. Nott —2H 47
Cincerhill Wlk. Nott —7H 31
Circe, The. Sin —4J 91
Citadel St. Nott —2A 64
Citrus Gro. Keg —7G 109
City Link. Nott —4F 65 (6H 5)
City Rd. Bees —1G 81
City Rd. Der —1A 74 (1E 6)
City Rd. Nott —6K 63

City Rd. Ind. Pk. Der —1A 74
City, The. Bees —2G 81
(in two parts)
Clandon Dri. Nott —4D 48
Clanfield Rd. Nott —7E 46
Clapgun St. Cas D —7K 107
Clapham St. Nctt —2A 64
Clara Mt. Rd. Hean —4J 27
Clarborough Dri. Arn —7J 33
Clare Clo. Nott —2A 48
Clarehaven. S'fd —3J 79
Claremont Av. Bees —7C 62
Claremont Av. Huck —7G 17
Claremont Dri. W Bri —5E 82
Claremont Gdns. Nott —5D 48
Claremont Rd. Nott —5D 48
Claremont Ter. Nott —1C 64 (1B 4)
Clarence Ct. Nott —2G 65 (3K 5)
Clarence Rd. Bees —6D 80
Clarence Rd. Der —7J 73
Clarence Rd. Long E —3G 97
Clarence St. Nott —2G 65 (2K 5)
Clarendon Chambers. Nott —2D 64 (2D 4)
Clarendon Ct. Nott —6D 48
Clarendon Pk. Nott —6D 48
Clarendon St. Nott —2D 64 (2C 4)
Clare St. Nott —2E 64 (3F 5)
Clare Valley. Nctt —3D 64 (5C 4)
Clarewood Gro. Nott —2A 100
Clarges St. Nott —7J 31
Clarke Av. Arn —5H 33
Clarke Av. Los —3E 26
Clarke Clo. C Bis —4G 87
Clarke Dri. Long E —5E 96
Clarke Rd. Nott —5G 65 (7J 5)
Clarkes La. Ast T —2D 106
Clarke's La. Bees —4C 80
Clarke St. Der —2B 74 (1G 7)
Clarkson Dri. Bees —2H 81
Claude St. Nott —6A 64
Claxton St. Hean —3F 27
Claxton Ter. Hean —3F 27
Clay Av. Nott —3J 49
Claye St. Long E —2J 97
Clayfield Clo. Nott —7G 31
Claygate. Nott —7J 49
Clay La. Hean —3H 27
Claypole Rd. Nott —7B 48
Clay St. Dray —2J 95
Clayton Ct. Bees —3G 81
Clayton Ct. Nott —2B 64
Clayton Gro. Los —1E 26
Claytons Dri. Nott —5A 64
Claytons Wharf. Nott —5A 64
Clement Rd. Hors W —6J 25
Clements Ga. Dis —5A 116
Clether Rd. Nott —1D 62
Cleve Av. Bees —5J 79
Cleveland Av. Chad —3H 75
Cleveland Av. Dray —2H 95
Cleveland Av. Long E —7K 79
Cleveland Clo. Nott —2A 64
Cleveley's Rd. Bees —5J 79
Clevely Way. Nott —5A 82
Cliff Boulevd. Kimb —6K 29
(in two parts)
Cliff Cres. Rad T —3K 67
Cliff Dri. Rad T —2A 68
Cliffe Hill Av. S'fd —1H 79
Cliffgrove Av. Bees —2D 80
Cliffhill La. Asl —2J 71
Cliffmere Wlk. Nott —7K 81
(in two parts)
Clifford Av. Bees —7E 62
Clifford Clo. Keyw —5D 102
Clifford Clo. Long E —5E 96
Clifford Ct. Nott —2B 64
Clifford St. Der —6D 74
Clifford St. Long E —2J 97
Clifford St. Nott —1B 64 (1A 4)
Cliff Rd. Cltn —1B 66
Cliff Rd. Nott —3F 65 (5G 5)
Cliff Rd. Rad T —3J 67
Cliffs, The. Rad T —2A 68
Cliff, The. Nott —2H 47
Cliff Way. Rad T —3K 67
Clifton Av. Long E —2A 98
Clifton Av. Rud —1E 100
Clifton Boulevd. Nott —5K 63
Clifton Cres. Bees —5E 80
Clifton Dri. Mick —5C 72
Clifton Grn. Nctt —6K 81
Clifton Gro. Ged —4C 50
Clifton La. Nott & Rud —1C 100
Clifton Leisure Cen. —7B 82
Clifton M. Nott —3C 64 (4A 4)
Clifton Rd. Alst —4H 55

Clifton Rd. *Nott* —3C **82**
Clifton Rd. *Rud* —2D **100**
Clifton St. *Bees* —2G **81**
Clifton St. *Der* —5C **74** (7H **7**)
Clifton Ter. *Nott* —4C **64** (6B **4**)
Clinton Av. *Brins* —6B **14**
Clinton Av. *Nott* —6D **48**
Clinton Ct. *Nott* —2E **64** (2E **4**)
Clinton St. *Arn* —6G **33**
Clinton St. *Bees* —1E **80**
Clinton St. *Der* —2D **74**
Clinton St. E. *Nott* —2E **64** (3F **5**)
Clinton St. W. *Nott* —2E **64** (3F **5**)
Clinton Ter. *Nott* —2C **64** (3A **4**)
Clipstone Av. *Map* —2J **49**
Clipstone Av. *Nott* —1E **64** (1D **4**)
Clipstone Clo. *Strel* —4D **46**
Clipstone Gdns. *Oak* —5H **57**
Clipston La. *Plum* —2D **102**
Clive Cres. *Kimb* —1A **46**
Cliveden Grn. *Nott* —7K **81**
**Clock Tower. —1A 64**
**(Nottingham)**
Clock Way. *Spon* —5B **76**
Clock Yd. *Der* —3J **73** (3A **6**)
Cloisters Ct. *Oak* —5F **57**
Cloister Sq. *Nott* —5A **64**
Cloisters, The. *Bees* —7G **63**
Cloister St. *Nott* —5A **64**
Close Quarters. *Bees* —7C **62**
Closes Side La. *E Bri* —3K **53**
Close, The. *Bees* —4D **80**
Close, The. *Dar A* —5K **55**
Close, The. *Der* —6H **73**
Close, The. *Nott* —3E **48**
Cloud Av. *S'fd* —1K **79**
Clouds Hill. *Nott* —1A **100**
Cloudside Ct. *Sand* —1F **79**
Cloudside Rd. *Sand* —1E **78**
Cloudwood Clo. *L'ver* —7F **73**
Clough Ct. *Nott* —7H **47**
Clover Clo. *Spon* —3B **76**
Clover Ct. *Shard* —7G **95**
Cloverdale. *Cotg* —6A **86**
Cloverdale Dri. *Sin* —7K **91**
Cloverfields. *C'tn* —4E **20**
Clover Grn. *Nott* —3K **47**
Cloverlands. *W Bri* —5E **82**
Cloverlands Ct. *Watn* —6A **30**
Cloverlands Dri. *Watn* —6A **30**
Clover Ri. *Newt* —4F **29**
Clover Slade. *Find* —7A **90**
Cloves Hill. *M'ly* —4J **41**
Club La. *Bar T* —5A **104**
Club Row. *Ilk* —6C **44**
Clumber Av. *Bees* —3D **80**
Clumber Av. *Brins* —3C **14**
(in two parts)
Clumber Av. *Map* —2J **49**
Clumber Av. *N'fld* —7E **50**
Clumber Av. *Sher R* —6D **48**
Clumber Clo. *Rip* —3A **12**
Clumber Ct. *Ilk* —1D **44**
Clumber Ct. *Nott* —4C **64** (6A **4**)
Clumber Cres. N. *Nott*
—3C **64** (5A **4**)
Clumber Cres. S. *Nott*
—4C **64** (6A **4**)
Clumber Dri. *Rad T* —2A **68**
Clumber Rd. *W Bri* —1H **83**
Clumber Rd. E. *Nott*
—3C **64** (5B **4**)
Clumber Rd. W. *Nott*
—3C **64** (5A **4**)
Clumber St. *Huck* —6J **17**
Clumber St. *Long E* —2H **97**
Clumber St. *Nott* —2E **64** (3F **5**)
Cluster Rd. *Belp* —1K **23**
Clusters Ct. *Belp* —1K **23**
Clyde Ter. *Nott* —1C **64** (1B **4**)
Coach Dri. *Eastw* —1D **28**
Coach Dri. *Quar* —7H **39**
Coachmans Cft. *Nott* —2G **63**
Coach Rd. *But* —1B **12**
Coach Rd. *Ridd* —1E **12**
Coachways. *M'ley* —3H **43**
Coates Av. *Huck* —3F **17**
Coatsby Rd. *Kimb* —6K **29**
Cobden Chambers. *Nott*
—3F **65** (4F **5**)
Cobden St. *Der* —3H **73**
(in three parts)
Cobden St. *Long E* —2H **97**
Cobden St. *Nott* —2A **64**
Cobden St. *Rip* —4B **11**
Cobham Clo. *Sten F* —6H **91**
Cobthorne Dri. *Alst* —3G **55**
Coburn Pl. *Der* —3K **73** (4C **6**)
Cockayne Clo. *Sand* —5F **79**

Cockayne St. N. *Altn* —3E **92**
Cockayne St. S. *Altn* —3E **92**
Cocker Beck. *Lamb* —6G **35**
Cockerhouse Rd. *Eastw* —1C **28**
Cockington Rd. *Nott* —2C **62**
Cockleys. *Long E* —3G **97**
Cock Pitt, The. *Der* —3B **74** (4F **7**)
Cockshut La. *Melb* —5F **113**
Cod Beck Clo. *Alv* —3J **93**
**Codnor Castle. —4G 13**
**(remains of)**
Codnor Denby La. *Den V* —1C **26**
Codnor Ga. *Cod* —3D **12**
Codnor Ga. Ind. Est. *Rip* —2D **12**
Codnor La. *Ridd* —1E **12**
Codrington Gdns. *Nott* —5E **32**
Cogenhoe Wlk. *Arn* —3H **33**
Cogley La. *Bing* —3G **97**
Cohen Clo. *Arn* —7K **33**
Cokefield Av. *Nut* —3F **47**
Coke St. *Der* —3H **73**
Colborn St. *Nott* —7H **49**
Colchester Rd. *Nott* —5E **46**
Coldstream Wlk. *Sin* —5J **91**
Coleby Av. *Nott* —5A **64**
Coleby Rd. *Nott* —4F **47**
Coledale. *W Bri* —2A **84**
Cole La. *Ock & Borr* —4E **76**
Coleman St. *Altn* —2E **92**
Coleraine Clo. *Chad* —4H **75**
Coleridge Cres. *Day* —6F **33**
Coleridge St. *Der* —2K **91**
Coleridge St. *Nott* —1A **64**
Coleridge St. *Sun* —4J **91**
(in two parts)
Colesbourne Rd. *Nott* —6B **82**
Coles Wlk. *Nott* —5C **32**
Colin Av. *Cod* —4D **12**
Colin Broughton Ct. *Nott* —6K **31**
Colindale Gdns. *Nut* —3D **46**
Colinwood Av. *Nott* —4A **32**
**Coliseum Cen. —5F 7**
Coliseum Cen. *Der* —4B **74** (5F **7**)
College Dri. *Nott* —5K **81**
(Clifton La.)
College Dri. *Nott* —6K **81**
(Village Rd.)
College M. *Der* —3J **73** (4A **6**)
College Pl. *Der* —2A **74** (2D **6**)
College Rd. *Bees* —3E **80**
College St. *E Bri* —3J **53**
College St. *Long E* —5F **79**
College St. *Nott* —2D **64** (3C **4**)
College, The. *Den* —2J **25**
Colley Moor Leys La. *Nott*
—6B **82**
Collier La. *Ock* —4E **76**
Colliers Way. *Nott* —2G **47**
Colliery Clo. *Nott* —6D **64**
Collin Av. *Sand* —4F **79**
Collingham Gdns. *Der* —3E **72**
Collin Grn. *Nott* —2F **49**
Collington St. *Bees* —2E **80**
Collington Way. *W Bri* —3F **83**
Collingwood Clo. *Nott* —4A **82**
Collingwood Rd. *Long E* —3H **97**
Collins Clo. *Nott* —1F **47**
Collins Homes. *Bees* —6E **62**
Collis Clo. *Altn* —2E **92**
Collison St. *Nott* —1B **64**
Collumbell Av. *Ock* —3E **76**
Collyer Rd. *C'tn* —4A **20**
Colly Ga. *Kimb* —1A **46**
Collygate Rd. *Nott* —6F **65**
Colmon Clo. *Nott* —6C **32**
Colmon Wlk. *Nott* —6C **32**
Colombo St. *Der* —7B **74**
Colonsay Clo. *Trow* —4H **61**
Colston Cres. *W Bri* —4F **83**
Colston Ga. *Cotg* —5K **85**
Colston Rd. *C Bis* —7F **87**
Colston Rd. *Nott* —5J **31**
Coltsfoot Clo. *Bing* —4J **69**
Coltsfoot Dri. *Sin* —7K **91**
Columbine Clo. *Oak* —6F **57**
Colville Ct. *Nott* —7D **48**
Colville St. *Der* —2H **73**
Colville St. *Nott* —7D **48**
Colville Ter. *Nott* —7D **48**
(in two parts)
Colville Vs. *Nott* —7D **48**
Colwell Dri. *Alv & Boul M* —4J **93**
**Colwick Country Pk. —4B 66**
Colwick Ind. Est. *Colw* —2D **66**
(in two parts)
Colwick Lodge. *Cltn* —1D **66**

Colwick Loop Rd. *Colw* —2C **66**
Colwick Mnr. Farm. *Colw* —2C **66**
Colwick Pk. Clo. *Colw* —2C **66**
Colwick Rd. *Nott* —4H **65** (6K **5**)
(in two parts)
Colwick Rd. *W Bri* —6G **65**
Colwick Wood Ct. *Nott* —3J **65**
Colwyn Av. *Der* —7H **73**
Colyear St. *Der* —3A **74** (4D **6**)
Comery Av. *Nott* —1J **65**
Comet Dri. *Eastw* —3E **28**
Comfrey Clo. *L'ver* —3D **90**
Comfrey Clo. *Nott* —6A **32**
Commerce Sq. *Nott* —3F **65**
(5G **5**)
Commerce St. *Der* —1F **93**
Commerce St. *Melb* —4G **113**
Commercial Av. *Bees* —2F **81**
Commercial Rd. *Keyw* —7C **102**
Commercial Rd. *Nott* —6H **31**
(in two parts)
Commodore Gdns. *Nott* —4J **47**
Common Clo. *Newt* —5E **28**
Common La. *Bees* —2A **80**
Common La. *Huck* —6D **16**
Common La. *Stan & Stan C*
—1D **58**
Common La. *Watn* —6B **30**
Comn. Piece La. *Find* —7C **90**
Commons Clo. *Newt* —5E **28**
Common, The. *Huck* —6C **16**
Common, The. *Quar* —6F **39**
Common, The. *Tickn* —6C **112**
Compton Acres. *W Bri* —2D **82**
Compton Acres Shop. Cen. *W Bri*
—3E **82**
Compton Av. *Ast T* —2C **106**
Compton Clo. *Alv* —3J **93**
Compton Rd. *Nott* —3D **48**
Comyn Gdns. *Nott* —1F **65** (1G **5**)
Condor Rd. *Quar H* —3D **60**
Conduit Clo. *Nott* —5E **64** (7F **5**)
Conery Gdns. *What* —4J **71**
Conery La. *What* —5G **71**
Coney Wlk. *Nott* —5B **32**
Conifer Cres. *Nott* —2A **100**
Conifer Wlk. *Nott* —7J **49**
Coningsby Gdns. E. *Wd'p* —2H **49**
Coningsby Rd. *Wd'p* —1H **49**
Coningswath Rd. *Cltn* —4A **50**
Conisborough Ter. *Nott* —6E **64**
Conisbrough Av. *Ged* —5F **51**
Coniston Av. *Nott* —4J **47**
Coniston Av. *Spon* —2A **76**
Coniston Clo. *Gam* —1A **84**
Coniston Cres. *Der* —5D **56**
Coniston Dri. *Ilk* —2B **60**
Coniston Rd. *Bees* —6D **62**
Coniston Rd. *Huck* —4F **17**
Coniston Rd. *Long E* —6E **78**
Connaught Rd. *Der* —4G **73**
Connelly Clo. *Arn* —7A **34**
Connelly Ct. *Bulw* —1K **47**
Connery. *Huck* —4G **17**
Connery M. *Bees* —7B **80**
Consett Clo. *Der* —6D **56**
Consort Gdns. *Arn* —4J **57**
Constable Av. *L'ver* —5G **73**
Constable Dri. *L'ver* —6F **73**
Constable La. *L'ver* —6G **73**
Constance St. *Nott* —5C **48**
Convent St. *Nott* —2F **65** (3G **5**)
Conway Av. *Borr* —6F **77**
Conway Av. *Cltn* —7E **50**
Conway Clo. *Nott* —7E **48**
Conway Cres. *Cltn* —6E **50**
Conway Gdns. *Arn* —7G **33**
Conway Rd. *Cltn* —7D **50**
Conway Rd. *Huck* —2D **30**
Conway St. *Long E* —1J **97**
Conway Wlk. *Nott* —7E **48**
Cook Clo. *Belp* —7E **10**
Cook Dri. *Ilk* —1E **60**
Cooke Clo. *Long E* —2F **97**
Cookfield. *Heag* —4E **10**
Cookham Clo. *Mick* —6A **72**
Cooks Dri. *Cas D* —7J **107**
Cookson Av. *Ged* —4B **50**
Coombe Clo. *Nott* —4J **63**
Coombe Rd. *Newt* —1F **29**
Co-operative Av. *Huck* —4H **17**
Co-operative St. *Der* —6K **73**
Co-operative St. *Long E* —2J **97**
Cooper Clo. *Arn* —7A **34**
Cooper Clo. *Nott* —7F **31**
Coopers Clo. *Borr* —7F **77**
Coopers Grn. *Nott* —5E **62**
Cooper St. *N'fld* —1E **66**

Cooper St. *Rip* —3K **11**
Copecastle Sq. *Der* —4B **74** (5F **7**)
Cope Clo. *Sin* —4A **92**
Copeland Av. *S'fd* —7J **61**
Copeland Gro. *Bing* —2J **69**
Copeland Rd. *Huck* —4J **17**
Copeland St. *Der* —4B **74** (5F **7**)
Copeland Wlk. *Der* —4B **74** (5F **7**)
Copenhagen Ct. *Nott* —5F **49**
Cope St. *Nott* —1B **64**
Copes Way. *Chad* —7G **57**
Copper Beeches. *Rip* —2J **11**
Copper Clo. *C Bis* —4G **87**
Copperleaf Clo. *Der*
—4K **73** (6B **6**)
Copper Yd. *Den V* —3B **26**
Coppice Av. *Ilk* —1B **44**
Coppice Clo. *Dar A* —6K **55**
Coppice Clo. *Huck* —7E **16**
Coppice Clo. *Klbrn* —5G **25**
Coppice Ct. *Hean* —6H **27**
Coppice Dri. *Eastw* —2B **28**
Coppice Dri. *Hean* —6H **27**
Coppice Ga. *Arn* —5H **33**
Coppice Gro. *Nott* —4H **49**
Coppice Rd. *Arn* —5H **33**
Coppicewood Dri. *L'ver* —7E **72**
Copplestone Dri. *Nott* —7A **34**
Copse Clo. *Bur J* —1K **51**
Copse Gro. *L'ver* —2E **90**
Copseside Clo. *Long E* —1E **96**
Copse, The. *Bees* —2C **80**
Copse, The. *Huck* —6J **17**
Copse, The. *Ilk* —1B **44**
Corbel Clo. *Oak* —5D **56**
Corben Gdns. *Nott* —6F **31**
Corbridge Gro. *L'ver* —2E **90**
Corby Clo. *Alv* —4F **93**
Corby Rd. *Nott* —5G **49**
Corden Av. *Mick* —6E **72**
Corden St. *Der* —6A **74**
Cordville Clo. *Chad* —3H **75**
Cordwell Clo. *Cas D* —6H **107**
Cordy La. *Brins* —5C **14**
Corfe Clo. *L'ver* —3H **91**
Corfield Av. *Hean* —6H **27**
Coriander Dri. *Nott* —3K **47**
Coriander Gdns. *L'ver* —5H **91**
Corinium Clo. *Alv* —4K **93**
Corinth Rd. *Nott* —6A **82**
Corn Clo. *Cotg* —6J **85**
Corncrake Av. *Nott* —3K **47**
Cornell Dri. *Arn* —5K **33**
Corner, The. *Low* —4D **36**
Cornfield Rd. *Kimb* —6J **29**
Cornfields, The. *Nott* —5D **32**
Cornflower Dri. *Oak* —4G **57**
Cornhill. *Alst* —3J **55**
Cornhill Rd. *Cltn* —6K **49**
Corn Mkt. *Der* —3A **74** (3E **6**)
Cornmill Clo. *Boul M* —4K **93**
Cornwall Av. *Bees* —4J **81**
Cornwall Av. *Long E* —1A **98**
Cornwall Clo. *W'wd* —1A **14**
Cornwallis Clo. *Long E* —3H **97**
Cornwall Rd. *Arn* —6E **32**
Cornwall Rd. *Der* —1D **74**
Coronation Av. *Alv* —4J **93**
Coronation Av. *Belp* —7A **10**
Coronation Av. *Nott* —7D **64**
Coronation Av. *Sand* —1E **78**
Coronation Clo. *Melb* —3G **113**
Coronation Rd. *B Vil* —7A **18**
Coronation Rd. *Coss* —4F **45**
Coronation Rd. *Huck* —4F **17**
Coronation Rd. *M'ley* —3H **43**
Coronation Rd. *Nott* —3H **49**
Coronation Rd. *Nut* —1B **46**
Coronation Rd. *Stan* —1E **58**
Coronation St. *Der* —1B **92**
Coronation St. *Ilk* —6D **44**
Coronation Wlk. *Ged* —5E **50**
Coronet Ct. *Oak* —4K **57**
Corporation Cotts. *Bul* —1B **52**
Corporation Oaks. *Nott* —7E **48**
Corporation Rd. *Ilk* —2E **60**
Corporation St. *Der*
—3A **74** (3E **6**)
Corsham Gdns. *Nott* —7J **49**
Cosby Rd. *Nott* —4H **65**
Cossall Ind. Est. *Coss* —4F **45**
Cossall Rd. *Trow* —7G **45**
Costock Av. *Nott* —2D **48**
Cotgrave Av. *Ged* —4D **50**
Cotgrave Clo. *Nott* —1E **46**
Cotgrave La. *Toll* —5D **84**
**Cotgrave Leisure and Cen., The.**
**—5A 86**
Cotgrave Rd. *Plum* —2D **102**

Cotgrave Shop. Cen. *Cotg* —5K **85**
Cotmanhay Rd. *Ilk* —3C **44**
Coton Clo. *Nott* —5C **82**
Cotswold Clo. *L'ver* —1G **91**
Cotswold Clo. *Long E* —1E **96**
Cotswold Ct. *Bees* —6D **62**
Cotswold Rd. *Nott* —5D **46**
Cottage Av. *What* —3H **71**
Cottage Clo. *Heag* —5E **10**
Cottage Clo. *Ilk* —3B **44**
Cottage Garden La. *Hean* —3F **27**
Cottage Mdw. *Colw* —3D **66**
Cottage Pasture La. *Gun* —6E **36**
Cottage Ter. *Nott* —2C **64** (3B **4**)
Cottam Dri. *Nott* —5B **32**
Cottam Gdns. *Nott* —5C **32**
Cottesmore Rd. *Nott* —3B **64**
Cottisford Clo. *L'ver* —1E **90**
Cotton Brook Rd. *Der* —1B **92**
Cotton La. *Der* —1B **92**
Countisbury Dri. *Oak* —5G **57**
County Bus. Pk. *Nott*
—4G **65** (7J **5**)
County Clo. *Bees* —3G **81**
**County House. —5G 5**
County Rd. *Ged* —3A **50**
County Rd. *Nott* —5G **65**
Coupe St. *Rip* —4B **12**
Court Cres. *Nott* —3F **63**
Courtenay Gdns. *Nott* —7F **49**
Court Gdns. *W Bri* —4D **82**
Courtland Dri. *Alv* —3H **93**
Courtland Gdns. *Alv* —2H **93**
Courtland Rd. *Etw* —6D **88**
Courtleet Way. *Nott* —1H **47**
Courtney Clo. *Nott* —2E **62**
Courtney Way. *Belp* —7D **10**
Court St. *Nott* —7B **48**
Court, The. *Alv* —3H **93**
Court, The. *Bees* —6A **80**
Court Vw. *Nott* —3C **64** (4B **4**)
Court Yd. *Bees* —7B **62**
Covedale Rd. *Nott* —1E **48**
Covent Gdns. *Rad T* —4E **68**
Coventry Ct. *Nott* —1H **47**
Coventry La. *Bees* —6K **61**
Coventry Rd. *Bees* —1G **81**
Coventry Rd. *Nott* —6H **31**
(in two parts)
Coverdale Wlk. *Alv* —3J **93**
(off Elvaston La.)
Covert Clo. *Bur J* —1J **51**
Covert Clo. *Huck* —6J **17**
Covert Clo. *Keyw* —5D **102**
Covert Cres. *Rad T* —4B **68**
Covert Rd. *W Bri* —2K **83**
Covert, The. *Spon* —4A **76**
Cowdray Clo. *Sten F* —7H **91**
Cowdrey Gdns. *Arn* —7K **33**
Cowen St. *Nott* —2F **65** (3G **5**)
Cowlairs. *Nott* —6A **32**
Cow La. *Bees* —7B **62**
Cowley St. *Der* —1J **73**
Cowley St. *Old B* —3K **47**
Cowlishaw Clo. *Shard* —1G **107**
Cowper Rd. *Newt* —5E **28**
Cowper Rd. *Wd'p* —2G **49**
Cowper St. *Sin* —4A **92**
Cowsley Rd. *Der* —7D **56** (1K **7**)
Cowslip Clo. *Bing* —3J **69**
**Coxbench Castle. —3F 41**
Coxbench Rd. *Der* —2E **40**
(in two parts)
Cox Grn. Ct. *Der* —2D **90**
Coxmoor Clo. *Edw* —4A **84**
Coxmoor Ct. *Nott* —4C **32**
Coxon St. *Spon* —3A **76**
Crabtree Clo. *Alst* —3G **55**
Crabtree Clo. *Cas D* —1J **115**
Crabtree Fld. *Colw P* —3B **66**
Crabtree Hill. *Der* —3G **55**
Crabtree Hill. *L Eat* —6C **40**
Crabtree Rd. *Nott* —7G **31**
Craddock Av. *Spon* —5A **76**
Cragdale Rd. *Nott* —1E **48**
Cragmoor Rd. *Bur J* —3J **51**
Craiglee Ct. *Sin* —5H **91**
Craig Moray. *Rad T* —3A **68**
Craig St. *Long E* —2J **97**
Crammond Clo. *Nott* —5D **64**
Crampton Ct. *Nott* —5C **32**
Cramworth Gro. *Nott* —3F **49**
Cranberry Clo. *W Bri* —2D **82**
Cranberry Gro. *L'ver* —3D **90**
Cranborne Clo. *Trow* —5H **61**
Cranbourne Gro. *Huck* —5E **16**
Cranbrook St. *Nott* —2F **65** (3G **5**)
Cranfield Wlk. *Nott* —6B **82**
Cranfleet Way. *Long E* —2E **96**

Cranford Gdns. *W Bri* —4E **82**
Cranhill Clo. *L'ver* —3D **90**
Cranleigh Dri. *Low* —4D **36**
Cranmer Av. *What* —4G **71**
Cranmer Gro. *Nott* —7E **48**
Cranmer Rd. *W Mead*
　　　　—3C **74** (3H **7**)
Cranmer St. *Ilk* —5D **44**
Cranmer St. *Long E* —1H **97**
Cranmer St. *Nott* —7E **48**
Cranmer Wlk. *Nott* —7E **48**
Cranmore Clo. *Arn* —3J **33**
Cranshaw Clo. *Long W* —7G **117**
Cransley Av. *Nott* —5D **62**
Cranston Av. *Arn* —4H **33**
Cranston Rd. *Bees* —6C **62**
Cranthorne Dri. *Nott* —1A **66**
Crantock Gdns. *Keyw* —6D **102**
Cranwell Ct. *Nott* —7F **31**
Cranwell Rd. *Nott* —5D **46**
Cranwood Clo. *Altn* —4D **92**
Craster Av. *Arn* —3J **33**
Craster Dri. *Nott* —5F **31**
Craven Rd. *Nott* —7A **48**
Crawford Av. *S'fd* —7H **61**
Crawford Clo. *Nott* —2E **62**
Crawford Ri. *Arn* —5A **34**
Crawley Rd. *Alv* —4F **93**
Crayford Rd. *Alv* —4G **93**
Crecy Clo. *Der* —5G **73**
Creeton Grn. *Nott* —1B **100**
Crescent Av. *Cltn* —5C **50**
Crescent, The. *Alv* —3E **92**
Crescent, The. *Bees* —5C **80**
　(Attenborough La. N.)
Crescent, The. *Bees* —6A **80**
　(Chetwynd Rd.)
Crescent, The. *Breas* —2A **96**
Crescent, The. *Chad* —3F **75**
Crescent, The. *Eastw* —3E **28**
Crescent, The. *Hors W* —6J **25**
Crescent, The. *Melb* —3H **113**
Crescent, The. *Nott* —6F **49**
Crescent, The. *Rad T* —4A **68**
Crescent, The. *Ris* —5B **78**
Crescent, The. *Stan C* —5D **42**
Crescent, The. *S'fd* —6J **61**
Crescent, The. *Wd'p* —2G **49**
Cressbrook Way. *Oak* —4H **57**
Cresswell Rd. *Bees* —3B **80**
Cressy Rd. *Nott* —6B **82**
Cresta Gdns. *Nott* —4F **49**
Crest, The. *Dar A* —5J **55**
Crest Vw. *Nott* —3D **48**
Crewe Clo. *Nott* —1B **64**
Crewe St. *Der* —7K **73**
Crewton Way. *Alv* —2F **93**
Cribb Clo. *Nott* —1D **82**
Crich Av. *L'ver* —6F **73**
Crich Circ. *L'ver* —6G **73**
Crich La. *Belp* —7A **10**
Crich Vw. *Nott* —4E **48**
Cricketers Ct. *L'ver* —1H **91**
Cricketers Ct. *W Bri* —6H **65**
Cricklewood Rd. *Der* —2F **73**
Criftin Rd. *Bur J* —2A **52**
Cringle M. *Oak* —5E **56**
Cripps Hill. *Nott* —5J **63**
Critchley St. *Ilk* —5D **44**
Critch's Flat. *Kimb* —7K **29**
Critch Vw. *Heag* —4D **10**
Crocus Pl. *Nott* —4F **65** (7G **5**)
Crocus St. *Nott* —5E **64** (7F **5**)
Croft Av. *Huck* —7G **17**
Croft Clo. *Dal A* —5H **59**
Croft Clo. *Ock* —4E **76**
Croft Clo. *Spon* —2B **76**
Croft Cres. *Aws* —1G **45**
Croft End. *L Eat* —6C **40**
Crofters Ct. *Oak* —5E **56**
Croft La. *Bread* —4C **56**
Crofton Clo. *Bees* —5D **80**
Crofton Clo. *Nott* —1H **63**
Crofton Rd. *Bees* —6D **80**
Croft Ri. *E Bri* —2J **53**
Croft Rd. *Arn* —5H **33**
Croft Rd. *Edw* —4J **83**
Croft Rd. *Keyw* —6B **102**
Crofts, The. *Bing* —3A **70**
Croft, The. *Barg* —4C **24**
Croft, The. *Dray* —3J **95**
Croft, The. *Heag* —3E **10**
Croft, The. *Keg* —1H **117**
Croft, The. *L'ver* —1H **91**
Croft, The. *Melb* —3G **113**
Croft, The. *M'ly* —4J **41**
Cromarty Clo. *Sin* —5J **91**
Cromarty Ct. *Nott* —5D **64**
Cromdale Clo. *Arn* —4A **34**

Cromer Clo. *Mick* —7A **72**
Cromer Rd. *Nott* —7G **49**
Cromford Av. *Cltn* —6B **50**
Cromford Clo. *Lan M* —1K **27**
Cromford Clo. *Long E* —4E **96**
Cromford Dri. *Mick* —4C **72**
Cromford Rd. *Chad* —7F **57**
Cromford Rd. *Lan M* —6G **13**
Cromford Rd. *Rip* —2K **11**
Cromford Rd. *W Bri* —2H **83**
Cromford Rd. Ind. Est. *Lan M*
　　　　—1K **27**
Crompton Rd. *Ilk* —5F **61**
Crompton Rd. Ind. Est. *Ilk*
　　　　—4F **61**
Crompton St. *Der* —4K **73** (5C **6**)
Cromwell Av. *Find* —7B **90**
Cromwell Av. *Ilk* —2E **60**
Cromwell Cres. *Lamb* —6F **35**
Cromwell Rd. *Bees* —1E **80**
Cromwell Rd. *Der* —6K **73**
Cromwell Rd. *What* —4G **71**
Cromwell St. *Cltn* —7C **50**
Cromwell St. *Gilt* —5F **29**
Cromwell St. *Nott* —2C **64** (2B **4**)
Cromwell Ter. *Ilk* —3D **44**
Crookdole La. *C'tn* —5D **20**
Cropston Clo. *W Bri* —4G **83**
Cropton Clo. *Alv* —3J **93**
Cropton Cres. *Nott* —1H **63**
Cropton Gro. *Bing* —3J **69**
Cropwell Bishop Rd. *C But*
　　　　—3H **87**
Cropwell Butler Rd. *C Bis*
　　　　—4H **87**
Cropwell Gdns. *Rad T* —5A **68**
Cropwell Grn. *Nott* —1H **65**
Cropwell Manor Ct. *C Bis*
　　　　—5H **87**
Cropwell Rd. *Rad T* —4K **67**
Crosby Rd. *W Bri* —6H **65**
Crosby St. *Der* —4H **73**
Cross Clo. *L'ver* —1G **91**
Cross Clo. Wlk. *L'ver* —1G **91**
Crossdale Dri. *Keyw* —5C **102**
Crossdale Gro. *Oak* —4J **57**
Crossdale Wlk. *Nott* —5A **32**
Crossfield Ct. *Nott* —5C **32**
Crossfield Dri. *Nott* —5C **32**
Crossgate Dri. *Q Dri & Nott*
　　　　—7C **64**
Crosshill. *Cod* —6D **12**
Crosshill. *Cotg* —5A **86**
Crosshill Dri. *Ilk* —2A **60**
Crosslands Mdw. *Colw* —3D **66**
Cross La. *Cod* —5D **12**
Cross La. *E Bri* —4K **53**
Cross Lea. *Dal A* —5H **59**
Crossley St. *Nott* —4D **48**
Crossley St. *Rip* —3K **11**
Crossman St. *Nott* —4D **48**
Cross St. *Arn* —5F **33**
Cross St. *Bees* —1F **81**
Cross St. *Cltn* —6B **50**
Cross St. *Der* —2H **73**
Cross St. *Eastw* —3E **28**
Cross St. *Long E* —1J **97**
Cross St. *N'fld* —7E **50**
Cross St. *Sand* —2G **79**
Cross, The. *Cotg* —5J **85**
Crossways Dri. *E Bri* —3K **53**
Crowborough Av. *Nott* —5E **62**
Crow Ct. *Bing* —3C **70**
Crowcroft Way. *Long E* —6F **79**
Crow Hill Rd. *Cltn* —7D **50**
Crowley Clo. *Nott* —1C **62**
Crown Clo. *Long E* —2E **96**
Crown Hill Way. *Stan C* —6D **42**
Crownland Dri. *Der* —7G **93**
Crown M. *Der* —5J **73** (7A **6**)
Crown St. *Der* —5J **73** (7A **6**)
Crown St. *Duf* —2J **39**
Crown Ter. *Belp* —1H **23**
Crown Wlk. *Der* —4A **74** (5E **6**)
Crow Pk. Dri. *Bur J* —3J **51**
Crowshaw St. *Der* —1B **92**
Crowthorne Clo. *Nott* —4A **32**
Crowthorne Gdns. *Nott* —4A **32**
Croxall Clo. *Nott* —4A **82**
Croxley Gdns. *Nut* —3D **46**
Croydon Rd. *Nott* —2A **64**
Croydon Wlk. *Der* —2D **72**
Crummock Clo. *Bees* —7C **62**
Crusader Ct. *Nott* —7J **81**
Cubley Wlk. *Der* —4G **91**
Cuckmere Clo. *Alst* —2B **56**
Cuillin Clo. *Long E* —7E **78**
Cuillin Clo. *Nott* —3B **32**
Culbert Lodge. *Nott* —5B **48**

Culbert Pl. *Nott* —5B **48**
Culdrose Wlk. *Nott* —5G **49**
Cullens Ct. *Nott* —4E **48**
Cullen Way. *Sin* —7J **91**
Culworth Clo. *Belp* —1D **24**
Culworth St. *Oak* —5H **57**
Cumberhills Rd. *Duf* —6D **38**
Cumberland Av. *Bees* —2D **80**
Cumberland Av. *Der* —2E **74**
Cumberland Clo. *Rud* —2E **100**
Cumberland Clo. *W'wd* —1A **14**
Cumberland Cres. *Borr* —7D **76**
Cumberland Pl. *Nott*
　　　　—3D **64** (4D **4**)
Cumbria Grange. *Gam* —1A **84**
Cumbria Wlk. *Mick* —7A **72**
Cummings St. *Der* —6A **74**
Curborough Dri. *Alv* —3K **93**
Curie Ct. *Nott* —5A **64**
Curlew Clo. *Nott* —2A **66**
Curlew Clo. *Sin* —5H **91**
Curlew Wharf. *Nott* —5C **64**
Cursley Way. *Bees* —6C **80**
Curtis St. *Huck* —6G **17**
Curzon Av. *Cltn* —7K **49**
Curzon Clo. *Alst* —3G **55**
Curzon Ct. *Duf* —3J **39**
Curzon Ct. *Mick* —7B **72**
Curzon Ct. *Nott* —1F **65** (1H **5**)
Curzon Gdns. *Nott* —1F **65** (1H **5**)
Curzon La. *Alv* —1G **93**
Curzon La. *Duf* —3H **39**
Curzon Pl. *Nott* —2F **65** (2G **5**)
Curzon Rd. *Chad* —1F **75**
Curzon St. *Der* —3K **73** (4B **6**)
　(in two parts)
Curzon St. *Got* —1H **111**
Curzon St. *Long E* —6F **79**
Curzon St. *N'fld* —7E **50**
Curzon St. *Nott* —2F **65** (2G **5**)
Cut La. *Der* —1B **74**
Cutthrough La. *Nott* —7H **63**
Cuttlebrook Clo. *Der* —2J **91**
Cuttle Hill Gdns. *E Bri* —3J **53**
Cuxton Clo. *Nott* —5D **46**
Cycle Rd. *Nott* —3A **64**
Cypress Ct. *Huck* —7C **16**
Cypress Wlk. *Chad* —3H **75**
Cyprus Av. *Bees* —1F **81**
Cyprus Ct. *Nott* —6E **48**
Cyprus Dri. *Bees* —1F **81**
Cyprus Rd. *Nott* —6E **48**
Cyril Av. *Bees* —1E **80**
Cyril Av. *Nott* —6K **47**
Cyril Av. *S'fd* —1H **79**
Cyril Rd. *W Bri* —7J **65**

**D**abell Av. *Nott* —5E **30**
Dagmar Gro. *Bees* —2G **81**
Dagmar Gro. *Nott* —5F **49**
Dahlia Dri. *Oak* —4J **57**
Dairy Ho. Rd. *Der* —7A **74**
Daisy Clo. *Cotg* —6J **85**
Daisy Farm Rd. *Newt* —4F **29**
Daisy Rd. *Nott* —5J **49**
Dakeyne St. *Nott* —2G **65** (3J **5**)
Dakota Rd. *Dis* —3K **115**
Dalbeattie Clo. *Arn* —4K **33**
Dalbury Wlk. *Der* —4G **91**
Dalby Sq. *Nott* —4J **63**
Daleacre Av. *Locki* —5D **108**
Dale Av. *Cltn* —7A **50**
Dale Av. *Long E* —7H **79**
Dale Av. *Map* —4J **49**
Dale Brook. *Hilt* —7A **88**
Dalebrook Cres. *Huck* —6C **16**
Dale Clo. *Breas* —1B **96**
Dale Clo. *Huck* —6C **16**
Dale Clo. *W Bri* —1K **83**
Dale Ct. *Klbrn* —5F **25**
Dale Farm Av. *Nott* —2J **65**
Dale Gro. *Nott* —3H **65**
Dalehead Rd. *Nott* —6K **81**
Dale La. *Bees* —2E **80**
Dalemoor Gdns. *Nott* —6H **47**
Dale Pk. Av. *Klbrn* —5G **25**
Dale Rd. *Alv* —2H **93**
Dale Rd. *Cltn* —7A **50**
Dale Rd. *Der* —6K **73**
Dale Rd. *Keyw* —6C **102**
Dale Rd. *Kimb* —1K **45**
Dale Rd. *Spon & Ock* —3B **76**
Dale Rd. *Stan* —2D **58**
Dale Rd. *Stan D* —5J **59**
Dalesgate Clo. *L'ver* —4F **91**
Daleside. *Cotg* —6J **85**
Daleside Rd. *Nott* —4H **65**
Daleside Rd. E. *Nott* —3K **65**

Dales Shop. Cen. *W Hal* —7G **43**
Dale St. *Ilk* —7D **44**
Dale St. *Nott* —3G **65** (5K **5**)
Dale Ter. *Nott* —3H **65**
Dale Vw. *Ilk* —1C **60**
Dale Vw. Gdns. *Klbrn* —5F **25**
Dale Vw. Rd. *Nott* —7K **49**
Dalkeith Av. *Alv* —4F **93**
Dalkeith Ter. *Nott* —7B **48**
Dallas-York Rd. *Bees* —2H **81**
Dalley Clo. *S'fd* —1J **79**
Dalley La. *Belp* —5G **9**
Dallimore Rd. *Ilk* —3B **60**
Dalness Ct. *Sin* —6H **91**
Dalton Av. *Der* —5G **73**
Dalton Clo. *S'fd* —3J **79**
Daltons Clo. *Lan M* —1J **27**
Dam Side. *Belp* —2A **24**
Damson Wlk. *Nott* —6K **49**
Danbury Mt. *Nott* —4F **49**
Danebridge Cres. *Oak* —6G **57**
Dane Clo. *Nott* —1F **65** (1G **5**)
Dane Ct. *Nott* —1F **65** (1G **5**)
Danesbury Cres. *Den* —4G **25**
Danesbury Ri. *Den* —4G **25**
Danes Clo. *Arn* —5F **33**
Danethorpe Va. *Nott* —2E **48**
Daniels Way. *Huck* —1E **30**
Dannah Cres. *Rip* —3B **12**
Dannah St. *Rip* —2A **12**
Darby St. *Der* —6K **73**
Darfield Dri. *Hean* —3J **27**
Darkey La. *S'fd* —3J **79**
　(in two parts)
Dark La. *Asl* —3J **71**
Dark La. *Bing* —3C **70**
Dark La. *C'tn* —6C **20**
Dark La. *Holb* —7A **24**
Dark La. *W Leak* —7E **110**
Darley Abbey Dri. *Dar A* —5K **55**
Darley Abbey Mills. *Dar A* —5A **56**
Darley Av. *Bees* —5J **79**
Darley Av. *Cltn* —5C **50**
Darley Av. *Nott* —7A **48**
Darley Dri. *Long E* —4E **96**
Darley Dri. *Rip* —1J **11**
Darley Dri. *W Hal* —6G **43**
Darley Gro. *Dar A* —6K **55**
Darley Gro. *Der* —7A **56** (1D **6**)
Darley La. *Der* —2A **74** (1D **6**)
Darley Pk. Dri. *Der* —6K **55**
Darley Pk. Rd. *Der* —6K **55**
Darley Rd. *Nott* —7A **48**
Darley Sq. *Ilk* —1C **44**
Darley St. *Dar A* —6A **56**
Darlton Dri. *Arn* —6J **33**
Darnall Clo. *Nott* —6A **32**
Darnhall Cres. *Nott* —7D **46**
Daron Gdns. *Nott* —6C **32**
Darsway. *Cas D* —6H **107**
Dartford Pl. *Alv* —4G **93**
Dartmeet Ct. *Nott* —7K **47**
Darvel Clo. *Nott* —1H **63**
Darwin Av. *Altn* —5D **92**
Darwin Av. *Ilk* —7C **44**
Darwin Clo. *Nott* —5A **32**
Darwin Pl. *Der* —3B **74** (3F **7**)
Darwin Rd. *Long E* —4F **97**
Darwin Rd. *Mick* —5C **72**
Darwin Sq. *Der* —4A **74** (5E **6**)
Dashwood St. *Der* —5A **74** (7D **6**)
Datchet Clo. *L'ver* —1E **90**
Davenport Rd. *Der* —1C **92**
Daventry Clo. *Mick* —5A **72**
David Gro. *Bees* —6E **62**
David La. *Nott* —3K **47**
David Lloyd Raquet &
　　Fitness Cen. —1D **24**
David's Clo. *Chel* —1F **105**
Davids La. *Gun* —1G **53**
Davidson Clo. *Arn* —6A **34**
Davidson St. *Nott* —4H **65**
Davies Rd. *W Bri* —1H **83**
Davy Clo. *L'by* —2H **17**
Dawlish Clo. *Huck* —6D **16**
Dawlish Ct. *Alv* —2J **93**
Dawlish Ct. *Eastw* —2B **28**
Dawlish Dri. *Nott* —1D **48**
Dawn Clo. *Huck* —3J **17**
Dawn's La. *Asl* —2J **71**
Dawn Vw. *Trow* —5H **61**
Dawsmere Clo. *Der* —6D **56**
Dawson Clo. *Newt* —4E **28**
Dawver Rd. *Kimb* —1K **45**
Daybrook Av. *Nott* —3E **48**
Daybrook Bus. Cen. *Nott* —7F **33**
Daybrook St. *Nott* —3E **48**
Daykins Row. *Cod* —5E **12**
Daylesford Clo. *L'ver* —1E **90**

Dales La. *Belp* —2K **23**
Dayton Clo. *Chad* —3J **75**
Dayton Ct. *Der* —7J **55**
Deabill St. *N'fld* —1E **66**
Deacon Clo. *Oak* —5E **56**
Dead La. *Coss* —5H **45**
Deadman's La. *Der* —6D **74**
Deakins Pl. *Nott* —2A **64**
Deal Gdns. *Nott* —6F **31**
Dean Av. *Nott* —4J **49**
Dean Clo. *L'ver* —6E **72**
Dean Clo. *Nott* —2D **62**
Dean Rd. *Ambgt* —2K **9**
Dean Rd. *Wd'p* —1G **49**
Deanscourt. *Cotg* —5A **86**
Deans Cft. *Bees* —6B **62**
Deans Dri. *Borr* —6D **76**
Dean St. *Der* —5J **73** (7A **6**)
Dean St. *Lan M* —2A **28**
Dean St. *Nott* —3F **65** (5H **5**)
Debdale La. *Keyw* —6B **102**
Deborah Dri. *Chad* —1G **75**
Deddington La. *Bees* —5B **62**
　(in two parts)
Dee Clo. *Sin* —6J **91**
Deepdale Av. *Ilk* —2B **60**
Deepdale Av. *S'fd* —2H **79**
Deepdale Clo. *Gam* —1K **83**
Deepdale Ct. *Hean* —4G **27**
Deep Dale La. *Sin & Bar T* —7J **91**
Deepdale Rd. *Beio* —7B **10**
Deepdale Rd. *Long E* —3E **96**
Deepdale Rd. *Nott* —3D **62**
Deepdale Rd. *Spon* —5B **76**
Deepdene Clo. *Nott* —4G **47**
Deepdene Way. *Nott* —4G **47**
Deep Furrow Av. *Cltn* —6B **50**
Deering Ct. *Nott* —6A **64**
Deerleap Dri. *Arn* —6E **32**
Deer Pk. *Nott* —3E **62**
Deer Pk. Dri. *Arn* —5D **32**
Deer Pk. Vw. *Spon* —2B **76**
De Ferrers Clo. *Duf* —3J **39**
Degge St. *Der* —4A **74** (5D **6**)
Deincourt Clo. *Spon* —2C **76**
Delamere Clo. *Breas* —1B **96**
Delamere Clo. *Oak* —6G **57**
Delia Av. *Huck* —3J **17**
Dell Way. *Nott* —6B **82**
Dellwood Clo. *Cltn* —4K **49**
Delta Ct. *Nott* —1D **64**
Delta St. *Nott* —5B **48**
Delven La. *Cas D* —7J **107**
Delves Ct. *Hean* —5G **27**
Delves Rd. *Hean* —5F **27**
Delville Av. *Keyw* —5C **102**
De Morgan Clo. *Und* —2E **14**
Denacre Av. *Long E* —7K **79**
Denarth Av. *Shel L* —6E **92**
Denbigh St. *Der* —1E **74**
Denby Comn. *Den V* —2B **26**
Denby La. *Cod* —4H **25**
Denby Pottery Vis. Cen. —2J **25**
Denehurst Av. *Nott* —5J **47**
Denewood Av. *Bees* —5C **62**
Denewood Cres. *Nott* —6E **46**
Denholme Rd. *Nott* —2D **62**
Denison Gdns. *Chad* —2H **75**
Denison St. *Bees* —1E **80**
Denison St. *Nott* —1B **64**
Denman St. Central. *Nott* —2A **64**
　(in three parts)
Denman St. E. *Nott*
　　　　—2B **64** (2A **4**)
Denmark Gro. *Nott* —5F **49**
Dennett Clo. *Nott* —1G **65** (1J **5**)
Dennis Av. *Bees* —7E **62**
Dennis Clo. *L'ver* —2C **90**
Dennison Way. *Rip* —4J **11**
Dennis St. *N'fld* —7E **50**
Denstone Dri. *Alv* —5G **93**
Denstone Rd. *Nott* —2G **65** (3K **5**)
Dentdale Ct. *Alv* —2J **93**
　(off Hodge Beck Clo.)
Dentdale Dri. *Nott* —3B **62**
Denton Av. *Sand* —2E **78**
Denton Dri. *W Eri* —4F **83**
Denton Grn. *Nott* —4F **47**
Denver Ct. *S'fd* —5J **61**
　(Crescent, The)
Denver Ct. *S'fd* —6J **61**
　(Melbourne Rd.)
Denver Rd. *Mick* —5B **72**
Depedale Av. *Borr* —5E **76**
Depot St. *Der* —6A **74**
Deptford Cres. *Nott* —7J **31**
　(in two parts)
Derby Canal Walkway. *Altn*
　　　　—2E **92**

Derby Canal Walkway. *Chel*
   —7E **92**
Derby Canal Walkway. *Der* —7F **75**
**Derby Cathedral. —3D 6**
**Derby City Mus. and Art Gallery.**
   **—3D 6**
**Derby County F.C. —5E 74**
   **(Pride Park Stadium)**
**Derby Gaol. —2B 6**
**Derby Golf Cen. —5B 76**
**Derby Golf Course. —5A 92**
Derby Gro. *Nott* —2B **64**
Derby Hills. *Tickn* —6D **112**
Derby Hills Ct. *Tickn* —6D **112**
Derby La. *Der* —1K **91**
**Derby Playhouse Theatre.**
   **—4B 74 (5F 7)**
**Derby Regional Swimming Pool.**
   **—3C 92**
Derby Rd. *Ambgt* —3K **9**
Derby Rd. *Ast T* —6C **94**
Derby Rd. *Bees & Nott*
   —7A **62** (4A **4**)
Derby Rd. *Belp & Milf* —3K **23**
Derby Rd. *Borr & Dray* —7F **77**
Derby Rd. *Chel* —6F **93**
   (in two parts)
Derby Rd. *Cox & L Eat* —1D **40**
Derby Rd. *Den* —4F **25**
Derby Rd. *Der & Stan* —4K **57**
Derby Rd. *Duf* —4K **39**
Derby Rd. *Etw & Etw* —7A **88**
Derby Rd. *Hean* —4F **27**
Derby Rd. *Ilk* —7A **44**
Derby Rd. *Keg* —7G **109**
Derby Rd. *Lan M* —2A **28**
Derby Rd. *Long E* —1E **96**
Derby Rd. *Lwr K & Klbrn* —7E **24**
Derby Rd. *Melb* —2G **113**
Derby Rd. *Milf* —1J **39**
Derby Rd. *Nott* —2C **64**
Derby Rd. *Ris & Sand* —4B **78**
Derby Rd. *Spon* —3H **75**
Derby Rd. *S'fd* —3G **79**
Derby Rd. Ind. Est. *Hean* —4F **27**
Derbyshire Av. *Trow* —3H **61**
Derbyshire Av. *W Hal* —6G **43**
Derbyshire Bus. Development Cen.
   *Der* —2D **74** (1K **7**)
Derbyshire Clo. *W Hal* —6G **43**
**Derbyshire Constabulary**
   **Memorabilia Mus.—3D 6**
**Derbyshire County Cricket**
   **Ground. —2C 74 (1H 7)**
Derbyshire Cres. *Nott* —2G **63**
Derbyshire Dri. *Ilk* —1C **60**
Derbyshire Dri. *W'wd* —1A **14**
Derbyshire La. *Huck* —5G **17**
Derby Small Bus. Cen. *Der* —6G **7**
Derby Southern By-Pass. *Der*
   —2A **104**
Derby Southern By-Pass.
   *Hilt & Etw* —6B **88**
Derby St. *Arn* —6H **33**
Derby St. *Bees* —1F **81**
Derby St. *Ilk* —6D **44**
Derby St. *Nott* —2D **64** (3C **4**)
**Derby Superbowl. —2A 92**
Derby Ter. *Nott* —2C **64** (3A **4**)
Derby Trad. Est. *Der* —7B **56**
Dereham Dri. *Arn* —7H **33**
Derrington Leys. *Alv* —3K **93**
Derry Dri. *Arn* —3H **33**
Derry Hill Rd. *Arn* —4G **33**
Derry La. *Bing* —4D **70**
Derventio Clo. *Der* —1A **74**
**Derventio Roman Fort. —7A 56**
   **(site of)**
Derwent Av. *Alst* —3A **56**
Derwent Av. *Borr* —5E **76**
Derwent Av. *Ilk* —4B **44**
Derwent Av. *Milf* —4K **23**
Derwent Av. *W Hal* —6G **43**
Derwent Bus. Cen., The. *Der*
   —2B **74** (1F **7**)
Derwent Clo. *Alst* —3A **56**
Derwent Clo. *Bees* —5E **80**
Derwent Clo. *Gam* —1A **84**
Derwent Ct. *Der* —3K **73** (4C **6**)
Derwent Ct. *Nott* —1C **64**
Derwent Cres. *Arn* —7J **33**
Derwent Dri. *Huck* —1G **31**
Derwent Dri. *Sten F* —7H **91**
Derwent Ho. *Der* —2C **74** (2J **7**)
Derwent Pde. *Pri P* —5D **74**
Derwent Ri. *Spon* —4B **76**
Derwent Rd. *Rip* —3J **11**
Derwent Rd. *Spon* —5K **75**
Derwent St. *Belp* —2J **23**

Derwent St. *Der* —3A **74** (3E **6**)
Derwent St. *Dray* —2J **95**
Derwent St. *Long E* —3F **97**
Derwent St. Ind. Est. *Long E*
   —3G **97**
Derwent Ter. *Nott* —4E **48**
Derwent Va. *Belp* —3K **23**
Derwent Vw. *Belp* —7K **9**
**Derwent Vis. Cen. —7K 9**
Desford Clo. *Nott* —2C **48**
Desmond Ct. *Und* —2E **14**
Devas Gdns. *Spon* —3K **75**
De Vere Gdns. *Wd'p* —1H **49**
Devitt Dri. *Huck* —3J **17**
Devon Cir. *Red* —4F **33**
Devon Clo. *Der* —1D **74**
Devon Clo. *Sand* —3F **79**
Devon Dri. *Nott* —4D **48**
Devon Dri. *Rud* —1F **101**
Devonshire Av. *Alst* —4K **55**
Devonshire Av. *Bees* —2E **80**
Devonshire Av. *Borr* —6E **76**
Devonshire Av. *Long E* —1A **98**
Devonshire Av. *Rip* —2J **11**
Devonshire Clo. *Ilk* —1C **44**
Devonshire Cres. *Nott* —4D **48**
Devonshire Dri. *Duf* —3H **39**
Devonshire Dri. *Eastw* —3D **28**
Devonshire Dri. *Mick* —5C **72**
Devonshire Dri. *S'fd* —5H **61**
Devonshire Promenade. *Nott*
   —4A **64**
Devonshire Rd. *Nott* —4D **48**
Devonshire Rd. *W Bri* —2G **83**
Devonshire St. *Ambgt* —1K **9**
Devonshire Wlk. *Der*
   —4A **74** (5E **6**)
Devon St. *Ilk* —2E **60**
Devon St. *Nott* —2H **65**
Dewberry La. *Rad T* —5B **68**
Dewchurch Dri. *Sun* —4J **91**
Dexter St. *Der* —6C **74**
Dial, The. *Cotg* —6J **85**
Diamond Dri. *Oak* —5F **57**
Dickens Ct. *Newt* —2F **29**
Dickens Sq. *Der* —2K **91**
Dickinson St. *Der* —6D **74**
Dickson Dri. *Rud* —3F **101**
Didcot Dri. *Nott* —5K **47**
Digby Av. *Nott* —3K **49**
Digby Av. *Woll* —3H **63**
Digby Ct. *Nott* —4B **64**
Digby Hall Dri. *Ged* —3A **50**
Digby St. *Ilk* —5E **44**
Digby St. *Kimb* —7H **29**
Dirac Clo. *Nott* —1J **99**
Diseworth Clo. *Chel* —7F **93**
Diseworth Gro. *Nott* —6F **65**
Diseworth Rd. *Cas D* —1J **115**
Distillery St. *Rud* —3E **100**
Dix Av. *Smal* —7B **26**
Dixie St. *Jack* —1K **13**
Djanogly Arts Cen. &
   **Recital Hall. —6K 63**
Dobbin Clo. *C Bis* —4H **87**
Dobholes La. *Smal* —7B **26**
Dockholm Rd. *Long E* —6G **79**
Dodburn Ct. *Sin* —5H **91**
Dodford Ct. *Hean* —4J **27**
Dog La. *Melb* —5A **114**
Dogwood Av. *Nott* —6F **31**
Doles La. *Find* —6B **90**
Dolley Av. *Belp* —6B **10**
Dolphin Clo. *Spon* —2B **76**
Dolphin Ct. *Nott* —5C **32**
Donald Hawley Way. *Duf* —3K **39**
Donbas Clo. *Bulw* —2H **47**
Doncaster Av. *Sand* —2F **79**
Doncaster Gro. *Long E* —7K **79**
Doncaster Ter. *Nott* —6E **64**
Donegal Wlk. *Chad* —4G **75**
Donington Clo. *Sun* —4H **91**
Donington Dri. *Sun* —4J **91**
Donington La. *Cas D* —3A **108**
**Donington Pk. —1D 114**
   **(Deer Park)**
**Donington Pk. Motor**
   **Racing Circuit. —3E 114**
**Donington Pk. Mus. —3F 115**
   **(Grand Prix Collection)**
Donington Rd. *Nott* —7A **82**
Donner Cres. *Ilk* —1C **44**
Dooland Dri. *Nott* —5H **49**
Dorchester Av. *Chad* —1E **74**
Dorchester Gdns. *W Bri* —5G **83**
Dorchester Rd. *Kimb* —6K **29**
Doris Ct. *Bees* —6A **80**
Doris Rd. *Ilk* —7E **44**
Dorket Clo. *Arn* —4J **33**

Dorket Dri. *Nott* —4K **63**
Dorket Ho. *Cltn* —6C **50**
   (off Foxhill Rd. E.)
Dorking Rd. *Der* —2F **73**
Dorking Rd. *Nott* —1A **64**
Dormy Clo. *Bees* —1C **80**
Dormy Clo. *Rad T* —4B **68**
Dormy Ct. *Nott* —6K **31**
Dornoch Av. *Nott* —4F **49**
Dorothy Av. *Huck* —3H **17**
Dorothy Av. *Newt* —2E **28**
Dorothy Av. *Sand* —3F **79**
Dorothy Boot Homes, The. *Nott*
   —7D **64**
Dorothy Courts. *Ilk* —6C **44**
Dorothy Gro. *Nott* —1J **63**
Dorrien Av. *Der* —2A **92**
Dorset Gdns. *W Bri* —3E **82**
Dorset St. *Der* —2D **74** (1K **7**)
Dorset St. *Nott* —2K **63**
Dorterry Cres. *Ilk* —2E **60**
Douglas Av. *Aws* —1G **45**
Douglas Av. *Cltn* —1B **66**
Douglas Av. *Hean* —3E **26**
Douglas Clo. *Rad T* —5K **67**
Douglas Ct. *Bees* —6A **80**
Douglas Cres. *Cltn* —1C **66**
Douglas Rd. *Bing* —3D **70**
Douglas Rd. *Long E* —6F **79**
Douglas Rd. *Nott* —2B **64** (3A **4**)
Douglas St. *Der* —6B **74**
Douro Dri. *Arn* —4K **33**
Dove Clo. *Bing* —4B **70**
Dove Clo. *Klbrn* —5G **25**
Dove Clo. *Mick* —5E **72**
Dovecote. *Cas D* —7K **107**
Dovecote. *Melb* —7D **114**
Dovecote Clo. *E Bri* —3J **53**
Dovecote Dri. *Borr* —6C **76**
Dovecote Dri. *Nott* —3E **62**
Dovecote La. *Bees* —2F **81**
Dovecote Rd. *Eastw & Newt*
   —3F **29**
Dovecotes, The. *Bees* —3F **81**
Dovecote, The. *Hors* —7F **25**
Dovedale Av. *Alv* —2J **93**
Dovedale Av. *Long E* —3E **96**
Dovedale Circ. *Ilk* —1C **44**
Dovedale Clo. *Rip* —6K **11**
Dovedale Ct. *Long E* —3F **97**
Dovedale Cres. *Belp* —1B **24**
Dovedale Ri. *Alst* —6H **55**
Dovedale Rd. *Nott* —1A **66**
Dovedale Rd. *Spon* —5B **76**
Dovedale Rd. *W Bri* —3J **83**
Dovedales, The. *Mick* —7B **72**
Dove La. *Long E* —7G **79**
Dovenby Rd. *Nott* —5B **82**
Dover Beck Clo. *C'tn* —5E **20**
Dover Beck Dri. *Wdbgh* —1G **35**
Dover Ct. *Der* —6A **74**
   (in two parts)
Doveridge Av. *Cltn* —6E **50**
Doveridge Rd. *Cltn* —6D **50**
Doveridge Wlk. *L'ver* —4G **91**
Dove Rd. *Dis* —3A **116**
Dove Rd. *Rip* —3J **11**
Dover St. *Der* —6A **74**
Dove St. *Nott* —6H **31**
Doveys Orchard. *C'tn* —5B **20**
Dower Clo. *Dar A* —5A **56**
Downes Clo. *Nott* —6G **31**
Downham Clo. *Arn* —7J **33**
Downham Clo. *Mick* —7C **72**
Downing Clo. *Der* —2D **72**
Downing Gdns. *Nott* —5H **31**
Downing Rd. *W Mead* —3D **74**
Downing St. *Nott* —5H **31**
Downmeadow. *Heag* —4E **10**
Downs, The. *Nott* —5C **82**
Dowson St. *Nott* —1H **65**
Doyne Ct. *Nott* —6E **64**
Drage St. *Der* —1B **74**
Dragwell. *Keg* —1H **117**
Drakemyre Clo. *Arn* —4K **33**
Drake Rd. *Cltn* —2F **67**
Draycott Clo. *Los* —1E **26**
Draycott Ct. *Ilk* —3D **44**
Draycott Dri. *Mick* —5A **72**
Draycott Rd. *Borr* —7E **76**
Draycott Rd. *Breas* —2A **96**
Draycott Rd. *Long E* —4D **96**
Draymans Ct. *Nott* —5B **48**
Drayton Av. *Der* —2D **72**
Drayton St. *Nott* —4E **48**
Dresden Clo. *Mick* —6A **72**
Drewry Ct. *Der* —3J **73** (5A **6**)
Drewry La. *Der* —4J **73** (5A **6**)
   (in three parts)

Dreyfus Clo. *Spon* —3B **76**
Drift, The. *Huck* —3H **17**
Drift, The. *Nott* —5A **82**
Drill Hall Cotts. *Der* —2G **73**
Dronfield Pl. *Ilk* —1C **44**
Drummond Av. *N'fld* —7F **51**
Drummond Dri. *Nut* —2E **46**
Drummond Rd. *Ilk* —5C **44**
Drury Av. *Spon* —4K **75**
Drury Wlk. *Nott* —3E **64** (5F **5**)
Dryden Ct. *S'fd* —6J **61**
Dryden St. *Der* —3K **91**
Dryden St. *Nott* —1D **64** (1D **4**)
Drysdale Clo. *Nott* —1H **47**
Drysdale Rd. *Mick* —5B **72**
Duchess Gdns. *Nott* —5H **31**
Duchess St. *Nott* —5H **31**
Duck Island. *Duf* —3J **39**
Duckworth Sq. *Der*
   —3A **74** (4D **6**)
Dudley Ct. *Bees* —7A **62**
Duesbury Clo. *Altn* —2E **92**
Duffield Clo. *Long E* —4E **96**
Duffield Ct. *Duf* —3K **39**
Duffield Ct. *Nott* —5B **32**
Duffield Rd. *Dar A & Der*
   —6K **55** (1C **6**)
Duffield Rd. *Der* —7A **40**
Duffield Rd. *L Eat* —6B **40**
Duffield Rd. Ind. Est. *L Eat*
   —1C **56**
Duke Clo. *Nott* —1F **47**
Duke Cres. *Gilt* —4G **29**
Dukeries La. *Oak* —5H **57**
Dukes Pl. *Ilk* —2C **44**
Dukes Pl. *Nott* —3F **65** (4H **5**)
Duke St. *Arn* —6H **33**
Duke St. *Bulw* —6H **31**
Duke St. *Der* —2A **74** (1E **6**)
Duke St. *Huck* —5H **17**
Duke St. *Ilk* —3D **44**
Duke St. *Nott* —6B **48**
Duke St. E. *Huck* —5H **17**
Duke William Mt. *Nott*
   —3C **64** (5A **4**)
Duluth Av. *Chad* —1G **75**
Dulverton Av. *Sten F* —7G **91**
Dulverton Va. *Nott* —3G **47**
Dulwich Rd. *Der* —2C **72**
Dulwich Rd. *Nott* —2A **64**
Dumbles Clo. *Ilk* —1A **60**
Dumbles La. *Den V* —3B **26**
Dumbles, The. *Lamb* —5F **35**
Dunbar Clo. *Long E* —5J **97**
Dunbar Clo. *Sin* —7J **91**
Dunblane Rd. *Rud* —3E **100**
Duncan Clo. *Belp* —6B **10**
Duncan Rd. *Der* —1K **91**
Duncombe Clo. *Nott* —7G **49**
Duncroft Av. *Ged* —5D **50**
Dundas Clo. *Nott* —1E **64** (1E **4**)
Dunedin Clo. *Mick* —5C **72**
Dunelm Dri. *C'tn* —5E **20**
Dungannon Rd. *Nott* —1A **100**
Dungley Hill. *Heag* —2D **10**
Dunholme Clo. *Nott* —5H **31**
Dunkery Ct. *Oak* —5G **57**
Dunkery Rd. *Nott* —1B **100**
Dunkirk. *Der* —4K **73** (5C **6**)
Dunkirk Rd. *Nott* —6A **64**
Dunlin Wharf. *Nott* —5C **64**
Dunlop Av. *Nott* —3A **64**
Dunnicliffe La. *Melb* —4G **113**
Dunoon Clo. *Nott* —3A **32**
Dunoon Clo. *Sin* —6J **91**
Dunsby Clo. *Nott* —7A **82**
Dunsford Dri. *Nott* —7A **34**
Dunsil Dri. *Q Dri* —7C **64**
Dunsil Rd. *Newt* —1F **29**
Dunsmore Clo. *Bees* —4H **81**
Dunsmore Dri. *Oak* —5E **56**
Dunstall Pk. Rd. *Der* —1D **92**
Dunstan St. *N'fld* —7E **50**
Dunster Rd. *Newt* —3F **29**
Dunster Rd. *W Bri* —2J **83**
Dunston Clo. *Long E* —2K **97**
Dunton Clo. *W Mead*
   —3C **74** (3H **7**)
Dunvegan Clo. *Sten F* —7H **91**
Dunvegan Dri. *Nott* —3B **32**
Durham Av. *Der* —2E **74**
Durham Av. *Nott* —3H **65**
Durham Chambers. *Nott*
   —3E **64** (4F **5**)
Durham Clo. *Nott* —3H **65**
Durham Cres. *Nott* —7J **31**
Durham St. *Ilk* —5D **44**
Durley Clo. *Alv* —2J **93**

Durlston Clo. *W Bri* —3D **82**
Durnford St. *Nott* —4B **48**
Dursley Clo. *Nott* —1H **47**
Durward Clo. *Altn* —2C **92**
Dyce Clo. *Nott* —6F **31**
Dylan M. *Nott* —6E **46**
Dylan Thomas Rd. *Nott* —5D **32**

**E**

Eagle Cen. *Der* —3A **74** (4E **6**)
Eagle Clo. *Arn* —6J **33**
Eagle Clo. *Bees* —7D **62**
Eagle Ct. *Nott* —6K **31**
Eagle Rd. *Quar H* —3D **60**
Eagle St. *Heag* —2E **10**
Ealing Av. *Nott* —2K **47**
Ealing Clo. *Der* —2F **73**
Eardley Clo. *Chad* —3H **75**
Eardley Rd. *Nott* —7A **32**
Earl Cres. *Ged* —3D **50**
Earl Dri. *Gilt* —4G **29**
Earls Clo. *Nott* —2C **62**
Earls Cres. *Oak* —5H **57**
Earlsfield Dri. *Nott* —4K **31**
Earlswood Clo. *Breas* —1B **96**
Earlswood Dri. *Edw* —4K **83**
Earlswood Dri. *Mick* —4D **72**
Easedale Clo. *Gam* —1A **84**
Easegill Ct. *Nott* —5B **32**
   (off Old Farm Rd.)
East Acres. *Cotg* —5K **85**
East Av. *Mick* —5B **72**
Eastbrae Rd. *Sun* —2H **91**
E. Circus St. *Nott* —3D **64** (4C **4**)
Eastcliffe Av. *Ged* —3B **50**
East Clo. *Dar A* —5J **55**
East Clo. *Keyw* —7C **102**
Eastcote Av. *Bees* —5B **62**
East Cres. *Bees* —3H **81**
East Cres. *Holb* —5C **24**
East Cft. *Nott* —4F **65** (7H **5**)
E. Croft Av. *L'ver* —4H **91**
Eastdale Rd. *Nott* —7A **50**
East Dri. *Nott* —6J **63**
Eastfield Rd. *Rip* —3C **12**
Eastgate. *Der* —2B **74** (2G **7**)
   (in two parts)
Eastglade Rd. *Nott* —7B **32**
East Gro. *Bing* —3B **70**
East Gro. *Nott* —6C **48**
Eastham Clo. *Nott* —1G **65** (1J **5**)
Eastham Rd. *Arn* —7K **33**
Eastholme Cft. *Colw P* —2B **66**
Easthorpe Cotts. *Rud* —2F **101**
Easthorpe St. *Rud* —2E **100**
East Lawn. *Find* —7B **90**
Eastleigh Dri. *Mick* —6C **72**
**East Midlands Aeropark &**
   **Vis. Cen. —3C 116**
East Moor. *Cotg* —6A **86**
Eastmoor Dri. *Cltn* —6D **50**
E. Nelson St. *Hean* —3G **27**
E. Service Rd. *Der* —6H **75**
East St. *Bing* —3B **70**
East St. *Der* —3A **74** (4E **6**)
East St. *Got* —1H **111**
East St. *Hean* —5J **27**
East St. *Ilk* —6D **44**
East St. *Long E* —1K **97**
East St. *Nott* —2F **65** (3G **5**)
East St. *Rud* —3E **100**
East Vw. *W Bri* —2F **83**
Eastview Rd. *Heag* —3E **10**
East Vw. Ter. *Lan M* —2K **27**
Eastway. *Cas D* —7K **107**
Eastwell St. *Huck* —4G **17**
Eastwold. *Cotg* —6A **86**
Eastwood Av. *L'ver* —6G **73**
Eastwood Clo. *Huck* —1E **30**
Eastwood Dri. *L'ver* —6G **73**
Eastwood Rd. *Kimb* —6H **29**
Eastwood Rd. *Rad T* —4A **68**
Eastwood St. *Nott* —1J **47**
Eaton Av. *Alst* —2A **56**
Eaton Av. *Arn* —6J **33**
Eaton Av. *Ilk* —1B **60**
Eaton Bank. *Duf* —4A **40**
Eaton Clo. *Alst* —2A **56**
Eaton Clo. *Bees* —2H **81**
Eaton Ct. *Der* —2J **73** (1A **6**)
Eaton Ct. *Duf* —4J **39**
Eaton Grange Dri. *Long E*
   —1E **96**
Eaton Pl. *Bing* —3A **70**
Eaton Rd. *Cas D* —7K **107**
Eaton St. *Nott* —2H **79**
Eaton St. *Nott* —3H **49**
Eaton Ter. *Nott* —4H **49**
Ebenezer St. *Ilk* —3D **44**

Ebenezer St. *Lan M* —2K **27**
Ebers Gro. *Nott* —6E **48**
Ebers Rd. *Nott* —5E **48**
Ebony Wlk. *Nott* —6K **49**
Ebury Rd. *Nott* —5D **48**
Ecclesbourne Av. *Duf* —3K **39**
Ecclesbourne Clo. *Duf* —3J **39**
Eckington Clo. *W Hal* —6G **43**
Eckington Ter. *Nott* —6E **64**
Ecton Clo. *Nott* —4B **32**
Edale Av. *Alv* —2H **93**
Edale Av. *Der* —6J **73**
Edale Av. *Mick* —6B **72**
Edale Av. *Alst* —6H **55**
Edale Clo. *Huck* —6C **16**
Edale Clo. *Long E* —3F **97**
Edale Dri. *Spon* —5B **76**
Edale Ri. *Bees* —5J **79**
Edale Rd. *Nott* —2J **65**
Edale Sq. *Ilk* —1C **44**
Edale Way. *Belp* —7K **9**
Eddlestone Dri. *Nott* —7B **82**
Eden Bank. *Ambgt* —2K **9**
Edenbridge Ct. *Nott* —5D **62**
Eden Clo. *Arn* —7H **33**
Edenhall Gdns. *Nott* —6B **82**
Eden Rd. *Chad* —4G **75**
Edensor Dri. *Belp* —7C **10**
Edensor Sq. *Der* —4J **73** (6B **6**)
Eden St. *Alv* —1G **93**
Edern Clo. *Nott* —6C **32**
Edern Gdns. *Nott* —6C **32**
Edgbaston Ct. *L'ver* —1G **91**
Edgbaston Gdns. *Nott* —6K **47**
Edgecote Way. *Nott* —7C **32**
Edge Hill. *Chel* —6F **93**
Edge Hill Ct. *Long E* —5J **97**
Edgelaw Ct. *Sin* —6H **91**
Edge Way. *Nott* —5D **46**
Edgewood Dri. *Huck* —7D **16**
Edgington Clo. *Cotg* —6A **86**
Edginton St. *Nott* —7H **49**
Edginton Ter. *Nott* —7H **49**
Edgware Rd. *Der* —2D **72**
Edgware Rd. *Nott* —6K **31**
Edgwood Rd. *Kimb* —7K **29**
Edinbane Clo. *Nott* —3B **32**
Edinboro Row. *Kimb* —6J **29**
Edinburgh Cres. *Altn* —5E **92**
Edinburgh Dri. *Bing* —2K **69**
Edingale Ct. *Bees* —3B **62**
Edingley Av. *Nott* —2E **48**
Edingley Sq. *Nott* —2D **48**
Edison Village. *Nott* —6A **64**
Edith Ter. *Nott* —1A **64**
Edith Wood Clo. *Alv* —4H **93**
Edlington Dri. *Nott* —4C **62**
Edmond Gro. *Huck* —4J **17**
Edmonds Av. *Arn* —3C **32**
Edmonton Ct. *W Bri* —2F **83**
Edmund Rd. *Spon* —5B **76**
Edmunds Sq. *Mick* —2K **89**
Ednaston Av. *L'ver* —4H **91**
Ednaston Rd. *Nott* —6K **63**
Edwald Rd. *Edw* —5K **83**
Edwalton Av. *W Bri* —1H **83**
Edwalton Clo. *Edw* —5K **83**
Edwalton Ct. *Nott* —7A **32**
Edwalton Lodge Clo. *Edw*
　　　　　　　　　—5J **83**
Edward Av. *Chad* —3G **75**
Edward Av. *Nott* —6K **47**
Edward Clo. *Huck* —1D **30**
Edward Rd. *Eastw* —3E **28**
Edward Rd. *Long E* —1H **97**
Edward Rd. *Nut* —1C **46**
Edward Rd. *W Bri* —6H **65**
Edwards Ct. *Nott* —1D **48**
Edwards Cres. *Klbrn* —5G **25**
Edwards La. *Nott* —7D **32**
　(in two parts)
Edward St. *Belp* —1A **24**
Edward St. *Der* —2A **74** (1C **6**)
Edward St. *Lan M* —1K **27**
Edward St. *S'fd* —1H **79**
Edwinstowe Av. *W Bri* —1H **83**
Edwinstowe Dri. *Nott* —2E **48**
Edwinstowe Rd. *Oak* —6G **57**
Edwin St. *Day* —7F **33**
Eelwood Rd. *Huck* —1D **30**
Egerton Dri. *S'fd* —5H **61**
Egerton Rd. *Wd'p* —2F **49**
Egerton St. *Nott* —7E **49**
Egerton Wlk. *Nott* —7E **48**
Eggesford Rd. *Sten F* —7H **91**
Egginton Rd. *Etw* —7D **88**
　(in two parts)
Egginton Rd. *Hilt* —7A **88**
Egling Cft. *Colw* —3D **66**

Egmanton Clo. *Oak* —6H **57**
Egmont Ct. *Nott* —5E **64**
Egreaves Av. *Los* —1E **26**
Egypt Rd. *Nott* —5B **48**
Eighth Av. *Lent* —3K **81**
Eisele Clo. *Nott* —7F **31**
Ekowe St. *Nott* —4B **48**
Eland Clo. *Spon* —2C **76**
Eland St. *Nott* —5B **48**
Elder Clo. *Arn* —4J **33**
Elder Gdns. *Nott* —5C **32**
Elder Gro. *Huck* —1H **31**
Eldon Chambers. *Nott*
　　　　　　—3E **64** (5E **4**)
Eldon Ho. *Der* —4A **74** (6D **6**)
Eldon Rd. *Bees* —7C **80**
Eleanor Av. *Ilk* —2E **60**
Eleanor Cres. *S'fd* —1K **79**
Electric Av. *Nott* —1C **82**
Eley Clo. *Ilk* —4A **44**
Eley Wlk. *Der* —4K **73** (6C **6**)
Elford Ri. *Nott* —3H **65** (4K **5**)
Elgar Dri. *Long E* —4F **97**
Elgar Gdns. *Nott* —1H **65**
Elgin Av. *L'ver* —1E **90**
Eliot Clo. *Long E* —4F **97**
Eliot Dri. *Ilk* —2B **60**
Eliot Rd. *L'ver* —1F **91**
Eliot Wlk. *Nott* —1J **99**
Elizabeth Clo. *Chad* —3H **75**
Elizabeth Clo. *Huck* —7E **16**
Elizabeth Clo. *W Hal* —6F **43**
Elizabeth Ct. *Ilk* —5B **44**
Elizabeth Gro. *Ged* —4C **50**
Elkstone Clo. *Oak* —5H **57**
Ella Bank Rd. *Hean* —4H **27**
Ella Rd. *W Bri* —6H **65**
Ellastone Av. *Nott* —5E **32**
Ellastone Gdns. *Alv* —2H **93**
Ellendale Rd. *Chad* —1H **75**
Ellerby Av. *Nott* —6A **82**
Ellerslie Gro. *Sand* —3E **78**
Ellesmere Av. *Der* —6D **74**
Ellesmere Bus. Pk. *Nott* —4C **48**
Ellesmere Clo. *Arn* —6K **33**
Ellesmere Dri. *Trow* —2G **61**
Ellesmere Rd. *W Bri* —4H **83**
Ellington Rd. *Arn* —3J **33**
**Elliot Durham Swimming Pool.**
　　　　　　　　　—5G **49**
Elliot St. *Nott* —2C **64** (3B **4**)
Ellis Av. *Huck* —6H **17**
Ellis Clo. *Long E* —3G **97**
Ellis Ct. *Nott* —1F **65**
Ellis Gro. *Bees* —3F **81**
Ellison Av. *Ast T* —3C **106**
Ellsworth Ri. *Nott* —7B **32**
Ellwood Cres. *Nott* —2G **63**
Elm Av. *Bees* —6D **80**
　(Long La.)
Elm Av. *Bees* —2E **80**
　(Newcastle Av.)
Elm Av. *Belp* —3B **24**
Elm Av. *Bing* —3C **70**
Elm Av. *Cltn* —7D **50**
Elm Av. *Huck* —7E **16**
Elm Av. *Keyw* —7D **102**
Elm Av. *Long E* —7G **79**
Elm Av. *Nott* —7E **48**
Elm Av. *Nut* —7B **30**
Elm Av. *Sand* —1F **79**
Elm Bank. *Nott* —6E **48**
Elm Bank Dri. *Nott* —6E **48**
Elmbridge. *Nott* —6D **32**
Elm Clo. *Keyw* —7D **102**
Elm Clo. *Nott* —7E **48**
Elmcroft. *Oxt* —1F **21**
Elmdale Gdns. *Nott* —6H **47**
Elm Dri. *Cltn* —7D **50**
Elm Dri. *Hilt* —7A **88**
Elm Gro. *Alst* —2H **55**
Elm Gro. *Arn* —4J **33**
Elm Gro. *Chad* —3H **75**
Elmhurst Av. *Nott* —4A **50**
Elmore Ct. *Nott* —1C **64** (1A **4**)
Elm Pk. Ct. *Der* —1K **73** (1B **6**)
Elms Av. *L'ver* —6F **73**
Elms Av. *Rip* —4K **11**
Elms Clo. *Rud* —3F **101**
Elmsdale Gdns. *Bur J* —2K **51**
Elms Dri. *L'ver* —7F **73**
Elms Farm Way. *L'ver* —1E **90**
Elmsfield Av. *Hean* —3J **27**
Elms Garden. *L'ver* —7F **73**
Elms Gdns. *Rud* —3E **100**
Elms Gro. *Etw* —6E **88**
Elmsham Av. *Nott* —4A **32**
Elms Pk. *Rud* —3F **101**
Elms St. *Der* —1K **73** (1B **6**)

Elms, The. *Colw* —1D **66**
Elms, The. *Watn* —6K **29**
Elmsthorpe Av. *Nott* —3A **64**
Elm St. *Borr* —6D **76**
Elmswood Gdns. *Nott* —3F **49**
Elmtree Av. *Der* —2B **92**
Elm Tree Av. *Klbrn* —6G **25**
Elm Tree Av. *W Bri* —1F **83**
Elmtree Rd. *C'tn* —5B **20**
Elm Vw. *Nott* —1B **64**
Elmwood Dri. *Bread* —5C **56**
Elnor St. *Lan M* —3A **28**
Elsecar Clo. *Belp* —7D **10**
Elson St. *Nott* —6B **48**
Elston Gdns. *Nott* —4A **82**
Elston M. *Nott* —7K **49**
Elstree Dri. *Nott* —1G **63**
Elswick Clo. *Nott* —5D **32**
Elswick Dri. *Bees* —4H **81**
Elterwater Dri. *Gam* —1A **84**
Eltham Clo. *Nott* —3F **47**
Eltham Dri. *Nott* —3F **47**
Eltham Rd. *W Bri* —1H **83**
Elton Clo. *S'fd* —7J **61**
Elton M. *Nott* —5D **48**
Elton Rd. *Der* —2B **92**
Elton Rd. N. *Nott* —5D **48**
Elton Ter. *Nott* —7B **48**
**Elvaston Castle Country Pk.**
　　　　**& Mus.** —2B **94**
Elvaston Ct. *Nott* —1B **48**
Elvaston Dri. *Long E* —5D **96**
Elvaston La. *Alv* —2H **93**
Elvaston Rd. *Nott* —2G **63**
Elvaston St. *Dray* —2K **95**
Elveden Dri. *Ilk* —3A **44**
Elwes Lodge. *Cltn* —1D **66**
Embankment Clo. *Der* —1D **72**
Emerald Clo. *Oak* —5F **57**
Emerson Sq. *Der* —3K **91**
Emerys Rd. *Ged* —6F **51**
　(in four parts)
Emmanuel Av. *Arn* —4C **32**
Emmanuel Av. *Nott* —5J **49**
Emmas Williams Ct. *Rip* —3K **11**
Emneth Clo. *Nott* —6H **49**
Empingham Clo. *Bees* —6B **80**
Empress Rd. *Der* —5K **73**
Emsworth Clo. *Ilk* —3B **44**
Ena Av. *Nott* —2H **65**
Enderby Gdns. *Red* —4G **33**
Enderby Sq. *Bees* —7F **63**
Endsleigh Gdns. *Bees* —1F **81**
Endsleigh Gdns. *Der* —2D **72**
Endsleigh Gdns. *Edw* —4J **83**
Enfield Chambers. *Nott*
　　　　—3E **64** (5F **5**)
Enfield Clo. *Hilt* —7A **88**
Enfield Rd. *Der* —2F **73**
Enfield St. *Bees* —2E **80**
Engine La. *Newt* —1F **29**
England Cres. *Hean* —3J **27**
Ennerdale Clo. *Gam* —1A **84**
Ennerdale Rd. *Long E* —6F **79**
Ennerdale Rd. *Nott* —1F **49**
Ennerdale Wlk. *Der* —5D **56**
Ennis Clo. *Chad* —1J **75**
Ennismore Gdns. *Nott* —1J **63**
Ennismore M. *W Bri* —5E **82**
Enoch Stone Dri. *Chad* —4H **75**
Enthorpe St. *Nott* —1H **63**
Epperstone By Pass. *Wdbgh*
　　　　　　　　　—6J **21**
Epperstone Ct. *W Bri* —7G **65**
**Epperstone Pk.** —3H **21**
Epperstone Rd. *Epp* —2F **21**
Epperstone Rd. *Low* —2D **36**
Epperstone Rd. *W Bri* —7G **65**
Epping Clo. *Der* —2C **72**
Epsom Rd. *Bees* —5J **79**
Epworth Dri. *Alv* —5G **93**
Erdington Way. *Bees* —5J **79**
Erewash Ct. *Long E* —7H **79**
Erewash Ct. *Man I* —5B **44**
Erewash Dri. *Ilk* —1E **60**
Erewash Gdns. *Nott* —5C **32**
Erewash Gro. *Bees* —6K **79**
　(in two parts)
**Erewash Mus.** —6D **44**
Erewash Sq. *Ilk* —1F **61**
Erewash St. *Long E* —1J **97**
**Erewash Valley Golf Course.**
　　　　　　　　　—7E **60**
Eric Av. *Huck* —3F **17**
Erith Clo. *Nott* —5D **46**
Ernest Rd. *Cltn* —6K **49**
Ernhale Ct. *Arn* —5G **33**
Erskine Rd. *Nott* —5D **48**
Esher Gro. *Nott* —5E **48**

Elms, The. *Colw* —1D **66**
Eskdale Clo. *Long E* —4F **97**
Eskdale Ct. *Gam* —1A **84**
Eskdale Dri. *Bees* —3A **80**
Eskdale Dri. *Nott* —6H **47**
Eskdale Wlk. *Alv* —3K **93**
　(off Whernside Clo.)
Esk Ho. Clo. *Edw* —4A **84**
Essex St. *Der* —2D **74** (1K **7**)
Essex St. *Eastw* —3D **28**
Essex St. *Ilk* —5D **44**
Estwic Av. *Eastw* —2D **28**
Ethel Av. *Huck* —3H **17**
Ethel Av. *Nott* —5J **49**
Etheldene. *C Bis* —4H **87**
Ethel Rd. *W Bri* —1H **83**
Ethel Ter. *Nott* —5C **48**
Eton Ct. *W Hal* —6F **43**
Eton Gro. *Nott* —3H **63**
Eton Rd. *W Bri* —2G **83**
Eton St. *Der* —7E **74**
Etrur a Gdns. *Der* —1A **74** (1E **6**)
Etta's Way. *Etw* —5D **88**
Ettrick Dri. *Sin* —7J **91**
Etwall By-Pass. *Etw* —5C **88**
Etwall La. *Burna* —4H **89**
**Etwa l Leisure Cen.** —4D **88**
Etwall Rd. *Mick* —2J **89**
Etwall St. *Der* —3H **73**
Eucalyptus Av. *Nott* —7J **81**
Eugene Gdns. *Nott* —5F **65**
Eugene St. *Nott* —4F **65** (7H **5**)
Europa Way. *Nott* —5E **82**
Euston Dri. *Der* —1B **74** (1G **7**)
Evans Av. *Alst* —2A **56**
Evans Rd. *Nott* —3K **47**
Evans St. *Altn* —3E **92**
Evanston Gdns. *Chad* —2H **75**
Evedon Wlk. *Nott* —4D **32**
Evelyn Gro. *Chad* —3G **75**
Evelyn St. *Bees* —1H **81**
Evelyn St. *Nott* —3G **65** (5J **5**)
Evergreen Clo. *Oak* —5G **57**
Eversley Wlk. *Nott* —5D **32**
Evesham Clo. *Der* —6E **56**
Evesham Ct. *Bees* —7A **80**
Ewart Rd. *Nott* —6B **48**
Ewe Lamb Clo. *Bees* —6K **61**
Ewe Lamb La. *Bees* —6K **61**
Ewel Rd. *Nott* —2E **62**
Exbourne Rd. *Nott* —5F **47**
Exbury Gdns. *W Bri* —4D **82**
Excelsior Av. *Alv* —3F **93**
Exchange Arc. *Nott* —4F **5**
Exchange Rd. *W Bri* —1H **83**
Exchange St. *Der* —3A **74** (4E **6**)
Exchange Wlk. *Nott*
　　　　—3E **64** (4F **5**)
Excise Chambers. *Nott* —4G **5**
Exeter Clo. *Ged* —4D **50**
Exeter Ho. *Der* —3B **74** (3F **7**)
Exeter Pl. *Der* —3B **74** (3F **7**)
Exeter Rd. *Nott* —6C **48**
Exeter Rd. *W Bri* —2H **83**
Exeter St. *Der* —2B **74** (2F **7**)
Extension St. *Ilk* —6D **44**
Exton Rd. *Nott* —3C **48**
Eyam Clo. *Bees* —4C **62**
Eyam Wlk. *Belp* —7A **10**
Eyes Ct. *Duf* —3J **39**
　(off Town St.)
Eyres Gdns. *Ilk* —4D **44**
Eyres La. *Got* —2G **111**
Eyre St. *Nott* —3G **65** (4J **5**)
Eyrie, The. *Sin* —7J **91**

**F**abis Dri. *Nott* —4A **82**
Factory La. *Bees* —3E **80**
Factory La. *Ilk* —4C **44**
Failsworth Clo. *Nott* —5A **82**
Fairbank Cres. *Nott* —4F **49**
Fairbourne Dri. *Mick* —4B **72**
Fairburn Clo. *Bramc* —1B **80**
Fairburn Clo. *Nott* —3C **62**
Faircroft Av. *Sand* —3F **79**
Fairdale Dri. *Newt* —3F **29**
Fairdene Ct. *Der* —6K **73**
Faires Clo. *Borr* —7F **77**
Faire St. *Der* —5J **73** (7A **6**)
Fairfax Clo. *Nott* —4B **48**
Fairfax Rd. *Der* —6K **73**
Fairfield Av. *Borr* —5E **76**
Fairfield Clo. *Nott* —3D **82**
Fairfield Cres. *Long E* —5E **96**
Fairfield Rd. *Der* —5D **56**
Fairfield Rd. *Hors W* —6J **25**
Fairfield St. *Bing* —3A **70**
Fairford Gdns. *L'ver* —3E **90**
Fairham Av. *Got* —1H **111**

**Fairham Brook Nature Reserve.**
　　　　　　　　　—1C **100**
Fairham Clo. *Rud* —1D **100**
Fairham Ct. *Nott* —5C **82**
Fairham Dri. *Nott* —3K **63**
Fairham Rd. *Keyw* —6B **102**
Fairholm Ct. *Nott* —1G **65** (1K **5**)
Fairisle Clo. *Nott* —7C **82**
Fairisle Clo. *Oak* —4J **57**
Fairland Cres. *W Bri* —4F **83**
Fairlawn Pl. *Sher* —4F **49**
Fairlawns. *Duf* —3H **39**
Fair Lea Clo. *Long E* —3H **97**
Fairlight Way. *Nott* —6D **32**
Fairmaid Gro. *Nott* —6A **82**
Fairmead Clo. *Nott* —6J **49**
Fairnley Rd. *Nott* —6D **46**
Fairview Av. *Und* —2D **14**
Fairview Clo. *Klbrn* —6H **25**
Fairview Clo. *L'ver* —1E **90**
Fairview Ct. *W Bri* —6F **83**
Fairview Grange. *Klbrn* —6H **25**
Fairview Rd. *Wd'p* —2G **49**
Fairway. *Keyw* —6D **102**
Fairway Clo. *Alst* —5H **55**
Fairway Cres. *Alst* —5H **55**
Fairway Cres. *Nwtn* —6H **53**
Fairway Dri. *Bees* —2D **80**
Fairway Dri. *Nott* —6K **31**
Fairway, The. *Ged* —3C **50**
Fairwood Dri. *Alv* —3K **93**
Falaise Way. *Hilt* —7A **88**
Falcon Clo. *Lent* —3A **64**
Falcon Ct. *Ilk* —5B **44**
Falconers Wlk. *Arn* —5E **32**
Falcon Gro. *Nott* —5C **48**
Falcons Ri. *Belp* —7C **10**
Falcon St. *Nott* —5C **48**
Falcon Way. *Sin* —7J **91**
Falconwood Gdns. *Nott* —7J **81**
Fallow Clo. *Nott* —6A **82**
Fallow Rd. *Spon* —2B **76**
Fall Rd. *Hean* —2G **27**
Falmouth Rd. *Alv* —4J **93**
Falstaff M. *New B* —5C **48**
Falston Rd. *Nott* —1G **63**
Faraday Building. *Nott* —6K **63**
Faraday Ct. *S'fd* —6J **61**
Faraday Rd. *Nott* —2A **64**
Far Cft. *Breas* —1B **96**
Farfield Av. *Bees* —7E **62**
Farfield Gro. *Bees* —7E **62**
Far La. *Ock* —3F **77**
Far Laund. *Belp* —7B **10**
Farley Rd. *Der* —6H **73**
Farleys La. *Huck* —6G **17**
　(in two parts)
Farley St. *Nott* —5H **31**
Farm Av. *Huck* —1D **30**
Farm Clo. *Belp* —1C **24**
Farm Clo. *E Bri* —3K **53**
Farm Clo. *Ilk* —6E **44**
Farm Clo. *Klbrn* —5G **25**
Farm Clo. *Long E* —4J **97**
Farm Clo. *Nott* —6A **82**
Farm Dri. *Alv* —4G **93**
Farmer St. *Bradm* —6G **101**
Farmhouse M. *Find* —7B **90**
Farmhouse Rd. *Sin* —7J **91**
Farmlands La. *L'ver* —3F **91**
Farm Rd. *Arn* —6K **33**
Farm Rd. *Bees* —3C **80**
Farm St. *Der* —4K **73** (6B **6**)
Farnah Grn. Rd. *Belp* —3H **23**
Farnborough Gdns. *Alst* —3B **56**
Farnborough Rd. *Nott* —1K **99**
Farncombe La. *Oak* —5F **57**
Farndale Clo. *Long E* —4E **96**
Farndale Ct. *Alv* —3J **93**
Farndale Dri. *Nott* —3B **62**
Farndon Dri. *Bees* —5K **79**
Farndon Grn. *Nott* —3J **63**
Farndon M. *Nott* —6J **49**
Far New Clo. *Sand* —3F **79**
Farneworth Rd. *Mick* —6B **72**
Farnham Clo. *Mick* —7A **72**
Farnham Wlk. *W Hal* —6F **43**
Farningham Clo. *Spon* —3B **76**
Farnsfield Av. *Bur J* —1A **52**
Farnsworth Clo. *Watn* —4A **30**
Farnway. *Dar A* —5J **55**
Far Pastures Clo. *Keyw* —7C **102**
Farrier Gdns. *L'ver* —2E **90**
Farriers Cft. *Ilk* —3A **44**
Farriers Grn. *Clif* —6J **81**
Farringdon Clo. *Der* —2D **72**
Farringdon Clo. *Nut* —3D **46**
Far Rye. *Nott* —1F **63**
Far St. *Bradm* —6G **101**

Farthing Ct. *Long E* —2F **97**
Farwells Clo. *Nott* —3J **47**
Faulconbridge Clo. *Nott* —7H **31**
Faversham Clo. *Alv* —4F **93**
Fearn Av. *Rip* —3A **12**
Fearn Chase. *Cltn* —7C **50**
Fearn Clo. *Breas* —2E **96**
Fearnleigh Dri. *Nott* —4K **47**
Fearon Clo. *Gun* —1F **53**
Featherstone Clo. *Ged* —3B **50**
Feignies Ct. *Keyw* —6C **102**
Felen Clo. *Nott* —6C **32**
Fellbarrow Clo. *W Bri* —3A **84**
Felley Clo. *Huck* —7E **16**
Felley Mill La. (North). *Und*
—1F **15**
Felley Mill La. (South). *Und*
—3E **14**
Fellow Lands Way. *Chel* —7G **93**
Fellows Rd. *Bees* —1E **80**
Fellows Yd. *Plum* —2C **102**
Fellside. *Belp* —1A **24**
Fellside. *Spon* —2B **76**
Fell Side. *Wd'p* —1J **49**
Fellside Clo. *Gam* —2A **84**
Felstead Ct. *Bees* —6C **62**
Felstead Rd. *Nott* —1G **63**
Felton Clo. *Bees* —3B **80**
Felton Rd. *Nott* —6F **65**
Fenchurch Clo. *Arn* —4C **32**
Fenchurch Wlk. *Der* —2F **73**
Fenimore Ct. *Rad T* —3B **68**
Fenroth Clo. *Nott* —5F **31**
Fenton Ct. *Nott* —2B **48**
Fenton Dri. *Nott* —3J **31**
Fenton Rd. *Mick* —6A **72**
Fenton Rd. *Nott* —2B **48**
Fenwick Clo. *Nott* —4F **47**
Fenwick Rd. *Nott* —4F **47**
Fenwick St. *Der* —2D **92**
Fergus Clo. *Nott* —1B **100**
Ferguson Clo. *Bees* —6C **80**
Fern Av. *Nott* —5D **48**
Fern Clo. *Bees* —1B **80**
Fern Cres. *Eastw* —2C **28**
Ferndale Clo. *Bees* —6D **80**
Ferndale Gro. *Nott* —1K **65**
Ferndale Rd. *Nott* —1K **65**
Ferndene Dri. *Long E* —2E **96**
Fernello Clo. *Bar T* —4A **104**
Ferngill Clo. *Nott* —6D **64**
Fernhill Ct. *Chel* —6G **93**
Fernilee Clo. *W Hal* —6G **43**
Fernilee Gdns. *Chad* —6F **57**
Fern Lea Av. *Cotg* —6J **85**
Fernleigh Av. *Nott* —4K **49**
Fern Rd. *C Bis* —4G **87**
Fernwood Clo. *L'ver* —1G **91**
Fernwood Cres. *Nott* —3C **62**
Fernwood Dri. *Rad T* —3K **67**
Fernwood Dri. *Watn* —5A **30**
Ferny Hollow Clo. *Nott* —5A **32**
Ferrers Clo. *Cas D* —7J **107**
Ferrers Cres. *Duf* —3H **39**
Ferrers Wlk. *Nott* —2G **65** (2J **5**)
Ferrers Way. *Der* —5J **55**
Ferrers Way. *Rip* —1J **11**
Ferriby Ter. *Nott* —6E **64**
Ferry Lodge. *Cltn* —1C **66**
Festival Av. *Breas* —2A **96**
Festival Rd. *Ilk* —2A **60**
Festus Clo. *Nott* —1F **65**
Festus St. *N'fld* —7E **50**
Field Av. *Huck* —1D **30**
Field Clo. *Bees* —4A **80**
Field Clo. *Borr* —5D **76**
Field Clo. *Breas* —2D **96**
Field Clo. *Ged* —4D **50**
Field Ct. *Klbrn* —6G **25**
Field Cres. *Alv* —4G **93**
Field Dri. *Alv* —4G **93**
Fieldfare Ct. *L'ver* —3E **90**
Fieldgate Dri. *Oak* —5F **57**
Field Head Way. *Oak* —4H **57**
Field Ho. Clo. *Nott* —2D **62**
Field La. *Alv* —3H **93**
Field La. *Bees* —4A **80**
Field La. *Belp* —1K **23**
Field La. *Chad* —1F **75**
Field La. *C Bis* —4G **87**
Field La. *Shelf* —6C **52**
Field La. *Wdbgh* —1G **35**
Field Ri. *L'ver* —2G **91**
Field Rd. *Ilk* —7D **44**
Field Row. *Belp* —1K **23**
Fields Av. *Rud* —4E **100**
Fields Dri. *Asl* —2H **71**
Fields Farm Rd. *Long E* —4G **97**
Field St. *Cod* —5D **12**

Fieldsway Dri. *Der* —5E **56**
Field Ter. *Rip* —3K **11**
Field, The. *Hean* —1H **43**
(in two parts)
Field Vw. Clo. *Alv* —5H **93**
Fieldway. *Nott* —4D **82**
Fiennes Cres. *Nott* —4C **64** (6A **4**)
Fife St. *Der* —1E **92**
Fifth Av. *Lent* —2J **81**
Filbert Wlk. *Chel* —2G **105**
Filey St. *Nott* —5J **31**
Filey Wlk. *Der* —6D **56**
Fincham Clo. *Der* —6D **56**
Finch Clo. *Nott* —7B **64**
Finch Cres. *Mick* —1A **90**
Finchley Av. *Der* —2D **72**
Finchley Clo. *Nott* —7J **81**
Findern Clo. *Alst* —3A **56**
Findern Clo. *Belp* —6B **10**
Findern Grn. *Nott* —1J **65**
Findern La. *Burna* —4J **89**
Findern St. *Der* —3H **73**
Fingal Clo. *Nott* —7B **82**
Finmere Clo. *L'ver* —1E **90**
Finningley Dri. *Alst* —5J **55**
Finsbury Av. *Der* —2F **73**
Finsbury Av. *Nott* —3H **65**
Finsbury Pk. Clo. *W Bri* —3E **82**
Finsbury Rd. *Arn* —3C **32**
Finsbury Rd. *Bees* —4C **62**
Finsley Wlk. *Der* —2J **91**
Firbank Ct. *Bees* —3B **80**
Firbeck Rd. *Arn* —5J **33**
Firbeck Rd. *Nott* —3B **62**
Fir Clo. *Huck* —1H **31**
Fir Clo. *Nott* —6F **31**
Fir Ct. *Rip* —3K **11**
Fircroft Av. *Nott* —6E **46**
Fircroft Dri. *Huck* —7C **16**
Fir Dale. *Cotg* —5A **86**
Firecrest Way. *Nott* —2K **47**
Firestone. *H'wod* —5G **23**
Firfield Av. *Breas* —1C **96**
Firs Av. *Bees* —1F **81**
Firs Av. *Rip* —3K **11**
Firsby Rd. *Nott* —4F **47**
Firs Cres. *Alst* —3J **55**
Firs Rd. *Edw* —4J **83**
Firs St. *Long E* —5E **96**
First Av. *Bees* —7E **62**
First Av. *Cltn* —7A **50**
First Av. *Colw* —2C **66**
First Av. *Ged* —5D **50**
First Av. *Ilk* —7D **44**
First Av. *Lent* —2J **81**
First Av. *Nott* —6D **48**
First Av. *Ris* —3D **78**
Firs, The. *Nott* —3F **49**
Firth Clo. *Arn* —4A **34**
Firth Dri. *Bees* —6C **80**
Firth Way. *Nott* —5F **31**
Firtree Gro. *Oak* —5H **57**
Fir Wlk. *Nott* —7K **49**
Fisher Av. *Wd'p* —1H **49**
Fisher Ct. *Ilk* —2D **44**
Fisher Ga. *Nott* —3F **65** (5H **5**)
Fisher La. *Bing* —3A **70**
Fisher La. *Duf* —2J **39**
Fisher St. *Altn* —3E **92**
Fisher St. *Nott* —6B **48**
Fishpond Dri. *Nott* —4C **64** (6B **4**)
Fiskerton Way. *Oak* —7H **57**
Five Acres. *Nott* —4C **82**
Five Lamps. *Der* —1K **73** (1C **6**)
Five Lamps Ct. *Der*
—2K **73** (1B **6**)
Flagholme. *Cotg* —6K **85**
Flake La. *Stan D* —6C **60**
Flamingo Ct. *Nott* —5C **64**
Flamstead Av. *Lamb* —6F **35**
Flamstead Av. *Los* —1E **26**
Flamstead La. *Den V* —4K **25**
Flamstead Rd. *Ilk* —5D **44**
Flamstead St. *Altn* —3E **92**
Flamsteed Rd. *Nott* —5D **46**
Flat, The. *Klbrn* —5F **25**
Flatts La. *C'tn* —4C **20**
Flatts La. *W'wd* —1B **14**
Flatts, The. *Bees* —3B **80**
Flawborough Ri. *W Bri* —5D **82**
Flawforth Av. *Rud* —2F **101**
Flawforth La. *Rud* —2F **101**
Flaxendale. *Cotg* —6A **86**
Flaxholme Av. *Duf* —5K **39**
Flaxton Way. *Nott* —6B **32**
Fleam Rd. *Nott* —4A **82**
Fleeman Gro. *W Bri* —6J **65**
Fleet Clo. *Nott* —1K **63**
Fleet Cres. *Belp* —2K **23**

Fleet Pk. *Belp* —2A **24**
Fleet St. *Der* —6A **74**
Fleet, The. *Belp* —3K **23**
Fleetway Clo. *Newt* —4F **29**
Fleetwith Clo. *W Bri* —3A **84**
Fleming Clo. *Watn* —5A **30**
Fleming Dri. *Cltn* —7A **50**
Fleming Gdns. *Nott* —7J **81**
Fletcher Ga. *Nott* —3E **64** (4F **5**)
Fletcher Rd. *Bees* —1G **81**
Fletcher's Row. *Rip* —2B **12**
Fletcher St. *Hean* —3G **27**
Fletcher St. *Long E* —1H **97**
Fletcher St. *Rip* —2A **12**
Fletcher Ter. *Nott* —4G **49**
Flewitt Gdns. *Nott* —1G **65** (1J **5**)
Flintham Dri. *Nott* —2D **48**
Flint St. *Altn* —3D **92**
Flixton Rd. *Kimb* —6K **29**
Flood St. *Ock* —4E **76**
Florence Av. *Long E* —7K **79**
Florence Boot Clo. *Nott* —7H **63**
Florence Ct. *Der* —4C **74** (6H **7**)
Florence Ct. *Ilk* —5D **44**
Florence Cres. *Ged* —6F **51**
Florence Gro. *Nott* —7J **49**
Florence Rd. *Ged* —5F **51**
Florence Rd. *Nott* —5J **49**
Florence Rd. *W Bri* —7H **65**
Florence St. *Huck* —7G **17**
Florey Ct. *Nott* —5A **64**
Florey Wlk. *Nott* —1J **99**
Florin Gdns. *Long E* —2F **97**
Flowers Clo. *Arn* —7K **33**
Flying Horse Wlk. *Nott*
—3E **64** (4F **5**)
Foljambe Ter. *Nott* —2F **65** (2H **5**)
Folkestone Dri. *Alv* —4G **93**
Folkton Gdns. *Nott* —5H **49**
Folly Rd. *Dar A* —63 **56**
Forbes Clo. *Long E* —4J **97**
**Forbes Hole Local Nature
Reserve. —4K 97**
Ford Av. *Los* —1E **26**
Ford Clo. *Rip* —4J **11**
Fordham Grn. *Nott* —1A **100**
Ford La. *Alst & L Eat* —2A **56**
(in two parts)
Ford St. *Belp* —1K **23**
Ford St. *Der* —3K **73** (3C **6**)
Ford St. *Nott* —5C **48**
Ford St. N. *Nott* —5C **48**
Fordwells Clo. *L'ver* —1E **90**
Foredrift Clo. *Got* —1H **111**
Foremark Av. *Der* —1J **91**
Forest Clo. *Belp* —7B **10**
Forest Clo. *Cotg* —5J **85**
Forest Cotts. *Nott* —4K **31**
Forest Ct. *Nott* —1C **64** (1A **4**)
(Gamble St.)
Forest Ct. *Nott* —7D **48**
(N. Sherwood St.)
Forester Clo. *Bees* —4C **80**
Forester Gro. *Cltn* —7B **50**
Forester Rd. *Nott* —6J **49**
**Forester's Leisure Pk. —2A 92**
Foresters Rd. *Rip* —2J **11**
Forester St. *Der* —4K **73** (5C **6**)
Forester St. *N'fld* —7E **50**
Forester's Way. *Der* —2A **92**
Forest Gro. *Nott* —7D **48**
(Colville St.)
Forest Gro. *Nott* —1C **64**
(Mt. Hooton Rd.)
Forest La. *Pap* —1K **17**
Forest Rd. *Bing* —3J **69**
Forest Rd. *C'tn* —4E **20**
Forest Rd. E. *Nott* —1C **64**
Forest Rd. W. *Nott* —1C **64** (1A **4**)
Forest Vw. Dri. *Huck* —5E **16**
Forest Vw. Ind. & Retail Est. *Nott*
—4J **31**
Forge Av. *C'tn* —4D **20**
Forge Hill. *Bees* —4D **80**
Forge Mill Gro. *Huck* —7K **17**
Forge Row. *Iron* —1H **13**
Forge, The. *Low* —3D **36**
Forge, The. *Trow* —2F **61**
Forman St. *Der* —3K **73** (4C **6**)
Forman St. *Nott* —2E **64** (3E **4**)
Forrester Av. *Wstn T* —5B **106**
Forster St. *Nott* —1A **64**
(in two parts)
Forsythia Gdns. *Nott* —5A **64**
Forty Foot La. *Melb* —5A **114**
Forty Horse Clo. *Rip* —3C **12**
Forum Clo. *Alv* —4K **93**
Fosbrook Dri. *Cas D* —6H **107**
Fosbrooke Dri. *Long E* —4H **97**

Fosse Clo. *Borr* —7E **76**
Fosse Rd. *Bing* —3H **69**
Fosse Wlk. *Cotg* —6A **86**
Foss Way. *Bing* —5G **69**
Foster Av. *Bees* —2F **81**
Foster Dri. *Nott* —2F **49**
Fosters La. *Bing* —3B **70**
Foston/Hatton/Hilton By-Pass.
*Hatt & Fos* —6A **88**
Fothergill Ct. *Nott* —7E **48**
Foundry La. *Milf* —5K **23**
Fountaindale Ct. *Nott* —7F **49**
Fountains Clo. *Alst* —3A **56**
Fountains Clo. *W Bri* —2K **83**
Fountains Ct. *Bees* —2G **81**
Fourth Av. *Cltn* —6K **49**
Fourth Av. *Lent* —2J **81**
Fourth Av. *Nott* —6D **48**
Fowler Av. *Spon* —4K **75**
Fowler St. *Der* —3J **73** (2A **6**)
Fowler St. *Dray* —2K **95**
Fox Clo. *Long E* —4H **97**
Fox Clo. *Sten F* —6H **91**
Fox Covert. *Colw* —3D **66**
Fox Covert La. *Nott* —1H **99**
**Fox Covert Local Nature Reserve.
—2H 97**
Foxdell Way. *Chel* —7G **93**
Foxearth Av. *Nott* —6C **82**
Foxes Clo. *Nott* —6B **4**
Foxes Wlk. *Alst* —3J **55**
Foxfields Dri. *Oak* —5E **56**
Foxglove Dri. *Oak* —5C **57**
Foxglove Rd. *Newt* —5F **29**
Foxgloves, The. *Bing* —4K **69**
Fox Gro. *Nott* —3A **48**
Fox Gro. Ct. *Nott* —3A **48**
Foxhall Rd. *Nott* —6C **48**
Fox Hill. *Cotg* —6J **85**
Foxhill Ct. *Cltn* —6C **50**
Foxhill Rd. *Bur J* —1J **51**
Foxhill Rd. *Cltn* —6A **50**
Foxhill Rd. Central. *Cltn* —6K **49**
Foxhill Rd. E. *Cltn* —6B **50**
Foxhill Rd. W. *Cltn* —6J **49**
Foxhills. *Keg* —2G **117**
Foxhollies Gro. *Nott* —3D **48**
Foxlands Av. *Dar A* —5K **55**
Foxley Ct. *Oak* —5G **57**
Fox Mdw. *Huck* —7F **17**
Fox Rd. *Cas D* —7H **107**
Fox Rd. *Nott & W Bri* —6H **65**
Fox St. *Der* —2A **74** (1E **6**)
Foxton Clo. *Ilk* —3A **44**
Foxton Clo. *Nott* —5F **31**
Foxton Gdns. *Nott* —7G **47**
Foxwood Gro. *C'tn* —5D **20**
Foxwood La. *Wdbgh* —6D **20**
Foyle Av. *Chad* —4G **75**
Fradley Clo. *Nott* —3J **31**
Frampton Gdns. *L'ver* —3D **90**
Frampton Rd. *Nott* —7G **47**
Frances Gro. *Huck* —3H **17**
Frances St. *Brins* —3B **14**
Franchise Ct. *Der* —4J **73** (5A **6**)
Franchise St. *Der* —4J **73** (5A **6**)
Francis Gro. *Nott* —3A **48**
Francis Rd. *Cltn* —6D **50**
Francis St. *Der* —2D **74** (2K **7**)
Francis St. *Nott* —1C **64** (1B **4**)
(in two parts)
Francklin Rd. *Low* —3D **36**
Franklin Clo. *Nott* —5E **32**
Franklin Rd. *Toll* —7B **84**
Franklyn Dri. *Alv* —3G **93**
Franklyn Gdns. *Keyw* —5C **102**
Franklyn Gdns. *Nott* —1J **63**
Fraser Cres. *Cltn* —5K **49**
Fraser Rd. *Cltn* —4K **49**
Fraser Rd. *Nott* —7F **65**
Fraser Sq. *Cltn* —5K **49**
Frazer Clo. *Spon* —2A **76**
Frearson Farm Ct. *Eastw* —4D **28**
Freckingham St. *Nott*
—2F **65** (3J **5**)
Freda Av. *Ged* —4B **50**
Freda Clo. *Ged* —3B **50**
Frederic Av. *Hean* —6H **27**
Frederick Av. *Alv* —3F **93**
Frederick Av. *Cltn* —7K **49**
Frederick Av. *Ilk* —2B **60**
Frederick Av. *Keg* —7G **109**
Frederick Gro. *Nott* —4B **64**
Frederick Rd. *S'fd* —1H **79**
Frederick St. *Der* —2H **73**
Frederick St. *Long E* —2K **97**
Freehold St. *Der* —4J **73** (6A **6**)
Freeland Clo. *Bees* —5K **79**

Freeman Av. *Sun* —3J **91**
Freemans Rd. *Cltn* —6E **50**
Freemans Ter. *Cltn* —6D **50**
Freemantle Wlk. *Nott* —5A **32**
Freesia Clo. *Mick* —7C **72**
Freeston Dri. *Nott* —5F **31**
Freeth Ct. *Nott* —5H **65**
Freeth St. *Nott* —5G **65**
Freiston St. *Nott* —7A **48**
Fremantle Rd. *Mick* —5C **72**
Fremount Dri. *Nott* —1F **63**
French La. *Hors* —1F **41**
French St. *Der* —6J **73**
French St. *Ilk* —1E **60**
Fresco Dri. *L'ver* —2D **90**
Freshwater Ho. *Alv* —2J **93**
(off Durley Clo.)
Fretwell St. *Nott* —7A **48**
Friar Ga. *Der* —3K **73** (2A **6**)
(in two parts)
Friar Ga. Ct. *Der* —3K **73** (3B **6**)
Friargate M. *Der* —3K **73** (4C **6**)
Friar La. *Nott* —3D **64** (5D **4**)
Friars Clo. *Dar A* —5K **55**
Friars Ct. *Ilk* —1A **60**
Friars Ct. *Nott* —4C **64** (6B **4**)
Friar St. *Long E* —2H **97**
Friar St. *Nott* —5A **64**
Friar Wlk. *Nwtn* —6J **53**
Friary Av. *Altn* —4E **92**
Friary Clo. *Nott* —5A **64**
Friary St. *Der* —3K **73** (4C **6**)
Friary, The. *Nott* —5A **64**
Friday La. *Ged* —4D **50**
**Friends Meeting House. —2C 4**
Friesland Dri. *Sand* —3D **78**
Frinton Rd. *Nott* —5E **46**
Frisby Av. *Long E* —3J **97**
Fritchley Clo. *Chad* —6G **57**
Frobisher Gdns. *Nott* —7F **33**
Froggatt Clo. *Alst* —2A **56**
Frogmore St. *Nott* —1E **64** (1E **4**)
Front St. *Arn* —6H **33**
Frost Av. *Lan M* —1J **27**
Fryar Rd. *Eastw* —1D **28**
Fulbrook Rd. *L'ver* —1E **90**
Fulforth St. *Nott* —1E **64** (1E **4**)
Fulham Rd. *Der* —3E **72**
Fuller St. *Rud* —3E **100**
Full St. *Der* —2A **74** (2D **6**)
Fullwood Av. *Ilk* —5C **44**
Fullwood St. *Ilk* —5C **44**
Fulmar Clo. *Mick* —5E **72**
Fulwood Clo. *Bees* —4C **80**
Fulwood Cres. *Nott* —5G **47**
Fulwood Dri. *Long E* —2E **96**
Furlong Av. *Arn* —5G **33**
Furlong Clo. *S'fd* —7H **61**
Furlong St. *Arn* —6G **33**
(in two parts)
Furnace La. *Los* —1E **26**
Furnace Rd. *Ilk* —7F **45**
Furness Clo. *W Bri* —1K **83**
Furness Rd. *Nott* —3J **47**
Furrows Clo. *Oak* —4J **57**
Furzebrook Rd. *Colw* —2C **66**
Furze Gdns. *Nott* —7F **49**
Fylde Clo. *Bees* —6J **79**
Fylingdale Way. *Nott* —4B **62**

**G**able Ct. *Mick* —1C **90**
Gables, The. *Nott* —5C **48**
Gabor Clo. *Nott* —7J **81**
Gabor Ct. *Nott* —7J **81**
Gabrielle Clo. *Nott* —2K **47**
Gadd St. *Nott* —1B **64**
Gadsby Clo. *Ilk* —3E **60**
Gadsby La. *Neth H* —2C **10**
Gadwall Cres. *Nott* —5C **64**
Gainsborough Clo. *Long E*
—4J **97**
Gainsborough Clo. *Oak* —6H **57**
Gainsborough Clo. *S'fd* —2J **79**
Gainsborough Ct. *Bees* —1G **81**
Gainsford Clo. *Nott* —1B **48**
Gainsford Cres. *Nott* —1B **48**
Gairloch Clo. *Sten F* —7H **91**
Gala Way. *Nott* —7A **32**
Gale Clo. *Bees* —2H **81**
Galena Dri. *Nott* —7J **49**
Galen Ct. *Nott* —5A **64**
Gallows Inn Clo. *Ilk* —2E **60**
Gallows Inn Ind. Est. *Ilk* —1F **61**
Galway Av. *Chad* —4H **75**
Galway Rd. *Arn* —5F **33**
Galway Rd. *Nott* —4B **64** (6A **4**)
Gamble St. *Nott* —1C **64** (1A **4**)
Gamston Cres. *Nott* —3E **48**

Gamston Lodge. *Cltn* —1C **66**
Ganton Clo. *Nott* —5H **49**
Garden Av. *Cltn* —7B **50**
Garden Av. *Ilk* —2D **60**
Garden City. *Cltn* —6C **50**
Garden Cres. *Cas D* —7K **107**
Gardendale Av. *Nott* —7K **81**
Gardenia Clo. *Bees* —6A **80**
Gardenia Cres. *Nott* —4K **49**
Gardenia Gro. *Nott* —4K **49**
Garden Rd. *Bing* —3K **69**
Garden Rd. *Eastw* —2D **28**
Garden Rd. *Huck* —5F **17**
Garden Rd. *S'fd* —2H **79**
Garden Row. *Keg* —7H **109**
Gardens Ct. *W Bri* —1J **83**
Gardens, The. *Los* —1E **26**
Gardens, The. *Mare* —5K **11**
Garden St. *Der* —2K **73** (1C **6**)
Garden St. *Nott* —2B **64**
Garfield Av. *Dray* —2J **95**
Garfield Clo. *C'tn* —3G **91**
Garfield Clo. *S'fd* —6J **61**
Garfield Ct. *Nott* —2B **64**
Garfield Rd. *Nott* —1B **64**
Garforth Clo. *Nott* —6A **48**
Garners Hill. *Nott* —3F **65** (5F **5**)
Garnet Ct. *Nott* —2G **65** (2K **5**)
Garnet St. *N'fld* —7D **50**
Garnett Av. *Hean* —3H **27**
Garrett Gro. *Nott* —6J **81**
Garrick St. *Alv* —2G **93**
Garry Clo. *Sten F* —7H **91**
Garsdale Clo. *Gam* —2A **84**
Garsdale Ct. *Alv* —3K **93**
Garsdale Dri. *Nott* —5C **82**
Garside Cres. *Cod* —4D **12**
Garth Cres. *Alv* —3H **93**
Garthorpe Ct. *Oak* —5F **57**
Garton Clo. *Bees* —3B **80**
Garton Clo. *Nott* —1H **47**
Gary Clo. *L'ver* —4H **91**
Gascoigne Dri. *Spon* —4K **75**
Gaskell Av. *Der* —2J **91**
Gasny Av. *Cas D* —5K **107**
Gas St. *Sand* —2G **79**
Gatcombe Clo. *Oak* —5H **57**
Gatcombe Clo. *Rad T* —4A **68**
Gatcombe Gro. *Sand* —5E **78**
Ga. Brook Clo. *Cod* —3D **12**
Gateford Clo. *Bees* —5B **62**
Gatehouse Ct. *Bees* —3D **80**
Gate Ind. Est. *Ilk* —4D **44**
Gateside Rd. *Q Dri* —6C **64**
Gatling St. *Nott* —2A **64**
Gaul St. *Nott* —6H **31**
Gauntley Ct. *Nott* —6B **48**
Gauntley St. *Nott* —6A **48**
Gautries Clo. *Nott* —5C **32**
Gavin M. *Nott* —6B **48**
Gawthorne St. *Nott* —5B **48**
Gayhurst Grn. *Nott* —1A **48**
Gayhurst Rd. *Nott* —1A **48**
Gaynor Ct. *Nott* —1H **63**
Gayrigg Ct. *Bees* —3B **80**
Gayton Av. *L'ver* —3H **91**
Gayton Clo. *Nott* —6D **46**
Gayton Thorpe Clo. *L'ver* —2D **90**
Gaywood Clo. *Nott* —1B **100**
Gedling Gro. *Arn* —6H **33**
Gedling Gro. *Nott* —1C **64** (1B **4**)
Gedling Rd. *Arn* —6H **33**
Gedling Rd. *Cltn* —6D **50**
Gedling St. *Nott* —3F **65** (4H **5**)
Gedney Av. *Nott* —6H **49**
Geldling Rd. *Arn* —7K **33**
Gell Rd. *Bees* —4A **80**
Gema Clo. *Alst* —3A **56**
George Av. *Bees* —3F **81**
George Av. *Long E* —7K **79**
George Ct. *Long E* —1J **97**
*George Grn. Ct. Snei* —3H **65**
(off Sneinton Boulevd.)
George Rd. *Cltn* —7C **50**
George Rd. *W Bri* —1G **83**
George's La. *C'tn* —7A **20**
George St. *Arn* —7G **33**
George St. *Belp* —1K **23**
George St. *Der* —3K **73** (3C **6**)
George St. *Huck* —4G **17**
George St. *Lan M* —2K **27**
George St. *Melb* —4G **113**
George St. *Nott* —2F **65** (3G **5**)
George Yd. *Der* —3A **74** (3D **6**)
Georgia Dri. *Arn* —3G **33**
Georgina Ct. *Cas D* —6K **107**
Georgina Rd. *Bees* —3F **81**
Gerard Clo. *Spon* —2B **76**
Gerard Ct. *Der* —4K **73** (5C **6**)

Gerard Gro. *Etw* —5E **88**
Gerard St. *Der* —4K **73** (4C **6**)
Gerrard Clo. *Arn* —3C **32**
Gerrard Cres. *Keg* —2H **117**
Gertrude Rd. *Chad* —7F **57**
Gertrude Rd. *Dray* —2J **95**
Gertrude Rd. *W Bri* —7J **65**
Gervase Gdns. *Nott* —6J **81**
Ghost Ho. La. *Bees* —3B **80**
Ghyll Clo. *Alv* —7G **75**
Gibbons Av. *S'fd* —2H **79**
Gibbons St. *Nott* —7A **64**
Gibb St. *Long E* —2J **97**
Gibfield La. *Belp* —3K **23**
Gibson Rd. *Nott* —6C **48**
Gifford Gdns. *Nott* —5E **64**
Gilbert Av. *Got* —1H **111**
Gilbert Clo. *Spon* —4K **75**
Gilbert Cres. *Duf* —4J **39**
Gilbert Gdns. *Nott* —1J **65**
Gilbert St. *Alv* —4H **93**
(in two parts)
Gilbert St. *Huck* —5G **17**
Gilderdale Way. *Oak* —4H **57**
Gilead St. *Nott* —6H **31**
Gillamoor Ct. *Alv* —3J **93**
Gillercomb Clo. *Edw* —4A **84**
Gillian Ct. *S'fd* —2J **79**
Gilliver Gdns. *Dray* —2J **95**
Gilliver La. *Clip* —7G **85**
Gillotts Clo. *Bing* —2A **70**
Gillott St. *Hean* —5J **27**
Gill St. *Nott* —1D **64** (1D **4**)
Gilpet Av. *Nott* —6H **49**
Giltbrook Cres. *Gilt* —5G **29**
Giltbrook Ind. Est. *Gilt* —6G **29**
Gilt Hill. *Kimb* —6H **29**
Giltway. *Gilt* —6G **29**
Gimson Clo. *Ilk* —3A **44**
Gin Clo. Way. *Aws* —7G **29**
Gipsy La. *Nott* —6J **81**
Girton Rd. *Nott* —3C **48**
Gisborne Clo. *Mick* —5C **72**
Gisborne Cres. *Alst* —3K **55**
Gisborne Grn. *Der* —2K **73** (1A **6**)
Gisburn Clo. *Nott* —4C **82**
Glade Av. *Nott* —2J **63**
Gladehill Rd. *Nott & Arn* —6E **32**
Glade, The. *Nott* —2A **100**
Gladstone Av. *Got* —1H **111**
Gladstone Av. *Hean* —3G **27**
Gladstone Clo. *Chel* —6F **93**
Gladstone Dri. *Brins* —5C **14**
Gladstone Rd. *Spon* —3A **76**
Gladstone St. *Bees* —3E **80**
Gladstone St. *Cltn* —7B **50**
Gladstone St. *Der* —7J **73**
Gladstone St. *Hean* —3G **27**
Gladstone St. *Ilk* —7D **44**
(in two parts)
Gladstone St. *Lan M* —2A **28**
Gladstone St. *Long E* —3H **97**
Gladstone St. *Nott* —6B **48**
Gladstone St. E. *Ilk* —6D **44**
Gladys St. *Nott* —5C **48**
Glaisdale Dri. E. *Nott* —1D **62**
Glaisdale Dri. W. *Nott* —2D **62**
Glaisdale Nook. *Alv* —3K **93**
(in two parts)
Glaisdale Pk. Ind. Est. *Nott*
—1D **62**
Glaisdale Parkway. *Nott* —2D **62**
Glamis Clo. *Oak* —5H **57**
Glamis Rd. *Nott* —4C **48**
Glanton Way. *Arn* —3J **33**
Glapton La. *Nott* —6K **81**
Glapton Rd. *Nott* —6E **64**
Glaramara Clo. *Nott* —6D **64**
Glasshouse Hill. *Cod* —3D **12**
Glasshouse St. *Nott* —2E **64** (2F **5**)
Glastonbury Rd. *Alv* —2J **93**
Gleadsmoss La. *Oak* —6G **57**
Glebe Av. *Rip* —2J **11**
Glebe Av. *Smal* —7B **26**
Glebe Cotts. *Nott* —7D **64**
Glebe Cres. *Ilk* —7E **44**
Glebe Cres. *Stan* —1D **58**
Glebe Dri. *Bur J* —3H **51**
Glebe Farm Clo. *W Bri* —4E **82**
Glebe Farm Vw. *Ged* —3D **50**
Glebe La. *Rad T* —4K **67**
Glebe Ri. *L'ver* —7G **73**
Glebe Rd. *Cltn* —4A **50**
Glebe Rd. *Nut* —7C **30**
Glebe Rd. *W Bri* —1H **83**
Glebe St. *Bees* —2E **80**
Glebe St. *Huck* —4G **17**
Glebe, The. *Coss* —2F **45**

Glen Av. *Eastw* —4F **29**
Glen Av. *Holb* —6C **24**
Glenbrook. *Cotg* —5A **86**
Glenbrook Cres. *Nott* —7G **47**
Glencairn Dri. *Nott* —6G **47**
Glencairn M. *Nott* —6G **47**
Glencoe Rd. *Nott* —7C **82**
Glencoyne Rd. *Nott* —1A **100**
Glencroft Dri. *Sten F* —6H **91**
Glendale Clo. *Cltn* —4B **50**
Glendale Ct. *Bees* —5E **80**
Glendale Dri. *Spon* —3B **76**
Glendale Gdns. *Arn* —4J **33**
Glendoe Gro. *Bing* —3J **69**
Glendon Dri. *Huck* —7G **17**
Glendon Dri. *Nott* —3C **48**
Glendon Rd. *Ilk* —3A **60**
Glendon Rd. *Sten F* —6H **91**
Glendon St. *Stan C* —4C **42**
Gleneagles Clo. *Mick* —6D **72**
Gleneagles Clo. *Edw* —5K **83**
Gleneagles Dri. *Arn* —4K **33**
Glenfield Av. *Kimb* —6H **29**
Glenfield Cres. *Mick* —6A **72**
Glenfield Rd. *Long E* —4H **97**
Glengarry Way. *Sin* —5J **91**
Glen Helen. *Colw* —1D **66**
Glenlivet Gdns. *Nott* —7B **82**
(in two parts)
Glenloch Dri. *Nott* —1B **100**
Glenmore Dri. *Sten F* —5H **91**
Glenmore Rd. *W Bri* —2K **83**
Glenmoy Clo. *Sun* —2J **91**
Glenn Way. *Shard* —1F **107**
Glenorchy Ct. *Oak* —4H **57**
Glenorchy Cres. *Nott* —5A **32**
Glenparva Av. *Red* —4G **33**
Glenridding Clo. *W Bri* —3B **84**
Glensford Gdns. *Nott* —3A **32**
Glen, The. *Bur J* —1J **51**
Glenside. *Wd'p* —1K **49**
Glenside Rd. *Bees* —6C **62**
Glenstone Ct. *Nott* —6B **48**
Glen, The. *Nott* —7A **82**
Glentworth Rd. *Nott* —1A **64**
Glen Vw. *Belp* —3K **23**
Glen Vine. *Rip* —3C **12**
Glenwood Av. *Nott* —3D **62**
Glenwood Rd. *Chel* —2G **105**
(in two parts)
Glins Rd. *Nott* —5B **32**
Glossop St. *Der* —2B **92**
Gloster St. *Der* —6E **74**
Gloucester Av. *Bees* —3F **81**
Gloucester Av. *Nott* —3A **64**
Gloucester Av. *Nut* —3F **47**
Gloucester Av. *Sand* —4E **78**
Glover Av. *Nott* —3D **62**
Glue La. *Los* —3E **26**
Goatchurch Ct. *Nott* —4C **32**
Goathland Clo. *Nott* —5D **32**
Goathland Rd. *Sten F* —7H **91**
Godber Rd. *Huck* —7E **16**
Godfrey Dri. *Ilk* —2A **60**
Godfrey Rd. *Hean* —4G **27**
(in two parts)
Godfrey St. *N'fld* —1E **66**
Godkin Dri. *Lan M* —1J **27**
Goldcrest Clo. *Bing* —4C **70**
Goldcrest Dri. *Spon* —2B **76**
Goldcrest Rd. *Nott* —2H **47**
Golden Valley. *Hors W* —6H **25**
Golden Valley. *Ridd* —1E **12**
**Golden Valley Country Pk.**
**—1D 12**
**Golden Valley Light Railway.**
**—1D 12**
Golders Grn. Wlk. *Der* —2E **72**
Goldham Rd. *Nott* —6D **46**
Gold La. *Der* —7C **54**
Goldsmith Sq. *Nott*
—2D **64** (2D **4**)
Goldsmith St. *Nott* —2D **64** (2D **4**)
Goldstone Ct. *Spon* —4A **76**
Goldswong Ter. *Nott* —7E **48**
Golf Clo. *L'ver* —7E **72**
Golf Club Rd. *Stan D* —6E **60**
Golf Course Rd. *Keyw* —7F **103**
Golf La. *Duf* —1J **39**
Golf Rd. *Rad T* —4A **68**
Gonalston La. *Epp* —1B **36**
Goodale St. *Der* —7A **74**
Goodall Cres. *Huck* —6J **17**
Goodall St. *Nott* —7B **48**
Goodliffe St. *Nott* —6B **48**
Goodman Clo. *Gilt* —5G **29**
Goodrington Rd. *Oak* —4J **57**
Goodsmoor Rd. *L'ver & Sin*
—4H **91**

Goodsmoor Rd. Ind. Est. *Sin*
—4J **91**
Goods Rd. *Belp* —3K **23**
Goodwin Clo. *Sand* —2E **78**
Goodwin Dri. *Kimb* —7J **29**
Goodwin's La. *H'wd* —4F **23**
Goodwin St. *Nott* —1C **64** (1B **4**)
Goodwood Av. *Arn* —5G **33**
Goodwood Cres. *Ilk* —3B **60**
Goodwood Dri. *Alv* —3J **93**
Goodwood Dri. *Bees* —6K **79**
Goodwood Rd. *Nott* —3D **62**
Goole Av. *Ilk* —2B **60**
Goosedale La. *B Vil* —5A **18**
**Goose Fair. —7C 48**
**(site of)**
Goosegate. *Cotg* —5J **85**
Goose Ga. *Nott* —3F **65** (4G **5**)
Goose La. *Cod* —4E **12**
Gordon Clo. *Bees* —6D **80**
Gordon Gro. *Nott* —5B **48**
Gordon Ri. *Nott* —4G **49**
Gordon Rd. *Borr* —7D **76**
Gordon Rd. *Bur J* —1A **52**
Gordon Rd. *Der* —5K **73**
Gordon Rd. *Nott* —1G **65** (1K **5**)
Gordon Rd. *W Bri* —1H **83**
Gordon Sq. *W Bri* —1H **83**
Gordon St. *Ilk* —5D **44**
Gordon St. *Nott* —2K **47**
Gorman Ct. *Arn* —6K **33**
Gorse Clo. *C'tn* —5B **20**
Gorse Clo. *L'ver* —3F **91**
Gorse Clo. *Long E* —6F **79**
Gorse Clo. *Newt* —4F **29**
Gorse Ct. *Nott* —1A **48**
Gorse Rd. *Keyw* —6B **102**
Gorse Wlk. *Nott* —7K **49**
Gorsey Clo. *Belp* —6J **9**
Gorsey Rd. *Nott* —7F **49**
Gorsty Leys. *Find* —7B **90**
Gosforth Ct. *Nott* —6F **65**
Gosforth Rd. *Der* —2E **92**
Goshawk Rd. *Quar H* —4E **60**
Gotham Rd. *E Leak* —6K **111**
Gotham Rd. *King S* —6A **110**
Gothic Clo. *Nott* —2A **48**
Goverton Sq. *Nott* —1K **47**
Gowan Clo. *Bees* —6C **80**
Gower St. *Der* —4A **74** (5D **6**)
Goyden Clo. *Nott* —5C **32**
G.P.T. Bus. Pk. *Bees* —3G **81**
Grace Av. *Bees* —3H **81**
Grace Cres. *Hean* —3H **27**
Grace Dri. *Nott* —6K **47**
Grafham Clo. *Chel* —6G **93**
Grafton Av. *Wd'p* —1G **49**
Grafton Ct. *Nott* —2C **64** (3A **4**)
Grafton St. *Der* —6J **73**
Graham St. *Ilk* —7D **44**
Graham St. *Nott* —2B **64**
Grainger Av. *W Bri* —5G **83**
Graingers Ter. *Huck* —7H **17**
Grainger St. *Nott* —5G **65** (7K **5**)
Grammer St. *Den V* —1C **26**
Grampian Dri. *Arn* —3D **32**
Grampian Way. *Long E* —1E **96**
Grampian Way. *Sten F & Sin*
—6H **91**
Granby Ct. *Bing* —3K **69**
Granby La. *Plun* —4F **71**
Granby St. *Ilk* —4D **44**
Granby Vs. *Nott* —3H **65**
Grandfield Av. *Rad T* —3K **67**
Grandfield Cres. *Rad T* —3K **67**
Grandfield St. *Los* —1E **26**
Grandstand Rd. *Der*
—2C **74** (1J **7**)
Grange Av. *Bees* —2F **81**
Grange Av. *Breas* —1B **96**
Grange Av. *Der* —2J **91**
Grange Av. *Rud* —1D **100**
Grange Clo. *Lamb* —6G **35**
Grange Clo. *Melb* —3H **113**
Grange Clo. *Nott* —7D **64**
Grange Clo. *Tickn* —7A **112**
Grange Cres. *Ged* —3D **50**
Grange Dri. *Cas D* —7J **107**
Grange Dri. *Long E* —1K **97**
Grange Farm. *Gam* —1A **84**
Grange Farm Clo. *Bees* —7A **80**
Grange Farm Clo. *H'ton* —5A **108**
Grangelea Gdns. *Bees* —7B **62**
Grangemoor. *Pap* —3K **17**
Grange Pk. *C But* —1G **87**
Grange Pk. *Long E* —1K **97**
Grange Pk. *W Bri* —3K **83**
Grange Rd. *Alv* —4H **93**
Grange Rd. *Edw* —4J **83**

Grange Rd. *Long E* —1K **97**
Grange Rd. *Stock* —3K **47**
Grange Rd. *Wd'p* —2G **49**
Granger Ter. *Brins* —4B **14**
Grange St. *Der* —6B **74**
(in two parts)
Grange, The. *Smal* —5E **26**
Grange Vw. *Eastw* —2D **28**
Grange Vw. Rd. *Ged* —4D **50**
Grangewood Av. *Ilk* —7D **44**
Grangewood Ct. *Nott* —4C **62**
Grangewood Dri. *Milf* —6A **24**
Grangewood Rd. *Nott* —4C **62**
Grannis Dri. *Nott* —6G **47**
Grant Av. *Chad* —3H **75**
Grantham Av. *Der* —6D **56**
Grantham Clo. *Gilt* —6G **29**
Grantham Rd. *Bing* —3B **70**
Grantham Rd. *Rad T* —5H **67**
Grantleigh Clo. *Nott* —2F **63**
(in two parts)
Granton Av. *Nott* —1B **100**
Grant St. *Nott* —2B **64** (2A **4**)
Granville Av. *Long E* —7H **79**
Granville Clo. *Duf* —3J **39**
Granville Ct. *Nott* —2H **65**
Granville Cres. *Rad T* —5J **67**
Granville Gro. *Nott* —2H **65**
Granville St. *Der* —3J **73**
Grasby Wlk. *Nott* —6K **81**
Grasmere Av. *Nott* —4J **47**
Grasmere Av. *Spon* —2A **76**
Grasmere Clo. *Huck* —4F **17**
Grasmere Ct. *Long E* —6F **79**
Grasmere Cres. *Sin* —5J **91**
Grasmere Gdns. *Got* —7H **99**
Grasmere Rd. *Bees* —7D **62**
Grasmere Rd. *Long E* —6F **79**
Grasmere St. *Sand* —3F **79**
Grassingdale Clo. *Cltn* —4B **50**
Grassington Rd. *Nott* —1K **63**
Grassmere. *Cotg* —5A **86**
Grass St. *Ilk* —3C **44**
Grassthorpe Clo. *Oak* —6H **57**
Grassy La. *Bees* —3G **81**
Grassy La. *Burna* —2J **89**
Grassy La. *Der* —2G **91**
Gravelly Hollow. *C'tn* —2H **19**
Gravel Pit La. *Spon* —3A **76**
Graveney Gdns. *Arn* —7K **33**
Graylands Rd. *Nott* —7D **46**
Grayling St. *Der* —6B **74**
Grays Clo. *Cas D* —7K **107**
Graystones Clo. *W Bri* —3A **84**
Grazingfield. *Nott* —4C **82**
Greasley Av. *Newt* —3G **29**
**Greasley Castle. —3H 29**
**(remains of)**
**Greasley Sports &**
**Community Cen. —3F 29**
Greasley St. *Nott* —6H **31**
Gt. Freeman St. *Nott*
—1E **64** (1F **5**)
Gt. Hoggett Dri. *Bees* —2A **80**
Gt. Northern Clo., The. *Nott*
—4F **65** (6H **5**)
Gt. Northern Cotts. *Huck* —3H **17**
Gt. Northern Rd. *Der*
—3J **73** (4A **6**)
Gt. Northern Rd. *Eastw* —3B **28**
Gt. Northern Way. *N'fld* —1F **67**
Greatorex Av. *Altn* —4E **92**
Greaves Clo. *Arn* —1K **49**
Greaves Clo. *Nott* —5D **46**
Greaves St. *Rip* —2A **12**
Greek St. *Nott* —2C **64** (3A **4**)
Greenacre. *Bur J* —1J **51**
Greenacre. *Edw* —4K **83**
Greenacre. *Nott* —2B **62**
Greenacre Av. *Hean* —2J **27**
Greenacres. *L'ver* —1F **91**
Greenacres Cvn. Pk. *W Bri*
—6A **66**
Greenacres Clo. *Newt* —3G **29**
Green Av. *Chel* —1G **105**
Green Av. *N'fld* —5D **50**
Greenbank. *Cltn* —1B **66**
Green Bank. *Spon* —4K **75**
Greenbank Ct. *Nott* —4E **48**
Greenburn Clo. *Gam* —2A **84**
Greenburn Clo. *L'ver* —3G **91**
Green Clo. *Huck* —7J **17**
Green Clo. *Plum* —5D **102**
Greencroft. *Nott* —6B **82**
Greendale Gdns. *Nott* —6H **47**
Greendale Rd. *Arn* —7H **33**
Greendale Rd. *Nott* —1A **66**
Greenfield Gro. *Cltn* —6K **49**
Greenfields. *Lan M* —1J **27**

Greenfields Av. *L'ver* —2F **91**
Greenfields Dri. *Cotg* —6K **85**
Greenfield St. *Nott* —6K **63**
Greenfinch Clo. *Spon* —2B **76**
Greenford Clo. *Nut* —3E **46**
Greengates Av. *Nott* —3H **49**
Greenhill Av. *Rip* —4A **12**
Greenhill Cres. *Cltn* —1C **66**
Greenhill Ri. *Cltn* —7C **50**
Greenhill Rd. *Cltn* —1C **66**
Greenhills Av. *Eastw* —2E **28**
Greenhills Rd. *Eastw* —2D **28**
Greenland Av. *Der* —3F **73**
Greenland Cres. *Bees* —4C **80**
Green La. *Alv* —1H **93**
Green La. *Bar T* —6A **104**
Green La. *Belp* —1K **23**
Green La. *Burna* —5H **89**
Green La. *Der* —3A **74** (6D **6**)
Green La. *Dis* —5K **115**
Green La. *Ilk* —7E **44**
Green La. *Lamb* —4F **35**
Green La. *Melb* —7K **113**
Green La. *Nott* —6K **81**
Green La. *Ock* —3E **76**
Green Leas. *Ast T* —2C **106**
Green Leys. *W Bri* —4E **82**
Greenmount Clo. *L'ver* —3E **90**
Green Pk. *Der* —2E **72**
Green Platt. *Cotg* —5J **85**
Greens Ct. *Ilk* —5B **44**
Greens Farm La. *Ged* —4E **50**
Greenside Clo. *Long E* —2J **97**
Greenside Ct. *Mick* —6A **72**
Greenside Wlk. *Nott* —1A **66**
Greens La. *Kimb* —7K **29**
**Green's Mill Mus.** —3H **65**
Green St. *Bar F* —5E **98**
Green St. *Nott* —6F **65**
Green, The. *Alst* —6H **55**
Green, The. *Ast T* —2D **106**
Green, The. *Bees* —4E **80**
*Green, The. Belp* —7A **10**
  (off Edale Way)
Green, The. *Breas* —1B **96**
Green, The. *Cas D* —7H **107**
Green, The. *Dis* —6K **115**
  (in two parts)
Green, The. *Dray* —2J **95**
Green, The. *Find* —7B **90**
Green, The. *King S* —6A **110**
Green, The. *Long W* —7G **117**
Green, The. *Low* —3K **35**
Green, The. *Mick* —7B **72**
Green, The. *Rad T* —4J **67**
Green, The. *Rud* —3E **100**
Green, The. *Tickn* —7A **112**
Green Wlk. *What* —3J **71**
Green Way. *Find* —7B **90**
Greenway Clo. *Borr* —5D **76**
Greenway Clo. *Rad T* —4J **67**
Greenway Dri. *L'ver* —7E **72**
Greenway, The. *Boul M* —4K **93**
Greenway, The. *Sand* —2F **79**
Greenwich Av. *Nott* —2J **47**
Greenwich Dri. N. *Der* —2F **73**
Greenwich Dri. S. *Der* —2F **72**
Greenwich Pk. Clo. *W Bri* —3E **82**
Greenwood Av. *Chad* —7F **57**
Greenwood Av. *Huck* —4F **17**
Greenwood Av. *Ilk* —7E **44**
Greenwood Av. *Nott* —2B **66**
**Greenwood Bonsai Studio.**
                            —5G **19**
Greenwood Ct. *Bees* —3D **80**
Greenwood Ct. *Der*
                   —2A **74** (2E **6**)
Greenwood Cres. *Cltn* —1C **66**
Greenwood Gdns. *Rud* —3F **101**
Greenwood Rd. *Nott & C'tn*
                            —2J **65**
Greenwood Va. *Huck* —4E **16**
Greet Ct. *Nott* —7K **47**
Greetwell Clo. *Nott* —1G **63**
Gregg Av. *Hean* —3H **27**
Gregory Av. *Breas* —1A **96**
Gregory Av. *Lan M* —2J **27**
Gregory Av. *Lent* —4B **64**
Gregory Av. *Map* —4J **49**
Gregory Boulevd. *Nott* —7A **48**
Gregory Clo. *S'fd* —7K **61**
Gregory Ct. *Bees* —4B **80**
Gregory Ct. *Nott* —4A **64**
  (Derby Rd.)
Gregory Ct. *Nott* —6B **48**
  (Noel St.)
Gregory St. *Ilk* —6C **44**
Gregory St. *Nott* —4A **64**
Gregorys Way. *Belp* —7C **10**

Gregory Wlk. *L'ver* —2C **90**
Gregson Gdns. *Bees* —7B **80**
Grenay Ct. *Rud* —1D **100**
  (in two parts)
Grendon Clo. *Belp* —6B **10**
Grenfell Av. *Sun* —3J **91**
Grenfell Ter. *Nott* —2A **48**
Grenville Dri. *Ilk* —3D **44**
Grenville Dri. *S'fd* —7J **61**
Grenville Ri. *Arn* —4H **33**
Grenville Rd. *Bees* —4H **81**
Grenvoir Dri. *Rip* —3C **12**
Gresham Clo. *W Bri* —1E **82**
Gresham Gdns. *W Bri* —1F **83**
Gresham Gdns. *Wd'p* —1J **49**
Gresham Rd. *Der* —1C **92**
Gresley Dri. *Nott* —4H **65** (6K **5**)
Gresley Rd. *Ilk* —5D **44**
Gretton Rd. *Nott* —2J **49**
Greyfriar Ga. *Nott* —4E **64** (6E **4**)
Greyhound St. *Nott* —3E **64** (3F **5**)
Greys Rd. *Wd'p* —2H **49**
Greystoke Dri. *Nott* —7C **46**
Grey St. *Der* —4K **73** (6C **6**)
Grey St. *Newt* —4E **28**
Greythorn Dri. *W Bri* —4F **83**
Grierson Av. *Nott* —5D **32**
Griffin Clo. *Alv* —2F **93**
Griffon Rd. *Quar H* —3D **60**
Griffs Hollow. *Cltn* —7C **50**
Grimes Ga. *Dis* —4A **116**
Grimesmoor Rd. *C'tn* —4E **20**
Grimsby Ter. *Nott* —1E **64** (1F **5**)
Grimshaw Av. *Alv* —2H **93**
Grimston Rd. *Nott* —1A **64**
Grindlow Rd. *Chad* —7G **57**
Grindon Cres. *Nott* —3J **31**
Grindslow Av. *W Hal* —6G **43**
Grinsbrook. *Lent* —3A **64**
Gripps Comn. *Cotg* —6K **85**
Gripps, The. *Cotg* —6K **85**
Grisedale Ct. *Bees* —4A **80**
Gritley M. *Nott* —5D **64**
Grizedale Gro. *Bing* —3H **69**
Groombridge Cres. *L'ver* —3E **90**
Groome Av. *Los* —1E **26**
Grosvenor Av. *Breas* —1D **96**
Grosvenor Av. *Long E* —5E **96**
Grosvenor Av. *Nott* —5E **48**
Grosvenor Clo. *Rad T* —4D **68**
*Grosvenor Ct. Nott* —6E **48**
  (off Elm Bank Dri.)
Grosvenor Dri. *L'ver* —3E **90**
Grosvenor Rd. *Eastw* —2D **28**
Grosvenor Rd. *Rip* —3K **11**
Grosvenor St. *Der* —7C **74**
Grouville Dri. *Wd'p* —1J **49**
Grove Av. *Bees* —2E **80**
Grove Av. *Nott* —1C **64** (1A **4**)
Grovebury Dri. *L'ver* —4G **91**
Grove Clo. *Bur J* —1K **51**
Grove Clo. *Thul* —5B **94**
Grove Ct. *Bees* —2D **80**
Grove Ct. *Rip* —4B **12**
Grove Ct. *Thul* —5B **94**
Grove Ho. *Der* —5A **74** (7E **6**)
Grove M. *Eastw* —4C **28**
Grove Pk. *Etw* —7D **88**
Grover Av. *Nott* —3J **49**
Grove Rd. *Bing* —2B **70**
Grove Rd. *Nott* —4B **64**
Groveside Cres. *Nott* —5J **81**
Groves Nook. *Chel* —1E **104**
Grove St. *Bees* —3G **81**
Grove St. *Der* —5A **74** (7E **6**)
  (in two parts)
Grove, The. *Breas* —1D **96**
Grove, The. *C'tn* —5E **20**
Grove, The. *Mick* —6C **72**
Grove, The. *Nott* —4D **48**
  (Haydn Av.)
Grove, The. *Nott* —1B **64**
  (Southey St.)
Grundy St. *Nott* —7A **48**
Guardian Ct. *Nott* —6J **47**
Guide Post. *Neth H* —2C **10**
**Guildhall Theatre.** —3E **6**
Guinea Clo. *Long E* —1E **96**
Gunhills La. *Wind* —6B **22**
Gun La. *Neth H* —1B **10**
Gunn Clo. *Nott* —6G **31**
Gunnersbury Way. *Nut* —3D **46**
Gunthorpe Clo. *Nott* —3D **48**
Gunthorpe Dri. *Nott* —3D **48**
Gunthorpe Rd. *Ged* —3A **50**
Gunthorpe Rd. *Low* —5E **36**
Gurney Av. *Sun* —3H **91**
Gutersloh Ct. *S'fd* —7K **61**
Guy Clo. *S'fd* —2J **79**

Gwenbrook Av. *Bees* —3E **80**
Gwenbrook Rd. *Bees* —3E **80**
Gwndy Gdns. *Nott* —6C **32**
**GX Superbowl.** —6A **64**
Gypsum La. *Got* —1G **111**
Gypsy La. *Dray* —1G **95**

**H**ackers Clo. *E Bri* —3J **53**
Hackworth Clo. *Newt* —2F **29**
Hadbury Rd. *Nott* —3B **48**
Hadden Ct. *Nott* —2D **62**
Haddon Clo. *Alst* —4H **55**
Haddon Clo. *Cltn* —4B **50**
Haddon Clo. *Huck* —6G **17**
Haddon Clo. *W Hal* —6G **43**
Haddon Cres. *Bees* —5C **80**
Haddon Dri. *Alst* —4H **55**
Haddon Dri. *L Eat* —4C **40**
Haddon Dri. *Mick* —5C **72**
Haddon Dri. *Spon* —4B **76**
Haddon Nurseries. *Ilk* —3C **44**
Haddon Rd. *W Bri* —2H **83**
Haddon St. *Der* —7J **73**
Haddon St. *Ilk* —3C **44**
Haddon St. *Nott* —4D **48**
Haddon Way. *Long E* —5D **96**
Haddon Way. *Rad T* —3A **68**
Hadleigh Clo. *Bees* —6J **79**
Hadley St. *Ilk* —2E **60**
Hadrian Gdns. *Nott* —3C **32**
Hadstock Clo. *Sand* —4F **79**
Hagg La. *Dal A* —2F **59**
  (in two parts)
Hag La. *Shot* —3A **22**
Hagley Clo. *Nott* —1J **65**
Haig St. *Der* —1F **93**
Haileybury Cres. *W Bri* —3H **83**
Haileybury Rd. *W Bri* —3H **83**
Hailsham Clo. *Mick* —5B **72**
Hains Clo. *Sin* —5K **91**
Haise Ct. *Nott* —1F **47**
Halberton Dri. *W Bri* —4F **83**
Hales Clo. *Cotg* —5J **85**
Haley Clo. *Kimb* —7H **29**
Halifax Clo. *Der* —6C **56**
Halifax Clo. *Hilt* —7A **88**
Halifax Ct. *Nott* —4D **46**
Halifax Pl. *Nott* —3F **65** (5G **5**)
Halina Ct. *Bees* —1F **81**
Hallam Ct. *Ilk* —3D **44**
Hallam Fields. *Cas D* —1J **115**
Hallam Fields Rd. *Ilk* —3E **60**
Hallam Rd. *Bees* —2E **81**
Hallam Rd. *Nott* —4J **49**
Hallam's La. *Arn* —6H **33**
Hallams La. *Bees* —4C **80**
Hallam Way. *W Hal* —6F **43**
Hall Clo. *Rad T* —4J **67**
Hall Ct. *W Hal* —7G **43**
Hall Cft. *Bees* —4D **80**
Hallcroft Rd. *Ilk* —6D **44**
Hall Dri. *Bees* —3C **80**
Hall Dri. *C Bis* —4G **87**
Hall Dri. *Got* —1G **111**
Hall Dri. *Nott* —4E **62**
Hall Dri. *Sand* —2F **79**
Hall Dyke. *Spon* —3K **75**
Hall Farm Clo. *Cas D* —7J **107**
Hall Farm Clo. *Toll* —7B **84**
Hall Farm Rd. *Duf* —4J **39**
Hallfields. *Edw* —5K **83**
Hall Gdns. *Bees* —1B **80**
Hall Ga. *Dis* —5K **115**
Hallgate Clo. *Oak* —4H **57**
Hallington Dri. *Hean* —4F **27**
Hall La. *Brins* —5A **14**
Hall La. *Neth H* —1C **10**
Hall La. *What* —7H **71**
Hall Leys La. *Melb* —1K **113**
Hallowell Dri. *Nott* —1F **63**
Hall Pk. *Bar T* —5A **104**
Hall Pk. Clo. *L'ver* —7F **73**
Hall Pk. Dri. *Eastw* —2C **28**
Hall Rd. *Lan M* —1A **28**
Halls La. *Newt* —5E **28**
Halls Rd. *S'fd* —2H **79**
Hall St. *Alv* —2G **93**
Hall St. *Nott* —3B **48**
Hall Vw. Dri. *Nott* —1D **62**
Halstead Clo. *Bees* —4C **80**
Halstead Clo. *Nott* —3H **47**
Halstock Dri. *Alv* —1J **93**
Haltham Wlk. *Nott* —1K **99**
Hambledon Dri. *Nott* —2H **63**
Hambledon Dri. *Sten F* —7H **91**
Hambleton Clo. *Long E* —7E **78**
Hamblin Cres. *Sin* —5K **91**
Hambling Clo. *Nott* —6G **31**

Hamilton Clo. *Arn* —4A **34**
Hamilton Clo. *Bees* —6K **79**
Hamilton Clo. *Mick* —5D **72**
Hamilton Ct. *Nott* —5B **82**
  (Farnborough Rd.)
Hamilton Ct. *Nott* —4D **64** (6C **4**)
  (Hamilton Dri.)
Hamilton Dri. *Nott* —4D **64** (6C **4**)
Hamilton Dri. *Rad T* —3K **67**
*Hamilton Gdns. Nott* —5D **48**
  (off Alexandra St.)
Hamilton Pl. *Nott* —3H **65**
Hamilton Rd. *Der* —6K **73**
Hamilton Rd. *Long E* —7H **79**
Hamilton Rd. *Nott* —6D **48**
Hamilton Rd. *Spon* —2B **76**
Hamilton, The. *Nott* —5A **64**
Hamlet, The. *Hean* —2G **27**
Hammersmith. *Rip* —1K **11**
Hammersmith Clo. *Nut* —2E **46**
Hammersmith Clo. *Rad T* —5D **68**
Hampden Gro. *Bees* —2E **80**
Hampden St. *Der* —1A **92**
Hampden St. *Gilt* —5F **29**
Hampden St. *Lan M* —2K **27**
Hampden St. *Nott* —1D **64** (1D **4**)
Hampshire Ct. *Jack* —1K **13**
Hampshire Dri. *Sand* —3F **79**
Hampshire Rd. *Der* —7C **56**
*Hampstead Ct. Nott* —3E **48**
  (off St Albans St.)
Hampstead Dri. *Der* —2E **72**
Hampstead Rd. *Nott* —5G **49**
Hampton Clo. *Bees* —5H **79**
Hampton Clo. *Spon* —3B **76**
Hampton Clo. *W Hal* —6F **43**
Hampton Ct. *Hean* —3F **27**
Hampton Rd. *W Bri* —2G **83**
Hanbury Rd. *Chad* —2E **74**
Handel St. *Der* —1C **92**
Handel St. *Nott* —2G **65** (3J **5**)
Handford Ct. *Der* —3J **73**
Handford St. *Der* —3H **73**
Hand's Rd. *Hean* —4H **27**
Handyside St. *Der* —2A **74** (1D **6**)
Hanger Bank. *Ast T* —2D **106**
Hankin Av. *Und* —2E **14**
Hankin St. *Huck* —6J **17**
Hanley Av. *Bees* —7B **62**
Hanley St. *Nott* —2D **64** (3D **4**)
Hannah Cres. *Nott* —1D **82**
Hanover Ct. *Nott* —1D **62**
Hanover Sq. *Der* —2E **72**
Hansard Ga. *W Mead*
                   —3C **74** (3H **7**)
Hanslope Cres. *Nott* —1D **62**
Hanslynn. *Thul* —5B **94**
Hanson Cres. *Huck* —5G **17**
Hanwell Way. *Der* —2F **73**
Hanworth Gdns. *Arn* —5F **33**
Harberton Clo. *Red* —4G **33**
Harby Dri. *Nott* —3J **63**
Harcourt Cres. *Nut* —3F **47**
Harcourt Pl. *Cas D* —6K **107**
Harcourt Rd. *Nott* —6C **48**
Harcourt St. *Bees* —2E **80**
Harcourt St. *Der* —4K **73** (6C **6**)
Harcourt Ter. *Nott* —2F **65** (2H **5**)
Hardacre Clo. *Melb* —3G **113**
Harden Ct. *Nott* —1J **99**
Hardhurst Rd. *Alv* —4H **93**
Hardigate Rd. *C But* —7F **69**
Hardstaff Almshouses. *Ged*
                            —4C **50**
Hardstaff Homes, The. *Gilt*
                            —5G **29**
Hardstaff Rd. *Nott* —2J **65**
Hardwick Av. *Alst* —4H **55**
Hardwick Av. *W Hal* —6G **43**
Hardwick Clo. *Rip* —1J **11**
Hardwick Ct. *Long E* —5D **96**
Hardwick Dri. *Mick* —6C **72**
Hardwicke Rd. *Bees* —5C **80**
Hardwick Gro. *Bing* —3K **69**
Hardwick Gro. *Nott*
                   —3C **64** (5A **4**)
Hardwick Gro. *W Bri* —6H **65**
Hardwick Pl. *Ilk* —2A **60**
Hardwick Rd. *Park T*
                   —4C **64** (6A **4**)
Hardwick Rd. *Sher* —3E **48**
Hardwick St. *Der* —1C **92**
Hardwood Clo. *Nott* —6G **31**
Hardy Barn. *Ship* —5J **27**
Hardy Clo. *Kimb* —6K **29**
Hardy Clo. *Long E* —1H **97**
Hardy Cres. *Cod* —4D **12**
Hardys Clo. *C Bis* —4H **87**
Hardy's Dri. *Ged* —5D **50**

Hardy St. *Kimb* —6K **29**
Hardy St. *Nott* —1C **64** (1A **4**)
Harebell Clo. *Oak* —4G **57**
Harebell Gdns. *Bing* —3J **69**
Harefield. *E Leak* —7K **111**
Harepit Clo. *Alv* —4G **93**
Harewood Av. *Nott* —1K **47**
Harewood Clo. *Belp* —7D **10**
Harewood Clo. *Rad T* —4A **68**
Harewood Clo. *Sand* —4E **78**
Hargrave Av. *Ock* —3E **76**
Hargreaves Clo. *L'ver* —3E **90**
Harkstead Rd. *Nott* —4D **32**
Harlaxton Dri. *Long E* —7A **80**
Harlaxton Dri. *Nott* —3B **64** (6A **4**)
Harlaxton Wlk. *Nott*
                   —1E **64** (1F **5**)
Harlech Clo. *Ilk* —3A **44**
Harlech Clo. *Spon* —3C **76**
Harlech Ri. *Bees* —4B **80**
Harlequin Clo. *Rad T* —4B **68**
Harlequin Ct. *Eastw* —2B **28**
Harlesden Av. *Der* —1E **72**
Harley St. *Nott* —4B **64**
Harlow Clo. *Alv* —5F **93**
Harlow Ct. *W Hal* —7F **43**
Harlow Gro. *Ged* —4C **50**
Harmston Ri. *Nott* —2B **48**
  (in two parts)
Harnett Clo. *Nott* —3F **65** (5G **5**)
Harold Av. *Lan M* —1K **27**
Harold Ct. *Der* —6B **74**
Harold St. *Nott* —3G **65** (4K **5**)
Harold St. *Nott* —3G **65** (4K **5**)
Harpenden Sq. *Nott* —3G **47**
Harpole Wlk. *Arn* —3H **33**
Harpswell Clo. *Alst* —5J **55**
Harpur Av. *L'ver* —2F **91**
Harpur Av. *Tickn* —7A **112**
Harrier Gro. *Huck* —1E **30**
Harrier Rd. *Belp* —7C **10**
Harrier Way. *Sin* —6J **91**
Harriet St. *Der* —5A **74**
Harriett St. *S'fd* —1H **79**
Harrimans Dri. *Breas* —1D **96**
Harrimans La. *Lent L* —1K **81**
Harringay Gdns. *Der* —2G **73**
Harrington Av. *Borr* —6E **76**
Harrington Clo. *Ged* —5F **51**
Harrington Dri. *Nott*
                   —3B **64** (5A **4**)
Harrington Rd. *L'ver* —7G **73**
Harrington St. *Altn* —3E **92**
Harrington St. *Dray* —2K **95**
Harrington St. *Long E* —4F **97**
Harrington St. *Pear T* —1A **92**
Harris Av. *Rip* —2J **11**
Harris Clo. *Nott* —2F **63**
Harris Clo. *Rip* —3J **11**
Harrison Ct. *Bing* —3J **69**
Harrison Rd. *S'fd* —7H **61**
**Harrison's Plantation Nature
                   Reserve.** —2G **63**
Harrison St. *Der* —5J **73** (7A **6**)
Harris Rd. *Bees* —2D **80**
Harrogate Cres. *Der* —6D **56**
Harrogate Rd. *Nott* —2A **66**
Harrogate St. *N'fld* —7D **50**
Harrowby Rd. *Nott* —3B **64** (5A **4**)
Harrow Dri. *Ilk* —3E **60**
Harrow Gdns. *Nott* —3J **63**
Harrow Rd. *Huck* —7D **16**
Harrow Rd. *Nott* —3G **63**
Harrow Rd. *W Bri* —2G **83**
Harrow St. *Der* —6E **74**
Harry Peel Ct. *Bees* —2G **81**
Harston Gdns. *W Bri* —5D **82**
Hart Av. *Sand* —2E **78**
Hartcroft Rd. *Nott* —7C **32**
Hartford Clo. *Nott* —5F **65**
Hartington Av. *Cltn* —5B **50**
Hartington Av. *Huck* —6C **16**
Hartington Clo. *W Hal* —6G **43**
Hartington Pl. *Ilk* —1C **44**
Hartington Rd. *Nott* —3E **48**
Hartington St. *Der*
                   —5A **74** (7E **6**)
Hartington Way. *Mick* —7B **72**
Hartland Dri. *Sun* —3J **91**
Hart Lea. *Sand* —2F **79**
Hartley Ct. *Nott* —1B **64**
Hartley Dri. *Bees* —2H **81**
Hartley Rd. *Nott* —1A **64**
Hartness Rd. *Nott* —7J **81**
Hartshay Hill. *Rip* —1H **11**
  (in two parts)
Hartshorne Rd. *Der* —3G **91**
Hartside Clo. *Gam* —1A **84**

Hartside Gdns. *Long E* —7E **78**
Hart St. *Lent* —4B **64**
Hartwell St. *Nott* —1F **65**
Hartwood Dri. *S'fd* —6H **61**
Harvest Clo. *Bing* —3K **69**
Harvest Clo. *Nott* —5B **32**
Harvest Way. *Oak* —4J **57**
Harvey Clo. *Rud* —4F **101**
Harvey Ct. *Cas D* —7K **107**
Harvey Ct. *Nott* —5A **64**
Harvey Cft. *Trow* —3G **61**
Harvey Hadden Stadium. —7F **47**
Harvey Rd. *Cas D* —1K **115**
Harvey Rd. *Der* —3E **92**
Harvey Rd. *Nott* —6F **47**
Harwich Clo. *Nott* —5G **31**
Harwill Cres. *Nott* —4H **47**
Harwood Clo. *Arn* —5K **33**
Hasgill Clo. *Oak* —4H **57**
Haslam's La. *Der* —6B **56**
Haslam St. *Nott* —4D **64** (6D **4**)
Haslemere Ct. *Der* —6B **74**
Haslemere Rd. *Long E* —1F **97**
Haslemere Rd. *Nott* —6K **47**
Hassock La. N. *Ship* —6K **27**
Hassock La. S. *Ship* —7A **28**
Hassocks La. *Bees* —1H **81**
Hassocks, The. *Bees* —1H **81**
Hassop Rd. *Chad* —7G **57**
Hastings St. *Cltn* —7A **50**
Hastings St. *Cas D* —1K **115**
Hastings St. *Der* —7A **74**
(in two parts)
Haswell Rd. *Nott* —1H **47**
Hatchard Wlk. *Hean* —3K **27**
Hatchmere Clo. *Oak* —6G **57**
Hatfield Av. *Sand* —4F **79**
Hatfield Dri. *W Bri* —4E **82**
Hatfield Rd. *Alv* —4F **93**
Hatfield Rd. *Nott* —5E **48**
Hatherleigh Clo. *Nott* —7A **34**
Hathern Clo. *Long E* —4H **97**
Hathern Clo. *Sun* —4K **81**
Hathern Grn. *Bees* —7G **63**
Hathersage Av. *Der* —1J **91**
Hathersage Av. *Long E* —4D **96**
Hatley Clo. *Nott* —6D **64**
Hatton Clo. *Arn* —3C **32**
Hatton Crofts. *Long E* —3G **97**
Hatton Gdns. *Nut* —3D **46**
Hattons Ct. *Melb* —4G **113**
Haulton Dri. *Cas D* —6J **107**
Havelock Rd. *Der* —1K **91**
Havelock St. *Ilk* —7D **44**
Havelock St. *Rip* —2A **12**
Haven Baulk Av. *L'ver* —2C **90**
Haven Baulk La. *L'ver & L'ver*
—2B **90**
Haven Clo. *W Bri* —3F **83**
Haven Ct. *Alv* —3K **93**
Havenwood Gro. *L'ver* —4G **91**
Havenwood Ri. *Nott* —1K **99**
Haverhill Cres. *Nott* —3K **31**
Haversham Clo. *Nott* —4K **47**
Hawarden Ter. *Nott* —7B **48**
Hawke St. *Der* —3G **73**
Hawkhurst Dri. *Nott* —5D **62**
Hawkins Ct. *Ilk* —2D **44**
Hawkins Dri. *Ambgt* —1B **10**
Hawkridge Gdns. *Nott*
—2G **65** (2J **5**)
Hawkridge St. *Nott* —2F **65** (2J **5**)
Hawksdale Clo. *Chel* —7G **93**
Hawkshead Av. *Der* —6D **56**
Hawkshead Clo. *W Bri* —3B **84**
Hawksley Gdns. *Nott* —6J **81**
Hawksley Rd. *Nott* —7B **48**
Hawks Wood Clo. *Bees* —4B **80**
Hawksworth Av. *Nott* —2F **49**
Hawksworth Rd. *W Bri* —6H **65**
Hawksworth St. *Nott*
—2G **65** (3K **5**)
Hawley Mt. *Nott* —3H **49**
Haworth Ct. *Nott* —7J **81**
Hawthorn Av. *Breas* —1D **96**
Hawthorn Av. *Cotg* —6K **85**
Hawthorn Av. *Huck* —5F **17**
Hawthorn Av. *Rip* —4K **11**
Hawthorn Clo. *Edw* —4K **83**
Hawthorn Clo. *Hilt* —7A **88**
Hawthorn Clo. *Keyw* —7C **102**
Hawthorn Clo. *Nott* —6D **64**
Hawthorn Clo. *Wdbgh* —1G **35**
Hawthorn Cres. *Arn* —4J **33**
Hawthorn Cres. *Find* —7B **90**
Hawthorne Av. *Alv* —2G **93**
Hawthorne Av. *Borr* —5D **76**
Hawthorne Av. *Long E* —3G **97**
Hawthorne Av. *S'fd* —2H **79**

Hawthorne Clo. *Klbrn* —3F **25**
Hawthorne Gro. *Bees* —2H **81**
Hawthorne Ri. *Aws* —2F **45**
Hawthorn Rd. *Cas D* —5K **107**
Hawthorns, The. *Belp* —7D **10**
Hawthorns, The. *L Eat* —6D **40**
Hawthorn St. *Der* —1C **92**
Hawthorn Vw. *Nott* —5D **64**
(in two parts)
Hawthorn Wlk. *Nott* —7K **49**
Hawton Cres. *Nott* —3J **63**
Hawton Spinney. *Nott* —3J **63**
Hawtrey Gdns. *Der* —3G **93**
Haycroft Way. *E Bri* —3J **53**
Hayden La. *Huck* —2H **17**
Haydn Av. *Nott* —4D **48**
Haydn Rd. *Chad* —7F **57**
Haydn Rd. *Nott* —4C **48**
Haydock Clo. *Kimb* —6K **29**
Haydock Pk. Rd. *Der* —1E **92**
Hayes Av. *Breas* —2K **95**
Hayes Av. *Der* —1H **91**
Hayes Clo. *W Hal* —6G **43**
Hayes Farm Ct. *Tickn* —7A **112**
Hayes Rd. *Keyw* —6B **102**
Hayes, The. *Find* —7A **90**
Hayes Wood Rd. *Stan C* —5C **42**
Hayfield Clo. *Belp* —7B **10**
Hayfield Gdns. *L'ver* —3F **91**
Hayles Clo. *Nott* —7D **32**
Hayley Cft. *Duf* —5K **39**
Hayling Clo. *Ilk* —3A **44**
Hayling Dri. *Nott* —5K **47**
Haymarket. *Der* —4D **6**
Haynes Av. *Trow* —2G **61**
Haynes Clo. *Nott* —5B **82**
Hay's Clo. *Ilk* —4B **44**
Haywood Clo. *Alv* —4G **93**
Haywood Ct. *Nott* —3G **65** (4J **5**)
Haywood Rd. *Nott* —4H **49**
Haywood St. *Nott* —3G **65** (4J **5**)
Hayworth Rd. *Sand* —3F **79**
Hazel Av. *L'ver* —3H **91**
Hazelbank Av. *Nott* —5H **49**
Hazel Clo. *Bing* —3C **70**
Hazel Clo. *Find* —7C **90**
Hazel Clo. *Hean* —4F **27**
Hazeldene Clo. *Duf* —1J **39**
Hazel Dri. *Nut* —7B **30**
Hazel Dri. *Spon* —2C **76**
Hazel Gro. *Duf* —3J **39**
Hazel Gro. *Huck* —7G **17**
Hazel Gro. *Map* —2J **49**
Hazel Hill Cres. *Nott* —5D **32**
Hazelhurst Gdns. *Nott* —6H **31**
Hazel Meadows. *Huck* —7G **17**
Hazelmere Gro. *Lent* —3A **64**
Hazelrigg Clo. *Cas D* —6H **107**
Hazel St. *Nott* —5H **31**
(in two parts)
Hazeltree Clo. *Rip* —4J **11**
Hazel Way. *L'by* —2H **17**
Hazelwood. *Cotg* —5A **86**
Hazelwood Clo. *Newt* —3F **29**
Hazelwood Hill. *H'wd* —5F **23**
Hazelwood Rd. *Chad* —7F **57**
Hazelwood Rd. *Duf* —6G **23**
Hazelwood Rd. *Nott* —7A **48**
Hazlewood Dri. *Huck* —6C **16**
Headingley Ct. *L'ver* —1G **91**
Headingley Gdns. *Nott* —6K **47**
Heafield Dri. *Keg* —1H **117**
Heage La. *Etw* —2E **88**
Heage Rd. *Rip* —3H **11**
Heage Rd. Ind. Est. *Rip* —3H **11**
Healey Clo. *Nott* —5E **64** (7F **5**)
Heanor & District Heritage Cen.
—5H **27**
Heanor Ga. Ind. Est. *Hean* —4F **27**
(in two parts)
Heanor Ga. Rd. *Hean* —4E **26**
Heanor Ho. *Spon* —5A **76**
Heanor Leisure Cen. —4H **27**
Heanor Rd. *Cod* —5D **12**
Heanor Rd. *Den V* —2C **26**
Heanor Rd. *Ilk* —1B **44**
Heanor Rd. *Los* —1E **26**
Heanor Rd. *Smal & Hean* —7B **26**
Heard Cres. *Bees* —7F **63**
Hearn La. *Arn* —5K **33**
Heath Av. *L'ver* —7G **73**
Heathcoat Building. *Nott* —6K **63**
Heathcoat St. *Nott* —3F **65** (4G **5**)
Heathcote Clo. *Alv* —4H **93**
Heathcotes Cotts. *Der* —5A **74**
Heath Ct. *Sin* —6J **91**
Heather Clo. *Newt* —4F **29**
Heather Clo. *Nott* —7F **49**
(Hungerhill Rd.)

Heather Clo. *Nott* —6H **31**
(Thames St.)
Heather Clo. *Sten F* —7H **91**
Heather Ct. *Hean* —4K **27**
Heather Cres. *Breas* —1D **96**
Heather Cres. *L'ver* —3G **91**
Heather Cft. *W Bri* —4E **82**
Heatherington Gdns. *Nott* —4C **32**
Heatherley Dri. *Nott* —2B **48**
Heathermead Clo. *Oak* —6F **57**
Heather Ri. *Bees* —6E **62**
Heather Rd. *Cltn* —5B **50**
Heather Va. *W Bri* —2D **82**
Heathfield Av. *Ilk* —6E **44**
Heathfield Gro. *Bees* —5C **80**
Heathfield Rd. *Nott* —2B **48**
Heath Gdns. *Breas* —1E **96**
Heath La. *Find* —7B **90**
(in two parts)
Heath Rd. *Rip* —3K **11**
Heath, The. *Gilt* —5F **29**
Heaton Clo. *Nott* —5H **49**
Heavenside. *E Leak* —7K **111**
Heavygate La. *Shot* —4C **8**
Hebden Clo. *L'ver* —3D **90**
Hebrides Clo. *Sin* —6H **91**
Heckington Dri. *Nott* —2H **63**
Hedderley Wlk. *Nott*
—1F **65** (1G **5**)
Heddington Gdns. *Arn* —5E **32**
Hedgebank Ct. *Oak* —4J **57**
Hedgerow Gdns. *Oak* —4J **57**
Hedgerows, The. *Hilt* —7A **88**
Hedges Dri. *Ilk* —3D **60**
Hedingham Way. *Mick* —7A **72**
Hedley St. *Nott* —6C **48**
Hedley Vs. *Nott* —5C **48**
Heigham Clo. *Der* —6D **92**
Heighington Gro. *Nott* —2A **48**
Helen Clo. *Bees* —2D **80**
Hellebore Clo. *Nott* —6A **32**
Helm Clo. *Nott* —6F **31**
Helmesdale. *Arn* —4K **33**
Helmsdale Gdns. *Nott* —4B **32**
Helmsley Dri. *Eastw* —2B **28**
Helston Clo. *Alv* —3H **93**
Helston Dri. *Nott* —4D **46**
Helvellyn Clo. *Nott* —5E **64**
Helvellyn Way. *Long E* —6F **79**
Hemington Ct. *H'ton* —6A **108**
Hemington Hill. *Cas D* —6A **108**
Hemington La. *Locki* —5C **108**
Hemingway Clo. *Cltn* —7A **50**
Hemingway Clo. *Newt* —4G **29**
Hemlock Av. *Long E* —7H **79**
Hemlock Av. *S'fd* —7J **61**
Hemlock Clo. *Oak* —4F **57**
Hemlock Gdns. *Nott* —7F **31**
Hemlock La. *Ilk* —2B **60**
Hempshill La. *Nott* —7F **31**
(Low Wood Rd.)
Hempshill La. *Nott* —7H **31**
(Sellers Wood Dri.)
Hemsby Gdns. *Nott* —5H **31**
(in two parts)
Hemscott Clo. *Nott* —5F **31**
Hemswell Clo. *Nott* —5F **31**
Hendon Ri. *Nott* —6H **49**
Hendon Way. *Der* —2F **73**
Hendre Gdns. *Nott* —6C **32**
Henley Clo. *N'fld* —1E **66**
Henley Gdns. *S'fd* —6J **61**
Henley Grn. *Der* —2D **72**
Henley Ri. *Nott* —3C **48**
Henley Way. *W Hal* —6F **43**
Henning Gdns. *Nott* —5C **32**
Henrietta St. *Nott* —7J **31**
Henry Ct. *Nott* —5E **64**
Henry Rd. *Bees* —2G **81**
Henry Rd. *Nott* —4B **64**
Henry Rd. *W Bri* —7G **65**
Henry St. *Der* —2K **73** (1C **6**)
(in two parts)
Henry St. *Huck* —6H **17**
Henry St. *Red* —3G **33**
Henry St. *Rip* —2K **11**
Henry St. *Snei* —3G **65** (4K **5**)
Henshaw Av. *Ilk* —2B **60**
Henshaw Pl. *Ilk* —2C **44**
Henson Clo. *Rad T* —4E **68**
Henson La. *Rad T* —3E **68**
Henson Sq. *Bees* —7B **62**
Hensons Row. *Nott* —4K **47**
Hepple Dri. *Nott* —6F **31**
Herald Clo. *Bees* —1H **81**
Herbert Buzzard Ct. *Huck* —6J **17**
(off Hankin St.)
Herbert Rd. *Nott* —5D **48**
Hereford Rd. *Chad* —7D **56**

Hereford Rd. *Ged* —3D **50**
Hereford Rd. *Nott* —2K **65**
Hereford Rd. *Wd'p* —1G **49**
Heritage Cen. —5E **6**
Heritage Ga. *Der* —3C **6**
Hermitage Av. *Borr* —6E **76**
Hermitage Ct. *Oak* —6H **57**
Hermitage Sq. *Nott* —3H **65**
Hermitage Wlk. *Ilk* —2D **60**
Hermitage Wlk. *Nott*
—4C **64** (6B **4**)
Hermor St. *Nott* —2C **64** (3A **4**)
Heron Dri. *Lent* —3A **64**
Herons Ct. *W Bri* —4A **84**
Heronswood Dri. *Spon* —2K **75**
Heron Way. *Mick* —6E **72**
Heron Wharf. *Nott* —5B **64** (7A **4**)
Hervey Grn. *Nott* —6A **82**
Heskey Clo. *Nott* —1E **64** (1F **5**)
Heskey Wlk. *Nott* —1E **64** (1F **5**)
Heslington Av. *Nott* —6A **48**
Hethbeth Ct. *Nott* —5B **64**
Hethersett Gdns. *Nott* —5H **31**
Hetley Rd. *Bees* —7F **63**
Hexham Av. *Ilk* —3E **60**
Hexham Clo. *W Bri* —2J **83**
Hexham Gdns. *Nott* —3C **32**
Hexham Wlk. *Der* —6E **56**
Heydor Clo. *Belp* —6B **10**
Heyford Ct. *Hean* —4J **27**
Hey St. *Long E* —5F **97**
Heyworth St. *Der* —2H **73**
Hickings La. *S'fd* —7J **61**
Hickleton Clo. *Rip* —3J **11**
Hickling Clo. *Shel L* —6D **92**
Hickling Rd. *Nott* —4J **49**
Hickling Way. *Cotg* —7A **86**
Hickton Dri. *Bees* —7B **80**
High Bank. *Den V* —3B **26**
Highbank Dri. *Nott* —1A **100**
Highbury Av. *Nott* —1J **47**
Highbury Clo. *Der* —2D **72**
Highbury Clo. *Nott* —3D **46**
Highbury Rd. *Keyw* —5C **102**
Highbury Rd. *Nott* —6J **31**
Highbury Wlk. *Nott* —7J **31**
High Chu. St. *Nott* —5B **48**
(in two parts)
Highclere Dri. *Cltn* —6D **50**
Highcliffe Rd. *Nott* —2J **65**
Highcroft. *Nott* —2H **49**
Highcroft Dri. *Nott* —2B **62**
Highcross Ct. *Nott* —1B **64**
High Cross Leys. *Nott*
—1E **64** (1F **5**)
Highcross St. *Nott* —2F **65** (3G **5**)
High Edge Dri. *Heag* —4E **10**
High Edge M. *Belp* —7A **10**
Highfield Clo. *Los* —7D **12**
Highfield Cotts. *Chad* —3E **74**
Highfield Ct. *Bees* —2F **81**
Highfield Dri. *Cltn* —7K **49**
Highfield Dri. *Ilk* —2K **59**
Highfield Dri. *Nut* —2F **47**
Highfield Gdns. *Der* —1K **73**
Highfield Gro. *W Bri* —1H **83**
Highfield La. *Chad* —3E **74**
Highfield M. *Der* —3E **74**
Highfield Rd. *Bees* —4A **80**
Highfield Rd. *Belp* —3K **23**
Highfield Rd. *Der* —1K **73**
Highfield Rd. *Keyw* —5C **102**
Highfield Rd. *Klbrn* —5F **25**
Highfield Rd. *L Eat* —7C **40**
Highfield Rd. *L'ver* —2G **91**
Highfield Rd. *Nott* —6K **63**
Highfield Rd. *Nut* —2E **46**
Highfield Rd. *W Bri* —1H **83**
Highfields. *Cod* —4D **12**
Highfields Science Pk. *Nott*
—6K **63**
Highfield St. *Long E* —6G **79**
Highfield Way. *Rip* —4J **11**
Highgate Clo. *Cltn* —4A **50**
Highgate Dri. *Ilk* —3A **44**
Highgate Grn. *Der* —3E **72**
Highgates. *Der* —4A **74** (6E **6**)
Highgrove Av. *Bees* —2D **80**
Highgrove Clo. *Hean* —4E **26**
Highgrove Dri. *Chel* —7F **93**
Highgrove Gdns. *Edw* —4J **83**
High Hazels Ct. *Newt* —1F **29**
High Hazels Rd. *Cotg* —4A **86**
High Hazles Clo. *Ged* —3C **50**
High Holborn. *Ilk* —3C **44**
High Holborn Rd. *Rip* —3C **12**
High Hurst. *C'tn* —5C **20**
High La. Central. *W Hal* —5H **43**

High La. E. *W Hal* —5J **43**
High La. W. *W Hal* —6E **42**
High Leys Rd. *Huck* —7F **17**
High Mdw. *Toll* —7B **84**
High Mdw. Clo. *Rip* —4K **11**
High Pk. Cotts. *Newt* —6H **15**
High Pavement. *Belp* —2A **24**
High Pavement. *Nott*
—3F **65** (5G **5**)
High Rd. *Bees* —2F **81**
(Acacia Wlk.)
High Rd. *Bees* —3E **80**
(Hall Dri.)
High Rd. *Bees* —6A **80**
(Rutland Av.)
High Spannia. *Kimb* —6K **29**
High St. *Arn* —6H **33**
High St. *Belp* —1A **24**
High St. *Brins* —3B **14**
High St. *Cas D* —1J **115**
High St. *Chel* —1F **105**
High St. *Cod* —4G **12**
High St. *Hean* —3G **27**
High St. *Huck* —5G **17**
High St. *Ilk* —6D **44**
High St. *Keg* —1G **117**
High St. *Klbrn* —5G **25**
High St. *Kimb* —7K **29**
High St. *Long E* —1J **97**
High St. *Los* —7E **12**
High St. *Melb* —4G **113**
High St. *Nott* —3E **64** (4F **5**)
High St. *Rip* —3K **11**
High St. *Rud* —2E **100**
High St. *S'fd* —1J **79**
High St. *Tickn* —7A **112**
High St. Av. *Arn* —6G **33**
High St. Pl. *Nott* —3E **64** (4F **5**)
Highurst Ct. *Nott* —2C **64** (2A **4**)
Highurst St. *Nott* —2C **64** (3A **4**)
High Vw. Av. *Keyw* —6D **102**
High Vw. Ct. *Nott* —6F **49**
Highwood Av. *Belp* —4B **24**
Highwood Av. *Nott* —6F **47**
Highwray Gro. *Nott* —7K **81**
Hilary Clo. *Belp* —7E **10**
Hilary Clo. *Nott* —4D **62**
Hilcot Dri. *Nott* —5H **47**
Hilderstone Clo. *Alv* —3K **93**
Hillary Pl. *Ilk* —2K **59**
Hillbeck Cres. *Nott* —3C **62**
Hillberry. *Rip* —3B **12**
Hill Brow. *Der* —4A **74** (5D **6**)
Hill Clo. *Newt* —4G **29**
Hill Clo. *Spon* —4A **76**
Hill Clo. *Stan C* —5C **42**
Hill Clo. *W Bri* —2K **83**
Hillcrest Clo. *Watn* —6A **30**
Hillcrest Dri. *Chel* —6F **93**
Hillcrest Dri. *Cod* —4D **12**
Hillcrest Dri. *Huck* —6D **16**
Hillcrest Dri. *Klbrn* —5G **25**
Hillcrest Gdns. *Bur J* —1J **51**
Hill Crest Gro. *Nott* —3D **48**
Hill Crest Pk. Ind. Est. *C'tn*
—3D **20**
Hill Crest Rd. *Der* —1D **74**
Hillcrest Rd. *Keyw* —5C **102**
Hillcrest Vw. *Cltn* —5K **49**
Hillcroft Dri. *Ock* —4E **76**
Hillcross Av. *L'ver* —2G **91**
Hillcross Dri. *L'ver* —2F **91**
Hill Dri. *Bing* —2K **69**
Hill Farm Ct. *Edw* —6J **83**
Hillfield Gdns. *Nott* —3A **32**
Hillfield Rd. *S'fd* —7K **61**
Hillgrove Gdns. *Nott* —5C **32**
Hilliers Ct. *Nott* —5B **32**
Hillingdon Av. *Nott* —3D **46**
Hillington Ri. *Nott* —6E **32**
Hill Nook Clo. *Chel* —2G **105**
Hill Ri. *Trow* —3G **61**
Hill Ri. Clo. *L'ver* —1H **91**
Hill Rd. *Bees* —5B **80**
Hill Rd. *B Vil* —1A **32**
Hill Rd. *Got* —3H **111**
Hill Rd. *Hean* —4F **27**
Hillsford Clo. *Nott* —2G **63**
Hillside. *Cas D* —6K **107**
Hillside. *Find* —7A **90**
Hillside. *Keg* —2H **117**
Hillside. *Lan M* —2J **27**
Hill Side. *Nott* —4K **63**
Hillside Av. *Chad* —3G **75**
Hillside Av. *Nott* —2J **49**
Hillside Cres. *Bees* —7E **62**
Hillside Cres. *Spon* —4B **76**
Hillside Dri. *Bur J* —1K **51**
Hillside Dri. *Long E* —1F **97**

Hillside Gro. *Sand* —2E **78**
Hillside Ri. *Belp* —3K **23**
Hillside Rd. *Bees* —5A **80**
  (Highfield Rd.)
Hillside Rd. *Bees* —6C **62**
  (Ullswater Cres.)
Hillside Rd. *Rad T* —4A **68**
Hillside Rd. *Spon* —4A **76**
Hills La. *Stan B* —7E **104**
Hill Sq., The. *Dar A* —6A **56**
Hills Rd. *Breas* —1K **95**
Hills Rd. *Wd'p* —2G **49**
Hill St. *Rip* —1K **11**
Hillsway. *Chel* —6F **93**
Hillsway. *L'ver* —7F **73**
Hill Syke. *Low* —3A **36**
Hill, The. *Dar A* —6A **56**
Hill Top. *Cas D* —2H **115**
Hill Top. *Oak* —4E **56**
Hilltop La. *Klbrn* —3E **24**
Hill Vw. *Duf* —3H **39**
Hillview Av. *Nott* —4F **49**
Hill Vw. Clo. *Hors W* —6H **25**
Hill Vw. Gro. *Spon* —3A **76**
Hillview Rd. *Bees* —6A **80**
Hill Vw. Rd. *Cltn* —5J **49**
Hilton Clo. *Long E* —5D **96**
Hilton Clo. *Mick* —7B **72**
Hilton Ct. *W Bri* —3K **83**
Hilton Cres. *W Bri* —3K **83**
Hilton Rd. *Etw* —5C **88**
Hilton Rd. *Nott* —4H **49**
Hinchin Brook. *Lent* —3A **64**
Hind Av. *Breas* —1A **96**
Hindscarth Cres. *Mick* —7C **72**
Hinshelwood Ct. *Nott* —1J **99**
Hinsley Clo. *Arn* —5K **33**
Hinsley Ct. *Nott* —2C **62**
Hirst Ct. *Nott* —2C **64** (2A **4**)
Hirst Cres. *Nott* —3F **63**
Hixon's La. *Dal A* —7K **59**
Hoare Rd. *Bees* —6B **80**
Hobart Clo. *Mick* —6D **72**
Hobart Clo. *Nott* —6E **64**
Hobart Dri. *S'fd* —6K **61**
Hob Hill. *H'wd* —5F **23**
Hobkirk Dri. *Sin* —7J **91**
Hobsic Clo. *Brins* —4B **14**
Hobson Dri. *Ilk* —1C **60**
Hobson's Acre. *Gun* —1F **53**
Hockerwood. *Nott* —4A **82**
Hockley. *Nott* —3F **65** (4H **5**)
Hodge Beck Clo. *Alv* —3J **93**
Hodgkin Clo. *Nott* —7J **81**
Hodgkinson St. *N'fld* —1E **66**
Hodson Ho. *Nott* —4E **48**
Hodthorpe Clo. *Oak* —6H **57**
Hoefield Cres. *Nott* —7G **31**
Hoe Hill Vw. *Toll* —7B **84**
Hoe La. *C But* —3G **87**
Hoe Nook. *C Bis* —4G **87**
Hoe Vw. Rd. *C Bis* —4G **87**
Hoewood Rd. *Nott* —6G **31**
Hogan Gdns. *Nott* —4C **32**
Hogarth Clo. *S'fd* —2J **79**
Hogarth St. *Nott* —1H **65**
Hoggbarn La. *Los* —1F **27**
Hoggetts Clo. *Bees* —2B **80**
Hogg La. *Rad T* —4J **67**
  (in two parts)
Hoggs Fld. *Eastw* —3D **28**
Holbeck Rd. *Huck* —3H **17**
Holbeck Rd. *Nott* —1K **63**
Holborn Av. *Nott* —2H **65**
Holborn Clo. *Nut* —3D **46**
Holborn Dri. *Der* —1E **72**
Holborn Pl. *Bulw* —6J **31**
Holborn Vw. *Cod* —4C **12**
Holbrook Ct. *Nott* —1A **100**
Holbrook Rd. *Alv* —4G **93**
Holbrook Rd. *Belp* —3K **23**
Holbrook St. *Hean* —3J **27**
Holbrook Vw. *Klbrn* —5G **25**
Holby Clo. *Nott* —5B **32**
Holcombe Clo. *Nott* —4H **47**
Holcombe St. *Der* —7B **74**
Holdale Rd. *Nott* —1K **65**
Holden Av. *Ast T* —2C **106**
Holden Ct. *Der* —1G **93**
Holden Ct. *Nott* —2C **64** (2A **4**)
Holden Cres. *Nut* —7C **30**
Holden Gdns. *S'fd* —2J **79**
Holden Rd. *Bees* —1E **80**
Holden St. *Nott* —2C **64** (2A **4**)
Holderness Clo. *Sten F* —7H **91**
Holgate. *Nott* —6J **81**
Holgate Rd. *Nott* —6E **64**
Holgate Wlk. *Huck* —6E **16**
Holkham Av. *Bees* —3C **80**

Holkham Clo. *Arn* —7J **33**
Holkham Clo. *Ilk* —3A **44**
Holland Clo. *Got* —1H **111**
Holland Mdw. *Long E* —4H **97**
Holland St. *Nott* —7B **48**
Holles Cres. *Nott* —4C **64** (6B **4**)
Hollies Dri. *Edw* —4J **83**
Hollies Rd. *Alst* —4H **55**
Hollies, The. *Eastw* —3D **28**
Hollies, The. *Sand* —3E **78**
Hollington Clo. *Chad* —1E **74**
Hollington Rd. *Nott* —1G **63**
Hollingworth Av. *Sand* —5F **79**
Hollins. The. *C'tn* —4E **20**
Hollinwell Av. *Nott* —2H **63**
Hollinwell Ct. *Edw* —5K **83**
Hollinwood La. *C'tn* —5K **19**
  (in two parts)
Hollis St. *Der* —1G **93**
Hollis St. *Nott* —5C **48**
Holloway Clo. *E Bri* —3K **53**
Holloway Rd. *Alv* —3F **93**
Holloway Rd. *Duf* —2H **39**
Hollowood Av. *L'ver* —1G **91**
Hollows, The. *Long E* —1A **98**
Hollows, The. *Nott* —4C **82**
Hollowstone. *Nott*
  —3F **65** (5H **5**)
Hollow, The. *Cas D* —7K **107**
Hollow, The. *L'ver* —7G **73**
Hollow, The. *Mick* —7B **72**
  (in two parts)
Holly Av. *Breas* —7D **78**
Holly Av. *Cltn* —7B **50**
Holly Av. *Nott* —7D **64**
Holly Av. *Rip* —4K **11**
Holly Av. *T'wd* —7J **49**
Hollybrook Gro. *Watn* —6B **30**
Hollybrook Way. *L'ver* —3D **90**
Holly Bush La. *Mak* —7A **24**
Holly Clo. *Bing* —3C **70**
Holly Clo. *Dray* —2J **95**
Holly Clo. *Huck* —7H **17**
**Holly Copse Nature Reserve.**
  **—4K 45**
Holly Ct. *Ast T* —3C **106**
Holly Ct. *Bees* —7C **62**
Holly Ct. *Mick* —7B **72**
Holly Ct. *Nott* —7H **49**
Hollycroft. *W Bri* —4J **83**
Hollydale Rd. *Nott* —1K **65**
Hollydene Clo. *Huck* —7C **16**
Hollydene Cres. *Nott* —2H **47**
Hollyfarm Ct. *Newt* —4G **29**
Holly Gdns. *Nott* —7H **49**
Hollygate Ind. Pk. *Cotg* —4A **86**
Hollygate La. *Cotg* —5K **85**
Holly La. *Bees* —3E **80**
Hollymoor Dri. *Chel* —7E **92**
Holly Rd. *Watn* —6K **29**
Hollythorpe Pl. *Huck* —7D **16**
Hollywell Av. *Cod* —5D **12**
Holm Av. *L Eat* —7B **40**
Holme Clo. *Ilk* —4B **44**
Holme Clo. *Wdbgh* —1H **35**
Holme Cft. *W Hal* —7G **43**
Holmefield Cres. *Ilk* —6E **44**
Holme Gro. *W Bri* —5K **65**
Holme La. *Hol P & Rad T* —4F **67**
Holme La. *Spon* —5J **75**
Holme Lea. *Sand* —2F **79**
Holme Lodge. *Cltn* —1C **66**
**Holme Pierrepont Country Pk.**
  **—4E 66**
**Holme Pierrepont Hall.** **—4F 67**
**Holme Pierrepont National**
  **Watersports Cen.** **—5C 66**
Holme Rd. *Bing* —3B **70**
Holme Rd. *W Bri* —6B **65**
Holmes Clo. *Lan M* —2J **27**
Holmesfield Dri. *Hean* —5H **27**
Holmesfield Dri. *Mick* —6D **72**
Holmes Rd. *Breas* —1B **96**
Holmes St. *Der* —4H **73**
Holmes St. *Hean* —3F **27**
Holme St. *Nott* —5G **65** (7K **5**)
Holmewood Cres. *Nott* —7C **32**
Holmewood Dri. *Gilt* —5F **29**
Holmfield. *Der* —2J **91**
Holmfield Rd. *Bees* —5C **80**
Holmleigh Way. *Chel* —1E **104**
Holmoak Clo. *Oak* —4H **57**
Holmsfield. *Keyw* —7C **102**
Holroyd Av. *Nott* —3H **65**
Holt Av. *Alv* —3J **93**
Holt Gro. *C'tn* —4D **20**
Holtlands Dri. *Alv* —4F **93**
Holwood Ct. *Nott* —7G **31**
Holyhead Dri. *Oak* —4H **57**

Holyoake Dri. *Long E* —2K **97**
Holyoake Rd. *Nott* —3J **31**
Holyrood Clo. *Spon* —3B **76**
Holyrood Ct. *Bees* —6C **62**
Holywell Rd. *Ilk* —3A **44**
Home Clo. *Arn* —6F **33**
Home Cft., The. *Bees* —1B **80**
Home Farm Clo. *Got* —1G **111**
Home Farm Clo. *Ock* —3E **76**
Home Farm Dri. *Alst* —3A **56**
Homefield Av. *Arn* —3J **33**
Homefield Rd. *Nott* —7K **47**
Homeleigh La. *Hov* —3K **37**
Homestead. *Lan M* —1J **27**
Homewell Wlk. *Nott* —5B **82**
Honeycroft Clo. *Belp* —3B **24**
Honeyfield Dri. *Rip* —4B **12**
Honeysuckle Clo. *Nott* —5E **46**
Honeysuckle Gro. *Bing* —4K **69**
Honeysuckle Gro. *Nott* —2H **47**
Honeywood Ct. *Nott* —7J **49**
Honeywood Dri. *Nott* —7J **49**
Honingham Clo. *Arn* —1H **49**
Honingham Rd. *Ilk* —3A **44**
Honister Clo. *Gam* —1A **84**
Honister Clo. *Nott* —2K **99**
Honiton Clo. *Bees* —6A **80**
Honiton Rd. *Nott* —5E **46**
Hood Cotts. *Nott* —4F **49**
Hood St. *Nott* —4F **49**
Hooley Clo. *Long E* —3F **97**
Hooley Pl. *Nott* —3F **49**
Hoopers Wlk. *Nott* —5E **64**
Hooton Rd. *Cltn* —7A **50**
Hooton St. *Nott* —2H **65**
Hope Av. *Mick* —6B **72**
Hope Clo. *Nott* —5D **64**
Hopedale Clo. *Nott* —2A **64**
Hope Dri. *Nott* —4D **64** (6C **4**)
Hope St. *Bees* —1E **80**
Hope St. *Der* —4B **74** (5F **7**)
Hope St. *Ilk* —7D **44**
Hope St. *Melb* —4F **113**
Hopetoun St. *Der* —1A **92**
Hopewell Clo. *Rad T* —2A **68**
Hopewell Wlk. *Ilk* —1D **44**
Hopkins Ct. *Eastw* —2D **28**
Hopping Hill. *Milf* —5K **23**
Hopping Hill Ter. E. *Milf* —6A **24**
Hopping Hill Ter. W. *Milf* —6A **24**
Hopton Clo. *Chad* —6G **57**
Hopwell Rd. *Dray* —5J **77**
Horace Av. *S'fd* —1G **79**
Horeston Cotts. *Hors W* —7H **25**
Hornbeam Clo. *Ilk* —7F **45**
Hornbeam Clo. *Oak* —5E **56**
Hornbeam Gdns. *Nott* —6F **31**
Hornbuckle Ct. *Nott* —2B **64**
Horncastle Rd. *Der* —6D **56**
Hornchurch Rd. *Nott* —6D **46**
Hornsby Wlk. *Nott* —5A **32**
Hornsea Rd. *Der* —6D **56**
Horridge St. *Ilk* —2D **44**
Horsecroft Clo. *Ilk* —4A **44**
Horsendale Av. *Nut* —2E **46**
Horse Shoes, The. *H'ton*
  —6A **108**
Horsham Dri. *Nott* —5B **32**
Horsley Cres. *Holb* —6C **24**
Horsley Cres. *Lan M* —2J **27**
Horsley La. *Cox* —2E **40**
Horsley Rd. *Hors* —7F **25**
Horton St. *Der* —6C **74**
Horwood Av. *Der* —6H **73**
Hoselett Fld. Rd. *Long E* —4J **97**
Hospital La. *Mick* —2K **89**
Hoten Rd. *Nott* —4H **65**
Hotspur Clo. *Nott* —1A **48**
Hotspur Rd. *Colw* —1C **66**
Houghton Clo. *Nut* —2E **46**
Houghton Ct. *Oak* —5F **57**
Houldsworth Ri. *Arn* —3G **33**
Hoult St. *Der* —4H **73**
Hound Rd. *W Bri* —7G **65**
Hounds Ga. *Nott* —3E **64** (5D **4**)
  (in two parts)
Hounslow Rd. *Der* —2F **73**
Houseman Gdns. *Nott* —5E **64**
Houston Clo. *Chad* —2H **75**
Houston Clo. *Nott* —4A **32**
Hovenden Gdns. *Nott* —7A **48**
Hoveringham Rd. *Cay* —5J **37**
Hove Rd. *Nott* —1A **48**
Hoveton Clo. *Shel L* —6D **92**
Howard Clo. *Long E* —7J **79**
Howard St. *Der* —6K **73**
Howard St. *Nott* —2E **64** (2F **5**)
Howarth Clo. *Long E* —2E **96**
Howbeck Rd. *Arn* —5K **33**

Howden Clo. *Mick* —7A **72**
Howden Rd. *Nott* —3J **31**
Howell Jones Rd. *Bees* —5B **80**
Howells Clo. *Nott* —5E **32**
Howe St. *Der* —3H **73**
Howick Dri. *Nott* —6F **31**
Howitt St. *Hean* —3H **27**
Howitt St. *Long E* —2J **97**
Howth Clo. *Chad* —4G **75**
Hoylake Ct. *Mick* —5A **72**
Hoylake Cres. *Nott* —7D **46**
Hoylake Dri. *Mick* —5A **72**
Hoylake Wlk. *Nott* —5C **32**
Hoyland Av. *Nott* —5A **64**
Hoyland Ct. *Belp* —7E **10**
Hoyle Rd. *C'tn* —3D **20**
Hubert Ct. *Nott* —1B **64**
Hubert Shaw Clo. *Shel L*
  —5E **92**
Hubert St. *Nott* —1B **64**
Huckerby Rd. *Ilk* —4A **44**
Hucklow Ct. *Oak* —4H **57**
**Hucknall Aerodrome.** **—3E 30**
Hucknall By-Pass. *Huck* —5E **16**
Hucknall Clo. *Strel* —4D **46**
Hucknall Cres. *Ged* —4C **50**
Hucknall Ind. Pk. *Huck* —1F **31**
Hucknall La. *Nott* —5J **31**
**Hucknall Leisure Cen.** **—4H 17**
Hucknall Rd. *Nott & Nott* —4K **31**
Hudson St. *Nott* —1H **65**
Hudson Way. *Pri P* —5C **74** (7J **7**)
Hufton's Ct. *Hean* —6J **27**
Hufton's Dri. *Hean* —6H **27**
Hugessen Av. *Huck* —4J **17**
Huggett Gdns. *Nott* —4C **32**
Hulland St. *Der* —5C **74** (7H **7**)
Hulland Vw. *Alst* —6H **55**
Humber Clo. *Alv* —3J **93**
Humber Clo. *Nott* —5E **64**
Humber Lodge. *Bees* —1G **81**
Humber Rd. *Bees* —1G **81**
Humber Rd. *Long E* —6G **79**
Humber Rd. S. *Bees* —2H **81**
Humberston Rd. *Nott* —4C **62**
Humbleton Dri. *Der* —3E **72**
Hungerhill La. *Wdbgh* —3D **34**
Hungerhill Rd. *Nott* —7F **49**
Hunger Hill Yd. *Ilk* —1E **60**
Hungerton St. *Nott* —4B **64**
Hunston Clo. *Nott* —7G **47**
Hunt Av. *Hean* —3G **27**
Hunter Dri. *Klbrn* —5F **25**
Hunter Rd. *Arn* —7A **34**
Hunter Rd. *Belp* —7D **10**
Hunters Clo. *Nott* —2C **82**
Hunters Cft. *Sten F* —7J **91**
Huntingdon Ct. *Melb* —3H **113**
Huntingdon Dri. *Cas D* —6J **107**
Huntingdon Dri. *Nott*
  —3D **64** (5C **4**)
Huntingdon Grn. *Der*
  —2C **74** (2J **7**)
Huntingdon St. *Nott*
  —1E **64** (1E **4**)
Huntingdon Wlk. *Sand* —3F **79**
Huntingdon Way. *Bees* —6K **79**
Huntley Av. *Spon* —2B **76**
Huntley Clo. *Nott* —7C **82**
Huntspill Rd. *Hilt* —7A **88**
Hurcomb St. *Nott* —7H **49**
Hurley Ct. *W Hal* —6G **43**
Hurst Dri. *Stan* —1E **58**
Hurts Cft. *Bees* —4D **80**
Hurt's Yd. *Nott* —2E **64** (3E **4**)
Huss's La. *Long E* —2K **97**
Hutchinson Grn. *Nott*
  —1F **65** (1G **5**)
Hutton Clo. *Bees* —6D **62**
Hutton St. *Altn* —3E **92**
Hutton St. *Nott* —4H **65**
Huxley Clo. *Der* —2K **91**
Huxley Clo. *Nott* —7D **46**
Hyam's La. *Dis* —5A **116**
Hyde Clo. *Nott* —4B **82**
Hyde Pk. Clo. *W Bri* —3E **82**
Hyde Pk. Rd. *Der* —2E **72**
Hyson Clo. *Nott* —6B **48**
Hyson St. *Nott* —7B **48**

**I**an Gro. *Cltn* —6D **50**
Ibsley Clo. *Alv* —3J **93**
Ikea Way. *Gilt* —6G **29**
Ilam Sq. *Ilk* —1C **44**
Ilford Clo. *Ilk* —3B **44**
Ilford Rd. *Der* —3E **72**
Ilford Wlk. *Der* —3E **72**
Ilkeston Rd. *Hean* —4H **27**

Ilkeston Rd. *Ilk* —4D **60**
Ilkeston Rd. *M'ly* —4A **42**
Ilkeston Rd. *Nott* —2K **63** (3A **4**)
  (in two parts)
Ilkeston Rd. *Sand & Sand*
  —6G **61**
Ilkeston Rd. *S'fd & Bees* —5J **61**
Ilkeston Rd. *Trow* —2F **61**
Imperial Av. *Bees* —2E **80**
Imperial Av. *Ged* —5C **50**
Imperial Ct. *Alst* —2H **55**
Imperial Rd. *Bees* —2E **80**
Imperial Rd. *Nott* —7K **31**
Inchwood Clo. *Bees* —6K **79**
Incinerator Rd. *Nott*
  —5G **65** (7J **5**)
Independent St. *Nott* —1B **64**
**Indoor Athletics Arena.** **—7F 47**
**Indoor Bowls Hall.** **—1A 98**
**Industrial Mus.** **—2E 6**
Industrial St. *Der* —6A **74**
**Info. Cen.** **—4F 5**
  **(Wilford)**
Ingham Dri. *Mick* —1B **90**
Ingham Gro. *Nott* —4A **64**
Ingham Rd. *Long E* —6G **79**
Ingleborough Gdns. *Long E*
  —1E **96**
Ingleby Av. *Der* —2J **91**
Ingleby Clo. *Cotg* —6K **85**
Ingleby Clo. *Nott* —3B **62**
Ingleby La. *Tickn* —6A **112**
Ingleby Rd. *Long E* —5D **96**
Ingleby Rd. *Stan B* —7B **104**
Ingle Clo. *Spon* —3A **76**
Ingledew Clo. *Oak* —6E **56**
Inglefield Rd. *Ilk* —1D **60**
Ingles Channel. *Belp* —1K **23**
Inglewood Av. *Mick* —5B **72**
Inglewood Rd. *Nott* —7A **82**
Ingliston Clo. *Alv* —3K **93**
Ingram Rd. *Nott* —7J **31**
Ingram Ter. *Nott* —7J **31**
Inham Cir. *Bees* —2C **80**
Inham Clo. *Bees* —3A **80**
Inham Rd. *Bees* —3A **80**
Inhams Fields Clo. *Gun* —1G **53**
Innes Clo. *Cltn* —7A **50**
Inn La. *Quar* —6F **39**
Instow Dri. *Sun* —4H **91**
Instow Ri. *Nott* —1F **65** (1H **5**)
Intake Rd. *Keyw* —6B **102**
**International Model Cen.** **—5C 18**
Inveraray Clo. *Sin* —6H **91**
Iona Clo. *Sin* —5J **91**
Iona Dri. *Trow* —4H **61**
Iona Gdns. *Nott* —4C **32**
Ipswich Cir. *Nott* —2J **65**
Ireland Av. *Bees* —3G **81**
Ireland Clo. *Bees* —3G **81**
Iremonger Rd. *Nott* —5F **65**
Irene Ter. *Nott* —4B **48**
Ireton Gro. *Bees* —6D **80**
Ireton Houses. *Belp* —2E **24**
Ireton St. *Bees* —2E **80**
Ireton St. *Nott* —2C **64** (2B **4**)
Iron Ga. *Der* —3A **74** (3D **6**)
**Iron Works.** **—5G 11**
  **(remains of)**
Irvine Clo. *Sten F* —6H **91**
Irving Pl. *Alv* —2F **93**
Irwin Dri. *Nott* —1F **47**
Isaac Newton Cen. *Nott* —6K **63**
Isaacs La. *S'fd* —1H **79**
Isabella St. *Nott* —4E **64** (6E **4**)
Isandula Rd. *Nott* —4B **48**
Island, The. *Eastw* —4D **28**
Islay Clo. *Arn* —4H **33**
Islay Clo. *Trow* —4H **61**
Islay Rd. *Sin* —5J **91**
Isleworth Dri. *Der* —2D **72**
Ismay Rd. *Chad* —2F **75**
Ivatt Dri. *Nott* —4H **65**
Ivernia Clo. *Sun* —4J **91**
Ives Clo. *W Bri* —4E **82**
Ivybridge Clo. *Oak* —4J **57**
Ivy Clo. *Watn* —4K **29**
Ivy Ct. *Etw* —5D **88**
Ivy Ct. *Mick* —7B **72**
Ivy Gro. *Cltn* —7B **50**
Ivy Gro. *Nott* —6C **48**
Ivy Gro. *Rip* —3K **11**
Ivy La. *Eastw* —3C **28**
Ivy Row. *What* —4K **71**
Ivy Sq. *Der* —6C **74**

**J**acklin Gdns. *Nott* —4C **32**
Jacksdale Clo. *Alst* —6H **55**

Jackson Av. Ilk —5C 44
Jackson Av. Mick —6E 72
Jackson Av. Sand —2E 78
Jacksons La. Etw —7D 88
Jackson's La. Heag —5D 10
Jacksons La. Heag —6J 23
Jackson St. Der —4J 73 (5A 6)
James Clo. Der —3J 73 (3A 6)
James St. Arn —5G 33
James St. Kimb —7K 29
Japonica Dri. Nott —2H 47
Jardine Ct. Dray —2K 95
Jardines, The. Bramc —6C 62
Jarrow Gdns. Nott —3B 32
Jarvey's La. Der —7C 54
Jarvis Av. Nott —1K 65
Jarvis Rd. Sten F —7J 91
Jasmine Clo. Bees —6D 62
Jasmine Clo. Chad —4H 75
Jasmine Clo. Clif —7J 81
Jasmine Clo. Strel —5E 46
Jasmine Ct. Hean —4A 28
Jasmine Rd. Nott —3A 48
Jasper Clo. Rad T —5J 67
Jawbone La. Melb —3J 113
Jayne Clo. Ged —4E 50
Jayne Clo. Nott —1E 62

J.B's Bingo & Entertainment Cen.
—7A 82

Jebb's La. Bing —3B 70
Jedburgh Clo. Kimb —6J 29
Jedburgh Clo. Nott —1F 65 (1H 5)
Jedburgh Clo. Sin —7J 91
Jedburgh Wlk. Nott
—1F 65 (1H 5)
Jeffares Clo. Keg —7G 109
Jefferson Pl. Alv —2F 93
Jemison Clo. L'ver —2C 90
Jenned Rd. Arn —3J 33
Jenner St. Nott —5D 48
Jenness Av. Nott —4A 32
Jennison St. Nott —6J 31
Jenny Burton Way. Huck —7J 17
Jenny's Ct. Belp —7C 10
Jermyn Dri. Arn —4C 32
Jersey Gdns. Nott —1G 65 (1K 5)
Jervis Ct. Ilk —3D 44
Jesmond Rd. Nott —7K 31
Jessamine Ct. Bees —2G 81
Jesses La. Belp —5G 9
Jessop Av. Iron —1H 13
Jessop Dri. Sten F —7J 91

Jessop Monument. —1G 13

Jessops La. Ged —3D 50
Jessop St. Cod —5D 12
Jessop St. Wain —5C 12
Joan Av. Hean —3G 27
Jodrell Av. Belp —1D 24
John Berrysford Clo. Chad
—3F 75
John Carroll Ct. Nott —1H 65

John Carrol Leisure Cen. —2B 64

John F. Kennedy Gdns. Chad
—2J 75
John Lombe Dri. Der
—1A 74 (1E 6)
John O'Gaunts Way. Belp —1C 24
John Port Clo. Etw —5E 88
John Quinn Ct. Nott —5B 48
Johnson Av. Altn —2E 92
Johnson Av. Huck —7H 17
Johnson Dri. Hean —3H 27
Johnson Rd. Nott —3A 64
John's Pl. Hean —4F 27
Johns Rd. Rad T —4A 68
John St. Der —4B 74 (6G 7)
John St. Hean —3F 27
John St. Ilk —5D 44
John St. New B —5B 48
Joseph Ct. Ilk —3C 44
Joseph St. Belp —1K 23
Joseph St. Der —7A 74
Joseph Wright Ter. Der —1D 6
Joyce Av. Bees —5K 79
Joyce Av. Nott —2F 49
Joyce Clo. Nott —2F 49
Jubalton Clo. Altn —3E 92
Jubilee Av. Rip —3J 11
Jubilee Clo. Melb —4H 113
Jubilee Ct. Belp —3A 24
Jubilee Ct. Nott —5D 46
Jubilee Rd. Day —7G 33
Jubilee Rd. Shel L —5E 92
Jubilee St. Kimb —6J 29
Jubilee St. Nott —3H 65
Judson Av. S'fd —2K 79
Julian Clo. Ilk —1F 61
Julian La. Shelf —5C 52
Julian Rd. W Bri —7K 65

Julie Av. Hean —4J 27
Jumelles Dri. C'tn —5B 20
Junction Rd. Long E —3A 98
Junction St. Der —4H 73
Juniper Clo. Nott —7J 81
Juniper Ct. Gilt —5G 29
Juniper Ct. Nott —1A 4
Juniper Gdns. Bing —3C 70
Jura Av. Rip —2K 11
Jury St. Der —3K 73 (3C 6)

Kappler Clo. N'fld —7E 50
Karen Ri. Arn —4J 33
Katherine Dri. Bees —5K 79
Katrine Wlk. Sin —5J 91
Kayes Ct. S'fd —1H 79
Kayes Wlk. Nott —3F 65 (5G 5)
Kean Pl. Alv —2F 93
Keats Av. L'ver —7E 72
Keats Clo. Day —6F 33
Keats Clo. Long E —4F 97
Keats Clo. Nut —7B 30
Keats Dri. Huck —6D 16
Keble Clo. Der —5B 74 (7G 7)
Kedleston Clo. Alst —6H 55
Kedleston Clo. Bees —3C 80
Kedleston Clo. Long E —4E 96
Kedleston Clo. Rip —1J 11
Kedleston Dri. Ilk —3B 44
Kedleston Dri. S. Ilk —3C 44
Kedleston Gdns. Der
—2K 73 (1B 6)

Kedleston Hall. —2C 54
Kedleston Old Rd. Der —7H 55
Kedleston Pk. —2C 54
Kedleston Pk. Golf Club. —1D 54
Kedleston Pk. Golf Course.
—1D 54

Kedleston Rd. Der —6D 38 (1B 6)
Kedleston St. Der —2K 73 (1B 6)
Keeling Clo. Newt —4F 29
Keepers Clo. B Vil —1A 32
Kegworth Av. L'ver —3G 91
Kegworth La. Long W —7F 117

Kegworth Mus. —1G 117

Kegworth Rd. Got —4D 110
Kegworth Rd. King S & Rat S
—6K 109
Keighton Dri. Nott —6J 63
Keilder Dri. Bing —3J 69
Keldholme La. Alv —2J 93
Kelfield Clo. Nott —1A 48
Kelham Grn. Nott —1H 65
Kelham M. Nott —6K 49
Kelham Way. Eastw —2C 28
Kelling Clo. Nott —7C 32
Kelly Wlk. Nott —1D 82
Kelmoor Rd. Alv —2H 93
Kelsey Clo. Bees —5E 80
Kelso Gdns. Nott —5D 64
Kelso Wlk. Sin —7J 91
Kelstern Clo. Nott —3H 47
Kelvedon Dri. L'ver —3E 90
Kelvedon Gdns. Nott
—1G 65 (1J 5)
Kelvin Clo. S'fd —3G 79
Kelvin Rd. Nott —7J 49
Kemble Pl. Alv —2F 93
Kemmel Rd. Nott —1K 47
Kempsey Clo. Nott —5A 32
Kempson St. Rud —2E 100
Kempton Clo. Kimb —6J 29
Kempton Dri. Arn —4J 33
Kempton Pk. Clo. Der —1D 92
Kendal Clo. Huck —4F 17
Kendal Ct. W Bri —7K 65
Kendal Dri. Bees —7D 62
Kendale Ct. Nott —5H 49
Kendal Rd. C Bis —4G 87
Kendal Wlk. Der —6D 56
Kendon Av. Sun —3J 91
Kendray Clo. Belp —7D 10
Kendrew Ct. Nott —7J 81
Kenia Clo. Cltn —6B 50
Kenilworth Av. Ilk —1K 91
Kenilworth Ct. Bees —7G 63
Kenilworth Ct. Nott —4D 64 (6C 4)
Kenilworth Dri. Ilk —2A 60
Kenilworth Rd. Bees —1G 81
Kenilworth Rd. Nott
—4D 64 (6C 4)
Kenilworth Rd. Rip —3J 11

Ken Martin Pool & Lido. —4J 31

Kenmore Gdns. Nott
—1F 65 (1H 5)
Kennedy Av. Long E —4G 97
Kennedy Clo. Chad —1G 75

Kennedy Clo. Day —6F 33
Kennedy Dri. S'fd —6J 61
Kennel La. Ann —1K 15
Kenneth Rd. Arn —3H 33
Kennington Rd. Nott —2K 63
Kenrick Rd. Nott —5J 49
(in two parts)
Kenrick St. N'fld —7E 50
Kensal Ct. W Bri —7G 65
Kensal Ri. Der —2F 73
Kensington Av. Hean —4E 26
Kensington Clo. Bees —7A 80
Kensington Ct. Nott —3E 48
(off St Albans St.)
Kensington Gdns. Cltn —7C 50
Kensington Gdns. Ilk —7E 44
Kensington Pk. Clo. W Bri
—3E 82
Kensington Rd. Sand —4E 78
Kensington St. Der —3K 73 (4B 6)
Kensington St. Ilk —1D 60
Kenslow Av. Nott —7A 48
Kent Av. Bees —4F 81
Kent Av. Jack —1K 13
Kentish Ct. Der —1B 74 (1F 7)
Kentmere Clo. Gam —1A 84
Kenton Av. Nut —3D 46
Kenton Ct. Nott —6F 65
Kent Rd. Gilt —4G 29
Kent Rd. Nott —4H 49
Kent Rd. S'fd —2H 79
Kent St. Der —1D 74 (1K 7)
Kent St. Nott —2F 65 (3G 5)
Kentwood Rd. Nott —3H 65
Kenyon Rd. Nott —4K 63
Keppel Ct. Ilk —3D 44
Kepple Ga. Rip —4B 12
Kerry Dri. Smal —7B 26
Kerry St. Der —1D 74 (1K 7)
Kerry's Yd. Klbrn —5F 25
Kersall Ct. Nott —1K 47
Kersall Dri. Nott —1K 47
Kersall Gdns. Huck —5H 17
Kersall Gdns. Cres. Huck —5H 17
Kershope Dri. Oak —4H 57
Kestrel Clo. Cltn —5K 49
Kestrel Clo. Quar H —3D 60
Kestrel Dri. Bing —4B 70
Kestrel Heights. Iron —1H 13
Kestrel Ho. Sin —7J 91
Kestrels Cft. Sin —6J 91
Keswick Av. Sun —3J 91
Keswick Clo. Bees —7D 62
Keswick Clo. Gam —1A 84
Keswick Clo. Ilk —2B 60
Keswick Ct. Long E —6F 79
Keswick St. Nott —3G 65 (4J 5)
Keswick St. Nott —3G 65 (4J 5)
Kett St. Nott —6H 31
Keverne Clo. Nott —4J 47
Kevin Clo. Chad —7H 57
Kevin Rd. Nott —5D 62
Kew Clo. W Bri —5E 82
Kew Cres. Hean —4K 27
Kew Gdns. Der —3F 73
Kew Gdns. Nott —3E 46
Keyhaven Clo. Der —7D 56
Keynsham Clo. Alv —1E 92
Keys Clo. Nott —6G 31
Keys St. Der —2B 74 (2F 7)
Key St. Nott —2H 65
Keyworth La. Bun —7H 101
Keyworth Rd. Ged —3B 50
Kibworth Clo. Nott —2B 48
(in two parts)
Kibworth Clo. Oak —6H 57
Kiddier Av. Arn —6K 33
Kilbourne Rd. Arn —4K 33
Kilbourn St. Nott —1E 64
Kilburn Clo. Bees —5B 62
Kilburn Dri. Ilk —3B 44
Kilburn La. Belp —2D 24
Kilburn Rd. Belp —1C 24
Kilburn Toll Bar. Klbrn —4F 25
Kilby Av. Nott —1J 65
Kilby Ho. Long E —1H 97
Kildare Rd. Chad —4H 75
Kildare Rd. Nott —6H 49
Kildonan Clo. Nott —4D 46
Killerton Grn. Nott —1B 48
Killerton Pk. Dri. W Bri —4D 82
Killingworth Av. Sin —5K 91
Killisick Ct. Arn —5K 33
Killisick La. Arn —5K 33
Killisick Rd. Arn —5J 33
Killis La. Klbrn —5D 24
Kilnbrook Av. Arn —4K 33
Kiln Clo. W Hal —5G 43

Kiln Cft. Etw —5E 88
Kilnsey Ct. L'ver —3D 90
Kilnwood Clo. Nott —7J 49
Kilsby Rd. Nott —6B 82
Kilverston Rd. Sand —2E 78
Kilverton Clo. Nott —3J 63
Kilvington Rd. Arn —6K 33
Kimber Clo. Nott —1D 62
Kimberley Clo. Kimb —1K 45
Kimberley Eastwood By-Pass.
Eastw —3B 28

Kimberley Recreation Cen.
—7A 30

Kimberley Rd. Borr —6D 76
Kimberley Rd. Nut —1B 46
Kimberley St. Nott —3J 65
Kimbolton Av. Nott —2B 64
Kinder Wlk. Der —4J 73
Kindlewood Dri. Bees —7B 80
King Alfred St. Der —4K 73 (5B 6)
King Charles St. Nott
—3D 64 (5D 4)
King Edward Ct. Nott
—2F 65 (3G 5)
King Edward Gdns. Sand —2F 79
King Edward St. Huck —6G 17
King Edward St. Nott
—2F 65 (3G 5)
King Edward St. Sand —2F 79
Kingfisher Clo. Bees —3H 81
Kingfisher Clo. Mick —2K 89
Kingfisher Clo. Nott —2K 47
Kingfishers Ct. W Bri —4A 84
Kingfisher Wlk. Sin —7J 91
Kingfisher Wharf. Nott
—5C 64 (7A 4)
King George Av. Ilk —6C 44
King John's Arc. Nott —4F 5
King John's Chambers. Nott
—4F 5
Kinglake Pl. Nott —5E 64 (7E 4)
Kingrove Av. Bees —2D 80
Kings Av. Ged —4C 50
Kingsbridge Av. Nott —7A 34
Kingsbridge Way. Bees —2C 80
Kingsbury Dri. Nott —6G 47
Kingsbury Rd. Der —2E 72
Kingsclere Av. Oak —5H 57
Kings Clo. Hean —4E 26
Kings Ct. Der —2A 74 (1D 6)
Kingscroft. Alst —3K 55
Kingsdale Clo. Long E —4E 96
Kingsdown Mt. Nott —5E 62
Kings Dri. Brins —5C 14
Kings Dri. L'ver & L'ver —6F 73
Kingsford Av. Nott —1A 64
Kingsgate. Locki —6D 108
Kings and Glo. Oak —5E 56
Kingsley Cres. Long E —5F 97
Kingsley Dri. N'fld —1E 66
Kingsley Rd. Alst —4H 55
Kingsley Rd. Nott —3J 65
Kingsley St. Sin —4K 91
Kingsmead Av. Trow —5H 61
King's Mead Clo. Der
—2K 73 (1C 6)
King's Mead Ho. Der —1K 73
Kingsmead Ind. Est. Der —2H 73
King's Mdw. Rd. Nott —5C 64
King's Mead Wlk. Der
—2K 73 (1C 6)
King's Mills La. Wstn T —5A 106
Kingsmoor Clo. Nott —6A 32
Kingsmuir Rd. Mick —5A 72
Kings Newton La. Melb —2G 113
King's Pl. Nott —3F 65 (4G 5)
Kings Rd. Sand —2F 79
Kingsthorpe Clo. Nott —5H 49
Kingston Av. Ilk —3E 60
Kingston Ct. Nott —3G 65 (4K 5)
Kingston Ct. W Hal —6F 43
Kingston Dri. Cotg —7K 85
Kingston La. King S —7J 109
Kingston Rd. W Bri —2G 83
Kingston St. Der —1K 73
King St. Bees —2G 81
King St. Belp —2K 23
King St. Der —2K 73 (1C 6)
King St. Duf —2J 39
King St. Eastw —3D 28
King St. Ilk —5D 44
King St. Long E —1H 97
King St. Nott —3E 64 (4E 4)
Kings Wlk. Nott —2E 64 (3E 4)
Kingsway. Der —3F 73
Kingsway. Hean —3F 27
Kingsway. Ilk —2D 60
Kingsway. Rad T —5J 67
Kingsway Gdns. Huck —1E 30

Kingsway Ind. Pk. Der —3G 73
Kingsway Pk. Clo. Der —3F 73
Kingsway Retail Pk. Der —4G 73
Kingsway Rd. Huck —1E 30
Kingswell Rd. Arn —6H 33
Kingswood Av. Belp —6C 10
Kingswood Clo. W Bri —3F 83
Kingswood Rd. Nott —2H 63
Kingswood Rd. W Bri —3F 83
Kinlet Rd. Nott —7C 32
Kinoulton Rd. C Bis —6F 87
Kinross Av. Der —7C 56
Kinross Cres. Nott —1G 63
Kinsale Wlk. Nott —6A 82
Kinsway Cres. Klbrn —5G 25
Kintyre Dri. Sin —6H 91
Kipling Clo. Nott —1J 99
Kipling Dri. Mick —7B 72
Kippis St. Nott —2F 65 (3G 5)
Kirby Clo. Newt —2E 28
Kirby Dri. Keg —2G 117
Kirby Rd. Newt —2E 28
Kirk Av. Keg —1H 117
Kirkbride Ct. Bees —4B 80
Kirk Bldgs. Cltn —7B 50
Kirkby Av. Ilk —1D 60
Kirkby Gdns. Nott —5F 65
Kirk Clo. Bees —4D 80
Kirk Clo. Rip —4J 11
Kirk Cotts. Nott —2A 48
Kirkdale Av. Spon —5B 76
Kirkdale Clo. Nott —3B 62
Kirkdale Gdns. Long E —3F 97
Kirkdale Rd. Long E —4F 97
Kirkdale Rd. Nott —1K 65
Kirkewhite Ct. Nott —5F 65
Kirkewhite St. W. Nott —5E 64
Kirkewhite Wlk. Nott —5E 64
Kirkfell Clo. W Bri —3A 84
Kirkfield Dri. Breas —1B 96
Kirkham Clo. Hean —4F 27
Kirkham Dri. Bees —6K 79
Kirkhill. Bing —2A 70
Kirk Hill. E Bri —4H 53
Kirkistown Clo. Alv —3J 93
Kirkland Clo. Cas D —7J 107
Kirkland Dri. Bees —6C 80
Kirkland Way. Sten F —6H 91
Kirk La. Rud —2E 100
Kirkley Gdns. Arn —5J 33
Kirk Leys Av. N. Spon —4A 76
Kirk Leys Av. S. Spon —4A 76
Kirkman Rd. Los —1E 26
Kirk Rd. Nott —4J 49
Kirk's La. Belp —2B 24
Kirkstead Clo. Oak —6H 57
Kirkstead Gdns. Nott —7B 48
Kirkstead St. Nott —7B 48
Kirkstone Ct. Long E —6F 79
Kirkstone Dri. Gam —1A 84
Kirk St. Der —1A 74
Kirkwhite Av. Long E —2H 97
Kirtle Clo. Nott —6H 47
Kirtley Dri. Nott —5C 64 (7B 4)
Kirton Av. Long E —2H 97
Kitchener Av. Der —2K 91
Kittiwake M. Lent —3A 64
Kiwi Clo. Huck —7D 16
Knapp Av. Eastw —4D 28
Kneesall Gro. Huck —5H 17
Kneeton Clo. Ged —2B 50
Kneeton Clo. Nott —2E 48
Kneeton Rd. E Bri —3J 53
Kneeton Va. Nott —2E 48
Knighton Av. Nott —1A 64
Knighton Rd. Wd'p —1F 49
Knightsbridge. Der —2E 72
Knightsbridge Ct. Nott —3E 48
(off Newstead St.)
Knightsbridge Dri. Nut —3E 46
Knightsbridge Dri. W Bri —4E 82
Knightsbridge Gdns. Huck
—2F 17
Knightsbridge Way. Huck —3E 16
Knights Clo. Bees —6K 79
Knights Clo. Nott —5B 32
Knights Clo. Sten F —7J 91
Knight's Clo. W Bri —5E 82
Knight St. N'fld —1D 66
Knightwood Dri. B Vil —7D 18
Kniveton Pk. Ilk —7B 44
Knole Rd. Nott —2E 62

Knole Street Baths. —6B 48

Knoll Av. Huck —7D 16
Knoll Clo. L'ver —1E 90
Knowl Av. Belp —6J 9
Knowle Hill. Kimb —1A 46
(in two parts)
Knowle La. Kimb —2A 46

Knowle Pk. *Kimb* —1A **46**
Knowles Wlk. *Arn* —5E **32**
Knutsford Grn. *Der* —5D **56**
Kozi Kots. *N'fld* —7D **50**
Krebs Clo. *Nott* —7J **81**
Kyle Gro. *Oak* —4H **57**
Kyle Vw. *Nott* —4C **32**
Kyme St. *Nott* —2B **64** (2A **4**)
Kynance Clo. *Alv* —4J **93**
Kynance Gdns. *Nott* —3D **82**

Labray Rd. *C'tn* —4C **20**
Laburnum Av. *Keyw* —7E **102**
Laburnum Clo. *Sand* —1F **79**
Laburnum Cres. *Alst* —2H **55**
Laburnum Gdns. *Nott* —1A **48**
Laburnum Gro. *Bees* —3H **81**
Laburnum Gro. *Huck* —7H **17**
Laburnum Gro. *Kgswy* —3E **72**
Laburnum St. *Nott* —7F **49**
Laburnum Way. *Etw* —6E **88**
Lace Cen. & Costume Mus.
        —5E **4**

Lace Hall Mus. —5G **5**
Lace Market. —4G **5**
Lace Market Theatre. —5G **5**
Lace Rd. *Bees* —1F **81**
Lace St. *Nott* —6K **63**
Lacey Av. *Huck* —7G **17**
Lacey Clo. *Ilk* —3A **44**
Lacey Fields Rd. *Hean* —4J **27**
Ladbroke Gdns. *Der* —2D **72**
Ladbrooke Cres. *Nott* —3J **47**
Ladybank Ri. *Arn* —5A **34**
Ladybank Rd. *Mick* —5A **72**
Lady Bay Av. *W Bri* —6H **65**
Lady Bay Bri. *Nott & W Bri*
        —5G **65**
Lady Bay Ct. *W Bri* —6J **65**
Lady Bay Rd. *W Bri* —6J **65**
Ladybower Rd. *Spon* —4B **76**
Ladybridge Clo. *Bees* —5E **80**
Ladycroft Av. *Huck* —5G **17**
Ladycroft Paddock. *Alst* —3J **55**
Lady Ga. *Dis* —6A **116**
Ladygrove Cotts. *Der* —5B **74**
Lady Lea Hill. *Hors* —7G **25**
Lady Lea Rd. *Hors* —7G **25**
Ladylea Rd. *Long E* —5E **96**
Lady Mantle Clo. *Chel* —7E **92**
Ladysmith Rd. *Borr* —6D **76**
Ladysmith St. *Nott* —3J **65**
Ladysmock Gdns. *Nott* —5F **65**
Ladywell Ct. *Belp* —2A **24**
Ladywood Av. *Belp* —7B **10**
Ladywood Rd. *Ilk* —3J **59**
Lake Av. *Los* —7E **12**
Lake Dri. *Der* —1K **91**
Lakehead Ho. *Nott* —7A **82**
Lakeland Av. *Huck* —7J **17**
Lakeside Av. *Long E* —5G **97**
Lakeside Bus. Cen. *Ship* —7J **72**
Lakeside Cres. *Long E* —4G **97**
Lakeside Dri. *L'ver* —2D **90**
Lake St. *Nott* —1B **64** (1A **4**)
Lamartine St. *Nott* —2F **65** (2H **5**)
Lamb Clo. *Eastw* —6F **15**
Lamb Clo. Dri. *Newt* —1E **28**
Lamb Cres. *Rip* —3B **12**
Lambe Ct. *Der* —5B **74** (7F **7**)
Lambert Cotts. *Nott*
        —2D **64** (3C **4**)
Lambert Gdns. *Nott* —6J **47**
Lambert St. *Nott* —7A **48**
Lambeth Ct. *Bees* —1H **81**
Lambeth Rd. *Arn* —3C **32**
Lambhouse La. *Shot G* —7C **8**
Lambie Clo. *Nott* —2J **63**
Lambley Almshouses. *Nott*
        —6F **49**
Lambley Av. *Nott* —3K **49**
Lambley Bridle Rd. *Bur J* —7H **35**
Lambley Ct. *Nott* —3H **49**
Lambley Dri. *Alst* —5G **55**
Lambley La. *Bur J* —1H **51**
Lambley La. *Ged* —3C **50**
Lambley Rd. *Low* —5A **36**
Lambley St. *Nott* —6H **31**
Lambourn Ct. *Der* —3A **56**
Lambourn Dri. *Alst* —3A **56**
Lambourne Cres. *Low* —4E **36**
Lambourne Dri. *Nott* —2F **63**
Lambourne Gdns. *Wd'p* —1J **49**
Lambrook Clo. *Mick* —6A **72**
Lambton Clo. *Ilk* —3C **44**
Lamcote Gdns. *Rad T* —4J **67**
Lamcote Gro. *Nott* —6F **65**
Lamcote M. *Rad T* —4J **67**

Lamcote St. *Nott* —6F **65**
Laming Gap La. *Cotg* —5G **103**
Lamins La. *B Vil* —7D **18**
Lammas Gdns. *E Bri* —2K **53**
Lammas Gdns. *Nott*
        —5F **65** (7G **5**)
Lammas La. *E Bri* —2K **53**
Lamorna Gro. *Nott* —2D **82**
Lampad Clo. *Melb* —3G **113**
Lampeter Clo. *Oak* —5H **57**
Lamplands. *Cotg* —5J **85**
Lamp Wood Clo. *C'tn* —5C **20**
Lanark Clo. *Nott* —4J **63**
Lanark St. *Der* —1E **74**
Lancaster Av. *Sand* —4E **78**
Lancaster Av. *S'fd* —2J **79**
Lancaster Ct. *Nott* —7K **49**
Lancaster Dri. *Hilt* —7A **88**
Lancaster Rd. *B Vil* —1A **32**
Lancaster Rd. *Huck* —1D **30**
Lancaster Rd. *Nott* —7K **49**
Lancaster Sports Cen. —2D **6**
Lancaster Wlk. *Spon* —2C **76**
Lancaster Way. *Nott* —4D **46**
Lancelot Dri. *Watn* —4K **29**
Lancelyn Gdns. *W Bri* —4G **83**
Landcroft Cres. *Nott* —7C **32**
Lander La. *Belp* —1A **24**
Landmere. *Sin* —6J **91**
Landmere Clo. *Ilk* —3A **44**
Landmere Gdns. *Nott* —5H **49**
Landmere La. *Rud & Edw* —6F **83**
  (in two parts)
Landmere La. *W Bri* —5D **82**
Landsdown Gro. *Long E* —7K **79**
Landseer Clo. *Nott* —1A **64**
Laneham Av. *Arn* —6J **33**
Laneside Av. *Bees* —6J **79**
Lane, The. *Aws* —2G **45**
Lane, The. *Rip* —2J **11**
Laneward Clo. *Ilk* —2B **44**
Langar Clo. *Nott* —2E **48**
Langar Rd. *Bing* —4A **70**
Langbank Av. *Nott* —4A **32**
Langdale Dri. *Bread* —6D **56**
Langdale Dri. *Long E* —3E **96**
Langdale Gro. *Bing* —3H **69**
Langdale Rd. *Nott* —2K **63**
Langden Ct. *Long E* —3J **97**
Langdon Clo. *Long E* —7E **78**
Langdown Clo. *Nott* —5G **31**
Langford Rd. *Arn* —6K **33**
Langford Rd. *Mick* —5B **72**
Langham Av. *Nott* —1J **65**
Langham Dri. *Bur J* —1K **51**
Langley Av. *Arn* —7H **33**
Langley Av. *Ilk* —1B **44**
Langley Dri. *Keg* —1G **117**
Langley Mill By-Pass. *Brins*
        —7J **13**
Langley Rd. *Spon* —5A **76**
Langley St. *Der* —3H **73**
Lang Rd. *Alv* —3F **93**
Langsett Dri. *Chel* —7G **93**
Langstrath Dri. *W Bri* —4A **84**
Langstrath Rd. *Nott* —7A **82**
Langton Clo. *Colw* —1C **66**
Langtree Gdns. *Bing* —2B **70**
Langtry Gro. *Nott* —5C **48**
Lanscombe Pk. Rd. *Alst* —6J **55**
Lansdown Clo. *Bees* —4B **80**
Lansdowne Av. *Alv* —4F **93**
Lansdowne Dri. *W Bri* —4F **83**
Lansdowne Rd. *Nott* —2A **48**
Lansic La. *Hov* —4J **37**
Lansing Clo. *Nott* —1B **100**
Lansing Gdns. *Chad* —2H **75**
Lanthwaite Clo. *Nott* —7B **82**
Lanthwaite Rd. *Nott* —7B **82**
Lapford Clo. *Nott* —7B **34**
Lapwing Clo. *Sin* —7J **91**
Larch Av. *Rip* —3K **11**
Larch Clo. *Alst* —4H **55**
Larch Clo. *Arn* —5E **32**
Larch Clo. *Bing* —3C **70**
Larch Clo. *Huck* —7H **17**
Larch Clo. *Nott* —1F **15**
Larch Cres. *Bees* —1E **80**
Larch Cres. *Eastw* —3C **28**
Larchdene Av. *Nott* —4D **62**
Larch Dri. *Sand* —7F **61**
Larch Gdns. *Nott* —6G **31**
Larch Rd. *Klbrn* —6H **25**
Larch Way. *Keyw* —7E **102**
Larges St. *Der* —3J **73** (3A **6**)
Largs Clo. *Nott* —3A **32**
Lark Clo. *Bees* —3A **80**
Lark Clo. *L'ver* —3G **91**
Larkdale St. *Nott* —1C **64** (1A **4**)

Larkfield Rd. *Nut* —1B **46**
Larkhill Cres. *Sin* —5K **91**
Larkin Clo. *Sin* —4A **92**
Larkland's Av. *Ilk* —7E **44**
Larkspur Av. *Red* —3G **33**
Larkspur Ct. *Oak* —4G **57**
Larwood Gro. *Nott* —2E **48**
Lascelles Av. *Ged* —4B **50**
Lashley Gdns. *Oak* —5F **57**
Latham St. *Nott* —6H **31**
Lathbury Clo. *Der* —6D **56**
Lathkill Av. *Alv* —2J **93**
Lathkill Av. *Ilk* —1C **44**
Lathkill Clo. *Nott* —6H **31**
Lathkill Clo. *W Hal* —6G **43**
Lathkilldale Cres. *Long E* —4E **96**
Lathkill Dri. *Rip* —6K **11**
Lathkill Rd. *Chad* —7F **57**
Latimer Clo. *L'ver* —2C **90**
Latimer Clo. *Nott* —7J **31**
Latimer Dri. *Bees* —4B **62**
Latimer St. *Der* —3D **92**
Latrigg Clo. *Mick* —7C **72**
Lauder Clo. *Sin* —7J **91**
Laughton Av. *W Bri* —4E **82**
Laughton Cres. *Huck* —1E **30**
Launceston Cres. *Nott* —4C **82**
Launceston Rd. *Alv* —4H **93**
Laund Av. *Belp* —6B **10**
Laund Clo. *Belp* —6B **10**
Launder St. *Nott* —5E **64**
Laund Hill. *Belp* —7A **10**
Laund Nook. *Belp* —7A **10**
Laurel Av. *Keyw* —7D **102**
Laurel Av. *Rip* —3K **11**
Laurel Cres. *Long E* —3G **97**
Laurel Cres. *Nut* —6B **30**
Laurel Cres. *Smal* —1B **42**
Laurel Rd. *Cltn* —6B **50**
Laurie Av. *Nott* —6C **48**
Laurie Clo. *Nott* —6C **48**
Laurie Pl. *Altn* —2E **92**
Lauriston Dri. *Nott* —2K **47**
Lavender Clo. *Nott* —5E **46**
Lavender Cres. *Cltn* —5B **50**
Lavender Gdns. *Hean* —4K **27**
Lavender Gro. *Bees* —3H **81**
Lavender Row. *Dar A* —6K **55**
Lavender Wlk. *Nott* —7F **49**
Laver Clo. *Arn* —6K **33**
Lawdon Rd. *Arn* —4J **33**
Lawley Av. *Bees* —6G **63**
Lawn Av. *Alst* —5H **55**
Lawn Av. *Etw* —4E **88**
Lawn Clo. *Hean* —3H **27**
Lawnheads Av. *L'ver* —6G **73**
Lawnlea Clo. *Sun* —4J **91**
Lawn Mill Rd. *Kimb* —6J **29**
Lawnside. *Spon* —3B **76**
Lawns, The. *Ast T* —2D **106**
Lawns, The. *What* —4J **71**
Lawnswood Clo. *L'ver* —1G **91**
Lawn Ter. *Ilk* —6C **44**
Lawrence Av. *Aws* —1G **45**
Lawrence Av. *Breas* —1B **96**
Lawrence Av. *Chad* —1H **75**
Lawrence Av. *Colw* —2C **66**
Lawrence Av. *Eastw* —3D **28**
Lawrence Av. *Rip* —4J **11**
Lawrence Clo. *Cotg* —5K **85**
Lawrence Dri. *Brins* —4B **14**
Lawrence Pk. *Und* —1F **15**
Lawrence St. *Der* —1K **91**
Lawrence St. *Long E* —1H **97**
Lawrence St. *Sand* —1F **79**
Lawrence St. *S'fd* —2H **79**
Lawrence Way. *Nott*
        —5C **64** (7A **4**)
Lawson Av. *Long E* —2J **97**
Lawson St. *Nott* —1C **64** (1A **4**)
Lawton Dri. *Nott* —4J **31**
Laxton Av. *Nott* —1K **47**
Laxton Dri. *Huck* —6E **16**
Leabrook Clo. *Nott* —5J **81**
Leabrook Gdns. *Huck* —4J **17**
Lea Clo. *Alst* —4J **55**
Leacroft Rd. *Der* —7B **74**
Leacroft Rd. *Nott* —7K **47**
Leadale Av. *Huck* —4J **17**
Lea Dri. *Chad* —2F **75**
Lea Dri. *Mick* —5B **72**
Leaf Clo. *Huck* —3H **17**
Leafe Clo. *Bees* —6C **80**
Leafenden Clo. *Dar A* —5A **56**
Leafgreen La. *L'ver* —3G **91**
Leafield Grn. *Nott* —6A **82**
Leafy La. *Hean* —4H **27**
Leahurst Gdns. *W Bri* —3K **83**

Leahurst Rd. *W Bri* —3J **83**
Leahy Gdns. *Nott* —7B **32**
Leake Rd. *Got* —1H **111**
Leake St. *Der* —3H **73**
Leamington Clo. *Der* —7H **73**
Leamington Dri. *Bees* —4C **80**
Leamington St. *Rip* —2A **12**
Leander Clo. *L'ver* —2H **91**
Leander Clo. *Nott* —2D **82**
Leaper St. *Der* —2J **73** (1A **6**)
Leas, The. *Bul* —1B **52**
Leatherlands. *Keg* —7H **109**
Leawood Gdns. *Oak* —4H **57**
Leche Cft. *Belp* —1D **24**
Lechlade Clo. *W Hal* —6F **43**
Lechlade Rd. *Nott* —7C **32**
Ledbury Chase. *Sten F* —7H **91**
Ledbury Pl. *Der* —6D **56**
Ledbury Va. *Nott* —6H **47**
Ledo Av. *Rip* —2K **11**
Leech Ct. *Gilt* —6F **29**
Lee Cres. *Ilk* —6F **45**
Leeds Pl. *Der* —4C **74** (6H **7**)
Lee Farm Clo. *Chel* —1F **105**
Lee La. *Hean* —4K **27**
Leen Clo. *B Vil* —1B **32**
Leen Clo. *Huck* —4J **17**
Leen Ct. *Nott* —5A **64**
Leen Dri. *Bulw* —4J **31**
Leen Dri. *Huck* —3H **17**
Leen Ga. *Nott* —5K **63**
Leen Mills La. *Huck* —3H **17**
Leen Pl. *Nott* —2A **64**
Leen Valley Golf Course. —5K **17**
Leen Valley Way. *Huck* —7J **17**
Leen Vw. Ct. *Nott* —7G **31**
Lee Rd. *Bur J* —1A **52**
Lee Rd. *C'tn* —4B **20**
Lees Barn Rd. *Rad T* —5H **67**
Lees Brook Ho. *Chad* —1G **75**
Lees Hill Footpath. *Nott*
        —4G **65** (6K **5**)
Lees Hill St. *Nott* —3G **65** (5K **5**)
Leeside. *Alv* —7G **75**
Lees Rd. *Nott* —5J **49**
Lees, The. *Boul M* —4K **93**
Leeway. *Spon* —4K **75**
Leicester Ho. *S'fd* —7K **61**
Leicester St. *Der* —5J **73**
Leicester St. *Long E* —3J **97**
Leigh Clo. *W Bri* —2E **82**
Leigh Rd. *Bees* —5K **79**
Leighton St. *Nott* —1H **65**
Leiston Gdns. *Nott* —5C **32**
Leisure Cen. —7A **82**
(Nottingham)
Leisure Cen. —5H **33**
(Rushcliffe Comp. Sch.)
Leivers Av. *Arn* —5H **33**
Lema Clo. *Nott* —5K **31**
Leman St. *Der* —5J **73** (7A **6**)
Lendal Ct. *Nott* —2C **64** (2A **4**)
Lendrum Ct. *Bur J* —2K **51**
Leniscar Av. *Los* —1E **26**
Len Maynard Ct. *Nott* —7J **49**
Lennox St. *Nott* —2F **65** (3H **5**)
Lens Rd. *Alst* —5G **55**
Lenton Av. *Chad* —2F **75**
Lenton Av. *Nott* —3C **64** (5A **4**)
Lenton Av. *Toll* —7A **84**
Lenton Baths. —4B **64**
Lenton Boulevd. *Nott* —2B **64**
Lenton Cir. *Toll* —7A **84**
Lenton Ct. *Nott* —4C **64** (6A **4**)
  (Lenton Av.)
Lenton Ct. *Nott* —3B **64**
  (Lombard Clo.)
Lenton Hall Dri. *Nott* —5J **63**
Lenton La. *Nott* —5B **64**
  (in two parts)
Lenton Mnr. *Nott* —4A **64**
Lenton Rd. *Nott* —4C **64** (6A **4**)
Lenton St. *Sand* —2G **79**
Leominster Dri. *Oak* —5H **57**
Leonard Av. *Nott* —4D **48**
Leonard Cheshire Clo. *Hean*
        —4K **27**
Leonard Clo. *Der* —5A **74** (7E **6**)
Leonard St. *Bulw* —1H **47**
Leonard St. *Der* —5B **74** (7F **7**)
Leonard Wlk. *Der* —5A **74** (7E **6**)
Leopold St. *Der* —5A **74** (7D **6**)
Leopold St. *Long E* —1H **97**
Le Page Ct. *Nott* —7G **47**
Leroy Wallace Av. *Nott* —1B **64**
Lerwick Clo. *Nott* —7C **82**
Leslie Av. *Bees* —3F **81**
Leslie Av. *Kimb* —1K **45**
Leslie Av. *Nott* —6C **48**

Leslie Clo. *L'ver* —2C **90**
Leslie Gro. *C'tn* —5D **20**
Leslie Rd. *Nott* —6C **48**
Letchworth Cres. *Bees* —4C **80**
Letcombe Rd. *Nott* —5A **82**
Leven Clo. *Sin* —7K **91**
Levens Clo. *W Bri* —3A **84**
Leveret Clo. *Chel* —7G **93**
Leverton Ct. *W Bri* —3H **83**
Leverton Grn. *Nott* —6A **82**
Leverton Wlk. *Arn* —5J **33**
Levick Ct. *Nott* —5E **64**
Lewcote La. *W Hal* —5J **43**
Lewindon Ct. *Wd'p* —2G **49**
Lewis Clo. *Nott* —1F **65** (1G **5**)
Lewis Ellise Home, The. *Der*
        —2F **73**
Lewis St. *Der* —7K **73**
Lewiston Rd. *Chad* —3H **75**
Lexington Gdns. *Nott* —2F **49**
Lexington Rd. *Chad* —2J **75**
Leybourne Dri. *Nott* —7A **32**
Leycote Way. *Belp* —7K **9**
Leyland Clo. *Bees* —6K **79**
Leyland Ct. *Der* —1J **73**
Leyland Gdns. *Der* —1J **73**
Leylands. *Der* —7J **55**
Leyland St. *Der* —1J **73**
Leys Ct. *Belp* —1D **24**
Leys Ct. *Rud* —3E **100**
Leys Fld. Gdns. *Chel* —7G **93**
Leys Rd. *Rud* —3E **100**
Leys, The. *Keyw* —2D **102**
Leys, The. *L Eat* —4D **40**
Leys, The. *Low* —3D **36**
Leys, The. *Nott* —7J **81**
Ley St. *N'fld* —7E **50**
Leyton Cres. *Bees* —3H **81**
Leytonstone Dri. *Der* —3E **72**
Library Rd. *Nott* —6J **63**
Lichfield Clo. *Bees* —5J **79**
Lichfield Clo. *Long E* —2K **97**
Lichfield Rd. *Nott* —3J **65**
Liddell Gro. *Nott* —2F **63**
Liddington St. *Nott* —5B **48**
Lidgate Clo. *Mick* —7A **72**
Lido. —5E **48**
Lilac Av. *Cltn* —6A **50**
Lilac Av. *Kgswy* —3E **72**
Lilac Clo. *Alv* —3G **93**
Lilac Clo. *Keyw* —7E **102**
Lilac Clo. *Nott* —5E **46**
Lilac Ct. *Alv* —3G **93**
Lilac Ct. *Nott* —7J **81**
Lilac Cres. *Bees* —3H **81**
Lilac Gro. *Bees* —3H **81**
Lilac M. *Ilk* —3B **44**
Lilac Rd. *Huck* —7H **17**
Lilacs, The. *Bees* —2G **81**
Lilac Way. *Alst* —5H **55**
Lilian Hind Ct. *Nott* —5F **31**
Lilian Prime Clo. *Alv* —1H **93**
Lilleker Ri. *Arn* —4G **33**
Lilley St. *Alv* —3H **93**
Lillie Ter. *Nott* —3H **65**
Lillington Rd. *Nott* —6H **31**
Lily Av. *N'fld* —7E **50**
Lily Gro. *Bees* —3H **81**
Lilypool, The. *Melb* —4H **113**
Lime Av. *Bread* —5D **56**
Lime Av. *Der* —5K **73** (7C **6**)
Lime Av. *Duf* —2J **39**
Lime Av. *Lan M* —3A **28**
Lime Av. *Rip* —3K **11**
Lime Clo. *Nut* —7A **30**
Lime Clo. *Rad T* —4K **67**
Lime Cres. *Belp* —3B **24**
Lime Cft. *Alst* —3K **55**
Limedale Av. *Oak* —4H **57**
Limefield Ct. *W Bri* —6J **65**
Lime Gro. *Chad* —3H **75**
Lime Gro. *Dray* —2H **95**
Lime Gro. *Long E* —1H **97**
Lime Gro. *Sand* —2F **79**
Lime Gro. *S'fd* —3H **79**
Lime Gro. Av. *Bees* —3E **80**
Limekiln Ct. *Nott* —5G **31**
Lime La. *Arn* —7G **19**
Lime La. *Oak & M'ly* —4G **57**
  (in two parts)
Limerick Rd. *Der* —4H **75**
Limes Av. *Mick* —7B **72**
Limes Pk. *Rip* —3J **11**
Limes, The. *Bar F* —3E **98**
Limes, The. *M'ley* —3G **43**
Lime St. *Ilk* —7D **44**
Lime St. *Nott* —6H **31**
Lime Ter. *Long E* —1H **97**
Lime Tree Av. *Der* —3K **73** (3B **6**)

Lime Tree Av. *Nott* —3H **47** (Broxtowe La.)
Lime Tree Av. *Nott* —4H **63** (Digby Av.)
Limetree Clo. *Keyw* —7D **102**
Lime Tree Ct. *Bees* —6G **63**
Limetree Ct. *Ilk* —1A **60**
Lime Tree Gdns. *Low* —4E **36**
Limetree Ri. *Ilk* —1A **60**
Lime Tree Rd. *Huck* —1H **31**
Lime Wlk. *L'ver* —7H **73**
Limmen Gdns. *Nott*
   —1G **65** (1J **5**)
Limpenny St. *Nott* —1C **64** (1A **4**)
Linacres Dri. *Chel* —7G **93**
Linby Av. *Huck* —5H **17**
Linby Clo. *Ged* —4C **50**
Linby Clo. *Nott* —1F **49**
Linby Dri. *Strel* —4D **46**
Linby Gro. *Huck* —4H **17**
Linby La. *L'by & Pap* —1H **17**
Linby Rd. *Huck* —4H **17**
Linby St. *Nott* —5J **31**
Linby Wlk. *Huck* —4G **17**
Lincoln Av. *Der* —1G **93**
Lincoln Av. *Sand* —4E **78**
Lincoln Cir. *Nott* —5C **64** (5A **4**)
Lincoln Clo. *S'fd* —6J **61**
Lincoln Ct. *Nott* —7E **46**
Lincoln Grn. *Chel* —7F **93**
Lincoln Gro. *Rad T* —4K **67**
Lincoln St. *Nott* —2E **64** (3F **5**)
Lincoln St. *Old B* —3A **48**
Lindale Clo. *Gam* —2A **84**
Lindbridge Rd. *Nott* —4F **47**
Linden Av. *Nott* —7J **81**
Linden Clo. *Klbrn* —5H **25**
Linden Ct. *Bees* —3G **81**
Linden Gro. *Bees* —3G **81**
Linden Gro. *Ged* —5F **51**
Linden Gro. *Sand* —1E **78**
Linden Gro. *S'fd* —2J **79**
Linden St. *Nott* —7F **49**
Lindfield Clo. *Nott* —4G **47**
Lindfield Rd. *Nott* —4F **47**
Lindford Clo. *Oak* —4F **57**
Lindisfarne Clo. *Sin* —6H **91**
Lindisfarne Gdns. *Nott* —4C **32**
Lindley St. *Newt* —1F **29**
Lindley Ter. *Nott* —7A **48**
Lindon Dri. *Alv* —3J **93**
Lindrick Clo. *Edw* —4A **84**
Lindrick Clo. *Mick* —6D **72**
Lindsay St. *Nott* —7B **48**
Lindsey Clo. *Der* —2E **74**
Lindum Gro. *Nott* —4H **65**
Lindum Rd. *Nott* —3K **47**
Linette Clo. *Nott* —4C **48**
Linford Ct. *Bees* —3B **62**
Ling Cres. *Rud* —1E **100**
Lingfield Ct. *Nott* —4D **62**
Lingfield Ri. *Mick* —5A **72**
Lingford. *Cotg* —5A **86**
Lingford St. *Huck* —6H **17**
Lingmell Clo. *W Bri* —2A **84**
Lingwood La. *Wdbgh* —3F **35**
Linkin Rd. *Bees* —2C **80**
Linkmel Clo. *Nott* —6C **64**
Linkmel Rd. *Eastw* —2A **28**
Links Clo. *Sin* —5K **91**
Linksfield Ct. *W Bri* —6E **82**
Linnell St. *Nott* —1H **65**
Linnet Clo. *Spon* —2B **76**
Linnet Hill. *Mick* —2K **89**
Linsdale Clo. *Nott* —2B **62**
Linsdale Gdns. *Ged* —2B **50**
Linton Ri. *Nott* —1J **65**
Linwood Cres. *Eastw* —4D **28**
Lion Clo. *Nott* —4J **47**
Liskeard Dri. *Alst* —3H **55**
Lismore Clo. *Nott* —2A **64**
Lismore Ct. *Sin* —6H **91**
Lissett Av. *Ilk* —7C **44**
Lister Clo. *Der* —5F **73**
Lister Ct. *Nott* —5A **64**
Listergate. *Nott* —3E **64** (5F **5**)
Listergate Sq. *Nott* —3E **64** (5F **5**)
Liston Dri. *Der* —7K **55**
Listowel Cres. *Nott* —1A **100**
Litchchurch St. *Der*
   —5B **74** (7G **7**)
Litchen Clo. *Ilk* —4D **44**
Litchfield Dri. *Der* —2G **93**
Litchfield Ri. *Arn* —3G **33**
Litchurch La. *Der* —6C **74**
Litchurch Plaza. *Der* —6C **74**
Littlebounds. *W Bri* —1F **83**
Lit. Bridge St. *Der* —2K **73** (2B **6**)
Littledale Clo. *Oak* —4J **57**

Lit. Eaton By-Pass. *H'brk & L Eat*
   —7E **24**
Lit. Eaton By-Pass. *L Eat* —2C **56**
Littlegreen Rd. *Wd'p* —1H **49**
Lit. Hallam Hill. *Ilk* —2C **60**
Lit. Hallam La. *Ilk* —1D **60**
Lit. Hayes. *W Bri* —4E **82**
Lit. John Wlk. *Nott* —7F **49**
Little La. *C'tn* —5B **20**
Little La. *Kimb* —1K **45**
Little La. *Toll* —5C **84**
Lit. Lime La. *Arn* —7G **19** (in two parts)
Lit. Longstone Clo. *Mick* —6D **72**
Lit. Lunnon. *Bar F* —3E **98**
Lit. Meadow. *Cotg* —6A **86**
Lit. Meadow Rd. *Chel* —7G **93**
Littlemore La. *Bradm* —6G **101**
Lit. Noel St. *Der* —2H **73**
Lit. Oakwood Dri. *Nott* —3K **31**
Littleover Cres. *Der* —1H **91**
Littleover La. *Der* —1H **91**
Lit. Ox. *Colw* —3D **66**
Lit. Parliament St. *Der*
   —4K **73** (6B **6**)
Lit. Tennis St. *Nott* —4J **65**
Lit. Tennis St. S. *Nott* —5J **65**
Littlewell La. *Stan D* —5D **60**
Lit. Woodbury Dri. *L'ver* —3D **90**
Lit. Wood Ct. *Huck* —7E **16**
Littlewood Gdns. *Nott* —2C **62**
Litton Clo. *Belp* —7B **10**
Litton Clo. *Ilk* —2C **44**
Litton Clo. *Wd'p* —2G **49**
Litton Dri. *Spon* —5B **76**
Liverpool St. *Der* —7E **56**
Liverpool St. *Nott* —2G **65** (3J **5**)
Liversage Almshouses. *Der*
   —4B **74** (6F **7**)
Liversage Ct. *Der* —4B **74** (6G **7**)
Liversage Pl. *Der* —4B **74** (6F **7**)
Liversage Rd. *Der* —4B **74** (6F **7**)
Liversage St. *Der* —4B **74** (5F **7**)
Liversage Wlk. *Der* —4B **74** (5G **7**)
Livingstone Rd. *Der* —7J **73**
Llanberis Gro. *Nott* —4J **47**
Lloyd St. *Der* —3H **73**
Lloyd St. *Nott* —4E **48**
Loach Ct. *Nott* —2J **63**
Lobelia Clo. *Nott* —7F **49**
Lochinvar Clo. *Spon* —4B **76**
Lock Clo. *Bees* —5G **81**
Lock Clo. *Ilk* —1A **60**
Lockerbie St. *Cltn* —1D **66**
Lockington Clo. *Chel* —7F **93**
**Lockington Pk. —5D 108**
Lockington Rd. *H'ton* —5B **108**
Lock La. *Long E* —5F **97**
Lock La. *Sand* —3F **79**
Locko Ct. *Spon* —3K **75**
**Locko Pk. —5B 58**
Locko Rd. *Der* —4K **57**
Locksley La. *Nott* —4A **82**
Lockton Av. *Hean* —5G **27**
Lock-up Yd. *Der* —3A **74** (4E **6**)
Lockwood Clo. *Bees* —4J **81**
Lockwood Clo. *Nott* —4C **32**
Lockwood Rd. *Alst* —3H **55**
Locomotive Way. *Pri P*
   —5D **74** (7K **7**)
Lodge Clo. *Duf* —3J **39**
Lodge Clo. *Etw* —5E **88**
Lodge Clo. *Nott* —6K **47**
Lodge Clo. *Red* —3G **33**
Lodge Dri. *Belp* —7J **9**
Lodge Est. *Ast T* —3D **106**
Lodge Farm La. *Arn* —4G **33**
Lodge La. *Der* —2K **73** (2C **6**)
Lodge La. *Lan M* —6G **13**
Lodge La. *Shot* —3B **8**
Lodge La. *Spon* —4K **75**
Lodge La. N. *Spon* —4K **75**
Lodge M. *Ast T* —3D **106**
Lodge Rd. *Long E* —4H **97**
Lodge Rd. *M'ley* —3G **43**
Lodge Rd. *Newt* —5E **28**
Lodge Row. *M'ley* —3G **43**
Lodge St. *Dray* —2J **95**
Lodge Way. *Mick* —7B **72**
Lodgewood Clo. *Nott* —7G **31**
Lodore Clo. *W Bri* —2A **84**
Logan Sq. *Nott* —2A **48**
Logan St. *Nott* —7J **31**
Lois Av. *Nott* —4B **64**
Lombard Clo. *Nott* —4B **64**
Lombard St. *Der* —2D **72**
Lombardy Lodge. *Bees* —7A **80**
Lomond Av. *Sin* —7K **91**
London Rd. *Der* —4A **74** (5E **6**)

London Rd. *Keg* —2H **117**
London Rd. *Nott* —3F **65** (6H **5**) (in two parts)
London Rd. *Shard* —7G **95**
Long Acre. *Bing* —3A **70**
Long Acre. *Huck* —5D **16**
Longacre. *Wd'p* —2H **49**
Long Acre E. *Bing* —3B **70**
Longbeck Av. *Nott* —5J **49**
Longbridge La. *Der* —1D **92**
Longbridge La. *Hean* —2F **27**
Longclose Ct. *Nott* —7G **31**
Long Cottage. *Ast T* —2D **106**
Long Cft. *Ast T* —2C **106**
Longdale Rd. *Nott* —7F **33**
Longden Clo. *Bees* —5K **61**
Longden St. *Nott* —2G **65** (3J **5**)
Longdon's Row. *Spon* —3K **75**
**Long Eaton Stadium. —1K 97**
Longfellows Clo. *Nott* —5D **32**
Longfield Cres. *Ilk* —2D **60**
Longfield La. *Ilk* —2D **60**
Longford Clo. *Alst* —6H **55**
Longford Cres. *Nott* —3J **31**
Longford St. *Der* —7H **55**
Long Hill Ri. *Huck* —6F **17**
Long Holden. *Dis* —6B **116**
Longlands Clo. *Bees* —4H **81**
Longlands Dri. *W Bri* —3B **84**
Longlands La. *Find* —7A **90**
Longlands Rd. *Bees* —4H **81**
Longlands Vs. *Ambgt* —1K **9**
Long La. *Bees* —6D **80**
Long La. *Keg* —4H **109**
Long La. *Ship* —7B **28**
Long La. *Watn* —4A **30**
Longleat Cres. *Bees* —3C **80**
Longley La. *Spon* —2K **75**
Longmead Rd. *Nott* —7E **32**
Longmead Dri. *Nott* —7E **32**
Long Mdw. Hill. *Low* —3K **35**
Long Mere La. *Belt* —7K **115**
Longmoor Av. *Low* —5E **36**
Longmoor Gdns. *Long E* —6E **78**
Longmoor La. *Breas* —7C **78**
Longmoor La. *Sand* —6E **78**
Longmoor Rd. *Long E* —6E **78**
Longore Sq. *Nott* —3K **63**
Longridge Rd. *Wd'p* —2H **49**
Long Row. *Belp* —1K **23**
Long Row. *King S* —6A **110**
Long Row. *Nott* —3E **64** (4E **4**)
Long Row. *Shard* —7K **95**
Long Row E. *Nott* —3E **64** (4F **5**)
Long Row W. *Nott* —3E **64** (4E **4**)
Long Stairs. *Nott* —3F **65** (5H **5**)
Longstock Clo. *Oak* —6E **56**
Longstone Ri. *Belp* —6B **10**
Longstone Wlk. *Der*
   —4K **73** (6C **6**)
Longthorpe Clo. *L'ver* —2E **90**
Longthorpe Ct. *Arn* —6H **33**
Longue Dri. *C'tn* —5B **20** (in two parts)
Longwall Av. *Q Dri & Nott* —6C **64**
Longwalls La. *Black* —5F **9**
Long W. Cft. *C'tn* —4A **20**
Long Whatton Rd. *Dis* —6A **116**
Longwood Ct. *Nott* —5B **32**
Lonscale Clo. *W Bri* —3A **84**
Lonsdale Dri. *Bees* —6J **79**
Lonsdale Pl. *Der* —4H **73**
Lonsdale Rd. *Nott* —1A **64**
Loom Clo. *Belp* —7C **10**
Lord Haddon Rd. *Ilk* —5C **44**
Lord Nelson St. *Nott* —3H **65**
Lord St. *Altn* —4D **92**
Lord St. *Nott* —3H **65** (4K **5**)
Lorimer Av. *Ged* —3D **50**
Lorna Ct. *Nott* —5F **49**
Lorne Clo. *Nott* —7E **48**
Lorne Gro. *Rad T* —4K **67**
Lorne St. *Der* —5K **73** (7B **6**)
Lorne Wlk. *Nott* —7E **48**
Lorraine Clo. *Shel L* —6E **92**
Lortas Rd. *Nott* —4B **48**
Loscoe-Denby La. *Den V & Los*
   —2C **26**
Loscoe Gdns. *Nott* —5D **48**
Loscoe Grange. *Los* —2E **26**
Loscoe Mt. Rd. *Nott* —4E **48**
Loscoe Rd. *Chad* —6G **57**
Loscoe Rd. *Hean* —2F **27**
Loscoe Rd. *Nott* —5E **48**
Lothian Pl. *Cas D* —7J **107**
Lothian Pl. *Der* —1D **74** (1K **7**)
Lothian Rd. *Toll* —7A **84**
Lothlorien Clo. *L'ver* —2F **91**
Lothmore Ct. *Nott* —5D **64**

Lotus Clo. *Nott* —7G **49**
Loudon St. *Der* —5A **74**
Loudoun Pl. *Cas D* —6J **107**
Loughborough Av. *Nott* —3H **65**
Loughborough Rd. *Bradm*
   —4F **101**
Loughborough Rd. *W Bri & Rud*
   —2G **83**
Loughrigg Clo. *Nott* —6D **64**
Louis Av. *Bees* —1E **80**
Louise Av. *N'fld* —6E **50**
Louise Greaves La. *Spon* —2A **76**
Louvain Rd. *Der* —5G **73**
Love I Clo. *Nott* —1F **47**
Lowater St. *Cltn* —7F **49**
Lowcroft. *Wd'p* —2H **49**
Lowcham La. *Wdbgh* —1H **35**
Lowcham Rd. *Epp* —1A **36**
Lowcham Rd. *Ged* —3A **50**
Lowcham Rd. *Low & Gun* —5E **36**
Lowcham St. *Nott* —2G **65** (3J **5**)
Lwr. Bagthorpe. *Bagt* —1D **14**
Lwr. Beauvale. *Newt* —2E **28**
Lwr. Bloomsgrove Rd. *Ilk* —4D **44**
Lwr. Brook St. *Long E* —2J **97**
Lwr. Canaan. *Rud* —1F **101**
Lwr. Chapel St. *Ilk* —5D **44**
Lwr. Clara Mt. Rd. *Hean* —4J **27**
Lower Ct. *Bees* —1G **81**
Lwr. Dale Rd. *Der* —6K **73**
Lwr. Dunstead Rd. *Lan M* —2J **27**
Lwr. Eldon St. *Nott*
   —3G **65** (5K **5**)
Lwr. Eley St. *Der* —5K **73** (7C **6**)
Lwr. Gladstone St. *Hean* —3G **27**
Lwr. Granby St. *Ilk* —4D **44**
Lower Grn. *Find* —7B **90**
Lwr. Hall Clo. *Holb* —7C **24**
Lwr. Maples. *Ship* —5J **27**
Lwr. Middleton St. *Ilk* —5E **44**
Lwr. Nelson St. *Hean* —3F **27**
Lwr. Orchard St. *S'fd* —1H **79**
Lwr. Park St. *S'fd* —2G **79**
Lwr. Parliament St. *Nott*
   —2F **65** (3F **5**)
Lwr. Regent St. *Bees* —2G **81**
Lower Rd. *Bees* —1H **81**
Lower Rd. *Mack* —7C **54**
Lwr. Stanton Rd. *Ilk* —1D **60**
Lwr. Whitworth Rd. *Ilk* —1D **60**
Lowes Hill. *Rip* —1K **11**
Low Row. *Nott* —3E **64** (4E **4**) (in two parts)
Lowes La. *Swar* —2C **104**
Lowe St. *Altn* —3E **92**
Loweswater Ct. *Gam* —1A **84**
Lowlands Dri. *Keyw* —5D **102**
Lowlands Lea. *Hean* —3H **27**
Lowlands Rd. *Belp* —7B **10**
Low Pavement. *Nott*
   —3E **64** (5F **5**)
Lows Ct. *Chel* —7H **93**
Lows La. *Stan D* —5D **60** (in two parts)
Low Wood Rd. *Nott* —1E **46**
Loxley Clo. *Oak* —5H **57**
Loxley Ct. *Nott* —6H **47**
Loxton Ct. *Mick* —5B **72**
Loyne Clo. *Sin* —7K **91**
Lucas La. *Hilt* —7A **88**
Luccombe Dri. *Alv* —4K **93**
Lucerne Clo. *Nott* —2D **82**
Lucerne Rd. *Oak* —4J **57**
Lucknow Av. *Nott* —6F **49**
Lucknow Ct. *Nott* —6F **49**
Lucknow Dri. *Nott* —6F **49**
Lucknow Rd. *Nott* —6F **49**
Ludford Rd. *Nott* —5J **31**
Ludgate Clo. *Arn* —3C **32**
Ludgate Dri. *E Bri* —4K **53**
Ludgate Wlk. *Der* —3C **72**
Ludham Av. *Nott* —5H **31**
Ludlam Av. *Gilt* —6E **28**
Ludlow Av. *W Bri* —1H **83**
Ludlow Clo. *Bees* —6D **62**
Ludlow Clo. *Spon* —3B **76**
Ludlow Hill Rd. *W Bri* —3H **83**
Lulworth Clo. *L'ver* —3H **91**
Lulworth Clo. *W Bri* —3E **82**
Lulworth Ct. *Kimb* —6K **29**
Lumb La. *H'wd* —3E **22** (in three parts)
Lundie Clo. *Sten F* —7H **91**
Lune Clo. *Bees* —5E **80**
Lupin Clo. *Nott* —7F **49**
Lupin Clo. *Oak* —4J **57**
Luther Clo. *Nott* —7G **49**
Luton Clo. *Nott* —5K **47**
Lutterell Ct. *W Bri* —3F **83**
Lutterell Way. *W Bri* —3K **83**

Lybster M. *Nott* —5D **64**
Lychgate Clo. *Oak* —5D **56**
Lychgate Ct. *Wat* —5K **29**
Lydia Gdns. *Eastw* —4C **28**
Lydney Pk. *W Bri* —2D **82**
Lydstep Clo. *Oak* —5J **57**
Lyle Clo. *Kimb* —6J **29**
Lyme Pk. *W Bri* —3D **82**
Lymington Gdns. *Nott* —1H **65**
Lymn Av. *Ged* —4D **50**
Lynam Ct. *Nott* —6H **31**
Lyncombe Gdns. *Keyw* —5D **102**
Lyncroft Av. *Rip* —2A **12**
Lyndale Dri. *Cod* —4D **12**
Lyndale Rd. *Bees* —7A **62**
Lynden Av. *Long E* —3H **97**
Lyndhurst Gdns. *W Bri* —4F **83**
Lyndhurst Gro. *Chad* —3G **75**
Lyndhurst Gro. *Long E* —7H **79**
Lyndhurst Rd. *Nott* —3H **65**
Lyndhurst St. *Der* —6A **74**
Lyngs, The. *E Bri* —4J **53**
Lynmouth Cres. *Nott* —7A **48**
Lynmouth Dri. *Ilk* —3B **44**
Lynncroft. *Eastw* —2E **28**
Lynstead Dri. *Huck* —7C **16**
Lynton Clo. *Rip* —1K **11**
Lynton Ct. *Nott* —7H **49**
Lynton Gdns. *Arn* —5J **33**
Lynton Rd. *Ambgt* —1A **10**
Lynton Rd. *Bees* —2C **80**
Lynton St. *Der* —4J **73** (6A **6**)
Lynwood Rd. *Sin* —5K **91**
Lyons Clo. *Rud* —1D **100**
Lytham Clo. *Der* —6D **56**
Lytham Dri. *Edw* —5A **84**
Lytham Gdns. *Nott* —4C **32**
Lythe Clo. *Nott* —3C **82**
Lyttelton St. *Der* —3G **73**
Lytton Clo. *Nott* —2G **65** (2J **5**)

**M**abel Gro. *W Bri* —7J **65**
Mabel St. *Nott* —5F **65** (7G **5**)
Macaulay St. *Sin* —4A **92**
Macauley Gro. *Nut* —7B **30**
Macdonald Sq. *Ilk* —2A **60**
Machins La. *Edw* —5J **83**
Mackenzie St. *Der* —2G **73**
Mackinley Av. *S'fd* —6J **61**
Macklin St. *Der* —3K **73** (4C **6**)
**Mackworth Castle. —7C 54 (remains of)**
Mackworth Rd. *Der*
   —2J **73** (1A **6**)
Maclaren Gdns. *Rud* —3F **101**
Maclean Rd. *Cltn* —7A **50**
Macmillan Clo. *Nott* —4H **49**
Macready Pl. *Alv* —2F **93**
Madeley Ct. *Mick* —7B **72**
Madeley St. *Der* —6A **74**
Madford Bus. Pk. *Day* —7F **33**
Madison Av. *Chad* —1E **74**
Madryn Wlk. *Nott* —6C **32**
Mafeking St. *Nott* —3J **65**
Magdala Rd. *Nott* —6E **48**
Magdalen Dri. *E Bri* —3K **53**
Magdalene Way. *Huck* —4G **17**
Magna Clo. *Low* —4E **36**
Magnolia Clo. *Nott* —5E **46**
Magnolia Ct. *Bees* —6D **62**
Magnolia Gro. *Huck* —1H **31**
Magnus St. *Bees* —2G **81**
Magnus Rd. *Nott* —3E **48**
Magson Clo. *Nott* —2G **65** (2K **5**)
Maiden La. *Nott* —3F **65** (4H **5**)
Maidens Dale. *Arn* —5F **33**
Maid Marian Way. *Nott*
   —3D **64** (4D **4**)
Maidstone Dri. *Alv* —4F **93**
Maidstone Dri. *Nott* —5D **62**
Maidwell Clo. *Belp* —6B **10**
Main Av. *Alst* —2K **55**
Maine Dri. *Chad* —2G **75**
Main Rd. *Cotg* —1H **85**
Main Rd. *Ged* —5D **50**
Main Rd. *Jack* —1K **13**
Main Rd. *Lent* —2J **81**
Main Rd. *Lwr H* —1F **11**
Main Rd. *M'ly & Smal* —3G **57**
Main Rd. *Plum* —1C **102**
Main Rd. *Rad T* —4J **67**
Main Rd. *Shelf* —6C **52**
Main Rd. *Thul* —3C **94**
Main Rd. *Und* —1C **14**
Main Rd. *Watn* —4D **29**
Main Rd. *Wilf* —2D **82**
Mainside Cres. *Und* —3E **14**
Main St. *Ambtn* —3F **95**

Main St. *Asl* —3J **71**
Main St. *Aws* —1G **45**
Main St. *Bradm* —6G **101**
Main St. *Breas* —1B **96**
Main St. *Bree H* —7B **114**
Main St. *Brins* —3B **14**
Main St. *Bulw* —7H **31**
(in two parts)
Main St. *Burna* —4H **89**
Main St. *Bur J* —2K **51**
Main St. *C'tn* —4K **19**
Main St. *C But* —1G **87**
Main St. *E Bri* —3J **53**
Main St. *Eastw* —4D **28**
Main St. *Epp* —6J **21**
Main St. *Etw* —5D **88**
Main St. *Find* —7B **90**
Main St. *Gam* —1A **84**
Main St. *Gun* —1F **53**
Main St. *H'ton* —6B **108**
Main St. *Hors W* —6H **25**
Main St. *Hov* —3K **87**
Main St. *Keyw* —7C **102**
Main St. *Kimb* —7K **29**
Main St. *Lamb* —6E **35**
Main St. *L'by* —1G **17**
Main St. *Locki* —6D **108**
Main St. *Long E* —2J **97**
Main St. *Long W* —7F **117**
Main St. *Low* —3D **36**
Main St. *M'ley* —3G **43**
Main St. *Melb* —5A **114**
(Dog La.)
Main St. *Melb* —2H **113**
(Kings Newton La.)
Main St. *Newt* —3G **29**
Main St. *Oxt* —1F **21**
Main St. *Pap* —1K **17**
Main St. *Shelf* —5C **52**
Main St. *Stan D* —7D **60**
Main St. *Strel* —4B **46**
Main St. *Tickn* —7A **112**
Main St. *Wstn T* —6A **106**
Main St. *What* —4K **71**
Main St. *Wdbgh* —1F **35**
Main St. Bulwell. *Bulw* —6H **31**
Maitland Av. *Wd'p* —2H **49**
Maitland Rd. *Wd'p* —2H **49**
Maize Clo. *L'ver* —3E **90**
Major St. *Nott* —2E **64** (2E **4**)
Makeney Rd. *Duf* —4K **39**
Makeney Rd. *Holb* —7B **24**
Makeney Rd. *Mak & Milf* —7A **24**
Malbon Clo. *Nott* —6H **49**
Malcolm Clo. *Nott* —7E **48**
Malcolm Gro. *L'ver* —1C **90**
Malcolm St. *Der* —6B **74**
Maldon Clo. *Bees* —4C **80**
Maldon Clo. *Long E* —4J **97**
Malham Rd. *L'ver* —3D **90**
Malin Clo. *Alv* —4H **93**
Malin Hill. *Nott* —3F **65** (5G **5**)
Malkin Av. *Rad T* —3A **68**
Mallard Clo. *Bing* —4C **70**
Mallard Clo. *Nott* —2B **48**
Mallard Ct. *Bees* —3G **81**
Mallard Rd. *Cltn* —1F **67**
Mallard Wlk. *Mick* —2A **90**
Malling Wlk. *Nott* —5G **49**
Mallow Way. *Bing* —3J **69**
(in two parts)
Malmesbury Rd. *Nott* —2J **49**
Maltby Clo. *Alst* —5K **55**
Maltby Clo. *Nott* —4H **47**
Maltby Rd. *Nott* —2J **49**
Malt Cotts. *Nott* —5B **48**

**Malt Cross Music Hall, The.**
—4E **4**

Malthouse Clo. *Eastw* —4D **28**
Malthouse Ct. *E Bri* —3J **53**
Malthouse La. *Neth H* —2B **10**
Malthouse Rd. *Ilk* —2D **60**
Malthouse Yd. *Rip* —3K **11**
Malting Clo. *Rud* —3E **100**
Maltings, The. *C Bis* —4G **87**
Maltings, The. *Der* —4A **74** (5E **6**)
Maltings, The. *Nott* —7H **49**
Maltings, The. *Shard* —1J **107**
Maltmill La. *Nott* —3F **65** (5F **5**)
Malton Pl. *Der* —6D **56**
Malton Rd. *Nott* —4B **48**
Malt St. *Got* —1H **111**
Malvern Clo. *Mick* —5B **72**
Malvern Clo. *Nott* —5G **49**
Malvern Ct. *Bees* —2H **81**
Malvern Cres. *W Bri* —3H **83**
Malvern Gdns. *Long E* —1E **96**
Malvern Rd. *Nott* —5G **49**
Malvern Rd. *W Bri* —3G **83**

Malvern Way. *Der* —6D **56**
Manchester St. *Der* —2H **73**
Manchester St. *Long E* —3H **97**
Mandalay St. *Nott* —2K **47**
Manesty Cres. *Nott* —2A **100**
Manifold Dri. *Alv* —1H **93**
Manifold Gdns. *Nott* —5E **64**
Manly Clo. *Nott* —5A **32**
Manners Av. *Ilk* —5B **44**
Manners Ind. Est. *Ilk* —5B **44**
Manners Rd. *Ilk* —5C **44**
Manners St. *Ilk* —1E **60**
Manning St. *Nott* —7F **49**
Manning Vw. *Ilk* —4D **44**
Mannion Cres. *Long E* —4F **97**
Manns Leys. *Cotg* —6J **85**
Mann St. *Nott* —6B **48**
Manor Av. *Bees* —2F **81**
(Dovecote La.)
Manor Av. *Bees* —5E **80**
(Kelsey Clo.)
Manor Av. *Der* —5G **73**
Manor Av. *Nott* —3G **65** (5K **5**)
Manor Av. *S'fd* —7H **61**
Manor Clo. *Belp* —3A **24**
Manor Clo. *Edw* —5K **83**
Manor Clo. *Long W* —7F **117**
Manor Ct. *Bar T* —5B **104**
Manor Ct. *Bees* —1B **80**
Manor Ct. *Breas* —1C **96**
Manor Ct. *Cltn* —7D **50**
Manor Cres. *Cltn* —6D **50**
Manor Cft. *Nott* —3A **48**
Manor Cft. *Rip* —1K **11**
Mnr. Farm La. *Nott* —6A **82**
Mnr. Farm M. *Burna* —4H **89**
Mnr. Farm Rd. *Ast T* —2D **106**
Mnr. Fields Dri. *Ilk* —7B **44**
Manor Grn. Wlk. *Cltn* —6D **50**
Manor Ho. Clo. *Low* —3D **36**
Manor Ho. Rd. *Long E* —2K **97**
Manor La. *Shelf* —5C **52**
Manor Leigh. *Breas* —1C **96**
Manor Pk. *Borr* —7C **76**
Manor Pk. *Rud* —2D **100**
Manor Pk. Ct. *Der* —5F **73**
Manor Pk. Way. *Der* —5F **73**
Manor Ri. *E Bri* —2J **53**
Manor Rd. *Bar F* —3E **98**
Manor Rd. *Belp* —2K **23**
Manor Rd. *Bing* —3B **70**
Manor Rd. *Borr* —7C **76**
Manor Rd. *C'tn* —5C **20**
Manor Rd. *Cltn* —6D **50**
Manor Rd. *Chel* —1F **105**
Manor Rd. *Der* —5G **73**
Manor Rd. *Eastw* —4D **28**
Manor Rd. *Ilk* —5C **44**
Manor Rd. *Keyw* —6C **102**
Manor Rd. *Nott* —3G **65** (6K **5**)
Manorwood Rd. *Cotg* —6K **85**
Mansell Clo. *Eastw* —4F **29**
Mansfield Ct. *Nott* —6D **48**
Mansfield Gro. *Nott*
—1D **64** (1D **4**)
Mansfield La. *C'tn* —3D **20**
Mansfield Rd. *Bread* —4F **57**
Mansfield Rd. *Der & Oak*
—2A **74** (1E **6**)
Mansfield Rd. *Eastw* —7C **14**
Mansfield Rd. *Hean* —3H **27**
Mansfield Rd. *Nott* —7D **48** (1E **4**)
Mansfield Rd. *Und* —3E **14**
Mansfields Cft. *Etw* —5D **88**
Mansfield St. *Der* —1A **74** (1E **6**)
Mansfield St. *Nott* —4E **48**
Manston M. *Nott* —1B **64**
Manthorpe Cres. *Nott* —3H **49**
Manton Cres. *Bees* —7F **63**
Manvers Av. *Rip* —3A **12**
Manvers Ct. *Nott* —3G **65** (4J **5**)
Manvers Gro. *Rad T* —4K **67**
Manvers Rd. *W Bri* —2H **83**
Manvers St. *N'fld* —1E **66**
Manvers St. *Nott* —3G **65** (4J **5**)
Manvers St. *Rip* —3A **12**
Manville Clo. *Bees* —4B **62**
Manville Clo. *Nott* —1J **63**
Maori Clo. *Huck* —7D **16**
Maple Av. *Bees* —3H **81**
Maple Av. *L'ver* —3H **91**
Maple Av. *Rip* —3J **11**
Maple Av. *Sand* —1F **79**
Maplebeck Ct. *Der* —2A **74** (1E **6**)
Maplebeck Rd. *Arn* —6J **33**
Maple Clo. *Bing* —3C **70**
Maple Clo. *Keyw* —7E **102**
Maple Clo. *Rad T* —5K **67**
Maple Ct. *Kimb* —7K **29**

Mapledene Cres. *Nott* —4C **62**
Maple Dri. *Alv* —3G **93**
Maple Dri. *Ast T* —4C **106**
Maple Dri. *Belp* —3B **24**
Maple Dri. *Chel* —1F **105**
Maple Dri. *Ged* —4F **51**
Maple Dri. *Huck* —7E **16**
Maple Dri. *Nut* —7B **30**
Maple Gdns. *Hean* —4F **27**
Maple Gro. *Alst* —2H **55**
Maple Gro. *Breas* —1B **96**
Maples St. *Nott* —7B **48**
Maplestead Av. *Nott* —2D **82**
Mapleton Av. *Chad* —6F **57**
Mapleton Rd. *Dray* —1J **95**
Mapletree Clo. *Nott* —6D **32**
Maple Way. *Nott* —4G **83**
Mapperley Brook. *M'ley* —4J **43**
Mapperley Cres. *Nott* —4G **49**

**Mapperley Golf Course.** —2K **49**
Mapperley Hall Dri. *Nott* —5E **48**
Mapperley Hall Gdns. *Nott*
—5F **49**
Mapperley La. *M'ley & W Hal*
—4G **43**
Mapperley Orchard. *Arn* —6K **33**
Mapperley Pk. Dri. *Nott* —6E **48**
Mapperley Plains. *Nott* —1K **49**

**Mapperley Reservoir Nature
Trail.** —2G **43**
Mapperley Ri. *Nott* —4G **49**
Mapperley Rd. *Nott* —7E **48**
Mapperley St. *Nott* —4E **48**
March Clo. *Nott* —6A **32**
Marchesi Clo. *Huck* —1E **30**
Marchington Clo. *Alst* —6J **55**
Marchwood Clo. *Nott* —2K **63**
Marcus St. *Der* —1A **74**
Mardale Clo. *W Bri* —3A **84**
Maree Clo. *Sin* —5J **91**
Marfleet Clo. *Mick* —5B **72**
Margaret Av. *Ilk* —6D **44**
Margaret Av. *Long E* —7K **79**
Margaret Av. *Sand* —4F **79**
Margaret Cres. *Ged* —4C **50**
Margaret Pl. *Bing* —2K **69**
Margarets Ct. *Bees* —7A **62**
Margaret St. *Der* —1A **74** (1D **6**)
Margreave Rd. *Chad* —1F **75**
Marham Clo. *Nott* —4G **65** (6K **5**)
Marhill Rd. *Cltn* —7D **50**
Maria Ct. *Park T* —4C **64** (6B **4**)
Marie Gdns. *Huck* —7G **17**
Marigold Clo. *Oak* —4H **57**
Marina Av. *Bees* —3F **81**
Marina Dri. *Altn* —4E **92**
Marina Dri. *Spon* —3K **75**
Marina Rd. *Smal* —5D **26**
Mariner Ct. *Nott* —7G **31**
Marion Av. *Huck* —3J **17**
Marion Murdoch Ct. *Ged* —4C **50**
Maris Clo. *Nott* —6J **81**
Maris Dri. *Bur J* —2J **51**
Marjorie Rd. *Der* —7E **56**

**Markeaton Craft Village.** —7G **55**
Markeaton La. *Der* —1E **72**

**Markeaton Pk.** —1G **73**
Markeaton St. *Der* —1H **73** (2A **6**)
Market Head. *Belp* —1A **24**
Market Pl. *Belp* —2A **24**
Market Pl. *Bing* —3F **70**
Market Pl. Bulw. —6H **31**
(off Main St., in two parts)
Market Pl. *Cod* —4E **12**
Market Pl. *Der* —3A **74** (3E **6**)
Market Pl. *Huck* —5G **17**
Market Pl. *Ilk* —6C **44**
Market Pl. *Iron* —1H **13**
Market Pl. *Keg* —1H **117**
Market Pl. *Long E* —1J **97**
Market Pl. *Melb* —4H **113**
Market Pl. *Rip* —3K **11**
Market Side. *Nott* —6H **31**
(off Bulwell High Rd.)
Market St. *Bing* —3A **70**
Market St. *Cas D* —7K **107**
Market St. *Der* —3A **74** (3E **6**)
Market St. *Dray* —2J **95**
Market St. *Hean* —3G **27**
Market St. *Ilk* —6D **44**
Market St. *Iron* —1G **13**
Market St. *Nott* —2E **64** (3E **4**)
Markham Ct. *Oak* —5E **56**
Markham Cres. *Nott* —2E **48**
Markham Rd. *Bees* —6D **62**
Mark's Clo. *Sun* —3H **91**
Mark St. *Sand* —3G **79**
Marlborough Ct. *Bees* —7F **63**

Marlborough Ct. *W Bri* —1H **83**
Marlborough Dri. *Belp* —7C **10**
Marlborough Rd. *Bees* —7F **63**
Marlborough Rd. *Breas* —2B **96**
Marlborough Rd. *Der* —2B **92**
Marlborough Rd. *Long E* —7K **79**
Marlborough Rd. *Wd'p* —1F **49**
Marlborough St. *Nott* —6A **64**
Marldon Clo. *Nott* —2B **62**
Marlow Av. *Nott* —4A **48**
Marlow Cres. *W Hal* —6F **43**
Marlowe Ct. *Der* —3K **91**
(in two parts)
Marl Rd. *Rad T* —4B **68**
Marlwood. *Cotg* —7A **86**
Marmion Rd. *Nott* —7J **49**
Marne Clo. *Ilk* —4D **44**
Marnham Dri. *Nott* —5G **49**
Marple Sq. *Nott* —7E **48**
Marriott Av. *Bees* —3A **80**
Marriott Clo. *Bees* —3A **80**
Marsant Clo. *Nott* —2J **63**
Marsden Clo. *Duf* —3J **39**
Marsden St. *Altn* —2E **92**
Marshall Dri. *Bees* —7K **61**
Marshall Hill Dri. *Nott* —5K **49**
Marshall Rd. *C Bis* —4G **87**
Marshall Rd. *Nott* —5J **49**
Marshall St. *Hean* —3H **27**
Marshall St. *Nott* —4E **48**
Marshall Way. *Ilk* —1B **60**
Marshaw Clo. *Mick* —7C **72**
Marshgreen Clo. *Alv* —4K **93**
Marsh La. *Belp* —7A **10**
Marsh La. Cres. *Belp* —1B **24**
Marston Brook. *Hilt* —7A **88**
Marston Clo. *Belp* —6C **10**
Marston Clo. *L'ver* —4H **91**
Marston Rd. *Nott* —7K **49**
Martell Ct. *Bees* —5C **80**
Martin Clo. *Blen I* —5F **31**
Martin Ct. *Blen I* —5F **31**
Martindale Clo. *Gam* —1A **84**
Martindale Ct. *Belp* —7D **10**
Martin Dri. *Chad* —7C **57**
Martin's Hill. *Cltn* —7C **50**

**Martin's Pond Nature Reserve.**
—2F **63**

Marton Rd. *Bees* —5C **80**
Marton Rd. *Nott* —4J **31**
Marvin Rd. *Bees* —2F **81**
Marwood Cres. *Cltn* —4A **50**
Marwood Rd. *Cltn* —5A **50**
Mary Ct. *Nott* —5G **49**
Maryland Ct. *S'fd* —6J **61**
Maryland Clo. *Chad* —2H **75**
Marylebone Cres. *Der* —2D **72**
Mary Rd. *Eastw* —4F **29**
Masefield Av. *Der* —2J **91**
Masonic Pl. *Nott* —2D **64** (3D **4**)
Mason Rd. *Ilk* —4B **44**
Mason Wlk. *Der* —4J **73** (6A **6**)
Massey Clo. *Bur J* —3J **51**
Massey Gdns. *Nott*
—1G **65** (1K **5**)
Masson Ct. *Nott* —4C **32**
Matlock Ct. *Long E* —4D **96**
Matlock Ct. *Nott* —2E **64** (2E **4**)
Matlock Ho. *Spon* —5A **76**
Matlock Rd. *Belp* —7K **9**
Matlock Rd. *Chad* —6F **57**
Matlock St. *N'fld* —7D **50**
Matthews Ct. *S'fd* —5K **61**
(in two parts)
Matthew St. *Alv* —3F **93**
Matthew Way. *L'ver* —2C **90**
Mattingly Rd. *Nott* —7G **31**
Maud St. *Nott* —5C **48**
Maun Av. *Nott* —1K **63**
Maun Gdns. *Nott* —1K **63**
Maurice Dri. *Nott* —4G **49**
Maws La. *Kimb* —6J **29**
Max Rd. *Chad* —7E **56**
Maxtoke Rd. *Nott* —4C **64** (6A **4**)
Maxwell Av. *Der* —7H **55**
Maxwell Clo. *Nott* —6B **64**
Maxwell St. *Breas* —1D **96**
Maxwell St. *Long E* —2J **97**
May Av. *Nott* —3E **62**
May Cotts. *Nott* —2A **48**
May Ct. *Nott* —5D **48**
Maycroft Gdns. *Nott* —7J **49**
Maydene Clo. *Nott* —7K **81**
Mayes Ri. *B Vil* —1A **32**
Mayfair. *Rad T* —4D **68**
Mayfair Ct. *Duf* —2J **39**
Mayfair Cres. *Der* —2C **72**
Mayfair Gdns. *Nott* —1B **48**

Mayfield Av. *Bur J* —1K **51**
Mayfield Av. *Hean* —4G **27**
Mayfield Av. *Klbrn* —5G **25**
Mayfield Ct. *Nott* —5B **48**
Mayfield Dri. *S'fd* —5K **61**
Mayfield Gro. *Long E* —7J **79**
Mayfield Rd. *Cltn* —7K **49**
Mayfield Rd. *Chad* —1E **74**
Mayflower Clo. *W Bri* —1J **83**
Mayflower Rd. *Newt* —5F **29**
Mayland Clo. *Nott* —1C **62**
Maylands. *Borr* —7D **76**
Maylands Av. *Breas* —1C **96**
Mayo Rd. *Nott* —5D **48**
Maypole. *Nott* —5A **82**
Maypole La. *L'ver* —2C **90**
Maypole Yd. *Nott* —2E **64** (3F **5**)
May's Av. *Cltn* —1A **66**
Mays Clo. *Cltn* —1A **66**
May St. *Der* —5K **73** (7A **6**)
May St. *Ilk* —2C **44**
Maythorn Clo. *W Bri* —5E **82**
Maythorne Wlk. *Nott* —5E **32**
Maytree Clo. *Oak* —4J **57**

**Maywood Golf Course.** —2C **78**
McGough M. *Sin* —4A **92**
McIntosh Rd. *Ged* —3B **50**
McNeil Gro. *Dray* —2J **95**
Mead Clo. *Sin* —5K **91**
Meadow Av. *Cod* —4D **12**
Meadowbank Ct. *Eastw* —2B **28**
Meadowbank Way. *Eastw* —2B **28**
Meadow Clo. *Asl* —2J **71**
Meadow Clo. *Breas* —2C **96**
Meadow Clo. *Dray* —2J **95**
Meadow Clo. *Eastw* —1D **28**
Meadow Clo. *Find* —7B **90**
Meadow Clo. *Ged* —7E **34**
Meadow Clo. *Hors W* —7K **25**
Meadow Clo. *Huck* —7D **16**
Meadow Clo. *Nott* —5G **65**
Meadow Clo. *Spon* —4A **76**
Meadow Cotts. *N'fld* —7D **50**
Meadow Ct. *Klbrn* —1K **23**
(Bridge St.)
Meadow Ct. *Klbrn* —6G **25**
(Dale Pk. Av.)
Meadow Ct. *Nott* —5H **65** (7K **5**)
(Brand St.)
Meadow Ct. *Nott* —5G **65**
(Meadow Clo.)
Meadow Cres. *Cas D* —1K **115**
Meadow Dri. *Keyw* —6E **102**
Meadow End. *Got* —1H **111**
Meadow End. *Rad T* —4C **68**
Meadow Gdns. *Bees* —4E **80**
Meadow Gdns. *Hean* —4K **27**
Meadowgrass Clo. *L'ver* —3F **91**
Meadow Gro. *Nott* —5G **65** (7K **5**)
Meadow La. *Alv* —7F **75**
Meadow La. *Bees* —3E **80**
Meadow La. *Bur J* —2K **51**
Meadow La. *Chad* —4F **75**
Meadow La. *C But* —2J **87**
Meadow La. *Long E* —2K **97**
(in two parts)
Meadow La. *Nott* —6G **65** (7K **5**)
Meadowlark Gro. *Oak* —6G **57**
Meadow Nook. *Boul M* —5J **93**
Meadow Ri. *Nott* —7F **31**
Meadow Rd. *Aws* —1G **45**
Meadow Rd. *Bees* —3G **81**
Meadow Rd. *Der* —3B **74** (3F **7**)
(in two parts)
Meadow Rd. *N'fld* —1D **66**
Meadow Rd. *Rip* —3A **12**
Meadows Cft. *Duf* —3H **39**
Meadows Ind. Est., The. *Der*
—3D **74** (4K **7**)
Meadows, The. *Aws* —1G **45**
Meadows, The. *Hean* —4G **27**
Meadows, The. *Wdbgh* —1F **35**
Meadow St. *Ilk* —5D **44**
Meadows Way. *Nott*
—6D **64** (7E **5**)
Meadowsweet Hill. *Bing* —3J **69**
Meadow Trad. Est. *Nott*
—4G **65** (7K **5**)
Meadow Va. *Duf* —3H **39**
Meadowvale Cres. *Nott* —7A **82**
Meadow Vw. *Belp* —2K **23**
Meadow Vw. Clo. *Oak* —4H **57**
Meadow Way. *Chel* —1G **105**
Mease, The. *Hilt* —7A **88**
Meath Av. *Chad* —4H **75**
Medawar Clo. *Nott* —7J **81**
Medbank Ct. *Nott* —3C **82**
Meden Clo. *Nott* —5A **82**
Meden Gdns. *Nott* —7K **47**

Medina Clo. *Alv* —4J **93**
Medina Dri. *Toll* —7B **84**
Medway Clo. *Bees* —3C **80**
Medway Dri. *Alst* —2A **56**
Medway St. *Nott* —2K **63**
Meeks Rd. *Arn* —5K **33**
Meerbrook Clo. *Oak* —6G **57**
Meerbrook Pl. *Ilk* —2A **60**
Meer Rd. *Bees* —3A **80**
Megaloughton La. *Spon* —5H **75**
Melandra Ct. *Der* —4J **73**
Melbourne Clo. *Alst* —5H **55**
Melbourne Clo. *Belp* —3A **24**
Melbourne Clo. *Duf* —4J **39**
Melbourne Clo. *Mick* —5D **72**
Melbourne Ct. *Long E* —5D **96**
Melbourne Ct. *Nott* —5J **47**

Melbourne Hall & Gardens.
—5H **113**

Melbourne Ho. *Spon* —5A **76**
Melbourne La. *Tickn* —6C **112**

Melbourne Parks. —7K **113**
Melbourne Ride. *Stan B* —4B **112**
Melbourne Rd. *Nott* —6H **47**
Melbourne Rd. *S'fd* —5J **61**
Melbourne Rd. *W Bri* —6H **65**
Melbourne St. *Der* —5A **74** (7E **6**)
Melbreak Clo. *Mick* —7C **72**
Melbury Rd. *Nott* —6D **46**
Melbury Rd. *Wd'p* —2H **49**
Meldreth Rd. *Nott* —1E **62**
Melford Hall Dri. *W Bri* —4E **82**
Melford Rd. *Nott* —6D **46**
Melfort Clo. *Sin* —7K **91**
Melksham Rd. *Nott* —5E **32**
Mellbreak Clo. *W Bri* —2A **84**
Mellers Ct. *Nott* —7J **49**
Mellon Ter. *Nott* —2C **64** (2B **4**)
Mellor's La. *Holb* —7C **24**
Mellors Rd. *Arn* —4H **33**
Mellors Rd. *W Bri* —3H **83**
Mellor St. *Altn* —3E **92**
Melrose Av. *Bees* —3G **81**
Melrose Av. *Nott* —3E **48**
Melrose Clo. *Sin* —7J **91**
Melrose Gdns. *W Bri* —4F **83**
Melrose St. *Nott* —3E **48**
Melton Av. *L'ver* —3G **91**
Melton Av. *Melb* —3G **113**
Melton Ct. *Sand* —3E **78**
Melton Gdns. *Edw* —4J **83**
Melton Gro. *W Bri* —1G **83**
Melton Rd. *Edw & Toll* —7J **83**
Melton Rd. *Plum* —2D **102**
Melton Rd. *W Bri & Edw* —1G **83**
Melville Clo. *Etw* —6D **88**
Melville Ct. *Nott* —6E **48**
Melville Gdns. *Nott*
—1G **65** (1K **5**)
Melville St. *Nott* —4E **64** (6F **5**)
Melvyn Dri. *Bing* —3A **70**
Memorial Rd. *Alst* —5G **55**
Mendip Clo. *Long E* —7E **78**
Mendip Ct. *Nott* —5B **32**
Mendip Ct. *Oak* —5E **56**
Menin Rd. *Alst* —5G **55**
Mensing Av. *Cotg* —5J **85**
Mercaston Rd. *Chad* —7F **57**
Merchant Av. *Spon* —4K **75**
Merchant St. *Der* —2J **73**
Merchant St. *Nott* —5H **31**
(in two parts)
Mercia Av. *C Bis* —4G **87**
Mercia Clo. *Gilt* —5E **28**
Mercian M. *Spon* —4K **75**
Mercury Clo. *Nott* —1A **48**
Mere Av. *C'tn* —5D **20**
Mere Clo. *C'tn* —5D **20**
Meredith Clo. *Nott* —6D **64**
Meredith Ct. *S'fd* —5K **61**
Mere Dri. *Borr* —7D **76**
Meregill Clo. *Nott* —4C **32**
Merevale Av. *Nott* —4B **82**
Merevale Clo. *Low* —4E **36**
Mere Way. *Rud* —5F **101**
Meriac Clo. *Nott* —5B **32**
Meriden Av. *Bees* —7G **63**
Meridian Ct. *Nott* —3C **48**
Merion Gro. *L'ver* —7E **72**
Merlin Clo. *Belp* —7C **10**
Merlin Clo. *Nott* —6A **82**
Merlin Dri. *Huck* —1E **30**
Merlin Grn. *Sin* —5H **91**
Merlin Way. *Mick* —2K **89**
Merlin Way. *Quar H* —3D **60**
Merridale Rd. *L'ver* —2G **91**
Merrill Way. *Altn* —4D **92**
(in two parts)
Merrivale Ct. *Nott* —6E **48**

Merrybower Clo. *Sten F* —6G **91**
Mersey St. *Nott* —6H **31**
Merthyr Ct. *Oak* —5H **57**
Merton Clo. *Arn* —4K **33**
Merton Ct. *S'fd* —6J **61**
Metcalfe Clo. *Alv* —1H **93**
Metcalf Rd. *Newt* —2F **29**
Meteor Cen., The. *Der* —6C **56**

Metro Cinema. —5D **6**
Mettham St. *Nott* —4B **64**
Mevell Ct. *Nott* —3C **64** (5B **4**)
Mews La. *C'tn* —5C **20**
Mews, The. *Duf* —3J **39**
Mews, The. *Melb* —4H **113**
Mews, The. *Nott* —6C **48**
Meynall Gro. *Nott* —5C **48**
Meynell Ct. *Alst* —5G **55**
Meynell Rd. *Long E* —4H **97**
Meynell St. *Der* —7K **73**

MGM Cinema. —4D **4**
Miall Ct. *Nott* —2A **64**
Miall St. *Nott* —2A **64**
Michael Gdns. *Nott* —5D **48**
Michael Rayner Ct. *Nott* —3K **47**
Michelle Clo. *Sten F* —6G **91**
Michigan Clo. *Chad* —3J **75**
Mickleborough Av. *Nott* —6H **49**
Mickleborough Way. *W Bri*
—5E **82**
Micklebring Clo. *Rip* —3H **11**
Micklecroft Gdns. *L'ver* —2C **90**
Mickledon Clo. *Long E* —1E **96**
Mickledon Clo. *Nott* —5D **64**
Mickleover By-Pass. *Mick*
—3B **90**

Mickleover Golf Course. —7D **72**
Mickleover Manor. *Mick* —7A **72**
Mickleross Clo. *Mick* —4B **72**
Middle Av. *Cltn* —6A **50**
Middlebeck Av. *Arn* —5A **34**
Middlebeck Clo. *Chel* —7F **93**
Middlebeck Dri. *Arn* —5K **33**
Middlebrook Rd. *Und* —1E **14**
Middledale Rd. *Cltn* —1A **66**
Middlefell Way. *Nott* —7K **81**
Middle Furlong Gdns. *Nott*
—5D **64**
Middle Furlong M. *Nott* —5D **64**
Middle Hill. *Nott* —3E **64** (5F **5**)
Middle La. *Bees* —3E **80**
Middle Nook. *Nott* —2E **62**
Middle Orchard St. *S'fd* —1H **79**
Middle Pavement. *Nott*
—3E **64** (5F **5**)
Middle St. *Bees* —2F **81**
Middleton Av. *Cod* —7D **12**
Middleton Av. *L'ver* —6G **73**
Middleton Boulevd. *Nott* —3J **63**
Middleton Clo. *Nut* —7C **30**
Middleton Cres. *Bees* —6E **62**
Middleton Dri. *L'ver* —6G **73**
Middleton Rd. *Ilk* —2E **60**
Middleton St. *Aws* —2G **45**
Middleton St. *Bees* —1E **80**
Middleton St. *Der* —7A **74**
Middleton St. *Ilk* —5E **44**
Middleton St. *Nott* —2A **64**
Midhurst Clo. *Bees* —6E **80**
Midhurst Way. *Nott* —6A **82**
Midlame Gdns. *Nott* —6F **31**
Midland Av. *N'fld* —7E **50**
Midland Av. *Nott* —4A **64**
Midland Av. *S'fd* —3G **79**
Midland Clo. *Nott* —1K **63**
Midland Cotts. *W Bri* —1H **83**
Midland Ct. *Nott* —5D **48**
(Edbury Rd.)
Midland Ct. *Nott* —2K **63**
(Midland Clo.)
Midland Cres. *Cltn* —7D **50**
Midland Gro. *N'fld* —6E **50**
Midland Ind. Est. *Ambgt* —1A **10**
Midland Pl. *Der* —4C **74** (6H **7**)
Midland Rd. *Cltn* —7D **50**
Midland Rd. *Der* —5B **74** (7G **7**)
Midland Rd. *Eastw* —3D **28**
Midland Rd. *Hean* —3G **27**
Midland St. *Long E* —1J **97**
Midland Ter. *Ambgt* —1K **9**
Midland Ter. *Long E* —7J **79**
Midway. *Dar A* —5J **55**
Midway, The. *Nott* —7A **64**
Mikado Rd. *Long E* —4G **97**

Mike Powers Pottery. —2E **100**
Milburn Gdns. *Oak* —4H **57**
Milburn Gro. *Bing* —3J **69**
Milbury Clo. *Oak* —5F **57**
Mildenhall Cres. *Nott* —5E **32**
Mileash La. *Dar A* —6K **55**

Mile End Rd. *Colw* —2C **66**
Milford Av. *Long E* —5F **79**
Milford Clo. *Nott* —5G **31**
Milford Ct. *Day* —7F **33**
Milford Dri. *Ilk* —3B **44**
Milford Dri. *Nott* —7A **50**
Milford Rd. *Duf* —1J **39**
Milford St. *Der* —1K **73**
Mill Acre Clo. *Ilk* —4B **44**
Millbank. *Hean* —4J **27**
(in two parts)
Millbank Av. *Belp* —3B **24**
Millbank Clo. *Der* —2C **72**
Millbank Clo. *Ilk* —3B **44**
Millbank Ct. *Nott* —7G **31**
Millbeck Av. *Nott* —3C **62**
Millbeck Clo. *Gam* —2A **84**
Mill Clo. *Borr* —7E **76**
Mill Clo. *Find* —7B **90**
Mill Clo. *Klbrn* —5G **25**
Mill Clo., The. *Old B* —3A **48**
Mill Cres. *Arn* —5G **33**
Mill Cft. *Nott* —4B **72**
Milldale Clo. *Nott* —6J **81**
Milldale Clo. *Rip* —6K **11**
Milldale Ct. *Belp* —2B **24**
Milldale Rd. *Long E* —3F **97**
Milldale Rd. *Spon* —5B **76**
Millenium Bus. Cen. *Pri P* —4E **74**
Millennium Ct. *Nott* —1K **47**
Millennium Way. *Nott* —2G **47**
Millennium Way. *Pri P* —4E **74**
Millennium Way E. *Nott* —2G **47**
Millennium Way W. *Nott* —2G **47**
Miller Hives Clo. *Cotg* —5J **85**
Millers Bri. *Cotg* —6J **85**
Millers Clo. *Shelf* —5C **52**
Millers Ct. *Der* —1D **6**
Millers Ct. *Nott* —1A **64**
Millers Dale Av. *Ilk* —1C **44**
Millersdale Clo. *Belp* —7B **10**
Millfield. *Shard* —7K **95**
Mill Fld. Clo. *Bur J* —3J **51**
Millfield Clo. *Ilk* —3A **44**
Millfield Rd. *Ilk* —7E **44**
Millfield Rd. *Kimb* —6J **29**
Mill Fleam. *Hilt* —7A **88**
Mill Ga. *E Bri* —4J **53**
Mill Heyes. *E Bri* —3K **53**
Mill Hill. *Boul M* —5J **93**
Mill Hill La. *Breas* —7C **78**
Mill Hill La. *Der* —5K **73** (7C **6**)
Mill Hill Rd. *Bing* —4K **69**
Mill Hill Rd. *Der* —5K **73** (7C **6**)
Millhouse Ct. *Dray* —2K **95**

Millicent Gro. *W Bri* —7H **65**
Millicent Rd. *W Bri* —7G **65**

Mill Lakes Country Pk. —1K **31**
Mill La. *Arn* —5G **33**
Mill La. *Belp* —2A **24**
Mill La. *Bradm* —5H **101**
Mill La. *Clip* —7H **85**
Mill La. *Cod* —4C **12**
Mill La. *Coss* —6F **45**
Mill La. *Cotg* —4J **85**
Mill La. *C Bis* —4G **87**
Mill La. *Keg* —1H **117**
Mill La. *Lamb* —6F **35**
Mill La. *Long W* —7G **117**
Mill La. *Mick* —4B **72**
Mill La. *Sand* —2G **79**
Mill Mdw. Way. *Etw* —5D **88**
Mill Moor Clo. *Chel* —7E **92**
Millom Pl. *Der* —6D **56**
Mill Rd. *Hean* —5J **27**
Mill Rd. *Newt* —2E **28**
Mill Rd. *S'fd* —7H **61**
Mill Row. *Spon* —3K **75**
Mills Clo. *Dray* —2J **95**
Mill St. *Belp* —1K **23**
Mill St. *Der* —2J **73** (2A **6**)
Mill St. *Ilk* —5D **44**
Mill St. *Nott* —3K **47**
Millview Clo. *Nott* —3H **65**
Mill Vw. Ct. *Nott* —3G **65** (5K **5**)
Mill Yd. *Huck* —5G **17**
Milner Av. *Cod* —4D **12**
Milner Av. *Dray* —2J **95**
Milner Ho. *Der* —1J **73** (1A **6**)
Milner Rd. *Long E* —1H **97**
Milner Rd. *Nott* —4E **48**
Milnhay Rd. *Lan M* —3A **28**
Milton Av. *Ilk* —2C **44**
Milton Clo. *Mick* —5A **72**
Milton Ct. *Arn* —6K **33**
Milton Ct. *Nott* —3D **48**
Milton Cres. *Bees* —6D **80**
Milton Ri. *Huck* —7D **16**
Milton Rd. *Ilk* —2C **44**

Milton St. *Der* —4J **73**
Milton St. *Ilk* —2D **44**
Milton St. *Long E* —2H **97**
Milton St. *Nott* —2E **64** (2F **5**)
Milton Ter. *Long E* —2H **97**
Milverton Rd. *Nott* —5E **32**
Milward La. *Burna* —4J **89**
Milward Rd. *Los* —3F **27**
Mimosa Clo. *Nott* —7J **81**
Mimosa Cres. *Sun* —4J **91**
Minerva St. *Nott* —5H **31**
(in two parts)

Miniature Railway. —7H **55**
(Abbey Pk.)
Minster Clo. *Huck* —4H **17**
Minster Ct. *Nott* —7D **48**
Minster Gdns. *Newt* —4F **29**
Minster Rd. *Oak* —5E **56**
Mint Gro. *Long E* —1E **96**
Minton Clo. *Bees* —7B **80**
Minton Rd. *Cas D* —6H **107**
Minver Cres. *Nott* —5G **47**
Mirberry M. *Nott* —4A **64**
Miriam Ct. *W Bri* —1G **83**
Misk Hollows. *Huck* —4F **17**
Misk Vw. *Eastw* —3F **29**
Miss on St. *Nott* —4G **49**
Misterton Clo. *Alst* —5J **55**
Mitcham Wlk. *Der* —2E **72**
Mitchell Av. *Lan M* —1J **27**
Mitchell Clo. *Nott* —7G **31**
Mitchell St. *Long E* —2J **97**
Mitchell Ter. *Ilk* —2E **60**
Moat, The. *Cas D* —6K **107**
Moffat Clo. *Nott* —7H **49**
Moira Clo. *Chad* —1G **75**
Moira Dale. *Cas D* —7K **107**
Moira Ho. *Arn* —6G **33**
Moira St. *Melb* —4G **113**
Molineux St. *Der* —6B **74**
Mollington Sq. *Nott* —2H **47**
Monarch Dri. *Oak* —4K **57**
Monarch Way. *Hean* —3E **26**
Mona Rd. *W Bri* —6J **65**
Mona St. *Bees* —2G **81**
Moncrieff Cres. *Chad* —7G **57**
Mondello Dri. *Alv* —3J **93**
Monks Clo. *Ilk* —6E **44**
Monks Clo. *Sten F* —6H **91**
Monk's La. *Got* —1H **111**
Monk St. *Der* —4K **73** (5B **6**)
Monksway. *Nott* —4C **82**
Monkton Clo. *Ilk* —3B **44**
Monkton Dri. *Nott* —7E **46**
Monmouth Clo. *Nott* —3B **62**
Monmouth St. *Der* —2D **74** (1K **7**)
Monroe Wlk. *Nott* —6C **32**
Monsaldale Clo. *Long E* —3F **97**
Monsal Dri. *Spon* —5B **76**
Monsall Av. *Ilk* —1C **44**
Monsall St. *Nott* —5B **48**
Monsell Dri. *Red* —4G **33**
Montague Rd. *Huck* —4G **17**
Montague St. *Bees* —1E **80**
Montague St. *Nott* —6J **31**
Monteith Pl. *Cas D* —6K **107**
Montford M. *Cas D* —6K **107**
Montfort Cres. *Nott* —2F **49**
Montfort St. *Nott* —2C **64** (3A **4**)
Montgomery Clo. *Bees* —6C **80**
Montgomery Clo. *Hilt* —7A **88**
Montgomery St. *Nott*
—1C **64** (1B **4**)
Montpelier. *Quar* —7H **39**
Montpelier Rd. *Ambgt* —1K **9**
Montpelier Rd. *Nott* —6A **64**
Montrose Clo. *Sin* —5J **91**
Montrose Ct. *S'fd* —6J **61**
Monument Hill. *Iron* —1H **13**
Monument La. *Iron* —2G **13**
(in three parts)
Monyash Clo. *Chad* —7G **57**
Monyash Clo. *Ilk* —3C **44**
Monyash Way. *Belp* —7B **10**
Moorbridge Cotts. *Nott* —3K **31**
Moorbridge La. *S'fd* —6H **61**
Moorbridge Rd. *Bing* —2A **70**
Moorbridge Rd. E. *Bing* —2A **70**
Moor Dri. *Alv* —4G **93**
Moore Av. *Keg* —7H **109**
Moore Clo. *W Bri* —6K **65**
Moore Ga. *Bees* —2F **81**
Moor End. *Spon* —3A **76**
Moore Rd. *Map* —4J **49**
Moores Av. *Sand* —1G **79**
Moore St. *Der* —5A **74**
Moor Farm Cvn. Pk. *C'tn* —6G **21**
Moor Farm Inn La. *Bramc* —5A **62**

Moorfield Ct. *S'fd* —6J **61**
Moorfield Cres. *Sand* —3F **79**
Moorfield Rd. *Holb* —6C **24**
Moorfields Av. *Eastw* —2D **28**
Moorgate. *Mack* —2C **72**
Moorgate St. *Nott* —2C **64** (2A **4**)
Moorgreen. *Newt* —7G **15**
Moorgreen Bus. Pk. *Newt* —1F **29**
Moorgreen Dri. *Strel* —4D **46**
Moorgreen Ind. Pk. *Newt* —7F **15**
Moorhead Av. *Alv* —4F **93**
Moorhouse Rd. *Nott* —1E **62**
Moorings, The. *Nott*
—5B **64** (7A **4**)
Moorland Av. *S'fd* —2H **79**
Moorland Clo. *Mick* —5B **72**
Moorlands Clo. *Long E* —6F **79**
Moor La. *Altn* —4C **92**
Moor La. *Asl* —2F **71**
Moor La. *Ast T* —2D **106**
Moor La. *Bar T* —7D **114**
Moor La. *Bees* —5B **62**
Moor La. *Bing* —2A **70**
Moor La. *Bradm* —7F **101**
Moor La. *C'tn* —6G **21**
Moor La. *Dal A* —5H **59**
Moor La. *Got* —1H **111**
Moor La. *L Eat* —5D **40**
(in three parts)
Moor La. *Ock* —1D **76**
Moor La. *Rud* —3E **100**
Moor La. N. *Bar T* —1B **104**
Moor La. S. *Bar T* —3B **104**
Moorpool Cres. *Holb* —6C **24**
Moor Ri. *Holb* —5C **24**
Moor Rd. *B Vil* —2K **31**
Moor Rd. *Bread* —3E **56**
Moor Rd. *Brins* —4C **14**
Moor Rd. *C'tn* —5E **20**
Moor Rd. *Pap* —2K **17**
Moor Rd. *Strel* —5D **46**
Moorsholm Dri. *Nott* —3C **62**
Moorside Cres. *Sin* —5K **91**
Moorside La. *Holb* —5C **24**
Moor St. *N'fld* —7D **50**
Moor St. *Spon* —3A **76**
Moor, The. *Trow* —1A **62**
Moorway. *Bread* —3E **56**
Moorway Cft. *L'ver* —2F **91**
Moorway La. *L'ver* —4E **90**

Moorways Sports Complex.
—3D **92**

Moray Ct. *Kimb* —6K **29**
Moray Wlk. *Der* —7C **56**
Morden Clo. *Nott* —6D **46**
Morden Grn. *Der* —2E **72**
Morden Rd. *Gilt* —5G **29**
Morefern Dri. *Oak* —5F **57**
Moreland Ct. *Cltn* —7A **50**
Moreland Ct. *Nott* —4H **65** (7K **5**)
Moreland Pl. *Nott* —4H **65** (7K **5**)
Moreland St. *Nott* —4H **65** (7K **5**)
Morello Av. *Cltn* —7D **50**
Moreton Rd. *Nott* —2A **100**
Morgan Ct. *Bees* —3H **81**
Morgan M. *Nott* —6K **81**
Morkinshire Cres. *Cotg* —4K **85**
Morkinshire La. *Cotg* —4J **85**
Morledge. *Der* —3A **74** (4E **6**)
Morleston St. *Der* —5B **74** (7F **7**)
Morley Av. *Nott* —4G **49**
Morley Clo. *Belp* —6E **10**
Morley Ct. *Nott* —3G **65** (3J **5**)
Morley Dri. *Ilk* —3B **44**
Morleyfields Clo. *Rip* —3B **12**
Morley Gdns. *Nott* —5D **48**
Morley Gdns. *Oak* —7H **57**

Morley Golf Course. —6F **41**
Morley La. *L Eat* —6D **40**
Morley La. *M'ly & Stan* —1C **58**
Morley Rd. *Chad & Oak* —1G **75**
Morley St. *Nott* —5J **49**
Morleys Clo. *Low* —4E **36**
Morley St. *Day* —7G **33**
Morley St. *Der* —2F **73**
Morlich Dri. *Sin* —5J **91**
Morningside Clo. *Altn* —5D **92**
Mornington Clo. *Sand* —2G **79**
Mornington Cres. *Der* —2E **72**
Mornington Cres. *Nut* —3D **46**
Morpeth Gdns. *Der* —5D **56**
Morrell Bank. *Nott* —7B **32**
Morrell Wood Dri. *Belp* —7D **10**
Morris Av. *Bees* —7B **80**
Morris Rd. *Nott* —5D **46**
Morris St. *N'fld* —7E **50**

Mortimer's Hole Cave. —4D **64**
(off Castle)
Mortimer St. *Der* —2C **92**

Morton Clo. *Rad T* —4C **68**
Morton Gdns. *Rad T* —4C **68**
Morval Rd. *Nott* —7E **46**
Morven Av. *Huck* —6H **17**
Moscow. *Milf* —1K **39**
Mosedale Clo. *Der* —1F **93**
Moseley St. *Rip* —2K **11**
Moses La. *Ilk* —1A **58**
Mosley St. *Huck* —6G **17**
Mosley St. *Nott* —6B **48**
Moss Clo. *Arn* —5E **32**
Moss Clo. *E Bri* —3K **53**
Mosscroft Av. *Nott* —7K **81**
Mossdale Rd. *Nott* —1E **48**
Moss Dri. *Bees* —1B **80**
Moss La. *Rip* —1K **11**
Moss Ri. *Nott* —4K **49**
Moss Rd. *Huck* —5F **17**
Moss Rd. *Ilk* —7C **44**
Moss Side. *Nott* —5C **82**
Moss St. *Der* —5J **73** (7A **6**)
Mossvale Dri. *L'ver* —3E **90**
Mosswood Cres. *Nott* —6D **32**
Mostyn Av. *Der* —7H **73**
Mottistone Clo. *Alv* —4K **93**
Mottram Rd. *Bees* —2C **80**
Moult Av. *Spon* —4A **76**
Moulton Clo. *Belp* —7D **10**
Mountbatten Clo. *Shel L* —5E **92**
Mountbatten Ct. *Ilk* —3D **44**
Mountbatten Gro. *Ged* —4C **50**
Mountbatten Way. *Bees* —6C **80**
Mt. Carmel St. *Der* —5K **73** (7C **6**)
Mountfield Av. *Sand* —4E **78**
Mountfield Dri. *Nott* —6C **32**
Mountfield Way. *Boul M* —5K **93**
Mountford Clo. *Oak* —5H **57**
Mt. Hooton. *Nott* —1C **64**
Mt. Hooton Rd. *Nott* —7C **48**
Mt. Pleasant. *Cltn* —7C **50**
Mt. Pleasant. *Cas D* —7K **107**
Mt. Pleasant. *Ilk* —2C **44**
Mt. Pleasant. *Keyw* —6D **102**
Mt. Pleasant. *Low* —3D **36**
Mt. Pleasant. *Nott* —4K **47**
Mt. Pleasant. *Rad T* —4J **67**
Mt. Pleasant. *Rip* —2K **11**
Mt. Pleasant Dri. *Rip* —7J **9**
Mt. Pleasant Dri. *Heag* —4E **10**
Mt. Sorrel Dri. *W Bri* —2K **83**
Mount St. *Breas* —2D **96**
Mount St. *Der* —5A **74** (7D **6**)
Mount St. *Hean* —4G **27**
Mount St. *New B* —5B **48**
Mount St. *Nott* —3D **64** (5D **4**)
(in two parts)
Mount St. *S'fd* —1J **79**
Mount St. Arc. *Nott* —4D **4**
Mount, The. *B Vil* —1A **32**
Mount, The. *Nott* —4A **50**
(Elmhurst Av.)
Mount, The. *Nott* —5E **46**
(Wyrale Dri.)
Mount, The. *Red* —4F **33**
Mount, The. *S'fd* —2H **79**
Mowbray Ct. *Nott* —2F **65** (2H **5**)
Mowbray Gdns. *Der* —2C **92**
Mowbray Gdns. *W Bri* —3H **83**
Mowbray Ri. *Arn* —5H **33**
Mowbray St. *Der* —1C **92**
Moy Av. *Sin* —7K **91**
Moyne Gdns. *Chel* —2G **105**
Moyra Dri. *Arn* —6E **32**
Mozart Clo. *Nott* —2A **64**
Mudpie La. *W Bri* —6K **65**
Muir Av. *Toll* —1B **102**
Muirfield Dri. *Mick* —6D **72**
Muirfield Rd. *Arn* —4B **32**
Mulberries Ct. *Alst* —3J **55**
Mulberry Clo. *Belp* —2B **24**
Mulberry Clo. *W Bri* —3D **82**
Mulberry Gdns. *Nott* —5G **31**
Mulberry Gro. *Huck* —1H **31**
Mulberry M. *Rip* —6J **11**
Mulberry Way. *Hilt* —7A **88**
Mull Ct. *Sin* —6H **91**
Mullion Pl. *Alv* —4H **93**
Mundella Rd. *Nott* —6F **65**
Mundy Clo. *Der* —2J **73** (1A **6**)
**Mundy Pleasure Ground. —1J 73**
Mundy's Dri. *Hean* —5H **27**
Mundy St. *Der* —2J **73** (1A **6**)
Mundy St. *Hean* —4G **27**
Mundy St. *Ilk* —4D **44**
Munford Cir. *Nott* —3G **47**
Munks Av. *Huck* —5F **17**
Munro Ct. *Sin* —5J **91**
Murby Cres. *Nott* —5H **31**
Murden Way. *Bees* —2H **81**

Muriel Rd. *Bees* —1F **81**
Muriel St. *Nott* —6B **31**
Murray Rd. *Mick* —4D **72**
Murray St. *Der* —1F **93**
**Museum of Nottingham Lace.**
**—5G 5**
Muskham Av. *Ilk* —3D **44**
Muskham St. *Nott* —6F **65**
Musters Ct. *Huck* —6J **17**
Musters Ct. *W Bri* —2G **83**
Musters Cres. *W Bri* —3H **83**
Musters Cft. *Colw* —4D **66**
Musters Rd. *Bing* —3G **51**
Musters Rd. *Rud* —3D **100**
Musters Rd. *W Bri* —7G **65**
Musters Wlk. *Nott* —5H **49**
Muston Clo. *Nott* —5H **49**
Muswell Rd. *Der* —2C **72**
Myers Clo. *Sin* —5K **91**
Myrtle Av. *Long E* —3G **97**
Myrtle Av. *Nott* —6D **48**
Myrtle Av. *S'fd* —2J **79**
Myrtle Gro. *Bees* —1G **81**
Myrtle Rd. *Cltn* —6A **50**
Myrtus Clo. *Nott* —6J **81**

**N**abarro Ct. *C'tn* —5C **20**
Nabbs La. *Huck* —6D **16**
Naburn Ct. *Nott* —5K **47**
Nailers Way. *Belp* —7C **10**
Nairn Av. *Der* —1D **74**
Nairn Clo. *Arn* —4K **33**
Nairn Clo. *Sten F* —6H **91**
Nairn M. *Cltn* —7C **50**
Namur Clo. *Der* —5G **73**
Nanranjan M. *Nott* —1C **64** (1B **4**)
Nansen Gdns. *Nott* —7B **32**
Nansen St. *Nott* —7J **31**
Naomi Ct. *Nott* —4J **31**
Naomi Cres. *Nott* —4J **31**
Napier Clo. *Mick* —4C **72**
Napier St. *Der* —3G **73**
Narrow La. *Belp* —4F **9**
Narrow La. *Tickn* —7A **112**
Narrow La. *Wat* —4K **29**
Naseby Clo. *Mick* —5A **72**
Naseby Clo. *Nott* —2B **48**
Naseby Dri. *Long E* —5J **97**
Naseby Rd. *Belp* —1D **24**
Nathaniel Rd. *Long E* —2K **97**
Nathans La. *Rad T* —1E **84**
**Nature Reserve. —5D 82**
**(Rushcliffe)**
Navenby Wlk. *Nott* —6A **82**
Navigation Home Pk. *Der*
—7E **74**
Naworth Clo. *Nott* —1A **48**
Naylor Av. *Got* —1H **111**
Neal Ct. *Lan M* —2J **27**
Neale St. *Long E* —2J **97**
Near Mdw. *Long E* —4J **97**
Nearsby Dri. *W Bri* —2K **83**
Nearwood Dri. *Oak* —4E **56**
Needham Rd. *Arn* —5J **33**
Needham St. *Bing* —3A **70**
Needham St. *Cod* —4D **12**
Needwood Av. *Trow* —5H **61**
Negus Ct. *Lamb* —7F **35**
Neighbours La. *Low* —4E **36**
Neighwood Clo. *Bees* —6J **79**
Neilson St. *Alv* —2F **93**
Nell Gwyn Cres. *Nott* —4E **32**
Nelper Cres. *Ilk* —2E **60**
Nelson Clo. *Mick* —5C **72**
Nelson Rd. *Bees* —4G **81**
Nelson Rd. *Day* —6G **33**
Nelson Rd. *Nott* —6J **31**
Nelson St. *Der* —5C **74** (7H **7**)
(in two parts)
Nelson St. *Ilk* —2D **44**
Nelson St. *Long E* —3H **97**
Nelson St. *Nott* —3F **65** (4H **5**)
Nene Clo. *Huck* —2E **30**
Nesfield Clo. *Alv* —2J **93**
Nesfield Ct. *Ilk* —5C **44**
Nesfield Rd. *Ilk* —5C **44**
Ness Wlk. *Alst* —4J **55**
Neston Dri. *Nott* —2H **47**
Nether Clo. *Duf* —1H **39**
Nether Clo. *Eastw* —1D **28**
Nether Clo. *Nott* —1J **65**
Netherclose St. *Der* —7A **74**
Netherfield La. *Locki* —3C **108**
Netherfield Rd. *Long E* —5F **97**
Netherfield Rd. *Sand* —3F **79**
Nethergate. *Nott* —6J **81**
(in two parts)
Nether La. *Holb* —1D **40**

Nether La. *Turn & H'wd* —7D **22**
Nether Pasture. *N'fld* —1E **66**
Netherside Dri. *Chel* —7G **93**
Nether St. *Bees* —2G **81**
Netherwood Ct. *Alst* —4G **55**
Nettlecliff Wlk. *Nott* —5A **32**
Nettlefold Cres. *Melb* —2H **113**
Neville Rd. *C'tn* —5D **20**
Neville Sadler Ct. *Bees* —1G **81**
Nevinson Av. *Sun* —2H **91**
Nevinson Dri. *Sun* —2H **91**
Nevis Clo. *Sten F* —7H **91**
Newall Dri. *Bees* —6C **80**
Newark Av. *Nott* —3G **65** (5K **5**)
Newark Ct. *Nott* —1B **48**
Newark Cres. *Nott*
—3G **65** (5K **5**)
Newark Rd. *Der* —5D **56**
Newark St. *Nott* —3G **65** (5J **5**)
Newberry Clo. *C Bis* —4G **87**
Newbery Av. *Long E* —3K **97**
Newbold Av. *Borr* —7E **76**
Newbold Clo. *Chel* —7H **93**
Newbold Dri. *Cas D* —5K **107**
Newborough Rd. *Alv* —3J **93**
New Breck Rd. *Belp* —2A **24**
New Brickyard La. *Long E* —2H **117**
Newbridge Clo. *W Hal* —6F **43**
Newbridge Cres. *Shel L* —5E **92**
Newbridge Rd. *Ambgt* —1K **9**
Newbury Clo. *Nott* —2J **49**
Newbury Ct. *Nott* —6D **48**
Newbury Dri. *Nut* —3D **46**
Newbury St. *Der* —1E **92**
Newcastle Av. *Bees* —2F **81**
Newcastle Av. *Ged* —5C **50**
Newcastle Chambers. *Nott*
—3E **64** (4E **4**)
Newcastle Cir. *Nott* —3C **64** (5A **4**)
Newcastle Ct. *Park T*
—3C **64** (5A **4**)
Newcastle Dri. *Nott*
—3C **64** (4A **4**)
Newcastle Farm Dri. *Nott* —5J **47**
Newcastle St. *Nott* —5J **31**
(Carey Rd.)
Newcastle St. *Nott* —2E **64** (3F **5**)
(Up. Parliament St.)
Newcastle Ter. *Nott*
(Newcastle Dri.) —2C **64** (3B **4**)
Newcastle Ter. *Nott* —5K **47**
(Nuthall Rd.)
Newchase Bus. Pk. *Der* —7C **74**
New Chester St. *Der* —7B **56**
Newcombe Dri. *Arn* —6A **34**
New Derby Rd. *Eastw* —2B **28**
Newdigate Rd. *Watn* —6A **30**
Newdigate St. *Der* —1A **92**
Newdigate St. *Ilk* —1E **60**
Newdigate St. *Kimb* —7K **29**
Newdigate St. *Nott* —2C **64** (2A **4**)
Newdigate St. *W Hal* —6E **42**
Newdigate Vs. *Nott*
—2C **64** (2A **4**)
New Eaton Rd. *S'fd* —3J **79**
Newel Wlk. *Mick* —7A **72**
New Farm La. *Nut* —7C **30**
Newfield Rd. *Nott* —3B **48**
Newgate Clo. *Cltn* —7C **50**
Newgate Clo. *Chel* —7H **93**
Newgate Ct. *Nott* —3B **64**
Newgate St. *Bing* —2A **70**
Newhall Gro. *W Bri* —6H **65**
Newham Clo. *Hean* —4J **27**
Newhaven Rd. *Chad* —2H **75**
Newholm Dri. *Nott* —3C **82**
New Inn La. *L Eat* —7C **40**
Newland Clo. *Bees* —6A **80**
Newland Clo. *Nott* —2J **63**
Newlands Clo. *Edw* —4A **84**
Newlands Dri. *Ged* —5D **50**
Newlands Dri. *Hean* —2G **27**
Newlands Rd. *Ridd* —1E **12**
Newland St. *Sher* —3A **73** (4C **6**)
New La. *Asl* —4F **71**
New Lawn Rd. *Ilk* —6C **44**
Newlyn Dri. *Der* —1K **91**
Newlyn Dri. *Nott* —6B **48**
Newlyn Gdns. *Nott* —6K **47**
Newmanleys Rd. *Eastw* —5C **28**
Newmanleys Rd. S. *Eastw*
—4C **28**
Newman Rd. *C'tn* —4C **20**
Newmarket Ct. *Der* —1D **92**
Newmarket Rd. *Der* —1D **92**
Newmarket Rd. *Nott* —7H **31**
Newmarket Way. *Bees* —6K **79**
Newmount Clo. *L'ver* —4H **91**
Newnham Av. *Rip* —3J **11**

New Normanton Mills Ind. Est. *Der*
—6A **74**
Newport Ct. *Alv* —4J **93**
Newport Dri. *Nott* —5K **47**
Newquay Av. *Nott* —7A **48**
Newquay Pl. *Alv* —4J **93**
New Rd. *Bar F* —3E **98**
New Rd. *Belp* —2K **23**
New Rd. *Dar A* —6A **56**
New Rd. *Heag* —5D **10**
New Rd. *Hilt* —7A **88**
New Rd. *Iron* —2E **12**
(Castle La.)
New Rd. *Iron* —1H **13**
(Station La.)
New Rd. *Newt* —1H **29**
New Rd. *Nott* —1K **63**
New Rd. *Oxt* —1F **21**
New Rd. *Rad T* —4K **67**
New Rd. *S'fd* —6H **61**
New Row. *Cltn* —7B **50**
Newstead Av. *Chad* —2F **75**
Newstead Av. *Nott* —4K **49**
Newstead Av. *Rad T* —3A **68**
Newstead Ct. *Nott* —1J **49**
Newstead Dri. *W Bri* —1K **83**
Newstead Gro. *Bing* —3J **69**
Newstead Gro. *Nott*
—1D **64** (1D **4**)
Newstead Ind. Est. *Arn* —6J **33**
Newstead Rd. *Long E* —5G **79**
Newstead Rd. N. *Ilk* —3B **44**
Newstead Rd. S. *Ilk* —3B **44**
Newstead St. *Sher* —3E **48**
Newstead Ter. *Huck* —4G **17**
Newstead Way. *Strel* —4D **46**
New St. *Der* —4B **74** (5G **7**)
New St. *Dray* —2J **95**
(in two parts)
New St. *Keg* —7J **109**
New St. *L Eat* —6C **40**
New St. *Long E* —1J **97**
New St. *Nott* —5D **48**
New St. *Ock* —4E **76**
New St. *Red* —4G **33**
New St. *Rip* —3A **12**
New St. *Stan* —1E **58**
New Ter. *Sand* —2F **79**
Newthorpe Comn. *Newt* —4E **28**
Newthorpe St. *Nott*
—5F **65** (7G **5**)
**Newton Airfield. —6G 53**
Newton Av. *Bing* —3K **69**
(in two parts)
Newton Av. *Rad T* —3A **68**
Newton Clo. *Arn* —7K **33**
Newton Clo. *Belp* —6C **10**
Newton Clo. *Low* —4E **36**
Newtondale Clo. *Nott* —5K **47**
Newton Dri. *S'fd* —2J **79**
Newton Dri. *W Bri* —4E **82**
Newton Gdns. *Nwtn* —1J **49**
Newton Rd. *Ged* —3B **50**
Newton's La. *Coss* —3F **45**
Newton St. *Bees* —2E **80**
Newton St. *Nott* —7A **64**
Newton's Wlk. *Der* —7J **55**
(in three parts)
New Tythe St. *Long E* —2K **97**
New Va. Rd. *Colw* —2B **66**
New Windmill Ct. *Nott* —3H **65**
New Works Cotts. *Bur J* —6G **51**
New Zealand La. *Duf* —4J **39**
New Zealand Sq. *Der* —3G **73**
Nicholas Clo. *Spon* —2A **76**
Nicholas Rd. *Bees* —6D **62**
Nicker Hill. *Keyw* —5C **102**
*Nicklaus Ct. Nott* —5C **32**
(off Crossfield Dri.)
Nicola Gdns. *Der* —5H **91**
Nidderdale. *Nott* —3C **62**
Nidderdale Clo. *Nott* —4C **62**
Nidderdale Ct. *Alv* —3K **93**
Nightingale Clo. *Nott* —6G **63**
Nightingale Clo. *Nut* —7D **30**
Nightingale Clo. *Rip* —3K **11**
Nightingale Rd. *Der* —2C **92**
Nightingale Way. *Bing* —4C **70**
Nile St. *Nott* —2F **65** (3H **5**)
Nine Acre Gdns. *Nott* —6F **31**
Nine Acres. *Keg* —1G **117**
Nine Corners. *Kimb* —7K **29**
Nixon Ri. *Huck* —7D **16**
Nobel Rd. *Nott* —1J **99**
Noble La. *Asl* —2H **71**
Noble St. *Der* —5C **74** (7H **7**)
Nodin Hill La. *Neth H* —1B **10**
Noel St. *Der* —2H **73**
Noel St. *Kimb* —7A **30**

Noel St. *Nott* —6B **48**
No Man's La. *Ris & Sand*
—7K **59**
Nook End Rd. *Hean* —4F **27**
Nook, The. *Bar T* —4A **104**
Nook, The. *Bees* —1G **81**
(Kenilworth Rd.)
Nook, The. *Bees* —4E **80**
(Meadow La.)
Nook, The. *C'tn* —5D **20**
Nook, The. *Holb* —6C **24**
Nook, The. *Kimb* —1A **46**
Nook, The. *Los* —1E **26**
Nook, The. *Nott* —3E **62**
Nooning La. *Dray* —2G **95**
Norbett Clo. *Bees* —5C **80**
Norbett Rd. *Arn* —4J **33**
Norbett Rd. *Arn* —5J **33**
Norbreck Clo. *Nott* —3H **47**
Norburn Cres. *Nott* —3B **48**
Norbury Clo. *Alst* —6H **55**
Norbury Ct. *Alst* —5H **55**
Norbury Cres. *L'ver* —4G **91**
Norbury Way. *Belp* —6C **10**
Norbury Way. *Sand* —2E **78**
Nordean Rd. *Nott* —1J **49**
Norfolk Av. *Bees* —7A **80**
Norfolk Clo. *Huck* —7D **16**
Norfolk Gdns. *Der* —7K **55**
Norfolk Pk. *Arn* —1K **49**
Norfolk Pl. *Nott* —2E **64** (3E **4**)
Norfolk Rd. *Long E* —7K **79**
Norfolk St. *Der* —6B **74**
Norfolk Wlk. *Sand* —3F **79**
Norland Clo. *Nott* —7G **49**
Norman Av. *Sun* —2J **91**
Normanby Rd. *Nott* —4C **62**
Norman Clo. *Bees* —3C **80**
Norman Clo. *Nott* —1E **64** (1F **5**)
Norman Ct. *Keg* —2H **117**
Norman Cres. *Ilk* —2C **44**
Norman Dri. *Eastw* —3F **29**
Norman Dri. *Huck* —1E **30**
Normandy Rd. *Hilt* —7A **88**
Norman Rd. *Nott* —6C **48**
Norman Rd. *Rip* —2J **11**
Norman St. *Ilk* —3C **44**
Norman St. *Kimb* —6K **29**
Norman St. *N'fld* —1E **66**
Norman St. N. *Ilk* —2C **44**
Normanton La. *Keyw* —6D **102**
Normanton La. *L'ver* —7G **73**
Normanton Rd. *Der*
—4A **74** (6D **6**)
Northacre Rd. *Oak* —5H **57**
Northall Av. *Nott* —7H **31**
Northam Dri. *Rip* —2J **11**
Northampton St. *Nott* —1G **65**
North Av. *Dar A* —4A **56**
North Av. *Mick* —5C **72**
North Av. *Sand* —2E **78**
N. Church St. *Nott* —2E **64** (2E **4**)
N. Circus St. *Nott* —3D **64** (4D **4**)
Northcliffe Av. *Nott* —4K **49**
North Clo. *Mick* —5C **72**
Northcote St. *Long E* —2J **97**
Northcote Way. *Nott* —1J **47**
Northdale Rd. *Nott* —7K **49**
Northdown Dri. *Bees* —4C **80**
Northdown Rd. *Nott* —1J **63**
North Dri. *Bees* —2E **80**
Northern Ct. *Nott* —2K **47**
Northern Dri. *B Vil* —1B **32**
Northern Dri. *Trow* —4H **61**
Northern Rd. *Hean* —3F **27**
Northfield. *Klbrn* —3F **25**
Northfield. *Sten F* —6H **91**
Northfield Av. *Ilk* —4C **44**
Northfield Av. *Long E* —5F **97**
Northfield Av. *Rad T* —3C **68**
Northfield Cres. *Bees* —4K **79**
Northfield Rd. *Bees* —4A **80**
Northfields. *Long E* —5F **97**
Northfields Way. *E Leak*
—7K **111**
North Ga. *Nott* —5K **81**
(College Dri.)
North Ga. *Nott* —5B **48**
(Radford Rd.)
*North Ga. Pl. Nott* —5B **48**
(off High Chu. St.)
Northgate St. *Ilk* —5C **44**
North Grn. *C'tn* —3B **20**
N. Hill Av. *Huck* —5F **17**
N. Hill Cres. *Huck* —5F **17**
North La. *Belp* —3H **23**
Northmead Dri. *Der* —5F **73**
Northolme Av. *Nott* —6J **31**
Northolt Dri. *Nut* —3D **46**

North Pde. *Der* —1A **74** (1D **6**)
North Rd. *Long E* —3G **97**
North Rd. *Nott* —3C **64** (3A **4**)
North Rd. *Rud* —1D **100**
North Rd. *W Bri* —2G **83**
North Row. *Dar A* —6A **56**
N. Sherwood St. *Nott*
—7D **48** (1E **4**)
Northside Wlk. *Arn* —3H **33**
North St. *Bees* —2E **80**
North St. *Der* —1K **73** (1C **6**)
North St. *Ilk* —5D **44**
North St. *Kimb* —1A **46**
North St. *Lan M* —2K **27**
North St. *L'ver* —6G **73**
North St. *Melb* —4G **113**
North St. *Newt* —3G **29**
North St. *Nott* —3G **65** (4J **5**)
Northumberland Clo. *Nott*
—1F **65** (1G **5**)
Northumberland St. *Der* —6K **73**
(in two parts)
North Vw. *Der* —7G **73**
Northville Ct. *Nott* —7F **49**
Northwold Av. *W Bri* —2F **83**
Northwood Av. *Chad* —1E **74**
Northwood Cres. *Nott* —7E **32**
Northwood Rd. *Nott* —7E **32**
Northwood St. *S'fd* —7H **61**
Norton St. *Nott* —1B **64**
(in two parts)
Norwich Gdns. *Nott* —4H **31**
Norwich St. *Der* —1D **74**
Norwood Clo. *Der* —3E **72**
Norwood Rd. *Nott* —2A **64**
Nothills Clo. *Chel* —1G **105**
Notintone Pl. *Nott* —3G **65** (4K **5**)
Notintone St. *Nott* —3G **65** (5K **5**)
Nottingham Airport. *Rad T*
—3D **84**
**Nottingham Archives. —4E 64**
**Nottingham Bowl. —4H 5**
**Nottingham Castle. —6D 4**
**Nottingham City Golf Course.**
**—4G 31**
**Nottingham East Midlands**
**International Airport. —3A 116**
**Nottingham Forest F.C. —6G 65**
**Nottingham Greyhound Stadium.**
**—4K 65**
**Nottingham Indoor Bowls Cen.**
**—7G 47**
**Nottingham Industrial Mus.**
**—4G 63**
Nottingham International Clothing
Cen. *Huck* —3E **16**
**Nottingham National Ice**
**Cen., The. —4H 5**
**Nottingham Race Course.**
**—4A 66**
Nottingham Rd. *Belp* —1A **24**
Nottingham Rd. *Bing* —3H **69**
Nottingham Rd. *Borr* —7D **76**
(in three parts)
Nottingham Rd. *Bul* —1A **52**
Nottingham Rd. *Bur J* —3H **51**
Nottingham Rd. *Cod* —5E **12**
Nottingham Rd. *C Bis* —4D **86**
Nottingham Rd. *Day* —7G **33**
Nottingham Rd. *Der*
(in four parts) —2A **74** (1E **6**)
Nottingham Rd. *Eastw & Newt*
—3D **28**
Nottingham Rd. *Got* —1H **111**
Nottingham Rd. *Hov* —1H **37**
Nottingham Rd. *Huck* —7J **17**
Nottingham Rd. *Ilk* —7D **44**
Nottingham Rd. *Keg* —7H **109**
Nottingham Rd. *Keyw* —7C **102**
Nottingham Rd. *Kimb* —7A **30**
Nottingham Rd. *Long E & Bees*
—1J **97**
Nottingham Rd. *Low* —4E **36**
Nottingham Rd. *Nott* —3A **48**
(in two parts)
Nottingham Rd. *Nut* —1D **46**
Nottingham Rd. *Rad T* —5H **67**
Nottingham Rd. *Rip* —2A **12**
Nottingham Rd. *Spon* —5K **75**
Nottingham Rd. *S'fd* —1H **79**
Nottingham Rd. *Trow* —3G **61**
Nottingham Rd. *Wdbgh* —3B **34**
Nottingham Rd. E. *Eastw* —4F **29**
Nottingham S. & Wilford Ind. Est.
*Nott* —4D **82**
**Nottingham Transport**
**Heritage Cen. —4E 100**
**Nottingham University**
**Sports Cen. —6G 63**

**O**adby Ri. *Sun* —3J **91**
Oak Acres. *Bees* —3A **80**
Oak Apple Cres. *Ilk* —1C **60**
Oak Av. *Bing* —3C **70**
Oak Av. *Lan M* —7K **13**
Oak Av. *Rad T* —3J **67**
Oak Av. *Rip* —5K **11**
Oak Av. *Sand* —1E **78**
Oak Clo. *Alst* —3J **55**
Oak Clo. *Duf* —3J **39**
Oak Clo. *Ock* —3E **76**
Oak Cres. *L'ver* —1G **91**
Oakdale Dri. *Bees* —4C **80**
Oakdale Gdns. *Oak* —4H **57**
Oakdale Rd. *Arn* —5K **33**
Oakdale Rd. *Cltn* —1B **66**
Oakdale Rd. *Nott* —1K **65**
Oak Dri. *Alv* —3G **93**
Oak Dri. *Eastw* —3C **28**
Oak Dri. *Hilt* —7A **88**
Oak Dri. *Mick* —6C **72**
Oak Dri. *Nut* —7B **30**
Oakenhall Av. *Huck* —5J **17**
Oakfield Clo. *Nott* —4C **62**
Oakfield Ct. *Stan C* —5C **42**
Oakfield Dri. *Sand* —5F **79**
Oakfield Rd. *Huck* —6H **17**
Oakfield Rd. *Nott* —4C **62**
Oakfield Rd. *S'fd* —1H **79**
Oakfields Rd. *W Bri* —6J **65**
Oak Flatt. *Bees* —3A **80**
Oakford Clo. *Nott* —4G **47**
Oak Gro. *Huck* —1H **31**
Oakham Clo. *Der* —6D **56**
Oakham Clo. *Nott* —6B **32**
Oakham Rd. *Rud* —6F **83**
Oakham Way. *Ilk* —3B **44**
Oakhurst Clo. *Belp* —6H **9**
Oakington Clo. *Nott* —1D **48**
Oakland Av. *Long E* —4G **97**
Oakland Ct. *Bees* —6A **62**
Oakland Gro. *C'tn* —5D **20**
Oaklands. *Den V* —4J **25**
Oaklands Av. *Hean* —3J **27**
Oaklands Av. *L'ver* —4G **91**
Oaklands Rd. *Etw* —5E **88**
Oakland St. *Nott* —7A **48**
Oaklands Way. *Melb* —3H **113**
Oakland Ter. *Long E* —4G **97**
Oakleigh Av. *Chad* —2F **75**
Oakleigh Av. *Nott* —4A **50**
Oakleigh St. *Nott* —2K **47**
Oakley M. *Nott* —7F **31**
Oakley's Rd. *Long E* —2J **97**
Oakley's Rd. W. *Long E* —3H **97**
Oak Lodge. *Bing* —3D **70**
Oak Lodge Dri. *Kimb* —6K **29**
Oakmead Av. *Nott* —6F **47**
Oakmere Clo. *Edw* —4A **84**
Oakover Dri. *Alst* —4H **55**
Oakridge. *Chad* —1H **75**
Oak Rd. *Thul* —5B **94**
Oakside Way. *Oak* —4H **57**
Oaks, The. *L Eat* —6C **40**
Oaks, The. *Nott* —2G **65** (2J **5**)
Oak St. *Der* —6A **74**
Oak St. *Nott* —5D **48**
Oaktree Av. *Der* —2B **92**
Oak Tree Av. *Rad T* —3K **67**
Oak Tree Clo. *Huck* —1D **30**
Oak Tree Clo. *W Bri* —7J **65**
Oak Tree Ct. *Borr* —7F **77**

Oak Tree Dri. *Ged* —4E **50**
Oakvale Ho. *Der* —6A **74**
Oak Vw. *Nott* —1B **64**
Oakwell Cres. *Ilk* —6C **44**
Oakwell Dri. *Ilk* —6C **44**
Oakwood Clo. *Sten F* —7H **91**
Oakwood Dri. *Nott* —7J **47**
Oakwood Dri. *Oak* —5H **57**
Oakwood Gdns. *Nut* —3D **46**
Oakwood M. *Der* —5F **57**
Oatfield La. *Rad T* —7D **52**
Oban Rd. *Bees* —2C **80**
Oberon Retail Pk. *Belp* —2K **23**
Occupation Dri. *Huck* —7G **17**
Occupation Rd. *Nott* —1H **47**
Ockbrook Ct. *Ilk* —3D **44**
Ockerby St. *Nott* —7J **31**
**Odeon Cinema. —4E 4**
Odesa Dri. *Bulw* —2H **47**
Offerton Av. *Der* —1J **91**
Ogdon Ct. *Nott* —1H **65**
Ogle Dri. *Nott* —4D **64** (6C **4**)
Ogle St. *Huck* —5G **17**
Okehampton Cres. *Nott* —7A **34**
Old Acres. *Wdbgh* —1H **35**
Old Bank Ct. *Nott* —4K **47**
Old Barn Clo. *L Eat* —6C **40**
Old Blacksmiths Yd. *Der* —3D **6**
Old Brickyard. *Nott* —7J **49**
Oldbury Clo. *Nott* —2K **99**
Oldbury Clo. *Oak* —5G **57**
Old Chapel La. *Und* —2E **14**
Old Chester Rd. *Der* —7A **56**
Old Chu. Clo. *Quar* —3G **55**
Old Chu. St. *Nott* —5A **64**
Old Coach Rd. *Nott* —1E **62**
(in three parts)
Old Coppice Side. *Hean* —5G **27**
(in two parts)
Old Derby Rd. *Eastw* —2B **28**
Old Dri. *Bees* —7D **62**
Old Epperstone Rd. *Low* —1A **36**
Oldershaw Av. *Keg* —1G **117**
Old Farm Ct. *Bar F* —3E **98**
Old Farm Rd. *Nott* —5B **32**
Old Ga. Av. *Wstn T* —5A **106**
Old Grantham Rd. *What* —3J **71**
Old Hall Av. *Alv* —2H **93**
Old Hall Av. *Duf* —3H **39**
Old Hall Av. *L'ver* —7F **73**
Old Hall Clo. *C'tn* —5C **20**
Old Hall Dri. *Nott* —5F **49**
Old Hall Mill Bus. Pk. *L Eat*
—7C **40**
Old Hall Rd. *L'ver* —7G **73**
Oldham Ct. *Bees* —4C **80**
Old Hartshay Hill. *Rip* —2J **11**
Old Hill La. *E Bri* —1K **53**
Oldknow St. *Nott* —1B **64**
Old La. *Dar A* —5A **56**
Old Lenton Clo. *C Bis* —4G **87**
Old Lenton St. *Nott* —2F **65** (3G **5**)
Old Lodge Dri. *Nott* —2F **49**
Old Main Rd. *Bul* —1A **52**
(in two parts)
Old Mnr. Clo. *Wdbgh* —1H **35**
Old Mansfield Rd. *Der* —6C **56**
**Old Market Square. —4E 4**
Old Mkt. Sq. *Nott* —4E **4**
Old Melton Rd. *Keyw* —2C **102**
Old Mill Clo. *Bees* —6A **80**
Old Mill Clo. *B Vil* —2K **31**
Old Mill Clo. *Duf* —3J **39**
Old Mill Clo. *Nott* —2B **64** (2A **4**)
Old Mill Ct. *Bing* —2A **70**
**Oldmoor Wood Nature Reserve.**
**—6K 45**
Old Oak Rd. *Nott* —6C **82**
Old Orchard Wlk. *Spon* —2B **76**
Old Park Clo. *Rat S* —4K **109**
Old Pk., The. *Cotg* —4K **85**
Old Pit La. *Smal* —7C **26**
Old Pond, The. *Hean* —5J **27**
Old Rd. *Heag* —3D **10**
Old Rd. *Rud* —7F **83**
Old Rufford Rd. *C'tn* —1K **19**
Old Sch. M. *Ast T* —2D **106**
Old School Clo. *Nott* —1A **100**
Old School Ho. Clo. *C But* —1H **87**
Old Stone Bri. *Iron* —1H **13**
Old St. *Nott* —2E **64** (2F **5**)
Old Tollerton Rd. *Gam* —1A **84**
Old Vicarage Clo. *L'ver* —7G **73**
Old Vicarage La. *Quar* —2G **55**
Olga Rd. *Nott* —1H **65**
Olive Av. *Long E* —7H **79**
Olive Gro. *Bur J* —1K **51**
Olive Gro. *Chad* —4F **75**
Oliver Clo. *Hean* —3K **27**

Oliver Clo. *Nott* —1C **64** (1B **4**)
Oliver Rd. *Ilk* —2A **60**
Oliver St. *Nott* —1C **64** (1B **4**)
Olive St. *Der* —4J **73** (6A **6**)
Olivier St. *Der* —7B **74**
Ollerton Rd. *Arn* —1G **33**
Olton Av. *Bees* —6F **63**
Olton Rd. *Mick* —4A **72**
Olympus Ct. *Huck* —2D **30**
Onchan Av. *Cltn* —1C **66**
Onchan Dri. *Cltn* —1C **66**
Onslow Rd. *Mick* —4B **72**
Opal Clo. *Oak* —5G **57**
Openwoodgate. *Belp* —2D **24**
Openwood Rd. *Belp* —2D **24**
Orange Gdns. *Nott* —5F **65**
Orby Clo. *Nott* —1H **65** (1K **5**)
Orby Wlk. *Nott* —2H **65**
Orchard Av. *Bing* —3K **69**
Orchard Av. *Cltn* —7C **50**
Orchard Av. *Cas D* —7J **107**
Orchard Bus. Pk. *Ilk* —5B **44**
Orchard Clo. *Boul M* —5K **93**
Orchard Clo. *Bread* —3D **56**
Orchard Clo. *Breas* —7D **56**
Orchard Clo. *Bur J* —1K **51**
Orchard Clo. *Dis* —6A **116**
Orchard Clo. *E Bri* —3K **53**
Orchard Clo. *Gun* —1G **53**
Orchard Clo. *Holb* —5B **24**
Orchard Clo. *L'ver* —2G **91**
Orchard Clo. *Melb* —4G **113**
Orchard Clo. *Nott* —6J **81**
Orchard Clo. *Ock* —4E **76**
Orchard Clo. *Rad T* —4J **67**
Orchard Clo. *Toll* —1B **102**
Orchard Clo. *Wain* —5C **12**
Orchard Clo. *W Hal* —7G **43**
Orchard Cotts. *Duf* —2J **39**
Orchard Ct. *Cltn* —7C **50**
Orchard Ct. *Ged* —4B **50**
Orchard Ct. *Huck* —6G **17**
Orchard Ct. *Lan M* —2K **27**
Orchard Ct. *Nott* —6A **48**
Orchard Ct. *Spon* —3A **76**
Orchard Cres. *Bees* —3C **80**
Orchard Dri. *C'tn* —5E **20**
Orchard Gro. *Arn* —7E **32**
Orchard Pk. Ind. Est. *Sand*
—2G **79**
Orchard Ri. *Hean* —3H **27**
Orchard Ri. *Lamb* —6G **35**
Orchard St. *Der* —2K **73** (2C **6**)
Orchard St. *Got* —1H **111**
Orchard St. *Huck* —6G **17**
Orchard St. *Ilk* —7D **44**
Orchard St. *Kimb* —7K **29**
Orchard St. *Lan M* —2K **27**
Orchard St. *Long E* —2J **97**
Orchard St. *Mick* —7B **72**
Orchard St. *Newt* —4E **28**
Orchard, The. *Belp* —1K **23**
Orchard, The. *Cod* —3D **12**
Orchard, The. *Hors W* —7K **25**
Orchard, The. *Stan D* —7D **60**
Orchard Way. *Chel* —7F **93**
Orchard Way. *Sand* —5E **78**
Orchid Clo. *W Bri* —4E **82**
Ordish Av. *Chad* —3F **75**
Ordnance Ct. *Bees* —5C **80**
Oregon Way. *Chad* —1H **75**
Orford Av. *Nott* —4B **82**
Orford Av. *Rad T* —5J **67**
Oriel Ct. *Der* —5B **74** (7G **7**)
Orion Clo. *Nott* —7E **46**
Orion Dri. *Nott* —7E **46**
Orkney Clo. *Sin* —6H **91**
Orlando Dri. *Cltn* —6D **50**
Orlock Wlk. *Nott* —1D **48**
Orly Av. *Cas D* —1J **115**
**Ormonde Fields Golf Course.**
**—5G 13**
Ormonde St. *Lan M* —1K **27**
Ormonde Ter. *Lan M* —1K **27**
Ormonde Ter. *Nott* —4E **48**
Ormskirk Ri. *Spon* —4B **76**
Ornsay Clo. *Nott* —4A **32**
Orpean Way. *Bees* —6J **79**
Orston Av. *Arn* —6J **33**
Orston Dri. *Nott* —3J **63**
Orston Grn. *Nott* —4K **63**
Orston La. *What* —4K **71**
Orston Rd. E. *W Bri* —6H **65**
Orston Rd. W. *W Bri* —6G **65**

Orton Av. *Bees* —2C **80**
Orton Way. *Belp* —6B **10**
Ortzen Ct. *Nott* —1B **64**
Ortzen St. *Nott* —1B **64** (1A **4**)
Orville Rd. *Nott* —1A **48**
Osborne Av. *Nott* —3E **48**
Osborne Clo. *Sand* —4F **79**
Osborne Gro. *Nott* —3E **48**
Osborne St. *Nott* —1A **64**
Osbourne Clo. *Watn* —6B **30**
Osgood Rd. *Arn* —1A **50**
Osier Rd. *Nott* —6E **64**
Osiers, The. *Keg* —1H **117**
Osman Clo. *Nott* —6D **64**
Osmaston Clo. *Long E* —4D **96**
Osmaston Pk. Ind. Est. *Der*
(Ellesmere Av.) —7D **74**
Osmaston Pk. Ind. Est. *Der*
—1E **92**
(Sandown Rd., in two parts)
Osmaston Pk. Rd. *Der* —2A **92**
(St Peter's St.)
Osmaston Rd. *Der* —4A **74** (5E **6**)
(Waverley St.)
Osmaston St. *Nott* —4B **64**
Osmaston St. *Sand* —3G **79**
Osnabruck Sq. *Der* —3A **74** (4E **6**)
Osprey Clo. *Bing* —4B **70**
Osprey Clo. *Nott* —7J **81**
Osprey Clo. *Sin* —7J **91**
Ossington Clo. *Nott* —1E **64** (1E **4**)
Ossington St. *Nott* —1B **64**
Osterley Grn. *Der* —3E **72**
Osterley Gro. *Nut* —4D **46**
Oswestry Clo. *Oak* —4H **57**
Otterburn Dri. *Alst* —5G **55**
Otter St. *Der* —1A **74**
Oulton Clo. *Arn* —7H **33**
Oulton Clo. *Shel L* —5D **92**
Oulton Lodge. *Nott* —4K **31**
Oundle Dri. *Ilk* —7F **45**
Oundle Dri. *Nott* —4J **63**
Ousebridge Cres. *Cltn* —6E **50**
Ousebridge Dri. *Cltn* —6E **50**
Outram Ct. *Rip* —2A **12**
Outram St. *Rip* —2A **12**
Outram Way. *Sten F* —7J **91**
Oval Ct. *L'ver* —1G **91**
Oval Gdns. *Nott* —6K **47**
Overdale Clo. *Long E* —3D **96**
Overdale Rd. *Der* —6J **73**
Overdale Rd. *Nott* —4J **47**
Over La. *Belp* —2D **24**
Over La. *H'wd* —2D **22**
Overstone Clo. *Belp* —1D **24**
Overstrand Clo. *Arn* —7H **33**
Owen Av. *Long E* —3A **98**
Owers Av. *Hean* —6H **27**
Owlers La. *L'ver* —6G **73**
Owlston Clo. *Eastw* —2D **28**
Owlswick Clo. *L'ver* —1E **90**
Owsthorpe Clo. *Nott* —5C **32**
Owthorpe Gro. *Nott* —4D **48**
Owthorpe Rd. *Cotg* —6K **85**
Oxborough Rd. *Arn* —6E **32**
Oxbow Clo. *Nott* —6E **64**
Oxbury Rd. *Watn* —5K **29**
Oxclose La. *Arn* —7D **32**
Oxendale Clo. *W Bri* —2A **84**
Oxengate. *Arn* —7E **32**
Oxenhope Clo. *L'ver* —2C **90**
Oxford Rd. *W Bri* —1J **83**
Oxford St. *Cltn* —5C **50**
Oxford St. *Der* —5B **74** (7G **7**)
Oxford St. *Eastw* —3D **28**
Oxford St. *Ilk* —7D **44**
Oxford St. *Long E* —1H **97**
Oxford St. *Nott* —3D **64** (4C **4**)
Oxford St. *Rip* —3K **11**
Oxford St. *Spon* —3A **76**
Oxton Av. *Nott* —2E **48**
**Oxton Bogs. —1C 20**
Oxton Rd. *Arn & C'tn* —5H **19**
Oxton Way. *Sin* —7K **91**
Oxwich Ct. *Oak* —4H **57**
Ozier Holt. *Colw* —3C **66**
Ozier Holt. *Long E* —3G **97**

**P**ack Horse Rd. *Melb* —2H **113**
Packington Hill. *Keg* —7G **109**
Packman Dri. *Rud* —1F **101**
Paddington M. *Nott* —1J **65**
Paddock Clo. *C'tn* —5D **20**
Paddock Clo. *Cas D* —7G **107**
Paddock Clo. *Nott* —1H **47**
Paddock Clo. *Rad T* —5J **67**
Paddock Cft. *Oak* —5E **56**

Paddocks, The. *Edw* —5K **83**
Paddocks, The. *Nut* —1B **46**
Paddocks, The. *Ock* —4E **76**
Paddocks, The. *Sand* —3E **78**
Paddocks Vw. *Long E* —1F **97**
Paddock, The. *Att* —6D **80**
Paddock, The. *Bing* —3A **70**
Paddock, The. *Boul M* —5K **93**
Paddock, The. *Holb* —7C **24**
Padge Rd. *Bees* —2H **81**
Padgham Ct. *Nott* —5C **32**
Padley Clo. *Alst* —2A **56**
Padley Clo. *Rip* —1J **11**
Padley Ct. *Nott* —7G **31**
Padleys La. *Bur J* —1J **51**
Padstow Clo. *Sten F* —6H **91**
Padstow Rd. *Alv* —4J **93**
Padstow Rd. *Nott* —7B **32**
Page La. *Dis* —6A **116**
Paget Cres. *Rud* —1E **100**
Paignton Clo. *Nott* —4H **47**
Paisley Gro. *Bees* —7C **80**
Palace La. *Shot* —3B **8**



Palatine Gro. *L'ver* —2D **90**
Palatine St. *Nott* —4D **64** (6C **4**)
Palerow La. *Shot* —1B **8**
Palin Ct. *Nott* —7B **32**
Palin Gdns. *Rad T* —4A **68**
Palin St. *Nott* —1B **64**
Palladium Dri. *L'ver* —3E **90**
Pall Mall. *Bread* —3E **56**
Palm Clo. *L'ver* —1E **90**
Palm Cotts. *Nott* —3F **49**
Palm Ct. Ind. Cen. *Nott* —5B **48**
Palmer Av. *Huck* —4G **17**
Palmer Cres. *Cltn* —7B **50**
Palmer Dri. *S'fd* —3H **79**
Palmerston Ct. *Melb* —4H **113**
Palmerston Gdns. *Nott*
(in two parts) —1E **64** (1F **5**)
Palmerston St. *Der* —7J **73**
Palmerston St. *Und* —2D **14**
Palm St. *Nott* —5B **48**
Palmwood Ct. *Nott* —1J **47**
Papplewick La. *Huck* —5H **17**
Parade, The. *Mick* —7B **72**
Parcel Ter. *Der* —3H **73**
Pares Way. *Ock* —3E **76**
Pargate Clo. *Mare* —7K **11**
Park Av. *Aws* —1F **45**
Park Av. *Bur J* —2K **51**
Park Av. *Cltn* —6D **50**
Park Av. *Cas D* —7H **107**
Park Av. *Eastw* —2C **28**
Park Av. *Huck* —5F **17**
Park Av. *Ilk* —6D **44**
Park Av. *Keyw* —6B **102**
Park Av. *Kimb* —2A **46**
Park Av. *Nott* —6E **48**
Park Av. *Plum* —5D **102**
Park Av. *Rip* —3B **12**
Park Av. *Stan* —1E **58**
Park Av. *W Bri* —7H **65**
Park Av. *Wdbgh* —1F **35**
Park Av. *Wd'p* —1G **49**
Park Av. E. *Keyw* —6B **102**
Park Av. W. *Keyw* —6B **102**
Park Chase. *Nott* —1H **47**
Park Clo. *Klbrn* —5G **25**
Park Clo. *L Eat* —6B **40**
Park Clo. *Nott* —6G **49**
Park Clo. *Stan D* —7D **60**
Park Ct. *Hean* —4H **27**
Park Ct. *Nott* —6A **64**
Park Cres. *Eastw* —1D **28**
Park Cres. *Heag* —4E **10**
Park Cres. *Ilk* —6E **44**
Park Cres. *Nott* —3C **62**
Parkcroft Rd. *W Bri* —2H **83**
Parkdale Rd. *Nott & Cltn* —1K **65**
Park Dri. *Huck* —7G **17**
Park Dri. *Ilk* —7D **44**
Park Dri. *L'ver* —7G **73**
Park Dri. *Nott* —3C **64** (5B **4**)
Park Dri. *Sand* —5E **78**
Parker Cen. *Der* —7B **56**
Parker Clo. *Arn* —5K **33**
Parker Clo. *Der* —2K **73** (1C **6**)
Parker Gdns. *S'fd* —7K **61**
Parker Ind. Est. *Der* —7B **56**
Parker St. *Der* —1K **73** (1A **6**)
Parker St. *Huck* —5H **17**
Pk. Farm Cen. *Alst* —5H **55**
Pk. Farm Dri. *Alst* —5H **55**
Parkfields Dri. *Der* —7J **55**
Parkgate. *Huck* —3H **17**
Park Gro. *Der* —1J **73**
Park Hall. *M'ley* —3F **43**

Park Hall La. *W Hal* —4F **43**
Park Hall Rd. *Den* —2G **25**
Parkham Rd. *Kimb* —6K **29**
Park Heights. *Nott*
—4C **64** (6A **4**)
Park Hill. *Aws* —1F **45**
Park Hill. *Nott* —2C **64** (3A **4**)
Pk. Hill Dri. *Der* —2K **91**
Park Homes. *Shel L* —6D **92**
Park Ho. Gates. *Nott* —5F **49**
Parking Clo. *C Bis* —4G **87**
Parkland Clo. *Nott* —5J **81**
Parkland Dri. *Chel* —2G **105**
Park La. *Alst* —3K **55**
Park La. *Cas D* —7D **106**
Park La. *Epp* —7K **21**
Park La. *Heag* —4E **10**
Park La. *Lamb* —6G **35**
Park La. *L'ver* —7G **73**
Park La. *Nott* —2A **48**
Park La. *Wstn T* —6A **106**
Park Leys Ct. *Spon* —4A **76**
Park M. *Nott* —6E **48**
Park Ravine. *Nott* —4C **64** (6B **4**)
Park Rd. *Bees* —2E **80**
(Bramcote Av.)
Park Rd. *Bees* —7K **61**
(Ewe Lamb La.)
Park Rd. *Belp* —3A **24**
Park Rd. *B Vil* —1A **32**
Park Rd. *C'tn* —7D **50**
Park Rd. *Cltn* —7D **50**
Park Rd. *Duf* —3H **39**
Park Rd. *Heag* —4E **10**
Park Rd. *Huck* —5F **17**
Park Rd. *Ilk* —7D **44**
Park Rd. *Mick* —6B **72**
Park Rd. *Nott* —4B **64** (7A **4**)
Park Rd. *Plum* —5D **102**
Park Rd. *Rad T* —3K **67**
Park Rd. *Rip* —3A **12**
Park Rd. *Spon* —3A **75**
Park Rd. *Wd'p* —1G **49**
Park Rd. E. *C'tn* —4D **20**
Park Rd. N. *Bees* —2E **80**
Park Row. *Nott* —3D **64** (5D **4**)
Park Side. *Belp* —2A **24**
Parkside. *Heag* —3E **10**
Parkside. *Nott* —4E **62**
Parkside. *Plum* —5D **102**
Parkside Av. *Long E* —1F **97**
Parkside Clo. *Iron* —1H **13**
Parkside Dri. *Iron* —1H **13**
Parkside Dri. *Long E* —1F **97**
Parkside Gdns. N. *Nott* —4E **62**
Parkside Gdns. S. *Nott* —5E **62**
Parkside Ri. *Nott* —5E **62**
Parkside Rd. *Chad* —3G **75**
Parkstone Clo. *W Bri* —3E **82**
Parkstone Ct. *Mick* —7A **72**
Park St. *Bees* —2E **80**
Park St. *Breas* —1D **96**
Park St. *Der* —4B **74** (6G **7**)
Park St. *Hean* —3F **27**
(in two parts)
Park St. *Long E* —7G **79**
Park St. *Nott* —3B **64**
Park St. *Rip* —3A **12**
Park St. *S'fd* —2G **79**
Park Ter. *Nott* —3D **64** (4C **4**)
Park Ter. *Plum* —4D **102**
Park, The. *Cotg* —4K **85**
Park, The. *Iron* —1G **13**
Park Valley. *Nott* —3D **64** (5C **4**)
Park Vw. *Ast T* —3D **106**
Park Vw. *Eastw* —4D **28**
Park Vw. *Hean* —4F **27**
Park Vw. *L Eat* —6C **40**
Park Vw. *Nott* —4G **49**
Pk. View Clo. *Alst* —3K **55**
Pk. View Ct. *Bees* —2D **80**
Pk. View Ct. *Nott* —2F **65** (3H **5**)
Parkview Dri. *Nott* —6C **32**
Pk. View Ho. *Der* —2C **74** (2J **7**)
Park Wlk. *Klbrn* —4F **25**
Parkway. *Chel* —1E **104**
Park Way. *Etw* —5E **88**
Parkway Ct. *Nott* —2D **62**
Parkwood Ct. *Nott* —1A **48**
Parkwood Cres. *Nott* —3G **49**
Parkyn Rd. *Day* —7F **33**
Parkyns St. *Rud* —2E **100**
Parliament Clo. *Der* —4J **73**
Parliament St. *Der* —4J **73** (6A **6**)
(in two parts)
Parliament St. Mills. *Der* —4J **73**
Parliament Ter. *Nott*
—2D **64** (3D **4**)

Parr Ga. *Bees* —3A **80**
Parrs, The. *Bees* —2H **81**
Parry Way. *Arn* —5K **33**
Parsons Gro. *Den V* —3K **25**
Parsons Mdw. *Colw* —3C **66**
Partridge Clo. *Bing* —4B **70**
Partridge Way. *Mick* —5E **72**
Parwich Cotts. *Der* —6A **74**
Pasteur Av. *Rip* —2J **11**
Pasteur Ct. *Nott* —5A **64**
Pasture Clo. *Colw P* —3C **66**
Pasture La. *C Bis* —5H **87**
Pasture La. *Long E* —3A **98**
Pasture La. *Rud* —3B **100**
Pasture Rd. *S'fd* —2G **79**
Pastures Av. *L'ver* —2D **90**
Pastures Av. *Nott* —1K **99**
**Pastures Golf Course. —2A 90**
Pastures Hill. *L'ver* —1E **90**
Pastures, The. *C'tn* —5B **20**
Pastures, The. *Duf* —2J **39**
Pastures, The. *Gilt* —5G **29**
Pasture Vw. *Gun* —1G **53**
Pateley Rd. *Nott* —2J **49**
Paterson Av. *Chad* —2H **75**
Patmore Sq. *Der* —2K **91**
Paton Rd. *Nott* —1A **48**
Patricia Dri. *Arn* —4J **33**
Patrick Rd. *W Bri* —7G **65**
Patten Ct. *Sin* —4A **92**
Patterdale Clo. *Gam* —1A **84**
Patterdale Ct. *Bees* —3A **80**
Patterdale Rd. *Alv* —7G **75**
Patterdale Rd. *Wd'p* —1H **49**
Patterson Rd. *Nott* —7B **48**
Pavilion Clo. *Nott* —6F **65**
Pavilion Ct. *Low* —5E **36**
Pavilion Rd. *Arn* —4D **32**
Pavilion Rd. *Ilk* —7C **28**
Pavilion Rd. *L'ver* —1G **91**
Pavilion Rd. *W Bri* —6G **65**
Paxton Clo. *Mick* —7A **72**
Paxton Gdns. *Nott*
—2G **65** (2J **5**)
Payne Rd. *Bees* —5A **80**
Payne St. *Der* —2H **73**
Paytons Rd. *Der* —5B **74** (7F **7**)
Peache Way. *Bees* —1B **80**
Peachey St. *Nott* —2E **64** (2E **4**)
Peach St. *Der* —3H **73**
Peach St. *Hean* —4F **27**
Peacock Clo. *Gun* —2G **53**
Peacock Clo. *Rud* —3D **100**
Peacock Cres. *Nott* —6A **82**
Peacock Gro. *L'ver* —3F **91**
Peacock Pl. *Ilk* —2B **44**
Peakdale Clo. *Long E* —3E **96**
Peakdale Clo. *Rip* —6K **11**
Peak Dri. *Der* —2B **92**
Peak Pk. *Der* —2B **92**
Pearce Dri. *Nott* —7H **47**
Pearl Clo. *Oak* —5G **57**
Pearmain Dri. *Nott* —7H **49**
Pearson Av. *Bees* —3B **80**
Pearson Clo. *Bees* —3B **80**
Pearson Ct. *Bees* —7B **62**
Pearson Ct. *Day* —6A **33**
Pearson St. *N'fld* —1E **66**
Pearson St. *Nott* —4B **48**
Pear Tree Av. *Rip* —4K **11**
Peartree Clo. *Cas D* —7J **107**
Peartree Ct. *Der* —6D **56**
Pear Tree Ct. *Etw* —5D **88**
Pear Tree Ct. *Nott* —2A **48**
Pear Tree Cres. *Der* —1A **92**
Pear Tree Ind. Est. *Der* —1B **92**
Pear Tree Orchard. *Rud* —2E **100**
Pear Tree Rd. *Der* —6A **74**
Pear Tree St. *Der* —1A **92**
Peary Clo. *Nott* —7B **32**
Peasehill. *Rip* —4B **12**
Peasehill Rd. *Rip* —4A **12**
Peas Hill Rd. *Nott* —1F **65** (1H **5**)
(in two parts)
Peatburn Av. *Hean* —3E **26**
Peatfield Ct. *S'fd* —6H **61**
Peatfield Rd. *S'fd* —6H **61**
Peat La. *Shot* —1B **8**
Peckham Gdns. *Der* —3E **72**
Peck La. *Gun* —1G **53**
(in two parts)
Peck La. *Nott* —3E **64** (4F **5**)
Pedestrian Way. *Nott* —5B **32**
Pedley St. *Ilk* —7D **44**
Pedmore Valley. *Nott* —6C **32**
Peebles Clo. *Sin* —5H **91**
Peel St. *Der* —2H **73**
Peel St. *Lan M* —2K **27**
Peel St. *Long E* —1J **97**

Peel St. *Nott* —1D **64** (1D **4**)
Peel Vs. *Nott* —4G **49**
Peers Clo. *Oak* —5H **57**
Peet St. *Der* —4J **73** (5A **6**)
Pegasus Way. *Hilt* —7A **88**
Peggs Wlk. *Der* —2J **91**
Pegwell Clo. *Sun* —2H **91**
Pelham Av. *Ilk* —5C **44**
Pelham Av. *Nott* —6D **48**
Pelham Cotts. *Nott* —5A **4**
Pelham Cres. *Bees* —1H **81**
Pelham Cres. *Nott* —3B **64** (4A **4**)
Pelham Rd. *Nott* —6D **48**
Pelham St. *Der* —4K **73** (6B **6**)
Pelham St. *Ilk* —5C **44**
Pelham St. *Nott* —3E **64** (4F **5**)
Pellham Ct. *Nott* —6D **48**
Pemberton St. *Nott*
—3F **65** (5H **5**)
Pembrey Clo. *Trow* —5H **61**
Pembridge Clo. *Nott* —4K **47**
Pembroke Dri. *Nott* —5E **48**
Pembroke St. *Der* —1D **74**
Pembury Rd. *Nott* —2E **62**
Penalton Clo. *Altn* —3E **92**
Penarth Gdns. *Nott* —3G **49**
Penarth Ri. *Nott* —3G **49**
Pencroft Gro. *L'ver* —4G **91**
Pendennis Clo. *Alv* —3H **93**
Pendennis Clo. *Ged* —5F **51**
Pendine Clo. *Red* —4F **33**
Pendlebury Dri. *Mick* —7C **72**
(in two parts)
Pendle Cres. *Nott* —5H **49**
Pendleside Way. *L'ver* —2C **90**
Pendock La. *Bradm* —7H **101**
Penge Rd. *Der* —1E **72**
Penhale Dri. *Huck* —7C **16**
Penhaligan's Clo. *Chel* —1F **105**
Penhaligan's Wlk. *Chel* —7F **93**
Penhurst Clo. *Nott* —4C **82**
Peniston Ct. *Melb* —5G **113**
Peniston Ri. *Melb* —5G **113**
Penllech Clo. *Nott* —6C **32**
Penllech Wlk. *Nott* —6C **32**
Pen Moor Clo. *Long E* —3E **96**
Pennant Rd. *Nott* —4K **47**
Pennard Wlk. *Nott* —1K **99**
Penn Av. *Nott* —4A **64**
Pennhome Av. *Nott* —4E **48**
Pennie Clo. *Long E* —5H **97**
Pennine Clo. *Arn* —4D **32**
Pennine Clo. *Long E* —7E **78**
Pennine Vw. *Heag* —4E **10**
Penn La. *Melb* —4G **113**
Penn St. *Belp* —1A **24**
Penshore Clo. *Nott* —7K **81**
Pentagon, The. *Der* —2C **74** (2J **7**)
Pentland Clo. *Oak* —5G **57**
Pentland Dri. *Arn* —3D **32**
Pentland Gdns. *Long E* —7E **78**
Pentrich Rd. *Rip* —2K **11**
Pentridge Dri. *Ilk* —3A **44**
Pentwood Av. *Arn* —3H **33**
Penzance Rd. *Alv* —4H **93**
Peoples Hall Cotts. *Nott*
—2F **65** (3G **5**)
(off Heathcoat St.)
Peppercorn Gdns. *Nott* —1J **63**
Pepper La. *Stan D* —7C **60**
Pepper Rd. *C'tn* —4C **20**
Peppers Dri. *Keg* —1F **117**
Pepper St. *Nott* —3E **64** (5F **5**)
Percival Rd. *Nott* —4D **48**
Percy Dri. *Der* —5J **73** (7A **6**)
Percy St. *Eastw* —3E **28**
Percy St. *Ilk* —7D **44**
Percy St. *Nott* —3K **47**
Peregrine Clo. *Lent* —3A **64**
Peregrine Clo. *Sin* —5H **91**
Peri Va. Clo. *Nut* —3B **46**
Perlethorpe Av. *Ged* —4B **50**
Perlethorpe Av. *Nott*
—3H **65** (5K **5**)
Perlethorpe Clo. *Ged* —4C **50**
Perlethorpe Cres. *Ged* —4C **50**
Perlethorpe Dri. *Ged* —4B **50**

Perlethorpe Dri. *Huck* —5H **17**
Perry Gdns. *Nott* —3D **48**
Perry Gro. *Bing* —3B **70**
Perry Rd. *Nott* —4B **48**
Perth Clo. *Mick* —4C **72**
Perth Dri. *S'fd* —6J **61**
Perth St. *Der* —6D **56**
Perth St. *Nott* —2E **64** (2F **5**)
Peter Baines Ind. Est. *Der*
—4K **73** (6C **6**)
Peterborough St. *Der* —7E **56**
Peterhouse Ter. *Der* —6A **74**
Peterlee Pl. *Alv* —4G **93**
Peters Clo. *Arn* —7A **34**
Peters Clo. *Melb* —7D **114**
Peters Clo. *Newt* —3G **29**
Petersfield Clo. *Nott* —6B **32**
Petersgate. *Long E* —7E **78**
Petersgate Clo. *Long E* —6E **78**
Petersham Dri. *Alv* —3J **93**
Petersham M. *Nott* —4B **64**
Petersham Rd. *Long E* —6E **78**
Petworth Av. *Bees* —5K **79**
Petworth Dri. *Nott* —2B **48**
Peveril Av. *Borr* —6E **76**
Peveril Ct. *Rip* —3J **11**
Peveril Ct. *W Bri* —1G **83**
Peveril Cres. *Long E* —4D **96**
Peveril Cres. *W Hal* —6G **43**
Peveril Dri. *Ilk* —4B **44**
Peveril Dri. *Nott* —4D **64** (6C **4**)
Peveril Dri. *W Bri* —5G **83**
Peveril M. *Nott* —5A **4**
Peveril Rd. *Bees* —7F **63**
Peveril St. *Der* —3D **92**
Peveril St. *Huck* —4G **17**
Peveril St. *Nott* —1B **64** (1A **4**)
**Pewit Golf Course. —7B 44**
Pheasant Fld. Dri. *Spon* —2C **76**
Philip Av. *Eastw* —4E **28**
Philip Av. *Nut* —7C **30**
Philip Gro. *Ged* —4C **50**
Philips Cft. *Duf* —2J **39**
Phoenix Av. *Ged* —4C **50**
Phoenix Cen. *Nott* —2G **47**
Phoenix Clo. *Nott* —5D **64**
Phoenix Ct. *Eastw* —3E **28**
Phoenix Ct. *Nott* —7B **64**
Phoenix Rd. *Newt* —1F **29**
Phoenix St. *Der* —2A **74** (2E **6**)
Phyllis Clo. *Huck* —3F **17**
Phyllis Gro. *Long E* —2K **97**
Piccadilly. *Nott* —7K **31**
Pickard La. *Heag* —3D **10**
Pickering Av. *Eastw* —3D **28**
Pickering Ri. *Der* —6C **56**
**Pickford's House Mus. —3B 6**
Pieris Dri. *Nott* —7J **81**
Pierrepont Av. *Ged* —5C **50**
Pierrepont Rd. *W Bri* —7J **65**
Pilcher Ga. *Nott* —3F **65** (4F **5**)
Pilgrims Way. *Sten F* —6G **91**
Pilkington Rd. *Nott* —5J **49**
Pilkington St. *Nott* —6H **31**
Pillar Ct. *Mick* —7C **72**
Pilsley Clo. *Belp* —6C **10**
Pimlico. *Der* —2F **73**
Pimlico. *Ilk* —6C **44**
Pimlico Av. *Bees* —4B **62**
Pinchom's Hill Rd. *Belp* —2B **24**
Pinder St. *Nott* —3F **65** (5H **5**)
Pine Av. *Lan M* —2J **27**
Pine Clo. *Chad* —4H **75**
Pine Clo. *Etw* —5E **88**
Pine Clo. *Rip* —3K **11**
Pine Clo. *Smal* —1B **42**
Pinecroft Ct. *Oak* —6H **57**
Pine Gro. *Huck* —1H **31**
Pine Hill Clo. *Nott* —4B **32**
Pinehurst Av. *Huck* —7C **16**
Pines, The. *Dray* —2K **95**
Pine Tree Wlk. *Eastw* —3C **28**
Pine Vw. *Nott* —1B **64**
Pinewood Av. *Arn* —4K **33**
Pinewood Av. *Cod* —5D **12**
Pinewood Gdns. *Nott* —1K **99**
Pinewood Rd. *Belp* —6J **9**
Pinfold. *Bing* —3B **70**
Pinfold Clo. *Cotg* —4K **85**
Pinfold Clo. *Wdbgh* —1G **35**
Pinfold Cres. *Wdbgh* —1G **35**
Pinfold La. *Nott* —2D **82**
Pinfold La. *Shelf* —5C **52**
Pinfold La. *S'fd* —1H **79**
Pinfold Rd. *Gilt* —4G **29**
Pinfold, The. *Belp* —7C **10**
Pinfold, The. *Thul* —5B **94**
Pingle. *Alst* —3J **55**
Pingle Cres. *Belp* —7K **9**

Pingle Cres. *Nott* —5B **32**
Pinglehill Way. *Chel* —7H **93**
Pingle La. *Belp* —7K **9**
Pingle La. *Heag* —2F **11**
Pingle, The. *Long E* —7H **79**
Pingle, The. *Melb* —4G **113**
Pingle, The. *Spon* —4A **76**
Pingreaves Dri. *Chel* —7G **93**
Pintail Clo. *Cltn* —2F **67**
Pintail Dri. *Sin* —5H **91**
**Pioneer Meadows Local Nature**
**Reserve. —3B 60**
Piper Clo. *Huck* —3H **17**
Pippin Clo. *Nott* —7H **49**
Pippin Hill. *Den V* —4A **26**
Pitcairn Clo. *Nott* —6E **64**
Pit Clo. La. *Chel* —1G **105**
Pit La. *Rip* —3A **12**
Pit La. *Ship* —7K **27**
Pit La. *Wain* —5C **12**
Pittar St. *Der* —5K **73** (7B **6**)
Plackett Clo. *Breas* —1B **96**
Plackett Clo. *S'fd* —7K **61**
Plains Farm Clo. *Nott* —3J **49**
Plains Gro. *Nott* —2J **49**
Plains La. *Black* —1F **23**
Plainspot Rd. *Brins* —3C **14**
Plains Rd. *Nott* —3H **49**
Plane Clo. *Nott* —6F **31**
Plantagenet Ct. *Nott*
—2F **65** (2H **5**)
Plantagenet St. *Nott*
—2F **65** (2H **5**)
Plantain Gdns. *L'ver* —4G **91**
Plantation Clo. *Arn* —4D **32**
Plantation Rd. *Keyw* —6B **102**
Plantation Rd. *Nott* —3C **62**
Plantation Side. *Nott* —7A **48**
Plantations, The. *Long E* —1E **96**
Plant La. *Long E* —5E **96**
Platt La. *Keyw* —5D **102**
Platts Av. *Hean* —4E **26**
Player St. *Nott* —1A **64**
**Play House. —4D 4**
Plaza Gdns. *Nott* —2B **48**
Pleasant Ct. *Nott* —7B **48**
Pleasant Pl. *Keg* —1H **117**
Pleasant Row. *Nott* —7B **48**
Plimsoll Ct. *Der* —5K **73** (7C **6**)
Plimsoll St. *Der* —2G **73**
Ploughfield Clo. *L'ver* —3F **91**
Ploughgate. *Dar A* —5K **55**
Plough La. *Low* —4D **36**
Plough La. *Nott* —3G **65** (5J **5**)
Ploughman Av. *Wdbgh* —1H **35**
Plover Wharf. *Nott* —5C **64**
Plowman Ct. *S'fd* —2G **79**
Plowright Ct. *Nott* —7F **49**
Plowright St. *Nott* —7F **49**
Plumb Rd. *Huck* —5F **17**
Plummer La. *Keg* —1G **117**
Plumptre Almhouses. *Nott* —5H **5**
Plumptre Clo. *Eastw* —4D **28**
Plumptre Pl. *Nott* —3F **65** (5G **5**)
Plumptre Rd. *Lan M* —7K **13**
Plumptre Sq. *Nott* —3F **65** (5H **5**)
Plumptre St. *Nott* —3F **65** (5G **5**)
Plumptre Way. *Eastw* —4D **28**
Plumtree Gdns. *C'tn* —5D **20**
Plumtree Rd. *Cotg* —6H **85**
Plungar Clo. *Nott* —1H **63**
Podder La. *Nott* —7A **34**
Pointers Ct. *Nott* —7J **49**
Point, The. *Nott* —6F **49**
Pollards Oaks. *Borr* —7E **76**
Polperro Way. *Huck* —7C **16**
Pond Hills La. *Arn* —5H **33**
Pond Rd. *Holb* —6C **24**
Ponsonby Ter. *Der* —3J **73** (4A **6**)
Pontefract St. *Der* —2D **92**
Pontypool Clo. *Oak* —5H **57**
Pool Clo. *Boul M* —5J **93**
Poole St. *Altn* —3E **92**
Pool Mdw. *Colw* —3D **66**
Pool Rd. *Melb* —4H **113**
Popham Ct. *Nott* —3F **65** (5G **5**)
Popham St. *Nott* —3F **65** (5G **5**)
Poplar Av. *Nott* —4C **48**
Poplar Av. *Rip* —4K **11**
Poplar Av. *Sand* —1E **78**
Poplar Av. *Spon* —3A **76**
Poplar Clo. *Alv* —2H **93**
Poplar Clo. *Bing* —3C **70**
Poplar Clo. *Cltn* —1B **66**
Poplar Cres. *Nut* —7A **30**
Poplar Nook. *Alst* —3A **56**
Poplar Row. *Dar A* —6A **56**
Poplars Av. *Bur J* —1A **52**

Poplars Clo. *Plum* —5D **102**
Poplars Rd. *Nott* —5B **64**
Poplars, The. *Alst* —3K **55**
Poplars, The. *Bees* —1F **81**
Poplars, The. *Plum* —3C **102**
Poplars, The. *W Bri* —1H **83**
Poplar St. *Nott* —3F **65** (5H **5**)
Poplar Way. *Ilk* —2B **60**
Porchester Clo. *Huck* —5J **17**
Porchester Rd. *Bing* —3K **69**
Porchester Rd. *Nott* —3H **49**
Porlock Clo. *Long E* —7E **78**
Porlock Clo. *Oak* —5G **57**
Portage Clo. *Rad T* —5J **67**
Port Arthur Rd. *Nott* —3J **65**
Porter Clo. *Nott* —1J **99**
Porterhouse Rd. *Rip* —3A **12**
Porter Rd. *Der* —7J **73**
Porter's La. *Find* —7A **90**
(in two parts)
Porter's La. *Oak* —4F **57**
Porters Wlk. *Nott* —1J **65**
Porthcawl Pl. *Oak* —5J **57**
Portico Rd. *L'ver* —3E **90**
Portinscale Clo. *W Bri* —3A **84**
Portland Clo. *Mick* —6B **72**
Portland Ct. *Nott* —1D **48**
Portland Cres. *S'fd* —2J **79**
Portland Gdns. *Huck* —5F **17**
Portland Grange. *Huck* —5E **16**
Portland Hill. *Nott* —6J **63**
**Portland Leisure Cen. —5F 65**
Portland Pk. Clo. *Huck* —5F **17**
Portland Rd. *Bees* —7K **79**
Portland Rd. *Cltn* —4A **50**
Portland Rd. *Gilt* —5F **29**
Portland Rd. *Huck* —5H **17**
Portland Rd. *Ilk* —3D **44**
Portland Rd. *Long E* —5E **96**
Portland Rd. *Nott* —2C **64** (2B **4**)
Portland Rd. *W Bri* —2H **83**
Portland St. *Bees* —1G **81**
Portland St. *Day* —7F **33**
Portland St. *Der* —7A **74**
Portland St. *Etw* —6E **88**
Portman Chase. *Sten F* —7H **91**
Portreath Dri. *Alst* —3J **55**
Portree Dri. *Nott* —4B **32**
Port Said Vs. *Nott* —5B **48**
Port Way. *Holb & Cox* —7C **24**
Portway Clo. *Alst* —3A **56**
Posey La. *Ast T* —3C **106**
Postern St. *Nott* —3D **64** (4D **4**)
Post Office Yd. *Hov* —3K **37**
Posts, The. *C But* —2G **87**
Potato Pit La. *Ilk* —6J **59**
Potomac M. *Nott* —3C **64** (5B **4**)
Potters Clo. *Nott* —6C **32**
Potters Ct. *Bees* —6D **62**
Potter St. *Melb* —4H **113**
Potter St. *Spon* —4K **75**
Potters Way. *Ilk* —6E **44**
Pottery Clo. *Belp* —7C **10**
Pottery La. *Den* —2J **25**
Poulter Clo. *Nott* —7K **47**
Poulton Dri. *Nott* —4H **65**
Poultry. *Nott* —3E **64** (4F **5**)
Poultry Arc. *Nott* —4F **5**
Powell St. *Der* —6J **73**
Powers Rd. *Nott* —6H **49**
Powis St. *Nott* —6H **31**
Powtrell Clo. *Ilk* —1F **61**
Poynter Clo. *Hean* —4E **26**
Poynton St. *Nott* —2D **64** (3D **4**)
Poyser Av. *Chad* —1G **75**
Poyser Clo. *New B* —5C **48**
Precinct, The. *Cotg* —5K **85**
Premier Rd. *Nott* —6C **48**
Prendwick Gdns. *Nott* —5D **32**
Prescot Clo. *Mick* —7A **72**
Prestbury Clo. *Oak* —6G **57**
Prestwick Clo. *Nott* —4D **46**
Prestwood Dri. *Nott* —7H **47**
Pretoria Vs. *Nott* —4J **47**
Previn Gdns. *Nott* —1H **65**
Pride Parkway. *Pri P*
—4B **74** (5H **7**)
Priestland Av. *Spon* —4K **75**
Primary Clo. *Belp* —1A **24**
Prime Enterprise Pk. *Der*
—2B **74** (1F **7**)
Prime Ind. Est. *Der* —6C **74**
Prime Parkway. *Der*
—1B **74** (1F **7**)
Primrose Av. *Und* —2D **14**
Primrose Bank. *Bing* —3K **69**
Primrose Bank. *Etw* —4E **88**
Primrose Clo. *Nott* —7F **49**
Primrose Clo. *Oak* —4F **57**

Primrose Cres. *Cltn* —7D **50**
Primrose Dri. *M'ly* —6J **41**
Primrose Hill. *Ilk* —3C **44**
Primrose Ri. *Newt* —5E **28**
Primrose St. *Cltn* —7D **50**
Primrose St. *Nott* —7D **31**
Primrose St. *Ilk* —3C **44**
Primula Clo. *Nott* —6J **81**
Primula Way. *L'ver* —5H **91**
Prince Charles Av. *Der* —2D **72**
Prince Edward Cres. *Rad T*
—5H **67**
Princess Alice Ct. *Der*
—2K **73** (2B **6**)
Princess Av. *Bees* —2G **81**
Princess Clo. *Ged* —4C **50**
Princess Clo. *Hean* —3F **27**
Princess Dri. *Borr* —6C **76**
Princess Dri. *Sand* —4F **79**
Princess St. *Long E* —1H **97**
Prince's St. *Der* —7A **74**
Princes St. *Eastw* —2D **28**
Prince St. *Ilk* —2C **44**
Prince St. *Long E* —1H **97**
Prioridge. *Cotg* —6A **86**
Prior Rd. *Day* —7F **33**
Priors Barn Clo. *Borr* —6F **77**
Priors Clo. *Bing* —2C **70**
Priors, The. *Low* —3D **36**
Priorway Av. *Borr* —7E **76**
Priorway Gdns. *Borr* —7E **76**
Priory Av. *Toll* —7A **84**
Priory Cir. *Toll* —7A **84**
Priory Clo. *Chel* —2G **105**
Priory Clo. *Ilk* —1A **60**
Priory Ct. *Ged* —4D **50**
Priory Ct. *Nott* —5G **49**
Priory Cres. *Ged* —5D **50**
Priory Gdns. *Oak* —5F **57**
Priory M. *Nott* —5A **64**
Priory Rd. *Eastw* —4D **28**
Priory Rd. *Ged* —5D **50**
Priory Rd. *Huck* —5E **16**
Priory Rd. *W Bri* —7H **65**
Priory St. *Nott* —5A **64**
Pritchard Dri. *S'fd* —2J **79**
Pritchett Dri. *L'ver* —1C **90**
Private Rd. *Huck* —5E **16**
Private Rd. *Sher & Map* —4E **48**
Private Rd. *Wdbgh* —7F **21**
Private Rd. 8. *Colw I* —2D **66**
Private Rd. 5. *Colw I* —2F **67**
Private Rd. 4. *Colw I* —2F **67**
Private Rd. 1. *Colw I* —1D **66**
Private Rd. 7. *Colw I* —1D **66**
Private Rd. 3. *Colw I* —2E **66**
Private Rd. 2. *Colw I* —2D **66**
Prize Clo. *Nott* —7J **81**
Promenade. *Nott* —2F **65** (2H **5**)
Prospect Dri. *Belp* —3K **23**
Prospect Pl. *Nott* —4B **64**
Prospect Rd. *Cltn* —5J **49**
Prospect Rd. *Den* —4F **25**
Prospect Rd. *Hean* —5J **27**
Prospect St. *Nott* —1A **64**
Prospect Ter. *Nott* —1A **64**
Providence Pl. *Ilk* —5C **44**
Providence St. *Rip* —4A **12**
Provident St. *Der* —6K **73**
Prudhoe Ct. *Nott* —5A **64**
Pulborough Clo. *Nott* —2B **48**
Pulborough Gdns. *L'ver* —3E **90**
Pullman Rd. *Der* —4F **75**
Pullman Rd. *Nott* —3H **65**
Pumping Sta. Cotts. *Nott*
—4J **65**
Purbeck Clo. *Long E* —1E **96**
Purbeck Dri. *W Bri* —3E **82**
Purchase Av. *Los* —3E **26**
Purdy Mdw. *Long E* —4D **96**
Putney Clo. *Der* —3C **72**
Pyatt St. *Nott* —6F **65**
Pybus St. *Der* —2H **73**
Pygall Av. *Got* —1G **111**
Pykestone Clo. *Oak* —5F **57**
Pym Leys. *Long E* —4D **96**
Pym St. *Nott* —1H **65** (1K **5**)
Pym Wlk. *Nott* —1G **65** (1J **5**)
Pytchley Clo. *Belp* —1D **24**

**Q**uaker Clo. *Melb* —3G **113**
Quantock Clo. *Arn* —3D **32**
Quantock Clo. *Sten F* —7H **91**
Quantock Gro. *Bing* —3J **69**
Quantock Rd. *Long E* —7E **78**
Quarndon Heights. *Alst* —5G **55**
Quarndon Vw. *Alst* —5G **55**
Quarn Dri. *Alst* —4G **55**

Quarn Gdns. *Der* —1K **73** (1B **6**)
Quarn St. *Der* —2K **73** (1A **6**)
(in two parts)
Quarn Way. *Der* —2K **73** (1B **6**)
Quarry Av. *Nott* —7H **31**
Quarrydale. *Huck* —3F **17**
Quarry Hill. *Stan D* —7D **60**
Quarry Hill Ind. Est. *Ilk* —2D **60**
Quarry Hill Rd. *Ilk* —2D **60**
Quarry Rd. *Belp* —3K **23**
Quarry Rd. *M'ly* —6H **41**
Quayside Clo. *Nott* —6G **65**
Queen Elizabeth Rd. *Bees* —4A **80**
Queen Elizabeth Way. *Ilk* —2A **60**
Queen Mary Ct. *Der* —1K **73**
Queen Mary's Clo. *Rad T* —5D **68**
Queens Av. *Ged* —4C **50**
Queens Av. *Hean* —3F **27**
Queens Av. *Ilk* —2E **60**
Queens Av. *Stan* —1E **58**
Queensberry St. *Nott* —2A **48**
Queen's Bower Rd. *Nott* —5E **32**
Queens Bri. Rd. *Nott*
—4E **64** (7F **5**)
Queensbury Av. *W Bri* —5E **82**
Queensbury Chase. *L'ver* —3E **90**
Queen's Ct. *Bing* —2K **69**
Queens Ct. *Der* —7J **55**
Queens Ct. *Dray* —2J **95**
Queen's Dri. *Bees* —2G **81**
Queen's Dri. *Belp* —7J **9**
Queens Dri. *Brins* —5C **14**
Queen's Dri. *Ilk* —6C **44**
Queen's Dri. *L'ver* —6G **73**
Queen's Dri. *Nott* —1C **82** (7D **4**)
Queens Dri. *Nut* —7C **30**
Queen's Dri. *Sand* —4F **79**
Queensferry Gdns. *Altn* —5E **92**
Queensland Clo. *Mick* —4C **72**
**Queen's Leisure Cen. —2D 6**
Queen's Rd. *Bees* —3G **81**
Queens Rd. *Keg* —7H **109**
Queens Rd. *Nott* —4E **64** (7F **5**)
Queen's Rd. *Rad T* —3K **67**
Queen's Rd. E. *Bees* —1H **81**
Queens Rd. N. *Eastw* —3D **28**
Queens Rd. S. *Eastw* —4D **28**
Queen's Rd. W. *Bees* —4D **80**
Queen's Sq. *Eastw* —3D **28**
Queen St. *Arn* —4H **33**
Queen St. *Belp* —2A **24**
Queen St. *Der* —2A **74** (2D **6**)
Queen St. *Huck* —4F **17**
Queen St. *Ilk* —6C **44**
Queen St. *Lan M* —2A **28**
Queen St. *Long E* —2J **97**
Queen St. *Nott* —2E **64** (3E **4**)
Queen St. *Wain* —5B **12**
**Queen Street Gallery. —2D 6**
Queens Vw. Dri. *Wain* —5C **12**
Queens Wlk. *Nott* —6D **64**
Queensway. *Cas D* —6H **107**
Queensway. *Der* —1H **73**
Queensway. *Melb* —3H **113**
Queen Ter. *Ilk* —6C **44**
Quenby La. *Rip* —3A **12**
Querneby Av. *Nott* —4G **49**
Querneby Rd. *Nott* —4G **49**
Quick Clo. *Melb* —4G **113**
Quick Hill Rd. *Sten F* —7H **91**
Quillings Way. *Borr* —7F **77**
Quinton Clo. *Nott* —3C **82**
Quintyn Rd. *Alv* —1G **93**
Quorn Clo. *Bees* —5E **80**
Quorn Cres. *Long E* —4H **97**
Quorn Gro. *Nott* —3C **48**
Quorn Ri. *Sun* —3J **91**
Quorn Rd. *Nott* —3C **48**

**R**abown Av. *L'ver* —1H **91**
Racecourse Pk. Ind. Est. *Der*
—7C **56**
Racecourse Rd. *Nott* —3K **65**
Radbourne La. *Kirk L & Der*
—3A **72**
Radbourne Rd. *Nott* —4H **65**
Radbourne St. *Der* —2G **73**
Radburn Ct. *S'fd* —6J **61**
Radcliffe Av. *Chad* —1F **75**
Radcliffe Dri. *Der* —5H **73**
Radcliffe Gdns. *Cltn* —6B **50**
Radcliffe Lodge. *Rad T* —4J **67**
Radcliffe Mt. *W Bri* —6H **65**
**Radcliffe on Trent Golf Course.**
**—5B 68**
Radcliffe Rd. *C But* —1F **87**
Radcliffe Rd. *Gam & Rad T*
—7B **66**

Radcliffe Rd. *W Bri & Gam*
—6G **65**
Radcliffe St. *Nott* —6F **65**
Radford Boulevd. *Nott* —1A **64**
Radford Bri. Rd. *Nott* —2J **63**
Radford Ct. *Nott* —2B **64**
Radford Ct. Ind. Est. *Nott* —2B **64**
Radford Cres. *Ged* —4C **50**
Radford Gro. La. *Nott* —1A **64**
Radford Rd. *Nott* —4A **48**
Radford Rd. *Smal* —7B **26**
Radford St. *Alv* —2F **93**
Radham Ct. *Nott* —4E **48**
Radley Sq. *Nott* —1K **47**
Radmarsh Rd. *Nott* —4A **64**
Rad Meadows. *Long E* —3G **97**
Radnor Gro. *Bing* —3J **69**
Radnor Pl. *Der* —7D **56**
Radstock Gdns. *Der* —6E **56**
Radstock Rd. *Nott* —7J **49**
Radstone Clo. *Oak* —5H **57**
Radway Dri. *Nott* —3C **82**
Raeburn Dri. *Bees* —6J **79**
Ragdale Rd. *Nott* —5H **31**
(in two parts)
Raglan Av. *Der* —3G **73**
Raglan Clo. *Nott* —7F **49**
Raglan Ct. *Bees* —6G **63**
Raglan Dri. *Ged* —5F **51**
Raglan St. *Eastw* —4E **28**
Raibank Gdns. *Wd'p* —1G **49**
Railway Cotts. *Kimb* —7K **29**
Railway Row. *Iron* —1H **13**
Railway Ter. *Der* —4C **74** (6H **7**)
Rainham Gdns. *Alv* —4G **93**
Rainham Gdns. *Rud* —3E **100**
Rainier Dri. *Chad* —2G **75**
Raithby Clo. *Nott* —7C **32**
Raleigh Clo. *Ilk* —3D **44**
Raleigh Clo. *Nott* —7J **81**
Raleigh Ct. *Nott* —1C **64** (1A **4**)
Raleigh M. *Nott* —2C **64** (2B **4**)
Raleigh St. *Der* —2G **73**
Raleigh St. *Nott* —2C **64** (2A **4**)
Ralf Clo. *W Bri* —4G **83**
Ramblers Clo. *Colw* —2C **66**
Ramblers Dri. *Oak* —4J **57**
Ramsdale Av. *C'tn* —4B **20**
Ramsdale Cres. *Nott* —3F **49**
**Ramsdale Pk. Golf Cen. —4K 19**
Ramsdale Rd. *Cltn* —5C **50**
Ramsdean Clo. *Der* —7D **56**
Ramsey Clo. *S'fd* —5J **61**
Ramsey Ct. *Nott* —5D **48**
Ramsey Dri. *Arn* —7K **33**
Ramshaw Way. *Der*
—4J **73** (6A **6**)
Ranby Wlk. *Nott* —1H **65**
Rancliffe Av. *Keyw* —5B **102**
Randal Gdns. *Nott* —7B **48**
Randal St. *Nott* —7A **48**
(in two parts)
Randolph Rd. *Der* —1K **91**
Ranelagh Gdns. *Der* —1F **73**
Ranelagh Gro. *Nott* —2G **63**
Rangemore Clo. *Mick* —4C **72**
Ranmere Rd. *Nott* —7G **47**
Ranmoor Rd. *Ged* —5D **50**
Ranmore Clo. *Bees* —5B **62**
Rannerdale Clo. *W Bri* —2A **84**
Rannoch Clo. *Alst* —4J **55**
Rannoch Clo. *Spon* —3B **76**
Rannoch Ri. *Arn* —4H **33**
Rannock Gdns. *Keyw* —6D **102**
Ranskill Gdns. *Nott* —5C **32**
Ransom Dri. *Nott* —5G **49**
Ransom Rd. *Nott* —5G **49**
Ranson Rd. *Bees* —7C **80**
Ranworth Clo. *Der* —6D **92**
Ratcliffe La. *Locki* —3F **109**
Ratcliffe St. *Eastw* —3D **28**
Rathgar Clo. *Nott* —3D **62**
Rathmines Clo. *Nott* —4A **64**
Rathvale Ct. *Bees* —4A **80**
Rauche Ct. *Der* —5B **74** (7F **7**)
Ravena Clo. *Colw* —1C **66**
Raven Av. *Nott* —2D **48**
Ravenhill Clo. *Bees* —4B **80**
Raven Oak Clo. *Belp* —3A **24**
Ravens Ct. *Nott* —1D **48**
Ravenscourt Rd. *Der* —1G **73**
Ravenscroft Dri. *Chad* —2F **75**
Ravensdale Av. *Long E* —6F **79**
Ravensdale Dri. *Nott* —4C **62**
Ravensdale Rd. *Alst* —4G **55**
Ravensdene Ct. *Nott* —6E **48**
Ravensmore Rd. *Nott* —4D **48**
Raven St. *Der* —5J **73** (7A **6**)
Ravenswood Rd. *Arn* —6H **33**

Ravensworth Rd. *Nott* —5H **31**
Rawdon Clo. *Cas D* —6J **107**
Rawdon St. *Der* —6K **73**
Rawlings Ct. *C Bis* —4H **87**
Rawlinson Av. *Der* —2A **92**
Rawson Grn. *Klbrn* —4F **25**
Rawson St. *Nott* —5B **48**
Raymede Clo. *Nott* —7B **32**
Raymede Dri. *Nott* —7A **32**
Raymond Dri. *Bing* —3C **70**
Rayneham Rd. *Ilk* —3A **44**
Rayner Ct. *Nott* —2B **64**
Raynesway. *Der* —1H **93**
Raynesway Pk. *Der* —7H **75**
Raynesway Pk. Dri. *Der* —7H **75**
Raynford Av. *Bees* —4D **80**
Rays Av. *Hean* —4G **27**
Ray St. *Hean* —4F **27**
Read Av. *Bees* —2G **81**
Reader St. *Spon* —3A **76**
Read Lodge. *Bees* —1G **81**
Readman Rd. *Bees* —5A **80**
Rearsby Clo. *Nott* —2D **62**
Rebecca Ct. *Der* —4H **73**
Rebecca Ho. *Der* —3J **73** (3A **6**)
Recreation Rd. *Sand* —2F **79**
Recreation St. *Long E* —1K **97**
Recreation Ter. *S'fd* —2H **79**
Rectory Ct. *Nott* —3E **62**
Rectory Ct. *Nott* —3F **63**
Rectory Ct. *W Bri* —1H **83**
Rectory Dri. *Ged* —4D **50**
Rectory Farm M. *Wstn T* —6A **106**
Rectory Gdns. *Ast T* —3C **106**
Rectory Gdns. *Nott* —3F **63**
Rectory La. *Bread* —2D **56**
Rectory M. *Ast T* —3C **106**
Rectory Pl. *Bar F* —3E **98**
Rectory Rd. *Breas* —1C **96**
Rectory Rd. *Colw* —2C **66**
Rectory Rd. *Cotg* —5J **85**
Rectory Rd. *W Bri* —1G **83**
Reculver Clo. *Sun* —2H **91**
Redbourne Dri. *Nott* —1J **63**
Redbridge Dri. *Nut* —3D **46**
Redbury Clo. *Der* —4J **73**
Redcar Clo. *Ged* —4C **50**
Redcar Gdns. *Der* —6D **56**
Redcliffe Gdns. *Nott* —6E **48**
Redcliffe Rd. *Nott* —6E **48**
Redfern Av. *Rip* —2A **12**
Redfield Rd. *Lent L* —7A **64**
Redfield Way. *Nott* —6A **64**
Redgates Ct. *C'tn* —4B **20**
Redhill Ct. *Belp* —3B **24**
Redhill Leisure Cen. —4G **33**
Redhill Lodge Dri. *Red* —4F **33**
Redhill Rd. *Arn* —4G **33**
Redland Av. *Cltn* —6D **50**
Redland Clo. *Bees* —4C **80**
Redland Clo. *Ilk* —3D **44**
Redland Clo. *Sin* —5K **91**
Redland Dri. *Bees* —5C **80**
Redland Gro. *Cltn* —6C **50**
Red La. *Brins* —4C **14**
Red La. *Low* —4D **36**
Red La. *Milf* —1A **40**
Red Lion Sq. *Hean* —3G **27**
Redmays Dri. *Bul* —7B **36**
Redmile Rd. *Nott* —4J **47**
Redmires Dri. *Chel* —7G **93**
Redmoor Clo. *Cod* —3D **12**
Redoubt St. *Nott* —2A **64**
Redruth Clo. *Nott* —1C **62**
Redruth Pl. *Alv* —4J **93**
Redshaw St. *Der* —1J **73**
Redstart Clo. *Spon* —2B **76**
Redway Cft. *Melb* —3G **113**
Redwing Cft. *Der* —2H **91**
Redwood. *W Bri* —2D **82**
Redwood Av. *Nott* —4D **62**
Redwood Ct. *Huck* —4F **17**
Redwood Cres. *Bees* —3G **81**
Redwood Rd. *Sin* —6J **91**
Reedham Wlk. *Nott* —5D **32**
Reedman Rd. *Long E* —5F **97**
Rees Gdns. *Nott* —4C **32**
Reeves Rd. *Der* —7B **74**
Regatta Way. *Nott* —7A **66**
Regency Clo. *L'ver* —2H **91**
Regency Ct. *Bees* —1G **81**
Regents Pk. Clo. *W Bri* —3E **82**
Regent St. *Bees* —1G **81**
Regent St. *Der* —5B **74** (7G **7**)
Regent St. *Ilk* —7D **44**
Regent St. *Kimb* —7K **29**
Regent St. *Lan M* —2B **58**
Regent St. *Long E* —1H **97**
Regent St. *New B* —5C **48**

Regent St. *Nott* —3D **64** (4C **4**)
Regent St. *Sand* —3G **79**
Regina Clo. *Rad T* —5J **67**
Reginald Rd. N. *Chad* —1F **75**
Reginald Rd. S. *Der* —2F **75**
Reginald St. *Der* —6B **74**
Regis Clo. *Oak* —5H **57**
Reid Gdns. *Watn* —6B **30**
Reigate Clo. *Bees* —6E **80**
Reigate Dri. *Bees* —6E **80**
Reigate Dri. *Der* —2D **72**
Reigate Rd. *Nott* —4B **48**
Rempstone Dri. *Nott* —1K **47**
Renals St. *Nott* —5A **74** (7D **6**)
Renals Way. *C'tn* —6D **20**
Renfrew Dri. *Nott* —3E **62**
Renfrew St. *Der* —1E **74**
Renne Hogg Rd. *Nott* —7C **64**
Repton Av. *Der* —7H **73**
Repton Dri. *Ilk* —7F **45**
Repton Rd. *Long E* —5D **96**
Repton Rd. *Nott* —7K **31**
Repton Rd. *W Bri* —3G **83**
Retford Clo. *Der* —5D **56**
Retford Rd. *Nott* —3C **48**
Retlaw Ct. *Bees* —3D **80**
Revelstoke Av. *Nott* —4K **31**
Revelstoke Way. *Nott* —4K **31**
Revesby Gdns. *Nott* —7J **47**
Revesby Rd. *Wd'p* —1H **49**
Revill Clo. *Ilk* —4A **44**
Revill Cres. *S'fd* —7K **61**
Reydon Dri. *Nott* —5K **47**
Reynolds Av. *Rip* —3B **12**
Reynolds Dri. *Nott* —2F **63**
Rhyl Cres. *Ged* —4D **50**
Rhymney Clo. *Oak* —5J **57**
Ribblesdale. *Ilk* —2A **60**
Ribblesdale Clo. *Alst* —5G **55**
Ribblesdale Ct. *Bees* —4A **80**
Ribblesdale Rd. *Long E* —4E **96**
Ribblesdale Rd. *Nott* —1E **48**
Ribble St. *Nott* —2K **63**
Riber Clo. *Long E* —4H **97**
Riber Clo. *W Hal* —6D **43**
Riber Cres. *Nott* —1B **48**
Richard Herrod Bowls Cen., The. —6A **50**
Richards Clo. *C Bis* —5G **87**
Richardson Clo. *Nott* —7J **81**
Richardson Dri. *Smal* —7B **26**
Richardson St. *Der* —2H **73**
Richborough Pl. *Nott* —5D **62**
Richey Clo. *Arn* —6K **33**
Richmond Av. *Breas* —1E **96**
Richmond Av. *C'tn* —4E **20**
Richmond Av. *Ilk* —2D **44**
Richmond Av. *L'ver* —1G **91**
Richmond Av. *Newt* —3F **29**
Richmond Av. *Nott* —7H **49**
Richmond Av. *Sand* —4E **78**
Richmond Clo. *L'ver* —2E **90**
Richmond Clo. *W Hal* —6F **43**
Richmond Ct. *Bees* —3E **80**
Richmond Dri. *Bees* —3E **80**
Richmond Dri. *Duf* —1H **39**
Richmond Dri. *Nott* —4F **49**
Richmond Dri. *Rad T* —3K **67**
Richmond Gdns. *Red* —4G **33**
Richmond Rd. *Chad* —2F **75**
Richmond Rd. *Der* —7A **74**
Richmond Rd. *W Bri* —6H **65**
Richmond Ter. *Rad T* —4K **67**
Ricklow Ct. *Nott* —1C **62**
Rick St. *Nott* —2F **65** (3G **5**)
Riddings. *Alst* —3J **55**
Riddings St. *Der* —5K **73** (7B **6**)
Ridding Ter. *Nott* —1E **64** (1F **5**)
Ridgedale Vw. *Rip* —2K **11**
Ridge Hill. *Low* —3D **36**
Ridge La. *Rad T* —2A **68**
Ridgeway. *Chel* —2G **105**
Ridgeway. *Hean* —5H **27**
Ridge Way. *Nott* —6A **32**
Ridgeway Av. *L'ver* —3G **91**
Ridgeway Dri. *Ilk* —2K **59**
Ridgeway La. *Neth H* —1B **10**
Ridgeway Wlk. *Nott* —5C **32**
Ridgewood Ct. *Oak* —5E **56**
Ridgewood Dri. *Bees* —4C **80**
Ridgmont Wlk. *Nott* —1K **99**
(in two parts)
Ridgway Clo. *Nott* —3A **84**
Ridgway St. *Nott* —1G **65** (1K **5**)
Riding Bank. *Melb* —4E **112**
Ridings, The. *Bul* —1A **52**
Ridings, The. *Keyw* —6E **102**
Ridings, The. *Ock* —2E **76**
Ridsdale Rd. *Nott* —1E **48**

Rifle St. *Nott* —2A **64**
Rigga La. *Duf* —4A **40**
Rigg Hill Ct. *Nott* —1G **47**
Rigley Av. *Ilk* —5D **44**
Rigley Dri. *Nott* —6A **32**
Rigsby Ct. *Mick* —5A **72**
Rimsdale Clo. *Sin* —5J **91**
Ring Leas. *Cotg* —6K **85**
Ringstead Clo. *W Bri* —3E **82**
Ringstead Wlk. *Nott* —5D **32**
Ringwood Clo. *Chad* —7E **56**
Ringwood Cres. *Nott* —2J **63**
Ringwood Rd. *Bing* —3J **69**
Ripley Ho. *Spon* —5A **76**
Ripley Leisure Cen. —3K **11**
Ripley Rd. *Heag* —2E **10**
Ripon Cres. *Chad* —7E **56**
Ripon Rd. *Nott* —2K **65**
Risborrow Clo. *Etw* —5G **89**
Rise Ct. *Nott* —6D **48**
Risegate. *Cotg* —5K **85**
Risegate Gdns. *Cotg* —5K **85**
Riseholme Av. *Nott* —4C **62**
Rise Pk. Rd. *Nott* —4K **31**
Rise, The. *Dar A* —5B **92**
Rise, The. *Nott* —3F **49**
Risley Ct. *Ilk* —3D **44**
Risley Dri. *Nott* —5D **64**
Risley La. *Breas* —5B **78**
Riste's Pl. *Nott* —3F **65** (4G **5**)
Ritchie Clo. *Cotg* —6A **86**
Ritson Clo. *Nott* —1F **65** (1H **5**)
Rivenhall Clo. *L'ver* —2D **90**
Riverdale Cvn. Pk. *Gun* —2G **53**
Riverdale Rd. *Bees* —6D **80**
Rivergreen. *Nott* —5A **82**
Rivergreen Clo. *Bees* —5C **62**
Rivergreen Cres. *Bees* —5C **62**
Rivermead. *Cotg* —5K **85**
Rivermead. *W Bri* —1F **83**
River Pk. Wlk. *Der* —7G **75**
River Rd. *Colw* —3C **66**
Riverside. *Bur J* —6K **51**
Riverside. *What* —3N **71**
Riverside Clo. *Bees* —5H **81**
Riverside Gardens. —3B **74** (3F **7**)
Riverside Ind. Pk. *Nott* —7C **64**
Riverside Rd. *Bees* —5G **81**
Riverside Rd. *Pri P* —4D **74** (6K **7**)
Riverside Way. *Nott* —6D **64**
River St. *Der* —2A **74** (1D **6**)
River Vw. *Milf* —6K **23**
Riverview. *Nott* —6F **65**
Riverway Gdns. *Nott* —5F **65**
Rivington Rd. *Bees* —6G **79**
Robbie Burns Rd. *Nott* —5D **32**
Robbinetts La. *Coss* —5H **45**
Roberts Clo. *Keg* —2H **117**
Roberts La. *Huck* —5F **17**
Roberts St. *Ilk* —1E **60**
Roberts St. *Nott* —3G **65** (4K **5**)
Robert St. *Der* —2B **74** (2F **7**)
Roberts Yd. *Bees* —1G **81**
Robey Clo. *L'by* —3H **17**
Robey Dri. *Eastw* —1D **28**
Robey Ter. *Nott* —7B **48**
Robina Dri. *Gilt* —5G **29**
Robin Cft. Rd. *Alst* —3J **55**
Robinet Rd. *Bees* —3F **81**
Robin Hood Chase. *Nott* —7F **49**
Robin Hood Clo. *Eastw* —4D **28**
Robin Hood Dri. *Huck* —1E **30**
Robin Hood Ind. Est. *Nott* —2G **65** (2J **5**)
Robin Hood Rd. *Arn* —4E **32**
Robin Hood St. *Nott* —2G **65** (3J **5**)
Robin Hood's Well. —5K **15**
Robin Hood Ter. *Nott* —2F **65** (2H **5**)
Robin Hood Way. *Nott* —6D **64**
Robinia Clo. *Oak* —4J **57**
Robinia Ct. *W Bri* —3J **83**
Robin Rd. *Der* —1K **73**
Robins Clo. *Boul M* —4K **93**
Robinscross. *Borr* —7D **76**
Robinson Gdns. *Nott* —7J **81**
Robinson Rd. *Nott* —3H **49**
Robinson's Hill. *Melb* —5F **113**
Robinsons Hill. *Nott* —6H **31**
Robinsons Ind. Est. *Der* —6B **74**
Robinswood Ho. *Nott* —7H **47**
Robins Wood Rd. *Nott* —1H **63**
Robin Wood. —3B **112**
Rob Roy Av. *Nott* —4B **64**
Robson Clo. *Alv* —2G **93**

Roby Lea. *Cas D* —6H **107**
Roche Clo. *Arn* —6A **34**
Rochester Clo. *Alv* —4G **93**
Rochester Ct. *Nott* —7F **31**
Rochester Dri. *Long E* —2E **96**
Rochester Wlk. *Nott* —7B **82**
Rochford Ct. *Edw* —5A **84**
Rochley Clo. *Oak* —5F **57**
Rockbourne Clo. *Alv* —3K **93**
Rock Ct. *Nott* —3K **47**
Rock Dri. *Nott* —4C **64** (6B **4**)
Rockford Ct. *S'fd* —6J **61**
Rockford Rd. *Nott* —3B **48**
Rockhouse Rd. *Alv* —3G **93**
Rockingham Clo. *Alst* —3A **56**
Rockingham Gro. *Bing* —3J **69**
Rockley Av. *Newt* —4E **28**
Rockley Av. *Rad T* —3K **67**
Rockley Clo. *Huck* —6C **16**
Rockleys Vw. *Low* —3A **36**
Rock Side. *Kimb* —7K **29**
Rockside Gdns. *Huck* —5E **16**
Rock St. *Nott* —5G **31**
Rockwell Ct. *S'fd* —1J **79**
Rockwood Cres. *Huck* —6D **16**
Rockwood Wlk. *Huck* —6E **16**
Rodel Ct. *Nott* —1F **65** (1G **5**)
Roden St. *Nott* —2G **65** (3J **5**)
Roderick St. *Nott* —2K **47**
Rodney Clo. *Hilt* —7A **88**
Rodney Ho. *Der* —3E **92**
Rodney Rd. *W Bri* —2J **83**
Rodney Wlk. *L'ver* —2C **90**
Rodney Way. *Ilk* —2A **44**
Rodsley Cres. *L'ver* —4H **91**
Rodwell Clo. *Nott* —1J **63**
Roebuck Clo. *Nott* —5D **32**
Roecliffe. *W Bri* —4G **83**
Roe Farm La. *Der* —1E **74**
Roehampton Dri. *Der* —1E **72**
Roehampton Dri. *Trow* —5H **61**
Roe Hill. *Wdbgh* —6G **21**
(in two parts)
Roe La. *Wdbgh* —1G **35**
Roes La. *C'tn* —5E **20**
Roe Wlk. *Der* —6A **74**
Roker Clo. *Nott* —5G **47**
Roland Av. *Nut* —2E **46**
Roland Av. *Wilf* —1D **82**
Rollerworld. —7C **56**
Rolleston Clo. *Huck* —7D **16**
Rolleston Cres. *Watn* —4K **29**
Rolleston Dri. *Arn* —6J **33**
Rolleston Dri. *Newt* —5E **28**
Rolleston Dri. *Nott* —3B **64** (6A **4**)
Roman Dri. *Nott* —2A **48**
Roman House. —3C **6**
Roman Rd. *Der* —1B **74**
Romans Ct. *Nott* —4A **48**
Roman Way. *Borr* —7E **76**
Romilay Clo. *Bees* —6G **63**
Romney Av. *Nott* —5D **62**
Romorantin Pl. *Long E* —2J **97**
Romsley Clo. *Mick* —4B **72**
Rona Clo. *Sin* —5J **91**
Rona Ct. *Nott* —1A **48**
Ronald Clo. *L'ver* —2C **90**
Ronald St. *Nott* —2B **64**
Rookery Gdns. *Arn* —5H **33**
Rookwood Clo. *Bees* —2E **80**
Roosa Clo. *Nott* —1F **47**
Roosevelt Av. *Chad* —2H **75**
Roosevelt Av. *Long E* —4G **97**
Roper Av. *Hean* —5G **27**
Ropewalk. *Keg* —1G **117**
Rope Wlk. *Rip* —4A **12**
Ropewalk Ind. Est. *Ilk* —5E **44**
Ropewalk, The. *Hean* —5H **27**
Ropewalk, The. *Ilk* —5E **44**
Ropewalk, The. *Nott* —2C **64** (3B **4**)
Ropewalk, The. *Stan C* —5D **42**
Ropsley Cres. *W Bri* —6J **65**
Rosamond's Ride. *Der* —1H **91**
Roscoe Av. *Red* —3G **33**
Roseacre. *Bees* —3G **81**
Rose Ash La. *Nott* —5D **32**
Rose Av. *Borr* —7E **76**
Rose Av. *Ilk* —4C **44**
Rosebank Dri. *Arn* —4K **33**
Roseberry Ct. *Oak* —6H **57**
Roseberry Gdns. *Huck* —6J **17**
Roseberry St. *Nott* —2A **48**
Rosebery Av. *W Bri* —6G **65**
Rose Clo. *Nott* —7F **49**
Rose Cotts. *Bur J* —1J **51**
Rose Ct. *Long E* —7F **79**

Rosecroft Dri. *Nott* —7E **32**
Rosedale Av. *Alv* —3G **93**
Rosedale Clo. *Long E* —3F **97**
Rosedale Rd. *Nott* —3B **62**
Rosegarth Wlk. *Nott* —4K **47**
Rose Gro. *Bees* —3H **81**
Rose Gro. *Keyw* —5D **102**
Rosegrove Av. *Arn* —4H **33**
Roseheath Clo. *Sun* —4J **91**
Rose Hill. *Keyw* —6C **102**
Rose Hill St. *Der* —6A **74**
Roseland Clo. *Keyw* —7C **102**
Rose La. *Tickn* —4A **112**
Roseleigh Av. *Nott* —4K **49**
Rosemary Clo. *Nott* —5E **46**
Rosemary Dri. *Alv* —4G **93**
Rosemoor La. *Oak* —6H **57**
Rosemount Ct. *Alst* —4G **55**
Roseneath Av. *Nott* —4A **32**
Rosengrave St. *Der* —4K **73** (6C **6**)
Rosetta Rd. *Nott* —5B **48**
(in two parts)
Rosette Ct. *Oak* —4J **57**
Rosewall Ct. *Arn* —6K **33**
Rosewood Clo. *Alv* —2J **93**
Rosewood Cres. *Hean* —3K **27**
Rosewood Gdns. *Nott* —6F **31**
Rosewood Gdns. *W Bri* —5E **82**
Roslyn Av. *Ged* —4C **50**
Ross Clo. *Low* —4E **36**
Rossell Dri. *S'fd* —3H **79**
Rossendale. *Ilk* —2C **44**
Rossett Clo. *Gam* —2B **84**
Rossington Dri. *L'ver* —3D **90**
Rossington Rd. *Nott* —2H **65**
Rossington Way. *L'ver* —3D **90**
Ross La. *Lamb* —6G **35**
Rosslyn Dri. *Huck* —4J **17**
Rosslyn Dri. *Nott* —4G **47**
Rosslyn Gdns. *Alv* —3G **93**
Ross Wlk. *Der* —6D **56**
Rosthwaite Clo. *W Bri* —3A **84**
Rothbury Av. *Trow* —5H **61**
Rothbury Gro. *Bing* —2J **69**
Rothbury Pl. *Der* —6E **56**
Rothesay Av. *Nott* —2B **64**
Rothesay Clo. *Sin* —5J **91**
Rothley Av. *Nott* —2H **65**
Rothwell Clo. *Nott* —4C **82**
Rothwell La. *Belp* —1B **24**
Rothwell Rd. *Mick* —5B **72**
Rough Heanor Rd. *Mick* —5E **72**
Roughs Woods. *Huck* —1D **30**
Roughton Clo. *Mick* —1B **90**
Roundhouse Rd. *Pri P* —4C **74** (6J **7**)
Roundwood Rd. *Arn* —6E **32**
Routh Av. *Cas D* —1K **115**
Rowan Av. *Klbrn* —5H **25**
Rowan Av. *Rip* —4K **11**
Rowan Av. *S'fd* —5J **61**
Rowan Clo. *Bing* —3C **70**
Rowan Clo. *C'tn* —5B **20**
Rowan Clo. *Chad* —3H **75**
Rowan Clo. *Ilk* —2D **60**
Rowan Clo. *Sten F* —6H **91**
Rowan Ct. *Nut* —7B **30**
Rowan Dri. *Keyw* —7E **102**
Rowan Dri. *Nott* —4C **82**
Rowan Gdns. *Nott* —6F **31**
Rowan Pk. Clo. *Der* —2H **91**
Rowan Wlk. *Nott* —6J **49**
Rowditch Av. *Der* —4H **73**
Rowditch Pl. *Der* —4H **73**
Rowe Gdns. *Nott* —7K **31**
Rowena Clo. *Alv* —2F **93**
Rowland Av. *Map* —4J **49**
Rowland M. *Nott* —7G **49**
Rowland St. *Altn* —3E **92**
Rowley Gdns. *L'ver* —2G **91**
Rowley La. *L'ver* —2G **91**
Rowsley Av. *Der* —1H **91**
Rowsley Av. *Long E* —4E **96**
Roxburgh Av. *Chad* —1E **74**
Roxley Ct. *Bees* —1E **80**
Roxton Ct. *Kimb* —6K **29**
Royal Av. *Long E* —7H **79**
Royal Cen. *Nott* —2D **64** (3E **4**)
Royal Clo. *Borr* —7D **76**
Royal Concert Hall. —3E **4**
Royal Ga. *Belp* —2D **24**
Royal Gro. *Oak* —4K **57**
Royal Hill Rd. *Spon* —2K **75**
(in two parts)
Royal M. *Bees* —5C **80**
Royal Standard Ct. *Nott* —3D **64** (5D **4**)

Royal Way. *Pri P* —5E **74**
Roy Av. *Bees* —4H **81**
Royce Av. *Huck* —1E **30**
Roydon Clo. *Mick* —4A **72**
Royston Clo. *Nott* —6D **64**
Royston Dri. *Belp* —7D **10**
Ruby Paddocks. *Kimb* —1K **45**
Ruddington Fields Bus. Pk. *Rud*
—4F **101**

Ruddington Framework
Knitters Mus. —3E **100**
Ruddington Grange Golf Course.
—7E **82**
Ruddington La. *Nott & Wilf*
—2D **82**

Ruddington Village Mus.
—2E **100**
Rudge Clo. *Nott* —2F **63**
Rudyard Av. *Spon* —2A **76**
Ruffles Av. *Arn* —1K **49**
Rufford Av. *Bees* —7A **62**
Rufford Av. *Ged* —4B **50**
Rufford Clo. *Huck* —6J **17**
Rufford Gro. *Bing* —3K **69**
Rufford Rd. *Long E* —5F **97**
Rufford Rd. *Nott* —3E **48**
Rufford Rd. *Rud* —2F **101**
Rufford Wlk. *Nott* —6H **31**
Rufford Way. *W Bri* —2K **83**
Ruffs Dri. *Huck* —7D **16**
Ruffstone Clo. *Holb* —6C **24**
Rugby Clo. *Nott* —6A **32**
Rugby Rd. *W Bri* —3E **82**
Rugby St. *Der* —7E **74**
Rugby Ter. *Nott* —7B **48**
Rugeley Av. *Long E* —2K **97**
Ruislip Clo. *Kimb* —6J **29**
Runcie Clo. *Cotg* —6K **85**
Runnymede Ct. *Bees* —3G **81**
Runnymede Ct. *Nott*
—2C **64** (2B **4**)
Runswick Dri. *Arn* —5H **33**
Runswick Dri. *Nott* —2G **63**
Runton Dri. *Nott* —2B **48**
Rupert Rd. *Bing* —3K **69**
Rupert Rd. *Chad* —1G **75**
Rupert St. *Ilk* —5E **44**
Ruscombe Pl. *Nott* —1F **65** (1H **5**)

Rushcliffe Arena. —2F **83**
Rushcliffe Av. *Cltn* —6B **50**
Rushcliffe Av. *Chad* —2F **75**
Rushcliffe Av. *Rad T* —4K **67**

Rushcliffe Country Pk. —4E **100**
Rushcliffe Ct. *Nott* —7K **31**
Rushcliffe Gdns. *Chad* —2F **75**

Rushcliffe Golf Course. —5K **111**
Rushcliffe Ri. *Nott* —1F **49**
Rushcliffe Rd. *Huck* —7E **16**
Rushdale Av. *L'ver* —3H **91**
Rushes, The. *Got* —1H **111**
Rushford Dri. *Nott* —3C **62**
Rush Leys. *Long E* —4H **97**
Rushmere Wlk. *Arn* —1H **49**
Rushton Gdns. *Nott* —7G **49**
Rushup Clo. *Alst* —2A **56**
Rushworth Av. *W Bri* —7G **65**
Rushworth Clo. *Nott* —7G **49**
(in two parts)
Rushworth Ct. *W Bri* —7G **65**
Rushy Clo. *Nott* —2D **62**
Rushy La. *Sand & Ris* —2C **78**
Ruskin Av. *Bees* —4D **80**
Ruskin Av. *Long E* —3E **96**
Ruskin Clo. *Day* —6F **33**
Ruskin Rd. *Der* —1K **73**
Ruskin St. *Nott* —2A **64**
Ruskin Way. *L'ver* —1F **91**
Russell Av. *Nott* —2F **63**
Russell Ct. *Long E* —7H **79**
Russell Cres. *Nott* —2F **63**
Russell Dri. *Nott* —2E **62**
Russell Gdns. *Bees* —6C **80**
Russell Pl. *Nott* —2D **64** (3D **4**)
Russell Rd. *Nott* —6B **48**
Russell St. *Der* —7C **74**
Russell St. *Long E* —7H **79**
Russell St. *Nott* —1C **64** (1B **4**)
Russet Av. *Cltn* —7C **50**
Russet Clo. *Oak* —6H **57**
Russey Clo. *Low* —4E **36**
Russley Rd. *Bees* —7A **62**
Ruth Dri. *Arn* —4J **33**
Rutherford Ho. *Nott* —6K **63**
Rutherford Ri. *Oak* —5F **57**
Ruthwell Gdns. *Nott* —3C **32**
Rutland Av. *Bees* —6A **80**
Rutland Av. *Borr* —6E **76**
Rutland Av. *Wain* —5C **12**
Rutland Ct. *Man I* —5B **44**

Rutland Dri. *Mick* —5C **72**
Rutland Gro. *Sand* —3G **79**
Rutland Rd. *Bing* —3B **70**
Rutland Rd. *Ged* —3B **50**
Rutland Rd. *W Bri* —6H **65**
Rutland St. *Der* —7A **74**
Rutland St. *Ilk* —5D **44**
Rutland St. *Nott* —3D **64** (5D **4**)
Rutland Ter. *Ilk* —4D **44**
Rutland Ter. *Kimb* —1A **46**
Rutland Vs. *Nott* —3H **65**
Ryal Clo. *Ock* —3E **76**
Ryan Clo. *Sin* —6J **91**
Rydal Av. *Long E* —6F **79**
Rydal Clo. *Alst* —3J **55**
Rydal Dri. *Bees* —7D **62**
Rydal Dri. *Huck* —4F **17**
Rydale Rd. *Nott* —1E **48**
Rydal Gdns. *W Bri* —3J **83**
Rydal Gro. *Nott* —3A **48**
Ryde Ho. *Alv* —2J **93**
Ryder St. *Nott* —2K **47**
Rye Butts. *Chel* —1E **104**
Rye Clo. *Oak* —4E **56**
Ryecroft Rd. *Cas D* —3B **108**
Ryecroft St. *S'fd* —6J **61**
Ryedale Gdns. *L'ver* —4G **91**
Ryegrass Clo. *Belp* —1D **24**
Ryegrass Rd. *Oak* —5J **57**
Ryehill Clo. *Nott* —5F **65**
Ryehill St. *Nott* —5F **65**
Ryeland Gdns. *Nott* —5E **64**
Ryemere Clo. *Eastw* —3C **28**
Rye St. *Nott* —5B **48**

Rykneld Bowling Club. —6H **73**
Rykneld Clo. *L'ver* —3C **90**
Rykneld Dri. *L'ver* —2D **90**
Rykneld Ho. *Mick* —5G **73**
Rykneld Rd. *Mick & L'ver* —4B **90**
Rykneld Way. *L'ver* —3C **90**
Ryknield Hill. *Den* —2H **25**
Ryknield Rd. *Klbrn* —6H **25**
Ryknild St. *Hors W* —7H **25**
Rylands Clo. *Bees* —4H **81**
Rylands Ct. *Bees* —3G **81**
Rymill Dri. *Oak* —6G **56**
Ryton Ct. *Nott* —6F **65**
Ryton Sq. *Nott* —5H **47**

**S**abina St. *Nott* —2F **65** (1H **5**)
Sacheverel St. *Der* —4A **74** (6D **6**)
Sackville St. *Der* —1K **91**
Saddlers Yd. *Plum* —2C **102**
Saddleworth Ct. *Nott* —1E **64**
Saddleworth Wlk. *Shel L* —6E **92**
Sadler Ga. *Der* —3A **74** (3D **6**)
Sadler Ga. Bri. *Der* —3A **74** (3D **6**)
Saffron Dri. *Oak* —6G **57**
Saffron Gdns. *Nott* —5D **64**
St Agnes Av. *Alst* —3J **55**
St Agnes Clo. *Nott* —6D **46**
St Aidans Ct. *Nott* —2A **48**
St Albans Clo. *Long E* —4J **97**
St Albans Ct. *Arn* —3D **32**
St Albans M. *Nott* —7K **31**
St Albans Rd. *Arn* —6F **33**
St Albans Rd. *B Vil* —1A **32**
St Alban's Rd. *Der* —5G **73**
St Albans Rd. *Nott* —5J **31**
St Albans St. *Sher* —3E **48**
St Alkmunds Clo. *Duf* —2J **39**
St Alkmund's Way. *Der*
—2K **73** (2C **6**)
St Alkmunds Way. *Duf* —2J **39**
St Andrew Clo. *Got* —1H **111**
St Andrews Clo. *Huck* —4G **17**
St Andrews Clo. *Nott* —6J **31**
St Andrews Ct. *Nott* —6K **31**
St Andrew's Dri. *Ilk* —6C **44**
St Andrews Ho. *Der*
—5C **74** (7H **7**)
St Andrew's Ri. *Keg* —2G **117**
St Andrew's Rd. *Nott* —7D **48**
St Andrew's Vw. *Der* —5D **56**
St Anne's Clo. *Der* —2J **73** (1A **6**)
St Anne's La. *Cas D* —7H **107**
St Ann's Gdns. *Nott* —7G **49**
St Ann's Hill. *Nott* —7E **48**
St Ann's Hill Rd. *Nott* —7E **48**
St Ann's St. *Nott* —2E **64** (2F **5**)
St Ann's Valley. *Nott* —1G **65**
St Ann's Way. *Nott* —1E **64** (1E **4**)
St Ann's Well Rd. *Nott*
—2F **65** (2G **5**)
St Anthony Ct. *Nott* —5A **64**
St Augustines Clo. *Nott* —5C **48**
St Augustine St. *Der* —7K **73**
St Austell Dri. *Nott* —3D **82**

St Austins Ct. *Cltn* —6D **50**
St Austins Dri. *Cltn* —6D **50**
St Barnabas R.C. Cathedral.
—3C **4**
St Bartholomew's Rd. *Nott*
—7H **49**
St Bride's Wlk. *Der* —2F **73**
St Catherines St. *Rad T* —5J **67**
St Cecilia Gdns. *Nott* —1F **65**
St Chads. *Cltn* —7D **50**
St Chads Clo. *Dray* —2J **95**
St Chad's Rd. *Der* —6J **73**
St Chad's Rd. *Nott* —2G **65** (3K **5**)
St Christopher St. *Nott* —3H **65**
St Clares Clo. *Der* —6H **73**
St Cuthbert's Rd. *Der* —5G **73**
St Cuthbert's Rd. *Nott*
—2G **65** (2K **5**)
St David's Clo. *Der* —5H **73**
St Edmunds Clo. *Alst* —3K **55**
St Edward's Rd. *Cas D* —1K **115**
St Ervan Rd. *Nott & Wilf* —2D **82**
St Georges Ct. *Huck* —4G **17**
St Georges Dri. *Bees* —6K **79**
St Georges Dri. *Nott* —5E **64**
St George's Pl. *Belp* —1K **23**
St Giles Rd. *Der* —7K **73**
St Giles Way. *C Bis* —4G **87**
St Helen's Cres. *Bur J* —2K **51**
St Helens Cres. *Trow* —3G **61**
St Helen's Gro. *Bur J* —3J **51**
St Helens Rd. *W Bri* —2H **83**
St Helen's St. *Der* —2K **73** (2C **6**)
St Helen's St. *Nott* —2C **64** (3B **4**)
St Helier. *Nott* —3C **64** (5B **4**)
St Hugh's Clo. *Dar A* —5K **55**
St James Av. *Ilk* —7E **44**
St James Clo. *Belp* —1D **24**
St James Ct. *Der* —3J **73** (3A **6**)
St James Ct. *Huck* —4G **17**
St James Ct. *Nott* —4K **49**
St James Ct. *Sand* —5F **79**
St James Dri. *Brins* —4B **14**
St James Rd. *Der* —7K **73**
St James's St. *Der* —3A **74** (4D **6**)
St James's St. *Nott*
—3D **64** (5D **4**)
St James's Ter. *Nott*
—3D **64** (5D **4**)
St James St. *S'fd* —2G **79**
St James Ter. *S'fd* —2G **79**
St John's Av. *Chad* —3H **75**
St John's Clo. *Alst* —4H **55**
St John's Clo. *Brins* —3B **14**
St John's Ct. *Cltn* —7B **50**
St John's Cres. *Huck* —7J **17**
St John's Dri. *Chad* —3G **75**
St John's Dri. *Klbrn* —5F **25**
St John's Rd. *Belp* —1A **24**
St John's Rd. *Ilk* —7E **44**
St John's Rd. *Rud* —2E **100**
St Johns Rd. *Smal* —1A **42**
St Johns St. *Long E* —2H **97**
St John's Ter. *Der* —2K **73** (2A **6**)
St Judes Av. *Nott* —4F **49**
St Laurence Ct. *Long E* —3J **97**
St Lawrence Boulevd. *Rad T*
—5H **67**
St Lawrence Clo. *Hean* —3H **27**
St Leonards Dri. *Nott* —3F **63**
St Leven Clo. *Nott* —6D **46**
St Lukes Clo. *W Bri* —3K **83**
St Luke's St. *Nott* —2G **65** (3J **5**)
St Lukes Way. *Bur J* —6K **51**
St Margaret's Av. *Nott* —6J **47**
St Mark's Rd. *Der* —1D **74** (1K **7**)
St Mark's St. *Nott* —2F **65** (2G **5**)
St Martins Clo. *Nott* —6E **46**
St Martin's Gdns. *Nott* —6D **46**
St Martin's Rd. *Nott* —6E **46**
St Mary's Av. *Dray* —2J **95**
St Mary's Av. *Ged* —4C **50**
St Mary's Bri. *Der* —2A **74** (1E **6**)
St Mary's Clo. *Alv* —3G **93**
St Mary's Clo. *Arn* —4H **33**
St Mary's Clo. *Bees* —7D **80**
St Mary's Clo. *Low* —3D **36**
St Mary's Ct. *Der* —2A **74** (1D **6**)
St Mary's Cres. *Rud* —2E **100**
St Mary's Ga. *Der* —3A **74** (3D **6**)
St Marys Ga. *Nott* —3F **65** (4G **5**)
St Mary's M. *Der* —2A **74** (1D **6**)
St Mary's Pl. *Nott* —3F **65** (4G **5**)
St Marys Rd. *Bing* —2B **70**
St Mary St. *Ilk* —6C **44**
St Mary's Wlk. *Jack* —1K **13**
St Marys Way. *Huck* —4F **17**
St Mary's Wharf Rd. *Der*
—1B **74** (1F **7**)

St Matthew's Wlk. *Dar A* —5K **55**
St Matthias Rd. *Nott*
—1G **65** (1K **5**)
St Mawes Av. *Nott* —2D **82**
St Mawes Clo. *Alst* —3H **55**
St Mellion Clo. *Mick* —7D **72**
St Michael's Av. *Ged* —4C **50**
St Michael's Av. *Nott* —6D **46**
St Michael's Clo. *Alv* —2J **93**
St Michael's Clo. *Holb* —7C **24**
St Michaels La. *Der*
—2A **74** (2D **6**)
St Michaels Sq. *Bees* —7B **62**
St Michaels Vw. *Alv* —2J **93**
(off Bransome Av.)
St Michaels Vw. *Huck* —3H **17**
St Nicholas Clo. *Alst* —5H **55**
St Nicholas Clo. *Arn* —6G **33**
St Nicholas M. *Der* —1K **73** (1C **6**)
St Nicholas Pl. *Der* —1K **73** (1C **6**)
St Nicholas St. *Nott*
—3E **64** (5E **4**)
St Norbert Dri. *Ilk* —2A **60**
St Osborne St. *Der* —5C **74** (7H **7**)
St Pancras Way. *Der*
—1B **74** (1F **7**)
St Patrick's Rd. *Huck* —5F **17**
St Patrick's Rd. *Nut* —7B **30**
St Pauls Av. *Nott* —7B **48**
St Paul's Rd. *Der* —1A **74**
St Paul's St. *Nott* —2K **63**
St Pauls Ter. *Nott* —7B **48**
St Peters Chambers. *Nott* —4F **5**
St Peter's Chu. Wlk. *Nott*
—3E **64** (4F **5**)
St Peter's Chyd. *Der*
—3A **74** (4D **6**)
St Peter's Clo. *Belp* —1K **23**
St Peters Cres. *Rud* —2E **100**
St Peter's Cft. *Belp* —1A **24**
St Peter's Ga. *Nott* —3E **64** (4F **5**)
St Peter's Rd. *Chel* —1G **105**
St Peter's Sq. *Nott* —4F **5**
St Peter's St. *Der* —3A **74** (4E **6**)
St Peters St. *Nott* —2A **64**
St Peter's Way. *Der* —4A **74** (5E **6**)
St Quentin Clo. *Der* —5G **73**
St Ronan's Av. *Duf* —4J **39**
St Saviours Gdns. *Nott* —5F **65**
St Stephen's Av. *Nott*
—3H **65** (6K **5**)
St Stephens Clo. *Borr* —7D **76**
St Stephen's Clo. *Sun* —3H **91**
St Stephen's Rd. *Nott*
—3G **65** (5K **5**)
St Swithins Clo. *Der* —5H **73**
St Thomas Dri. *Asl* —2J **71**
St Thomas Rd. *Der* —1G **91**
St Vincent Clo. *Long E* —3J **97**
St Werburgh's Chyd. *Der* —3C **6**
St Werburgh's Cloisters. *Der*
—3C **6**
St Werburgh's Vw. *Spon* —3K **75**
St Wilfrid's Rd. *W Hal* —7G **43**
St Wilfrid's Sq. *C'tn* —5D **20**
St Wystan's Rd. *Der* —5G **73**
Salamander Clo. *Cltn* —4B **50**
Salcey Dri. *Trow* —5H **61**
Salcombe Cir. *Red* —4F **33**
Salcombe Clo. *Newt* —4G **29**
Salcombe Cres. *Rud* —1F **101**
Salcombe Dri. *Red* —4F **33**
Salcombe Rd. *Nott* —3B **48**
Sale St. *Der* —6B **74**
Salford Gdns. *Nott* —2F **65** (2H **5**)
Salisbury Ct. *Nott* —4G **49**
Salisbury Dri. *Belp* —7D **10**
Salisbury La. *Melb* —4H **113**
Salisbury Sq. *Nott* —3A **64**
Salisbury St. *Bees* —1G **81**
Salisbury St. *Der* —5A **74** (7D **6**)
Salisbury St. *Long E* —2J **97**
Salisbury St. *Nott* —3A **64**
(in two parts)
Sallywood Clo. *Sten F* —7H **91**
Salmon Clo. *Nott* —6F **31**
Salop St. *Day* —6F **33**
Saltburn Clo. *Der* —6C **56**
Saltburn Rd. *Nott* —1G **63**
Saltby Grn. *W Bri* —5D **82**
Salter Clo. *Cas D* —6H **107**
Salterford Av. *C'tn* —4D **20**
Salterford Rd. *Huck* —7E **16**
Saltford Clo. *Ged* —4D **50**
Salthouse Clo. *Bees* —2C **80**
Salthouse Ct. *Bees* —1G **81**
Salthouse La. *Bees* —7G **63**
Saltney Way. *Nott* —5C **82**
Salvin Clo. *C Bis* —4G **87**

Samantha Ct. *Oak* —6H **57**
Samson Ct. *Oak* —6H **57**
Samson Ct. *Rud* —1D **100**
Samuel Ct. *Rip* —4K **11**
Sancroft Ct. *L'ver* —2F **91**
Sancroft Rd. *Spon* —2A **76**
Sandale Clo. *Gam* —2A **84**
Sandalwood Clo. *Alv* —2J **93**
Sandays Clo. *Nott* —6E **64**
Sandbach Clo. *Oak* —6G **57**
Sandbed La. *Belp* —4C **24**
Sandby Ct. *Bees* —3C **80**
(in two parts)
Sanders Clo. *Ilk* —4A **44**
Sanderson Ct. *Belp* —1K **23**
Sanderson Rd. *Chad* —2H **75**
Sandfield Clo. *Oak* —6H **57**
Sandfield Ct. *Nott* —7G **31**
Sandfield Rd. *Arn* —7H **33**
Sandfield Rd. *Bees* —6J **79**
Sandfield Rd. *Nott* —3B **64**
Sandford Av. *Long E* —2J **97**
Sandford Rd. *Nott* —4H **49**
Sandgate. *Bees* —6D **62**
Sandgate Clo. *Alv* —3G **93**
Sandham La. *Rip* —3J **11**
Sandham Wlk. *Nott* —5A **82**
Sandhill Rd. *Und* —1F **15**
Sandhurst Dri. *Bees* —6C **80**
Sandhurst Dri. *Rud* —3D **100**
Sandhurst Rd. *Nott* —4H **31**

Sandiacre Friesland Sports Cen.
—3D **78**
Sandiacre Rd. *S'fd* —2G **79**
Sandon St. *Nott* —5C **48**
Sandown Av. *Mick* —5A **72**
Sandown Rd. *Bees* —5K **79**
Sandown Rd. *Der* —1D **92**
Sandpiper Way. *Lent* —3A **64**
Sandringham Av. *W Bri* —7G **65**
Sandringham Cres. *Nott* —2C **62**
Sandringham Dri. *Bees* —6C **62**
Sandringham Dri. *Hean* —3E **26**
Sandringham Dri. *Spon* —4B **76**
Sandringham Pl. *Huck* —4H **17**
Sandringham Pl. *Ilk* —2B **60**
Sandringham Rd. *Der* —6E **56**
Sandringham Rd. *Nott* —3H **65**
Sandringham Rd. *Sand* —5F **79**
Sands Clo. *Colw* —2C **66**
Sandside. *Cotg* —6K **85**
Sandwell Clo. *Long E* —3E **96**
Sandyford Clo. *Nott* —3J **47**
Sandyhill Clo. *Chel* —7G **93**
Sandy La. *Bees* —5D **62**
Sandy La. *Cox* —2F **41**
Sandy La. *Hol P* —5F **67**
Sandy La. *Huck* —5G **17**
Sandy La. *Oxt* —1G **21**
Sandypits La. *Etw* —5E **88**
(in two parts)
Sanger Clo. *Nott* —1J **99**
Sanger Gdns. *Nott* —1J **99**
Sankey Dri. *Nott* —6G **31**
Santolina Dri. *Oak* —6F **57**
Sapele Clo. *Ged* —4E **50**
Sapperton Clo. *L'ver* —4H **91**
Sargent Gdns. *Nott* —1H **65**
Saskatoon Clo. *Rad T* —5J **67**
Saunby Clo. *Arn* —6K **33**
Saundersfoot Way. *Oak* —5H **57**
Saunders Yd. *Klbrn* —5F **25**
Saunten Clo. *Edw* —4A **84**
Savages Rd. *Rud* —1E **100**
Savages Row. *Rud* —1E **100**
Save Penny La. *Duf* —2A **40**
Saville Clo. *S'fd* —7J **61**
Saville Rd. *Wd'p* —1H **49**
Savoy Workshops. *Lent* —4B **64**

Sawley Bridge Marina. —7E **96**
Sawley Rd. *Breas* —2C **96**
Sawley Rd. *Dray* —2K **95**
Sawmand Clo. *Long E* —3G **97**
Sawmills Ind. Pk. *Los* —2F **27**
Saxelby Gdns. *Nott* —5H **31**
Saxondale Av. *Mick* —4A **72**
Saxondale Dri. *Nott* —1K **47**
Saxondale Dri. *Rad T* —3D **68**
Saxon Grn. *Nott* —4A **64**
Saxon Way. *Cotg* —7K **85**
Saxton Av. *Hean* —3H **27**
Saxton Clo. *Bees* —1H **81**
Scafell Clo. *W Bri* —3A **84**
Scafell Way. *Nott* —2K **99**
Scalby Clo. *Eastw* —3B **28**
Scalford Dri. *Nott* —3J **63**
Scarborough Av. *Ilk* —6B **44**
Scarborough Ri. *Der* —6C **56**
Scarborough St. *Nott*
—2F **65** (2H **5**)

Scarcliffe Clo. *Shel L* —6E **92**
Scarf Wlk. *Nott* —1D **82**
Scargill Av. *Newt* —4F **29**
Scargill Clo. *Newt* —4F **29**
Scargill Rd. *W Hal* —6G **43**
Scargill Wlk. *Eastw* —2D **28**
Scarrington Rd. *W Bri* —6H **65**
Scarsdale Av. *Alst* —4G **55**
Scarsdale Av. *L'ver* —6G **73**
Scarsdale Rd. *Duf* —3J **39**
Sceptre St. *Nott* —4E **48**
School Av. *Huck* —1D **30**
School Clo. *Nott* —6F **65**
Schoolhouse Hill. *Heag* —3D **10**
School La. *Asl* —2J **71**
School La. *Bees* —4C **80**
School La. *Bing* —2A **70**
School La. *Cas D* —6J **107**
School La. *Chel* —1G **105**
School La. *Heag* —2D **10**
School La. *Rip* —3J **11**
School La. *Stan D* —1D **78**
School La. *What* —4K **71**
School Rd. *Und* —1E **14**
School Sq. *W Hal* —7G **43**
School Wlk. *B Vil* —1A **32**
School Way. *Nott* —6F **65**
Science Rd. *Nott* —6K **63**
Scotches, The. *Belp* —7K **9**
Scotholme Av. *Nott* —6B **48**
Scotland Bank. *Cotg* —5K **85**
Scotland Rd. *Nott* —3B **48**
Scott Av. *Bees* —2F **81**
Scott Clo. *Nott* —1F **47**
Scott Dri. *Belp* —7E **10**
Scottsdale Wlk. *Nott* —5G **49**
Scott St. *Der* —7K **73**
Scrimshire La. *Cotg* —5J **85**
Script Dri. *Nott* —2A **48**
Scrivelsby Gdns. *Bees* —4D **80**
Scrooby Row. *Nott* —5C **32**
Scropton Wlk. *Shel L* —6E **92**
Seaburn Rd. *Bees* —5J **79**
Seaford Av. *Nott* —2H **63**
Seaford Way. *Ilk* —1D **44**
Seagrave Clo. *Oak* —1H **57**
Seagrave Ct. *Nott* —6G **33**
Seagrave Rd. *Nott* —5D **46**
Seale St. *Der* —1A **74** (1E **6**)
Seamer Rd. *Kimb* —6K **29**
Searl St. *Der* —2K **73** (2B **6**)
Seascale Clo. *Der* —6D **56**
Seatallan Clo. *W Bri* —2A **84**
Seathwaite Clo. *Edw* —4A **84**
Seatoller Clo. *W Bri* —3A **84**
Seaton Clo. *Mick* —5A **72**
Seaton Cres. *Nott* —5G **47**
Second Av. *Bees* —7E **62**
Second Av. *Cltn* —7A **50**
Second Av. *Chel* —2G **105**
Second Av. *Ged* —5D **50**
Second Av. *Ilk* —7D **44**
Second Av. *Lent* —2J **81**
Second Av. *Nott* —6D **48**
Second Av. *Ris* —4D **78**
Sedgebrook Clo. *Nott* —3J **47**
Sedgebrook Clo. *Oak* —5F **57**
Sedgefield Grn. *Mick* —7A **72**
Sedgeley Rd. *Toll* —1B **102**
Sedgemoor Rd. *Long E* —4J **97**
Sedgewood Gro. *Nott* —5A **82**
Sedgley Av. *Nott* —2H **65**
Sedgwick St. *Jack* —1K **13**
Sedgwick St. *Lan M* —2K **27**
Sedley Av. *Nut* —7C **30**
Seely Av. *C'tn* —4B **50**
Seely Rd. *Nott* —2B **64** (3A **4**)
Sefton Av. *S'fd* —7J **61**
Sefton Dri. *Nott* —5F **49**
Sefton Rd. *Chad* —2F **75**
Selbourne St. *Der* —6D **74**
Selby Clo. *Bees* —5J **79**
Selby La. *Keyw* —7C **102**
Selby Rd. *W Bri* —2H **83**
Selhurst Ct. *Nott* —7B **48**
Selhurst St. *Nott* —7B **48**
Selina Clo. *Cas D* —6J **107**
Selina St. *Melb* —4G **113**
Selkirk St. *Der* —1E **74**
Selkirk Way. *Nott* —5D **48**
Sellars Av. *Rud* —3E **100**
Sellers Wood Dri. *Blen I* —5F **31**
Sellers Wood Dri. W. *Bulw* —6E **31**
Seller's Wood Nature Reserve.
—6E **30**
Selside Ct. *Bees* —4A **80**
Selston Dri. *Nott* —4J **63**
Selston Rd. *Jack* —1K **13**
Selworthy Clo. *Oak* —5G **57**

Selwyn Clo. *Nott* —1A **48**
Selwyn St. *Der* —2G **73**
Senna Ct. *Bees* —1H **81**
Serina Av. *Der* —1H **91**
Serina Ct. *W Bri* —1G **83**
Serlby Ri. *Nott* —1H **65**
Serlby Rd. *Newt* —2E **28**
Serpentine Clo. *Rad T* —5D **68**
Service Rd. *Arn* —6E **32**
Settlement, The. *Ock* —3E **76**
Sevenlands Dri. *Boul M* —5J **93**
Sevenoaks Av. *Der* —3D **72**
Seven Oaks Cres. *Bees* —6B **62**
Seven Oaks Rd. *Ilk* —6E **60**
Seventh Av. *Lent* —3J **81**
Severals. *S'fd* —1K **79**
Severn St. *Der* —1F **93**
Severn St. *Nott* —6H **31**
Severnvale Clo. *Alst* —2B **56**
Seymour Clo. *Der* —2G **73**
Seymour Rd. *Eastw* —4D **28**
Seymour Rd. *Huck* —7E **16**
Seymour Rd. *W Bri* —7K **65**
Seymour St. *Nott* —2G **65** (2K **5**)
Shacklecross Clo. *Borr* —7E **76**
Shackleton Clo. *Nott* —4D **46**
Shacklock Clo. *Arn* —3C **32**
Shadwell Gro. *Rad T* —4J **67**
Shady La. *Bees* —6D **80**
Shaef Clo. *Hilt* —7A **88**
Shaftesbury Av. *Bur J* —1A **52**
Shaftesbury Av. *Long E* —5F **97**
Shaftesbury Av. *Rad T* —4D **68**
Shaftesbury Av. *Sand* —3E **78**
Shaftesbury Cres. *Der* —7B **74**
Shaftesbury Sports Cen. —7B **74**
Shaftesbury St. *Der* —7C **74**
Shaftesbury St. *New B* —5C **48**
Shaftesbury St. S. *Der* —1B **92**
Shakespeare Clo. *Colw* —2C **66**
Shakespeare Dri. *Dis* —6A **116**
Shakespeare St. *Long E* —7G **79**
Shakespeare St. *Nott*
—2D **64** (2D **4**)
Shakespeare Vs. *Nott*
—2E **64** (2E **4**)
Shaldon Clo. *Nott* —4B **32**
Shaldon Dri. *L'ver* —7H **73**
Shalfleet Dri. *Alv* —3J **93**
Shamrock St. *Der* —7J **73**
Shandwick Clo. *Arn* —3K **33**
Shandwick Ct. *Sin* —6H **91**
Shanklin Dri. *S'fd* —1H **79**
Shanklin Ho. *Alv* —2J **93**
Shannon Clo. *Sun* —3H **91**
Shannon Sq. *Chad* —4H **75**
Shanwell Clo. *Nott* —4D **46**
Shardale Gdns. *Nott* —2K **47**
Shardlow Heritage Cen. —1J **107**
Shardlow Rd. *Alv* —2H **93**
Shardlow Rd. *Ast T* —3D **106**
Sharnford Way. *Bees* —3B **62**
Sharp Clo. *Ilk* —1A **60**
Sharp Clo. *Long E* —3G **97**
Sharphill Rd. *Edw* —4K **83**
Sharrard Clo. *Und* —2E **14**
Shaw Cres. *Huck* —1E **30**
Shaw Gdns. *Nott* —1J **99**
Shaw La. *Milf* —5K **23**
Shaws Grn. *Der* —2H **73**
Shaw St. *Der* —2J **73**
Shaw St. *Rud* —2E **100**
Shaw St. E. *Ilk* —1E **60**
Shaw St. W. *Ilk* —1E **60**
Shaw's Yd. *Klbrn* —5F **25**
Shearing Clo. *Ged* —5E **50**
Shearing Hill. *Ged* —5E **50**
Shearwater Clo. *Der* —2H **91**
Sheepfold La. *Rud* —3E **100**
Sheet Stores Ind. Est. *Long E*
—4H **97**
Sheffield Pl. *Der* —4C **74** (6H **7**)
Shelby Clo. *Lent* —3A **64**
Sheldon Clo. *Long E* —5F **79**
Sheldon Ct. *Shel L* —6E **92**
Sheldon Rd. *Los* —7E **12**
Shelford Clo. *Bees* —4D **80**
Shelford Clo. *Mick* —5A **72**
Shelford Clo. *Rad T* —3A **68**
Shelford Cres. *Bur J* —1A **52**
Shelford Dri. *Bing* —3K **69**
Shelford Hill. *Shelf* —6C **52**
Shelford Ri. *Nott* —1J **65**
Shelford Rd. *Ged* —3A **50**
Shelford Rd. *Nwtn* —5G **53**
Shelford Rd. *Rad T & Shelf*
—4K **67**

Shellburne Clo. *Nott* —5A **32**
Shelley Av. *Nott* —5A **82**
Shelley Clo. *Huck* —6D **16**
Shelley Clo. *Nut* —7B **30**
Shelley Dri. *Sin* —3A **92**
Shelley Rd. *Day* —6F **33**
Shelmory Clo. *Altn* —4E **92**
Shelt Hill. *Wdbgh* —1H **35**
Shelton Av. *Huck* —1J **31**
Shelton Dri. *Der* —1E **92**
Shelton Gdns. *Rud* —2D **100**
Shelton St. *Nott* —1E **64** (1F **5**)
Shenfield Gdns. *Nott* —4K **31**
Shenington Way. *Oak* —5H **57**
Shepard Clo. *Nott* —7F **31**
Shepherd Ct. *Huck* —1D **30**
Shepherds Clo. *Nott* —7G **47**
Shepherd's La. *Tickn* —5D **112**
Shepherd St. *L'ver* —7G **73**
Shepherds Wood Dri. *Nott*
—7J **47**
Shepherd Wlk. *Keg* —2G **117**
Shepton Clo. *Ilk* —3B **44**
Shepton Cres. *Nott* —4H **47**
Sheraton Dri. *Nott* —4E **62**
Sherborne Rd. *Nott* —5G **47**
Sherborne Rd. *W Bri* —3H **83**
Sherbourne Dri. *Belp* —7D **10**
Sherbrook Av. *Day* —7F **33**
Sherbrooke Clo. *C'tn* —4C **20**
Sherbrooke Rd. *Nott* —5D **48**
Sherbrooke Ter. *Nott* —5D **48**
Sherbrook Rd. *Day* —7E **32**
Sherbrook Ter. *Day* —7F **33**
Sheridan Ct. *Nott* —1E **4**
Sheridan Ct. *S'fd* —3J **79**
Sheridan St. *Sin* —4K **91**
Sheriffs Lea. *Bees* —6J **79**
Sheriffs Way. *Nott* —5E **64** (7F **5**)
Sheringham Clo. *Arn* —7H **33**
Sherman Clo. *Hilt* —7A **88**
Sherman Dri. *Bees* —6C **80**
Sherrington Clo. *Nott* —1J **99**
Sherston Clo. *Oak* —5H **57**
Sherwin Clo. *Nott* —1E **64** (1F **5**)
Sherwin Gro. *Nott* —4A **64**
Sherwin Rd. *Nott* —4A **64**
Sherwin Rd. *S'fd* —6K **61**
Sherwin Sports Cen. —1B **92**
Sherwin St. *Der* —7J **55**
Sherwin Wlk. *Nott* —1E **64** (1E **4**)
Sherwood Av. *Borr* —6F **77**
Sherwood Av. *C'tn* —4B **20**
Sherwood Av. *Chad* —1F **75**
Sherwood Av. *L'ver* —4H **91**
Sherwood Av. *Nott* —3F **49**
Sherwood Av. *Bees* —5C **80**
Sherwood Gro. *Bing* —3K **69**
Sherwood Gro. *C'tn* —4D **20**
Sherwood Lodge Dri. *Arn*
—2E **18**
Sherwood Ri. *Eastw* —4D **28**
Sherwood Ri. *Nott* —5C **48**
Sherwood St. *Der* —5J **73** (7A **6**)
Sherwood St. *Huck* —6J **17**
Sherwood Va. *Nott* —4F **49**
Sherwood Wlk. *L'by* —2G **17**
Shetland Clo. *Der* —1C **74**
Shields Cres. *Cas D* —7H **107**
Shilling Way. *Long E* —2E **96**
Shipley Comn. La. *Ilk* —2A **44**
Shipley Country Pk. & Vis. Cen.
—6G **27**
Shipley Ct. *Ilk* —5B **44**
Shipley Ga. *Eastw* —6C **28**
Shipley Hall. —1H **43**
(remains of)
Shipley La. *Hean* —1H **43**
Shipley La. *Shot* —2D **22**
Shipley Ri. *Cltn* —7C **50**
Shipley Rd. *Nott* —4F **47**
Shipley Vw. *Smal* —7B **26**
Shipley Wlk. *Shel L* —6E **92**
Shipstone St. *Ilk* —1F **61**
Shipstone St. *Nott* —6B **48**
Shipstones Yd. *Nott* —5J **31**
Shirebrook Clo. *Nott* —3J **47**
Shire Hall & Galleries. —5G **5**
Shireoaks. *Belp* —7H **9**
Shireoaks Clo. *L'ver* —2G **91**
Shirland Ct. *Shel L* —6E **92**
Shirley Clo. *Cas D* —6J **107**
Shirley Cres. *Breas* —1B **96**
Shirley Dri. *Arn* —6K **33**
Shirley Pk. *Ast T* —3D **106**
Shirley Rd. *Chad* —6F **57**
Shirley Rd. *Nott* —6E **48**
Shirley Rd. *Rip* —3K **11**

Shirley St. *Long E* —5E **96**
Shop La. *Neth H* —2C **10**
Shop Stones. *Ock* —3E **76**
Shores Wood Clo. *Nott* —5D **32**
Short Av. *Alst* —2K **55**
Shortcross Av. *Nott* —2H **49**
Short Hill. *Melb* —5A **114**
Short Hill. *Nott* —3F **65** (5G **5**)
Short Lands. *Belp* —1A **24**
Short La. *Cas D* —6H **107**
Short Row. *Belp* —1K **23**
Short Stairs. *Nott* —3F **65** (5H **5**)
Short St. *Belp* —1B **24**
Shortwood Av. *Huck* —7F **17**
Shortwood Clo. *Nott*
—3F **65** (5G **5**)
Shorwell Gdns. *Alv* —4J **93**
Shorwell Rd. *Nott* —7A **50**
Shottle Wlk. *Shel L* —6E **92**
Shotton Dri. *Arn* —3J **33**
Showcase Cinemas. —7A **64**
Shrewsbury Clo. *Oak* —5H **57**
Shrewsbury Rd. *Nott* —3J **65**
Shrimpton Ct. *Rud* —3F **101**
Shropshire Av. *Der* —1E **74**
Shropshire Av. *W'wd* —1A **14**
Sibson Dri. *Keg* —1F **117**
Sibson Wlk. *Arn* —3H **33**
Siddals La. *Alst* —3K **55**
Siddals Rd. *Der* —3B **74** (4F **7**)
Siddons St. *Alv* —2G **93**
Side Ley. *Keg* —7G **109**
Sidings, The. *Asl* —3J **71**
Sidings, The. *Der* —4G **75**
Sidings, The. *Low* —5E **36**
Sidlaw Ri. *Arn* —3D **32**
Sidmouth Clo. *Alv* —2J **93**
Sidmouth Clo. *Keyw* —5C **102**
Sidney Ho. *Der* —7G **73**
Sidney Rd. *Bees* —1E **80**
Sidney St. *Der* —5B **74**
Sidney St. *Kimb* —7K **29**
Sidney St. *Long E* —3H **97**
Silbury Clo. *Nott* —2K **99**
Silver Birch Clo. *Nott* —2H **47**
Silverburn Dri. *Oak* —5F **57**
Silverdale. *S'fd* —3J **79**
Silverdale Rd. *Nott* —4B **48**
Silverhill Clo. *Strel* —4D **46**
Silver Hill Rd. *Der* —6A **74**
Silverhill Rd. *Spon* —5A **76**
Silverhow Clo. *W Bri* —3A **84**
Silver La. *Thul* —4B **94**
Silverton Dri. *Sten F* —7G **91**
Silverwood Rd. *Bees* —2E **80**
Silvey Gro. *Spon* —4K **75**
Simcoe Leys. *Chel* —7F **93**
Simkin Av. *Nott* —5J **49**
Simone Gdns. *Nott* —6B **82**
Simon Fields Clo. *Stan C* —4C **42**
Simons Ct. *Bees* —6D **62**
Simon Wlk. *Sten F* —6G **91**
Simpson St. *Altn* —3E **92**
Sims Av. *Der* —3J **73** (3A **6**)
Sinclair Clo. *Hean* —5F **27**
Sinclair Clo. *Sin* —6J **91**
Sinfin Av. *Shel L* —5D **92**
Sinfin Central Ind. Pk. *Sin*
—4K **91**
Sinfin District Cen. *Sin* —6J **91**
Sinfin Fields Cres. *Altn* —4D **92**
Sinfin La. *Bar T* —4A **104**
Sinfin La. *Sin & Der* —5K **91**
Sinfin La. Ind. Est. *Sin* —4K **91**
Sinfin Moor La. *Sin & Chel*
(in two parts) —6K **91**
Sinfin Moor Pk. —6A **92**
Sir Francis Ley Ind. Est. *Der*
—7B **74**
Sir Frank Whittle Rd. *Der*
—7C **56** (1H **7**)
Sir Henry's La. *Melb* —7G **113**
Sir John Robinson Way. *Arn*
—6F **33**
Siskin Clo. *Mick* —2K **89**
Siskin Dri. *Sin* —5H **91**
Sisley Av. *S'fd* —2J **79**
Sisters La. *Ock* —3E **76**
Sitwell Clo. *Spon* —4K **75**
Sitwell Dri. *Klbrn* —5G **25**
Sitwell St. *Der* —4A **74** (5E **6**)
Sitwell St. *Spon* —4K **75**
Sixth Av. *Lent* —3J **81**
Skeavingtons La. *Ilk* —1C **44**
Skelwith Clo. *W Bri* —3A **84**
Sketchley Ct. *Nott* —6G **31**
Sketchley St. *Nott* —1H **65** (1K **5**)
Skiddaw Clo. *W Bri* —3A **84**
Skiddaw Dri. *Mick* —7C **72**

Skipton Cir. *Nott* —1J **65**
Skipton Clo. *Ilk* —3B **44**
Skipton Grn. *Der* —6C **56**
Skithorne Ri. *Low* —5D **36**
Skylark Clo. *Bing* —4B **70**
Skylark Dri. *Nott* —2K **47**
Skylark Way. *Sin* —5H **91**
Slack Av. *Rip* —3K **11**
Slack La. *Dar A* —5K **55**
Slack La. *Der* —3H **73**
Slack La. *Hean* —5G **27**
Slack La. *Neth H* —2C **10**
Slack La. *Rip* —3K **11**
Slack Rd. *Ilk* —3H **43**
Slade Clo. *Etw* —5E **88**
Slade Clo. *Ilk* —2D **60**
Sladelands Dri. *Chel* —1G **105**
Slade La. *Melb* —5B **114**
Slade Rd. *Bees* —3B **80**
Slaidburn Av. *Nott* —3C **82**
Slaidburn Clo. *Mick* —7C **72**
Slaney Clo. *Altn* —2E **92**
Slater Av. *Der* —3J **73** (2A **6**)
Sledmere Clo. *Alv* —2J **93**
Sleepy La. *Melb* —2H **113**
Slindon Cft. *Alv* —3K **93**
Sloan Dri. *Bees* —4B **62**
Sloane Ct. *W Bri* —5E **82**
Sloane Rd. *Der* —2E **72**
Sloethorne Gdns. *Arn* —5F **33**
Smalley Clo. *Und* —2E **14**
Smalley Dri. *Oak* —4H **57**
Smalley Mill Rd. *Hors* —1G **41**
Small Meer Clo. *Chel* —1E **104**
Small's Cft. *Wdbgh* —1G **35**
Smeath Rd. *Und* —2D **14**
Smedley Av. *Ilk* —7E **44**
Smedley Clo. *Nott* —4H **47**
Smedley's Av. *Sand* —3F **79**
Smeeton St. *Hean* —4K **27**
Smisby Way. *Shel L* —6E **92**
Smite Clo. *What* —3H **71**
Smite Ct. *Nott* —1K **63**
Smith Av. *Cod* —3D **12**
Smith Av. *Melb* —2H **113**
Smith Dri. *Lan M* —2J **27**
Smithfield Av. *Trow* —3H **61**
Smiths Clo. *C Bis* —4G **87**
Smithurst Rd. *Gilt* —5E **28**
Smithy Clo. *Nott* —6K **81**
Smithy Cres. *Arn* —5H **33**
Smithy La. *Long W* —7E **116**
Smithy Row. *Nott* —3E **64** (4F **5**)
Smithy Vw. *C'tn* —5C **20**
Smythson Dri. *Nott* —3E **62**
Snake La. *Duf* —3H **39**
Snape Nook Ct. *Nott* —6F **31**
Snape Wood Rd. *Nott* —6F **31**
Snead Ct. *Nott* —4C **32**
Sneinton Boulevd. *Nott* —3H **65**
Sneinton Dale. *Nott* —3H **65**
Sneinton Hermitage. *Nott*
—4G **65** (6K **5**)
Sneinton Hollows. *Nott*
—3H **65** (5K **5**)
Sneinton Rd. *Nott* —3G **65** (4J **5**)
Snelsmoor La. *Chel* —1H **105**
Snelston Cres. *L'ver* —6H **73**
Snowberry Av. *Belp* —2B **24**
Snowdon Clo. *Nott* —4D **32**
Soarbank Clo. *Kimb* —6J **29**
Soar La. *Sut B* —3J **117**
Sobers Gdns. *Arn* —7K **33**
Society Pl. *Der* —6A **74**
Softwood Clo. *Nott* —6F **31**
Soloman Rd. *Coss* —4F **45**
Solway Clo. *Bees* —3E **80**
Solway Clo. *Oak* —5G **57**
Somerby Clo. *Bees* —3B **62**
Somerby Way. *Oak* —5F **57**
Somersal Clo. *Shel L* —6D **92**
Somersby Rd. *Wd'p & Map*
—1H **49**
Somerset Clo. *Long E* —1A **98**
Somerset St. *Der* —1D **74**
Somerton Av. *Nott* —4C **82**
Somme Rd. *Alst* —4F **55**
Songthrush Av. *Nott* —2K **47**
Sophie Rd. *Nott* —1B **64**
Sorrel Dri. *Bing* —3J **69**
Soudan Dri. *Nott* —6D **64**
Southampton St. *Nott*
—1G **65** (1J **5**)
South Av. *Chel* —6F **93**
South Av. *Dar A* —4A **56**
South Av. *L'ver* —7H **73**
South Av. *Rad T* —3B **68**
South Av. *Spon* —4A **76**
S. Brae Clo. *L'ver* —2H **91**

**South Charnwood Swimming Pool. —5G 49**
Southchurch Ct. *Nott* —5B **82**
Southchurch Dri. *Nott* —7A **82**
Southcliffe Rd. *Cltn* —7B **50**
South Ct. *Bees* —4H **81**
South Ct. *Mick* —7B **72**
Southcroft. *L'ver* —4H **91**
Southdale Dri. *Cltn* —7B **50**
Southdale Rd. *Cltn* —7B **50**
 (in two parts)
S. Devon Av. *Nott* —4K **49**
S. Down Clo. *Sten F* —7G **91**
South Dri. *Chad* —3G **75**
South Dri. *Chel* —6F **93**
South Dri. *Der* —1K **73**
South Dri. *Mick* —6E **72**
Southey St. *Nott* —1B **64** (1A **4**)
Southfield Rd. *Nott* —1K **63**
Southfields. *Long E* —2J **97**
Southfields Ct. *Bees* —3B **80**
Southgate Clo. *Mick* —5A **72**
Southglade Rd. *Nott* —7A **32**
**Southglade Sports Cen. —7B 32**
Southlea Rd. *Cltn* —7B **50**
Southmead Way. *Der* —5F **73**
South Pde. *Nott* —3E **64** (4E **4**)
South Pl. *Rip* —3K **11**
Southport Ter. *Nott* —7A **48**
South Rd. *Bees* —4G **81**
South Rd. *Nott* —4C **64** (5B **4**)
South Rd. *W Bri* —2G **83**
S. Sherwood St. *Nott*
 —2E **64** (2E **4**)
Southside. *Arn* —5A **34**
S. Snape Clo. *Nott* —6F **31**
South St. *Der* —3J **73** (3A **6**)
South St. *Dray* —2J **95**
South St. *Eastw* —3C **28**
South St. *Gilt* —5G **29**
South St. *Huck* —5G **17**
South St. *Ilk* —7D **44**
South St. *Long E* —2J **97**
South St. *Melb* —4G **113**
South Vw. *Der* —7G **73**
South Vw. *Milf* —6A **24**
S. View Rd. *Cltn* —4B **50**
Southwark Clo. *Der* —3F **73**
Southwark St. *Nott* —3A **48**
Southwell Ri. *Gilt* —6F **29**
Southwell Rd. *Low* —4E **36**
Southwell Rd. *Nott* —3F **65** (4J **5**)
Southwell Rd. *Oxt* —1G **21**
Southwold Dri. *Nott* —2J **63**
Southwood St. *Der* —1F **93**
Sovereign Ct. *Bees* —3G **81**
Sovereign Gro. *Long E* —2F **97**
Sovereign Way. *Oak* —4J **57**
Soverign Way. *Hean* —4E **26**
Sowbrook La. *Dal A* —3B **60**
Sowter Rd. *Der* —2A **74** (2E **6**)
Spa La. *Der* —5K **73** (6C **6**)
Spalding Rd. *Nott* —2G **65** (3K **5**)
Spaniel Row. *Nott* —3E **64** (5E **4**)
Spanker La. *Neth H* —2B **10**
Spanker Ter. *Neth H* —2C **10**
Sparrow Clo. *Ilk* —3D **60**
Sparrow Clo. *Sin* —5H **91**
Spean Ct. *Nott* —2G **63**
Spean Dri. *Nott* —7H **47**
Speedwell Clo. *Bing* —5J **69**
Speedwell Clo. *Oak* —4J **57**
Speedwell La. *Kimb* —7J **29**
Spenbeck Dri. *Alst* —2A **56**
Spencer Av. *Altn* —5D **92**
Spencer Av. *Belp* —1B **24**
Spencer Av. *Map* —1A **50**
Spencer Av. *Sand* —1F **79**
Spencer Clo. *Rud* —2D **100**
Spencer Cres. *S'fd* —7K **61**
Spencer Dri. *Nut* —7C **30**
Spencer Rd. *Belp* —1A **24**
Spencer St. *Der* —1G **93**
Spencer St. *Stan C* —5C **42**
Spey Clo. *Huck* —2D **30**
Spicer Clo. *Bees* —6C **80**
Spindle Gdns. *Nott* —6G **31**
Spindle La. *C'tn* —2A **20**
Spindletree Dri. *Oak* —5E **56**
Spindle Vw. *C'tn* —6D **20**
Spinners Way. *Belp* —6C **10**
Spinney Clo. *Cotg* —6K **85**
Spinney Clo. *Dar A* —5A **56**
Spinney Clo. *W Bri* —4K **83**
Spinney Cres. *Bees* —5K **79**
Spinney Dri. *Long E* —6G **79**
Spinney Hill. *Melb* —3G **113**
Spinney Ri. *Bees* —5J **79**
Spinney Rd. *Bing* —3K **69**

Spinney Rd. *Chad* —1F **75**
Spinney Rd. *Der* —5J **73**
Spinney Rd. *Ilk* —1C **60**
Spinney Rd. *Keyw* —6B **102**
Spinney Rd. *Long E* —6G **79**
Spinney, The. *Belp* —6A **10**
Spinney, The. *B Vil* —7A **18**
Spinney, The. *Borr* —7E **76**
Spinney, The. *Bul* —1B **52**
Spinney, The. *Cas D* —6J **107**
Spinney, The. *Ilk* —1C **60**
Spinney, The. *Nut* —3F **47**
 (Harcourt Cres.)
Spinney, The. *Nut* —7B **30**
 (Laurel Cres.)
Spinney, The. *Rip* —1K **11**
Spinney, The. *Stan D* —7D **60**
Spinney, The. *Wd'p* —2G **49**
Spinney Way. *Nott* —4C **82**
Spinningdale. *Arn* —4K **33**
Spital Hill. *Cas D* —6J **107**
Spital, The. *Cas D* —6J **107**
Spondon St. *Nott* —4E **48**
 (in two parts)
Spoonley Wood Ct. *L'ver* —2D **90**
**Sports Cen. —3D 92 (Derby)**
Spot, The. *Der* —4A **74** (5E **6**)
Spout La. *Shot* —1A **8**
Spray Clo. *Colw* —2C **66**
Spridgeon Clo. *Long E* —6F **79**
Spring Clo. *Belp* —6J **9**
Spring Clo. *Breas* —1A **96**
Spring Clo. *Watn* —6A **30**
Springdale Ct. *Mick* —7C **72**
Springdale Gdns. *Trow* —5H **61**
Springdale La. *E Bri* —4K **53**
Springfield. *Keg* —1F **117**
Springfield. *L'ver* —6F **73**
Springfield Av. *Eastw* —3E **28**
Springfield Av. *Long E* —1K **97**
Springfield Av. *Los* —7D **12**
Springfield Av. *Sand* —5E **78**
Springfield Clo. *C Bis* —4H **87**
Springfield Ct. *S'fd* —6K **61**
Springfield Dri. *Duf* —3B **93**
Springfield Dri. *Nott* —7F **31**
Springfield Gdns. *Ilk* —4D **44**
Springfield Retail Pk. *Nott*
 —4K **31**
Springfield Rd. *Chad* —3H **75**
Springfield Rd. *Chel* —7E **92**
Springfield Rd. *Etw* —6D **88**
Springfield Rd. *Huck* —6D **16**
Springfield Rd. *Red* —4G **33**
Springfields. *W Bri* —2F **83**
Springfield St. *Nott* —5B **48**
Springfield Ter. *Rip* —3A **12**
Springfield Vw. *Rip* —2K **11**
Spring Gdns. *Chad* —1F **75**
Spring Garden Ter. *Ilk* —4D **44**
Spring Grn. *Nott* —2A **100**
Springhead Clo. *Bulw* —7G **31**
Spring Hill. *Kimb* —1K **45**
Springhill Clo. *Nott* —4H **31**
Springhill Way. *Cod* —4C **12**
Spring Hollow. *H'wd* —6G **23**
Springland Farm Cotts. *Nut*
 (off Watnall Rd.) —7D **30**
Spring La. *Hean* —4G **27**
Spring La. *Nott & Lamb* —7A **34**
Spring Mdw. *Cotg* —5A **86**
Springmoor. *Colw P* —2B **66**
Spring Rd. *Nott* —6J **31**
Spring St. *Der* —4K **73** (6B **6**)
Spring St. *Huck* —4G **17**
Spring Ter. *Nut* —1D **46**
Spring, The. *Long E* —4H **97**
Springwood Clo. *C'tn* —5E **20**
Springwood Dri. *Oak* —5G **57**
Springwood Gdns. *Wd'p* —3H **49**
**Springwood Leisure Cen.**
 —5G **57**
Spruce Gdns. *Nott* —6G **31**
Spruce Gro. *Huck* —7H **17**
Sprydon Wlk. *Nott* —1B **100**
Squares Dri. *B Vil* —6D **18**
Square, The. *Bees* —2F **81**
Square, The. *B Vil* —1A **32**
Square, The. *Der* —6A **56**
Square, The. *Got* —1H **111**
Square, The. *Keyw* —7C **102**
Square, The. *Mick* —7B **72**
Square, The. *Woll* —3E **62**
Squires Av. *Nott* —4H **31**
Squires Clo. *C Bis* —4H **87**
Squires Way. *L'ver* —2E **90**
Squires Way. *W Bri* —2F **83**
Squirrel La. *Bree H* —7A **114**

Stable Clo. *E Bri* —3K **53**
Stables St. *Der* —3H **73**
Stacey Av. *Nott* —6B **32**
Stadium Ind. Pk. *Long E* —1K **97**
Stadium Vw. *Pri P* —5E **74**
Stadmoor Ct. *Chel* —1F **105**
Stafford Av. *Nott* —7H **31**
Stafford Clo. *Smal* —7B **26**
Stafford Ct. *Cltn* —7E **50**
Stafford Ct. *Nott* —1F **47**
Staffords Acre. *Keg* —1G **117**
Stafford St. *Der* —3K **73** (4B **6**)
Stafford St. *Long E* —1K **97**
Stagsden Cres. *Nott* —2C **62**
Staindale Ct. *Nott* —5J **47**
Staindale Dri. *Nott* —5J **47**
Staines Clo. *Mick* —6A **72**
Stainmore Gro. *Bing* —3J **69**
Stainsborough Rd. *Huck* —6C **16**
Stainsby Av. *Hean* —4G **27**
Stainsby Av. *Hors W* —7A **26**
Staithes Wlk. *Der* —6C **56**
Staker La. *Mick* —4B **90**
Staker Way. *Mick* —2B **90**
Stamford Clo. *Long E* —5J **97**
Stamford Ct. *Nott* —5J **47**
Stamford Rd. *W Bri* —2J **83**
Stamford St. *Altn* —3D **92**
Stamford St. *Aws* —2G **45**
Stamford St. *Hean* —3G **27**
Stamford St. *Ilk* —5C **44**
Stamford St. *Newt* —4G **29**
Stanage Grn. *Mick* —6D **72**
Stancliffe Av. *Nott* —6A **30**
Standard Ct. *Nott* —3D **64** (5D **4**)
Standard Hill. *Nott*
 —3D **64** (5D **4**)
Standhill Av. *Cltn* —6K **49**
Standhill Rd. *Cltn* —5J **49**
Stanesby Ri. *Nott* —6A **82**
Stanford Gdns. *Rad T* —3K **67**
Stanford St. *Nott* —3E **64** (5E **4**)
Stanhome Ct. *W Bri* —4F **83**
Stanhome Dri. *W Bri* —4F **83**
Stanhome Sq. *W Bri* —4F **83**
Stanhope Cres. *Arn* —5G **33**
Stanhope Cres. *Bur J* —7K **51**
Stanhope Rd. *Arn* —5G **33**
Stanhope Rd. *Ged* —2B **50**
Stanhope Rd. *Mick* —6G **72**
Stanhope St. *Der* —6K **73**
Stanhope St. *Ilk* —1E **60**
Stanhope St. *Long E* —1H **97**
Stanhope St. *Nott* —3G **65** (4H **5**)
Stanhope St. *Stan D* —7D **60**
Stanhope Way. *Bing* —3A **70**
Stanier Way. *Chad* —5G **75**
Staniland Clo. *Bees* —6C **80**
Stanley Av. *Nott* —6C **48**
Stanley Av. *Rip* —2A **12**
Stanley Clo. *Der* —7K **55**
Stanley Clo. *Ilk* —7C **44**
Stanley Ct. *Eastw* —4D **28**
Stanley Dri. *Nott* —7A **62**
Stanley Pl. *Nott* —2D **64** (3D **4**)
Stanley Rd. *Alv* —3E **92**
Stanley Rd. *Chad* —3G **75**
Stanley Rd. *For F* —6C **48**
 (in two parts)
Stanley Rd. *Map* —4J **49**
Stanley Rd. *W Bri* —2H **83**
Stanley St. *Der* —3H **73**
Stanley St. *Ilk* —7D **44**
Stanley St. *Long E* —2J **97**
Stanmore Clo. *Nut* —3E **46**
Stanmore Gdns. *Arn* —7G **33**
 (in two parts)
Stansfield St. *Nott* —2A **64**
Stanstead Av. *Nott* —4K **31**
Stanstead Av. *Toll* —1B **102**
Stanstead Rd. *Mick* —5A **72**
Stanthorne Clo. *Nott* —4C **82**
Stanton Av. *Belp* —1B **24**
Stanton Clo. *Keyw* —7G **103**
Stanton Ga. *Stan D* —6G **61**
Stanton Hill. *Tickn* —6C **112**
Stanton La. *Keyw* —7F **103**
Stanton Rd. *Ilk* —1D **60**
Stanton Rd. *Sand* —1D **78**
Stanton St. *Der* —7K **73**
Stanway Clo. *Nott* —1A **66**
Stanwick Clo. *Nott* —6E **46**
Stapleford By-Pass. *Sand & S'fd*
 —4E **78**
Stapleford La. *Bees* —4K **79**
Stapleford Rd. *Trow* —3G **61**
Staplehurst Dri. *Nott* —2C **48**
Staples St. *Nott* —4G **49**
Stapleton Rd. *Ilk* —2C **44**

Starch La. *Sand* —1F **79**
Starcross Ct. *Mick* —5A **72**
Starkie Av. *Cas D* —7H **107**
Starthe Bank. *Hean* —3H **27**
Starthwood Rd. *Huck* —1D **30**
Statham St. *Der* —1J **73**
Station App. *Der* —3B **74** (4G **7**)
 (in two parts)
Station App. *Duf* —2K **39**
Station Av. *Ged* —5E **50**
Station Clo. *Chel* —1F **105**
Station Ct. *Ilk* —5C **44**
Station La. *Cod* —6D **12**
Station La. *Iron* —1H **13**
Station Rd. *Ambgt* —1K **9**
Station Rd. *Aws* —1G **45**
Station Rd. *Bees* —2F **81**
 (in two parts)
Station Rd. *Borr* —7D **76**
Station Rd. *Bread* —3D **56**
Station Rd. *Bulw* —7J **31**
Station Rd. *Bur J* —3K **51**
Station Rd. *Cas D* —6K **107**
Station Rd. *Chel* —1F **105**
Station Rd. *Den* —2H **25**
Station Rd. *Dray* —2K **95**
Station Rd. *Duf* —2K **39**
Station Rd. *H'ton* —4A **108**
Station Rd. *Huck* —5H **17**
Station Rd. *Ilk* —5D **44**
 (in three parts)
Station Rd. *Keg* —7H **109**
Station Rd. *Kimb* —7K **29**
Station Rd. *King S* —6A **110**
Station Rd. *Lan M* —3J **27**
Station Rd. *L Eat* —7C **40**
Station Rd. *Long E* —1K **97**
Station Rd. *Low* —4E **36**
Station Rd. *Mick* —6B **72**
Station Rd. *Nott* —7F **33**
Station Rd. *Plum* —3C **102**
Station Rd. *Sand* —3G **79**
Station Rd. *Spon* —5K **75**
Station Rd. *Stan* —6J **41**
Station Rd. *W Hal* —2D **58**
Station St. *Bing* —2B **70**
Station St. *Ilk* —4E **44**
Station St. *Long E* —2J **97**
Station St. *Nott* —4E **64** (6F **5**)
Station Ter. *Huck* —5H **17**
Station Ter. *Rad T* —4K **67**
Station Vs. *Bees* —3G **81**
Staunton Av. *Sun* —3J **91**
Staunton Clo. *Cas D* —6J **107**
Staunton Dri. *Nott* —2E **48**
Staveley Clo. *Shel L* —6E **92**
Staverton Dri. *Mick* —4B **72**
Staverton Rd. *Nott* —1D **62**
Steacfold Clo. *Nott* —7H **31**
Steacs Clo. *Cltn* —7B **50**
Steam Mill La. *Rip* —4C **12**
Steecman Av. *Nott* —2J **49**
Steeles Way. *Lamb* —6F **35**
Steeple Clo. *Oak* —5E **56**
Steinbeck Rd. *Cltn* —7A **50**
Stella Av. *Toll* —1B **102**
Stella Gro. *Toll* —1B **102**
Stenson Av. *Sun* —3J **91**
Stenson Ct. *Rip* —3B **12**
Stenson Rd. *Sten F & Der*
 —7F **91**
Stephensons Way. *Chad* —5G **75**
Steprey Ct. *Nott* —5F **47**
Stepping Clo. *Der* —3J **73**
Stepping La. *Der* —3H **73** (3A **6**)
Sterndale Ho. *Der* —4A **74** (5D **6**)
Sterndale Rd. *Long E* —3F **97**
Stevenage Clo. *Alv* —4F **93**
Steven Clo. *Bees* —4K **79**
Stevenholme Cres. *Nott* —7C **32**
Steven's La. *Breas* —1B **96**
Stevenson Av. *Breas* —1K **95**
Stevenson Gdns. *Rud* —3F **101**
Stevenson Pl. *L'ver* —1F **91**
Stevens Rd. *Sand* —3E **78**
Stewart Clo. *Spon* —2A **76**
Stewarton Clo. *Arn* —4K **33**
Stiles Rd. *Alv* —2H **93**
Stiles Rd. *Arn* —7A **34**
Stiles Wlk. *Duf* —2J **39**
Stinsford Clo. *Nott* —5E **32**
Stirland St. *Cod* —3D **12**
Stirling Clo. *Der* —7C **56**
Stirling Gdns. *Bees* —6C **80**
Stirling Gro. *Kimb* —6J **29**
Stirling Gro. *Nott* —1B **100**
Stockbrook Rd. *Der* —5H **73**

Stockbrook St. *Der* —4J **73** (6A **6**)
Stockdale Clo. *Arn* —3C **32**
Stockdove Clo. *Sin* —5H **91**
Stocker Av. *Alv* —2J **93**
Stockgill Clo. *W Bri* —2A **84**
Stockhill Cir. *Nott* —3J **47**
Stockhill La. *Nott* —3J **47**
Stocking La. *E Leak* —6K **111**
Stocks Rd. *Kimb* —6J **29**
Stockton St. *Nott* —6H **31**
Stockwell. *Nott* —7H **31**
Stockwell La. *C Bis* —4H **87**
Stoddard Dri. *Hean* —3H **27**
Stoke Clo. *Belp* —1D **24**
Stoke Ferry La. *Shelf* —5K **51**
Stoke La. *Bur J* —3K **51**
Stoke La. *Ged & Bur J* —5F **51**
Stolle Clo. *Arn* —7A **34**
Stoneacre. *Nott* —5D **32**
Stonebridge Rd. *Nott*
 —2G **65** (2J **5**)
Stonebroom Wlk. *Shel L* —6E **92**
Stonechat Clo. *Mick* —6E **72**
Stone Clo. *Spon* —2A **76**
Stonehaven Clo. *Arn* —4K **33**
Stonehill. *Cas D* —1H **115**
Stonehill Rd. *Der* —6K **73**
Stonehills. *Keg* —1G **117**
Stoneleigh Clo. *Bees* —3C **80**
Stoneleigh St. *Nott* —2C **64** (2B **4**)
Stone Meadows. *Long E* —4J **97**
Stonepit Clo. *Nott* —5H **49**
Stonesby Clo. *Oak* —5F **57**
Stonesby Va. *W Bri* —5D **82**
Stonesdale Ct. *Alv* —3J **93**
Stoney Bank. *Low* —3D **36**
Stoneycroft Rd. *Nott* —1A **48**
Stoney Cross. *Spon* —5A **76**
Stoney Cross Ind. Pk. *Spon*
 —5K **75**
Stoney Flatts Cres. *Chad* —7G **57**
Stoney Ga. Rd. *Spon* —5K **75**
Stoney Houghton Gdns. *Nott*
 —5F **31**
Stoneyhurst Ct. *Shel L* —6E **92**
Stoney La. *Belp* —1A **24**
Stoney La. *Brins* —7A **14**
 (in two parts)
Stoney La. *Holb* —7C **24**
Stoney La. *Spon* —3A **76**
Stoney La. *Trow* —1F **61**
Stoney La. *Wain* —5C **12**
Stoney St. *Bees* —1F **81**
Stoney St. *Nott* —3F **65** (4G **5**)
**Stony Clouds Local Nature Reserve. —7F 61**
Stoodley Pike Gdns. *Alst* —5G **55**
Stoppard Clo. *Ilk* —4B **44**
Stores Rd. *Der* —7B **56** (1G **7**)
Storey Av. *Ged* —4C **50**
**Storm Extreme Sports Cen.**
 —7C **74**
Stornoway Clo. *Sin* —6H **91**
Stornoway Ct. *Bees* —3G **81**
Storth Av. *Huck* —6G **17**
Story Gdns. *Huck* —7J **17**
Stotfield Rd. *Nott* —2B **62**
Stourdale Clo. *Long E* —3E **96**
Stourport Dri. *Chel* —6G **93**
Stowe Av. *W Bri* —3F **83**
Stowmarket Dri. *Der* —6D **56**
Stragglethorpe La. *Rad T* —6G **67**
Strand. *Der* —3A **74** (3D **6**)
Strand Arc. *Der* —3A **74** (3D **6**)
Strand, The. *Att* —7D **80**
Stratford Clo. *Colw* —2C **66**
Stratford Rd. *Der* —5D **56**
Stratford Rd. *W Bri* —1H **83**
Stratford St. *Ilk* —2D **44**
Strathaven Ct. *Spon* —3A **76**
Strathglen Clo. *Kimb* —6J **29**
Strathmore Av. *Alv* —3F **93**
Strathmore Clo. *Huck* —7E **16**
Strathmore Rd. *Arn* —4K **33**
**Straws Bridge Open Space.**
 —7A **44**
Straw's La. *E Bri* —3K **53**
Streatham Rd. *Der* —2E **72**
Street La. *Rip* —4H **11**
Strelley Av. *Rip* —4J **11**
Strelley La. *Nott* —7B **46**
Strelley Rd. *Nott* —6C **46**
Strelley St. *Nott* —6H **31**
Stretton Clo. *Mick* —7B **72**
Striding Edge Clo. *Long E*
 —6F **79**
Stripes Vw. *C'tn* —6D **20**
Stroma Clo. *Sin* —5K **91**
Strome Clo. *Nott* —5E **64**

Strome Ct. *Nott* —5E **64**
Strutt St. *Belp* —2K **23**
Strutt St. *Der* —6A **74**
Stuart Clo. *Arn* —5K **33**
Stuart St. *Der* —2A **74** (2E **6**)
Studbrook Clo. *Cas D* —7H **107**
Studland Way. *W Bri* —3E **82**
Sturgeon Av. *Nott* —4B **82**
Sturges La. *Thul* —5B **94**
Sturton St. *Nott* —6C **48**
Styring St. *Bees* —2F **81**
Sudbury Av. *Ilk* —7E **44**
Sudbury Av. *Sand* —1E **78**
Sudbury Clo. *Der* —3J **73** (4A **6**)
Sudbury Clo. *Long E* —5D **96**
Sudbury M. *Eastw* —4C **28**
Sudbury St. *Der* —3J **73** (4A **6**)
Suez St. *Nott* —5B **48**
Suffolk Av. *Bees* —4J **81**
Suffolk Av. *Der* —1E **74**
Suffolk Av. *Huck* —7C **16**
Sulleys Fld. *Quar* —7H **39**
Sullivan Clo. *Nott* —7H **49**
Sumburgh Rd. *Nott* —7C **82**
Summerbrook Ct. *Der*
    —4J **73** (6B **6**)
Summerfields Way. *Ilk* —2A **44**
Summerfields Way S. *Ilk* —4B **44**
Summer Leys Rd. *Nott*
    —4F **65** (7G **5**)
Summers Ct. *Spon* —4K **75**
Summer Way. *Rad T* —3J **67**
Summer Wood Ct. *Der* —2H **91**
Summerwood La. *Nott* —1K **99**
Sunart Clo. *Sin* —7K **91**
Sunbeam St. *What* —3K **71**
Sunbourne Ct. *Nott* —1B **64**
Sunbury Gdns. *Arn* —4J **33**
Sunderland Gro. *Nott* —4D **46**
Sundew Clo. *Spon* —4B **76**
Sundown Av. *L'ver* —3H **91**
Sundridge Pk. Clo. *W Bri*
    —3E **82**
Sunflower Clo. *Alv* —7G **75**
Sunlea Cres. *S'fd* —3K **79**
Sunnindale Dri. *Toll* —7B **84**
Sunningdale Av. *Hean* —5H **27**
Sunningdale Av. *Spon* —3K **75**
Sunningdale Dri. *Ilk* —2K **59**
Sunningdale Dri. *Wdbgh* —7G **21**
Sunningdale Rd. *Nott* —7A **32**
Sunninghill Clo. *W Hal* —6F **43**
Sunninghill Dri. *Nott* —5A **82**
Sunninghill Ri. *Arn* —4J **33**
Sunny Bank Gdns. *Belp* —3K **23**
Sunnydale Rd. *Nott* —1K **65**
Sunny Gro. *Chad* —3G **75**
Sunny Hill. *Milf* —6K **23**
Sunnyhill Av. *Der* —3J **91**
Sunnyside Rd. *Bees* —2C **80**
Sunridge Ct. *Nott* —6E **48**
Sunrise Av. *B Vil* —7D **18**
Sunrise Av. *Nott* —1B **48**
Sun St. *Der* —4K **73** (6B **6**)
Surbiton Clo. *Der* —2E **72**
Surbiton Ct. *Nott* —5G **49**
Surbiton Ct. *W Hal* —6F **43**
Surbiton Sq. *Nott* —3H **47**
Surfleet Clo. *Nott* —4C **62**
Surgey's La. *Arn* —4H **33**
Surrey Ct. *Nott* —5G **49**
Surrey St. *Der* —2H **73**
Susan Clo. *Huck* —3H **17**
Susan Dri. *Nott* —2K **47**
Sussex Cir. *Der* —7E **56**
Sussex St. *Nott* —3E **64** (5F **5**)
Sussex Way. *Sand* —3F **79**
Sutherland Dri. *W Bri* —4J **83**
Sutherland Rd. *Der* —7K **73**
Sutherland Rd. *Nott* —7K **49**
Suthers Rd. *Keg* —1F **117**
Sutton Av. *Chel* —6F **93**
Sutton Clo. *Der* —2H **73**
Sutton Ct. *Eastw* —3D **28**
Sutton Dri. *Shel L* —5E **92**
Sutton Gdns. *Rud* —3E **100**
Sutton Ho. *Alv* —4J **93**
Sutton La. *Etw* —4D **88**
Sutton Passeys Cres. *Nott*
    —3H **63**
Sutton Rd. *Arn* —3H **33**
Sutton Rd. *Keg* —2G **117**
Swab's La. *C Bis* —7F **87**
Swains Av. *Nott* —1J **65**
Swaledale Clo. *Nott* —5K **47**
Swaledale Ct. *Alv* —3J **93**
Swallow Clo. *Mick* —6E **72**
Swallow Clo. *Nott* —2K **47**
Swallowdale Rd. *Sin* —5H **91**

Swallow Dri. *Bing* —4B **70**
Swallow Gdns. *Cltn* —5K **49**
Swan Mdw. *Colw* —3C **66**
Swanmore Rd. *L'ver* —1E **90**
Swansdowne Dri. *Nott* —6B **82**
Swanwick Gdns. *Chad* —6F **57**
Swarkestone Dri. *L'ver* —4G **91**
**Swarkestone Old Hall. —4E 104
(remains of)**
Swarkestone Rd. *Bar T* —4A **104**
    (in two parts)
Swarkestone Rd. *Chel* —1F **105**
Swarkestone Rd. *Swar* —4D **104**
Swayfield Clo. *Mick* —6A **72**
Sweeney Ct. *Nott* —5C **32**
Sweetbriar Clo. *Alv* —4G **93**
Sweet Leys Rd. *Nott* —6E **64**
Swenson Av. *Nott* —4A **64**
Swift Clo. *Mick* —5E **72**
Swift Ct. *Eastw* —3D **28**
Swigert Clo. *Nott* —1F **47**
Swildon Wlk. *Nott* —5B **32**
Swinburne St. *Der* —5A **74** (7D **6**)
Swinburne St. *Nott* —1H **65**
Swinburne Way. *Day* —6E **32**
Swinderby Dri. *Oak* —6H **57**
Swindon Clo. *Gilt* —6G **29**
Swiney Way. *Bees* —6K **79**
Swingate. *Kimb* —1A **46**
Swinney Bank. *Belp* —7A **10**
Swinney La. *Belp* —7A **10**
Swinscoe Gdns. *Nott* —5B **32**
Swinscoe Ho. *Der* —4K **73** (5D **6**)
Swinstead Clo. *Nott* —1F **63**
Swithland Dri. *W Bri* —4G **83**
Sycamore Av. *Alst* —4H **55**
Sycamore Av. *Find* —7B **90**
Sycamore Av. *Rip* —4K **11**
Sycamore Clo. *Bing* —3C **70**
Sycamore Clo. *Etw* —5E **88**
Sycamore Clo. *Huck* —7E **16**
Sycamore Clo. *M'ley* —3H **43**
Sycamore Clo. *Rad T* —5K **67**
Sycamore Ct. *Bees* —1G **81**
Sycamore Ct. *Spon* —3A **76**
Sycamore Cres. *Kimb* —2A **46**
Sycamore Cres. *Sand* —1E **78**
Sycamore Dri. *Ilk* —7F **45**
Sycamore Gro. *Nott* —5H **49**
Sycamore Pl. *Nott* —6E **48**
Sycamore Ri. *Nott* —2H **47**
Sycamore Rd. *Aws* —1F **45**
Sycamore Rd. *Cas D* —5K **107**
Sycamore Rd. *Long E* —4G **97**
Sycamores, The. *Eastw* —5C **28**
Sydenham Ct. *Nott* —5A **64**
Sydenham Rd. *Der* —1E **72**
Syderstone Wlk. *Arn* —1H **49**
Sydney Clo. *Mick* —5D **72**
Sydney Gro. *Rad T* —4J **67**
Sydney Rd. *Dray* —2J **95**
Sydney Rd. *Nott* —2H **63**
Syke Rd. *Nott* —5B **32**
Synge Clo. *Nott* —1J **99**
Syon Pk. Clo. *W Bri* —3E **82**

**T**addington Clo. *Chad* —7E **56**
Taddington Rd. *Chad* —6E **56**
Taft Av. *Sand* —2F **79**
Talbot Ct. *Rad T* —4J **67**
Talbot Dri. *S'fd* —5H **61**
Talbot St. *Der* —4K **73** (4B **6**)
Talbot St. *Nott* —2D **64** (3C **4**)
**Tales of Robin Hood.—5D 4**
Talgarth Clo. *Oak* —5J **57**
Tamar Av. *Alst* —3H **55**
Tamarix Clo. *Ged* —4E **50**
Tambling Clo. *Arn* —7K **33**
Tame Clo. *Nott* —4A **82**
Tamworth Gro. *Nott* —6B **82**
Tamworth Ri. *Duf* —2J **39**
Tamworth Rd. *Cas D & Shard*
    (in two parts) —3A **108**
Tamworth Rd. *Long E* —5F **97**
    (in two parts)
Tamworth Rd. *Shard* —2B **108**
Tamworth St. *Duf* —2J **39**
Tamworth Ter. *Duf* —2J **39**
Tangmere Cres. *Nott* —5E **46**
Tanners Wlk. *Nott* —3E **64** (5F **5**)
Tansley Av. *Stan C* —5C **42**
Tansley Ri. *Chad* —6F **57**
Tansy Way. *Bing* —4J **69**
Tants Mdw. *Lwr K* —7E **24**
Tantum Av. *Los* —1E **26**
Tanwood Rd. *Bees* —7B **80**
Tanyard Clo. *Cas D* —6K **107**
Taplow Clo. *Mick* —6A **72**

Tarbert Clo. *Nott* —5D **64**
Target St. *Nott* —2A **64**
Tarina Clo. *Chel* —1G **105**
Tasman Clo. *Mick* —5D **72**
Tatham's La. *Ilk* —4C **44**
    (in two parts)
Tattershall Dri. *Bees* —1H **81**
Tattershall Dri. *Nott*
    —3C **64** (4A **4**)
Tattle Hill. *Dal A* —5G **59**
Taunton Clo. *Alv* —2J **93**
Taunton Rd. *W Bri* —2H **83**
Taupo Dri. *Huck* —7C **16**
Tavern Av. *Nott* —6A **48**
Taverners Cres. *L'ver* —1G **91**
Tavistock Av. *Nott* —5E **48**
Tavistock Av. *Rip* —1K **11**
Tavistock Clo. *Huck* —7D **16**
Tavistock Clo. *Sten F* —6H **91**
Tavistock Ct. *Nott* —5E **48**
Tavistock Dri. *Nott* —5E **48**
Tavistock Rd. *W Bri* —2H **83**
Tawny Way. *L'ver* —2E **90**
Tay Clo. *Sten F* —7H **91**
Taylor Clo. *Nott* —3J **65**
Taylor Cres. *S'fd* —7K **61**
Taylor La. *Los* —1F **27**
Taylor Pk. *Und* —1F **15**
Taylors Cft. *Wdbgh* —1F **35**
Taylor St. *Der* —6D **74**
Taylor St. *Ilk* —5D **44**
Tayside Clo. *Sten F* —6H **91**
Tay Wlk. *Alst* —4J **55**
TDG Pinnacle. *W Hal* —1G **59**
Teak Clo. *Nott* —7F **49**
Tealby Clo. *Nott* —6F **31**
Teal Clo. *Cltn* —1F **67**
Teal Wharf. *Nott* —5C **64**
Teasels, The. *Bing* —4K **69**
Technology Dri. *Bees* —3G **81**
Tedworth Av. *Sten F* —7H **91**
Teesbrook Dri. *Nott* —3B **62**
Teesdale Ct. *Bees* —4A **80**
Teesdale Rd. *Long E* —3E **96**
Teesdale Rd. *Nott* —4C **48**
Telford Clo. *Mick* —7C **72**
Telford Dri. *Newt* —2F **29**
Templar Clo. *Sten F* —6G **91**
Templar Lodge. *Bees* —2H **81**
Templar Rd. *Bees* —2H **81**
Templebell Clo. *L'ver* —3E **90**
Temple Cres. *Nut* —2D **46**
Temple Dri. *Nut* —2E **46**
Templeman Clo. *Rud* —1D **100**
Templeoak Dri. *Nott* —4C **62**
Temple St. *Der* —5A **74**
Tenant St. *Der* —3A **74** (3E **6**)
Tenbury Cres. *Nott* —5H **47**
Tenby Dri. *Oak* —4J **57**
Tene Clo. *Arn* —3H **33**
Tennessee Rd. *Chad* —1G **75**
Tennis Ct. Ind. Est. *Nott* —4J **65**
Tennis Dri. *Nott* —3C **64** (4B **4**)
Tennis M. *Nott* —3C **64** (4B **4**)
Tennis Vw. *Nott* —3C **64** (4B **4**)
Tennyson Av. *Ged* —5D **50**
Tennyson Ct. *Huck* —6D **16**
Tennyson Ct. *Nott* —3D **48**
Tennyson Dri. *Bees* —6D **80**
Tennyson Rd. *Wd'p* —2G **49**
Tennyson St. *Der* —2D **92**
Tennyson St. *Ilk* —3C **44**
Tennyson St. *Nott* —1C **64** (1A **4**)
    (in two parts)
Tenter Clo. *Long E* —4H **97**
Tenter Clo. *Nott* —5B **32**
Tenter La. *Heag* —3D **10**
Terrace St. *Nott* —7B **48**
Terrian Cres. *W Bri* —1H **83**
Terry Pl. *Alv* —3F **93**
Terton Rd. *Nott* —5B **32**
Tetney Wlk. *Nott* —7G **47**
Tettenbury Rd. *Nott* —3B **48**
Teversal Av. *Nott* —3B **64**
Tevery Clo. *S'fd* —7J **61**
Teviot Pl. *Oak* —5G **57**
Teviot Rd. *Nott* —1B **48**
Tewkesbury Clo. *W Bri* —2J **83**
Tewkesbury Cres. *Der* —7D **56**
Tewkesbury Dri. *Kimb* —6J **29**
Tewkesbury Dri. *Nott* —2A **48**
Tewkesbury Rd. *Long E* —5J **97**
Thackeray's La. *Wd'p* —1F **49**
Thackeray St. *Nott* —2B **64** (2A **4**)
Thackeray St. *Sin* —4A **92**
Thames Clo. *Der* —3D **72**
Thames St. *Nott* —6H **31**
Thane Rd. *Nott* —2K **81**
Thanet Dri. *Alv* —3G **93**

Thatch Clo. *Der* —5K **55**
Thaxted Clo. *Nott* —1D **62**
**Theatre Royal. —3E 4**
Theatre Sq. *Nott* —2E **64** (3E **4**)
Theatre Wlk. *Der* —3B **74** (4F **7**)
Thelda Rd. *Keyw* —6C **102**
Thetford Clo. *Arn* —7J **33**
Third Av. *Cltn* —6K **49**
    (in two parts)
Third Av. *Ged* —5D **50**
Third Av. *Ilk* —7D **44**
Third Av. *Lent* —2J **81**
Third Av. *Nott* —6D **48**
Thirlbeck. *Cotg* —6A **86**
Thirlmere. *W Bri* —3A **84**
Thirlmere Av. *Alst* —4J **55**
Thirlmere Clo. *Long E* —6F **79**
Thirlmere Clo. *Nott* —7H **49**
Thirlmere Rd. *Long E* —6F **79**
Thirsk Pl. *Der* —2D **92**
Thirston Clo. *Nott* —6F **31**
Thistle Bank. *E Leak* —7K **111**
Thistle Clo. *Newt* —5F **29**
Thistledown Clo. *Dar A* —5A **56**
Thistledown Rd. *Nott* —2A **100**
Thistle Grn. Clo. *Hean* —4K **27**
Thistle Rd. *Ilk* —3E **60**
Thomas Av. *Rad T* —3C **68**
Thomas Clo. *Nott* —1F **65** (1H **5**)
Thomas Cook Clo. *Melb* —4G **113**
Thomas Rd. *Keg* —2G **117**
Thompson Clo. *Bees* —5C **80**
Thompson Gdns. *Nott* —4C **32**
Thompson St. *Lan M* —2K **27**
Thomson Dri. *Cod* —4D **12**
Thoresby Av. *Ged* —4B **50**
Thoresby Av. *Nott* —4H **65**
Thoresby Clo. *Oak* —6H **57**
Thoresby Clo. *Rad T* —3A **68**
Thoresby Clo. *Rip* —3A **12**
Thoresby Ct. *Nott* —6F **49**
Thoresby Cres. *Dray* —2H **95**
Thoresby Dale. *Huck* —5H **17**
Thoresby Rd. *Bees* —6C **62**
Thoresby Rd. *Bing* —3J **69**
Thoresby Rd. *Long E* —3F **97**
Thoresby St. *Nott* —3G **65** (5J **5**)
Thor Gdns. *Nott* —4B **32**
Thorncliffe Rd. *Nott* —6E **48**
Thorncliffe Rd. *Nott* —6E **48**
Thorn Clo. *Alst* —3H **55**
Thorndale Rd. *C'tn* —5D **20**
Thorndale Rd. *Nott* —4J **47**
Thorndike Av. *Alv* —2F **93**
Thorndon Clo. *Mick* —1B **90**
Thorn Dri. *Newt* —5F **29**
Thorndyke Clo. *Bees* —4H **81**
Thorner Clo. *Nott* —1A **48**
Thorness Clo. *Alv* —4J **93**
Thorney Hill. *Nott* —7H **49**
Thorneywood Mt. *Nott* —7H **49**
Thorneywood Ri. *Nott* —7H **49**
Thorneywood Rd. *Long E* —1K **97**
Thornfield Ind. Est. *Nott* —2H **65**
Thorn Gro. *Huck* —1H **31**
Thornhill Clo. *Bees* —5B **62**
Thornhill Rd. *Der* —4G **73**
Thornhill Rd. *L'ver* —7G **73**
Thornley St. *Nott* —7A **48**
Thorn St. *Der* —6K **73**
Thornthwaite Clo. *W Bri* —2A **84**
Thornton Av. *Red* —4F **33**
Thornton Clo. *Nott* —3E **62**
Thorntons Clo. *Cotg* —5A **86**
Thornton Ter. *Nott* —7B **48**
Thorntree Clo. *Breas* —7D **78**
Thorn Tree Gdns. *Eastw* —1D **28**
Thorntree La. *Der* —3A **74** (4E **6**)
Thorold Clo. *Nott* —6A **82**
Thoroton Av. *W Bri* —6H **65**
Thoroton St. *Nott* —2C **64** (2A **4**)
Thorpe Clo. *Nott* —5B **32**
Thorpe Clo. *S'fd* —1G **79**
Thorpe Cres. *Nott* —4K **49**
Thorpe Dri. *Mick* —5C **72**
Thorpe Hill Dri. *Hean* —6G **27**
Thorpelands Dri. *Alst* —6J **55**
Thorpe Lea. *Gun* —1F **53**
Thorpe Leys. *Long E* —4D **97**
Thorpe Rd. *Eastw* —1D **28**
Thorpe's Rd. *Hean* —4F **27**
Thorpes Rd. Ind. Est. *Hean*
    —5F **27**
Thorpe St. *Ilk* —3C **44**
Thorpe Way. *Belp* —7B **10**
Thrapston Av. *Arn* —3H **33**
Thraves Yd. *Rad T* —4J **67**
Three Gates. *Belp* —3K **23**

Three Tuns Rd. *Eastw* —3E **28**
Threlkeld Clo. *W Bri* —2A **84**
Thrumpton Av. *Long E* —2K **97**
Thrumpton Dri. *Nott* —6D **64**
**Thrumpton Pk. —7A 98**
Thrushton Clo. *Find* —7A **90**
Thruxton Clo. *Alv* —3J **93**
Thurcroft Clo. *Der* —2G **73**
Thurgarton Av. *Nott* —3H **65**
Thurgarton La. *Hov* —1K **37**
Thurgarton St. *Nott* —3H **65**
Thurland St. *Nott* —3E **64** (3F **5**)
Thurlby Clo. *C Bis* —4G **87**
Thurlby La. *Keyw* —7F **103**
Thurlestone Dri. *Nott* —7A **34**
Thurloe Ct. *W Bri* —5E **82**
Thurlow Ct. *Oak* —6G **57**
Thurman Dri. *Cotg* —5K **85**
Thurman St. *Ilk* —1E **60**
Thurman St. *Nott* —1B **64**
Thurmans Yd. *Nott* —1B **64**
Thurrows Way. *Chel* —7H **93**
Thursby Rd. *Nott* —5A **82**
Thurstone Furlong. *Chel* —7E **92**
Thyme Clo. *L'ver* —4H **91**
Thymus Wlk. *Nott* —7J **81**
Thyra Ct. *Nott* —5G **49**
Thyra Gro. *Bees* —2G **81**
Thyra Gro. *Nott* —5F **49**
Tiber Clo. *Alv* —4K **93**
Tickham Av. *Sten F* —7H **91**
Ticknall La. *Den* —3H **25**
Ticknall Wlk. *Son* —3J **91**
Tideswell Rd. *Chad* —6F **57**
Tidworth Clo. *Nott* —1G **63**
Tilberthwaite Clo. *Gam* —2A **84**
Tilbury Pl. *Alv* —4G **93**
Tilbury Ri. *Nott* —3G **47**
Tilford Gdns. *S'fd* —2J **79**
Tiller Clo. *L'ver* —3F **91**
Tilstock Ct. *Watn* —5A **30**
Tilton Gro. *Ilk* —2A **60**
Timbersbrook Clo. *Oak* —6G **57**
Tim La. *Bur J* —2K **51**
Timsbury Ct. *Oak* —5E **56**
Tinderbox La. *Burna* —4H **89**
Tinker Cft. *Ilk* —7C **44**
Tinsley Rd. *Eastw* —4B **28**
Tintagel Clo. *Der* —6B **74**
Tintagel Grn. *Nott* —4A **82**
Tintern Dri. *Nott* —4K **47**
Tipnall Rd. *Cas D* —7J **107**
Tippett Ct. *Nott* —1H **65**
Tip Tree Clo. *Kimb* —6K **29**
Tiree Clo. *Sin* —5K **91**
Tiree Clo. *Trow* —4H **61**
Tishbite St. *Nott* —6H **31**
Tissington Clo. *Nott* —6C **48**
Tissington Dri. *Oak* —4H **57**
Tissington Rd. *Nott* —6C **48**
Titchfield Ct. *Huck* —6G **17**
Titchfield St. *Huck* —5H **17**
Titchfield Ter. *Huck* —5H **17**
Tithby Dri. *Nott* —2F **49**
Tithby Rd. *Bing* —4A **70**
Tithby Rd. *C But* —2H **87**
Tithe Gdns. *Nott* —4C **32**
Tithe La. *C'tn* —5D **20**
Tiverton Clo. *Huck* —7D **16**
Tiverton Clo. *Mick* —4B **72**
Tiverton Clo. *Nott* —4H **47**
Tivoli Gdns. *Der* —1J **73**
Toad La. *Der* —4D **40**
Toadmoor La. *Ambgt* —1K **9**
Tobermory Way. *Sin* —6H **91**
Tobias Clo. *Nott* —5B **32**
Todd Clo. *Nott* —1J **99**
Todd Ct. *Nott* —1J **99**
Toft Clo. *Cotg* —6J **85**
Toft Rd. *Bees* —5A **80**
Token Ho. Yd. *Nott* —4F **5**
Tollerton Grn. *Nott* —1K **47**
Tollerton La. *Toll* —1B **102**
Tollerton Rd. *Rad T* —2B **84**
Tollhouse Hill. *Nott*
    —2D **64** (3D **4**)
Tomlinson Av. *Got* —1G **111**
Tomlinson Ct. *Der* —2F **93**
Tomlinson Ind. Est. *Der* —5B **56**
Tonbridge Dri. *Alv* —4G **93**
Tonbridge Mt. *Nott* —5D **62**
Tonge La. *Bree H* —7B **114**
Ton La. *Low* —3D **36**
Tonnelier Rd. *Nott* —6A **64**
Top Farm Ct. *Klbrn* —5F **25**
Top La. *Shot* —5A **8**
Topley Gdns. *Chad* —5F **57**
Top Mnr. Clo. *Ock* —3E **76**
Top Rd. *Rud* —3E **100**

Top Row. *Bur J* —7H **51**
Top Valley Dri. *Nott* —5A **32**
Top Valley Way. *Nott* —6A **32**
Torbay Cres. *Nott* —7D **32**
Torkard Dri. *Nott* —5B **32**
Torridon Clo. *Sin* —5J **91**
Torrington Ct. *Nott* —4F **49**
Torvill Dri. *Nott* —2D **62**
Toston Dri. *Nott* —3J **63**
Totland Dri. *Nott* —4K **47**
Totland Rd. *Bees* —5C **62**
Totley Clo. *Nott* —3J **31**
Totnes Clo. *Huck* —6D **16**
Totnes Rd. *Nott* —6K **65**
Toton La. *S'fd* —1H **79**
Tottle Gdns. *Nott* —1K **63**
Tottle Rd. *Nott* —7C **64**
Tourist Info. Cen. —4F **5**
(Nottingham)
Tourist Info. Cen. —2K **11**
(Ripley)
Tower Cres. *Kimb* —2A **46**
Tower St. *Der* —2D **92**
Towe's Mt. *Cltn* —7C **50**
Towle Clo. *Borr* —7D **76**
Towles Pastures. *Cas D* —7J **107**
Towle St. *Long E* —5E **96**
Towlson Ct. *Bees* —5D **80**
Towlsons Cft. *Nott* —3K **47**
Town End Rd. *Dray* —6K **95**
Townsend Ct. *Nott* —4C **32**
Townsend Gro. *Chel* —7G **93**
Townside Clo. *Long E* —5F **97**
Town St. *Bees* —7B **62**
Town St. *Duf* —3J **39**
Town St. *Holb* —7C **24**
Town St. *Sand* —3F **79**
Town, The. *L Eat* —7C **40**
Town Vw. *Kimb* —6K **29**
Towson Av. *Lan M* —3A **28**
Towyn Ct. *Nott* —6C **32**
Tracy Clo. *Bees* —6E **62**
Trafalgar Clo. *Nott* —1B **64**
Trafalgar Rd. *Bees* —4G **81**
Trafalgar Rd. *Long E* —3H **97**
Trafalgar Sq. *Long E* —2H **97**
Trafalgar Ter. *Long E* —2J **97**
Traffic St. *Der* —4B **74** (6F **7**)
Traffic St. *Nott* —4E **64** (7E **4**)
Trafford Gdns. *Nott* —7K **47**
Trafford Way. *L'ver* —1G **91**
Tranby Gdns. *Nott* —3F **63**
Travers Rd. *Sand* —2E **78**
Tredegar Dri. *Oak* —5H **57**
Treegarth Sq. *Nott* —4D **32**
Tree Vw. Clo. *Arn* —4E **32**
Trefoil Clo. *Bing* —4K **69**
Tregaron Clo. *Oak* —5J **57**
Tregony Way. *Sten F* —6H **91**
Trelawn Clo. *Nott* —4F **49**
Tremadoc Ct. *Nott* —6D **48**
Tremayne Rd. *Nott* —1C **62**
Trenchard Clo. *Nwtn* —7H **53**
Trent Av. *Rud* —1E **100**
Trent Boulevd. *W Bri* —6H **65**
Trent Bri. *Nott* —6G **65**
Trent Bri. Bldgs. *W Bri* —6G **65**
Trent Bri. Ct. *L'ver* —1G **91**
Trent Clo. *Sten F* —7H **91**
Trent Cotts. *Long E* —5G **97**
Trent Ct. *W Bri* —6J **65**
Trent Cres. *Bees* —5E **80**
Trentdale Rd. *Cltn* —1B **66**
Trent Dri. *Huck* —2D **30**
Trent Dri. *L'ver* —3H **91**
Trent Gdns. *Bur J* —2A **52**
Trentham Dri. *Nott* —7J **47**
Trentham Gdns. *Bur J* —3H **51**
Trentham Gdns. *Nott* —7J **47**
Trent Ho. *Long E* —5E **96**
Trent La. *Bur J* —2K **51**
Trent La. *Cas D* —5J **107**
Trent La. *E Bri* —2G **53**
Trent La. *Long E* —6J **97**
Trent La. *Melb* —1J **113**
Trent La. *Nott* —4H **65**
Trent La. *Wstn T* —6A **106**
Trent La. Ind. Est. *Cas D* —5K **107**
Trent Lock Golf Course. —5G **97**
Trenton Clo. *Bees* —6A **62**
Trenton Dri. *Chad* —2H **75**
Trenton Dri. *Long E* —1A **98**
Trenton Grn. *Chad* —2H **75**
Trent Ri. *Spon* —4B **76**
Trent Rd. *Bees* —4G **81**
Trent Rd. *Ilk* —3B **60**
Trent Rd. *Nott* —3H **65**

Trentside. *Bees* —5G **81**
Trentside. *Gun* —2G **53**
Trentside. *Swar* —4D **104**
Trentside. *W Bri* —7G **65**
Trentside N. *W Bri* —6G **65**
Trent S. Ind. Pk. *Nott* —4J **65**
Trent St. *Alv* —2G **93**
Trent St. *Long E* —1J **97**
Trent St. *Nott* —4F **65** (6G **5**)
Trent Va. Rd. *Bees* —4G **81**
Trent Valley Vw. *Nott* —5J **49**
Trent Valley Way. *Nwtn* —4G **53**
Trentview Ct. *Nott* —5H **65** (7K **5**)
Trent Vw. Gdns. *Rad T* —2A **68**
Tresillian Clo. *Dar A* —5J **55**
Tressall Clo. *Ilk* —6E **44**
Trevelyan Rd. *W Bri* —6H **65**
Treveris Clo. *Spon* —4B **76**
Trevino Gdns. *Nott* —5C **32**
Trevone Av. *S'fd* —2J **79**
Trevone Ct. *Alv* —4J **93**
Trevor Rd. *Bees* —3F **81**
Trevor Rd. *W Bri* —2J **83**
Trevose Gdns. *Nott* —3F **49**
Treyford Clo. *Nott* —4C **82**
Triangle, The. *Ilk* —1E **60**
(in two parts)
Tricornia Dri. *Nott* —2H **47**
Trigg Ct. *Los* —1E **26**
Tring Va. *Nott* —2C **48**
Trinity Av. *Nott* —4A **64**
Trinity Clo. *Ilk* —3C **44**
Trinity Cres. *Lamb* —6G **35**
Trinity Row. *Nott* —2E **64** (3E **4**)
Trinity Sq. *Nott* —2E **64** (3F **5**)
Trinity St. *Der* —4B **74** (6G **7**)
Trinity Wlk. *Nott* —2E **64** (3F **5**)
Trinstead Way. *Nott* —6E **32**
Triumph Rd. *Nott* —2K **63**
Trivett Sq. *Nott* —3F **65** (5H **5**)
Troon Clo. *Kimb* —6J **29**
Troon Clo. *L'ver* —1E **90**
Trough La. *Watn* —5K **29**
Trough Rd. *Watn* —5K **29**
Troutbeck. *Cotg* —5A **86**
Troutbeck Cres. *Bees* —7C **62**
Troutbeck Gro. *L'ver* —2E **90**
Trowbridge Clo. *Oak* —5E **56**
Trowell Av. *Ilk* —2E **60**
Trowell Av. *Nott* —2B **62**
Trowell Gdns. *Nott* —2C **62**
Trowell Gro. *Long E* —6F **79**
Trowell Gro. *Trow* —4H **61**
Trowell Pk. Dri. *Trow* —5H **61**
Trowell Rd. *Nott* —3B **62**
Trowell Rd. *S'fd* —5J **61**
Trowels La. *Der* —4G **73**
Trueman Gdns. *Arn* —7K **33**
Trueman St. *Ilk* —2D **44**
Truman Clo. *Nott* —1F **65** (1G **5**)
Truman Dri. *Huck* —6G **17**
Trumans Rd. *Nott* —6F **65**
Truman St. *Kimb* —6H **29**
Truro Cres. *Chad* —7E **56**
Truro Cres. *Nott* —7A **48**
Trusley Gdns. *L'ver* —4H **91**
Tudor Clo. *Colw* —2C **66**
Tudor Clo. *Long E* —7H **79**
Tudor Ct. *Huck* —7C **16**
Tudor Ct. *S'fd* —3H **79**
Tudor Falls. *Hean* —2G **27**
Tudor Fld. Clo. *Chel* —1G **105**
Tudor Gro. *Nott* —7D **48**
Tudor Rd. *Chad* —2G **75**
Tudor Rd. *W Bri* —1H **83**
Tudor Sq. *W Bri* —1H **83**
Tudwal Clo. *Nott* —6C **32**
Tudwal Wlk. *Nott* —6C **32**
Tufnell Gdns. *Der* —1F **73**
Tulip Av. *Nott* —7F **49**
Tulip Rd. *Aws* —1F **45**
Tulla Clo. *Sten F* —7J **91**
Tunnel Rd. *Nott* —3C **64** (5A **4**)
Tunstall Cres. *Nott* —5G **47**
Tunstall Dri. *Nott* —2B **48**
Tunstall Rd. *Wd'p* —2H **49**
Tuphall Clo. *Chel* —7A **88**
Turnbarrel. *Melb* —4H **113**
(off Castle La.)
Turnberry Clo. *Bees* —2C **80**
Turnberry Clo. *Ilk* —4A **44**
Turnberry Ct. *Edw* —5A **84**
Turnberry Rd. *Nott* —7K **31**
Turner Av. *Lan M* —2J **27**
Turner Clo. *S'fd* —2J **79**
Turner Dri. *Gilt* —6F **29**
Turner Rd. *Long E* —5G **97**

Turner's Almshouses. *Der* —2H **73**
Turner St. *Altn* —3E **92**
Turner St. *Huck* —5G **17**
Turneys Ct. *Nott* —5G **65**
Turney St. *Nott* —6F **65**
Turnpike La. *Bees* —7G **63**
Turnstone Wharf. *Nott* —5B **64**
Turpin Av. *Ged* —3B **50**
Turrell Ct. *Bramc* —6D **62**
Turton Clo. *Lan M* —2J **27**
Tuxford Clo. *Oak* —6H **57**
Tuxford Wlk. *Nott* —1H **65**
Tweedsmuir Clo. *Oak* —5F **57**
Twells Clo. *Nott* —7H **49**
Twickenham Dri. *Der* —2E **72**
Twin Oaks Clo. *L'ver* —2D **90**
Twitchell, The. *Bees* —4E **80**
Twycross Rd. *Nott* —5K **47**
Twyford Clo. *Hean* —5E **26**
Twyford Clo. *W Hal* —6F **43**
Twyford Gdns. *Nott* —4A **82**
Twyford Rd. *Bar T* —4A **104**
Twyford Rd. *Long E* —5D **96**
Twyford St. *Der* —5A **74** (7E **6**)
Tyburn Clo. *Arn* —4C **32**
Tynedale Chase. *Sten F* —7G **91**
Tynedale Clo. *Long E* —3E **96**
Tynedale Clo. *Nott* —5K **47**
Tynefield Ct. & M. *Etw* —7D **88**
Tyne Gdns. *Huck* —2D **30**

**U**CI Cinemas. —6C **56**
Uffa Magna. *Mick* —7B **72**
Ulldale Ct. *Bees* —4B **80**
Ullscarf Clo. *W Bri* —3A **84**
Ullswater Clo. *Der* —5D **56**
Ullswater Clo. *Gam* —2B **84**
Ullswater Clo. *Ged* —4D **50**
Ullswater Cres. *Bees* —6C **62**
Ullswater Dri. *Huck* —5F **17**
Ullswater Dri. *Spon* —2A **76**
Underhill Av. *Der* —2K **91**
Underhill Clo. *Der* —3J **91**
Underpass, The. *Der*
—2B **74** (2F **7**)
Union Clo. *L'by* —2G **17**
Union Rd. *Ilk* —7C **44**
Union Rd. *Nott* —2E **64** (2F **5**)
(in two parts)
Union St. *Bees* —2F **81**
Union St. *Bing* —3A **70**
Union St. *Long E* —1J **97**
Union St. *Melb* —4G **113**
Unity Cres. *Nott* —4A **50**
University Boulevd. *Bees & Nott*
—7H **63**
**University Pk.** —7J **63**
Upchurch Clo. *Mick* —5A **72**
Uplands Av. *L'ver* —3G **91**
Uplands Ct. *Nott* —1F **63**
Uplands Gdns. *Der* —6J **73**
Upminster Dri. *Arn* —4H **33**
Upminster Dri. *Nut* —2D **46**
Up. Bainbrigge St. *Der* —6K **73**
Up. Barn Clo. *Hean* —3H **27**
Up. Boundary Rd. *Der* —4J **73**
Up. Canaan. *Rud* —1F **101**
Up. College St. *Nott*
—2D **64** (3C **4**)
Up. Dale Rd. *Der* —7K **73**
Up. Dunstead Rd. *Lan M* —2K **27**
Up. Eldon St. *Nott* —3G **65** (4K **5**)
Up. Hall Clo. *Holb* —7C **24**
Up. Hollow. *L'ver* —7G **73**
Up. Marehay Rd. *Rip* —6J **11**
Up. Moor Rd. *Altn* —3E **92**
Up. Nelson St. *Hean* —3F **27**
Up. Orchard St. *S'fd* —1J **79**
Up. Parliament St. *Nott*
—2D **64** (3D **4**)
Up. Wellington St. *Long E* —7G **79**
Uppingham Cres. *W Bri* —3F **83**
Uppingham Gdns. *Nott*
—5F **65** (7H **5**)
Upton Clo. *Hean* —4J **27**
Upton Dri. *Nott* —1F **49**
Upton M. *Nott* —6K **49**
Utah Clo. *Hilt* —7A **88**
Utile Gdns. *Nott* —6G **31**
Uttoxeter New Rd. *Der*
—5F **73** (5A **6**)
Uttoxeter Old Rd. *Der*
—4H **73** (3A **6**)
Uttoxeter Rd. *Mick* —7B **72**

**V**ale Clo. *Asl* —3J **71**
Vale Clo. *Eastw* —3F **29**

Vale Cres. N. *Nott* —1K **63**
Vale Cres. S. *Nott* —1K **63**
Vale Gdns. *Colw* —2B **66**
Vale Mills. *Der* —5K **73** (7B **6**)
Valerian Way. *Bing* —3J **69**
Valerie Rd. *Ast T* —3B **106**
Vale Rd. *Colw* —2C **66**
Valeside Gdns. *Colw* —2C **66**
Vale St. *Der* —6A **74**
Vale, The. *Ilk* —3C **44**
Valetta Rd. *Arn* —6K **33**
Valley Ct. *Nott* —1F **49**
Valley Dri. *Newt* —4F **29**
Valley Farm Ct. *Nott* —5C **32**
Valley Gdns. *W Bri* —3A **84**
Valley Rd. *Bees* —3A **80**
Valley Rd. *Cltn* —5K **49**
(in two parts)
Valley Rd. *Chad* —2H **75**
Valley Rd. *Ilk* —2C **60**
Valley Rd. *Kimb* —6H **29**
Valley Rd. *L'ver* —7H **73**
Valley Rd. *Nott* —4B **48**
Valley Rd. *Rad T* —2A **68**
Valley Rd. *W Bri* —3J **83**
Valley Vw. *Belp* —3A **24**
Valley Vw. *Ilk* —2C **60**
Valley Vw. Dri. *Stan C* —5D **42**
Valmont Rd. *Bees* —7A **62**
Valmont Rd. *Nott* —3C **48**
Vancouver Av. *Rad T* —5J **67**
Vancouver Av. *Spon* —5K **75**
Vanguard Rd. *Dis* —3J **115**
Vanguard Rd. *Long E* —4J **97**
Vardon Av. *Bees* —6G **63**
Varley St. *Der* —2D **92**
Varney Rd. *Nott* —5B **82**
Vaughan Av. *Huck* —3J **17**
Vaughan Rd. *Bees* —4A **80**
Vauxhall Av. *Der* —1E **72**
Vedonis Pk. *Huck* —7G **17**
Venn Ct. *Bees* —2F **81**
Ventnor Ho. *Alv* —2J **93**
Ventnor Ri. *Nott* —2B **48**
Venus Clo. *Nott* —1A **48**
Verbena Clo. *Nott* —7F **49**
Verbena Dri. *L'ver* —5H **91**
Verder Gro. *Nott* —5A **32**
Vere St. *Nott* —6H **31**
Vermont Dri. *Chad* —2J **75**
Verne Clo. *Cltn* —7A **50**
Vernon Av. *Bees* —2F **81**
Vernon Av. *Cltn* —6D **50**
Vernon Av. *Nott* —7D **64**
Vernon Av. *Old B* —3A **48**
Vernon Ct. *Nut* —3F **47**
Vernon Dri. *Nut* —3F **47**
Vernon Dri. *Spon* —4B **76**
Vernon Ga. *Der* —3J **73** (3A **6**)
(in two parts)
Vernon Pk. Dri. *Nott* —3A **48**
Vernon Pl. *Nott* —2K **47**
Vernon Rd. *Nott* —2K **47**
Vernon St. *Der* —3J **73** (3A **6**)
Vernon St. *Ilk* —2D **44**
Vernon St. *Nott* —2D **64** (3C **4**)
Verona Av. *Colw* —1D **66**
Veronica Dri. *Cltn* —5B **50**
Veronica Dri. *Gilt* —5G **29**
Veronica Wlk. *Nott* —7J **81**
Vestry Rd. *Oak* —5E **56**
Vetchfield Clo. *Sin* —7K **91**
Vicarage Av. *Der* —6J **73**
Vicarage Av. *Ilk* —2B **44**
Vicarage Clo. *Belp* —1A **24**
Vicarage Clo. *Nott* —3B **48**
(Perry Rd.)
Vicarage Clo. *Nott* —1E **64** (1E **4**)
(St Anne's Way)
Vicarage Clo. *Smal* —7B **26**
Vicarage Ct. *Mick* —7B **72**
Vicarage Dri. *Bur J* —2J **51**
Vicarage Dri. *Chad* —1G **75**
Vicarage Gdns. *Hean* —4H **27**
Vicarage Grn. *Edw* —5A **83**
Vicarage La. *Duf* —2J **39**
Vicarage La. *Iron* —1H **13**
Vicarage La. *L Eat* —6B **40**
Vicarage La. *Rad T* —4A **68**
Vicarage La. *Rud* —2E **100**
Vicarage Rd. *Chel* —7F **93**
Vicarage Rd. *Mick* —6A **72**
Vicarage Rd. *Milf* —5K **23**
Vicarage St. *Bees* —2E **80**
Vicarage St. *Ilk* —2B **44**
Vicarwood Av. *Dar A* —6K **55**
Vicarwood Av. *Holb* —6C **24**
Vickers St. *Nott* —6F **49**
Victor Av. *Der* —7K **55**

Victor Cres. *Sand* —4G **79**
Victoria Av. *Borr* —6D **76**
Victoria Av. *Dray* —2J **95**
Victoria Av. *Hean* —4F **27**
Victoria Av. *Low* —5E **36**
Victoria Av. *Nott* —6C **64**
Victoria Bus. Pk. *N'fld* —1F **67**
Victoria Cen. East.
(off Willow Row) —2K **73** (2C **6**)
Victoria Cen. E. *Nott* —2E **64**
(off Clinton St. E.)
Victoria Cen. S. *Nott*
(off Lincoln St.) —2E **64** (3F **5**)
Victoria Clo. *Arn* —3H **33**
Victoria Clo. *Mick* —4C **72**
Victoria Ct. *Ilk* —5C **44**
Victoria Ct. *Long E* —1J **97**
Victoria Cres. *Nott* —4F **49**
Victoria Embkmt. *Nott* —6E **64**
Victoria Gdns. *Watn* —4A **30**
Victoria Gro. *L'by* —2H **17**
Victoria Leisure Cen. —3H **5**
Victoria Pk. Leisure Cen. —5C **44**
Victoria Pk. Way. *N'fld* —1F **67**
Victoria Rd. *Bing* —2C **70**
Victoria Rd. *Dray* —2J **95**
Victoria Rd. *N'fld* —7D **50**
Victoria Rd. *Nott* —3D **48**
Victoria Rd. *Rip* —2K **11**
Victoria Rd. *Sand* —3F **79**
Victoria Rd. *W Bri* —1G **83**
Victoria Shop. Cen. *Nott*
—2E **64** (3F **5**)
Victoria St. *Cas D* —5K **107**
Victoria St. *Der* —3A **74** (4D **6**)
Victoria St. *Eastw* —2D **28**
Victoria St. *Ged* —5D **50**
Victoria St. *Huck* —4F **17**
Victoria St. *Ilk* —3D **44**
Victoria St. *Kimb* —3A **30**
Victoria St. *Lan M* —2A **28**
Victoria St. *Long E* —4F **97**
Victoria St. *Melb* —4G **113**
Victoria St. *Nott* —3E **64** (4F **5**)
Victoria St. *Rad T* —4K **67**
Victoria St. *Rip* —2B **12**
Victoria St. *S'fd* —1H **79**
Victoria Ter. *Nott* —3G **65** (4K **5**)
Victor Ter. *Nott* —4E **48**
Victory Av. *Rip* —3B **12**
Victory Clo. *Long E* —3J **97**
Victory Rd. *Bees* —4G **81**
Victory Rd. *Der* —2B **92**
Vigar Ct. *Bees* —2G **81**
Village Clo. *Edw* —5K **83**
Village Rd. *Clif* —6J **81**
Village St. *Der* —1J **91**
Village St. *Edw* —5J **83**
Village, The. *Dal A* —5H **59**
Village, The. *W Hal* —7F **43**
Villa Rd. *Keyw* —5D **102**
Villa Rd. *Nott* —7E **48**
Villas Rd. *Ambgt* —1K **9**
Villa St. *Bees* —1F **81**
Villa St. *Dray* —2K **95**
Villiers Rd. *W Bri* —2J **83**
Villiers Rd. *Wd'p* —2F **49**
Vincent Av. *Bees* —3F **81**
Vincent Av. *Ilk* —6D **44**
Vincent Av. *Spon* —5A **76**
Vincent Clo. *Klbrn* —5G **25**
Vincent Gdns. *Nott* —7A **48**
Vincent St. *Der* —7K **73**
Vine Clo. *L'ver* —2F **91**
Vine Cres. *Sand* —2F **79**
Vine Farm Clo. *Cotg* —5J **85**
Vine Farm Clo. *Ilk* —1B **60**
Vines Cross. *Nott* —5E **62**
Vine Ter. *Huck* —5H **17**
Viola Clo. *Oak* —4J **57**
Violet Av. *Newt* —5F **29**
Violet Clo. *Nott* —3K **47**
Violet Rd. *Cltn* —4B **50**
Violet Rd. *W Bri* —7J **65**
Violet St. *Der* —7K **73**
Viscount Rd. *Dis* —4K **115**
Vista, The. *S'fd* —3J **79**
Vivian Av. *Nott* —6D **48**
Vivian St. *Der* —7B **56**
Vulcan Clo. *Nott* —2A **48**
Vulcan St. *Der* —7B **74**
Vyse Dri. *Long E* —3F **97**

**W**addington Dri. *W Bri* —4F **83**
Wade Av. *Ilk* —7E **44**
Wade Av. *L'ver* —1G **73**
Wadebridge Gro. *Alv* —4J **93**
Wade Dri. *Mick* —6C **72**

Wade St. *L'ver* —7G **73**
Wades Way. *Bing* —4C **70**
Wadham Rd. *Wd'p* —1G **49**
Wadhurst Gdns. *Nott*
　　　　　—1G **65** (1H **5**)
Wadhurst Gro. *Nott* —5D **62**
Wadsworth Rd. *S'fd* —7K **61**
Wagstaff La. *Jack* —1K **13**
Wagtail Clo. *Sin* —5H **91**
Wainfleet Clo. *Ilk* —3A **44**
Waingrove. *Nott* —5C **82**
Waingroves Rd. *Rip* —4B **12**
Waingroves Rd. *Wain* —6D **12**
Wakami Cres. *Chel* —6G **93**
Wakefield Av. *Rad T* —3A **68**
Wakefield Ct. *Cas D* —6A **108**
Wakefield Cft. *Ilk* —3A **44**
Wakelyn Clo. *Shard* —1H **107**
Walbrook Clo. *Nott* —3G **47**
Walbrook Rd. *Der* —7K **73**
Walcote Clo. *Belp* —7C **10**
Walcote Dri. *W Bri* —4E **82**
Walcott Grn. *Nott* —7K **81**
Waldeck Rd. *Nott* —5D **48**
Waldemar Gro. *Bees* —2G **81**
Waldene Dri. *Alv* —3G **93**
　　(in two parts)
Waldorf Av. *Alv* —2G **93**
Waldorf Clo. *Alv* —2G **93**
Waldron Clo. *Nott* —5F **65**
Walesby Cres. *Nott* —1J **63**
Walgrave Clo. *Belp* —6B **10**
Walgrave Wlk. *Nott* —6D **32**
Walk Clo. *Dray* —2J **95**
Walker Av. *Rip* —2A **12**
Walker Bldgs. *Chel* —1G **105**
Walker Clo. *Ilk* —3E **60**
Walker Gro. *S'fd* —2J **79**
Walker La. *Der* —2K **73** (2C **6**)
Walkers Clo. *Bing* —4B **71**
Walker's La. *Tickn* —7A **112**
Walker St. *Eastw* —3E **28**
Walker's Yd. *Rad T* —4K **67**
Walk Mill Dri. *Huck* —3H **17**
Walk, The. *Der* —4J **91**
Wallace Av. *Cltn* —7D **50**
Wallace Gdns. *Bees* —6K **79**
Wallace St. *Der* —3G **73**
Wallace St. *Got* —7H **99**
Wallan St. *Nott* —1A **64**
Wallet St. *N'fld* —7E **50**
Wallet St. *Nott* —5F **65** (7H **5**)
Wallett Av. *Bees* —7F **63**
Wallfields Clo. *Find* —6B **90**
Wallis Clo. *Dray* —2J **95**
Wallis St. *Nott* —2A **48**
Wallk, The. *Klbrn* —5H **25**
Wall St. *Rip* —2K **11**
Walnut Av. *Alv* —2H **93**
Walnut Clo. *Asl* —2K **71**
Walnut Clo. *Ast T* —2D **106**
Walnut Clo. *Bar T* —4A **104**
Walnut Clo. *Chel* —2G **105**
Walnut Clo. *Ilk* —7E **44**
Walnut Cft. *Burna* —4H **89**
Walnut Dri. *Bees* —7B **62**
Walnut Gro. *C'tn* —6D **20**
Walnut Gro. *E Bri* —4J **53**
Walnut Gro. *Rad T* —4K **67**
Walnut Rd. *Belp* —2B **24**
Walnut St. *Der* —2C **92**
Walnut Tree Gdns. *Nott* —6F **31**
Walnut Tree La. *E Bri* —4J **53**
Walpole St. *Der* —2D **74**
Walsham Clo. *Bees* —6C **80**
Walsham Ct. *Der* —6D **56**
Walsingham Rd. *Wd'p* —1J **49**
Walters Av. *Brins* —6C **14**
Walter St. *Der* —1J **73** (1A **6**)
Walter St. *Dray* —1H **95**
Walter St. *Nott* —1C **64** (1B **4**)
Waltham Av. *Sin* —5K **91**
Waltham Clo. *W Bri* —2K **83**
Walthamstow Dri. *Der* —2F **73**
Walton Av. *Altn* —5E **92**
Walton Av. *Nott* —2H **65**
Walton Ct. *Cltn* —7C **50**
　　(in two parts)
Walton Ct. *Keg* —7G **109**
Walton Ct. *W Hal* —6F **43**
Walton Cres. *Cltn* —7C **50**
Walton Dri. *Der* —2J **91**
Walton Dri. *Keyw* —6D **102**
Walton Hill. *Cas D* —6J **107**
　　(Darsway)
Walton Hill. *Cas D* —4F **115**
　　(Hill Top)
Walton M. *Nott* —7H **49**

Walton Rd. *Arn* —4J **33**
Walton Rd. *Chad* —3F **75**
Walton St. *Long E* —1H **97**
Wansbeck Clo. *Nott*
　　　　　—2C **64** (2A **4**)
Wansfell Clo. *Mick* —7C **72**
Wansford Av. *Arn* —4H **33**
Wansley La. *Bagt* —1C **14**
Wanstead Way. *Nott* —4A **32**
Ward Av. *Huck* —3F **17**
Ward Av. *Nott* —3K **49**
Wardle Gro. *Arn* —5J **33**
Wardlow Av. *Chad* —7G **57**
Wardlow Rd. *Ilk* —3C **44**
Wardwick. *Der* —3A **74** (3C **6**)
Wareham Clo. *Nott* —3G **47**
Wareham Clo. *W Bri* —3E **82**
Warksworth Rd. *Turn & Duf*
　　　　　—6C **22**
Warkton Clo. *Bees* —3C **80**
Warmwells La. *Rip* —5K **11**
Warner St. *Der* —5K **73** (7B **6**)
Warner St. *Mick* —7B **72**
Warner St. *Nott* —2A **64**
Warren Av. *Nott* —4C **48**
Warren Av. *S'fd* —1H **79**
Warren Ct. *S'fd* —1H **79**
Warrendale Ct. *Chel* —7G **93**
Warrender Clo. *Bees* —6C **62**
Warrener Gro. *Nott* —5A **32**
Warrenhill Clo. *Arn* —6E **32**
Warren La. *Locki* —7E **96**
　　(in two parts)
Warren Rd. *Huck* —7D **16**
Warren St. *Der* —1F **93**
Warren, The. *Cotg* —6K **85**
Warrington Rd. *Nott* —6J **31**
Warser Ga. *Nott* —3F **65** (4G **5**)
Warsick La. *Stan B* —3A **112**
Warsop Clo. *Strel* —4D **46**
Warton Av. *Nott* —6H **49**
Warwick Av. *Bees* —7F **63**
Warwick Av. *Der* —4J **73**
Warwick Av. *Wd'p* —1G **49**
Warwick Dri. *Ilk* —3A **44**
Warwick Gdns. *Belp* —7D **10**
Warwick Gdns. *Cotg* —7K **85**
Warwick Rd. *Long E* —2K **97**
Warwick Rd. *Nott* —4F **49**
Warwick St. *Der* —6D **74**
Warwick St. *Nott* —5A **64**
Wasdale Clo. *W Bri* —3A **84**
Washdyke La. *Huck* —3D **16**
Washington Av. *Chad* —1H **75**
　　(in two parts)
Washington Clo. *Melb* —4G **113**
Washington Cotts. *Borr* —7F **77**
Washington Ct. *Arn* —6H **33**
Washington Dri. *S'fd* —6K **61**
Wash Pit La. *Cols B* —7K **87**
Wasnidge Clo. *Nott*
　　　　　—2F **65** (2H **5**)
Wasnidge Wlk. *Nott*
　　　　　—2F **65** (1H **5**)
Watchwood Gro. *C'tn* —4D **20**
Watcombe Cir. *Nott* —4D **48**
Watcombe Rd. *Nott* —5E **48**
Watendlath Clo. *W Bri* —3A **84**
Waterdown Rd. *Nott* —7K **81**
Waterford Dri. *Chad* —4G **75**
Waterford St. *Nott* —3A **48**
Waterfurrows La. *Shelf* —5D **52**
Watergo La. *Mick* —2B **90**
Waterhouse La. *Ged* —4E **50**
Watering La. *Holb* —7D **24**
Water La. *Oxt* —1F **21**
Water La. *Rad T* —4J **67**
Water La. *Shelf* —5C **52**
Waterloo Ct. *Der* —1B **74** (1F **7**)
Waterloo Cres. *Nott*
　　　　　—1C **64** (1A **4**)
Waterloo La. *Trow* —1K **61**
Waterloo Promenade. *Nott*
　　(in two parts) —1C **64** (1A **4**)
Waterloo Rd. *Bees* —3G **81**
Waterloo Rd. *L'by* —2G **17**
Waterloo Rd. *Nott* —1C **64** (1A **4**)
Watermeadow Rd. *Alv* —4G **93**
Watermeadows, The. *Long E*
　　　　　—1F **97**
Watermeadows, The. *Swar*
　　　　　—4D **104**
Water Orton Clo. *Bees* —5J **79**
Waterside Clo. *Dar A* —5A **56**
Waterside Clo. *Gam* —2A **84**

Waterside Clo. *Sand* —5F **79**
Waterside Gdns. *Nott* —6A **64**
Waterway St. *Nott* —5F **65** (7G **5**)
　　(in two parts)
Waterway St. W. *Nott*
　　　　　—5E **64** (7E **4**)
Waterway, The. *Sand* —4G **79**
Watford Rd. *Nott* —4H **47**
Watkinson St. *Hean* —3F **27**
Watkin St. *Nott* —1E **64** (1F **5**)
Watnall Rd. *Huck* —3D **30**
Watnall Rd. *Nut* —7C **30**
Watney Factory Units. *Huck*
　　　　　—7F **17**
Watson Av. *Hean* —3H **27**
Watson Av. *Nott* —5H **33**
Watson Gdns. *Der* —2K **73** (1B **6**)
Watson St. *Der* —1J **73** (1A **6**)
　　(in two parts)
Watten Clo. *Sin* —7K **91**
Waveney Clo. *Alst* —2B **56**
Waveney Clo. *Arn* —7J **33**
Waverley Av. *Bees* —2G **81**
Waverley Av. *Ged* —5E **50**
Waverley Mt. *Nott* —1C **64**
Waverley St. *Der* —2C **64**
Waverley St. *Long E* —1J **97**
Waverley St. *Nott* —1C **64** (1C **4**)
Waverley Ter. *Nott* —2D **64** (2C **4**)
Wayfaring Rd. *Oak* —6G **57**
Wayford Wlk. *Nott* —5H **31**
Wayne Clo. *Nott* —7A **82**
Wayson Rd. *Ilk* —4A **44**
Wayte Ct. *Rud* —7G **83**
Wayzgoose Dri. *Der*
　　　　　—2C **74** (2J **7**)
Weardale Rd. *Nott* —4C **48**
Wearmouth Gdns. *Nott* —4C **32**
Weaver Row. *Ilk* —6D **44**
Weavers Clo. *Nott* —7C **10**
Weavers Clo. *Borr* —7F **77**
Weavers Grn. *Mick* —7A **72**
Weaver's La. *Ann & Ann* —2J **15**
Weaverthorpe Rd. *Wd'p* —1J **49**
Webb Rd. *Nott* —7H **47**
Webster Av. *Eastw* —4D **28**
Webster St. *Der* —4K **73** (6C **6**)
Weedon Clo. *Nott* —1J **65**
Weekday Cross. *Nott*
　　　　　—3E **64** (5F **5**)
Weetman Gdns. *Nott* —5C **32**
Weightman Dri. *Gilt* —6F **29**
Weirfield Rd. *Dar A* —5A **56**
Welbeck Av. *Der* —4B **50**
Welbeck Av. *Ilk* —2B **60**
Welbeck Clo. *Nott* —1E **64**
Welbeck Gdns. *Bees* —5K **79**
Welbeck Gdns. *Wd'p* —2J **49**
Welbeck Gro. *Alst* —4G **55**
Welbeck Gro. *Bing* —3J **69**
Welbeck Rd. *Long E* —5F **79**
Welbeck Rd. *Rad T* —3A **68**
Welbeck Rd. *W Bri* —7G **65**
Welbeck Wlk. *Nott* —1E **64** (1F **5**)
Welby Av. *Nott* —3B **64**
Welch Av. *S'fd* —7K **61**
Weldbank Clo. *Bees* —4B **80**
Welham Cres. *Arn* —6J **33**
Welland Clo. *Mick* —4B **72**
Welland Ct. *Nott* —1H **65** (1K **5**)
Welland Rd. *Hilt* —7A **88**
Welldon St. *Den V* —1C **26**
Wellesley Av. *Sun* —2H **91**
Wellesley Cres. *Nott* —4D **46**
Wellin Clo. *Edw* —5K **83**
Wellin Ct. *Edw* —5K **83**
Wellington Cir. *Nott*
　　　　　—3D **64** (4C **4**)
Wellington Ct. *Belp* —2K **23**
Wellington Ct. *Eastw* —3D **28**
Wellington Cres. *Der*
　　　　　—4B **74** (6H **7**)
Wellington Cres. *W Bri* —1H **83**
Wellington Pl. *Eastw* —3D **28**
Wellington Rd. *Bur J* —1A **52**
Wellington Sq. *Nott*
　　　　　—2C **64** (3A **4**)
Wellington St. *Der* —5B **74** (7G **7**)
Wellington St. *Eastw* —2D **28**
Wellington St. *Hean* —3F **27**
Wellington St. *Long E* —5G **79**
Wellington St. *Nott* —1E **64** (1F **5**)
Wellington St. *Rip* —3A **12**
Wellington St. *S'fd* —2G **79**
Wellington Ter. *Nott*
　　　　　—2C **64** (3A **4**)
Wellington Vs. *Nott*
　　　　　—2C **64** (3A **4**)
Wellin La. *Edw* —5K **83**

Well La. *Milf* —6K **23**
Wells Ct. *Der* —2C **90**
Wells Gdns. *Nott* —6H **49**
Wellspring Dale. *S'fd* —3J **79**
Wells Rd. *Mick* —6C **72**
Wells Rd., The. *Nott* —7H **49**
Well St. *Der* —1A **74** (1D **6**)
Well St. *Rip* —3K **11**
Well Yd. *Holb* —7C **24**
Welney Clo. *Mick* —1B **90**
Welshpool Rd. *Der* —6D **56**
Welstead Av. *Nott* —4G **47**
Welton Gdns. *Nott* —5G **31**
Welwyn Av. *Alst* —4H **55**
Welwyn Av. *Shel L* —5E **92**
Welwyn Rd. *Nott* —2E **62**
Wembley Gdns. *Bees* —5B **62**
Wembley Gdns. *Der* —2E **72**
Wembley Rd. *Arn* —7K **33**
Wemyss Gdns. *Nott* —4K **63**
Wendling Gdns. *Nott* —6D **32**
　　(in two parts)
Wendover Clo. *Mick* —7A **72**
Wendover Dri. *Nott* —4H **47**
Wenlock Clo. *Gilt* —5G **29**
Wenlock Clo. *Mick* —7C **72**
Wensleydale Clo. *Nott* —5K **47**
Wensleydale Rd. *Long E* —3F **97**
Wensleydale Wlk. *Alv* —2J **93**
Wensley Dri. *Spon* —5B **76**
Wensley Rd. *Wd'p* —1G **49**
Wensor Av. *Bees* —7F **63**
Wentworth Clo. *Mick* —7D **72**
Wentworth Ct. *Kimb* —7J **29**
Wentworth Cft. *Hean* —2J **27**
Wentworth Rd. *Bees* —2C **80**
Wentworth Rd. *Nott* —4D **48**
Wentworth St. *Ilk* —4E **44**
Wentworth Way. *Edw* —5K **83**
Werburgh Clo. *Spon* —4K **75**
Werburgh St. *Der* —4K **73** (5B **6**)
Wesleyan Chapel Wlk. *S'fd*
　　　　　—1H **79**
*Wesley Ct. Nott* —4E **48**
　　(off Drayton St., in two parts)
Wesley Gro. *Nott* —5D **48**
Wesley La. *Der* —3E **76**
Wesley Pl. *S'fd* —7J **61**
Wesley Rd. *Alv* —4H **93**
Wesley Rd. *Ambgt* —1K **9**
Wesley St. *Ilk* —2C **44**
Wesley St. *Lan M* —2A **28**
Wesley St. *Nott* —5D **48**
Wesley Way. *Rud* —3F **101**
Wessex Way. *Gilt* —5E **28**
Wessington M. *Alst* —6J **55**
West Av. *Der* —2K **73** (1B **6**)
West Av. *Dray* —1H **95**
West Av. *Rip* —3J **11**
West Av. *Sand* —2E **78**
West Av. *S'fd* —7J **61**
West Av. *W Bri* —1G **83**
West Av. N. *Chel* —6E **92**
West Av. S. *Chel* —7E **92**
West Bank. *Ambgt* —2A **10**
W. Bank Av. *Der* —7J **55**
W. Bank Clo. *Der* —7J **55**
West Bank M. *Keg* —1G **117**
W. Bank Rd. *Alst* —2J **55**
Westbourne Ct. *Bees* —6K **61**
Westbourne Pk. *Der* —2D **72**
Westbourne Rd. *Und* —2E **14**
West Bridgford Green Line Walk.
　　　　　—3H **83**
Westbury Clo. *Bees* —4C **80**
Westbury Ct. *Der* —5J **73**
Westbury Gdns. *Belp* —7C **10**
Westbury Rd. *Nott* —4B **48**
Westbury St. *Der* —5H **73**
Westby La. *Aws* —2G **45**
Westcliffe Av. *Ged* —3B **50**
Westcliffe Av. *Rad T* —3A **68**
West Clo. *Dar A* —5J **55**
West Clo. *Keyw* —7C **102**
West Cres. *Bees* —4H **81**
W. Croft Av. *L'ver* —4H **91**
Westcross Av. *S'fd* —7J **61**
Westdale Clo. *Long E* —4E **96**
Westdale Ct. *Cltn* —4B **50**
Westdale Cres. *Cltn* —5C **50**
Westdale La. E. *Cltn* —4A **50**
Westdale La. W. *Map* —3J **49**
Westdene Av. *Altn* —4D **92**
West Dri. *Mick* —6A **72**
West Dri. *Nott* —7H **63**
West End. *Bees* —3F **81**
West End. *C'tn* —4A **20**
West End. *Long W* —7D **116**
W. End Arc. *Nott* —3D **64** (4D **4**)

W. End Cres. *Ilk* —6B **44**
W. End Dri. *Ilk* —6B **44**
W. End Dri. *Shard* —1G **107**
W. End St. *S'fd* —2G **79**
W. End Vs. *Rad T* —4J **67**
Westerfield Way. *Nott* —4C **82**
Westerham Clo. *Nott* —7D **46**
Westerham Rd. *Rud* —3D **100**
Westerhope Clo. *Edw* —4A **84**
Westerlands. *S'fd* —3K **79**
Western Av. *Bing* —2K **69**
Western Av. *Rud* —6J **47**
Western Dri. *Hean* —5H **27**
Western Fields. *Rud* —3D **100**
Western Gdns. *Nott* —6K **47**
Western Rd. *Der* —5K **73**
Western Rd. *Mick* —6B **72**
Western St. *Nott* —2F **65** (3G **5**)
Western Ter. *Nott*
　　　　　—3C **64** (4A **4**)
*Western Vs. Ambgt* —1K **9**
　　(off Villas Rd.)
Westfield Av. *Hean* —5H **27**
Westfield Clo. *Ilk* —1A **60**
Westfield Dri. *Ilk* —4B **44**
Westfield Gro. *Bing* —3K **69**
Westfields La. *Wdbgh* —1E **34**
W. Furlong. *Cotg* —6A **86**
West Ga. *Long E* —2J **97**
Westgate Ct. *Bees* —3E **80**
Westgate St. *Nott* —1G **65**
Westgreen Av. *Altn* —4D **92**
West Gro. *Altn* —4D **92**
Westhall Rd. *Mick* —5B **72**
Westhay Ct. *Nott* —2J **63**
West Hill. *Cod* —5D **12**
Westholme Gdns. *Nott* —1J **63**
Westhorpe Av. *Nott*
　　　　　—2H **65** (3K **5**)
Westhorpe Dri. *Long E* —1G **97**
Westland Av. *Huck* —1D **30**
West Lawn. *Find* —7B **90**
W. Leake La. *Thrum* —1C **110**
Westleigh Av. *Der* —2G **73**
Westleigh Rd. *Nott* —4E **46**
Westley Cres. *L Eat* —4D **40**
W. Manor Ct. *Bees* —3D **80**
Westmeadow La. *Long W*
　　　　　—7C **116**
W. Meadows Ind. Est. *Der*
　　　　　—3C **74** (3H **7**)
Westminster Av. *Sand* —3G **79**
Westminster Clo. *Nott* —7G **49**
Westminster Dri. *Rad T* —4D **68**
Westminster St. *Der* —1F **93**
West Moor. *Nott* —3B **66**
Westmoore Clo. *Nott* —3K **49**
Westmoore Ct. *Nott* —3K **49**
Westmoreland Ct. *Nott* —5D **48**
Westmorland Clo. *Der*
　　　　　—2C **74** (1J **7**)
Westmorland Way. *Jack* —1K **13**
Weston Av. *Nott* —1C **64**
Weston Clo. *Wd'p* —2G **49**
Weston Cotts. *Nott* —1A **64**
Weston Ct. *Shel L* —6D **92**
Weston Ct. *Wstn T* —6A **106**
Weston Cres. *Long E* —5D **96**
Weston Pk. Av. *Shel L* —6D **92**
Weston Pk. Gdns. *Shel L* —6D **92**
Weston Ri. *Chel* —2G **105**
Weston Rd. *Wstn T & Ast T*
　　　　　—4B **106**
Weston Spot Clo. *Rip* —5K **11**
Weston St. *Hean* —5J **27**
Weston Ter. *Nott* —3E **48**
West Pk. Ct. *Long E* —2H **97**
West Pk. Leisure Cen. —2F **97**
West Pk. Rd. *Der* —7J **55**
Westray Clo. *Bees* —4B **62**
West Rd. *Spon* —3K **75**
West Row. *Dar A* —6A **56**
W. Service Rd. *Der* —6G **75**
West St. *Arn* —6G **33**
West St. *Hean* —3F **27**
West St. *Huck* —5G **17**
West St. *Ilk* —7C **44**
West St. *Kimb* —2A **46**
West St. *Lan M* —2K **27**
West St. *Nott* —3G **65** (4J **5**)
West St. *Shelf* —5C **52**
West Ter. *Huck* —5G **17**
West Ter. *Ilk* —5D **44**
West Vw. *W Bri* —3F **83**
W. View Av. *L'ver* —2F **91**
Westview Ct. *Cltn* —6D **50**
W. View Rd. *Cltn* —6D **50**
Westville Dri. *Huck* —2E **30**
Westville Gdns. *Nott* —7F **49**

West Wlk. *Nott* —3G **65** (4J **5**)
Westward Av. *Bees* —2G **81**
Westway. *Cotg* —6K **85**
Westwick Rd. *Nott* —1C **62**
Westwick St. *Ilk* —1E **60**
Westwood Dri. *Altn* —4D **92**
Westwood Gdns. *Jack* —1A **14**
Westwood Rd. *Nott* —3H **65**
Wetherby Clo. *Kimb* —7J **29**
Wetherby Clo. *Nott* —5H **47**
Wetherby Rd. *Der* —2D **92**
Wetherlam Clo. *Nott* —5E **64**
Weyacres. *Borr* —7E **76**
Weybridge Clo. *W Hal* —6F **43**
Wharfedale. *Nott* —4B **62**
Wharfedale Clo. *Alst* —3B **56**
Wharfedale Rd. *Long E* —3E **96**
Wharf La. *Rad T* —4J **67**
Wharf Rd. *Nott* —4D **64** (6D **4**)
Wharf, The. *Shard* —1J **107**
  (in two parts)
Wharncliffe Rd. *Ilk* —6C **44**
Whateley Ct. *Nun* —2E **90**
Whatton Dri. *W Bri* —5D **82**
Whatton Ri. *Nott* —2D **48**
Whatton Rd. *Keg* —2G **117**
Whatton Towerhill. —4J **71**
Wheatacre Rd. *Nott* —7B **82**
Wheat Clo. *Nott* —2D **62**
Wheatcroft Vw. *W Bri* —5E **82**
Wheatcroft Way. *Der* —5C **56**
Wheatfields Rd. *Nott* —7J **49**
Wheatgrass Rd. *Bees* —3B **80**
Wheathill Gro. *L'ver* —3E **90**
Wheatland Clo. *Sten F* —7G **91**
Wheatley Clo. *Rud* —4E **100**
Wheatley Dri. *Cltn* —7A **50**
Wheatley Gro. *Bees* —4F **81**
Wheatsheaf Clo. *Oak* —5J **57**
Wheatsheaf Ct. *Bur J* —2K **51**
Wheeldale Clo. *Nott* —3B **62**
Wheeldon Av. *Belp* —1B **24**
Wheeldon Av. *Der* —1J **73**
Wheeldon Ct. *Nott* —5B **48**
Wheeldon Mnr. *Der* —7J **55**
Wheeler Av. *Eastw* —4F **29**
Wheeler Ga. *Nott* —3E **64** (4E **4**)
Wheeler Ga. *Nott* —2E **14**
Wheelwright Way. *Pri P*
  —5D **74** (7K **7**)
Wheldon Av. *Cltn* —4A **50**
Whenby Clo. *Mick* —6A **72**
Whernside Clo. *Alv* —3K **93**
Whernside Rd. *Wd'p* —1G **49**
Whetstone Clo. *Nut* —3D **46**
Whickham Ct. *Nott* —6F **65**
Whilton Ct. *Belp* —1D **24**
Whilton Cres. *W Hal* —6F **43**
Whimsey Pk. *Cltn* —1D **66**
Whinbush Av. *Altn* —4E **92**
Whinfell Clo. *Nott* —6B **82**
Whinlatter Dri. *W Bri* —2A **84**
Whiston Clo. *Nott* —7C **32**
Whiston St. *Der* —6A **74**
Whitaker Gdns. *Der* —6J **73**
Whitaker Rd. *Der* —6H **73**
Whitaker St. *Der* —6A **74**
Whitbread St. *Nott* —6B **48**
Whitburn Rd. *Bees* —5J **79**
Whitby Av. *Der* —6C **56**
Whitby Clo. *Nott* —3B **62**
Whitby Cres. *Wd'p* —1J **49**
Whitby Rd. *Newt* —2E **28**
Whitchurch Clo. *Nott* —5C **32**
Whitcombe Gdns. *Nott* —5C **32**
Whitcombe Pl. *Rip* —2K **11**
Whiteacre. *Bur J* —1J **51**
Whitebeam Gdns. *Nott* —6F **31**
Whitechapel St. *Nott* —4K **47**
White City Trad. Est. *Nott* —4J **65**
Whitecross Gdns. *Der*
  —1J **73** (1A **6**)
Whitecross Ho. *Der*
  —1J **73** (1A **6**)
White Furrows. *Cotg* —6J **85**
White Gates. *Cod* —4D **12**
Whitegate Va. *Nott* —7K **81**
Whitehall Ct. *Rad T* —4E **68**
White Hart Yd. *Klbrn* —5F **25**
Whitehead Clo. *Ilk* —4B **44**
Whitehead Dri. *Brins* —4B **14**
Whitehouse Clo. *Shel L* —6D **92**
Whitehouse Ri. *Belp* —6J **9**
Whitehurst St. *Altn* —2D **92**
Whitelands. *Cotg* —6A **86**
White La. *Shot* —2B **22**
Whiteley Clo. *S'fd* —7J **61**
Whiteley Rd. *Rip* —5A **12**
White Lion Sq. *Ilk* —7D **44**

White Lodge Gdns. *Nott* —7D **46**
Whitemoor Av. *Nott* —5K **47**
Whitemoor Ct. *Nott* —6K **47**
  (in two parts)
Whitemoor Ct. Ind. Est. *Nott*
  —6K **47**
Whitemoor Hall. *Belp* —7D **10**
Whitemoor La. *Belp* —1C **24**
Whitemoor Rd. *Nott* —4K **47**
Whitemoss Clo. *Nott* —4E **62**
White Rd. *Nott* —3A **48**
White's Av. *Nott* —1K **65**
Whites Cft. *Wdbgh* —1F **35**
Whitestone Av. *S'fd* —2J **79**
White St. *Der* —1J **73**
Whiteway. *Dar A* —5J **55**
Whiteways Ct. *Nott* —7A **82**
Whitewells La. *Belp* —4G **9**
Whitfield Clo. *Nott* —2D **82**
Whiting Av. *Bees* —6K **79**
Whitmore Rd. *Chad* —2F **75**
Whitstable Clo. *Der* —2H **91**
Whittaker La. *L Eat & L Eat*
  (in two parts)
  —4A **40**
Whittaker Rd. *Bees* —5A **80**
Whittier Rd. *Nott* —4J **65**
Whittingham Rd. *Nott* —3J **49**
Whittington St. *Altn* —4D **92**
Whittlebury Dri. *L'ver* —2D **90**
Whitton Clo. *Bees* —6C **80**
Whitton Clo. *Nott* —4D **32**
Whitwell Clo. *Nott* —5F **47**
Whitwell Gdns. *Alv* —4J **93**
Whitwell Rd. *Nott* —4E **46**
Whitworth Dri. *Ged* —4G **51**
Whitworth Dri. *Rad T* —5J **67**
Whitworth Ri. *Nott* —5B **32**
Whitworth Rd. *Ilk* —1D **60**
Whyburn La. *Huck* —5C **16**
Whyburn St. *Huck* —6J **17**
Whysall St. *Hean* —3G **27**
Whyston Ct. *Huck* —7C **16**
Whyteleafe Gro. *Oak* —6H **57**
Wichnor Clo. *Nott* —4A **82**
Wickens Wlk. *Nott* —1G **65**
Wickersley Clo. *Alst* —5J **55**
Wicket Gro. *Lent* —3A **64**
Wickstead Clo. *Wd'p* —3H **49**
Wicksteed Clo. *Belp* —7D **10**
Widdowson Clo. *Blen I* —5F **31**
Widdowson's Row. *Rud* —2E **100**
  (off Cumberland Clo.)
Widdybank Clo. *Alst* —5G **55**
Widecombe La. *Nott* —1K **99**
Wighay Rd. *Huck* —3F **17**
Wigley Clo. *Nott* —1G **65** (1K **5**)
Wigman Rd. *Nott* —6D **46**
Wigmore Clo. *Mick* —5A **72**
Wigwam Gro. *Huck* —5J **17**
Wigwam La. *Huck* —5J **17**
Wilcox Dri. *Und* —3E **14**
Wilden Cres. *Nott* —5A **82**
Wilderbrook La. *Shot* —4D **8**
Wilders Lea Ct. *Belp* —3A **24**
Wildman St. *Nott* —1C **64** (1A **4**)
Wildsmith St. *Der* —1G **93**
Wild St. *Der* —3H **73**
Wilford Cres. *Rud* —1E **100**
Wilford Cres. E. *Nott* —6F **65**
Wilford Cres. W. *Nott* —6E **64**
Wilford Gro. *Nott* —5E **64**
  (in two parts)
Wilford La. *Wilf & W Bri* —2D **82**
Wilford Rd. *Nott* —5D **64** (7D **4**)
  (in two parts)
Wilford Rd. *Rud* —5D **82**
Wilford Sports Complex. —2F **83**
Wilford St. *Nott* —4E **64** (6E **4**)
Wilfred St. *Der* —6B **74**
Wilfrid Gro. *W Bri* —5G **83**
Wilhallow La. *Jack* —1C **14**
Wilkins Dri. *Altn* —2E **92**
Wilkins Gdns. *Nott* —7J **81**
Wilkinson Av. *Bees* —2F **81**
Wilkinson St. *Nott* —5K **47**
Willaston Clo. *Nott* —2J **47**
Willbert Rd. *Arn* —5J **33**
Willerby Rd. *Wd'p* —1J **49**
Willersley Dri. *Nott* —5E **64**
Willesden Av. *Der* —1E **72**
Willesden Grn. *Nut* —3D **46**
Willetts Rd. *Chad* —1G **75**
Willey La. *Und & Newt* —3E **14**
William Av. *Eastw* —3D **28**
William Booth Birth Place Mus.
  —4K **5**
William Booth Rd. *Nott* —3J **65**
William Clo. *Ged* —6F **51**
William Lee Bldgs. *Nott* —7K **63**

William Olds Ct. *Nott* —2G **63**
William Rd. *S'fd* —1H **79**
William Rd. *W Bri* —7G **65**
Williams Rd. *Bees* —5A **80**
William St. *Belp* —1K **23**
William St. *Der* —2K **73** (1A **6**)
William St. *Huck* —5G **17**
William St. *Long E* —6G **79**
Willington Rd. *Etw* —5D **88**
Willn St. *Der* —7K **73**
Willoughby Av. *Long E* —6G **79**
Willoughby Av. *Nott* —3B **64**
Willoughby Clo. *Breas* —1D **96**
Willoughby Ct. *Nott* —7H **63**
Willoughby Ct. *Nott* —4B **64**
Willoughby Rd. *W Bri* —2H **83**
Willoughby St. *Bees* —1F **81**
Willoughby St. *Nott* —4B **64**
Willow Av. *Cltn* —6E **50**
Willow Av. *Huck* —1D **30**
Willow Av. *Long E* —7H **79**
Willow Av. *Rip* —5K **11**
Willow Av. *S'fd* —2H **79**
Willow Brook. *Keyw* —7E **102**
Willowbrook Ct. *Nott* —6E **64**
Willowbrook Grange. *Chel*
  —1G **105**
Willow Clo. *Ast T* —2D **106**
Willow Clo. *Bur J* —1K **51**
Willow Clo. *Dar A* —5K **55**
Willow Clo. *Lamb* —6E **35**
Willow Clo. *Rad T* —5K **67**
Willow Clo. *Stan C* —4C **42**
Willow Cotts. *Nott* —7G **47**
Willow Ct. *Und* —3E **14**
Willow Ct. *W Bri* —3F **83**
Willow Cres. *Ged* —4E **50**
Willow Cft. *Boul M* —5J **93**
Willowcroft Rd. *Spon* —5K **75**
Willowdene. *Cotg* —5A **86**
Willow Farm Ct. *Find* —7B **90**
Willowfields. *Hilt* —7A **88**
Willow Gro. *Belp* —3A **24**
Willowherb Clo. *Sin* —7K **91**
Willow Hill Clo. *Bulw* —7G **31**
Willow Holt. *Low* —4E **36**
Willow Ho. *Der* —2C **74** (2J **7**)
Willow Ind. Est. *Nott* —5J **31**
Willow La. *Ged* —4D **50**
Willow Pk. La. *Ast T* —4C **106**
Willow Pk. Way. *Ast T*
  —3C **106**
Willowpit La. *Hilt* —2A **88**
Willow Ri. *Sand* —3F **79**
Willow Rd. *Bing* —3D **70**
Willow Rd. *Cltn* —6E **50**
Willow Rd. *Cas D* —5K **107**
Willow Rd. *Nott* —6A **64**
Willow Rd. *W Bri* —4G **83**
Willow Row. *Der* —2K **73** (2C **6**)
  (in two parts)
Willows Ct. *Rip* —2K **11**
  (off Cromford St.)
Willowsend Clo. *Find* —7B **90**
Willow Sports Cen. —2C **6**
Willows, The. *Bees* —2F **81**
Willow Vw. *Nott* —1B **64**
Willow Wong. *Bur J* —1K **51**
Willson Av. *L'ver* —1G **91**
Willson Rd. *L'ver* —2G **91**
Willwell Dri. *W Bri* —5E **82**
Wilmington Av. *Alv* —4H **93**
Wilmington Gdns. *Nott* —7F **33**
Wilmore Rd. *Der* —4A **92**
Wilmorton Link. *Der* —6E **74**
Wilmot Av. *Chad* —7F **57**
Wilmot Av. *Wstn T* —5A **106**
Wilmot Dri. *Smal* —1B **42**
Wilmot Ho. *Long E* —4E **96**
Wilmot La. *Bees* —3F **81**
Wilmot Rd. *Belp* —1A **24**
Wilmot St. *Der* —4A **74** (6D **6**)
Wilmot St. *Hean* —4G **27**
Wilmot St. *Ilk* —5C **44**
Wilmot St. *Long E* —4E **96**
Wilmslow Dri. *Oak* —6G **57**
Wilne Av. *Long E* —5E **96**
Wilne Clo. *Long E* —5E **96**
Wilne La. *Dray & Long E* —5A **96**
Wilne La. *Shard* —1J **107**
Wilne Rd. *Dray* —3J **95**
Wilne Rd. *Long E* —5D **96**
Wilson Av. *Los* —1D **26**
Wilson Clo. *Arn* —7K **33**
Wilson Clo. *Mick* —1A **90**
Wilson Ri. *Melb* —5A **114**
Wilson Rd. *Chad* —7F **57**
Wilson Rd. *Eastw* —4D **28**
Wilsons Ct. *Rud* —2E **100**

Wilson St. *Der* —4K **73** (5C **6**)
Wilsthorpe Rd. *Breas* —1C **96**
Wilsthorpe Rd. *Chad* —1F **75**
Wilsthorpe Rd. *Long E* —1F **97**
Wiltor Clo. *Sten F* —7G **91**
Wiltor Pl. *Ilk* —5D **44**
Wiltor Rd. *Nott* —1A **64**
Wiltor St. *Ilk* —5D **44**
Wiltor St. *Nott* —2A **48**
Wiltor Ter. *Nott* —2A **48**
Wiltra Gro. *Duf* —3K **39**
Wiltshire Av. *Jack* —1K **13**
Wiltshire Rd. *Der* —7D **56**
Wimbledon Dri. *Nut* —3E **46**
Wimbledon Rd. *Der* —2E **72**
Wimbledon Rd. *Nott* —3C **48**
Wimbourne Clo. *W Bri* —3E **82**
Wimbourne Clo. *Chel* —1G **105**
Wimbourne Rd. *Nott* —1B **64**
Wimpole Gdns. *Der* —2F **73**
Wimpole Rd. *Bees* —6D **62**
Wincanton Clo. *Der* —7D **74**
Winchcombe Way. *Oak* —5G **57**
Winchester Av. *Bees* —7E **62**
Winchester Ct. *Nott* —3G **49**
Winchester Cres. *Chad* —7D **56**
Winchester Cres. *Ilk* —6E **44**
Winchester St. *Nott* —3E **48**
Winchester Ter. *Nott* —3E **48**
Windermere Av. *Ilk* —2A **60**
Windermere Clo. *Gam* —1A **84**
Windermere Clo. *Ged* —4D **50**
Windermere Cres. *Alst* —4J **55**
Windermere Dri. *Spon* —3A **76**
Windermere Gdns. *Long E*
  —6F **79**
Windermere Rd. *Bees* —6D **62**
Windermere Rd. *Huck* —5F **17**
Windermere Rd. *Long E* —6E **78**
Windermere Rd. *Nott* —6C **48**
Windles Sq. *C'tn* —5E **20**
Windley Cres. *Dar A* —6K **55**
Windley Dri. *Ilk* —3B **44**
Windley La. *Turn* —7C **38**
Windmill Av. *Huck* —6G **17**
Windmill Clo. *Boul M* —5K **93**
Windmill Clo. *Cas D* —1K **115**
Windmill Clo. *Nott* —2H **65**
Windmill Clo. *Ock* —3E **76**
Windmill Ct. *Keyw* —7D **102**
Windmill Gro. *Huck* —5G **17**
Windmill Hill. *Oxt* —1G **21**
Windmill Hill La. *Der* —2G **73**
Windmill Hill Wlk. *Der* —3C **72**
Windmill La. *Belp* —1A **24**
Windmill La. *Nott* —3G **65** (5K **5**)
Windmill Ri. *Belp* —7A **10**
Windmill Rd. *Etw* —6D **88**
Windmill Vw. *Heag* —4E **10**
Windmill Vw. *Nott* —3J **65**
Windmill Way. *Keg* —1F **117**
Windrush Clo. *Alst* —2B **56**
Windrush Clo. *Bees* —6D **62**
Windsmoor Rd. *Brins* —3B **14**
Windsor Av. *L'ver* —1F **91**
Windsor Av. *Melb* —3G **113**
Windsor Clo. *Borr* —7E **76**
Windsor Clo. *Hean* —2G **27**
Windsor Clo. *Huck* —4H **17**
Windsor Clo. *Trow* —2F **61**
Windsor Ct. *Bing* —3J **69**
Windsor Ct. *Mick* —5B **72**
Windsor Ct. *Sand* —4F **79**
Windsor Ct. *W Hal* —6F **43**
Windsor Cres. *Ilk* —2B **60**
Windsor Cres. *S'fd* —1J **79**
Windsor Cres. *Wd'p* —7J **33**
Windsor Dri. *Spon* —2B **76**
Windsor St. *Bees* —2G **81**
Windsor St. *S'fd* —1J **79**
Windy La. *L Eat* —5C **40**
Wing All. *Nott* —3F **65** (4G **5**)
Wingate Clo. *Nott* —1F **63**
Wingbourne Wlk. *Nott* —4J **31**
Wingerworth Pk. Rd. *Spon*
  —3A **76**
Wingfield Dri. *Bees* —6G **63**
Wingfield Dri. *Chad* —6F **57**
Wingfield Dri. *Ilk* —3B **44**
Wings Dri. *Huck* —1D **30**
Winifred Cres. *Bur J* —2K **51**
Winifred St. *Huck* —6H **17**
Winrow Gdns. *Nott* —3J **47**
Winscale Av. *Nott* —5C **32**
Winscale Gdns. *Nott* —5C **32**
Winscombe Mt. *Nott* —1K **99**
Winsford Clo. *Nott* —4H **47**
Winslow Grn. *Chad* —2J **75**

Winster Av. *Cltn* —5B **50**
Winster Clo. *Bees* —6F **63**
Winster Clo. *Belp* —7B **10**
Winster Clo. *Chad* —6E **56**
Winster Way. *Long E* —4D **96**
Winston Clo. *Map* —7A **34**
Winston Clo. *S'fd* —7J **61**
Winterbourne Dri. *S'fd* —6J **61**
Winter Closes. *Und* —3D **14**
Wintergreen Dri. *L'ver* —3D **90**
Winterton Clo. *Arn* —7H **33**
Winterton Ri. *Nott* —6D **32**
Winthorpe Rd. *Arn* —6J **33**
Wintringham Cres. *Wd'p*
  —1J **49**
Wirksworth Rd. *Duf* —3H **39**
Wirksworth Rd. *Ilk* —2K **59**
Wirksworth Rd. *Shot* —1A **22**
Wisa Ter. *Nott* —3F **49**
Wisgreaves Rd. *Der* —1F **93**
Wishford Av. *Nott* —4A **64**
Wisley Clo. *W Bri* —5E **82**
Wistow Clo. *Nott* —6A **48**
Witham Clo. *Hilt* —7A **88**
Witham Dri. *L'ver* —3H **91**
Withern Rd. *Nott* —5F **47**
Witney Clo. *Der* —1C **92**
Witney Clo. *Nott* —5A **32**
Wittering Clo. *Long E* —4J **97**
Witton Ct. *Sten F* —6H **91**
Wiverton Rd. *Bing* —3A **70**
Wiverton Rd. *Nott* —6C **48**
Woburn Clo. *Edw* —4A **84**
Woburn Cft. *Sand* —4E **78**
Woburn Pl. *Der* —3F **73**
Woburn Ri. *Wd'p* —1K **49**
Wodehouse Av. *Got* —7H **99**
Wolds Dri. *Keyw* —7D **102**
Wolds La. *Clip* —1H **103**
Wolds La. *Keyw* —2F **103**
Wolds Ri. *Keyw* —6D **102**
Wolfa St. *Der* —4K **73** (5B **6**)
Wollaton Av. *Ged* —3B **50**
Wollaton Ct. *Nott* —7A **32**
Wollaton Cres. *Bees* —7E **62**
Wollaton Hall Dri. *Nott* —4K **63**
Wollaton Hall Natural History
  Mus. —4G **63**
Wollaton Paddocks. *Nott* —3C **62**
Wollaton Pk. —4H **63**
Wollaton Ri. *Nott* —5B **62**
Wollaton Rd. *Bees* —6E **62**
Wollaton Rd. *Chad* —7F **57**
Wollaton Rd. *Nott* —3E **62**
Wollaton Rd. N. *Chad* —6F **57**
Wollaton St. *Huck* —5H **17**
Wollaton St. *Nott* —2D **64** (3C **4**)
Wollaton Va. *Nott* —3B **62**
Wolsey Av. *Nott* —2B **64**
Wolverley Grange. *Alv* —3K **93**
Woodale Clo. *L'ver* —3D **90**
Wood Av. *Sand* —2E **78**
Woodbank Dri. *Nott* —5D **62**
Woodbeck Ter. *Oak* —5H **57**
Woodborough La. *Arn & Wdbgh*
  —2K **33**
Woodborough Rd. *Nott*
  —1E **64** (1F **5**)
Woodbridge Av. *Nott* —5A **82**
Woodbridge Clo. *Chel* —1E **104**
Woodchester Dri. *Alv* —3K **93**
Woodchurch Rd. *Arn* —4D **32**
Woodcote Way. *L'ver* —2E **90**
Wood Cft. *L'ver* —1H **91**
Woodcroft, The. *Dis* —6A **116**
Wood End Rd. *Hean* —3G **27**
Woodfall La. *Quar* —2B **38**
Woodfield Dri. *Rip* —4C **12**
Woodfield Rd. *Nott* —5E **46**
Woodford Clo. *Nott* —4A **32**
Woodford Rd. *Der* —1E **72**
Woodford Rd. *Huck* —6H **17**
Woodford Rd. *Wd'p* —1J **49**
Woodgate Clo. *Cotg* —5J **85**
Woodgate Ct. *Nott*
  —2C **64** (3A **4**)
Woodgate Dri. *Chel* —1G **105**
Woodgate La. *Cotg* —4H **85**
Wood Gro. *C'tn* —4D **20**
Woodhall Dri. *L'ver* —1C **90**
Woodhall Rd. *Nott* —2H **63**
Woodhedge Dri. *Nott* —6J **49**
Woodhouse Rd. *Klbrn* —5F **25**
Woodhouse St. *Nott*
  —2H **65** (2K **5**)
Woodhouse Way. *Nott* —6D **46**
Woodhurst Clo. *Der* —7D **56**
Woodkirk Rd. *Nott* —6B **82**
Woodland Av. *Borr* —6E **76**

Woodland Av. *Breas* —1D **96**
Woodland Av. *Ilk* —2B **44**
Woodland Av. *Nott* —1J **47**
Woodland Clo. *Cotg* —6K **85**
Woodland Clo. *Rad T* —4B **68**
Woodland Dri. *Nott* —5F **49**
Woodland Dri. *Nut* —2F **47**
Woodland Farm Clo. *Huck* —1D **30**
Woodland Gro. *Bees* —3D **80**
Woodland Gro. *Colw* —1D **66**
Woodland Gro. *Wd'p* —2F **49**
Woodland Rd. *Der* —7J **55**
Woodland Rd. *W Bri* —6H **65**
Woodlands. *Wat* —6A **30**
Woodlands Av. *Shel L* —5E **92**
Woodlands Clo. *L Eat* —6B **40**
Woodlands Clo. *Melb* —2G **113**
Woodlands Gro. *Huck* —1D **30**
Woodlands La. *Bees* —2G **105**
Woodlands La. *Quar* —7H **39**
Woodlands Pk. *Dray* —6K **77**
Woodlands Pl. *Melb* —3G **113**
Woodlands Rd. *Alst* —2J **55**
Woodlands, The. *Melb* —3G **113**
Woodlands, The. *Rad T* —4J **67**
Woodlands Way. *Melb* —3G **113**
Woodlands Yd. *Chel* —2H **105**
Woodland Way. *Eastw* —3C **28**
Wood La. *Ged* —5E **50**
Wood La. *Got* —2F **111**
Wood La. *Hors W & M'ly* —7K **25**
Wood La. *Huck* —5E **16**
Wood La. *Milf* —6K **23**
Woodlane Gdns. *Nott* —7H **49**
Woodlark Ho. *Nott* —7H **49**
Woodlea Gro. *L Eat* —5C **40**
Wood Leigh. *Keyw* —7C **102**
Woodleigh Gdns. *Nott* —4K **49**
Woodleys. *Nott* —7J **49**
Woodley Sq. *Nott* —3J **31**
Woodley St. *Rud* —2E **100**
Wood Link. *Nott* —6E **30**
Woodminton Dri. *Chel* —6F **93**
Woodpecker Clo. *Bing* —4B **70**
Woodpecker Hill. *Dal A* —5J **59**
Woodrising Clo. *Oak* —4H **57**
Wood Rd. *Chad* —6F **57**
Wood Rd. *Spon* —2C **76**
Woodroffe Wlk. *Der* —2J **91**

Woodsend Clo. *Bur J* —2K **51**
Woodsford Gro. *Nott* —6A **82**
Woodshop La. *Swar* —4D **104**
Woodside. *Eastw* —3C **28**
Woodside. *M'ly* —3K **41**
Woodside Av. *Nut* —7A **30**
Woodside Av. *Rip* —4K **11**
Woodside Clo. *Rad T* —4B **68**
Woodside Cres. *Ilk* —1B **44**
Woodside Cres. *Long E* —1F **97**
Woodside Dri. *Alst* —3A **56**
Woodside Dri. *Arn* —5F **33**
Woodside Rd. *Bees* —6F **63**
  (Audley Dri.)
Woodside Rd. *Bees* —4A **80**
  (Gell Rd.)
Woodside Rd. *Bur J* —3H **51**
Woodside Rd. *Rad T* —4B **68**
Woodside Rd. *Sand* —3E **78**
Woods La. *C'tn* —5C **20**
Woods La. *Der* —5K **73** (7A **6**)
Woods Mdw. *Boul M* —4K **93**
Woodsorrel Dri. *Oak* —4H **57**
Woodstock Av. *Nott* —1A **64**
Woodstock Clo. *Alst* —3H **55**
Woodstock Rd. *Bees* —5J **79**
Woodstock St. *Huck* —6H **17**
Woodstock St. W. *Huck* —6H **17**
Woodston Wlk. *Arn* —3J **33**
Wood St. *Arn* —5H **33**
Wood St. *Cod* —4D **12**
Wood St. *Der* —2B **74** (1F **7**)
Wood St. *Eastw* —3D **28**
Wood St. *Ilk* —5D **44**
Wood St. *Nott* —2C **64** (3A **4**)
Wood St. *Rip* —2K **11**
Woodthorne Av. *Shel L* —5E **92**
Woodthorpe Av. *Chad* —2F **75**
Woodthorpe Av. *Wd'p* —2G **49**
Woodthorpe Ct. *Nott* —3G **49**
Woodthorpe Dri. *Wd'p & Map*
  —2F **49**
Woodthorpe Gdns. *Nott* —3H **49**
Woodthorpe Grange Pk. —3G 49
Woodthorpe Rd. *Nott* —3H **49**
Woodvale. *Nott* —3C **62**
Woodview. *Cotg* —5A **86**
Wood Vw. *Edw* —5K **83**
Woodview Bus. Cen. *Arn* —4C **32**

Woodview Ct. *Nott* —2A **66**
Woodville Clo. *Bees* —2C **80**
Woodville Dri. *Nott* —3E **48**
Woodville Rd. *Nott* —4E **48**
Woodwards Clo. *Borr* —7F **77**
Woodward St. *Nott* —6F **65**
Woodyard La. *Nott* —2G **63**
Woolacombe Clo. *Nott* —1B **50**
Wooliscroft Way. *Ilk* —4A **44**
Woolmer Rd. *Nott* —6E **64**
Woolpack La. *Nott* —3F **65** (4G **5**)
  (in two parts)
Wool Pk. La. *Nott* —3F **65** (4H **5**)
Woolrych St. *Der* —6K **73**
Woolsington Clo. *Nott* —4D **46**
Woolsthorpe Clo. *Nott* —1F **63**
Woolsthorpe Cres. *Ilk* —3B **60**
Wootton Clo. *Nott* —7D **46**
Worcester Clo. *Low* —4E **36**
Worcester Cres. *Der* —7D **56**
Worcester Gdns. *Wd'p* —7G **33**
Worcester Rd. *Wd'p* —1G **49**
Wordsworth Av. *Huck* —6D **16**
Wordsworth Dri. *Sin* —4J **91**
Wordsworth Dri. *Sin* —4A **92**
Wordsworth Rd. *Aws* —1G **45**
Wordsworth Rd. *Day* —6F **33**
Wordsworth Rd. *Nott* —1A **64**
Wordsworth Rd. *W Bri* —2G **83**
Worksop Rd. *Nott* —2H **65** (2K **5**)
Worrall Av. *Arn* —6H **33**
Worrall Av. *Long E* —7J **79**
Worth St. *Cltn* —6C **50**
Wortley Av. *Trow* —4H **61**
Wortley Clo. *Ilk* —6E **44**
Wortley Hall Clo. *Nott* —5J **63**
Worwood Dri. *W Bri* —4E **82**
Wossock La. *W Leak* —7E **110**
Woulds Fld. *Cotg* —7K **85**
Wragley Way. *Sten F* —7G **91**
Wray Clo. *Nott* —2G **65** (2K **5**)
Wren Pk. Clo. *Belp* —7H **9**
Wren Pk. Clo. *Find* —7B **90**
Wrenthorpe Va. *Nott* —7A **82**
Wretham Clo. *Mick* —1B **90**
Wright Av. *Rip* —3B **12**
Wrights Orchard. *Keyw*
  —7C **102**
Wright St. *Cod* —4D **12**

Wright St. *N'fld* —7E **50**
Wroughton Ct. *Eastw* —3E **28**
Wroxham Clo. *Shel L* —5D **92**
Wroxham Dri. *Nott* —4D **62**
Wyaston Clo. *Alst* —6J **55**
Wychwood Dri. *Trow* —5H **61**
Wychwood Rd. *Bing* —3J **69**
Wycliffe Gro. *Nott* —4G **49**
Wycliffe St. *Nott* —5B **48**
Wycombe Clo. *Nott* —1K **99**
Wye Gdns. *Nott* —1K **63**
Wye St. *Alv* —1G **93**
Wykeham Rd. *Wd'p* —1J **49**
Wykes Av. *Ged* —4D **50**
Wymondham Clo. *Arn* —7J **33**
Wynbreck Dri. *Keyw* —6D **102**
Wyndale Dri. *Ilk* —1A **60**
Wyndham Ct. *Bees* —4B **80**
Wyndham M. *Nott* —7D **48**
Wyndham St. *Alv* —2G **93**
Wyndings, The. *Wd'p* —2H **49**
Wynhill Ct. *Bing* —2J **69**
Wynndale Dri. *Nott* —3C **48**
Wynton Av. *Alv* —1F **93**
Wynwood Clo. *Bees* —7B **80**
Wynwood Rd. *Bees* —7B **80**
Wynyard Clo. *Ilk* —3B **44**
Wyrale Dri. *Nott* —5E **46**
Wysall La. *Keyw* —7C **102**
Wysall Rd. *Bun* —7K **101**
Wyton Clo. *Nott* —1C **48**
Wyvelle Cres. *Keg* —7G **109**
Wyver La. *Belp* —5K **9**
Wyvern Av. *Long E* —3H **97**
Wyvern Bus. Pk. *Der* —5G **75**
Wyvern Clo. *Newt* —5E **28**
Wyvern Retail Pk. *Der* —4G **75**
Wyvern Way. *Chad* —4F **75**
Wyville Clo. *Nott* —2A **64**

**Y**alding Dri. *Nott* —3C **62**
Yalding Gdns. *Nott* —3C **62**
Yardley Way. *Belp* —1D **24**
*Yarmouth Ho. Alv* —2J **93**
  *(off Durley Clo.)*
Yarrow Clo. *Sin* —7J **91**
Yarwell Clo. *Der* —6D **56**
Yarwell Clo. *Nott* —7A **50**

Yates Av. *Ast T* —3C **106**
Yatesbury Cres. *Nott* —6E **46**
Yates Clo. *Long E* —2K **97**
Yates Dri. *Der* —7A **74**
Yates Gdns. *Nott* —5C **32**
Yates St. *Der* —7A **74**
Yeoman Av. *B Vil* —1B **32**
Yeovil Clo. *Alv* —2J **93**
Yewbarrow Clo. *W Bri* —3A **84**
Yew Clo. *Nott* —4F **49**
Yewdale Clo. *Clif* —1K **99**
Yewdale Clo. *W Bri* —3A **84**
Yewdale Gro. *Oak* —4H **57**
Yews Dri. *Chel* —1G **105**
Yew Tree Av. *Nott* —5E **48**
Yew Tree Av. *Ock* —3F **77**
Yew Tree Clo. *Alv* —2J **93**
Yew Tree Clo. *Rad T* —4H **67**
Yew Tree Ct. *Bees* —2F **81**
Yew Tree La. *Ged* —4E **50**
Yew Tree La. *Nott* —6J **81**
Yew Tree La. *Thul* —5B **94**
Yew Tree Rd. *Huck* —7H **17**
Yonge Clo. *Rad T* —5J **67**
York Av. *Bees* —4F **81**
York Av. *Sand* —3E **78**
York Bri. *Der* —4C **74** (5H **7**)
York Clo. *Ged* —4D **50**
York Dri. *Nott* —4D **46**
Yorke St. *Huck* —5G **17**
York House. —2F 5
York Rd. *Chad* —1F **75**
York Rd. *Long E* —7G **79**
York St. *Der* —3J **73** (3A **6**)
York St. *N'fld* —7E **50**
York St. *Nott* —1E **64** (1F **5**)
Youlgreave Clo. *Chad* —6F **57**
Young Clo. *Nott* —1F **47**
Young St. *Der* —7K **73**
Ypres Rd. *Alst* —5G **55**
Yvonne Cres. *Cltn* —7D **50**

**Z**etland Cres. *Sten F* —7G **91**
Zulla Rd. *Nott* —6E **48**
Zulu Rd. *Nott* —5B **48**